BREAKING THE ZERO-SUM GAME

Transforming Societies through Inclusive
Leadership

Building Leadership Bridges

The International Leadership Association (ILA) series, *Building Leadership Bridges*, brings together leadership coaches and consultants, educators and students, scholars and researchers, and public leaders and executives working around the globe to create unique topical volumes on contemporary leadership issues. This cross-sector, cross-cultural, cross-disciplinary series contributes to more integrated leadership thinking, practices, and solutions that can positively impact our complex local and global environments. The world needs better leadership and ILA's mission of promoting a deeper understanding of leadership knowledge and practice for the greater good aims to make a difference. Learn more at www.ila-net.org.

Forthcoming Titles:

Global and Culturally Diverse Leaders and Leadership: New Dimensions and Challenges for Business, Education and Society, edited by Jean Lau Chin, Joseph E. Trimble, Joseph E. Garcia (2017), ISBN: 978-1787434967

Recent Titles:

Grassroots Leadership and the Arts for Social Change, edited by Susan J. Erenrich and Jon F. Wergin (2017), ISBN: 978-1786356888

Creative Social Change: Leadership for a Healthy World, edited by Kathryn Goldman Schuyler, John Eric Baugher, Karin Jironet (2016), ISBN: 978-1786351463

Leadership 2050: Critical Challenges, Key Contexts, and Emerging Trends, edited by Matthew Sowcik, Anthony C. Andenoro, Mindy McNutt, and Susan Elaine Murphy (2015), ISBN: 978-1785603495

BREAKING THE ZERO-SUM GAME

Transforming Societies through Inclusive Leadership

Edited by

Aldo Boitano de Moras
Executive Development, ILA, Santiago, Chile

Raúl Lagomarsino Dutra
ESE Business School, Universidad de Los Andes, Santiago, Chile

H. Eric Schockman
Department of Leadership and Center for Leadership, Woodbury University, Burbank, CA, USA

United Kingdom – North America – Japan – India – Malaysia – China

Emerald Publishing Limited
Howard House, Wagon Lane, Bingley BD16 1WA, UK

First edition 2017

British Library Cataloguing in Publication Data
A catalogue record for this book is available from the British Library

ISBN: 978-1-78743-186-7 (Print)
ISBN: 978-1-78743-185-0 (Online)
ISBN: 978-1-78743-237-6 (Epub)

ISSN: 2058-8801 (Series)

ISOQAR certified
Management System,
awarded to Emerald
for adherence to
Environmental
standard
ISO 14001:2004.

Certificate Number 1985
ISO 14001

INVESTOR IN PEOPLE

Contents

Part 4 Inclusiveness and Diversity in Higher Education

Part 5 Inclusiveness in the Field

List of Contributors

Niels Agger-Gupta — School of Leadership Studies, Royal Roads University, Victoria, Canada

Barbara A. Baker — Women's Leadership Institute, Auburn University, Auburn, AL, USA

Maria Basualdo — Ontario Public Interest Research Group, Ottawa, Canada

Aldo Boitano de Moras — Executive Development, ILA, Santiago, Chile

Juana Bordas — Mestiza Leadership International, Denver, CO, USA

Ethan Brownell — University of Minnesota – Twin Cities, Minneapolis, MN, USA

Gloria J. Burgess — Seattle University, Edmonds WA, USA

Mecca Antonia Burns — Presence, Earlysville, VA, USA

Michael R. Carey — Organizational Leadership, Gonzaga University, Spokane, WA, USA

Robin E. S. Carter — Alvernia University, Reading, PA, USA

Chris Cartwright — Intercultural Communication Institute, Portland, OR, USA

Helen Caton-Hughes — The Forton Group, Willoughby, UK

Sarah Chace — Department of Leadership and American Studies, Christopher Newport University, Newport News, VA, USA

William Clark — Eli Patrick & Co, Windsor, CT, USA

Claire Delisle — Department of Criminology, University of Ottawa, Ottawa, Canada

Raúl Lagomarsino Dutra	ESE Business School, Universidad de Los Andes, Santiago, Chile
Brighid Dwyer	Villanova University, Villanova, PA, USA
Leigh E. Fine	Kansas State University, Manhattan, KS, USA
Tami J. France	Leadership and Organization Development, Mayo Clinic, Rochester, MN, USA
Christopher Gergen	Forward Impact, Durham, NC, USA
Cheryl Getz	Department of Leadership Studies, University of San Diego, San Diego, CA, USA
Ralph A. Gigliotti	Rutgers University, New Brunswick, NJ, USA
Malcolm E. Glover	University of Central Arkansas, Conway, AR, USA
Miriam Gosling	Centre for Peace and Global Studies, Sidcot School, Winscombe, UK
Maura Harrington	Center for Nonprofit Management, Los Angeles, CA, USA
Brigitte Harris	Faculty of Social and Applied Science, Royal Roads University, Victoria, Canada
Andrea Hughes	Independent Researcher, Taipei City, Taiwan
Bob Hughes	The Forton Group, Willoughby, UK
Adina Ilea	Department of Criminology, University of Ottawa, Ottawa, Canada
Zhi Luan	Department of Leadership Studies, University of Central Arkansas, Conway, AR, USA
Ebere Morgan	Deztiny Strategics Inc., Milton, Ontario, Canada
Bernard Mukisa	Budondo Intercultural Center and Suubi Health Project, Budondo, Uganda

Denis Muwanguzi   Budondo Intercultural Center and
                         Suubi Health Project, Budondo,
                         Uganda

Lyndon Rego   Leadership Beyond Boundaries,
                         Center for Creative Leadership,
                         Greensboro, NC, USA

Colleen Rigby   Waikato Management School,
                         University of Waikato, Hamilton,
                         New Zealand

Jill Robinson   University of Redlands, Redlands,
                         CA, USA

Elisa Sabatini   Via International, San Diego, CA, USA

Lydia Sanyu   Budondo Intercultural Center and
                         Suubi Health Project, Budondo,
                         Uganda

H. Eric Schockman   Department of Leadership and Center
                         for Leadership, Woodbury University,
                         Burbank, CA, USA

Lorraine Stefani   Faculty of Education and Social
                         Work, University of Auckland,
                         Auckland, New Zealand

Leonard D. Taylor Jr.   Mississippi State University,
                         Mississippi State, MS, USA

Randal Joy Thompson   Dream Connect Global, Reno, NV,
                         USA

Dung Q. Tran   School of New and Continuing
                         Studies, Seattle University, Seattle,
                         WA, USA

Rouxelle de Villiers   Waikato Management School,
                         University of Waikato, Hamilton,
                         New Zealand

Joyce de Vries   Auburn University, Auburn, AL, USA

Jennifer Walinga   School of Communications and
                         Culture, Royal Roads University,
                         Victoria, BC, Canada

Kevin Walsh   Phillips Graduate University,
                         Chatsworth, CA, USA

Preface

This book was intended to create a dialogue around the question: What does an inclusive society look like, and more specifically, how do future leaders and followers personify inclusiveness?

We live in a fractured world: from widening income disparities, to religious zealots, to the polarization resulting from elections and campaigning in developed democracies across the planet. The idea that for some to "win," others must "lose" is prevalent. We too often today glorify victors as "heroes" relegating the opposition as the "other" which we then demonize. Events such as: the Occupy Wall Street or Black Lives Matter movements; Arab Spring; the political tide from left to right in Europe; the throngs of refugees fleeing from war-torn societies; and racial strife in the United States …. all are signs that people are tired of living in a zero-sum world. This book provides a powerful antidote, revolving around new cutting-edge theories and best practices, which can be applied to transform societies into more inclusive, diverse, and democratic entities.

Every chapter in this volume is a journey into a different type of society, one with alternative paradigms and thinking, inspired by our commonalities, rather than forces that divide us. This volume is an attempt to build symbolic and real bridges to inclusion by understanding ourselves and the "other." Instead of competition, selfishness, and control (which have supported suprastructures of racism, inequality, and xenophobia), this volume is a living testimony that a functioning alternative reality does exist. Each author contributing to this volume insightfully probes the relationship between leaders and followers as positive change agents whom together can solve the "wicked" problems facing us today and bring forth a more inclusive society. Using the lens of inclusiveness, this volume also brings a global perspective that transcends cultures, disciplines, nation states, and other artificial boundaries.

Inclusive leadership may or may not be the silver bullet to get us to a Maslowian state of self-actualization, but it definitely can be viewed and studied as a transformative formula that can drive catalytic positive change. Edwin P. Hollander (2009) posits that inclusive leadership should be seen as an interpersonal process that entails mutual relationships with share goals and a common vision of the future. Hollander's true genius was to shift away from leader-centric analysis to a persistent focus on followership. From that perspective, he argues we need to build an inclusive culture of legitimacy through the ethical nourishing of "idiosyncrasy credits" as a basis by which followers are able to evaluate the leader's performance. For Hollander "leadership is doing things with people, not to people." As Donald Hantula (2009) summarizes Hollander's work, "inclusive leadership is for every man and every woman. Along a leader's thorny journey, beauty, strength and other traits depart quickly and knowledge can fade, leaving only the leader's good deeds, building idiosyncrasy credits among the followers and gaining their support."

We leave the reader with some profound questions the book raises: How do leaders and followers find new collaborations to supplant or improve upon top-down or bottom-up change? How does the next generation of inclusive leaders bring better tools and new technologies to move beyond hatred and division into forgiveness and reconciliation? In the era of post-globalization, how does inclusiveness work in bringing poor and underprivileged people into the development process? Have global organizations been able to maximize diversity to create a unified and inclusive global culture? Do the effects of governmental policy outputs include all stakeholders of society vis-à-vis race, gender, ethnicity, sexual orientation, and disability status?

These questions are just some lingering thoughts the editors and authors of this volume wish to leave the reader not only to ponder but activate upon.

THE DESIGN OF THIS VOLUME

Breaking the Zero-Sum Game: Transforming Societies Through Inclusive Leadership is composed of five parts and a short introduction to each section. We move from the more theoretical (Part I: Pushing the Boundaries of Inclusiveness) into a more pragmatic overview (in Part II: Trials of Breaking the Zero-Sum Game). In Part III: Spiritual Inclusiveness examines in more depth how faith and spirituality may evolve into a more harmonious plateau using inclusiveness as a bridge to our collective souls. Part IV: Inclusiveness and Diversity in Higher Education brings together some of the best practices in leadership education and higher education administration to demonstrate how equality and justice can radiate from global campuses into their respective societies. Lastly, Part V: Inclusiveness in the Field presents several authors' writings about very specific case examples of applied inclusivity: from village women in sub-Sahara Africa; to the work of a leading NGO, Heifer International; to a global student-based organized campaign to stop 'blood minerals' exported from the Democratic Republic of the Congo into our mobile cellular devices used around the globe.

These are but tidbits of what awaits the reader as one delves into the richness of each chapter of this volume. We hope the overall take-away message is that inclusive leadership and follow-ership matters, and that this book has been a catalyst in raising core questions and awareness leading to both continued dialogue and ultimately concerted action.

Aldo Boitano de Moras
Raúl Lagomarsino Dutra
H. Eric Schockman
Editors

References

Hollander, E. P. (2009). *Inclusive leaders: The essential leader-follower relationship*. New York: NY: Routledge.

Hantula, D. A. (2009). Book review: Hollander's inclusive leadership. *Psychological Record*, 59, 701–704.

Dr. Edwin P. Hollander, a pioneering visionary of inclusive leadership

Acknowledgements from the Editors

An endeavor such as this can only be created with the participation and support of many individuals all rowing in the same direction.

We deeply appreciate the nourishment and hard work from all those who contributed chapters to this volume. The editors have collectively learned much from each author in this journey and we thank you for your openness to dig deeper intellectually and envision with us the end goal of inclusiveness as a dynamic process.

The editors also owe a huge debt of eternal gratitude to Debra DeRuyver, Communications Director of the International Leadership Association (ILA). Debra was with us every step of the way – offering sound advice, unconditional accessibility day or night (hopefully without too much stress on her family life), and overall a consummate professional cheerleader for the editorial team, that coincidentally she managed to assemble. We also thank the staff of ILA for their faith in us and support for our work. Kudos goes out particular to Cynthia Cherry, CEO; Shelly Wilsey, COO; and Bridget Chisholm, Director of Conferences. They and the rest of the ILA staff were the cementing blocks and foundation that enabled us to build an architecture of this book.

The editors would also like to thank our readers who are making the real difference daily in a myriad of ways towards a more holistic and inclusive world. We hope in our own small way that we have prepared you with the pragmatic tools, best practices, and theoretical justifications to continue to strive for justice and diversity in your own finite orbits. Taken together, we can transform societies and break the chains of zero-sum scenarios that lay before us.

Additionally, Eric would like to thank his co-editors, Aldo and Raúl for providing the intellectual comradeship, plus plenty of beers, long Skype sessions, and a pending trip to Patagonia that sustained my enthusiasm for the gestation of this endeavor. Thank you as well to: Dean Douglas Cremer, Marlene Noonan, Steven Henry Crithfield, Michael Brett Mason, Elizabeth "Lisa" Cooper, Dr. Ariane David, Dr. Elizabeth Trebow, my chocolate lab Brixton who was my comfort partner always at my side, and our research assistants: Kevin Tamaki and Cody Thompson. And, Raúl would like to thank everyone at ESE Business School for their continuous support, and especially his wife Mariana, for everything, every day.

About the Editors

Aldo Boitano is the founder/Executive Director of Executive Development. He serves on the boards of ILA and Electra, a renewable energy company. He currently teaches on international business, leadership and building high performance teams at ESE-Universidad Los Andes and at the School of Business Universidad de Chile both at corporate programs and at postgraduate and MBA level. He normally lectures and consults on leadership, teamwork, business models, and technology topics. He is a former Associate Professor on international business at the University of North Carolina-Charlotte Belk School. Aldo is a world-class mountaineer and active philanthropist as well as a seasoned lecturer and consultant to companies and world forums. He has 20 years of experience in senior level leadership positions including CEO of Vertical Chile and CEO of El-Colorado/Farellones Ski resorts.

Raúl Lagomarsino Dutra is Professor and Department Head, Organizational Behavior/Human Resources Management at ESE Business School, Universidad de Los Andes, Chile. He has almost 20 years of experience in executive education in some of the most prestigious business schools in Latin America. He has an MBA and a PhD from IESE Business School and is the co-founder of Emergap, a business consulting firm specialized in cultural transformation and innovation in emerging markets. He has collaborated with more than 100 companies in consulting projects and is a guest speaker at several leadership, strategy, and innovation forums.

H. Eric Schockman is Associate Professor, Chair of the Department of Leadership and Director for the Center for Leadership at Woodbury University. He also teaches in the PhD program in global leadership and change at Pepperdine University and previously served as Associate Dean and Associate Adjunct Professor at the Sol Price School of Public Policy at the University of Southern California. He is president and founder of the Global Hunger Foundation, dedicated to helping women in the developing world. He was a top consultant to the California State Assembly and the Los Angeles City Council. He served in the Peace Corps in Sierra Leone, West Africa, and taught agricultural and sustainable development. Eric holds a PhD in political science and international relations from the University of California.

Foreword

I t is a pleasure to introduce this volume of *Breaking the Zero-sum Game: Transforming Societies Through Inclusive Leadership*. The chapters in this volume reflect contemporary applications of inclusive leadership. They point to ways that inclusiveness can be significant in contributing to leadership research and practice.

Over 60 years ago, I began studying what was known about desirable qualities of leader–follower relations. Those of participation, support, and information flow showed greater overall benefits than traditional top-down forms. After many decades of research, I arrived at inclusive leadership as the best way to meet most criteria for effective leadership. It is opposed to authoritarian rule, as summed up in my phrase "doing things with people, not to people" (2009, 2013–2014). The emphasis is on listening in each role. It is conceptually derived from Mary Parker Follett's 1930s (Graham, 1996) advocacy of "power with." It is essential to processes of emergent leadership and intended social change.

Contemplating my personal history, as I approach age 90, I delight in recalling how new concepts challenged old "leader-centric" ones, like having "charisma" that actually depends on follower perceptions. The "situational view" of leadership arrived in the 1950s. The work and views of Hemphill (1949), Gouldner (1950), and Sanford (1950), among others, engaged me. I wanted to study and understand the leader–follower relationships. Among the research techniques I used are experiments, peer nominations, and "critical incidents" obtained in writing from respondents with work experience.

In my 1978 book, *Leadership Dynamics*, I offered a practical guide drawn from what I'd learned as a leader–follower, including as a Provost. I brought out essentials of leader–follower interdependence that are distinctly "relational," such as followers accepting a leader's legitimacy, an essential matter, to my advocacy of inclusive leadership.

Looking back 70 years, at age 19 I served as an Army private in 1946–1947 doing diagnostic testing in a psychiatric unit. I had completed 2 years of courses at Western Reserve, then given up a draft deferment. I returned to finish, and graduated in 1948 with Calvin Hall, and Daniel Levinson as mentors. Back on duty in the Korean War, I served for 3 years as a Naval Aviation Psychologist starting early in 1951, after earning a Master's degree in 1950 at Columbia in psychological measurement, assisting Robert Thorndike. He and four other professors named here made lasting, and appreciated, impressions on my values, and career.

Conceptually, inclusive leadership drew on the work of George Homans (1961, 1974), whom I enjoyed when on a sabbatical at Harvard, with my wife and son, in 1969–1970. I was congenial with Homans' view of leadership through the "social exchange theory" that he propounded, stressing the "norm of reciprocity." Also, I used "systems theory" concepts, from contact with Herbert Simon, when working on his decision-making project at Carnegie Tech (now Carnegie Mellon University) leading to his Nobel Economics Prize two decades later. In 1954–1957 I taught there. I went on leave to teach at Istanbul University as a Fulbright Professor in 1957–1958.

While at Carnegie Tech, I also started doing small-group leadership experiments, with support from the Office of Naval Research (ONR). That led to the 20-year leadership research program I directed at SUNY-Buffalo, while serving in academic and professional leadership roles, including provost of social sciences and administration and earlier, as long-time director of the PhD program in social and organizational psychology, with National Institute of Mental Health (NIMH) support. Raymond Hunt and I began it in 1962, with two other faculty members, when I arrived. With a core faculty of six, and leadership well-covered, we had 72 doctoral graduates when I retired 27 years later to join the CUNY doctoral faculty. The SUNY-Buffalo program alumni include a former State University President, Dean of Social Work at another public one, consulting firm heads, and a deceased Past-President of the Australian Psychological Society among others who have had productive academic careers.

As a leadership researcher in the early 1950s, studying training "sections" of Naval Aviation Cadets, I primarily used peer nominations. Among the findings using this sociometric technique was how well even early nominations predicted future leader performance. In addition to high validity, and reliability, nominations for leader and follower were highly correlated, and not significantly affected by friendship. In this study I did with Webb (1955), we first introduced "followership" as a term in the research literature. It was a reminder that leaders originate as followers, who showed such qualities as communications skills and dependability. I earned my PhD from Columbia in 1952, having done my courses before, and taking those in social psychology from Otto Klineberg and Goodwin Watson, both of whom were on my dissertation committee, with Thorndike. The main finding was that cadets nominated highest on leadership were not high on authoritarianism (F Scale), even in this military setting. Similar result was found with emergent college student leaders who were "moderates" on the Machiavellianism Scale (*Psychological Reports*, 1979).

Prior research of mine found nominations made after early contact among cadets, three weeks, highly predictive of later performance ratings as an officer. These and many other findings, with emergent leadership implications, are presented in my 1964 book. My comparable follow-up study at the Newport Officer Candidate School (OCS) found similar validity and reliability (*Journal of Applied Psychology*, 1968).

My interest continued in gathering and analyzing good and bad leadership from the perspective of the followers' experiences, and their written accounts provided an abundance of findings about them (2013, 2014a, 2014b).

Eventually, other colleagues, such as notable scholars James Burns and John Gardner, came to state more about followers and their perceptions of leaders. That came about 20 years after what I termed "Idiosyncrasy Credit" (1958). That is a follower-oriented concept of what leaders can and cannot do, as a result of follower perceptions of the leader. It becomes essential in understanding a deeper sense of this symbiotic relationship. Credits can provide a leader with greater latitude for expression, including flagrant deviation.

Credits are also based upon formal legitimacy of holding an office, but can impose restraint on latitude. Gaining credits that could allow one to be a bold leader may bring about change, but not always in followers' interests. Alternatively, failing to use one's credits can deplete them and, it becomes a test of a leader's legitimacy with his or hers' followers.

Lao Tzu, in 6th Century B.C. China, wrote, "The wise leader settles for good work, then lets others have the floor... and does not take all the credit for what happens." Trust and loyalty regarding a leader arise from the needs and expectations of followers, and their views of a leader's actions, attitudes, and motives.

As the field of leadership has developed, it is still dominated by leader centrism. This appeal reveals the continuing attraction of the major actor. But it reveals a failure to recognize the importance of follower perceptions and demands, as interdependent feedback operating between leaders and followers.

While "transformational leadership" also implicates system relations, it is with less follower feedback on the leader. But, Burns does allude to participative leadership, in a gesture toward inclusiveness that brings the maximum number of individuals to the common table. Top-down, non-participative leadership still prevails, perpetuating the dichotomy of those who hold power and those who do not. Transformational and inclusive leadership styles both involve moral and ethical concerns (2015), which allow for future leaders to emerge. Leader attention to democratic practice, and collective interests, is essential, without marginalizing any of the populace. A "servant" commitment, as in Greenleaf's concept, could bring leaders and followers to a higher plane.

As the field of inclusive leadership evolved, it has gained acceptance as a standard of conduct. For example, in higher educational institutions, student participation in a share of decision processes has occurred as they serve as elected representatives, with faculty and staff, on all committees, with benefits achieved.

Taking account of diversity is another ethical responsibility. Inclusion applies as well in such practices as with "employee stock ownership programs," board membership, constituents as voters and advocates, indeed, all entitled as "stakeholders." Autocrats who rule with absolute authority have shown their ability to crush aspirations of social movements like Arab Spring and Occupy Wall Street. Eventually, greater political legitimacy can flow from inclusive leadership, as it has evolved from age, gender, immigration status and everywhere different cultures and arenas exist.

In conclusion, seen in a larger perspective, various streams of thought have converged on the concept of leadership as a process rather than a person or state. This process is essentially a shared experience, a voyage through time, with benefits to be gained and hazards to be surmounted by the parties involved. A leader is not a sole voyager, but a key figure whose actions or inactions can determine others' well-being and the broader good. It is not too much to say that communal social health, as well as achieving a desired destination, is largely influenced by a leader's decisions and the information and values upon which based, so as to "perform and inform" at both ends. When pressed on the leader's "accountability," consider that participative decision-making is not "weaker" for taking in information and views, in contrast to just the leader doing it alone (2013–2015).

New York, New York, October, 2016

Acknowledgments: Many thanks to H. Eric Schockman and Debra DeRuyver who provided the impetus to do this and to Cynthia Cherry for her encouragement and support. I am also grateful to our son, Peter Hollander, for his aid in processing this section, and thankful to be asked and able to contribute to this important book.

Edwin P. Hollander
Distinguished Professor of Psychology Emeritus,
College and the Graduate Center,
City University of New York

References

Burns, J. M. (1978). *Leadership*. New York, NY: Harper and Row.

Gardner, J. W. (1990). *On leadership*. New York, NY: Free Press/Macmillan.

Gouldner, A. W. (1950). *Studies in leadership*. New York, NY: Harper.

Graham, P. (1996). *Mary Parker Follett. Prophet of management*. Boston, MA: Harvard University Press.

Hemphill, J. (1949). *Situational factors in leadership*. Columbus, OH: Ohio State University, Personnel Research Board.

Hollander, E. P. (1958). Conformity, status, and idiosyncrasy credit. *Psychological Review, 65*, 117–127.

Hollander, E. P. (1964). *Leaders, groups, and influence*. New York, NY: Oxford University Press.

Hollander, E. (1967/1981) Principles and methods of social psychology, 4th ed New York and Oxford: Oxford University Press.

Hollander, E. P. (1978). *Leadership dynamics*. New York, NY: Free Press/Macmillan, (Paperback ed., 1984, Simon & Schuster. Korean ed. Seoul, 2005).

Hollander, E. (2012) Inclusive Leadership: The essential leader-follower relationship. New York: Routledge.

Hollander, E. P. (2013). Inclusive leadership and idiosyncrasy credit in leader-follower relations. Leadership in higher education. Chapters 8 and 17.

In M. G. Rumsey (Ed.). *The Oxford Handbook of Leadership*. New York, NY: Oxford University Press.

Hollander, E. P. (2014a). Barack Obama and inclusive leadership in engaging followership. In D. D. Sharma & U. Gielen (Eds.), *The global Obama: Crossroads of leadership in the 21st century*. New York, NY: Routledge. Chapter 4.

Hollander, E. P. (2014b). Leader-follower dynamics and the role of idiosyncrasy credit and inclusion. In G. Goethals, S. Allison, R. Kramer, & D. Messick (Eds.), *Conceptions of leadership: Enduring ideas and emerging insights*. London: Palgrave Macmillan. Chapter 12.

Hollander, E. P. (2015). Further ethical challenges in the leader-follower relationship. In J. Ciulla (Ed.), *Ethics, the heart of leadership* (3rd ed., pp. 70–100). Westport, CT: Praeger.

Hollander, E. P. & Webb, W. B. (1955). Leadership, followers, and friendship: An analysis of peer nominations. *Journal of Abnormal and Social Psychology*, *50*, 163–167.

Homans, G. C. (1961, 1974 Rev.). *Social behavior its elementary forms*. New York, NY: Harcourt.

Sanford, F. H. (1950). *Authoritarianism and leadership*. Philadelphia, PA: Institute for research in Human Relations.

PART 1
Pushing the Boundaries of Inclusiveness

Introduction

The authors of these chapters show us how the boundaries of inclusive leadership have been expanded past their previous confines — not only in geographic or demographic terms but also in terms of the core ideas and beliefs of what inclusiveness means.

The notions of democratizing leadership and of servant leadership are both tied to inclusiveness and are explored along with examples of the results of their application around the world. The idea of inclusive leadership starting first within a geographic community and then evolving with different views and perspectives into more of a regional and global movement that shares values, a common background, and world view is just one example of how, in the times we live in, ideas and social movements can start anywhere and also reach everyone.

1

Breaking the Zero-Sum Game: Transforming Societies through Inclusive Leadership

Ebere Morgan

Keywords: Leadership; inclusive leadership; diversity; inclusion; outcomes; benefits

'Beyond the horizon of time is a changed world, very different from today's world. Some people see beyond that horizon and into the future. They believe that dreams can become reality. They open our eyes and lift our spirits. They build trust and strengthen our relationships. They stand firm against the wind of resistance and give us the courage to continue the quest. We call these people leaders'

Kouzes and Posner (1995, p. 317)

In contemporary times, rapidly changing demographics due to increase in women and ethnic minorities joining the workforce has incited changes in how organizations address and tackle with diversity and its frameshift processes. Other drivers of diversity across organizational workforce include disability, age, sexual orientation and race. These combine together in creating the need to appreciate both the diversity of our workplace and the world at large, especially in response to the globalization trends in the recent times (Salib, 2014).

Contemporaneously, there exists a strong shift in global economic power from industrialized Western nations to the developing East, along with the increasing population and diversity in countries like Canada, which has created complex social environments. This also has mounted much pressure on leaders to meet their respective organizational goals — while fostering the effective achievement and advancing the development of their constituents at the individual level (Bishop & Mahoney, 2009; Lugg & Shoho, 2006; Salib, 2014).

Scientific researchers and practitioners continue to debate and deliberate on the most effective means of dealing with these resultant changes on all fronts and levels. These range from the macro to the micro social consequences, such as the definition of the terms 'inclusion', 'diversity' and 'inclusive leadership'. This chapter attempts to examine theories, models and mechanisms of inclusion and inclusive leadership (IL), as well as the effective implementation processes by which they can be made practical and applicable in organizations.

According to Langdon, McMenamin, and Krolik (2002), labour force projections that predict of greater numbers of women and minorities moving into the workforce, both nationally and globally, have prompted organizations to begin focusing their efforts on managing the effects of this demographic shift.

The Question of Leadership

Leadership has been under intense and rigorous study for the past few decades. Its importance and significance are difficult to overstate. Nevertheless, researchers and authorities do not seem any closer to an agreement on the essential underpinnings and substantive nature of leadership (MacLean, 2008). The nature of both work and the workplace, as well as people and places, has changed drastically (Billett, 2006). The recent state of corporate scandals (Wong, 2002), the increasing diversity of the workforce and the quickening pace of social and technological change require a fundamental rethinking in leadership research (Wong, 2007).

In recent years, leading researchers have dealt on the subject of leadership in various dimensions. For example, Northouse (2007) contends that leadership is 'a process whereby an individual influences a group of individuals to achieve a common goal' (p. 3). Bolman and Deal (2008) propose that good leaders have a clear vision, make their expectations known and direct organizations towards attaining desired goals; they must be goal-focused and keep their staff on track, despite distractions that may occur. Although a scholarly consensus on the definition of leadership has proven challenging due to its complexity, researchers, however, conclude that 'leadership is the ability to influence, motivate, and enable others to contribute toward the effectiveness and success of the organizations of which they are members' (McShane, 2004, p. 400).

Conversely, Drucker (1993) believed that the quality of product/service and performance of managers are deciding factors of organizational success. Bass (1990), in a study, concluded that 45% to 65% of the total factors that cause success or failure of an organization are decided by leaders. Thus, it is important to note that the leadership style, theory, framework or model adopted by a leader has the key relationship with the success of an organization.

Legends and myths about the characteristic distinctions between 'great leaders' and 'commoners' have always had a huge magnetic attraction to people and societies. Bass (1990) notes: 'The study of leadership rivals in age the emergence of civilization, which shaped its leaders, as much as it was shaped by them. From its infancy, the study of history has been the study of leaders — "what they did and why they did it"' (p. 3). Leadership still fascinates scholars, as well as the general public. However, the term 'leadership' means different things to different people. Definitions of leadership vary in terms of emphasis on leader abilities, personality traits, influence relationships, cognitive versus emotional orientation, individual versus group orientation, and appeal to self- versus collective interests (Den Hartog & Koopman, 2001, p. 166). Definitions also vary in whether they are primarily descriptive or normative in nature, as well as in their relative emphasis on behavioural styles (Den Hartog & Koopman, 2001; Den Hartog et al., 1997). For example, leadership is described as the process of influencing the activities of an organized group towards goal achievement (Rauch & Behling, 1984), the influence processes affecting the interpretation of events for followers, the choice of objectives for the group or organization, the organization of work activities to accomplish the objectives, the motivation of followers to achieve the objectives, the maintenance of cooperative relationships and teamwork and the enlistment of support and cooperation from people outside the group or organization (Yukl, 1994, 1998); and in terms of a process of social influence whereby a leader steers members of a group towards a goal (Bryman, 1992).

Hernandez, Eberly, Avolio, and Johnson (2011) observe that it is not uncommon for both leadership practitioners and academics to lament the range of definitions that are typically used in the literature to describe leadership. The differences in how leadership has been defined have resulted in disparate approaches to conceptualizing, measuring, investigating and critiquing leadership. For example, some authors have focused solely on the leader to explain leadership, whereas others have examined leadership from a relational, group or follower-centred perspective. To add to the differentiation that has emerged in the leadership literature, other authors have focused on examining leader traits versus behaviours, while still others have drawn from the cognition and affect literatures to explicate leadership and its effects (p. 1165).

Summarily, influence, people, group, goal and objectives are the underlying recurrent themes and concepts that reverberate in leadership theory and research studies (Bryman, 1992; Parry & Bryman, 2006). Nonetheless, far too many leading scholars recognize the reality that the concept of leadership remains in its growing stages and lacks a grand, unifying theory to provide general direction to thinkers and researchers (Burns, 2003, p. 2).

Perspectives of Leadership — A Comprehensive Review

According to Boyce (2006), the quest to classify, catalogue, sort and understand the breadth of leadership scholarship and practice is not new. The works of Stogdill (1981), Kellerman (1984), Bass (1990) and Northouse (2001) represent well-known writings that provide a broad perspective on the theory and practice of leadership, and are frequently cited in leadership literature reviews (p. 71).

St-Hilaire (2008) points out that among the copious literature on leadership theory, several overarching trends can be distinguished, sifted and differentiated. He argues that there is no
agreed upon classification among researchers. However, he suggests drawing up a picture of the major trends: An early period,
consisting of such well-known theories as Traits Theory,
Behaviour Theory and Contingency/Situational Theory; a second
period, consisting of Multilevel Approaches; the New Leadership
period, which emerged in the 1980s and included both
Transformational and Charismatic theories; and finally, Post-
Charismatic and Post-Transformational Leadership Approaches,
which emerged in reaction to New Leadership theories. St-Hilaire
also contends that although the above mentioned approaches are
presented chronologically, some approaches (e.g. Leader-
Member Exchange, one of the Multilevel Approaches) are still
relevant to current empirical and theoretical works (p. 5).

Den Hartog and Koopman (2001, p. 167) suggested that
another way to view leadership is in terms of the different
domains which leadership encompasses. Most approaches to
leadership have been leader-centred. They also observe that one
can distinguish between the leader, follower and relationship
domain of leadership (Graen & Uhl-Bien, 1995). In all three
domains, different levels of analysis (i.e. individual, dyad, group
or larger collectivities) can be the focus of investigation in leadership research (e.g. Yammarino & Bass, 1991).

Graen and Uhl-Bien (1995) propose that leader behaviour,
characteristics and their effects are the primary issues of concern
in the leader-based (leader-centric) domain. A follower-based
(follower-centric) approach would lead to hypotheses focusing
on follower issues such as follower characteristics, behaviours,
and perceptions or topics such as empowerment (Hollander,
1992a, 1992b; Meindl, 1990). Further, a relationship-based
model takes the relationship between leader and follower as the
starting point for research and theory building. Issues of concern
are reciprocal influence and the development and maintenance of
effective relationships (e.g. Bryman, 1992; Den Hartog &
Koopman, 2001; Graen & Scandura, 1987, p. 167).

Diversity and Inclusion

Diversity has become a topical research theme in the recent past.
Initially, it was dominated by a focus on the 'problems'

associated with diversity, such as discrimination, bias, affirmative action and tokenism (Shore et al., 2009, 2011). Nevertheless, this research area has and continues to spawn numerous significant and insightful body of knowledge through empirical research undertakings (Jackson & Joshi, 2011). Interestingly, as the diversity field of study continues to evolve, researchers have adaptively poised themselves and focused on ways in which diversity may enhance work processes and organizational mechanisms that promote the potential value in diversity (Gonzalez & DeNisi, 2009; Homan et al., 2008; Shore et al., 2011). As set forth by Cox (1991) and his views on the multicultural organization, there exists a strong measure of consistency with scholars and their bid in researching ways to incorporate and integrate diverse individuals in organizations (Thomas & Ely, 1996). One of such emerging research efforts is directed towards creating work environments where people of diverse backgrounds feel included in social and organizational settings (Bilimoria, Joy, & Liang, 2008; Roberson, 2006; Shore et al., 2011).

According to Roberson (2006), the concept of inclusion has been nascent in the organizational literature for the past decade, with comparable avenues of research occurring earlier in areas such as social work and social psychology. However, while this concept has recently gained mounting recognition, as yet, inclusion remains a fairly new concept without consensus on the nature of this construct or its theoretical underpinnings. This crucial lack of consensus hampers the utility of inclusion, both theoretically and practically (Shore et al., 2011, p. 1263).

As earlier indicated, research on diversity and its extensions has concentrated on understanding both positive and negative outcomes associated with difference (Shore et al., 2009). However, according to Cottrill, Lopez, and Hoffman (2014), concepts of diversity and inclusion are fundamentally distinct but interconnected (p. 275). They posit that while definitions of diversity focus on demographic make-up of groups and organizations, the definitions of inclusion underscore systematic participation and moving beyond appreciating diversity towards leveraging and integrating diversity into everyday work life (Roberson, 2006; Stevens, Plaut, & Sanchez-Burks, 2008). Additionally, some scholars opined that the concepts of diversity and inclusion are rooted in social justice, which seeks to eliminate oppressive marginalization by creating systems in which all people can participate and thus experience equality and equity in regard to distribution of organizational resources (Cottrill et al., 2014; Plummer, 2003).

In the recent past, several scholars, through research, have accentuated the critical importance of leadership in diversity and inclusion (e.g. Cox, 2001; Podsiadlowski, Gröschke, Kogler, Springer, & van der Zee, 2013). They contend that leaders of diverse and inclusive organizations must, as a matter of fact, exemplify a welcoming comfort with diversity, ensure its broad utility and application, create opportunities for dialogue about and across various divides, as well as, demonstrate strong authenticity in driving effective leadership (Cottrill et al., 2014; Wasserman, Gallegos, & Ferdman, 2007).

Thematically, organizational research literature has defined diversity in several ways. Largely, it focuses on the composition of work groups through the lens of (1) distinguishing factors that set aside individuals from one another (Kreitz, 2008), (2) observable individualities such as gender, race, ethnicity and age or (3) non-observable elemental distinctives such as education or socio-economic status (Milliken & Martins, 1996; Roberson, 2006). Resultantly, Thomas and Ely (1996) describe diversity as 'the varied perspectives and approaches to work that members of different identity groups bring' (p. 80). Overall, diversity has its direct implications on individual, group and organizational behaviour and performance (Cottrill et al., 2014, p. 277).

INCLUSION FRAMEWORK

In their work, *Inclusion and diversity in work groups*, Shore et al. (2011) defined inclusion as 'the degree to which an employee perceives that he or she is an esteemed member of the work group through experiencing treatment that satisfies his or her needs for belongingness and uniqueness' (p. 1265). The scholars contended that even though the themes of belongingness and uniqueness were apparent in the diversity and inclusion literature, existent research had not focused on the need to balancing them in order to foster inclusion (p. 1265).

Thus, the authors advanced a framework to support their definition of inclusion. The framework proposes that uniqueness and belongingness work together to produce feelings of inclusion in people. They also suggested that that uniqueness provides opportunities for improved group dynamics and performance when a unique individual is an accepted member of the group and the group values the particular unique characteristic (p. 1265);

thus indicating that both aspects can occur simultaneously. For instance, minority members (who are unique) with developed networks (and thus a sense of belongingness) report a high level of career optimism (Friedman, Kane, & Cornfield, 1998; Shore et al., 2011).

A combination of other facets of the framework, as expressed in Figure 1, creates the descriptive results of Assimilation, Differentiation and Exclusion. For example, at polar end of the spectrum is the low-belongingness/low-uniqueness combination labelled exclusion. The authors also proposed that this typified a situation where the individual is ill-treated as an organizational outsider with unique value in the work group, as opposed to other employees or groups who are considered insiders. Some scholars argue that when the need for belongingness is frustrated, there will exist harmful cognitive, emotional, behavioural and health outcomes (Baumeister, DeWall, Ciarocco, & Twenge, 2005; Blackhart, Nelson, Knowles, & Baumeister, 2009; DeWall, Maner, & Rouby, 2009; Shore et al., 2011).

INCLUSIVE LEADERSHIP

Broadly speaking, diversity, while being the multidimensional admixture of people, attributes, perspectives and input, inclusion is the systematic means of making the resulting admixture work homogenously. IL, on the other hand, is the capability needed in managing the diverse perspectives and leading out the desired effective outcomes.

IL means not just accepting, but actively seeking out diverse viewpoints and making sure everyone on your team feels their voice is heard. It means not just paying lip service to concepts like equality and engagement, but actually implementing them and believing in them. Inclusive leaders ask people what they think, stop to listen to the answers and actively engage through positive participative implementation.

Hollander (2008) declared that IL is essentially about relationships that can accomplish significant objectives for mutual benefit between leaders and followers. This leadership attainment or achievement level entails 'doing things with people, rather than to people', which is the core and essence of inclusion. Additionally, improving decision making and achieving desired ends are part of its goals and objectives, without the sole reliance on just one person's capabilities alone. Hollander (2008) suggested that IL also ensures a climate that installs fairness of input and output to all participants, while respecting and promoting competition and cooperation as part of the participative process (p. 3).

Hollander (2008) also emphasized that IL can find expression in political circles, where its influence is significantly centred on the 'consent of the governed' and taking responsibility, as well as being accountable to them. Here, a greater degree of leader-centric notions of leadership continue to stress and highlight traditional leader qualities such as character and charisma, which in themselves have limited effects by neglecting the essential relationship with followers (p. 3).

It is to be understood that an important objective of IL is to demonstrate how followers can be actively included in leadership, with a role in an effective mutual process. Nonetheless, the primary goal of IL is to positively enhance the understanding and practice of effective leadership. It is also important to note that leaders commonly possess greater initiative. However, followers are critical for success, as they too can become leaders in the long term (Hollander, 2008). The author also stresses on the notion that leadership, at all levels, benefits from active followers, in a unity, including 'upward influence' on a two-way, rather than a one-way street (Hollander, 1992, 1992, 2004).

Fundamentally, this two-way operation of leadership and followership is founded on the four Rs of IL that are vital to successful practice, namely: Respect, Recognition, Responsiveness and Responsibility, both ways (Hollander, 2008). This suggests that a leader's vision, or cognitive acumen, alone will not suffice. According to Byrne, Symonds, and Silver (1991), this phenomenon is called 'CEO Disease' due to shortcomings associated with power and insularity observed oftentimes in leadership that is less inclusive.

Further, Mor Barak's (2005, 2011) inclusion model categorizes the leader as a key factor in influencing the employee or follower experience of inclusion. Correspondingly, Shore et al.'s (2011) theoretical framework of inclusion classifies leader philosophy, values, strategies, decisions and practices as antecedents of perceived work group inclusion. Overall, leadership commitment to diversity is important in diversity management (Gavino, Eber, & Bell, 2010; Podsiadlowski et al., 2013) and inclusive workplaces (Roberson, 2006). Additionally, in order to create a culture of inclusion, some authors suggest that leaders must view and treat others as unique and different, engage individuals and groups in genuine dialogue, model appropriate behaviours and actively address resistance to diversity efforts (Cottrill et al. 2014; Wasserman et al., 2007, p. 277).

INCLUSIVE LEADERSHIP COMPETENCIES

McClelland (1973) defines leadership competency as 'a set of underlying characteristics that an individual or team possesses which have been demonstrated to predict superior or effective performance in a job' (Mendenhall, Osland, Bird, Oddou, & Maznevski, 2008, p. 64). The evolution from exclusion to IL requires leaders with global mindsets and skill sets. These global analytical skills are essential part of a global mindset that is able to use global logic for understanding the global dimensions of customers, standards, industry, competition, environmental challenges, and differences in leadership practices (Jeannet, 2000).

Jokinen (2005) defined global leadership competency as: [A set of] universal qualities that enable individuals to perform their job outside their own national, as well as, organizational culture no matter what their educational or ethnic background is, what functional area their job description represents, or what organization they come from (p. 200).

Fundamentally, IL is a team process. According to Kouzes and Posner (2012), 'Collaboration is a critical competency for achieving and sustaining high performance. As organizations become increasingly diverse, collaborative skills are essential to navigating conflicting interests and natural tensions that arise' (p. 218).

Global Mindset

Jeannet (2000) considers global mindset as a 'state of mind that is able to understand a business, industry, or particular market on a global basis' (p. 46). In Dalton et al.'s (2002) work, a global mindset is measured by an assessment of a series of cross-cultural skills (mastering foreign languages) and behaviours (extensive international travel and global assignments). The authors argued that a global mindset can lead to superior overall firm's performance. Calori, Johnson, and Sarmin (1994) refer to global mindset as a 'cognitive structure or mental map that allows the leader to understand the complexity of the firm's global environment' (p. 68). Therefore, the global mindset is a necessity for global leadership and an essential competency that aids in advancing them to achieve competitiveness in the current dynamic business environment (Konyu-Fogel, 2011).

Self-Awareness

Stein and Book (2011) asserted, 'Emotional self-awareness is crucial for success, whatever our role' (p. 63). Campbell (2002), in support contended that, 'Self-awareness of one's leadership style is an essential first step in identifying key strengths, targeting areas for improvement, and creating a successful action plan for development'. (p. 92). According to Mavrinac (2005), effective leadership development starts with self, specifically self-awareness. The author identified this self-awareness process as crucial success factor achieved through reflection and insight that will lead to development and change.

Mavrinac (2005) submitted that reflecting is a key strategy to gaining insight and knowledge about patterns of behaviour, emotions and perceptions to determine their appropriateness in relation to the context or situation at hand (Mavrinac, 2006; Schon, 1987). Effective reflection can lead to intrinsic and extrinsic change through adopting new patterns of behaviour and discontinuing undesirable ones (Argyris, 1999). This entire process is essential in the process of leadership development (Mavrinac, 2005).

Empathy

According to Geller (2000) the term 'empathic leadership' embodies a leader who takes time to thoroughly understand the perspective of another person before giving advice or direction (Wan, 2012). Everding and Huffaker (1998) asserted that a significant benefit to greater empathic skill, from an organizational leadership perspective, is 'an increased ability for leaders to become aware of the similarities and differences in relationships and to acquire the capability to act on those differences appropriately' (Washington, 2004, p. 24). Empathy is an important element of emotional intelligence (Goleman, Boyatzis, & McKee, 2002). The scholars contended that leaders with higher emotional intelligence have deeper understanding, are more sensitive, and are more likely to have higher awareness about their employees' feelings.

Cultural Intelligence

According to Earley, Ang, and Tan (2006), cultural intelligence (CQ) encompasses not only cultural awareness or cultural sensitivity, but also an individual's capability for successful adaptation to new and unfamiliar cultural settings. Some authors hold that CQ is a person's capability to function effectively in settings characterized by cultural diversity (Ang et al., 2007; Van Dyne & Ang, 2005).

Earley and Peterson (2004) assert that CQ reflects one's capacity for adapting across cultures and for gathering, interpreting, and acting upon 'radically different' (p. 105) cultural cues to function effectively in another cultural setting or multicultural situation (Tan, 2004). According to Dean (2007), culturally intelligent persons can see the importance of building relationships that bridge the differences among various cultural perspectives.

Similarly, development in CQ equips leaders with a better understanding of cultural difference and the reasons for valuing cultural distinctives (Earley & Ang, 2003; Earley & Mosakowski, 2004; Earley et al., 2006). Thus, CQ affords major organizational benefits as a tool for understanding, identifying, and developing global leadership (Alon & Higgins, 2005; Earley & Mosakowski, 2000, 2004; Earley et al., 2006). Organizations can thus benefit significantly by embracing CQ as a part of their global leadership selection and development programs (Alon & Higgins, 2005; Earley & Peterson, 2004; Earley et al., 2006).

Janssens and Brett (2006) declared that the principles of CQ can also guide leaders in the process of building well-performing global teams. Other researchers posit that CQ is important because it provides a useful means of evaluating and developing intercultural competency at all levels of an organization (Earley & Ang, 2003; Earley et al., 2006; Van Dyne & Ang, 2005) and enabling cross-cultural relationships and extensive team building and teamwork dynamics.

Collaborative Teamwork

Inclusive leaders are successful at building relationships at varied levels. They understand that 'Paying attention, personalizing recognition, and creatively and actively appreciating others increase their trust in you. This kind of relationship is even more critical as work forces are becoming increasingly global and diverse' (Kouzes & Posner, 2012, p. 288). Researchers proposed that an important incentive for creating and developing multicultural teams is that they possess an enormous potential wealth of resources from which to create innovative approaches to complex challenges and to provide a broad range of ways to implement solutions (e.g. Distefano & Maznevski, 2000; Janssens & Brett, 2006). Another significant motivation for expanding the use of global teams is the recognition that the creative value afforded by high-performing global teams is indispensable (Distefano & Maznevski, 2000). Janssens and Brett (2006) declared that, the quality of a global team's decisions is closely related to the degree to which the team utilizes the members' unique perspectives in the team tasks of information extraction and decision making.

INCLUSIVE LEADERSHIP BENEFITS AND OUTCOMES

Salib (2014) categorized IL into two broad outcomes — servant leadership outcomes and inclusion outcomes.

Servant Leadership Outcomes

Salib (2014) contends that organizational and team citizenship is considered an extra role, helping behaviour that positively affects the workplace (p. 13). The author maintains that although these behaviours are not the main job or task, they support overall organizational/team functioning. Several studies suggest that servant leadership positively influences employee engagement in citizenship behaviours (Ebener & O'Connell, 2010; Ehrhart, 2004; J. Hu & Liden, 2011; Liden, Wayne, Zhao, & Henderson, 2008; Walumbwa, Hartnell, & Oke, 2010).

Inclusion Outcomes

As discussed earlier, the theory of inclusion predicted that both creativity and citizenship are consequences of inclusion (Shore et al., 2011). According to Salib (2014), evidence of inclusion, and the proposed model of inclusion, increasing creativity and citizenship behaviours was present in organizational research literature. By the same token, Carmeli, Reiter-Palmon, and Ziv (2010) also found that IL positively impacted self-reported creativity in the workplace.

According to Cottrill et al. (2014, p. 278), some perspectives underscore the information-processing and problem-solving benefits of heterogeneous groups (Mannix & Neale, 2005; Williams & O'Reilly, 1998) and argue that diverse organizations offer the potential for greater creativity, innovation, organizational adaptability, recruitment and retention of better employees and enhanced profit and corporate image (Acquavita, Pittman, Gibbons, & Castellanos-Brown, 2009; Holvino, Ferdman, & Merrill-Sands, 2004; Phillips, Kim-Jun, & Shim, 2011).

Conversely, theoretical paradigms such as similarity-attraction theory (Newcomb, 1961) self-categorization (Turner, 1985), suggest negative implications for diverse organizations, such as personnel issues and financial costs due to harassment and discrimination, lower commitment, greater turnover and inhibited decision making and change processes (Cottrill et al., 2014; Cox, 2001; Stevens et al., 2008, p. 278).

Organizational Culture and Change

Some researchers assume that change in organizational culture occurs by means of interventions at three levels: individual, group/organizational, or societal. While it is unclear which level of intervention is most effective at producing organizational change under a given set of conditions (Dansereau & Alutto, 1990), Burke (2002) concluded that change efforts are best directed at the systemic, rather than at the individual, level. This is because 'the objective for (organizational) change is systemic; that is, some aspect of the (organizational) system is pinpointed for change' (p. 50). Therefore, the appropriate level for examining culture's role in organizational change is likely at the organizational level as well (Wildenberg, 2006).

According to Lijewski (2013), change is defined as moving from an existing state to an altered or different state. Hoyte and Greenwood (2006) defined organizational change as 'a transformation which moves an organization from an existing condition to a future state that represents a targeted strategic ideal' (p. 92). A chief component of the internal structure is the organization's human capital. As Ian Smith (2005) stated, 'The people in the organizations can be either the key to achieving effective change, or the biggest obstacles to success' (p. 411). Therefore, resulting organizational change is a functional transformation of both the internal business structure and its human capital (Lijewski, 2013).

One of culture's most evident roles in organizations lie in resisting change, with research (Campbell, 2002) demonstrating culture's ability to hold organizational values stable, despite extensive, changes in top organizational leadership and environmental pressure to change. According to Weick (2001), organizational culture advances as a force that holds together the organization or its subgroups and increases the tightness of the organizational coupling. Such organizational cohesion protects the organization from external environmental pressures, but at the same time makes the organization less adaptable to future environmental changes. Consequently, the organization's culture can be seen as a source of high organizational reliability, but also the source of resistance to change (Wildenberg, 2006). This is quite profound in organizations, especially, in accommodating inclusion that extends to a section of under-represented people groups, for example, the aging, disability and LGBT communities.

According to Hewlett and Yoshino (2006), LGBT inclusion is top of mind for the business community — and not just because it's the right thing to do. The Center for Talent Innovation's newest report, 'Out in the World: Securing LGBT Rights in the Global Marketplace', demonstrates that countering LGBT discrimination makes an organization competitive in three areas, namely: Fostering an LGBT-inclusive workplace helps a company (1) attract and retain top talent, (2) woo and win critical consumer segments and (3) innovate for underserved markets.

In confronting the complexities that surround such issues, it is critical to gain the unique insights on the specific barriers to inclusion which comprehensive diversity and inclusion strategies must address as a means and way forward.

Inclusive Leadership — Why Does It Matter?

The contemporary human and business ecosystems are rife with the constant pressure of change (Anderson, 2014). This presents a significant challenge for leaders of the 21st century in every framework of human activity and social exchange. It has become imperative that surviving and thriving under the immensity of such change pressures demand the skillset and competencies that transcend beyond the norm as was readily obtainable a few decades ago. Resultantly, today, personal and corporate successes require a whole new mindset, toolset and skillset.

Ryan (2000) submits that IL is an approach in which leaders include staff, community members, students and stakeholders in organizational processes to create socially just organizations through 'meaningful' participation — not simply by integrating marginalized groups for the sake of the satisfying the status quo. Another researcher suggests that IL is an interactive management of diversity and difference in organizations and social exchange groups (Rayner, 2009).

Essentially, IL matters because we increasingly live in a deeply interconnected, global environment and also research suggests that inclusive organizations with diverse workforce perform better financially than those without (Shore et al., 2011). As the organizations strive to become more inclusive, it is important that they focus on issues of inclusive climate, inclusive practices and IL.

References

Acquavita, S. P., Pittman, J., Gibbons, M., & Castellanos-Brown, K. (2009). Personal and organizational diversity factors' impact on social workers' job satisfaction: Results from a national internet-based survey. *Administration in Social Work, 33*(2), 151-1.

Alon, I., & Higgins, J. M. (2005). Global leadership success through emotional and cultural intelligences. *Business Horizons, 48,* 501–512.

Anderson, D. L. (2014). *Organization development: The process of leading organizational change* (3rd ed.). Thousand Oaks, CA: Sage.

Ang, S., Van Dyne, L., Koh, C., Ng, K. Y., Templer, K. J., Tay, C., & Chandrasekar, N. A. (2007). Cultural intelligence: Its measurement and effects on cultural judgment and decision making, cultural adaptation, and task performance. *Management and Organization Review, 3*(3), 335–371.

Argyris, C. (1999). *On organizational learning* (2nd ed.). Malden, MA: Blackwell.

Bass, B. M. (1990). *Bass and Stodgill's handbook of leadership.* New York, NY: Free Press.

Baumeister, R. F., DeWall, C. N., Ciarocco, N. J., & Twenge, J. M. (2005). Social exclusion impairs self-regulation. *Journal of Personality and Social Psychology, 88,* 589–604.

Bilimoria, D., Joy, S., & Liang, X. (2008). Breaking barriers and creating inclusiveness: Lessons of organizational transformation to advance women faculty in academic science and engineering. *Human Resource Management, 47,* 423–441.

Billett, S. (2006). *Work, change, and workers.* Dordrecht, The Netherlands: Springer.

Bishop, P. W., & Mahoney, H. (2009). Improving the social capital of students in high-poverty schools: What will it take? In M. S. Khine & I. M. Saleh (Eds.), *Transformative leadership and educational excellence: Learning organizations in the information age* (pp. 309–331). Rotterdam, NL: Sense Publishers.

Blackhart, G. C., Nelson, B. C., Knowles, M. L., & Baumeister, R. F. (2009). Rejection elicits emotional reactions but neither causes immediate distress nor lowers self-esteem: A meta-analytic review of 192 studies on social exclusion. *Personality and Social Psychology Review, 13,* 269–309.

Bolman, L. G., & Deal, T. E. (2008). *Reframing organizations: Artistry, choice, and leadership* (4th ed.). San Francisco, CA: Jossey-Bass.

Boyce, K. (2006). Using a comprehensive leadership framework as a scholarship and teaching tool. *Journal of Leadership Education, 5*(2), 69–79.

Bryman, A. (1992). *Charisma and leadership in organizations.* London: Sage.

Burke, W. W. (2002). *Organization change: Theory and practice.* Thousand Oaks, CA: SAGE Publications.

Burns, J. M. (2003). *Transforming leadership.* New York, NY: Grove/Atlantic.

Byrne, J. A., Symonds, W. C., & Silver, J. F. (1991). CEO disease. *The training and development sourcebook,* 263. Retrieved from https://www.academia.edu/17794841/Analysis_of_Inclusive_Leadership

Calori, R., Johnson, G., & Sarmin, P. (1991). CEO's cognitive maps and the scope of the organization. *Strategic Management Journal, 15* (6), 437–457.

Campbell, D. (2002). *Campbell leadership descriptor: Facilitator's guide.* San Francisco, CA: Jossey-Bass/Pfeiffer.

Carmeli, A., Reiter-Palmon, R., & Ziv, E. (2010). Inclusive leadership and employee involvement in creative tasks in the workplace: The mediating role of psychological safety. *Creativity Research Journal, 22*(3), 250–260. doi:10.1080/10400419.2010.504654

Cottrill, L., Lopez, P. D., & Hoffman, C. C. (2014). How authentic leadership and inclusion benefit organizations. *Equality, Diversity and Inclusion: An International Journal, 33*(3), 275–292. Retrieved from http://www.eeotrust.org.nz/content/docs/information/research/authentic%20leadership%202014%20issue%203.pdf

Cox, T. Jr. (2001). *Creating the multicultural organization: A strategy for capturing the power of diversity.* San Francisco, CA: Duarte-Carmen.

Cox, T. H. (1991). The multicultural organization. *Academy of Management Executive, 5,* 34–47.

Dalton, M., Ernst, C., Deal, J., & Leslie, J. (2002). *Success for the new global manager: What you need to know to work across distances, countries, and cultures.* San Francisco, CA: Jossey-Bass and the Center for Creative Leadership.

Dansereau, F., & Alutto, J. (1990). Levels of analysis issues in climate and culture research. In B. Schneider (Ed.), *Organizational climate and culture* (pp. 193–236). San Francisco, CA: Jossey-Bass.

Dean, B. P. (2007). *Cultural intelligence in global leadership: A model for developing culturally and nationally diverse teams* (Order No. 3292256). Available from ProQuest Dissertations & Theses Global. Retrieved from http://search.proquest.com/pqdtglobal/docview/304713848/74C94F272B9041ACPQ/1?accountid=165104

Den Hartog, D. N., & Koopman, P. (2001). *Leadership in Organizations. Handbook of Industrial, Work & Organizational Psychology: Volume 2.* Sage Publications. Retrieved from http://www.libvolume7.xyz/psychology/bsc/semester5/foundationsoforganizationalbehavior/leadershipinorganization/leadershipinorganizationnotes2.pdf

Den Hartog, D. N., Koopman, P. L., Thierry, Hk., Wilderom, C. P. M., Maczynski, J., & Jarmuz, S. (1997). Dutch and Polish perceptions of leadership and national culture: The GLOBE project. *European Journal of Work and Organizational Psychology, 6*(4), 389–415.

DeWall, C. N., Maner, J. K., & Rouby, D. A. (2009). Social exclusion and early-stage interpersonal perception: Selective attention to signs of acceptance. *Journal of Personality and Social Psychology, 96,* 729–741.

Distefano, J. J., & Maznevski, M. L. (2000). Creating value with diverse teams in global management. *Organizational Dynamics, 29*(1), 45–63.

Drucker, P. F. (1993). *Post-capitalist society.* New York, NY: HarperCollins Publishers.

Earley, P. C., & Ang, S. (2003). *Cultural intelligence: Individual interactions across cultures.* Stanford, CA: Stanford Business Books.

Earley, P. C., Ang, S., & Tan, J. (2006). *CQ: Developing cultural intelligence at work.* Stanford, CA: Stanford Business Books.

Earley, P. C., & Mosakowski, E. (2000). Creating hybrid team cultures: An empirical test of transnational team functioning. *Academy of Management Journal, 43*(1), 26–49.

Earley, P. C., & Mosakowski, E. (2004). Cultural intelligence. *Harvard Business Review, 82*(10), 139–146.

Earley, P. C., & Peterson, R. S. (2004). The elusive chameleon: Cultural intelligence as a new approach to intercultural training for the global manager. *Academy of Management Learning and Education, 3*(1), 100–115.

Ebener, D. R., & O'Connell, D. J. (2010). How might servant leadership work? *Nonprofit Management and Leadership, 20*(3), 315–335. doi:10.1002/nml.256

Everding, H. E., & Huffaker, L. A. (1998). Educating adults for empathy: Implications of cognitive role taking and identity formation. *Religious Education, 93*(4), 413–431.

Friedman, R., Kane, M., & Cornfield, D. B. (1998). Social support and career optimism: Examining the effectiveness of network groups among Black managers. *Human Relations, 51*, 1155–1177.

Gavino, M. C., Eber, J. E., & Bell, D. (2010). Celebrating our diversity: Creating an inclusive climate in a US university. *Equality, Diversity and Inclusion, 29*(4), 395–405.

Geller, E. S. (2000). *Empathic leadership.* Retrieved from http://www.safetyperformance.com/pdf/Articles/2000/EmpathicLeadership.pdf

Goleman, D., Boyatzis, R. E., & McKee, A. (2002). *Primal leadership: Realizing the power of emotional intelligence.* Boston, MA: Harvard Business School Press.

Gonzalez, J. A., & DeNisi, A. S. (2009). Cross-level effects of demography and diversity climate on organizational attachment and firm effectiveness. *Journal of Organizational Behavior, 30*, 21–40.

Graen, G. B., & Scandura, T. (1987). Toward a psychology of dyadic organizing. *Research in Organizational Behaviour, 9*, 175–208.

Graen, G. B., & Uhl-Bien, M. (1995). Relationship-based approach to leadership: Development of leader-member exchange (LMX) theory of leadership over 25 years: Applying a multi-level multi-domain perspective. *Leadership Quarterly, 6*, 219–247.

Hernandez, M., Eberly, M. B., Avolio, B. J., & Johnson, M. D. (2011). The loci and mechanisms of leadership: Exploring a more comprehensive view of leadership theory. *The Leadership Quarterly, 22*, 1165–1185.

Hewlett, S. A., & Yoshino, K. (2006). LGBT-Inclusive Companies Are Better at 3 Big Things. *Harvard Business Review.* Retrieved from https://hbr.org/2016/02/lgbt-inclusive-companies-are-better-at-3-big-things

Hollander, E. P. (1992a). Leadership, followership, self, and others. *Leadership Quarterly, 3*(1), 43–54.

Hollander, E. P. (1992b). The essential interdependence of leadership and followership. *Current Directions in Psychological Science, 1,* 71–75.

Hollander, E. P. (2004). Idiosyncrasy credit; upward influence. In G. R. Goethals, G. J. Sorenson, & J. M. Burns (Eds.), *Encyclopedia of leadership* (pp. 695–700; 1605-1609). Great Barrington, MA: Berkshire/SAGE.

Hollander, E. P. (2008). *Inclusive leadership: The essential leader-follower relationship.* New York, NY: Routledge.

Holvino, E., Ferdman, B. M., & Merrill-Sands, D. (2004). Creating and sustaining diversity and inclusion in organizations: Strategies and approaches. In M. S. Stockdale & F. J. Crosby (Eds.), *The psychology and management of workplace diversity* (pp. 245–276). Malden, MA: Blackwell Publishing.

Homan, A. C., Hollenbeck, J. R., Humphrey, S. E., van Knippenberg, D., Ilgen, D. R., & Van Kleef, G. A. (2008). Facing differences with an open mind: Openness to experience, salience of intragroup differences, and performance of diverse work groups. *Academy of Management Journal, 51,* 1204–1222.

Hoyte, D. S., & Greenwood, R. A. (2006). Journey to the north face: A guide to business transformation. *Academy of Strategic Management Journal, 6,* 91–104.

Hu, J., & Liden, R. C. (2011). Antecedents of team potency and team effectiveness: An examination of goal and process clarity and servant leadership. *Journal of Applied Psychology, 96*(4), 851–862. doi:10.1037/a0022465

Jackson, S. E., & Joshi, A. (2011). Work team diversity. In S. Zedeck (Ed.), *APA handbook of industrial and organizational psychology: Vol. 1. Building the organization* (pp. 651–686). Washington, DC: American Psychological Association.

Janssens, M., & Brett, J. M. (2006). Cultural intelligence in global teams: A fusion model of collaboration. *Group & Organization Management, 31*(1), 124–153.

Jeannet, J. (2000). *Managing with a global mindset.* London: Pearson Education.

Jokinen, T. (2005). Global leadership competencies: A review and discussion. *Journal of European Industrial Training, 29* (2/3), 199–216.

Kellerman, B. (1984). *Leadership: Multidisciplinary approaches.* Englewood Cliffs, NJ: Prentice Hall.

Konyu-Fogel, G. (2011). *Exploring the effect of global mindset on leadership behavior: An empirical study of business leaders in global organizations* (Order No. 3444218). Available from ProQuest Dissertations & Theses Global. (857921579). Retrieved from http://search.proquest.com/docview/857921579?accountid=165104

Kouzes, J. M., & Posner, B. Z. (1995). *The leadership challenge: How to keep getting extraordinary things done in organizations.* San Francisco, CA: Jossey-Bass.

Kouzes, J. M., & Posner, B. Z. (2012). *The leadership challenge* (5th ed.). San Francisco, CA: Jossey-Bass.

Kreitz, P. A. (2008). Best practices for managing organizational diversity. *The Journal of Academic Librarianship, 34*(2), 101–120.

Langdon, D. S., McMenamin, T. M., & Krolik, T. J. (2002). Labor market in 2001: Economy enters a recession. *Monthly Labor Review, 125*(2), 3–33.

Liden, R. C., Wayne, S. J., Zhao, H., & Henderson, D. (2008). Servant leadership: Development of a multidimensional measure and multi-level assessment. *The Leadership Quarterly, 19*(2), 161–177. doi:10.1016/j.leaqua.2008.01.006

Lijewski, J. S. (2013). *Exploring implementation of organizational change toward environmental sustainability* (Order No. 3557291). Available from ProQuest Dissertations & Theses Global. (1335138398). Retrieved from http://search.proquest.com/docview/1335138398?accountid=165104

Lugg, C. A., & Shoho, A. R. (2006). Dare public school administrators build a new social order?: Social justice and the possibly perilous politics of educational leadership. *Journal of Educational Administration, 44*(3), 196–208.

MacLean, R. C. (2008). What is leadership and why is there leadership instead of none (Order No. 3338095). Available from ProQuest Dissertations & Theses Global (304381590). Retrieved from https://search.proquest.com/docview/304381590?accountid=165104

Mannix, E., & Neale, M. A. (2005). What differences make a difference? The promise and reality of diverse teams in organizations. *Psychological Science in the Public Interest, 6*, 31–55.

Mavrinac, M. A. (2005). Transformational leadership: Peer mentoring as a values-based learning process. *Portal: Libraries and the Academy, 5*(3), 391–404.

Mavrinac, M. A. (2006). *The dynamics of protecting self: Experiencing organizational change, a grounded theory.* (Unpublished doctoral dissertation), Fielding Graduate University, Santa Barbara, CA.

McClelland, D. C. (1973). Testing for competence rather than testing for "intelligence". *American Psychologist, 28*(1), 1–14.

McShane, S. L. (2004). *Canadian organizational behavior* (5th ed.). Toronto, ON: McGraw-Hill Ryerson.

Meindl, J. R. (1990). On leadership: An alternative to the conventional wisdom. *Research in Organizational Behavior, 12*, 159.

Mendenhall, M. E., Osland, J. S., Bird, A., Oddou, G., & Maznevski, M. (2008). *Global leadership: Research, practice and development.* Routledge Global Human Resource Management Series, New York: NY: Taylor & Francis, 15–17.

Milliken, F. J., & Martins, L. L. (1996). Searching for common threads: understanding the multiple effects of diversity in organizational groups. *The Academy of Management Review, 21*(2), 402–433.

Mor Barak, M. E. (2005). *Managing diversity: Toward a globally inclusive workplace.* Thousand Oaks, CA: Sage.

Mor Barak, M. E. (2011). *Managing diversity: Toward a globally inclusive workplace.* Thousand Oaks, CA: Sage Publications.

Newcomb, T. M. (1961). *The acquaintance process.* New York, NY: Holt, Rinehart, and Winston.

Northouse, P. G. (2001). *Leadership: Theory and practice* (2nd ed.). Thousand Oaks, CA: Sage Publications.

Northouse, P. G. (2007). *Leadership: Theory and practice* (4th ed.). Thousand Oaks, CA: Sage.

Parry, K. W., & Bryman, A. (2006). Leadership in organization. In S. T. Clegg, C. Harry, T. B. Lawrence, & W. R. Nord (Eds.), *The Sage handbook of organization studies* (pp. 447–468). London: Sage Publications.

Phillips, K. W., Kim-Jun, S. Y., & Shim, S. (2011). The value of diversity in organizations: A social psychology perspective. In D. De Cremer, R. van Dick, & J. K. Murnighan (Eds.), *Social psychology and organizations* (pp. 253–271). New York, NY: Routledge.

Plummer, D. L. (2003). Overview of the field of diversity management. In D. L. Plummer (Ed.), *Handbook of diversity management: Beyond awareness to competency based learning* (pp. 1–50). Lanham, MD: University Press of America Inc.

Podsiadlowski, A., Gröschke, D., Kogler, M., Springer, C., & van der Zee, K. (2013). Managing a culturally diverse workforce: Diversity perspectives in organizations. *International Journal of Intercultural Relations, 37*(2), 159–175.

Rauch, C. F., & Behling, O. (1984). Functionalism: Basis for an alternate approach to the study of leadership. In J. G. Hunt, D. M. Hosking, C. A. Schriesheim, & R. Stewart (Eds.), *Leaders and managers: International perspectives on managerial behavior and leadership*. Elmsford, NY: Pergamon Press.

Rayner, S. (2009). Educational diversity and learning leadership: a proposition, some principles and a model of inclusive leadership? *Educational Review, 61*(4), 433–447.

Roberson, Q. M. (2006). Disentangling the meanings of diversity and inclusion in organizations. *Group and Organization Management, 31*, 212–236.

Ryan, J. (2000). Inclusive leadership and social justice. *Leadership and Policy in Schools, 5*(3), 3–17.

Salib, E. R. (2014). *A model of inclusion and inclusive leadership in the U.S.* (Order No. 3643345). Available from ProQuest Dissertations & Theses Global. (1617960042). Retrieved from http://search.proquest.com/docview/1617960042?accountid=165104

Schon, D. A. (1987). *Educating the reflective practitioner*. San Francisco, CA: Jossey-Bass.

Shore, L. M., Chung, B., Dean, M. A., Ehrhart, K. H., Jung, D., Randel, A., & Singh, G. (2009). Diversity and inclusiveness: Where are we now and where are we going? *Human Resource Management Review, 19*, 117–133.

Shore, L. M., Randel, A. M., Chung, B. M., Dean, M. A., Ehrhart, K. H., & Singh, G. (2011). Inclusion and diversity in work groups: A review and model for future research. *Journal of Management, 34*(4), 1262–1289.

Smith, I. (2005). Achieving readiness for organizational change. *Library Management, 26*(6), 408–412.

Stein, S. J., & Book, H. E. (2011). *The EQ edge: Emotional intelligence and your success* (3rd ed.). Mississauga, ON: Jossey-Bass, ISBN: 978-0-470-68161-9.

Stevens, F. G., Plaut, V. C., & Sanchez-Burks, J. (2008). Unlocking the benefits of diversity: All-inclusive multiculturalism and positive organizational change. *Journal of Applied Behavioral Science, 44*(1), 116–133.

St-Hilaire, F. (2008). Leadership theories: Towards a relational model, Collegerisquespesychosociaux-travail.fr. Retrieved from: http://www.college-risquespsychosociauxtravail.fr/site/exam_retrospectif_final_fsth.pdf

Stogdill, R. M. (1981). *Stogdill's handbook of leadership: A survey of theory and research.* New York, NY: Free Press.

Tan, J. (2004). Cultural intelligence and the global economy. *Leadership in Action, 24*(5), 19–21.

Thomas, D. A., & Ely, R. D. (1996). Making differences matter: A new paradigm for managing diversity. *Harvard Business Review, 74*(5), 79–90.

Turner, J. (1985). Social categorization and the self concept: A social cognitive theory of group behavior. In T. Postmes & N. R. Branscombe (Eds.), *Rediscovering social identity* (pp. 243–272). New York, NY: Psychology Press.

Van Dyne, L., & Ang, S. (2005, June 30). *Cultural intelligence: An essential capability for individuals in contemporary organizations.* Retrieved from http://globaledge.msu.edu/KnowledgeRoom/FeaturedInsights/Cultural%20Intelligence.pdf

Walumbwa, F. O., Hartnell, C. A., & Oke, A. (2010). Servant leadership, procedural justice climate, service climate, employee attitudes, and organizational citizenship behavior: A cross-level investigation. *Journal of Applied Psychology, 95*(3), 517–529. doi:10.1037/a0018867

Wan, A. R. (2012). *A study to determine the impact of empathy on leadership effectiveness among business leaders in the united states and Malaysia* (Order No. 3547703). Available from ProQuest Dissertations & Theses Global. (1277649988). Retrieved from http://search.proquest.com/docview/1277649988?accountid=165104

Washington, G. G. (2004). *An analysis of the impact of empathy on propensity to lead* (Order No. 3129927). Available from ProQuest Dissertations & Theses Global. (305045488). Retrieved from http://search.proquest.com/docview/305045488?accountid=165104

Wasserman, I. C., Gallegos, P. V., & Ferdman, B. M. (2007). Dancing with resistance: Leadership challenges in fostering a culture of inclusion. In K. M. Thomas (Ed.), *Diversity resistance in organizations* (pp. 175–199). New York, NY: Taylor & Francis Group, LLC.

Weick, K. E. (2001). *Making sense of the organization.* Malden, MA: Blackwell Publishers, Inc.

Wildenberg, G. J. (2006). *The culturally aligned change message: How knowledge of organizational culture can improve support for organizational change* (Order No. 3274581). Available from ProQuest Dissertations & Theses Global. (304908776). Retrieved from http://search.proquest.com/docview/304908776?accountid=165104

Williams, K., & O'Reilly, C. (1998). The complexity of diversity: A review of forty years of research. In B. Staw & R. Sutton (Eds.), *Research in organizational behavior* (Vol. 21, pp. 77–140). Greenwich, CT: JAI Press.

Wong, P. T. P. (2002). Creating a positive, meaningful work place: New challenges in management and leadership. In B. Pattanayak & V. Gupta (Eds.), *Creating performing organizations.* New Delhi, India: Sage.

Wong, P. T. P. (2007). Best practices in servant leadership. *Servant Leadership Research Roundtable*, 7, 1–15. Retrieved from: http://www.regent.edu/acad/global/publications/sl_proceedings/2007/wong-davey.pdf

Yammarino, F. J., & Bass, B. M. (1991). Person and situation views of leadership: A multiple levels of analysis approach. *Leadership Quarterly*, 2, 121–139.

Yukl, G. (1994). *Leadership in organizations* (3rd ed.). Englewood Cliffs, NJ: Prentice Hall.

Yukl, G. (1998). *Leadership in organizations* (4th ed.). Englewood Cliffs, NJ: Prentice-Hall.

2

What's in a Word? Troubling and Reconstructing the Discourse of Inclusion

Leigh E. Fine

Keywords: Inclusion; leadership; inclusive leadership; discourse; leadership discourse

---

When thinking about teaching, writing about, or living the principles of inclusive leadership, I found myself engaged in the intellectual exercise of defining the concept frequently enough to make me uncomfortable. Inclusive leadership is a phrase that connotes a particular form of the exercise of leadership, one that I — nor others — have interrogated closely. This revelation became more disturbing as I thought about the course I teach on multicultural leadership: the phrase *inclusive leadership* serves as an intellectual cornerstone for its learning objectives. If I hope that my students grow in their capability to practice inclusive leadership, just what does that mean? What are the implications if I, as the instructor and the positional authority in the room, am unsure what that means? Just what is inclusion, and how does it relate to the practice of leadership?

Foucault uses the term *discourse* to describe the "authorized vocabulary" (1978, p. 17) that surrounds a concept. In my estimation, the field has done a respectable job contesting the discourse surrounding leadership: examining alternate definitions, expanding the definition of who is able to become a leader, and highlighting different leadership contexts are now the standard in the field (Peck & Dickinson, 2009; Rumens, 2016). The fact that few have explored the discourse of *inclusive* leadership is problematic, particularly because the field could benefit immensely from a critical interrogation thereof — and has already engaged in similar work of troubling the discourse of leadership generally.

Words matter, as language is one way in which discourse exerts social power (Butler, 2005), and there is indeed a language surrounding the word inclusion that is present in the field of leadership studies. Whenever I ask my students to define inclusion, there is no shortage of efforts to engage in the task: most definitions encompass variations of "making sure everyone has a place at the table," "listening to everyone's opinion," "making sure all types of people are represented," and "not leaping to judgments." Others support my students' narratives: inclusion is a term with a strong aura of discourse that generally refers to permitting equal access to resources and a general recognition of rights (Oxoby, 2009; Phelan, 2001).

Few that study and practice leadership would find such aims objectionable; therefore, if it appears we're all on the same linguistic page, what's the problem with using the phrase *inclusive leadership*? Writing on the discourse surrounding the concept of inclusion, Choo and Ferree (2010) point out that "inclusion sometimes fetishizes the study of 'difference' without necessarily giving sufficient attention to its relation to unmarked categories, especially to how the more powerful are defined as normative standards" (p. 133). That is to say, although the discourse of inclusion supports a generalized form of human dignity, *it also has the potential to absorb and erase the complex power relations that constitute its very necessity as a leadership concept.* If the goal is to bring everyone to the proverbial table, as my students offer, is inclusive leadership doing enough to ask whose table at which we hope to convene, why we're not all at that table in the first place, or what keeps some of us from joining that table even if we would like to do so?

Queer and critical race theorists illuminate this tension: the act of inclusion is one that can be assimilationist, erasing and subsuming difference instead of interrogating and truly celebrating it. If we use the phrase *inclusive leadership* to mean access and tacit recognition, but not disruption and redefinition, does it simply reinforce the power status quo and foreclose opportunities for diverse people to access the power and potential of leadership?

I write this piece with two aims. The first is to problematize and trouble the concept of inclusion (Ford, Harding, & Learmonth, 2008). This volume, much like my institution and my course, uses the phrase *inclusive leadership* to deploy a set of generally progressive values. However, a critical interrogation of this term can illuminate the theoretical and practical limitations of relying on this tacit understanding. I draw upon literature related to discourse, queer theory, race, and tokenism to support the argument that the term inclusion in its current discursive form is problematic.

In so doing, I support my second aim: the reconstruction of inclusion (discourse) as a term that more accurately encapsulates its progressive goals while leaving increased space for a broader range of intelligible subjects-as-leaders. Although the current discourse surrounding the phrase *inclusive leadership* may be assimilationist if left uninterrogated, I believe it is not beyond redemption. Engaging in a critical re-envisioning of the phrase may still render it useful. I use Alvesson and Spicer's (2012) critical leadership approach to provide a path forward for this new inclusive leadership that simultaneously honors and transcends multiple social identities in its practice.

Queering the Discourse of Inclusion

What is fascinating about the definitions of inclusion my students develop is that they view it as a largely individually contingent process instead of nesting it in more complex social relations. Left unsaid in their definitions is the subject, *I: I* make sure everyone is included, *I* make sure everyone has a place at the table. The ability to recognize others, to allow them to be intelligible, is power indeed. Butler (2005) troubles this idea through exploring the limits of self-narration. Often inclusive leadership projects center on listening to the stories of diverse others in an attempt to build empathy and understanding (Fine, 2015; Scharmer,

2009). Butler, though, discusses the limits of language and discourse in creating new realities. For instance, the phrase, "I include you," may seem to be a simple statement of togetherness and coalition building that is tautologically inclusive. Butler would ask, though: who is the "I" that is doing the including? The fact that "I" have the power or social authority to "include" you indicates that a reversal of this script — "You include me" — may be unimaginable. And if the reverse is unimaginable, what does that mean for the role power will play in moderating the leadership relationship "you" and "I" hope to create through our interaction?

Butler illustrates one way in which a queering leadership approach can articulate limitations to our contemporary inclusive leadership discourse. The project of queering leadership refers to "look[ing] at this thing called leadership as if it were odd or queer. As soon as we start thinking about what we regard as normal we find how peculiar the 'normal' is" (Ford et al., 2008, p. 92). The act of queering leadership helps to articulate why relying on discourse to guide collective action can propagate a status quo understanding of leadership that leaves some new, exciting, beneficial realities unrealized or even unspeakable. Engaging in a queering of leadership helps to articulate why a consensus definition of inclusion that erases structure is problematic, as it supports and neglects to interrogate a particular set of normative power relations.

In this continued spirit of questioning the reigning discourse of inclusion, it is worthwhile to define the word inclusion itself, then evaluate whether this definition is problematic. Exploring the dynamics of social inclusion, Oxoby (2009, p. 1136) describes how the term refers to both "access to rights and resources," but also "the presence of obstacles to social institutions without directly defining the rights or institutions in question." If this is a suitable working definition, it is notable that those that study inclusive leadership tend to focus on the first part of Oxoby's definition — access — and neglect to explore the obstacles to access that permeate social structure, much as my students tend to do. For instance, Bennett's (2004) model of ethnorelativism is used frequently in leadership to help stakeholders analyze their responses to cross-cultural encounters and the role one's own cultural identity plays in moderating them (Fine, 2015; Nevarez & Wood, 2010). However, like most psychosocial models, Bennett paints ethnorelativism as a linear, developmental process, with more enlightened attitudes farther along the spectrum of his model (Zafar, Sandhu, & Khan, 2013). This has the side effect of locating the power to include *on the individual*: if one simply develops the skills and awareness to engage with "other" cultures, then one has become an ethnorelative person. We know, though, that inclusion is not a solo process. The other is necessary to generate the social interaction needed to push one's own cultural boundaries (Butler, 2005).

This is further complicated by our predilection for looking at the phrase inclusive leadership as an adjective/noun pairing instead of as an adverb/verb pairing. That is, one way of queering the discourse around inclusive leadership is to examine it as a process rather than as a state of being. Some scholars are attempting to engage in this project with leadership. Peck and Dickinson (2009) describe how leadership is inherently performative. Drawing on constructionist and postmodern literature, the authors argue that the act of engaging in leadership draws on social scripts, roles, and even props that constrain our available repertoires for engaging in social change and incorporating diverse voices. Ford et al. (2008) point out that leadership discourse relies on an archetypal leader that discourse gives the power to render others' contributions as valuable within a group setting. This also distances the performance of inclusion from the social context in which it is nested, rendering inequality and privilege largely invisible.

We have reason to believe that inclusion is a more problematic term than we might think it to be: namely, because the discourse surrounding leadership is still propped up by an overriding definition of what leadership is, a dominant discourse surrounding who is allowed to enact leadership behaviors, and a persistent belief that leadership development is contingent on individual development. That is, the discourse surrounding the idea of inclusion is one that creates an end point — "I am inclusive," "I include you" — as well as a concrete means of getting there — "I have made progress," "I included you." Queering our mutual definition of inclusion can reveal limitations to this subject-based, structure-devoid assumed consensus of what inclusion is and how it can most effectively be practiced.

Race, Assimilationism, and Inclusion Discourse in Leadership

Audre Lorde was invited to speak at a humanities conference on the role of difference in constructing feminism, and used her time on the panel to excoriate the conference for relegating her — and the narratives of queer women, women of color, and queer women of color — to a token spot on a panel: "I stand here as a Black lesbian feminist, having been invited to comment within the only panel at this conference where the input of Black feminists and lesbians is represented" (1984/2007, p. 110). Were we to ask the conveners of the panel, I am sure they believed they were doing due diligence in "including" the voice of Black women (or, rather, a singular Black woman), recognizing that race also played a role in modern feminism. Lorde's point, though, is that if inclusion is thought of as simply providing access or indulging a single voice, that is not enough. Lorde took the audience to task for not living up to its ideals of engaging meaningfully and consistently with the populations the conference purported to embrace.

Few examples could illustrate the limits of inclusion discourse more than the exploration of the scholarship — or lack thereof — on race and leadership. In articulating how inclusive leadership conjures up an archetypal (read: cisgendered, heterosexual, male) leader who has the power to do the including, literature on race and its relationship to leadership, likewise, can point to the limits of constructing inclusive leadership. Kanter's (1977) work on tokenism has long been a standard in exploring how the presence of those from diverse social identities is insufficient to catalyze social change. As the discourse in American business began to shift and these organizations felt pressured to diversify their workforces, the token women and people of color discovered that their presence alone did little to challenge to pre-existing social norms that relegated them to secondary status.

Those who have studied the relationship between race and leadership indicate that this problem from the late 70s is still present for those who struggle with questions of leadership and diversity (Gooden, 2012). Ospina and Foldy (2009) explore why those who study leadership have been slow relative to other disciplines in bringing questions of race to bear in their scholarship. They note that many works that explore leadership either neglect to directly engage with issues of race or tend to adopt a color-blind approach that vaguely urges leaders to transcend racial differences. Such approaches, Ospina and Foldy argue, have the side effect of leaving leadership discourse in place without critically interrogating the very real effects of race within leadership relationships. Instead, the authors suggest an approach that "grappl[es] with the social reality of race/ethnicity" (Ospina & Foldy, 2009, p. 890) that overtly engages with the complexities of race as a potentially transformative construct. Instead of thinking of race to be something that must be overcome, inclusive leaders might think about how to welcome the ways in which racial differences can lead to new, exciting, change-based social realities.

A holistic analysis of the role race plays in the negotiation of leadership relationships cannot ignore the psychic energy needed to fully engage in the project of inclusion. Muñoz (1999) explores the phenomenon of disidentification: the process minority persons engage in as they decide which aspects of discourse they will adhere to, and which they — by choice or necessity — will contest. The existence of a dominant discourse surrounding leadership gives voice to the dilemma minority subjects face as they engage in leadership relationships. Because the dominant discourse upholds a particular form of leadership that is raced, classed, gendered, and sexualized, those that do not conform to such ideals often find they must choose to either comply with these unjust power structures or agitate — and, thus, risk — to create more expansive leadership realities. Instead of putting the burden of disidentification on those who are not intelligible according to contemporary leadership discourse, an inclusive leadership would find ways to make this a collective project to help everyone access the promise of leadership.

Our identities — including race, gender, and sexuality, among others — mutually constitute one another and affect our social interactions (Collins, 1993; Hames-García, 2011). The same is true for leadership. Bringing our full selves to bear in a truly inclusive leadership relationship means an acknowledgment that of these social and personal identities in governing how we experience, deploy, and respond to leadership, and that such differences are not inherently more useful or valid than another if all else is equal. If the predominant discourse surrounding inclusion stops short of providing full, critical, meaningful access to diverse others, then it has the potential to be tantamount to an "add Black people and stir" (Dreger, 2006) conceptualization of leadership relationships. (We could substitute many other social identities in the above quote — women, queer people, Muslims, etc. — and the argument that such discourse is problematic still stands.) Such conceptualizations are assimilationist (Hornsey & Hogg, 2000), setting up a discourse ideal that leadership as practiced by those in the dominant group is authentic, and that any deviation thereof is an imitation (Ford et al., 2008).

The Baby and the Bathwater of Inclusive Leadership

Clearly, there are limits to assuming that there exists a common, desirable definition of the phrase *inclusive leadership*. Calling oneself inclusive simultaneously places the implicit locus of power on oneself, denying the other the ability to be a leadership subjects themselves and overlooking the role of sociohistorical forces. It has the potential to be assimilationist, erasing the diversity that has the potential to trouble and enrich existing leadership discourse. How, then, can we begin to trouble this discourse, creating a new discourse that holds promise for a truly inclusive leadership accessible by a multitude of subjects?

This past fall, I attended a talk at my university given by Lourdes Ashley Hunter, a Black transwoman activist. Ms. Hunter was unapologetic, passionate, and incisive, sharing her story about her struggles engaging in political activism for transwomen of color. Following her talk, a student in the audience approached the microphone during the question and answer period. She thanked Ms. Hunter for sharing her story, acknowledging her vulnerability and her power. The student then noted that she has encountered no transgender people since coming to college, which made her feel like she was not doing her part to reach out to others and make them feel welcome. She asked Ms. Hunter how she could best include transgender people in her life.

Ms. Hunter, without missing a beat, said, "Well, first off, I don't believe in using the word 'inclusion.' I find that's a word that white people use to make themselves feel better."

Ms. Hunter's response gave me pause. To be sure, the student still cast herself as the active party in her question: what could *she do* to build coalitions with trans people. At the same time: does not such a question acknowledge the very real phenomenon of power that moderates our social interactions? Should not the onus of building such coalitions or convening such conversations be placed on those whose identities carry more social currency? Upon further reflection, I have come to realize that Ms. Hunter's response succinctly and powerfully encapsulated a tension in my own scholarship and teaching of inclusive leadership. Although I believe that inclusion as a term still remains a meaningful construct that indicates a desire to hear and be with others, it is not completely devoid of the power relations that continue to constitute our relations to one another that leave some at a disadvantage.

At the risk of falling prey to *argumentum ad temperantiam*, I believe the concept of inclusive leadership is not beyond hope. Alvesson and Spicer (2012) share a framework they call critical leadership studies to carefully explore both the limitations and strengths of particular approaches to understanding leadership. They suggest employing a "tactic of *progressive pragmatism.* This entails pragmatically, but critically, working with already accepted discourses... in the service of broadly emancipatory goals" (2012, p. 377, emphasis authors'). In other words, those who study leadership should be open to exploring alternative, troubling, disruptive interpretations, but can also feel free to acknowledge what pieces of discourse are functional or beneficial. Applied to the discourse surrounding inclusion, a critical approach would seek to identify what aspects of discourse serve ethically desirable aims, as well as what aspects could afford re-examination and contestation.

So what does inclusion under the current inclusion discourse regime get right? There is reason to believe that the phrase *inclusive leadership* represents noble ideals in its common usage (e.g., Fierke, Lui, Lepp, & Baldwin, 2014; Hollander, 2012; Komives, Wagner, & Associates, 2009). Underpinning this intent, I would argue, is a belief in pluralism and the value of listening (Scharmer, 2009; Wheatley, 2002). I would like to think that the field of leadership studies — at least, more so than many other fields of academic inquiry — displays a willingness to hear, entertain, and wrestle with unique stories, controversial narratives, and conflicting interpretations. Those who purport to be inclusive leaders articulate the desire to hear multiple and diverse voices, which is one way to start critical cross-cultural dialogues (Heifitz, Grashow, & Linsky, 2009; Wheatley, 2002).

But noble intentions are worth nothing without meaningful social action to back them up; indeed, they can frequently end up reproducing the discourse status quo (Butler, 2004; Jezebel Staff, 2016). Inclusive leadership discourse still needs to reconcile with two critical questions to reach its full emancipatory potential. Fortunately, both questions can be engaged with through leveraging pre-existing strengths of inclusive leadership discourse.

First, we as inclusive leaders must ask: who is doing the including? This question has obvious power implications for setting the tone in leadership relationships. If inclusion is thought of as a benevolent act, then there is inherent inequality built into the relationship from the outset. Instead of thinking of inclusion as an endpoint, as a requirement, or as a vaguely desirable good, leadership systems should be willing to engage with the potentially awkward and potentially painful questions of what the purpose of inclusion is within that particular context. If such questions are left unspeakable, then the leadership system is free to perpetuate the status quo of power relations which does not disturb the very cross-cultural gulfs of understanding that were meant to be addressed in the first place (Foucault, 1978; Heifitz et al., 2009). Fortunately, the pieces of inclusion discourse related to valuing diversity can serve as a starting point for such conversations. If diversity is important, then compelling the group to articulate why it is important can only help to surface conflicting interpretations and work toward a more pluralist approach to practicing leadership.

I believe that, through judicious, careful, honest, and painful exploration, our field is uniquely poised for the task of encouraging communal, cooperative action to reimagine discourse (Alvesson & Spicer, 2012). Two prominent leadership approaches, the Social Change Model (Astin, 1996; Komives et al., 2009) and civic leadership (Chrislip & O'Malley, 2013), advocate for putting into practice mobilization, community building, and listening to diverse others as cornerstones in the practice of radical, change-based leadership. Leadership has the tools in place to transform inclusion from passive to active: challenging one's own place in sociohistorical cultural systems, and creating positive change that broadens all subjects' ability to be intelligible as leaders.

Second, practitioners of inclusive leadership should ask what role structure plays in moderating inclusive leadership relationships (Choo & Ferree, 2010). If exploring inclusive leadership focuses solely on self-reflection or small group process, but neglects to address sociohistorical barriers to inclusion, then these explorations could negate the very real pain, misunderstanding, and inequality that creates gulfs between those from different cultural backgrounds in the first place (Collins, 1993). Again, civic leadership (Chrislip & O'Malley, 2013) and the Social Change Model of Leadership (Komives et al., 2009) demonstrate the importance of social action in dismantling pernicious discourse and addressing systemic barriers to inclusion, challenging us to look beyond the individual as the locus for inclusive leadership.

Our current discourse surrounding inclusion in the field of leadership largely advocates for broadening our mutual definitions of leader and leadership while being mindful of the role of social structure. In other words, inclusive leadership works are troubling the very ideas of leader and leadership themselves, which then could have the potential effect of reconstituting how we conceptualize of inclusive leadership in particular (Ford et al., 2008; Peck & Dickinson, 2009). By contesting hierarchical conceptualizations of leadership and differentiating leadership from management, many leadership scholars have already troubled the discourse's status quo and its relationship to the social (Peck & Dickinson, 2009; Rost, 1991). As such, this field may already be "queered" — that is, open to conversations of troubling and contesting prevailing patterns of thought related to what leadership is and who is a leader (Lee, Learmonth, & Harding, 2008). If many of us are already committed to expanding the bounds of who is a leader, I am confident that we are up to the task of critically examining how and to what degree we are complicit in upholding forms of discourse that marginalize others.

Fig. 1 summarizes how I have conceptualized of the discourse surrounding inclusive leadership, critiques of existing discourse, and our potential to revise our collective understanding of inclusive leadership. Although the current inclusive leadership discourse may obscure power relations and sociohistorical forces, the field of leadership studies has the tools to counter this status quo. In so doing, we may be able to explore new leadership realities that help the phrase better represent our mutually intended ideals.

What's in a Word?

In her goal to practice what we might term inclusive leadership, the student in the audience at Ms. Hunter's talk that night cast herself as the active party, the one with power, the savior. Ms. Hunter challenged her definition and delicately rebuked her approach, but not her intent. Although intent alone is not sufficient, in this case it was a starting point: both the student and Ms. Hunter were able to hear one another and transform the discourse around inclusion in our shared space. Even more than that, the student was given concrete, attainable, and difficult

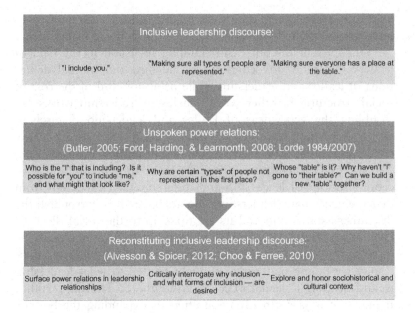

Fig. 1. Contesting and Reconstituting Inclusion Discourse.

steps to take on should she truly desire to enact the change she wished to see.

Though leadership should be wary of the potential for inclusion discourse to push for assimilation, the activity of critically interrogating it and reconstructing it is perhaps the ultimate practice of its — and our — ideals. If we can bring ourselves as aspiring practitioners of inclusive leadership to engage with such questions, we have the potential to rebuild the discourse surrounding the term. Inclusion does not have to be a zero-sum game wherein those with structural privilege are the only ones who can give the narrative of including, nor a space that reproduces problematic power relations. Inclusion can yet become a concept that embodies a dramatic reimagining of the term that allows us to make manifest new, exciting, equitable, and empathetic leadership realities.

References

Alvesson, M., & Spicer, A. (2012). Critical leadership studies: The case for critical performativity. *Human Relations*, *65*(3), 367–390.

Astin, H. S. (1996). Leadership for social change. *About Campus*, *1*, 4–10.

Bennett, M. J. (2004). Becoming interculturally competent. In J. S. Wurzel (Ed.), Toward multiculturalism: A reader in multicultural education (pp. 62–77). Newton, MA: Intercultural Resource Corporation.

Butler, J. (2004). *Undoing gender*. New York, NY: Routledge.

Butler, J. (2005). *Giving an account of oneself*. New York, NY: Fordham University Press.

Choo, H. Y., & Ferree, M. M. (2010). Practicing intersectionality in sociological research: A critical analysis of inclusions, interactions, and institutions in the study of inequalities. *Sociological Theory*, 28(2), 129–149.

Chrislip, D. D., & O'Malley, E. (2013). *For the common good: Redefining civic leadership*. Wichita, KS: KLC Press.

Collins, P. H. (1993). Toward a new vision: Race, class, and gender as categories of analysis and connection. *Race, Sex & Class*, 1(1), 25–45.

Dreger, A. (2006, August 1). *Add Black people and stir?* Retrieved from http://alicedreger.com/diversity. Accessed on April 20, 2016.

Fierke, K. K., Lui, K. W., Lepp, G. A., & Baldwin, A. J. (2014). Teaching inclusive leadership through student-centered practices. *Journal of the Academy of Business Education*, 15, 51–65.

Fine, L. E. (2015). Teaching multicultural leadership using a social constructionist approach. *Journal of Leadership Education*, 14(2), 209–217.

Ford, J., Harding, N., & Learmonth, M. (2008). *Leadership as identity: Constructions and deconstructions*. Basingstoke, UK: Palgrave MacMillan.

Foucault, M. (1978). *The history of sexuality: Volume 1: An introduction* (R. Hurley, trans.). New York, NY: Random House.

Gooden, M. A. (2012). What does racism have to do with leadership? Countering the idea of color-blind leadership: A reflection on race and the growing pressures of the urban principalship. *Educational Foundations*, 26(1-2), 67–84.

Hames-García, M. (2011). *Identity complex: Making the case for multiplicity*. Minneapolis, MN: University of Minnesota Press.

Heifitz, R., Grashow, A., & Linsky, M. (2009). *The practice of adaptive leadership: Tools and tactics for changing your organization and the world*. Boston, MA: Harvard Business Press.

Hollander, E. P. (2012). *Inclusive leadership: The essential leader-follower relationship*. New York, NY: Routledge.

Hornsey, M. J., & Hogg, M. A. (2000). Assimilation and diversity: An integrative model of subgroup relations. *Personality and Social Psychology Review*, 4(2), 143–156.

Jezebel Staff & Contributors. (2016). Why do white liberals fear Mackelmore? Retrieved from http://themuse.jezebel.com/what-do-white-liberals-fear-about-macklemore-1754974465. Accessed on April 20, 2016.

Kanter, R. M. (1977). Some effects of proportions on group life: Skewed sex ratios and responses to token women. *American Journal of Sociology*, 82(5), 965–990.

Komives, S. R., Wagner, W., & Associates (2009). *Leadership for a better world: understanding the Social Change Model of leadership development*. San Francisco, CA: Jossey-Bass.

Lee, H., Learmonth, M., & Harding, N. (2008). Queer(y)ing public administration. *Public Administration, 86*(1), 149–167.

Lorde, A. (2007). The master's tools will never dismantle the master's house. In N. K. Bereano (Ed.), *Sister outsider: Essays and speeches by Audre Lorde* (pp. 110–113). New York, NY: Ten Speed Press (Original work published 1984).

Muñoz, J. E. (1999). *Disidentifications: Queers of color and the performance of politics.* Minneapolis, MN: University of Minnesota Press.

Nevarez, C., & Wood, L. J. (2010). *Community college leadership and administration: Theory, practice, and change.* New York, NY: Peter Lang.

Ospina, S., & Foldy, E. (2009). A critical review of race and ethnicity in the leadership literature: Surfacing context, power and the collective dimensions of leadership. *The Leadership Quarterly, 20,* 876–896.

Oxoby, R. J. (2009). Understanding social inclusion, social cohesion and social capital. *International Journal of Social Economics, 36*(12), 1133–1152.

Peck, E., & Dickinson, H. (2009). *Performing leadership.* London, UK: Palgrave – McMillan.

Phelan, S. (2001). *Sexual strangers: Gays, lesbians, and the dilemmas of citizenship.* Philadelphia, PA: Temple University Press.

Rost, J. C. (1991). *Leadership for the twenty-first century.* Westport, CT: Praeger.

Rumens, N. (2016). Towards queering the business school: A research agenda for advancing lesbian, gay, bisexual, and trans perspectives and issues. *Gender, Work, and Organisation, 23*(1), 36–51.

Scharmer, C. O. (2009). *Theory U: Leading from the future as it emerges.* San Francisco, CA: Barrett-Koehler.

Wheatley, M. (2002). *Turning to one another: Simple conversations to restore hope to the future.* San Francisco, CA: Barrett-Koehler.

Zafar, S., Sandhu, S. Z., & Khan, Z. A. (2013). A critical analysis of "Developing intercultural competence in the language classroom" by Bennett, Bennett, and Allen. *World Applied Sciences Journal, 21*(4), 565–571.

3

Fostering Inclusive Innovation Ecosystems

Lyndon Rego and Christopher Gergen

Keywords: Inclusive innovation; collective leadership; collective impact; community transformation; social capital

As we peer into the fog of the future, we see a world shrouded in volatility, change, and conflict. The problems that bedevil us today are wrapped in layers of complexity that defy simple solutions. Yet one thing is clear: We're all in it together. Our futures are bound to each other.

Long ago, our ancestors saw the world as connected. They envisioned humans as intertwined in the web of life where interdependent relationships between people and nature were assumed and appreciated, even if the actual cause and effect was not quite apparent. Huddled around nighttime campfires, they told tales of people, gods, and animals who interacted and impacted each other, and sometimes even traded identities. These tales shaped cultures and provided a code of conduct for everyday life, often based on values of respect, unity, and harmony.

As we evolved, our ancestors moved toward greater degrees of power and separation, dividing into nations and hierarchies, carving knowledge into disciplines, and exercising ever-greater mastery over each other and their environments. The industrial and scientific revolutions gave human beings great power and hubris.

Now, as we step into yet another new global age, we recognize that we live in a world that is deeply connected and completely interdependent. Our individual actions impact our collective future. For instance, carbon emissions in the industrial world and deforestation of rainforests drive climate change. This triggers drought and desertification, and leads to the displacement of people and political instability. Just as actions in the global village cause far-reaching consequences, so too do ideas. Ideas — whether in service of democracy, capitalism, radicalism, or revolution — can quickly turn into movements that ripple across our planet today through the hyper speed of instant messaging and social media.

Unlike our ancestors who intuited the web of connections, we increasingly have the data and tools to trace the web of cascading effects. What we then lack is not the ability to see these connections but to effectively channel our individual abilities in service of our collective good. We urgently need to build our capacity for thinking and acting holistically. We need to apply the great knowledge, tools, and capabilities we've developed through our human journey in service of our common good, for both humans and the planet. The words Martin Luther King, Jr. offered were never more relevant, "We must live together as brothers or perish as fools."

The authors have been part of the wider quest for collective action, working on the fronts of community and economic development using the tools of leadership and innovation. We believe the path of inclusive innovation and collective leadership provides a way for us to transform communities in effective ways. This chapter offers methods we have developed and learning we have acquired. While certainly not a magic recipe for resolving our challenges, we hope it offers insights that others on the quest may find useful.

Defining Leadership and Innovation

It may be helpful to define what we mean by leadership and innovation. Leadership is defined by the Center for Creative Leadership as the process of creating shared direction, alignment, and commitment (Drath et al., 2008). Direction is charting a course for where the group is going. Alignment is about creating shared understanding of the roles the parties will play in working together. Commitment signals the readiness of the parties to work together. Together, these three elements represent the ability of groups to coalesce in action. Collective leadership favors the kind of leadership that is shaped and owned by all stakeholders, rather than behaviors that are enforced or coerced. The task of orchestrating leadership becomes more complex with greater group size and diversity. This makes the challenges of creating shared direction, alignment, and commitment more difficult.

Innovation is the ability to shape new things that create greater value (Horth & Vehar, 2015). Without innovation, we slip into stagnation or atrophy. Innovation emphasizes value creation over and above newness and creativity, though these are enablers of innovation. Innovation also differs from invention that often is associated with new discoveries. It may not require fresh discovery, only fresh insight about how needs can be addressed or problems can be solved. Driving innovation becomes more challenging when it entails more significant departures from what exists. Incremental and evolutionary innovations are less challenging to undertake than radical or revolutionary innovation, which require new models and methods.

Innovation	*High*	Creative Chaos	Inclusive Innovation & Collective Leadership
	Low	Atrophy	Cohesion & Stagnation
		Low	*High*
		Collective Leadership	

We developed the model above to illustrate that innovation and leadership are symbiotic. Innovation is inherently about change and requires leadership to enact and create value. Established systems tend to resist change. Without effective leadership to unite the new with the old, we get chaos. Leadership, unless it is dynamically oriented toward change, recedes to the maintenance of the existing order. Both innovation and leadership spring from empathy and understanding human needs; both push outward from stagnation, stemming from the belief that better outcomes are possible.

Innovation and leadership are essential in our fast-changing world but they are not easy to enact and sustain. They cannot be "one and done" efforts and must be baked into a culture to foster continual adaptation and renewal. Creating embedded and sustained capacity in organizations and communities requires engagement and inclusion. Sustained outcomes are elusive when they do not include all community stakeholders in shaping and implementing solutions. The need to forge solutions with all stakeholders — even adversaries — is embodied in a statement by leadership scholar Bill Torbert who flipped the polarizing refrain, "If you're not part of the solution, you're part of the problem" to "If you're not part of the problem, you can't be part of the solution" (Kahane, 2004).

Our colleagues from the Center for Creative Leadership have framed a declaration of interdependence to call out the need for collective leadership (Palus, McGuire, & Ernst, 2012). They write "the enormous challenges we face — climate, war, disease, prosperity, justice — can only be solved by groups working collaboratively together. We need a new kind of leadership, one more concerned with solving big challenges for all our futures than with winning the next political battle that the other group loses. We need a declaration of interdependence."

The need for interdependent leadership is especially great in fostering societal impact. Asif and Palus from the Center for Creative Leadership (CCL) state that societal impact "requires an evolution to more interdependent cultures and mindsets among the collaborating organizations and their members" (Asif & Palus, 2013). These interdependent leadership cultures, they explain, are characterized by practices that see leadership as a collective activity that requires mutual inquiry and learning.

So too, globalization requires that local communities find ways to bridge their internal divisions to thrive in a competitive environment (Gergen & Rego, 2016). In our connected world, the sharp, bony fingers of competition push into every soft corner of the globe. To compete, communities everywhere need to find ways to drive innovation that stimulates economic growth and community wellbeing. Nurturing a local innovation and entrepreneurial environment requires inclusive approaches that unite sectors and community stakeholders in common purpose, fostering greater social capital.

Social capital represents what we can do because of our relationships. Networks are at the heart of social capital (Willburn & Cullen, 2014). We enhance social capital when we see and understand the connections between ourselves and others. These network connections form the bridges that span boundaries and enable collective action. Networks are strong when they are deep, open, and inclusive. When we integrate and harness the diversity in our communities, we enhance our collective social consciousness and capital, as well as our potential for innovation.

Fostering Inclusive Innovation

In this chapter, we share approaches from our work in the United States, Latin America, Africa, and Asia that focus on shaping inclusive innovation ecosystems. These efforts have shaped practices that foster inclusion and build collective commitment toward concerted action. Through the ensuing pages, we will trace the logic, approach, and outcomes of these initiatives and how they relate to:

- Identity and empathy
- Relationships, networks, and movements
- Entrepreneurship and innovation
- Broadening and sustaining innovation
- Capacity development

IDENTITY AND EMPATHY

Identity is an important starting point in leadership development. It is important that each individual's identity is recognized and valued in order to foster true relationships and collaboration. Often this step of relationship-building is left out in change efforts as the focus leaps ahead to framing goals and shaping strategies. The lack of awareness of the identity of the other thrusts each side into missteps as they engage in the change process from their own values, aspirations, and world views, which may be in turn, invisible or mysterious to others and can result in longer-term disconnect and mistrust.

In Ghana, we worked with the Ministry of Agriculture and agricultural extension workers to help them engage with farmers in a new way. These government workers provided technical support to farmers in rural villages. Change was elusive and farmers often resisted changing the methods they've always used. We equipped the extension workers with a tool called the "tree of life." Using the tool, participants draw a tree. The roots represent identity and values. The branches, stretching upward, represent hopes and aspirations for the future. The trunk of the tree connects the roots and branches, evoking an exploration of how our identities enable us to create our futures. After the training, the government workers took this tool into the villages, working with groups of farmers to draw their trees. The activity revealed the struggles of the villagers and the hopes they had for the lives, often simple things like a school for their children or better farm tools. The extension workers were moved by what they learned about the complexity and challenge of the villager's lives. They had previously operated in isolation of the farmers' fuller lives, which had been invisible to them. The villagers now said to them, "we want you to come back because now you understand us." The encounter had fostered understanding and empathy. Understanding the lives of the farmers enhanced the ability of the extension workers to speak in meaningful ways to the farmers and connect the actions they advocated to the outcomes the villagers wanted.

Half a world away, the Foundation for the Alleviation of Poverty in Chile works to enable the poor to develop the skills and processes to rise out of poverty. The Foundation's Servicio Pais program places college graduates on extended service assignments in rural areas. One remarkable outcome of the program is that half of these participants choose, on completion of their assignments, to continue work in the challenging rural regions they served in rather than return to the comfort of city life. They are highly sought after by government, corporate, or nonprofit organizations for the abilities they have acquired for how to consistently engage with the local communities, to listen, to balance different opinions, and to work to unify the needs of different groups.

In these examples, we see how being immersed in another's world changes our view of them. When we understand others, we invariably seek to bridge our differences. Nobel Prize winner Amartya Sen in his book *Identity and Violence* observed that much of the conflict in the world stems from polarization around a single aspect of identity, be it religion, race, language, or class (Sen, 2006). When we unpack our identities, we find that we share many commonalities that can be the basis for connection and relationship.

RELATIONSHIPS, NETWORKS, AND MOVEMENTS

A critical driver in achieving collective efforts is building relationships and networks. Relationships are the glue of leadership. They represent bonds that hold things together and enable work to be accomplished over the bumpy road of difference.

In any given civic ecosystem, government, business, and civil society actors may find themselves working at cross-purposes even as they pursue similar aims such as attracting talent, creating jobs, and protecting the environment. What hinders collaboration is often the lack of connection, understanding, and trust. Without this foundation, group efforts can quickly degrade into competition. Focusing on building an empathetic relationship at the outset establishes the foundation for collective impact later. This serves to humanize interactions and create mutual appreciation. A second stage is to target areas of common ground to weave the new personal relationships into working relationships. From there, progress can be made on a set of strategic actions that foster sustained economic and community impact.

This pattern represents a process the Center for Creative Leadership calls boundary-spanning leadership. Boundary-spanning leadership is about establishing direction, alignment, and commitment service of a higher vision or goal (Ernst & Chrobot-Mason, 2010). Boundary-spanning leadership is a sequenced process. The initial cross-boundary efforts foster trusting relationships that blossom into greater integration and collective action.

An example of this approach was embodied in our work in El Salvador focused on driving economic development in the nation via cross-sector collaborations in 50 municipalities. A grounding intervention was a two-day leadership program where we brought leaders together from government, civil society, and business to share personal stories, struggles, hopes, and aspirations. Using tools such as social identity maps (http://www. leadingeffectively.com/interdependent-leadership/wp-content/uploads/ 2013/11/MOOC-Social-Identity-workbook.pdf), these leaders got to know each other at a personal level. These exchanges built trust and relationships, and helped them see that the essence of what they wanted was not very different from what the other desired, preparing them to engage with greater mutual understanding and respect on the difficult road ahead.

Another parallel practice called polarity management resulted in enhanced relationships between the police and the community in Charleston, South Carolina (Berry Hawes, 2016). Here the police and the community engaged in a process that traced the upsides and downsides of active and passive policing in communities. Through the process, the police and community understood each other's perspectives and needs, and were able to arrive at a shared understand of the behaviors that provided both safety and liberty to the community. Polarity management treats deep-seated differences not as a problem to solve but a tension to manage. This distinction focuses on understanding opposing perspectives and working to create shared outcomes that both sides want and can support. The power of the investment in building relationships between the police and the community was evident in the wake of the racially motivated shootings of nine African-American worshippers at the Emanuel African Methodist Episcopal Church in the city. Rather than take to the street in rage as may have been expected, the community engaged peacefully with the police to create space for both mourners and protestors.

Challenges can only be truly addressed by bringing to the table all parties that are enmeshed in the conflict. Boundary-spanning and polarity management are methods that bring disconnected groups that are distrustful of each other to engage in a process of building mutual understanding and finding common ground.

Achieving a higher order of change requires building movements that span boundaries and catalyze broad-based action. During the US civil rights struggle, success came from the shared efforts of a large coalition of people and organizations — spanning class and color lines — coming together to seek change. What is fundamental in these transformational efforts is that the push for change offers compassion rather than aggression toward opponents. The goal is to turn away from polarization toward unity. Martin Luther King expressed this sentiment in an evocative way, "Love is creative, understanding goodwill for all men. It is the refusal to defeat any individual."

Movements hinge on a common purpose but advance through grassroots agents and the innovations they produce. In the US civil rights efforts, actors experimented independently with a variety of protest forms, from marches, rallies, sit-ins, and boycotts. Successful practices were shared and emulated, enabling their impact to ripple across regions. When movements gain momentum, more people join in, pushing change toward the tipping point. A tipping point occurs when people from the other side join in the struggle. In the civil rights struggle for equal rights in the United States, White marchers joined in marches and sit-ins, signaling that the struggle was not a cause just for Black people but one in service of our common humanity.

Ultimately, practices such as boundary-spanning leadership and polarity management suggest that groups have common interests that are often hidden in misunderstanding. Transcending differences requires a foundation of trust but finding transformational outcomes is the work of entrepreneurial action and innovation.

ENTREPRENEURSHIP AND INNOVATION

Christopher's efforts have focused on launching two multi-year, multi-city learning collaboratives operating across distressed cities in the United States focused on fostering inclusive entrepreneurial innovation called Forward Cities (www.forwardcities. org) and InnovateNC (www.innovatenc.org). Much of the world's people today live in sprawling metropolises. These cities are complex aggregations of people, cultures, and histories. In many cities, the affluent and the poor live apart, seldom interacting even as their futures are tied together. In other cities, distress is broad-based as legacy businesses succumb to global competition, seeing the shuttering of factories, loss of jobs, and the wholesale flight of talent and investment.

A case in point is Durham, North Carolina, once a booming hub for tobacco and textiles, as well as home to one of the nation's foremost African-American business communities called the "Black Wall Street." As the city hit tough times at the close of the century, the downtown saw an exodus of young entrepreneurial talent. Bull City Forward (BCF) was launched to create conditions to attract creative and entrepreneurial talent back to the city. Supported by the city, university partners, and investors, BCF helped trigger a downtown revitalization, reclaiming the beautiful brick warehouses and transforming them into trendy new workspaces for entrepreneurs and startups.

The effort leveraged and integrated learning from communities across the nation. Communities like Indianapolis are doing a great job developing and recruiting a strong pipeline of entrepreneurial talent. New Orleans, Pittsburgh, and London built strong entrepreneurial support systems. San Francisco, Toronto, and Boston created thriving incubator/accelerator spaces. Others, like Providence and Pittsburgh, tap local universities for talent, research, and new venture possibilities. Yet, it was quickly apparent that no community was taking a truly comprehensive approach to intentionally fostering, developing, and scaling high-impact, high-growth social enterprises. Efforts like BCF sought to aggregate effective practices for collective community-building efforts.

Through this work, five key levers to developing inclusive innovation ecosystems were identified, including: (1) building talent pipelines through local education efforts, recruitment, and retention; (2) creating strong enabling environments to connect emerging problem solvers with the resources and relationships they need to grow (access to capital, collaborative workspaces, and mentorship); (3) developing robust data gathering efforts to measure the economic and community impact being created through entrepreneurial and innovation actions, (4) fostering a supportive community and economic development policy environment to bring public support to these efforts, and (5) shining a light on these efforts through story-telling. These together provide a pathway for communities to catalyze a local innovation economy that ideally benefits all citizens.

BROADENING AND SUSTAINING

Innovation has a short shelf-life. Competitive advantage is fleeting as effective practices are quickly emulated elsewhere and better value propositions are continually birthed by competitors. For innovation to be a sustained capability, it must be deeply embedded in the DNA of a community. It must be widespread, entrenched, and inclusive across race, gender, and demographic lines.

The Forward Cities effort launched in Durham, North Carolina, is helping spark a broader statewide effort that is now underway. In Greensboro, North Carolina, which is one of the InnovateNC sites, the authors are working on an effort to create an inclusive innovation ecosystem in a diverse and stratified community. A starting point, we built a broad network of representatives of all stakeholder groups — senior leaders in major companies, top governmental officials, grassroots NGO leaders, and leaders from immigrant and refugee communities. In bringing them together through a local Innovation Council, we asked each party to not just represent their own stakeholder groups but also to raise their vision to encompass the entire community. Rather than attempt to unravel knotty problems of the present, we turned toward the future to envision the community we wanted to build and the drivers that would enable them.

A key element of the effort focused on job creation and the development of skills that would be needed in the future. Because the effort included all sectors and stakeholders, we were able to think and act expansively with regard to community needs and assets. Rather than seeing this as a role for education or training entities, we saw that businesses had a valuable role to play in providing internships that would let student build practical job skills. So too, recognizing that established educational institutions may not be places where those who haven't been part of these environments will feel welcome, we are working to bring development into their communities. Our belief is that if we nurture an intertwined, integrated collaborative environment, more entrepreneurs will rise, gain support, create new businesses and jobs, and transform the communities they live in.

CAPACITY DEVELOPMENT

While not everyone is an entrepreneur, everyone can develop an entrepreneurial mindset (Gergen & Vanourek, 2008). Indeed, the volatile future we face requires all people to be agile learners who can spot opportunities and position themselves to seize them. Building this capability is the work of capacity development. Our efforts focus on development on two fronts — horizontal development and vertical development (Petrie, 2011). Horizontal development focuses on acquiring a broader base of *skillsets* that enhance and extend capability to increase effectiveness. Vertical development in contrast focuses on shifting *mindset* — how we think about issues determines how we work to address them. It is about cultivating a bigger mind that enables us to act from a perspective that is more holistic and that seeks to harmonize a broader array of system inputs and human needs. Great leaders create more transformational outcomes because of this breadth of perspective, rather than because they have a wider array of skills. It is their ability to integrate and unite people and perspectives that represents the impact they are able to create.

In India, CCL has launched the Global Citizen Leader (GCL) initiative with business schools to develop critical job-related skills that extend beyond technical competencies to developing a greater degree of vertical leadership capability. The ability to work in teams and tackle unfamiliar challenges is essential on the job. It is not, however, what traditional classroom-based educational models are geared to deliver. The GCL effort provides a foundation in leadership and innovation for all first-year students through a combination of classroom learning and team-based projects for community organizations, government, and business.

Through GCL, students embark on this journey with the tools of design thinking — spending half their time and effort to deeply understand the environment, needs, and aspirations of the people and organizations they were assigned to help. In working with rural communities, they found that people are poor not because they are lazy but because of deep-seated barriers. Teenage girls drop out of rural schools not because they do not want to learn but because of the lack of toilets at schools. In understanding these barriers, students are able to shape solutions that can truly make a difference. The projects provide the students with experiences that put them in zones they would ordinarily not find themselves in. As with the Servicio Pais program, it engenders a sense of empathy for marginalized populations and a sense of empowerment stemming from the student's first-hand experience that they can make things better. Working with organizations on the ground in these communities on the projects provides both the opportunity for students to gain real work experience and for employers to play an active role as partners and mentors in grooming future talent.

This form of project-based capacity building that brings together youth, organizations, and social challenges represents a compelling win-win arrangement that we believe represents where education needs to turn at large. Students are engaged in practical projects that enable active learning. Engagement with real-world problems builds both commitment and capability for students to make a difference in the lives of others. The practical job experience acquired through these projects closes the gap between education and employer needs. By starting early with young people in educational systems, we can scale and "democratize" leadership capacity and help ensure that our communities have an abundance of creative, connected, empathetic, and subsequently committed leaders for the future.

Into the Future

The emerging future presents reasons for hope and concern. We're headed into an era where Millennials and Generation Z are eager to express their voice and claim their power (Gergen & Rego, 2014). Wired with devices, they have a deeper sense of what's going on and a desire for purpose. They also collaborate in ways that are agile and peer-based, organizing quickly using social media. These shifts have been manifest in a suite of start-ups like Facebook, Uber, and Airbnb that are scaling quickly and changing the competitive landscape. They are also manifest in the youth-driven Arab Spring and the Occupy Movement. While the capacity of the youth to organize and challenge the entrenched system is evident, these movements have locked horns with the establishment, turned violent, and have often been crushed (Malsin, 2012). Using techniques such as boundary spanning and polarity management can help build pathways for youth movements to bridge differences from the existing order to the new. Formal systems must also proactively engage young people to tap their aspirations, leverage their talents and passions, and invite them as partners in shaping change. The integration of youth energy and voice into existing business, social, and political spheres represents a singular opportunity for the society at large.

In Closing

The patterns we have traced in this chapter emphasize the value of all people and underscores that the greatest impact comes when we are able to work together. Uniting diverse people and agendas together in common purpose is a complex and difficult challenge but not an insurmountable one. As we lean into the future, we must seek and advance our capacity for inclusive and collective action. The practices we have shared in this chapter — identity development and empowerment; boundary-spanning leadership and polarity management; broadening and sustaining networks; and developing capacity — are approaches that we need to amplify. We must move these efforts into more educational environments across the world and apply them in our communities to build coalitions for broad-based collective action that includes all people. The future will demand the best of all of us. An old African proverb states, "If you want to walk fast walk alone, if you want to walk far walk together." In our modern world, we have the ability and need to work on both sides of this equation. We can go both fast and far by aggregating our collective abilities to build inclusive innovation ecosystems that create good for all.

References

Asif, V., & Palus, C. J. (2013). *Leadership strategies for societal impact.* Greensboro, NC: Center for Creative Leadership.

Berry Hawes, J. (2016). *From tragedy to trust: Can Charleston achieve unity after the Emanuel AME Church shooting?* The Post and Courier. Published Jun 15, 2016. Retreived from http://data.postandcourier.com/saga/oneyearlater/page/6

Drath, W. H., McCauley, C. D., Palus, C. J., Van Velsor, E., O'Connor, P. M. G., & McGuire, J. B. (2008). Direction, alignment, commitment: Toward a more integrative ontology of leadership. *Leadership Quarterly, 19,* 635–653.

Ernst, C., & Chrobot-Mason, D. (2010). *Boundary spanning leadership: Six practices for solving problems, driving innovation, and transforming organizations.* New York: McGraw-Hill Professional.

Gergen, C., & Rego, L. (2014). *Educating a new generation of entrepreneurial leaders.* Stanford Social Innovation Review.

Gergen, C., & Rego, L. (2016). *Making beautiful places: Fostering inclusive innovation through place-based ecosystem development.* Innovations: Technology, Governance, Globalization. Special Edition for Global Entrepreneurship Congress 2016.

Gergen, C., & Vanourek, G. (2008). *Life entrepreneurs: Ordinary people creating extraordinary lives.* San Francisco, CA: Jossey-Bass.

Horth, D., & Vehar, J. (2015). *Becoming a leader who fosters innovation.* Greensboro, NC: Center for Creative Leadership.

Kahane, A. (2004). *Solving tough problems: An open way of talking, listening, and creating new realities.* San Francisco: Berrett-Koehler.

Malsin, J. (November 13, 2012). Best of enemies: Why occupy activists are working with New York City's government. Time.

Palus, C. J., McGuire, J. M., & Ernst, C. (2012). Developing interdependent leadership. *In the handbook for teaching leadership: Knowing, doing, and being.* S. Snook, N. Nohria, & R. Khurana (Eds.), Sage Publications with the Harvard Business School.

Petrie, N. (December 2011). *Future trends in leadership development: A white paper.* Greensboro, NC: Center for Creative Leadership.

Sen, A. (2006). *Identity and violence: The illusion of destiny.* New York: W.W. Norton & Co.

Willburn, P., & Cullen, K. (2014). *A leader's network: How to help your talent invest in the right relationships at the right time.* Center for Creative Leadership.

4

Toward the "Other": Followership Justice and Leadership Reach

Robin E. S. Carter

Keywords: Other; zero-sum; inclusion; community leadership; spatial; place leadership theory

Introduction

Inclusion has varied meanings to countless places and people (World Bank, 2013; Young, 1990). To distressed communities and marginalized populations, the concept of inclusion captures the lack of societal protective factors that leadership decisions around distribution or policy might intentionally promote or ignore. For at-risk populations, it is a sense of fairness that "others" enjoy. For the privileged, this exclusion of the "other," knowingly or not, contributes to increased social injustice, thus promoting the zero-sum game. These opposing forces advancing "otherness" complicated by the bordered, yet, connected binaries of local or global, inclusion or exclusion, and leader or follower require a transdisciplinary discourse that broad societal leadership and followership can leverage as postmodernism fades.

This quest begins with the understanding of two, postmodern, societal processes. First, the contemporary zero-sum game is no longer as materially and spatially obvious as the affluent taking from the poor; or the socioeconomic divide between global north and south. Second, efforts to understand inclusion are further complicated by leadership's often limiting scope of characteristics, styles, and organizational change theories predictably found within business sectors. Combined, removing the contemporary zero-sum game is about shifting governance and tolerance perspectives in an effort to positively impact all societal dimensions. In sketching these complex activities, followership voice is equally necessary toward informing leadership theory and practice. I term this *followership justice*.

While the transformational turn (Avolio & Bass, 1994; Avolio & Gibbons, 1988; Bass, 1995, 2008; Bass & Avolio, 1990) in the 1980s was most valuable in enacting change *and* legitimizing leadership as a discipline, this enduring dimension has unintentionally limited leadership efforts toward uncovering less linear, more abstract, spatial understandings "in-between" leader–follower relationships, transactions, and roles preventing what I term as *leadership reach*. At the leadership core, societal powers that worsen the conditions of or coercively deprive "other" are common, hidden activities. This inclusive expression increases less effective community development rather than centering.

This concern for "other" is more clearly organized in extending leadership borders toward human geography, education, and social justice with a phenomenological stance (Heil, 2010; Küpers, 2010). Here, spatial and social relationships, open access to knowledge, social justice dimensions, and meaning over measurement further leadership theory. Next, the practical implications for leadership are briefly discussed toward how we can begin spatializing these sovereignties. Finally, demonstrating how leadership scholarship has begun shifting toward advancing the nonzero-sum game within place leadership theory is synthesized. This framework collectively contributes to deepening an alternative leadership lens, away from the often hidden agendas that leaders are privileged to govern. Rather, followers, citizens, and members often marginalized as "other" are at the center of this dialogue.

Observing Leadership from a Distance

In a similar vein, a significant difference between this essay and other leadership platforms is that these representations are by a nonleader. Through varied lived experiences my followership position of observing and studying leadership is most valuable from a distance as the inner circles where leadership is managed and debated is in close proximity to privilege where "others" including myself are excluded from participation or worse, "included" as a token symbol to advance leaderships' inclusionary image. Therefore, I am upfront about my membership of uncovering solutions toward removing antiquated, judgmental, societal games. A participants gain or loss, whether social or material, should not be the result of community leaders discussing opportunities of a binary framework. Whom deserves a home, opportunity, employment advancement, or a "hand up" more? Is it the medaled veteran returning from combat, struggling, unemployed, and exhausted? Is it the lone mother balancing countless responsibilities under the scrutiny of societal pressures of a higher standard than two parent or two income households? Or, is it the immigrant or visibly unfamiliar family seeking to improve their lives by seeking refuge from danger or poverty? In a world where plentiful resources abound, why are we trying to make ourselves feel better by strategically selecting a demographic that is popular to help while simultaneously ignoring a group that is politically acceptable to ignore? This contemporary, feel good, welfare no longer needs to be a conversation on a planet that has an abundance of wealth, resources, and talent to provide justice for all its citizens. Rather, it is a process that leadership consciousness has marketed and branded, thus, silencing the "other."

Shifting this sovereignty begins with a wider perspective of "otherness" features outside leadership literature to include human geography, education, and social justice. This includes injustices within developing countries and those within the United States, European Union, and other hegemonies, as "othering" is not confined to place, people, situation, or process. Other" can include identity of culture, ethnicity, heritage, disability, capability, incarceration, health inequality, birth place, religion, philosophy, age, mobility, migration, socioeconomic status, title, gender, sexual orientation, or any visual or verbal difference we as humanity label (see Fig. 1).

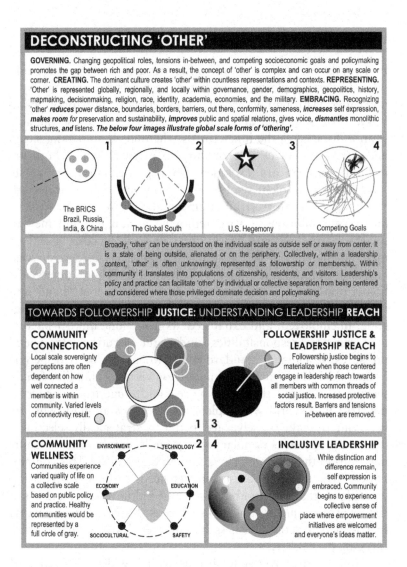

DECONSTRUCTING 'OTHER'

GOVERNING. Changing geopolitical roles, tensions in-between, and competing socioeconomic goals and policymaking promotes the gap between rich and poor. As a result, the concept of 'other' is complex and can occur on any scale or corner. **CREATING.** The dominant culture creates 'other' within countless representations and contexts. **REPRESENTING.** 'Other' is represented globally, regionally, and locally within governance, gender, demographics, geopolitics, history, mapmaking, decisionmaking, religion, race, identity, academia, economies, and the military. **EMBRACING.** Recognizing 'other' *reduces* power distance, boundaries, borders, barriers, out there, conformity, sameness, *increases* self expression, *makes room* for preservation and sustainability, *improves* public and spatial relations, gives voice, *dismantles* monolithic structures, *and* listens. *The below four images illustrate global scale forms of 'othering'.*

The BRICS Brazil, Russia, India, & China   The Global South   U.S. Hegemony   Competing Goals

OTHER Broadly, 'other' can be understood on the individual scale as outside self or away from center. It is a state of being outside, alienated or on the periphery. Collectively, within a leadership context, 'other' is often unknowingly represented as followership or membership. Within community it translates into populations of citizenship, residents, and visitors. Leadership's policy and practice can facilitate 'other' by individual or collective separation from being centered and considered where those privileged dominate decision and policymaking.

TOWARDS FOLLOWERSHIP **JUSTICE:** UNDERSTANDING LEADERSHIP **REACH**

COMMUNITY CONNECTIONS
Local scale sovereignty perceptions are often dependent on how well connected a member is within community. Varied levels of connectivity result.

FOLLOWERSHIP JUSTICE & LEADERSHIP REACH
Followership justice begins to materialize when those centered engage in leadership reach towards all members with common threads of social justice. Increased protective factors result. Barriers and tensions in-between are removed.

COMMUNITY WELLNESS
Communities experience varied quality of life on a collective scale based on public policy and practice. Healthy communities would be represented by a full circle of gray.

ENVIRONMENT — TECHNOLOGY
ECONOMY — EDUCATION
SOCIOCULTURAL — SAFETY

INCLUSIVE LEADERSHIP
While distinction and difference remain, self expression is embraced. Community begins to experience collective sense of place where empowerment initiatives are welcomed and everyone's ideas matter.

Fig. 1.   Deconstructing "Other," Toward Followership Justice and Leadership Reach. © Robin E. S. Carter

Why Leadership?

Before grappling with this win-win societal solution we must ask: *Why is the discipline of leadership so useful in uncovering solutions of how to break the zero-sum game?* After all, while leadership scholarship is oriented in transcending the broad social sciences where all societal issues can legitimately be debated, it should not be considered a landfill for solving every historical or contemporary complexity. So, while the boundaries of leadership must be reconsidered, saturating every conversation creates the very authoritative symbol this essay attempts to dismantle.

While the transformational turn in the 1980s highlighted how useful leadership scholarship is, transformation should no longer be the "go to" solution for every human condition. Reacting to the now prevalent economic crisis of postindustrial dying towns or solving issues within rapidly, demographically changing communities predictably promotes revenue for the elite and only possible recovery for the rest. Where the leadership conversation can be most useful is in shifting the leadership lens inward toward leadership practice to sincerely examine how the "other" lives:

> ...in the state and in society; we belong to a social circle which jostles against its members and is jostled by them; we feel the social pressure from all sides and we react against it with all our might; we experience a restraint to our free activities and we struggle to remove it; we require the services of other [people] which we cannot do without; we pursue our own interests and struggle for the interests of other social groups, which are also our interests. In short, we move in a world which we do not control, but which controls us, which is not directed toward us and adapted to us, but toward which we must direct and adapt ourselves.
>
> (Gumplowicz, 1963, p. 6)

Leadership, studied and developed by leaders *only* is similar to feminist theory solely analyzed and explained by the opposing gender. Or, in keeping with the zero-sum game theme, it is similar to asking: *Whose ideas matter more?*

To be fair, this conversation needs to highlight the often helpless thinking pattern of the disadvantaged. Combined, leader and follower contribute toward "othering." Individually, this often surfaces as a follower or member lacking a sense of place within community, the confidence to voice valid concerns, or the myth that education ends in youth where career and income are often dictated. This tiny box many followers operate in, equally promotes socioeconomic competition.

A critical theory understanding of adult learning should investigate how people learn to recognize the flow of power in their lives and communities, how they come to appreciate that power as inscribed ...in their everyday reasonings and actions, and how they try to redirect it to serve the interests of the many rather than the few.

(Agger, 2006, p. 47)

On a larger, more visible scale, the turn of the most recent century, social justice, water crisis in Bolivia highlights this necessary shift.

Bolivia granted a 40 year privatization lease to a subsidiary of the Bechtel Corporation, giving it control over the water on which more than half a million people survive. Immediately the company raised rates by an average of 50% and in many cases much more.

(*The Democracy Center*, 2000, n.p.)

Here, corporate greed sparked collective, peaceful, organized protest that caused a little known country to experience global attention. This injustice further evolved when the peaceful protestors were confronted with unwarranted, authoritative police brutality. Despite, local leader's skewed perceptions and practice, citizens collectively shifted role from follower to leader in enacting necessary transformation. Transformation did not begin with leadership. Often, however, voices from the margins are simply viewed as rebellious and misinformed within leadership circles. Until leadership spheres include "others," lateral hierarchies will continue to create zero-sum processes that benefit the already "haves" and ignore the increasing "have nots." Going beyond predictable leadership discussions this essay asks: *What does it mean to shift from follower to leader?* This is a process and relationship yet to be meaningfully advanced within leadership theory and practice.

Similarly, grassroots efforts, social movements, and immigration activities such as *Arab Spring, Black Lives Matter, Economy for the Common Good, Occupy Movement*, and the recent refugee crisis in Europe most dramatically and spatially emphasize "otherness." On the leadership level, these uprisings underscore that leadership, examined as management, knowledge, skill, or craft will predictably continue to promote competition, influence, domination, authority, and silencing of the "other."

While deconstructing leadership is too broad a topic here, the postmodern narrative of marginalized landscapes and individual and collective voices requires leaders to shift perspective toward progress and collaboration *and* followers to lead – breaking free of labels and tolerance. The beauty of leadership and followership, if realized, are the combined efforts toward a shared vision, where leader's undue privilege and follower's increased ownership blend together toward effective change. What underpins these changes are the often abstract, spatial relationships and social transactions "in-between" the leader–follower roles.

Therefore, the primary reason why societal, public, civic, or community leadership is a valid perspective from which to examine breaking the zero-sum game are power dynamics such as proximity and distance that allow for inclusion or exclusion to operate (Bachelard, 1994; Massey, 2010; Rushing, 2004; Tuan, 2002). Leaders must design thoughtful, inclusive places that preserve heritage, embrace evolving demographics, ultimately serving future needs, while followers must similarly look toward self-sustaining, empowerment activities. Here is where the non-zero-sum process begins to crystalize. With this as the starting point, exclusion is further explained from human geography, education, and social justice where spatial relationships and social transactions surface.

Human Geography: Borders, Boundaries, and Barriers

Doreen Massey (2010) speaks to "other" as a process that "Visiting a place is a practice of engagement an encounter with others. It is in that process of establishing a relation that the 'cost' (and the value) can be measured" (n.p.). Yi-Fu Tuan (1996) explains self as a "member" of a community that can also be alienated by feeling homeless, isolated, or alone in a vibrant lived or worked place as "tangible adversaries" (p. 188). The focus of this aspect of "other" is on the social and spatial distance and proximity to power that heightened globalization of conflicting mobility and limitations has promoted despite the myth of increased, effective connectedness. Rather, Wilbur Zelinsky suggests that *two* opposing forces are at work: homogenization and difference both have increased.

> While virtually all American places are participating to some degree or other in nationwide homogenization, as well as globalization and transnational acculturation,

many are nevertheless able to invent or assert autonomy,
to nurture a set of local variations on a cultural theme.
(Zelinsky, 2011, p. 220)

Additionally, outside the more clearly defined human geography discussion, the Commons includes shared concerns with human geography such as land use, food adequacy, knowledge sharing, removal of defined borders, boundaries, forestry, access to water, and open access resources mostly funded by tax payers, yet, most often not accessible to global citizens. Antoni Negri and Michael Hardt (2009) explain that sovereignties are dismantled and collaborated citizenship is effectively celebrated in this context. In direct opposition to the Commons is the growing popularity of gated communities within the United States. Here, the Commons free exchange of goods and knowledge versus the bordered community landscapes, the United States continues to construct the zero-sum game with varied local scale contexts. Rather, removing "other" involves belonging, caring, and awareness that allows all to feel connected locally and globally. More specifically, people can have diverse backgrounds and beliefs and also share commonalities within a defined place as Anssi Paasi suggests (2002, 2003, 2011). Additionally, Massey explains that there is a popular misunderstanding that space no longer matters as travel and technology have "shortened" distances (2010). She promotes that boundaries are equally defined as a dimension of stories and social transactions. For community leaders this emphasizes new narratives that Paasi (2002) explains as an identity to society not only attached to one's birth, but, also involving mobile spaces, immigration, and mobility. Exclusionary perspectives and policy that some belong more than "others" based on birth place fosters exclusion and has furthered the zero-sum game within increased migration and mobility.

Returning to the refugee crisis, Pope Francis publically removed the zero-sum game when he generously provided refuge for displaced families. Void of hidden agendas or political stance this humanitarian effort is a symbolic representation of *leadership reach* when the Pope widened his arms toward embracing strangers within nonbirth borders.

With a strong focus on social and material bounded spaces within human geography and varied cartographies such as the Commons and gated communities, there is a need "...to create and preserve places, rituals, and events that foster greater attachment to the social fabric of the community." (Beatley & Manning, 1997, p. 32). Many care, most want to help, but because of the homogenization process that global connectivity promotes, and the either exclusionary or cookie cutter policymaking that often results, meaningfully connecting at the local level has been eroded or ignored by community leadership scholarship.

Like it or not, this *is* leadership. While humans have traveled to outer-space and cyber-space, spatial analysis of leadership, governance, and sovereignty seldom includes this, now, once again, popular re-emergence of place analysis.

Education: Open and Free

Viewing lack of access to learning as an exclusionary leadership process, this section directly challenges the current restrictive educational, both public and at the university level; within the United States and then extends it globally. Since the 1990s of heightened network and connectivity, educational leadership strategically restricts access to research as well as isolates worldwide educational access between the global north and south. Additionally, the United States segregates access to quality education based on property tax.

In the United States the problem begins with federally appointed and elected officials *and equally includes* local public school administrators (societal leaders) whom casually submit to these discriminatory, federal mandates. Public school administrators that are nicely compensated within underperforming schools with often higher, mismanaged property taxes do not live where they work, but, are financially free to select what school district to send their children for academic opportunity. In turn, school leaders criticize the disadvantaged families for not attending "well-designed programs" in the precious evening hours that administrators strategically create without community feedback or concern. Because public school administrators are not on the receiving end of educational *in*equity they are not only *un*aware of the very root of the problem, but, also incapable of solving it. The income gap continues to widen; educational inequity goes unnoticed by most because the poor are voiceless. The zero-sum game not only continues, but, increases.

Something needs to change. The information infrastructure in place since the 1990s offers a solution to not only provide educational equity within *developed* countries such as the United

States, but, also *under*developed states - *globally* (Apple, 2011; Atkins, Brown, & Hammond, 2007; Attwood, 2009; Camilleri, Ehlers, & Pawlowski, 2014; Hylén, 2007; Johnstone, 2005; Kauppinen, 2013; Santoro, 2009; Wiley, 1998, 2006). For example, recently, underdeveloped countries lacked desktop and laptop resources to tap into this informational network. Bypassing the wired age, most now have smart phones and are networked unlike never before (*United Nations News Centre*, 2013). In the United States the educational apartheid we experienced mid-century has resurfaced despite *Brown vs. Board of Education* in 1964. Jonathan Kozol has visited "approximately 60 schools in 30 districts, situated in 11 states" (2005, p. 135) mostly from 2000 to 2005 documenting this trend.

> ...the demarcations between separate worlds of education are assuming sharper lines. There is a new emboldenment among the relatively privileged to isolate their children as so completely as they can from more than token numbers of the children of minorities. In some cities, as we've seen, young middle-class white families have successfully been pressuring their school boards to carve out almost entirely separate provinces of education for their children, ...
>
> (Kozol, 2005, p. 135)

> Those that defend the bifurcated system ... make the familiar argument, "Don't change our schools; make the others better." These people "fail to see," he wrote, "that the two systems are inextricably linked; each exists, in part, because of the other."
>
> (Kozol, 2005, p. 141)

While there is an overwhelming amount of change that needs to occur, open access to educational resources is a necessary beginning toward justice. Despite the removal of borders and increased mobility, education is divided between the "us" and the "them."

"Other" surfaces in educational apartheid with little or no challenge from public school administrators when policy attempts to "include" with mismanaged programs. This nicely packaged "othering" takes the form of profiling any population other than two parent, middle class or upper class Caucasian families to include: non-whites, families speaking two or more languages, and lone parent households to name only a few. Here, every child or family that is defined by the government as "minority" or disadvantaged receives a special, exclusionary invitation to participate in a program that provides unimaginative solutions to what those at center believe is the problem. Rather, members are voiceless in what could be meaningful dialogue. The public school system must require education equity for all regardless of how much one pays in property taxes, whether or not they receive free or reduced lunches, or have the intellectual or cultural ability to speak a second language. Standardized testing created by those at center with little regard for cultural difference, unquestionably has additionally continued to orient those whom have been at center to retain their socioeconomic standing.

While the process of globalization within the postmodern is often examined from the perspective of a market system, addition of the educational system adds clarity that people are now not only competing for profit, but, for educational justice that in turn makes improved socioeconomic attainment less possible for those marginalized at birth. Educational inequity is no longer an unconscious bias. Governments and administrative public school leadership alike enable it. The educational system requires renewed leadership, unattached to political objectives and undue privilege. It can no longer be ignored.

Local Scale Social Justice

Although this essay recognizes that broad social justice agendas should remain at the global level such as gender inequality, racism, child labor laws, and peacebuilding, a dimension not typically discussed is the *in*justice that can occur as a result of globally applied justice policy when local distinctiveness may not represent universal norms. One such issue is human security that addresses the unfair re-distribution of wealth as the increasing, income gap widens. This essay takes up the issue that globally applied socioeconomic factors have negatively impacted local self-sufficiency because the *meaning* of social justice changes from place to place. It dismisses the wide acceptance of implementing social theories as a universal solution to all human rights issues.

One way to remove "other" involves listening to the margins. Jean-François Lyotard (1984) and Richard Rorty (1998) describe the importance of understanding varied justice situations as a direct result of governance. Rorty proposes that "hearing sad and sentimental stories" (p. 167) that help people imagine the suffering of others considered "not like us" (p. 167) allows for less generic interpretation. Additionally, Lyotard states that "…if we want to be just we must create an idea and practice of justice that is not linked to that of consensus." (p. 66). The constant struggles of African-Americans in the United Sates, indigenous peoples in Australia and Americas, conflicts in Ireland and Israel, gender inequality, health inequality, social welfare in the East, and the ongoing Middle Eastern religious, economic, and political struggles and refugee crisis in Europe are representations of "othering" that limits participation and opportunity on varied scales. While leadership must understand broad policy networks, narrowing focus toward the lived experience is equally needed. In an era of globalization, local community leaders must be concerned for the varied, countless systems that impact and influence each local system and work toward horizontal, less governed "leadership." Additionally, as is increasingly the case, the Caucasian, middle class family often not associated with "othering" might more easily within the twenty-first century transition into "otherness" with an unexpected, life changing event such as a fire destroying their primary residence or poor health. Global think tanks where policy gridlock can occur often overlook local scale issues such as this.

While listening to the margins often suggests a rebellious perspective of protest and resistance as discussed earlier with the water war in Bolivia, leadership should interpret this necessary noise as a legitimate response to leadership's lack of governance. Just as global influence is developing in ways unprecedented, so too is the local scale system experiencing heightened mobility, migration, diversity, and difference. This speaks to how community leadership must expand its scope to assist in removing the zero-sum game.

"Other": Implications for Leadership

While the term "other" is found in human geography, education, and social justice, and beyond, it is rarely used within leadership scholarship. In some instances, (Conger, 1990; Hollander, 1992; Kipnis, 1976) "other" is discussed as a follower role involving various processes of authority, power, misunderstanding, and in some situations manipulation in an effort to obtain a specific goal. While Hollander (1992) and Hollander and Offermann (1990) decades ago, advanced the importance of the follower role, the progressive focus of leadership characteristics and styles since, has over powered this necessary social justice concern.

"Other": Space and Practice

Though awareness of these spatial relationships and social transactions is useful in understanding this phenomenon of *followership justice* and *leadership reach*, it does not fully explain the complexity of bordered, yet, connected binaries of global or local, inclusion or exclusion, and leader or follower dynamics. Of the three disciplinary features of "other" examined, efforts to include "other" within leadership is further complicated by its abstractness. While understanding of the: "out there," "here," "near," "far," "distant," "close," "at borders," and "in-between" is necessary, such a journey may not be an approach that current leadership welcomes, or values. Therefore, the chapter questions became: *What leadership scholarship might community leadership and followership collectively and positively respond to in an effort to remove the zero-sum game on a local scale? What emergent leadership theory provides solutions for inclusionary practice that synch with the abstract tensions around social barriers and material borders?*

Place Leadership Theory

Putting this together, a vision for the future toward breaking the zero-sum game involves borderless contexts; open, fluid, and free access to knowledge; and listening to voices from peripheries. A common thread here is the need for local leadership to broadly understand global activities while focusing on local connectivity and relationships. Based on place leadership theory, Chris Collinge, John Gibney, and Christopher Mabey (2010) from the University of Birmingham suggest that relying on national programs to impact economic recovery is insensitive and not applicable to locale (Collinge et al., 2010). Without a truly transformational approach, community will continue to lose sight of the cultural, competitive advantage in understanding and sustaining a locale's unique sense of place.

Accurately measuring community wellness is needed so that locales are better positioned to be economically strong as they simultaneously operate in a global marketplace and work toward local social justice. Leadership of place connects place, policy, leadership, and followership in response to policy weakness within the context of globalization. Place leadership is not about reacting or responding to crisis, but averting social, cultural, political, and environmental issues before exclusion occurs (Collinge & Gibney, 2010). Rather, it encourages and develops sustainable policy for all members. Examining the intersection of placemaking and policymaking offers a catalyst for positive change in promoting increased community wellness.

Spatially, place leadership theory promotes leveraging horizontal resources rather than the traditional top down leadership approach toward local policymaking (Collinge & Gibney; Collinge, et al.; Mabey & Freeman, 2010). Chris Collinge and John Gibney suggest it will create a more "fair, sustainable and yet competitive economic development" (p. 379) for communities that have experienced significant change and challenges as a result of increased global connectivity. This intersection of placemaking and policymaking begins by first developing a strong understanding of place that results in more effective policymaking for all members.

> Place becomes the nexus for the delivery of an improved integration of vertical, horizontal and cross-boundary public service delivery across spatial scales and economic development, planning and regeneration policy themes.
>
> (Collinge & Gibney, 2010, p. 387).

The full impact that place leadership can have on removing the zero-sum game *and* leadership scholarship is far from realized. What is known is that community concept of place and followership tolerance are changing. In response, governance must also keep pace and equally evolve. Reacting to crisis rather than fostering proactive change is not the solution as the transformational style promotes. Moving beyond the long-standing silo thinking of traditional community leadership and replacing it with a leadership style that offers a place-based approach can only push removal of the zero-sum game forward.

Summary: "Other" as Postmodernism Fades

By reaching beyond leadership scholarship toward *followership justice* and *leadership reach*, challenging traditional transformational change approaches, transdisciplinary dissecting of concept of "other," equally holding leaders and followers accountable, and weaving postmodern binaries throughout and then replacing these concepts together again by funneling this through place leadership theory, we can begin to see the complexity and range of the moving parts. Combined, the ever growing leadership discipline and complex geopolitical and economic powers briefly introduced here, operating at global and regional levels while impacting countless locales, concept of "other," *followership justice*, and *leadership reach* requires continued inquiry. Put another way, it is an awareness and acceptance of the need to embed *followership justice* and *leadership reach* within the wider leadership scholarship and the abstract concept of "other" that underpins and explains them that will position leadership theory and practice at the forefront of removing the zero-sum game as postmodernism fades.

Where do we go from here? This begins with introducing unresolved questions with possible solutions for further exploration, investigation, and debate.

1. *What does it mean to move from a followership position to a leadership role?*
   When one shifts from the periphery toward center, the newly promoted leader is in a unique position to remove inequality. They can act as a mediator and articulate concerns of the voiceless to policy and decision makers. Ideally, *followership justice* can now be placed on the agenda and demand accountability from governance. However, as is often the case, these bold leaders lose influence when their concerns are not shared by the elite. Moving from followership to leadership, therefore, often does not translate into effective change.
2. *How can society accept and reward duality of leader–follower roles?*
   People participate in different roles within various contexts. One might perform a support role for an employer, yet, is conversely perceived as leader within community. Society

often does not make room for these conflicting titles. Leadership scholarship should advance exploring roles beyond the "what do you do for a living?" context as this acceptance begins to remove leadership inequalities by rewarding critical, behind the scenes activities that often act as more authentic change agents.

3. *Is leadership reach a process that leadership theory is willing to embrace? In other words, are leaders willing to give up some pie?*

One percenters serve as the unprecedented population where wealth hording has significantly widened the income gap. With the exception of a few sacrificial philanthropists, this increasing inequality is a direct result of "leaders" not willing to give up some of the pie. Change can occur through improved educational contexts and social advocacy efforts where people are reached with knowledge of how the world is geopolitically and economically organized. This empowerment process will begin to reverse this trend of undue wealth and begins with increased followership engagement that academia is equipped to promote as the twenty-first century progresses.

4. *How might this interrelated process of often worsening conditions for the disadvantaged become more recognized in leadership circles?*

Increased exposure to diversity and difference and increased accountability and transparency around financial related practices of elected and appointed community leaders where this information becomes publically available will empower membership. Equally, citizens and residents must commit to seeking this knowledge, thus, equipping themselves toward challenging ineffective policy toward cultural sustainability for the future.

5. *How can these coercively deepening and widening structures within society be examined and resolved?*

Negotiation and conflict resolution models should be mutually developed and implemented for community leaders and members to leverage.

6. *Where are the leader and follower boundaries?*

Leaders must understand regional contexts where less defined areas have meaning without shared governance. This can be seen in the global south that includes various countries, urban fear as shared across cities, educational apartheid shared by New York City and developing countries, and access to clean water or adequate resources experienced in California and third world countries. Leadership theory and practice must either embrace these regionally connected social spheres or clearly define where implied borders between leader and follower should live and operate. This research suggests that leadership should not define these borders.

7. *How can the binary activities of governance and tolerance be further explained?*

Leaders govern and followers often tolerate. This dual process promotes the zero-sum game. However, in an age of surveillance, binaries can no longer be suppressed or ignored. Rather, peaceful dialogue between opposing experiences emerges as a political space for solutions. Mutually agreeing to listen regardless of stance or position will correctly shift unfair governance and the tolerance that passively enables it.

8. *What does the bridge between the leader and the follower look like?*

This bridge can only be represented horizontally and void of fear as a regional balance between the local and global scales. Hierarchies and monolithic structures must be dismantled as society seeks *followership justice* and *leadership reach*.

Acknowledgments

I acknowledge that my concepts are inspired by varied lived experiences. The natural, built, and human landscapes that have shaped my discourse — in chronological order are artistic expression; spatial analysis; Pennsylvania German (Dutch) sensibilities; geographies of the Oley Valley in Berks County, Pennsylvania; cityscapes of Philadelphia; tensions in-between; the Harriet Sartain Travel Fellowship from Moore College of Art & Design to observe and experience modern architecture and urban planning and development in the cities of Houston, Dallas, San Francisco, and Chicago; my adult and teen aged daughters Sian, Joi, Kallan, and Liya; ignoring pedestrian American parenting; slipping from middle class into poverty; losing a home; independently reaching for once familiar socioeconomic stability; tolerating countless injustices; advocating for justice, beige cubicles, Alvernia University in Reading, Pennsylvania and the Franciscan intellectual tradition as a non-Catholic; concepts of place and space, hex signs; and the barn and skyscraper as leadership–followership metaphor. I am grateful to the International Leadership Association and the editors of this book for allowing such a way of thinking to contribute toward this inclusionary text. The terms *followership justice* and *leadership reach* are mine as the result of my combined lived experience and encouragement of my daughters.

References

Agger, B. (2006). *Critical social theories* (2nd ed.). Boulder, CO: Paradigm.

Apple, M. W. (2011). Global crises, social justice, and teacher education. *Journal of Teacher Education, 62*(2), 222–234.

Atkins, D. E., Brown, J. S., & Hammond, A. L. (February 2007). *A review of the open educational resources (OER) movement: Achievements, challenges, and new opportunities* (Vol. 13). Menlo Park, CA: The William and Flora Hewlett Foundation.

Attwood, R. (2009). Get it out in the open. *Times Higher Education (London).*

Avolio, B. J., & Bass, B. M. (1994). *Transforming communities through effective leadership*. Final report to the W.K. Kellogg Foundation. Binghamton, NY: State University of New York at Binghamton.

Avolio, B. J., & Gibbons, T. C. (1988). Developing transformational leaders: A life span approach. In J. A. Conger & N. Rabindra Kanungo (Eds.), *Charismatic leadership: The elusive factor in organizational effectiveness* (Vol. xii, Issue 352, pp. 276–308). San Francisco, CA: Jossey-Bass.

Bachelard, G. (1994). *The poetics of space*. Boston: Beacon Press.

Bass, B. M. (1995). Theory of transformational leadership redux. *The Leadership Quarterly, 6*(4), 463–478.

Bass, B. M. (2008). *The Bass handbook of leadership; Theory, research & managerial applications* (4th ed.). New York, NY: Free Press.

Bass, B. M., & Avolio, B. J. (1990). Training and development of transformational leadership: Looking to 1992 and beyond. *European Journal of Industrial Training, 14*(5), 21–27.

Beatley, T., & Manning, K. (1997). *The ecology of place: Planning for environment, economy, and community*. Washington, DC: Island Press.

Camilleri, A. F., Ehlers, U. D., & Pawlowski, J. (2014). *State of the art review of quality issues related to open educational resources (OER)*. Luxembourg: Publications Office of the European Union.

Collinge, C., & Gibney, J. (2010). Place-making and the limitations of spatial leadership: Reflections on the Øresund. *Policy Studies, 31*(4), 475–489.

Collinge, C., Gibney, J., & Mabey, C. (2010). Leadership and place. *Policy Studies, 31*(4), 367–378.

Conger, J. A. (1990). The dark side of leadership. *Organizational Dynamics, 19*(2), 44–55.

Gumplowicz, L. (1963). *Outlines of sociology* (2nd ed.). New York, NY: Paine-Whitman.

Heil, D. (2010). Understanding and leading organizations: A hermeneutic phenomenological investigation. *Philosophy Today, spring*, 7–17.

Hollander, E. P. (1992). Leadership, followership, self, and others. *The Leadership Quarterly, 3*, 43–54.

Hollander, E. P., & Offermann, L. (1990). Relational features of organizational leadership and followership. In K. E. Clark & M. B. Clark (Eds.), *Measures of leadership* (pp. 83–97). West Orange, NJ: Leadership Library of America.

Hylén, J. (2007). *Giving knowledge for free: The emergence of open educational resources*. Paris, France: OECD Publishing.

Johnstone, S. M. (2005). Open educational resources serve the world. *Educause Quarterly, 28*(3), 15–18.

Kauppinen, I. (2014). Different meanings of 'knowledge as commodity' in the context of higher education. *Critical Sociology, 40*(3), 393–409.

Kipnis, D. (1976). *The Powerholders*. Chicago, IL: University of Chicago Press.

Kozol, J. (2005). *The shame of a nation: The restoration of apartheid schooling in America*. New York, NY: Three Rivers Press.

Küpers, W. (2010). 'Inter-Place' - Phenomenology of embodied space and place as basis for a relational understanding of leader-followership in organizations. *Environment, Space, Place, 2*(1), 81–121.

Lyotard, J.-F. (1984). *The postmodern condition: A report of knowledge*. Minneapolis, MN: University of Minnesota Press.

Mabey, C., & Freeman, T. (2010). Reflections on leadership and place. *Policy Studies, 31*(4), 505–522.

Massey, D. (2010). *Is the world getting larger or smaller? Open Democracy*. Retrieved from http://www.open.democracy.net/print/4354. Accessed on March 2016.

Negri, A., & Hardt, M. (2009). *Commonwealth*. Cambridge, MA: Harvard University Press.

Paasi, A. (2002). Bounded space in the mobile world: Deconstructing 'regional identity'. *Tijdschrift voor Economische en Sociale Geografie, 93*(1), 137–148.

Paasi, A. (2003). Region and place: Regional identity in question. *Progress in Human Geography, 27*, 475–485.

Rorty, R. (1998). *Truth and progress: Philosophical papers, 3*. Cambridge, UK: Cambridge University Press.

Rushing, W. (2004). Globalization and the paradoxes of place: Poverty and power in Memphis. *City & Community, 3*, 65–81.

Santoro, D. (2009). Teaching to save the world: Avoiding circles of certainty in social justice education. *Philosophy of Education, 6*, 241–249.

The Democracy Center. (2000). *Bolivia's war over water: Dispatches from the scene: February – April 2000*. Retrieved http://democracyctr.org/bolivia/investigations/bolivia-investigations-the-water-revolt/bolivias-war-over-water/

Tuan, Y.-F. (1996). *Cosmos and hearth: A cosmopolite viewpoint*. Minneapolis, MN: University of Minnesota Press.

Tuan, Y.-F. (2002). Community, society, and the individual. *Geographical Review, 92*(3).

United Nations News Centre. (2013). *Speakers at UN event urge stronger leadership, or financing to ensure education for all.* Retrieved from http://www.un.org/apps/nres/story.asp?NewsID=46003

Wiley, D. (1998). Open Content. Retrieved from OpenContent.org.

Wiley, D. (2006). *The current state of open educational resources.* Paper for Expert Meeting on Open Educational Resources.

World Bank. (2013). *Inclusion matters: The foundation for shared prosperity.* Washington, DC: World Bank.

Young, I. M. (1990). *Justice and the politics of difference.* Princeton, NJ: Princeton University Press.

Zelinsky, W. (2011). *Not yet a placeless land: Tracking an evolving American geography.* Boston, MA: University of Massachusetts Press.

5

Denizen Leaders as Radical Negotiators of Third Alternatives in Complex Societies: Not Yours, Not Mine, But Ours

Rouxelle de Villiers and Colleen Rigby

Keywords: Contextual intelligence; equity; persuading

Denizen Leaders in Just Societies

Socially just leadership ensures equal participation and resources for all, and thus requires a clear set of principles (Noble, 2015a, 2015b). Socially just leaders are proactive, engage in transformative behaviours and are acutely aware of societal issues (Snyder, 2013). They show courage, persistence and commitment to a social justice agenda; encourage participation; rely on inclusive communication and examine their own assumptions and biases (Bogotch, 2002).

Leaders in complex societies are negotiators between opposing parties, using processes and principles to reach 'third alternatives' (Covey, 2011) — not win-lose, lose-lose or impasse — to
resolve conflict. Negotiators need to see the problem from a
different perspective than that of the opposing parties (Fisher,
Ury, & Patton, 1987, 2011). This requires denizen leadership —
people who are of that place, but whose world view differs from
that of their colleagues, competitors and foes.

Nelson Mandela aimed to resolve issues through negotiation
rather than civil war; he was both a citizen and an alien within
his own society. This alienation enabled him to see the third
alternative, which enabled a peaceful transition and showed how
to challenge dangerous assumptions that reinforced the status
quo. This chapter expands on the concepts of denizen leaders,
the elements underlying negotiation in complex situations and
considers how inclusive theory applies (Declerck, 1986; Koenig-
Archibugi & Zürn, 2006). Inclusive theory stresses the use of
social power and influence to bring all parties to a common goal.

We examine the *principles of negotiation* to reach a third
alternative, the *assumptions of key parties* where social justice
issues are at stake, the *capabilities* shown by a denizen leader to
reach radical alternatives and the *behaviours* denizen leaders use
to overcome assumptions and biases (Larson & Luthans, 2006;
Luthans, Youssef, & Avolio, 2007) (Fig. 1).

We examine the assumptions of one party (OP) and the other
party (TOP) based on the work of negotiation and leadership
authorities (Bass & Riggio, 2006; Brett, 2007; Covey, 2011;
Fisher & Ury, 1982; Goleman, Boyatzis, & McKee, 2003;

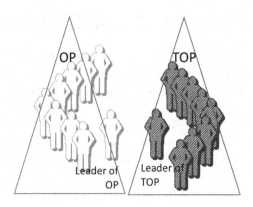

Fig. 1.   Two-Party Negotiations: One Party (OP) Versus TOP (About Here).

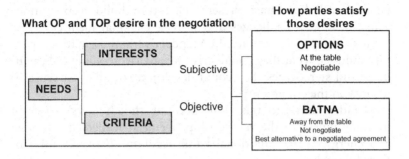

Fig. 2.   What Parties Desire in Negotiation and Methods to Satisfy Their Desires. *Source*: Adapted from Grande and Wanis-Saint (2003).

Pruitt & Carnevale,1993; Woodside, 2012; Weick, 1995) and our study of Nobel Laureates (Rigby & De Villiers, 2014)

We also consider the behaviours and characteristics of denizen leaders as radical negotiators, in situations where agreement has previously been unable to be reached (Fig. 2).

The 3rd Alternative: Negotiating Beyond 'Yours' or 'Mine'

BE TOUGH ON THE PROBLEM AND SOFT ON THE RELATIONSHIP

Negotiation involves allocating resources including people, money, equipment, time, political or social power and status. Negotiators have to consider conflicting interests to find a 'net value outcome: an agreement that is better than an alternative of no agreement' (Brett, 2007, p. 7) or what Roger Ury (2007) calls the third alternative. In negotiation dilemmas, 'no agreement' may be unacceptable or disastrous. The needs of OP and TOP and the minimum requirements to reach an agreement must be identified, and help must be given for leaders to engage inclusively and move beyond satisficing (accepting a barely acceptable agreement) to ensure satisfaction for both OP and TOP.

Balance Interest in Task and Relational Outcomes

Eric Klinger's (1977) motivational theory is that humans pursue issues that are emotionally important to them. The key difference between happiness and meaningfulness lies in people being givers rather than takers (Parker, 2014). Meaningfulness occurs when people can link the past, present and future, build deep relationships, deal with challenges and have a personal identity in the context of their community. In Mandela's 'rainbow nation', people could see what they could strive for; by overcoming old prejudices and stereotypes they could develop a socially just sense of identity in the community.

Leaders have to take into account stakeholders' sense of meaningfulness in the relationship. Denizen leaders invest time and energy in the 'emotional bank accounts' (Covey, 2007) of their followers.

Leadership scholars report that leaders need to build inspiring relationships to get things done (Boyatzis, Jack, Cesaro, Passarelli, & Khawaja, 2010; Goleman, Boyatzis, & McKee, 2005). Effective leaders do not focus on outcomes and measures too soon, as this may result in closed minds and strong negative 'dissonance' (Boyatzis, 2016).

While attending to TOP's inter-personal priorities, interests and positions, leaders have to consider the strategic outcome, aiming to generate high net value for all parties by finding a balance between the relationships and the task outcomes for both parties.

Consider and Uncover Multiple Interests, Including Cultural Differences and Basic Human Needs

In today's complex societies and business contexts, cultural sensitivity is vital for building strong, lasting relationships. Balancing relationships and tasks is at the core of effective leadership. A hazard in negotiated outcomes is assuming all participants have the same cultural values, beliefs or norms. Suggested outcomes need to be explained and accepted at individual-level negotiations (Fisher et al., 1987).

Fisher and Shapiro (2005) define the core concerns in negotiation as appreciation, affiliation, autonomy, status and role. Leaders who deliver upon these fundamental interests generate buy-in for their ideas.

Individuals are guided by beliefs, the most important of which is trust. We adopt the definition of trust, stated by Audun Josong and Stephane Presti (2004, p. 1) as *'the extent to which one party is willing to depend on somebody or something in a given situation with a feeling of relative security, even though negative consequences are possible'*. Since trusting OP makes TOP vulnerable, leaders demonstrate trust and act in a trustworthy manner by giving information in order to receive information.

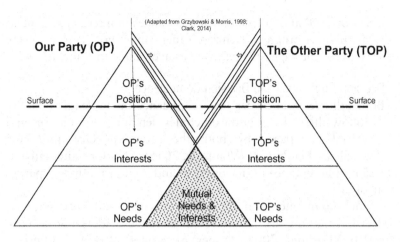

Fig. 3.   Position versus Interest in Negotiation.

Denizen leaders seeking social justice or buy-in to proposals are aware of the importance of small talk, acts of service, patience and goodwill and the role these actions and attributes will play in generating and demonstrating trust.

Standards of appropriate and inappropriate behaviour in a given context are termed 'norms' (Brett, 2007, p. 39). Communication norms reduce the number of choices we have when deciding how to behave and provide guidance on how we can expect others to behave. To negotiate suitable third alternatives, leaders must know if they are dealing with high-context cultures, where the unspoken contextual meaning of the communication has great weight, or low-context cultures, where meaning is based mostly on words. Denizen leaders need to understand the norms, beliefs, interests and priorities of TOP in high-context cultures, to see which norm is guiding the conversation (Brett, 2007) (Fig. 3).

Listening and Seeing with Your Mind and Your Heart

Denizen leaders need to understand many aspects of TOP in order to reach a common purpose or agreed outcome. Denizen leadership calls for mindful observation of verbal and non-verbal gestures and communication. Denizen leaders focus on clarifying expectations and assumptions, and are willing to change as the negotiations proceed. According to Kathleen Reardon (2005, p. 17), communication improves if both parties 'articulate the type of interaction they intend to have', but unfortunately this is seldom done. Leaders need to declare their intent, ascertain the intent of TOP and keep monitoring changes in interests and intent as discussions progress. Denizen leaders' main goal is to persuade TOP to see the suggested pathway as acceptable to some degree.

Decision Confidence and Decision Competence

Both follower and leader need confidence in the leader's ability to follow through, so good outcomes demand good choices and perceived confidence by both the proposer (OP) and TOP (De Villiers, Hankin, & Woodside, 2015). The third alternative is a sign of acceptance of, inclusion in and admiration for all parties involved.

Self-confidence and the ability to deal with ambiguity in decision making are important in effective leaders (Goldsmith, 2010; Khurana, 2002; Stoner & Stoner, 2013), leading to higher levels of persistency when faced with adversity (Hollenbeck & Hall, 2004; Stoner & Stoner, 2013). Confidence in one's own ability (also known as efficacy) is often a result of 'successive successes' (Bandura, 1998; Gist, 1987; Stoner & Stoner, 2013). Finding a senior mentor as role model is one effective way to develop confidence and accept ambiguity in decision making (Goldsmith, 2003). Within an organization, inexperienced leaders can benefit from observing the actions and decisions of more experienced staff.

A third way to improve self-efficacy is positive reinforcement — praise and encouragement from respected others. The praise-giver must however be credible and that 'praise and encouragement must be perceived as realistic' (Stoner & Stoner, 2013, p. 47). A fourth method to assist emerging leaders is by investing in personal psychological capital (Luthans & Youssuf, 2004; Luthans, Avolio, Avey, & Norman, 2007) — a state characterized by self-confidence, optimism, perseverance and resilience — which can be developed through training (Boyatzis, Smith, & Blaize, 2006) where emerging leaders face their fears and reframe adversities as challenges (Stoner & Gilligan, 2002).

IDEATION AND MULTIPLE POSSIBLE ALTERNATIVES FOR MUTUAL GAIN

Beyond Zero-Sum or Fixed Pie: From Problem Solving to Futuring or Forward-Flecting

When conflicting parties realize their futures are inter-dependent, a dramatic shift of awareness occurs, away from inter-personal relationships and conflicts, towards shared values and mutual interest (a 'win-win' situation), taking into account the importance of creating value for all stakeholders, identifying objective standards to allow claimants to focus on the interests, and not separating the people and the problem (Lax & Sebenius, 1986).

Purposeful action is where the future can be created intentionally and aligned with values When parties are asked to imagine themselves in the future looking back 'scenarios become more creative, more collaborative and [...] more actionable in the short run'. (Lindaman & Lippitt, 1979).

Mandela and Aung San Suu Kyi were both capable of 'forward-flexing' — projecting from the present into the future and 'almost being able to stand at that future point and look back on the effect of a decision' (Gerwel in Higgins, 2013, p. 13). Of his prolonged imprisonment, Mandela said: 'It was a tragedy to lose the best days of your life, but you learned a lot. You had time to think — to stand away from yourself, to look at yourself from a distance, to see contradictions in yourself' (Lieberfeld, 2004, p. 390.)

Reframing, Re-diagnosing the Problem; Intelligence Gathering

A major task of leaders is to transform organizations and lead followers towards new visions, even though this may involve highly invasive changes (Liu, 2010). To achieve disruptive innovations or alterations, leaders have to persuade followers that the suggested path is worth following, by finding a mental mode TOP can embrace and accept 'without losing face'.

Do you prefer six eggs or half a dozen? The way you describe a situation reflects your framing of the situation. If TOP accepts the frame without question, the discussion will proceed within that defined perspective (Fisher et al., 1987). The framing of an issue has four major attributes (Knight, 1999): a description of the problem; an identification of the cause of the problem; a recommended solution; and a moral evaluation of the causal agent and its relation to the problem. Of the four, problem identification is probably the most important, using five framing devices: metaphors, exemplars, catch phrases, depictions and visual images. Leaders hone their ability to frame and reframe a problem; when skilfully applied, this can shift the focus away from conflict and result in negotiations towards possible solutions (Kahneman & Tversky, 1984).

Denizen leaders consider TOP's attitudes, fears and natural risk aversion (O'Neill, 2001) and frame issues to help avert or negate those fears and risks.

Denizen leaders realize that the way they ask questions, encode assumptions and behave, will frame how people think about a situation or plan. In the words of Joseph Jaworski (1998, p. 168):

> ... it is through language that we create the world, because it's nothing until we describe it. And when we describe it, we create distinctions that govern our actions. To put it another way, we do not describe the world we see, but we see the world we describe.

By using analogies, stories, metaphors and symbols that help demonstrate common interests (rather than differences), denizen leaders can frame more persuasive and convincing arguments to make TOP more willing to consider alternatives they might have otherwise ignored (Reardon, 2005).

Rules of Engagement and Decisions

Adrian McLean (2013, p. 23) writes that 'meaning is neither universal nor fixed'. He supports his arguments with various examples of non-verbal language such as the gesture of 'thumbs up' which is seen as an expression of hope or good luck in the UK, but as friendship or copulation in Corfu or Turkey. Leaders must be interested in and sensitive to the meanings held by gestures, words and symbols to ensure that assumptions do not lead to misunderstandings. All humans use heuristics or mental short cuts — ways to observe, make sense of their environments and make decisions — in order to deal with the daily overload of information they face (Gigerenzer, 2004; Todd, 2001; Weick, 1995, 1998, 2007). We 'see what we normally see or are trained to see'. For example, in some organizations punctuality will be noticed, recorded and rewarded. In others the emphasis might be on accuracy or innovation or collaboration. These cultural foci or organizational norms generate the unconscious and deliberate culture of the organization (Hofstede, 2001), so that staff and stakeholders learn what is important and 'how it is done here'.

Jeanne Brett (2007, p. 217) reports on the difficulty of managing and leading multi-cultural teams and suggests that an important resource provided by leaders is organizational support for the team. A leader's role is to provide support for team activities, define clear tasks and roles and offer support for collaboration models, norms and decision rules.

Denizen leaders need to get all parties to address conflict. Negotiation and leadership experts (Brett, 2007; Reardon, 2005) suggest four important strategies: (i) build inter-personal trust, dignity and respect; (ii) focus energy on the same task; (iii) build diversity and tolerance of differences and (iv) develop and set norms for interaction and decision rules that everyone is willing to abide by. Leaders need to have an understanding, respect and tolerance for the communication, decision and confrontational structures of TOPs, balanced by clear moral and ethical standards that 'will carry them and their followers through situations of corruption, bribery, and extortion' (Brett, 2007, p. 282).

Wear TOP's Shoes for a Day; Join Them 'at ground zero' — Total Immersion

To achieve integrative solutions, where all parties believe the suggested path/plan is fair, leaders need familiarity with the approaches, interests, values and 'unwritten rules' of TOP and need to be sensitive to signals of distrust; status symbols; who holds the power of veto and who pretends to be in charge; which mistakes will be tolerated and which are intolerable to TOP.

To understand the real meanings of the communicated messages of TOP, denizen leaders must be able to read the unspoken messages; uncover the hidden agendas; and make qualified guesses at the unexpressed desires and interests of all stakeholders (Geertz, 1973; Marshall & McLean, 1985). Mindful denizen leaders consciously pursue interpretive frameworks to understand TOP, while carefully persuading TOP (including their own employees) to accept the suggested pathway/third alternative. In leadership and negotiation training, the importance of the written word and the spoken word are emphasized, but impromptu or rehearsed gestures and the use of symbols will affect 'new understanding' and 'new meanings' in a major way.

Leaders need to stay in touch where 'touch simply means being present and available to your people' (Stoner & Stoner, 2013, p. 181). They relate the story of how New York mayor, Giuliani spent days at Ground Zero following the 9/11 attacks on New York City in 2001. Denizen leaders model the behaviour they expect and by doing that, 'enhance constituents' ability to thrive' (Jackson & Daly, 2011, p. 22). They are not only inclusive; they seek to be included.

Nobel laureate Nelson Mandela spent much time during his incarceration talking to his white jailers, attending various church functions, reading the oppressors' daily newspaper and spending time with other inmates of various political viewpoints (Mandela, 2008). As a denizen leader, Mandela knew to don the symbol of the Springbok rugby jersey early in his term as president to show solidarity with his new white followers (Lieberfeld, 2009).

Matters of Trust

TRUST

There are three types of trust (Folger, Poole, & Stutman, 2013). In a Promotive or Cooperative interdependence, the parties can open up to others knowing this will be supported and feelings can be expressed safely. Power is not used indiscriminately and shared power is favoured so that all parties work towards a unified solution, so a future together as a social unit is possible.

On the other hand in Competitive and Individualistic types of trust, where power is used individualistically and it is unsafe to express feelings, the outcome may have little future. To build a climate of trust in social justice issues, the leader needs to demonstrate empathy to others' views no matter how at odds they might be with their own. Change of any sort brings uncertainty and while one way to reduce this uncertainty is to make assumptions, this may not be the best option. Other ways include open discussion of what people expect of the negotiation climate, what would be needed for it to change and ways to create a positive climate (Fig. 4).

COLLABORATION

Negotiation may result in destructive adversarial processes, or relationship-building process (Claremont & Davies, 2005). The former occurs when a single issue escalates and conflict then spirals, individuals are scapegoated and new problems are added to the original issue. Collaboration, on the other hand, involves guiding, encouraging and empowering TOP — not imposing values or judgements to reach an agreed outcome. The collaborative denizen leader is impartial, able to set aside assumptions and personal beliefs during the negotiation process. Denizen leaders understand the various sources of power that may arise, and handle them in a strategic and empathic way. Active listening, reflection and open-ended questioning are significant competencies of the collaborative leader.

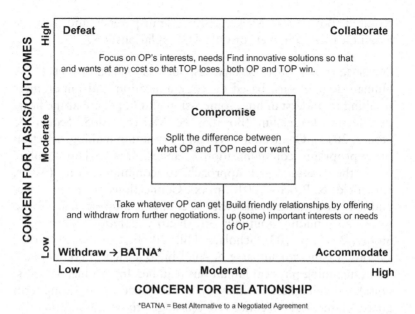

Fig. 4. Five alternative outcomes in negotiations. *Source:* Adapted from Grzybowski and Morris (1998), Thomas and Kilmann (1978).

CONSIDER AND UNCOVER MULTIPLE INTERESTS

Transparency, Self-Awareness and Balanced Processing

Psychologists believe that attitudes are composed of feelings, knowledge and action intent. Business consultants call this the ABC of attitude: affect (feelings and emotions), beliefs (thoughts, also called cognition) and conation (intentions). Denizen leaders are aware of the importance of attitudes, and manage their own by reflecting on their feelings, intentions and cognitions in an organized and structured manner. They also aim to build the ABC of attitudes of TOPs and followers.

Influencing attitudes means intentionally influencing the beliefs of TOP, which form the basis of TOP's attitude towards leaders' suggestions and plans. Often feelings precede beliefs, because feelings can arise automatically, whereas beliefs take conscious effort. However, TOP's attitudes can be better understood and influenced when both feelings and beliefs are considered. Leaders' actions 'speak louder than words'. Thus, denizen leaders need social intelligence, excellent communication skills and the ability to influence inter-personal interactions to effect the change required (Boyatzis & McKee, 2005). Transparency and trust are vital in leader–follower (or OP–TOP) relationships.

Combined Forces: Hope, Mindfulness, Compassion and Resilience

Human connections, based on communication and mindfulness resulting in understanding, compassion and hope, are at the heart of effective leadership (Boyatzis & McKee, 2005; Stoner & Stoner, 2013). Connections depend on meaning making, selection of appropriate communication channels, and what scholars term 'the transactional approach to communication' (Adler, Rosenfeld, & Proctor, 2013, p. ix). Connections are about 'give-and-take communications' with a common interest in resolving issues and finding mutually satisfactory solutions (Stoner & Stoner, 2013, p. 103). Scholars (Hill, 2003; Reardon, 2005) list various reasons for impasse or total break-down in communications, including physical limitations (e.g. hearing problems, stress, noise); unwillingness or inability to recognize mutual long-term goals; biases and preconceived blockages to collaboration; and low levels of cultural and inter-organizational sensitivity. The single most important skill for an emerging leader is 'attunement' — the ability to listen for underlying meaning (Bernard, 2009; Lax & Sebenius, 2013; Stoner & Stoner, 2013), cultural nuances, and reflections of interests and intentions aimed at understanding TOP, rather than merely making one's own point (Goleman, 2006; Johnson & Beechler, 1998, p. 86). When such skills are consistently practiced, long-term, trusting networks result.

Promise-keeping, truth-telling and unwavering fairness build ethics and hope. Mandela felt that 'honesty, sincerity, simplicity, humility, pure generosity, absence of vanity, readiness to serve others — qualities which are within easy reach of every soul are the foundation of one's spiritual life' (Mandela, 1975, p. iii in Nwagbara, 2013).

MAINTAINING 'FACE' — A CONCERN FOR BOTH PARTIES

Denizen leaders are able to maintain 'face' (Ting-Toomey, 1998). The idea of 'face' is based on the dual Chinese concepts of loss of face with accompanying feelings of shame, and gaining/restoring face through status, recognition, influence and power. To build face, leaders use clusters of behaviours that uphold and support TOP's face throughout the negotiation, even if OP disagrees with TOP's stance. Face can be lost when identity is at risk, cultural norms are not taken into account or intercultural communication is poor. Face plays a significant role in conflict behaviour (Ting-Toomey & Oetzel, 2003). In low-context cultures, individuals might behave competitively if they feel their self-image is threatened, whereas in high-context cultures, conflict may be avoided to save face. The leader may need to use preventative or restorative strategies to restore face.

Vision: A Primer for Efficacy and Optimism

MAKING THE VISION VISIBLE

When leaders can articulate a vision, such as Mandela's 'Rainbow Nation', and reflect this in artefacts (a new flag for the new nation), optimism for a collaborative and socially just outcome is more likely to exist. As Richard Rorty (in Bennett, 2015, p. 25) noted: 'To retain social hope, members of a society need to be able to tell themselves a story about how things might get better, and see no insuperable obstacle to this story's coming true'.

Once a leader has established the hope that justice will prevail, the next step is to establish feasibility. Denizen leaders need to speak the 'language of possibility' (Freire, 2003, p. 87). They need to not only articulate current limitations, but to imagine a reality that lies beyond such limitations and act 'to create contexts of freedom and dignity for all'.

INSPIRING OTHERS TO GREATNESS: DREAMING BIG

When seeking social justice, denizen leaders need to inspire people to dream big. This often requires dialogue with people at all levels to build the feasibility of the vision. Victories for social justice and human rights happen because of collaborative efforts (Kauffman & Wolff, 2010, p. 168). It takes openness on the leader's part to hear the naysayers and to engage with the limiting conditions, finding ways to remove roadblocks.

Denizen leaders move followers to act in ways they didn't dream possible. Great leaders unite opposing parties in a common vision, helping onlookers to become followers.

Dangerous Assumptions of 'Ineffective' Leaders Versus Sensitive Assumptions of 'Effective' 3rd Alternative Leaders

Assumptions can arise as a response to a perceived threat. Those perceiving a threat make inferences and reach conclusions — often attributing blame to TOP, followed by a sense that TOP should be punished. Fear and anger escalate and can cause further negative thinking about the situation, making it more difficult to respond constructively and regulate emotions (Goleman, 2006).

Past experiences give all parties to a negotiation a set of assumptions that may guide their choices (Zhou, Zhang, & Xie, 2014). Denizen leaders must be aware that their own and TOP's mindset(s) can influence the outcome. The negotiator can either focus on TOP's feelings or assumptions to create value for all, or focus on win-lose outcomes (Xie & Zhou, 2012). Assumptions in social justice negotiations can become a barrier to interpretation and problem solving. In negotiation it is important to consider 'the Who' (relationships), 'the What' (emotional perceptions, relationship, status, power and external effects) and 'the When' (one-off events, distinct phases, and multiple rounds within ongoing relationships (Bendersky & McGinn, 2010, p. 781)

Leaders who do not tap into the unstated assumptions may inadvertently perpetuate inequities. For a collaborative outcome, leaders need to see the negotiation topic as a problem that can be solved. 'Negotiators usually assume that conflicts are more competitive than they are' (Lewicki & Hiam, 2006, p. 129).

GETTING PAST ASSUMPTIONS AND BARRIERS TO INSIGHTS

The assumptions of OP and TOP may differ (Bass & Riggio, 2006). One party may see themselves as the saviour in terms of self-concept, while another has the perception that they are fighting for liberty or democracy. As an example, South Africa's apartheid government saw itself keeping communism at bay, while the African National Council (ANC) framed their struggle as a democratic vote for all. The words used by parties to label each other may be emotive. Labelling (e.g., those fighting for a cause may be labelled freedom fighters or terrorists) may pigeon-hole TOP and build fear or support amongst constituents.

Silence by the parties may also play a role in outcomes. The assumption might be that the silent person in a negotiation is the one who holds the power when TOP is out of the room, or that the silent person is irrelevant to TOP. This creates further assumptions about power, teamwork and relationships.

Getting past assumptions often requires the leader to ask some key questions to determine how TOP might have ... At this point the leader may ask TOP if there are other ways to see the issue; what the event/issue might have looked like had parties not been acting with any malevolent intent, and how personally important the situation is now. This opens up the possibility that there is an alternative construal of the event or issue. Give this open discussion, tensions are likely to ease (Runde & Flanagan, 2010).

Characteristics and Traits of Denizen Leaders

There are seven characteristics of denizen leaders (see Fig. 5) that can help to create, maintain or promote social justice: contextual

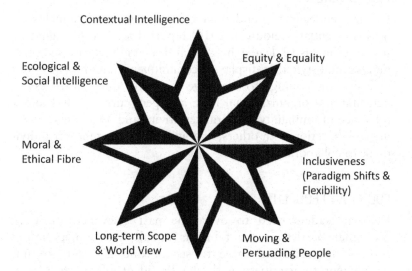

Fig. 5. Denizen leadership star of characteristics and traits.

intelligence, ecological and social intelligence, inclusiveness, moral and ethical fibre, a long-term scope and world view, the ability to move and persuade people, the ability to shift a pattern of thinking and the ability to deal with others equitably and equally. These are discussed in more depth below:

CONTEXTUAL INTELLIGENCE

Leaders with contextual intelligence can differentiate and integrate complex information (Coren & Suedfeld, 1990; Suedfeld & Coren, 1992). They can interpret information in complex situations holistically, taking into account all aspects and all stakeholders, while differentiating between multiple aspects of the system without stereotyping or showing prejudice. Leaders dealing with social justice can stay focused on the evolving social system in which negotiation takes place.

ECOLOGICAL AND SOCIAL INTELLIGENCE

Denizen leaders can operate within a complex and sometimes chaotic environment, but remain steadfast on achieving the vision. With contextual intelligence they can finely balance the needs of the environment, social justice and TOP.

INCLUSIVENESS

For denizen leaders to undertake effective negotiations, inclusiveness is essential. Deloitte's (2016) report describes the signature traits of inclusive leadership. Such leaders have an inclusive mindset and style that displays a commitment to and inclusion of diversity; the courage to challenge the status quo; awareness of personal and organizational bias; an open, curious mind and a tolerance of ambiguity; cultural sensitivity and awareness; ongoing collaboration with others; and willingness to empower individuals to collaborate.

EQUITY AND EQUALITY

Denizen leaders need to overcome past grievances to treat the other parties at the table as equals in the negotiation process. Mandela was able to see beyond 27 years of imprisonment to negotiate with the President of South Africa, De Klerk, to reach an equitable agreement. Similarly Aung San

Suu Kyi[1] had to overcome the issues of prolonged home detention to negotiate with the military. Both have done this in the interests of democracy for their people.

TOP might try to increase their equity by building bigger delegations. Denizen leaders must apply procedural rules to ensure equity and equality at the negotiation table, despite group size or past resource controls.

Despite being confronted with 'us and them' stereotypes of OP and TOP, denizen leaders see beyond the stereotypes. They do not fall into the trap of using a common enemy to reach resolution. They aim to be inclusive of all parties, no matter what the past has brought. Denizen leadership often requires the ability to see a pattern that could exist outside of the current framework (Freire, 2003). A paradigm is a pattern of thinking, which may be held by an individual or a group. Denizen leaders can reframe the problem in a different pattern and engage others with this new pattern of thinking.

MORAL AND ETHICAL FIBRE

Denizen leaders have the moral and ethical fibre to step outside of the typical corruption and tyranny that accompanies social injustice. They remain morally uncorrupted and maintain a clear vision of the future in broad terms, with minimal deviation from that vision, while keeping TOP on board.

PERSUASION: MOVING PEOPLE

Denizen leaders use the power of persuasion (Cialdini, 2001) to influence people to move from fixed positions. It is the ability to talk about what parties might lose if they do not go along with a proposed solution that may persuade, rather than what they might gain. Other factors that persuade are the ability to seek a high goal but retreat to a fallback position during negotiation, the power of reciprocity and keeping people aware of what other parties are doing.

---

[1]*Nobel Peace Prize* laureate *Aung San Suu Kyi* is a Burmese social democratic stateswoman, politician and diplomat who serves as Leader of the National League for Democracy (NLD). *Aung San Suu Kyi* led the NLD to a majority win in Myanmar's first openly contested election in 25 years in November 2015. The win came five years to the day since she was released from 15 years of house arrest.

LONG-TERM SCOPE AND WORLD VIEW

Denizen leaders see solutions like stargazers looking through a telescope. They know that want they need to achieve is not a short-term option. It requires patience and long-term vision. They focus on building the feasibility of the vision in the long term, bringing in whomever it takes to turn the vision into reality. Mandela built relationships with western powers, but also with those who had supported the struggle, such as Gaddafi in Libya and Castro in Cuba.

Denizen leaders can step out of their own circumstances and see a global view. Their mental model of reality is based on a theory that encompasses a macro view of the situation, and lets them keep the end goal in sight.

Conclusion

We have focused on denizen leaders who bring about social justice; however, it is also important to consider how this applies to leaders of global enterprises. Consider Tim Cook of Apple's stand against the FBI on phone hacking and Google's decision not to be censored in China (Knijnik, 2013). These leaders can be seen as aliens within their core business, fighting for social justice.

The characteristics and processes outlined here could apply equally to denizen leaders within organizations. Many of the characteristics that apply to denizen leaders fighting for social justice in the political and social world apply also to denizen leaders in global organizations. So what can organizations do to develop denizen leadership for just and socially responsible leadership? By formally assessing leadership negotiation styles and capabilities, organizations can identify gaps and strengths, then actively develop the characteristics and traits of denizen leaders willing to open their minds to the long-term social, economic and socio-cultural benefits of third alternatives. Integrating such skills and attributes into formal and informal development plans for emerging and advanced leaders will benefit global organizations. Leaders should be encouraged to reflect on their practices and to pursue feedback from their constituents and stakeholders on their capacities as denizen leaders. Leadership mentors, coaches, trainers and consultants should convince leaders to practice denizen leadership. They can then optimize the use of talent, support greater involvement of and responsibility towards all constituents, and act as radical negotiators for third alternatives in complex societies to the greater good of all.

References

Adler, R. B., Rosenfleld, L. B., & Proctor, R. F. (2013). *Interplay: The process of interpersonal communication.* New York, NY: McGraw-Hill.

Bandura, A. (1998). Personal and collective efficacy in human adaptation and change. In J. G. Adair, D. Belanger, & K. L. Dion (Eds.), *Advances in psychological science: Vol. 1. Personal, social and cultural aspects* (pp. 51–71). Hove, UK: Psychology Press.

Bass, B. M., & Riggio, R. E. (2006). *Transformational leadership.* Boston, MA: Psychology Press.

Bendersky, C., & McGinn, K. L. (2010). Open to negotiation: phenomenological assumptions and knowledge dissemination. *Organisation Science, 21*(3), May-June, 781–797.

Bennett, O. (2015). Cultures of optimism: *The institutional promotion of hope.* Hampshire, GBR: Palgrave MacMillan.

Bernard, P. E. (2009). Bringing soul to international negotiation. *Negotiation Journal, 25*(2), 147–159.

Bogotch, I. E. (2002). *Educating for eco-justice and community.* Athens, GA: University of Georgia Press.

Boyatzis, R. E. (2016). *Neuroscience and leadership*: The promise of insights. The Kenscho Search Advantage. Retrieved from https://www.researchgate.net/publication/265068320_Neuroscience_and_Leadership_The_Promise_of_Insights. Accessed on August 20, 2016.

Boyatzis, R. E., Jack, A., Cesaro, R., Passarelli, A., & Khawaja, M. (2010). *Coaching with Compassion: An fMRI Study of Coaching to the Positive or Negative Emotional Attractor.* Presented at the Annual Meeting of the Academy of Management, Montreal. Neuroscience and Leadership: The Promise of Insights. Retrieved from https://www.researchgate.net/publication/265068320_Neuroscience_and_Leadership_The_Promise_of_Insights. Accessed on August 20, 2016.

Boyatzis, R. E., & McKee, A. (2005). *Resonant leadership: Renewing yourself and connecting with others through mindfulness, hope, and compassion.* Boston, MA: Harvard Business Press.

Boyatzis, R. E., Smith, M. L., & Blaize, N. (2006). Developing sustainable leaders through coaching and compassion. *Academy of Management Learning & Education, 5*(1), 8–24. doi:10.5465/AMLE.2006.20388381.

Brett, J. M. (2007). *Negotiating globally. How to negotiate deals, resolve disputes, and make decisions across cultural boundaries.* San Francisco, CA: John Wily & Sons, Inc.

Cialdini, R. B. (2001). Harnessing the science of persuasion. *Harvard Business Review, 79*(9), 72–81.

Claremont, R., & Davies, L. (2005). *Collaborative conflict management.* Sydney: Lansdowne.

Coren, S., & Suedfeld, P. (1990). A power test of conceptual complexity: Textual correlates. *Journal of Applied Psychology, 20*(3) 357–367.

Covey, S. R. (2007). *The seven habits of highly effective people*. Sydney, Australia: Simon & Schuster.

Covey, S. R. (2011). *The 3rd alternative: Solving life's most difficult problems*. New York, NY: Simon and Schuster.

De Villiers, R., Hankin, R., & Woodside, A. G. (2015). *Decision Confidence and Decision Competence*. Paper presented at the ANZAM, Queenstown, New Zealand.

Declerck, R. (1986). Definiteness and inclusive reference. *Journal of Literary Semantics, 16*(1), 12–29.

Deloitte. (2016). The Six Signature Traits of Inclusive Leadership: Thriving in a diverse new world. Deloitte University Press. Deloitte Touche Tohmashu Sydney, Australia.

Fisher, R., & Shapiro, D. (2005). *Beyond reason: Using emotions as you negotiate*. New York, NY: Penguin Group.

Fisher, R., & Ury, W. (1982). *Getting to yes*. London: Hutchinson.

Fisher, R., Ury, W., & Patton, B. (1987). *Getting to yes*. New York, NY: Simon & Schuster Sound Ideas.

Fisher, R., Ury, W. L., & Patton, B. (2011). *Getting to yes: Negotiating agreement without giving in*. New York, NY: Penguin books.

Folger, J., Poole, M. S., & Stutman, R. K. (2013). *Working through conflict: Strategies for relationships, groups, and organizations*. (7th Ed.). Boston, MA: Pearson.

Freire, P. (2003). *Pedagogy of the oppressed*. New York, NY: Continuum.

Geertz, C. (1973). *The interpretation of cultures: Selected essays*. New York, NY: Basic Books.

Gigerenzer, G. (2004). Fast and frugal heuristics: The tools of bounded rationality. In D. Koehler & N. Harvey (Eds.), *Blackwell handbook of judgment and decision making* (pp. 62–88). Oxford, UK: Blackwell.

Gist, M. E. (1987). Self-efficacy: Implications for organizational behaviour and human resource management. *Academy of Management Review, 12*(3), 472–485.

Goldsmith, M. (2003). Helping successful people get even better! *The Journal for Quality and Participation, 26*(1), 4.

Goldsmith, M. (2010). *What got you here won't get you there: How successful people become even more successful*. New York, NY: Hyperion.

Goleman, D. (2006). *Social intelligence: The revolutionary new science of human relationship*. New York, NY: Bantam Books.

Goleman, D., Boyatzis, R., & McKee, A. (2003). *The new leaders*. London, UK: Little, Brown.

Grande, L., & Wanis-Saint, J. A. (2003, June 2016). ICON for Negotiation Advice. Retrieved from http://www.mediate.com/articles/thoughtbridge4.cfm. Accessed on November 15, 2015.

Grzybowski, A., & Morris, C. (1998). Canadian negotiation, mediation and communication training materials. Victoria, British Columbia, Canada. *Institute for Dispute Research, University of Victoria and Pacific Resolutions*.

Higgins, J. (2013). Living out our differences: Reflections on Mandela, Marx and my country: An interview with Jakes Gerwel. *Thesis Eleven, 115*(1), 7–24.

Hill, L. A. (2003). *Becoming a Manager: How New Managers Master the Challenges of Leadership.* Boston, MA: Harvard Business School Press.

Hofstede, G. (2001). *Culture's consequences: Comparing values, behaviors, institutions and organizations across nations.* New York, NY: Sage Publications, Inc.

Hollenbeck, G. P., & Hall, D. T. (2004). Self-confidence and leader performance. *Organizational Dynamics, 33*(3), 254–269.

Jackson & Daly. (2011). All things to all people: Adversity and resilience in leadership. *Nurse Leader, 21,* 22–30.

Johnson, S. D., & Beechler, C. (1998). Examining the relationship between listening effectiveness and leadership emergence: Perceptions, behaviours, and recall. *Small Group Research, 29,* 452–471.

Jøsang, A., & Presti, S. L. (2004, March). Analysing the relationship between risk and trust. In *International Conference on Trust Management* (pp. 135–145). Berlin, Heidelberg: Springer.

Kahneman, D., & Tversky, A. (1984). Choices, values, and frames. *American Psychologist, 39*(4), 341–350. doi:10.1037/0003-066X.39.4.341. Accessed on December 5, 2015.

Kauffman, P., & Wolff, E. A. (2010). Playing and protesting: Sport as a vehicle for social change. *Journal of Sport and Social Issues, 34*(2), 154–175.

Khurana, R. (2002). The curse of the superstar. *Harvard Business Review, 30,* 60–66.

Klinger, E. (1977). *Meaning and void: Inner experience and the incentives in people's lives.* Minneapolis, MN: University of Minnesota Press.

Knight, M. G. (1999). Getting past the impasse: Framing as a tool for public relations. *Public Relations Review, 25*(3), 381–398. doi:10.1016/S0363-8111 (99)00016-8.

Knijnik, J. (2013). Visions of gender justice: Untested feasibility on the football fields of Brazil. *Journal of Sport and Social Issues, 37*(1), 8–30.

Koenig-Archibugi, M., & Zürn, M. (2006). New modes of governance in the global system: exploring publicness, delegation and inclusiveness theory. *Journal of the Motherhood Initiative for Research and Community Involvement, 8*(1), 55–69.

Larson, M., & Luthans, F. (2006). Potential added value of psychological capital in predicting work attitudes. *Journal of Leadership & Organizational Studies, 13*(2), 75–92.

Lax, D. A., & Sebenius, J. K. (1986). *The manager as negotiator.* New York, NY: Free Press.

Lax, D. A., & Sebenius, J. K. (2013). *3-D Negotiation: Powerful tools to change the game in your most important deals.* Boston, MA: Harvard Business Press.

Lewicki, R. J., & Hiam, A. (2006). *Mastering business negotiation: A working guide to making deals and resolving conflict.* San Francisco, CA: Jossey-Bass.

Lieberfeld, D. (2004). Peace profile: Nelson Mandela. *Peace Review: A Journal of Social Justice, 16*(3), 387–392.

Lieberfeld, D. (2009). Lincoln, Mandela, and qualities of reconciliation-oriented leadership. *Peace and Conflict: Journal of Peace Psychology, 15*(1), 27–47.

Lindaman, E. B., & Lippitt, R. O. (1979). *Choosing the future you prefer. A goal setting guide.* Ann Arbor, MI: Human Resource Development Associates.

Liu, H. (2010). When leaders fail: A typology of failures and framing strategies. *Management Communication Quarterly, 24*(2), 232–259.

Luthans, F., Avolio, B. J., Avey, J. B., & Norman, S. M. (2007). Positive psychological capital: Measurement and relationship with performance and satisfaction. *Personnel psychology, 60*(3), 541–572.

Luthans, F., Youssef, C. M., & Avolio, B. J. (2007). *Psychological capital: Developing the human competitive edge.* Oxford, United Kingdom: Oxford University Press.

Luthans, F., & Youssuf, C. M. (2004). Human, social and now psychological capital management. *Organizational Dynamics, 32*(2), 143–160.

Mandela, N. (2008). *Long walk to freedom: The autobiography of Nelson Mandela.* Hachette Digital, Inc.

Marshall, J., & McLean, A. (1985). Exploring organisation culture as a route to organisational change. In V. Hammond (Ed.), *Current research in management* (pp. 2–20). London: Francis Pinter.

McLean, A. (2013). *Leadership and cultural webs in organisations: Weavers'. Tales:* Emerald Group Publishing.

Noble, D. J. (2015a). Pratfalls, pitfalls, and passion: The melding of leadership and social justice. *Creighton Journal of Interdisciplinary Leadership, 1*(2), 107–119.

Noble, D. J. (2015b). Leading for tomorrow in a world yearning for justice. In M. Sowcik, A. Andenoro, M. McNutt, & E. Murphy (Eds.), *Leadership 2050: Critical challenges, key contexts and emerging trends* (pp. 43–58). Bingley, UK: Emerald Group Publishing Limited. Ch.3.

Nwagbara, U. (2013). The human side of political leadership: Conversations with Myself (2010) as a reflection of servant -leadership Nelson Mandela. *Leadership, 9,* 141–144.

O'Neill, B. (2001). Risk aversion in international relations theory. *International Studies Quarterly, 45*(4), 617–640.

Parker, C. B. (2014). *Stanford research: The meaningful life is a road worth travelling.* Stanford Report. Retrieved from http://news.stanford.edu.news/2014/January/meaningful-happy-life-010114.html. Accessed on August 20, 2016.

Pruitt, D. G., & Carnevale, P. J. (1993). *Negotiation in social conflict.* Salt Lake City, UT: Thomson Brooks/Cole Publishing Co.

Reardon, K. (2005). Becoming a *skilled negotiator.* Danvers, MA: Wiley and Sons, Inc.

Rigby, C., & De Villiers, R. (2014). Bringing about Global Change through Reconciliation Leadership. *Paper presented at the International Leadership Association's 16th Annual Global Conference. San Diego,* 30 October-2 November 2014.

Runde, C. E., & Flanagan, T. A. (2010). *Developing your conflict competence. A hands —on guide for leaders, managers, facilitators and teams.* San Francisco, CA: John Wiley & Sons.

Snyder, S. (2013). *Leadership and the art of struggle: How great leaders grow through challenge and adversity.* Oakland CA: Berrett-Koehler Publishers.

Stoner, C. R., & Gilligan, J. F. (2002). Leader rebound: How successful managers bounce back from the tests of adversity. *Business Horizons, 45*(6), 17–24.

Stoner, C. R., & Stoner, J. S. (2013). *Building leaders: Paving the path for emerging leaders.* New York, NY: Routledge.

Suedfeld, P., & Coren, S. (1992). Cognitive correlates of conceptual complexity. Personality *and Individual Differences, 13*, 1193–1199.

Thomas, K. W., & Kilmann, R. H. (1978). Comparison of four instruments measuring conflict behavior. *Psychological Reports, 42*(3), 1139–1145.

Ting-Toomey, S. (1998). Intercultural conflict styles: A face negotiation theory. In Y. Y. Kim & W. B. Gudykunst (Eds.), *Theories in intercultural communication* (pp. 213–238). Newbury Park, CA: Sage.

Ting-Toomey, S., & Oetzel, J. (2003). Face concerns in interpersonal conflict: A cross-cultural empirical test of face negotiation theory. *Communication Research, 30*(6), 599–624.

Todd, P. M. (2001). Fast and frugal heuristics for environmentally bounded minds. In G. Gigerenzer & R. Selten (Eds.), *Bounded rationality: The adaptive toolbox* (Vol. Dahlem Workshop Report, pp. 51–70). Cambridge, MA: MIT Press.

Ury, W. (2007). *Getting past no: Negotiating in difficult situations.* New York, NY: Bantam.

Weick, K. E. (1995). *Sensemaking in organizations.* Thousand Oaks, CA: Sage.

Weick, K. E. (1998). The attitude of wisdom: Ambivalence as the optimal compromise. Organizational Wisdom and Executive Courage, 40–64.

Weick, K. E. (2007). Drop your tools: On reconfiguring management education. *Journal of Management Education, 31*(1), 5–16. doi:10.1177/1052562906293699.

Woodside, A. G. (2012). Incompetency training: Theory, practice and remedies. *Journal of Business Research, 65*, 279–293. doi:10.1016/j.jbusres.2011.10.025.

Xie, T., & Zhou, J. (2012). Feelings and comparisons in negotiation: One subjective outcome, two different mechanisms. *Public Personnel Management, 41*(5), 21–33.

Zhou, J., Zhang, Z. -R., & Xie, T. (2014). Making collaborators happy: The outcome priming effect in integrative negotiation. *Public Personnel Management, 43*(3), 290–300.

6

Exploring Inclusive Leadership through the Lens of a Collaborative Structure

William Clark

Keywords: Self-leadership; inclusive leadership; collaboratives; nonprofit leadership; community leadership; strategy development; change management

Introduction

The financial and political interests of the powerful few seem to overshadow the needs of local communities. These same individuals hold positions of significant leadership that embolden the behavior that causes harm to the unpowered many. This creates, what many unpowered communities view as a zero-sum world where they see themselves as the losers. Consequently, these communities struggle to piece together its precious resources to maintain their dignity.

Community members must be empowered to develop the skills to fortify itself from pilfering. Through inclusive leadership, community leaders can build their capacity to maximize and leverage the diverse talents, backgrounds, and perspectives of all community members (Janakiraman, 2011). The principles of inclusive leadership are important for community leaders to embrace, as they take on meaningful leadership roles in their communities that will have a sustainable impact. While inclusive leadership can be applied to the type of leaders that have a broader sphere of influence, inclusive leadership can be readily applied to community leaders to develop their capacity to influence change from the bottom up.

Inclusive leaders have the capacity to cause meaningful changes in our community. Inclusive leadership seeks to engage the relevant thoughts, feelings, emotions, and values of others to make the right and best decision that benefits the community. The leadership decisions that are made as a result of inclusive leadership behaviors are made for more than just influencing people to achieve a common goal. The focus of an inclusive leader is on arriving at a decision that is responsive to the feedback received from the community. The final decision, although flawed in some instances and limited due to the reality that everyone's feedback will not be included, is inclusive by way of hearing people in an honest and sincere way that lets them feel like they are a part of the process and made a meaningful contribution.

In this chapter, you will learn the important lesson of what it means to be inclusive and how to develop those skills within collaborative structures. Communities are depending upon emerging leaders to embrace the principles of inclusive leadership and apply those lessons in a way that will contribute to the resolution of the most pressing issues facing the community.

What Is Inclusive Leadership?

THE BASICS OF INCLUSIVE LEADERSHIP

Many practitioners and theorist define leadership as the process of influencing a group of people to achieve direction, alignment, and commitment toward a goal (Northouse, 2013; Van Velsor, McCauley, & Ruderman, 2010). Through leadership, organizations create the infrastructure needed to establish market positioning. Leadership studies have a host of subsidiary theories that explain a variety of leadership styles. One such style is inclusive leadership.

Inclusive leadership is a "distributed approach" to leadership that seeks to engage members of the team and key stakeholders in the process of designing a specific future or set of goals (Alimo-Metcalfe, 2010). Inclusive leadership is the antithesis of common practices of leadership that hoards the responsibility of developing and casting a vision within a limited scope of influencers. Central to the ideals of inclusive leadership is embracing the diversity of the team. Diversity can be defined by a number of identifiers — culture, place of birth, language, experience, worldview, etc. An inclusive leader embraces these identifiers as an opportunity to influence individual followers.

The diversity of an individual creates an opportunity for effective influence. This is important for leaders of all types because researchers believe the methods of influence used by a leader have a long-lasting impact on the follower (Chong, 2014). A positive or negative experience can have a ripple effect in the life and career of a follower for years. The driving force behind diversity practices of inclusive leadership is to leverage the strengths and potential of each team member to inch closer to the goal of the team (Alimo-Metcalfe, 2010).

INCLUSIVE LEADERSHIP WITHIN A COLLABORATIVE STRUCTURE

While a collaborative organization establishes its market position, the collaborative will begin to walk through developing its capacity to operate as a market influencer. As a market influencer, the collaborative is choosing to use its collaborative muscles to achieve a full-range of goals. As a market influencer, a collaborative should have the following characteristics to ensure its goals are achieved (Hall, 2013).

- The organization is honest and does business the right way
- The organization is a trusted source of information
- The executives of the organization are thought leaders
- The organization has a meaningful relationship with consumers
- Key employees are considered experts in the field
- The organization receives awards for its work
- The organization is known for treating people well
- The organization shows up in the top search results of customers
- The organization has a positive online reputation
- The organization has a presence at major industry events

Collaborative members bring their cultures and ways of doing business to the collaborative. This can create challenges as the collaborative seeks to operate as a single new organization.

Staffs of the collaborative spend the majority of the time navigating the diversity that exists within the structure. This challenge takes an inordinate amount of time of the staff because managing the egos and business interests of each member must be weighed against the interests of other members, all the while synthesizing all interests toward a set of common goals. The best practices of managing this structure and its variety of nuances emanate from the foundation of inclusive leadership practices.

Inclusion is typified by the acceptance of the diverse backgrounds, skills, and contributions of a variety of people who can help an organization achieve its ultimate goal. Through inclusion, an organization avoids any appearance of exiling any ideas from persons that can potentially add value in the future. Inclusive organizations feed off of the new energy and competency of the persons that are invited into the strategy development process (Simmons, 1995).

INCLUSIVE LEADERSHIP APPLIED

Collaborative structures are a ripe foundation for creating and strengthening inclusive leadership practices because a collaborative cannot survive on the single contributions of one member. Since the contributions of all members are needed for the success of the collaborative, staff of a collaborative naturally executes inclusive leadership. There are a variety of models that explain inclusive leadership in ways that are relevant to organizations, countries, and individuals, however, Charlie Marrow presents a model of inclusive leadership that is grounded in three core areas of practice — leading self, leading culture, and leading relationships. Below is a deeper dive into each element (Morrow, 2015).

Leading self, also known as self-leadership, is the focus on leading self to achieve a personal set of goals (Houghton & Neck, 2002). While most leadership theories focus on the leadership of others, self-leadership encourages leaders to focus on their own leadership development. The foundations of self-leadership are three strategies for personal development — cognitive strategies, behavioral strategies, and natural reward strategies. Leading self is a natural fit within the inclusive leadership paradigm. Self-leaders set goals they are looking to achieve as an individual. These goals vary based on the context with which these goals are set. Within the parameters of inclusive leadership, self-leaders know the importance of engaging all partners to ensure the collaborative incorporates these voices within its operations.

A self-leader who is leading a collaborative structure knows the importance of personal humility, individual consideration, and middle of the road management practices (Northouse, 2013). As a result, all three of these practices become the goals of a self-leader and all of their cognitive and behavioral strategies are recalibrated to achieve these goals.

Leading culture is the process of providing direction to the practices, values, believes, and underlying assumptions of an organization (Rashid, Sambasivan, & Rahman, 2004; Russell, 2001). An organization's culture is a reflection of how they historically responded to past experiences to preserve the values of the organization and create default mechanisms that ensure continuation of a desired behavior (Lim, 1995). Inclusive leaders are continuously looking for opportunities to expand buy-in to the culture so more members become owners of the culture and make it ubiquitous. To deepen the infusion of the culture within individual members, inclusive leaders utilize several tactics that include the alignment of individual goals with the goals of the organization and continuous exposure to the culture. Both approaches seek to sustain these standards through individual commitments and consensus.

Leading relationships are the power skill of influencing people to do something that serves the greater good of the organization and their personal goals. Transformational leadership is one such mechanism that helps inclusive leaders build meaningful relationships that result in the common good for the organization and individuals (Northouse, 2013). Transformational leaders elevate the needs and interests of others ahead of making self-serving decisions. It is segmented into four quadrants, otherwise known as the four I's. The four I's of transformational leadership are Idealized influence, Inspirational motivation, Intellectual stimulation, and Individualized consideration (ibid). Transformational leaders build personable relationships with followers and create an equitable culture that transcend beyond their self-interest to meet a higher level of needs (Bass, 1985).

Collaborative Self-Leadership

The overlap between self-leadership and inclusive leadership within a collaborative structure is the development of organizational behaviors that result in self-directed teams, self-managing teams, and high-performing teams (Neck & Manz, 2013). This is essential for collaboratives because they are comprised of many members who bring their unique organizational perspective to the collaborative. Since this perspective is not guaranteed to be checked at the door when engaging in collaborative work, the value that is placed on self-directed teams within a collaborative is even more important. The goal of these self-directed teams forces the collaborative to develop behaviors that are unique to the collaborative and not a reflection of the values of a single member.

A closer look at organizational self-leadership shows that it is more of a reflection of inclusive leadership. When you consider the behavior of a self-leading organization, you will see the bubbling of inclusive behaviors that creates a solid mix of the partners that are a part of a collaborative relationship. As a reminder, self-leadership is undergirded by three strategies. Those strategies are cognitive strategies, behavioral strategies, and natural reward strategies.

COGNITIVE STRATEGIES

Cognitive strategies are the creation of thought patterns that influence behaviors (Houghton & Neck, 2002). Within a collaborative structure, partners come together to establish a unique way of thinking that is a mishmash of all of the collective values and goals of the partners involved. Collectively, a collaborative organization comes together to shape belief systems, vision, and values (Neck & Manz, 2013). The belief systems of a self-leading collaborative include the mission and goals. The mission and goals of the collaborative do not represent the interest of a single member; rather, it's the collective representation of what all members of the partnership value. Secondly, a specific design of the future is what drives the creation of collaborative relationships. The future is what members of the collaborative latch on because what results from a collaborative can have long-term benefits toward the personal interests of each member. Lastly, the values of the collaborative allow the collaborative to remain focused on what initially brought them together. This helps members of the collaborative work together to pursue common goals and filter out ideas that do not help the collaborative reach these goals.

BEHAVIORAL STRATEGIES

Behavioral strategies are the execution of cognitive strategies (Houghton & Neck, 2002). Behavioral strategies are the results of the belief systems, visions of the future, and reaffirmation of values a collaborative organization has established. When a collaborative organization has thought through how it will function as a unified body, the behavioral strategies that are implemented provide the necessary support to sustain the decision that has been made. Those sustainable approaches include the following (Neck & Manz, 2013).

Self-observation: A collaborative that observes its behavior keeps track of how well it is doing according to the cognitive approaches it has developed. One such approach includes being aware of the performance of the collaborative according to its cognitive standards. This observation helps the collaborative to determine if it is on the correct pathway forward.

Self-goal setting: When organizational goals are set, it is incumbent upon the organization to permeate these goals into the work of every organizational member. Personal goals are established so individuals can measure their contribution to the goals of the collaborative.

Self-rewards: Rewards are mechanisms that are used to highlight achievements that align with the goals of an organization. A collaborative structure can have a reward system that notifies each member that the collaborative is performing as planned. It is important that these self-rewards are routinely shared among collaborative members.

Practice: Practice is when an individual or team improves their ability to perform a task before executing the task in a public domain. During practice an individual or group learns how to perform the task as second nature to their core functions. It is during this time of preparation alternative plans are created to confront challenges that will arise.

NATURAL REWARDS

Natural reward strategies are the elements of a task that are enjoyable and elevate one's interest in the task (Houghton & Neck, 2002). Natural rewards are achievable within collaborative organizations. To encourage team members to find natural rewards as they engage in the work of the collaborative, these rewards must be clearly defined based upon the interests of each member and integrated into the strategy of the collaborative. For example, if a youth serving organization is energized (or receives natural rewards) by developing strategies to better serve youth, a collaborative that is comprised of members that serve youth will find their connection to the collaborative via any youth centered strategy and is likely to best inform the collaborative's strategy relative to youth. If the youth serving organization is able to develop a strategy for the collaborative that aligns with their own strategy to serve youth, they are rewarded with the natural excitement of knowing they have increased their impact in partnership with the collaborative.

Collaborative Structures or Networks

Collaborative structures are a network of businesses or organizations that work together, in some capacity, to increase the competitiveness of the entire network of partners (Lam, Chan, Ip, & Lau, 2008). While the partners in the collaborative may be competitors in the open market, they leverage the benefits of being in a collaborative to lower overhead costs, pursue a common strategic agenda, and other joint interest to extend their resources. The National Fund for Workforce Solutions (National Fund), a leader in the development and formation of collaborative structures, invested in the operations of 35 collaboratives across 26 states since 2007 with a focus on workforce development. As a result of their investment, 53,000 individuals completed an occupational skill training and 75% of those individuals earned an industry-approved credential. The National Fund also actively supports 2,300 employers in 85 active industry partnerships to employ over 1 million workers.

The National Funds' work has led to the development of nationally recognized guidelines of a high-performing collaborative (*Characteristics of a high-performing funders collaborative*, 2014).

- Share a strategic vision
- Operates with a clear and compelling purpose
- Generates financial support from partners
- Works under strong management
- Advocates for evidence-based decision making

- Ensures sustainability
- Communicates effectively

These characteristics are critical to validating the strength of a collaborative structure. The absence of any of these characteristics can lead to a breakdown in trust and will subsequently impact the market and upset customers.

Organizations enter collaborative relationships for business benefits, but maintaining a collaborative structure requires intermittent pulse checks in the following areas (Parung & Bititci, 2008).

- Commitment: Members of the collaborative are focused on the goals that are developed by the group. Members are not frazzled by the challenges that arise and are not threatened by the success of the collaborative.
- Coordination: Because the collaborative is made of members that do not typically work together, the collaborative must be held together through the coordination of all of its activities. The strategic interests, communication, and collaborative activities much are coordinated to ensure that one voice emanates from the collaborative on behalf of every member. Even though every member may not agree with all of the decisions of the collaborative, the outputs from the collaborative are aligned with the collective interest of all members.
- Trust: Collaborative structures are formed because of similar business interests. In some cases, this means, competitors in the same market working together even though they compete for the same market share. The collaborative relationship is the opportunity for competitors to put aside their competitive interest and focus on building a relationship based on mutual interests. Through this relationship, trust is developed and is earned, which can result in mutual respect and understanding outside of the collaborative relationship.
- Communication: The communication between collaborative partners is vital to the smooth functionality of the collaborative. A collaborative structure inherently presents communication challenges because each partner comes to the relationship with their own communication styles and mechanisms that works within their respective organization. Organizational representatives use terms and acronyms familiar to them to describe persons, places, or things. Without explaining the meaning of these terms, partners may

misinterpret those words. Subsequently, the partnership will have to develop a shared understanding of those terms to move their joint business interests forward.

- Conflict Resolution: Similar to the challenges partners face as they grapple with their communication challenges, partners of a collaborative will also have to work through how to resolve conflicts as they arise. Conflict can show up when a major decision has to be made. Since partners of a collaborative are within the same market and compete for the same book of business, conflict may be inevitable within a collaborative. Conflict can stem from unique ways of handling decision-making, strategy development, and execution of tasks. However, the greater interest for partners is how the collaborative will benefit their respective businesses. While the collaborative is meant to be a neutral zone for competitors, who are now joining forces, organizational representatives are continuously mindful of the competitive advantage they can gain by the decisions made within a collaborative structure. It becomes extremely important to have a neutral collaborative staff that can help navigate through the complexities of this new partnership and the self-interests that are represented by each organization.

Removing the Zero-Sum for Struggling Communities through Collaborative Structures

CREATE A COLLABORATIVE

Research has proven that collaborative structures are useful in developing inclusive leadership practices and behaviors. If there is any possibility of developing a win-win for helping communities overcome their challenges while encouraging government intervention and the investment of large and small businesses, that possibility begins with the development of effective collaborative relationships between the community, government, and business owners. Developing a collaborative is hard work but it can be done if the joint interest of all parties remains the focus of the collaborative.

Collaborative structures are effective tools for leveraging their internal assets and joining larger communities for greater impact. Collaborative structures can be comprised of members of multiple communities that add value to the conversation of economic development and community development. Members of the collaborative may include politicians, businesses, organizations, and the community itself.

Before establishing a collaborative with members of influence, it stands to reason that communities that are looking to overcome economic devastation should establish smaller collaboratives to develop and model inclusive leadership. Proving success on a smaller scale will generate trust and interest from potential members who may want to create a larger collaborative, in partnership with several smaller collaboratives, to have a larger impact.

Establishing a new collaborative can be fun and exciting because the energy around a new project is infectious. Although this work can be exciting, it is imperative to ensure that the collaborative is staffed with strong leadership to keep the collaborative going even during its toughest times. This is where the application of inclusive leadership comes into play. Inclusive leadership is a critical element for any collaborative to survive.

INCLUSIVE LEADERSHIP EXAMPLE THROUGH A COLLABORATIVE

An example of a collaborative organization that has exhibited the elements of inclusive leadership practices is a case study about a service-oriented collaborative that serves youth (the Collaborative). The Collaborative's mission is to create a successful future for youth. This collaborative is comprised of over 30 partners that come together to inform and execute the strategy of the Collaborative. Members of the Collaborative agree to take an active role in a strategy group.

The strategy groups aforementioned require effort from partners. These working groups develop strategies that push the Collaborative forward and must be strong enough to attract funding from philanthropic sources. Therefore, members that decide to join a strategy group are also deciding to make an investment in the forward progress of the collaborative and success of their own organization. The Collaborative has exhibited best practices in developing a strong sustainable collaborative through inclusive leadership. Below is the framework for how inclusive leadership impacted the Collaborative.

LEADING SELF

The Executive Director of the Collaborative exhibits self-leadership, which has set the tone for how she leads the culture and relationships of the collaborative. The Executive Director has established meaningful cognitive goals such as recognizing each member of the collaborative as co-leaders and responsible partners. This type of thinking perpetuates a servant leadership posture.

Secondly, The Executive Director translates cognitive strategies of servant leadership into action. The servant leadership behaviors that extend cognitive strategies into action include frequent communication, inclusion on grant applications, and soliciting guidance and feedback. The combination of these cognitive strategies maintains a focus on being a servant leader, which lays a foundation for an inclusive leadership culture.

LEADING CULTURE

Leading the culture of the collaborative is essential to making each member feel that their interests are met as a result of their membership. The Executive Director has rallied collaborative members around the goal of improving the lives of local residents from birth to the age of 24 to ensure they have what they need to be successful in school, career, and life. In addition, The Executive Director is responsible for making sure the collaborative establishes achievable goals, facilitating the development of a plan of action, hiring core staff to run the operations of the collaborative, managing and disseminating data to members of the collaborative, and raising the profile of the collaborative to attract new partners. Not all members of the collaborative have the same exact goals but they have determined that there is enough overlap with their own goals and the collaborative offers a great opportunity to advance these goals.

The Executive Director manages the convening of a partnership of over 30 organizations by engaging them to take an active role in drafting the action plan of the collaborative. This action plan was divided into four categories: early learning and school readiness, connecting families, health and wellness, and youth and workforce development. Members of the collaborative volunteered to contribute to one of these four strategy areas where they believed they could add the most value.

The Executive Director supports the action plan and the goals of the collaborative with a core staff. The staffing model

The Executive Director opted for focuses on supporting the core functions of the collaborative. This includes a focus on data, operations management, and communication. These core functions of the collaborative support its members. For example, the data staff monitors the progress of the action plan and provides collaborative members with data. Available data include information about the city of children, youth, young adults, and more. There are instances when data are used to coordinate a collective effort to pursue resources.

LEADING RELATIONSHIPS

The structure of a high-performing collaborative calls for strong management. In the case of the Collaborative, their core leadership team extends beyond the role of The Executive Director. The core leadership team includes a chairperson of the collaborative along with a vice-chairperson, the chairs of the strategy groups and committees and funders. The size of a core leadership team varies from one collaborative to the next, but there are no rules on what the best size of a core team should be. However, the size of a core leadership team should be appropriately sized to support the needs of collaborative members.

While the core leadership team provides strategic direction for the collaborative, the work of the collaborative's grassroots stakeholders is synonymous with the philosophy of the collaborative's core leadership team. These stakeholders are not only members for the sake of accessing data; they become members because of the outcomes the collaborative is able to yield. Outcomes that benefit the entire collaborative include the strength of the collaborative when pursuing a funding opportunity, the collective strength of collaborative members to execute on funding obligations, and the collective data of stakeholders, that have similar strategic interests, to make data-driven decisions.

OTHER EMPIRICAL EXAMPLES OF INCLUSIVE LEADERSHIP THROUGH COLLABORATIVES

There are countless examples that can be drawn from to outline the role collaborative structures play in developing inclusive leadership practices. One example is collaborations between service providers and serve clients through specific access points. Within this type of collaborative, the executive director must operate with a strong sense of purpose (or vision) for how services are provided as a collective group. This particular self-leadership strategy plays a critical role in influencing how the executive director manages and coordinates relationships between the members of the collaborative. This is vital because each service provider has a set of standard operating procedures by which they conduct their work, but in this case, each partner must be convinced to adjust their procedures to mesh with other members. Secondly, the executive director must create a collective impact culture among partners. Each partner must agree to adjust their normal services to fit the context of the collective services that will be provided by the collaborative. Each member must also agree to have their services supervised by staff from the collaborative when they engage a client of the collaborative to ensure operational consistency. Lastly, the executive director must manage relationships between each member of the collaborative. Each member agrees to be a part of this collaborative because they see an alignment with their strategic plans. Maintaining these relationships ensures the collaborative can have the desired impact in the community it is serving.

Another example of a collaborative structure that yields inclusive leadership is collaborations between the public sector and philanthropy. In these collaborations, both entities work together to leverage public resources and the public will along with the less restricted resources of philanthropy to target specific outcomes. The executive director of this collaborative has to utilize self-leadership practices to negotiate between restricted resources that come along with public resources. The critical self-leadership skill in this collaborative structure is cognitive — specifically the emergence of the thought patterns of the executive director regarding the use of public and philanthropic resources to meet a joint need. In an environment where the use of both public and private dollars is under scrutiny, an inclusive leader must figure out the leverage points of each resource to accomplish the goals of each. The subsequent approaches to inclusive leadership — leading culture and leading relationships — are vital, the role of the leader in leading self is the antecedent to any positive outputs from the culture and relationships that emerge from this collaboration.

SUSTAINING THE CHANGES WITHIN ZERO-SUM COMMUNITIES

The context in which a collaborative operates requires its leaders to embody the principles of inclusive leadership. Inclusive leadership opens the tent of the collaborative for its members to influence its strategic direction. In order for inclusive leadership to have a systemic effect within the collaborative, executive staff and executive committee members must establish a culture of inclusion that is visible, measurable, and replicable by collaborative members. Communities that are looking to overcome the zero-sum challenges within their community can look to the Collaborative as an example of how inclusive leadership can grow out of a collaborative structure. Sustaining a collaborative effort is challenging. Equally, it is challenging to maintain inclusive leadership practices. These challenges should be welcomed experiences for members of the collaborative to realize consistent results from the partnership that will benefit them and the stakeholders they represent.

Acknowledgments

I would like to thank my wife and my three children for their support. I would also like to thank my parents, my extended family, and colleagues for inspiring me.

References

Alimo-Metcalfe, B. (2010). Developments in gender and leadership: Introducing a new "inclusive" model. *Gender in Management: An International Journal*, 25(8), 630−639.

Bass, B. M. (1985). *Leadership and performance beyond expectations*. New York, NY: Free Press.

Characteristics of a high-performing funders collaborative. (2014). Retrieved from http://nfwsolutions.org/sites/nfwsolutions.org/files/publications/Characteristics_of_a_High-Performing_Regional_Funder_Collaborative_single_pages_12.29.14.pdf. Accessed on May 1, 2016.

Chong, M. (2014). Influence behaviors and organizational commitment: A comparative study. *Leadership & Organization Development Journal*, 35(1), 54−78.

Hall, J. (2013). Is your company an industry leader? Retrieved from http://www.forbes.com/sites/johnhall/2013/08/06/10-factors-to-crown-you-an-industry-leader/#216e9003452c. Accessed on May 01, 2016.

Houghton, J., & Neck, C. (2002). The revised self-leadership questionnaire: Testing a hierarchical factor structure for self-leadership. *Journal of Managerial Psychology*, 17(8), 672−691.

Janakiraman, M. (2011). Inclusive leadership: Critical for a competitive advantage. Retrieved from http://www.berlitz.com/SiteData/docs/BerlitzWPI/2b6dd531f5ed23d1/BerlitzWP_InclusiveLeadershipFinal.pdf.

Lam, C., Chan, S., Ip, W., & Lau, C. (2008). Collaborative supply chain network using embedded genetic algorithms. *Industrial Management & Data Systems*, *108*(8), 1101–1110.

Lim, B. (1995). Examining the organizational culture and organizational performance link. *Leadership & Organization Development Journal*, *16*(5), 16–21.

Morrow, C. (2015). Moving the dial: Measuring inclusive leadership. Retrieved from http://www.diversityjournal.com/13313-moving-dial-measuring-inclusive-leadership. Accessed on July 24, 2016.

Neck, C., & Manz, C. (2013). *Mastering self-leadership: Empowering yourself for personal excellence* (6th ed.). Upper Saddle River, NJ: Pearson Education.

Northouse, P. (2013). *Leadership: Theory and practice* (6th ed.). Thousand Oaks, CA: Sage.

Parung, J., & Bititci, U. (2008). A metric for collaborative networks. *Business Process Management Journal*, *14*(5), 654–656.

Rashid, M., Sambasivan, M., & Rahman, A. (2004). The influence of organizational culture on attitudes toward organizational change. *Leadership & Organization Development Journal*, *25*(2), 161–179.

Russell, R. (2001). The role of values in servant leadership. *Leadership & Organization Development Journal*, *22*(2), 76–84.

Simmons, M. (1995). Building an inclusive organization. *Empowerment in Organizations*, *3*(3), 11–18.

Van Velsor, E., McCauley, C. D., & Ruderman, M. N. (2010). *The Center for Creative Leadership handbook of leadership development* (3rd ed.). San Francisco, CA: Jossey-Bass.

PART 2
Trials of Breaking the Zero-Sum Game

Introduction

Mixing practical narratives with a strong theoretical background, these chapters illustrate how ideas and practices derived from Peter Senge, Otto Scharmer, Betty Sue Flowers, and Joseph Jaworski, among others, have mixed and influenced each other. Trials of communities working to break the zero-sum game, the notion that in order to win someone else has to lose, show the challenges faced by real people and provide a historical perspective. These examples create a storyline of civil and human rights and the evolution of leadership to shape an inclusive, just, and compassionate society. The section's contributions from diverse fields and backgrounds provide a strong foundation upon which we all can build.

7 Inclusive Leadership for a New Social Order: Dr. A.T. Ariyaratne

Cheryl Getz and Elisa Sabatini

Keywords: Sri Lanka; Sarvodaya; inclusive leadership; social movements; conscious leadership; Buddhist principles

Introduction

In 1958 an economics teacher thought to take his students out to the rural area to engage with villagers and learn more about them, their living conditions, and the reality of the many challenges of village life. This simple process of bridging the village with volunteers has led to a nationwide phenomena where, "we build the road, the road builds us," is no longer a simple aphorism, it is a way of life for thousands of people. Known to many as the Gandhi of Sri Lanka, this man of small stature is Dr. Ahangamage Tudor Ariyaratne, the founder, leader, and spiritual guide of the Sarvodaya Shramadana Movement, the largest established nongovernmental organization in Sri Lanka, which has expanded to over 15,000 villages and engages thousands of families in their own development as well as the development of the community.

Dr. Ari, as he is affectionately known, followed primarily Buddhist principles of compassion, loving kindness, goodness and tranquility, and Gandhian values such as truthfulness, nonviolence, and self-sacrifice; and combined these with action to create highly participatory programs that have fundamentally improved the wellbeing of village life in Sri Lanka. Believing always in inclusivity and participation, Sarvodaya engages all Sri Lankan villagers be they Buddhist, Muslim, Hindu, or Christian.

Dr. Ari in the diverse community of Sri Lanka 2016

Sarvodaya is Sanskrit for *Awakening of All*, and Shramadana means *the sharing of labor, thought and energy*, and combined create a development movement that enables community participation to ensure that everyone's basic human needs are met. Essential to the movement's relevancy and expansion has been the participation of all village society: mothers, farmers, youth, children, and elders. It is the careful representation of these groups that provide the leadership and engagement for both social and material development in the villages.

Sarvodaya was founded during a time of great civil unrest and much violence with the goal of bringing people from all ethnic and religious groups together to build villages to live peacefully and safely. The civil war which endured until 2002 with a ceasefire agreement was renewed again in 2005 by hostilities between the mostly Buddhist government and the (mostly Hindu) Liberation Tigers of Tamil Eelam (LTTE). By 2009 the government took control of all LTTE areas amidst accusations of human rights violations on both sides. Despite these differences, Sarvodaya has led humanitarian efforts to support displaced Tamil and Sinhalese communities throughout and following the violence. The overall success of the Sarvodaya model of inclusive and adaptive leadership led by Dr. Ariyaratne demonstrates a spirit of generosity, and reflects his belief in the dignity and respect for all living beings.

It is well understood by scholars and practitioners alike that leadership is a process that involves relationships between leaders and followers who, when effective, work together and with a common purpose (Burns, 1978; Heifetz, 1994; Hollander, 2009; Rost, 1991). Inclusive leadership then is pursuing leadership in community with others, or "doing this with people rather than to people, which is the essence of inclusion" (Hollander, 2009, p. 3).

Dr. Ari and Sarvodaya demonstrate inclusive leadership not only in the actions of their leader, but in the form that the organization has taken over time as a result of Dr. Ari's lifetime commitment to ensuring that all Sri Lankans, regardless of race, religion, or culture have food, shelter, and other basic needs. In fact, the basis of the movement is that it meets 10 basic human needs that were identified by the villagers shaping the overall Sarvodaya movement. They are: clean and beautiful environment, drinking water, minimal clothing, nutrition, simple housing, basic health care, communication facilities, energy, holistic education, and cultural and spiritual needs. These basic needs have continued to be emblematic of the movement, even as it has grown and adapted over time. In a discussion about social movements Grant said (2009), "Leadership is accepting responsibility to create conditions that enable others to achieve shared purpose in the face of uncertainty. Leaders accept responsibility not only for their individual 'part' of the work, but also for the collective 'whole'" (p. 527). While Sarvodaya is much more now than a social movement, it began when Dr. Ari saw a need and was able to enlist other more privileged Sri Lankans to join villagers as a way to begin to bridge this divide, and address a deeply entrenched social problem within the country. He later continued this effort beyond and during a time of much civil unrest. With respect to the collective whole, Dr. Ari was drawn to Gandhian thought and principles.

In this chapter we discuss how one's life experiences shape their leadership capacity, and specifically how Dr. Ari has been able to empower others toward real change. We begin with how history shapes experience, then a discussion of the role of charismatic and servant leadership in the early years when starting the movement. We then describe elements of adaptive leadership and how Dr. Ari exemplifies each, and we conclude with a discussion about generative leadership and looking toward the future of how his leadership legacy will continue long beyond his life.

Early Years Shaping Leadership

Wijesingha (2008) described Dr. Ari's early years as the son of a wealthy merchant. His early life was oriented around his studies at the nearby temple where he early on was inculcated with Buddhist philosophy as a way of being. After high school some family illness and economic problems meant that his university studies were delayed. A singular event during this period formed his early inquisitiveness and leadership quality.

One evening when he was walking along the beach, he spotted a woman spinning, and he recognized her as someone who used to plead on the road for money to buy bread. He asked how much she earned for her labors, and she told him she got only three rupees each week. This sad story motivated Dr. Ari to learn more about the industry in the area. He held a meeting where about 80 exploited women aired their grievances, and basic machinery was installed, and funds were secured from wealthy benefactors, and the production of coir (rope woven from coconut fiber) began. The Unawatuna Coir Workers Co-operative emerged, and he worked tirelessly to get the society registered, but to no avail. He learned that the Sri Lankans in power who replaced the British were even more arrogant and treated ordinary people with scant respect. This contributed to Dr. Ari's aversion toward the party system that he felt eroded basic human values, and motivated him to study economics at Vidyodaya University (Wijesingha, 2008).

As a young man, Dr. Ari (1998) was highly influenced by the life, writings, and teachings of Mahatma Gandhi, he said: "I knew very little about Mahatma Gandhi's teaching but on February 1, 1948, I saw a crowd of people in my village peeping at a newspaper and crying aloud as if a national calamity had occurred. This unforgettable experience of his assassination stirred me to read whatever material written by him I could find" (p. 91). At Vidyodaya University he organized a Social Service Unit and began to provide field trips to support rural development of the most underprivileged villages. And upon completion of his university degree in Economics, he was hired to teach in a high school and he began to organize teachers and students to support village necessities. One of the most powerful and revolutionary activities was his strong desire to work with the poorest of the poor, the classes and castes equivalent to the untouchables in India (Wijesingha, 2008, pp. 55–65). His studies and his passion for serving the poorest village communities shaped a leadership philosophy that would later empower millions of villagers to become self-reliant, thus ensuring that those in neglected communities could develop their own solutions to achieve their basic needs.

Dr. Ari's vision and connection to Gandhian teachings led him to the founding of Sarvodaya, a term coined by Mahatma Gandhi to describe a new social order which he envisioned as being very different from the capitalist or communist systems prevalent at that time. He said, "I first heard the word Sarvodaya, literally, it means the 'welfare of all.' We have interpreted it as meaning the 'awakening of all through sharing.' It awoke in me the ideal to which I have dedicated my life" (Ariyaratne, 1998, p. 92).

Servant Leadership and Compassionate Action

The premise of the Sarvodaya philosophy, which is based on Buddhist principles, is that everyone is included, irrespective of religious or cultural beliefs, and everyone has gifts and talents that should be valued and respected. The Sarvodaya Movement is truly an example of inclusive leadership and compassionate action that depends first on the transforming of oneself through meditation and awakening of the person, then the family, village, national, and final global awakening. Dr. Ari's life has been dedicated to the service of others, and as a practicing Buddhist he understands that all sentient beings are interconnected. People, nature, and the environment hold a symbiotic relationship, which deserves dignity and respect. Thus all sentient beings are at some level of awakening and all have a right to achieve an optimal level of development. He believes that what happens in society will depend on how many people are awakened, and to do this people must be empowered to see themselves as their own best resource. These principles of awakening have been alive in the movement for over 60 years, and are as strong today as they were in the beginning.

Many would say Dr. Ari is a charismatic leader in the sense that he is a mythic character within his country of Sri Lanka. However, as Paulo Freire notes, "if the leader discovered he is becoming charismatic not because of his or her qualities but because mainly he or she is able to express the expectations of a great mass of people, then he or she is much more of a translator of the aspirations and dreams of the people, instead of being the creator of the dreams...." (Horton & Friere, 1990, p. 111). In fact, Dr. Ari's humility would not allow him to see himself as a charismatic leader, but he more closely embodies the characteristics of a servant leader of the people, who systemized a simple philosophy into action that transforms communities.

This life dedication to service versus identifying as a *leader* is described in the work of Robert Greenleaf (1991). "The difference manifests itself in the care taken by the servant first to make sure that other people's highest priority needs are being served. The best test, and difficult to administer, is: Do those served grow as persons? Do they, while being served, become healthier, wiser, freer, more autonomous, more likely themselves to become servants? And, what is the effect on the least privileged in society?" (p. 7). Dr. Ari is well known in Sri Lanka for working side-by-side with villagers addressing the needs as defined within each community. He continues to dedicate his life to empowering others through compassionate action. Dr. Ari (1998) states, "Ultimately compassion, cooperation, equanimity, morality, forgiveness and selflessness are most effectively practiced in small communities; they cannot be centralized or manifested through large structures. What Sarvodaya is trying to do is to develop such communities, link them together, nationally and globally." "We must overcome our greed for power and wealth, master our own minds to establish self-governing communities, learn the joy of living" (Ariyaratne, 1998, p. 97).

Noteworthy is that Dr. Ari, while dutifully practicing servant leadership, also was observing and formalizing simple methodologies of action that could be followed by all members of the community no matter their age or level of education. This is what forged a system that allowed all to be followers and all to be leaders. This system became the Movement that was formed by networking together the village societies. The genius of working with people whatever their level of human development was made more challenging as Sri Lanka experienced a 26-year civil war.

Adaptive Leadership During Tumultuous Times

Adaptive leadership begins with the authenticity of a leader, and is essential in order to build trust and respect among followers. Anderson and Williams (2016) have worked with hundreds of highly successful leaders from across the globe, and they remind us that leaders who exercise great leadership have a strong reflective capacity that is connected to their deepest inner knowing. When describing exemplary leaders they use words like, "integrity, honesty, passion, vision, risk-taking, fearlessness, compassion, courage, authenticity, collaboration, self-awareness, selflessness, purposefulness, intuition, and wisdom" (p. 29). In many ways, these characteristics describe Dr. Ari, who as a practicing Buddhist, has led thousands of people in meditation and prayer. He speaks about the importance of loving-kindness and seeking nonviolent resolutions to difficult challenges. He continued to organize and engage through all the years of civil war in his country, and he and his family have been in danger on more than one occasion. What is striking when speaking with him and his grown children is how they have maintained these values over the years and through extremely difficult times where confrontations with elected officials and law enforcement were commonplace. These examples are far too many for the scope of this chapter, but each time the response was one of compassion and loving-kindness. As participants in several group meditations with Dr. Ari, we understand the power of the example he continues to set, and how he has become an established, well-known, and respected leader in Sri Lanka. He engages groups toward the possibility of working together regardless of religion or cultural identity. In addition to setting the direction, understanding systems, and giving the work back to the group, adaptive leaders are centered, tethered to purpose at all times, and able to be mindful enough to hold steady despite the chaos and disequilibrium around them.

In exercising adaptive leadership Dr. Ari began with understanding the importance of identifying values and a connection to a deeper purpose. Adaptive leadership means working on behalf of something that is worth the time, energy, and life commitment. "One distinct aspect of leading adaptive change is that you must connect with the values, beliefs, and anxieties of the people you are trying to move" (Heifetz, 2009, p. 38). Dr. Ari stayed true to his desire to help those in need, and adhered to simple Buddhist principles to frame the Sarvodaya Movement. This seemingly simple systemic organizing has resulted in the national network of over 15,000 villages all interconnected through Sarvodaya, yet each at their own stage of development. From the beginning and in a highly stratified society, and then through civil war and great instability, Dr. Ari held steady, often taking a balcony perspective in order to realize the larger vision for the country. His keen insight and capacity to navigate through extremely tumultuous times in a period of overwhelming systemic imbalance for nearly 60 years is an extraordinary illustration of adaptive leadership.

The Sarvodaya philosophy is grounded in four individual and four community principles that he adhered to personally and then collectively with those he worked with. The four individual or personality awakening practices are: loving-kindness, compassion, altruistic joy, and equanimity. And the four community principles are giving or sharing, pleasant language, constructive activity for the benefit of others, and treating everyone equally (Macy, 1983). These are not just theoretical concepts but have become and continue to be actionable ways of living for thousands of villagers in Sri Lanka, through mass mobilization of voluntary actions. Empowering villagers by the mobilization of people from all walks of life was done by giving them positions of leadership within the village. Dr. Ari recognized by talking with village elders that the people could be their own best resource — and he had the foresight to organize them based on what they identified as village needs. His efforts went from those simple work projects with students to organizing groups of people from the village to address their own needs, thus avoiding dependency on others. He was doing work similar to asset based community development, and he knew intuitively the benefits, long before this was studied in the United States, in the late 1980s and 1990s. Each group (committee) represents a specific faction in the village: children, youth, mothers, farmers, and elders which gives each group a platform and way to voice their needs within the community. This is a powerful example of bottom up leadership where, as Heifetz would say mobilizing the people and giving the work back is essential for moving groups toward a common goal. This process is open to everyone in the village and "permits the emergence of local leadership that is an alternative to the power customarily exerted by the larger landowners and merchants" (Macy, 1983, p. 27). The next step in the process is when the five groups are functional they are ready to form their own "Village Awakening Council, which serves as an autonomous legal entity designing its own developmental program" (Macy, 1983, p. 27). This is an example where people take responsibility for joining in the process and for sharing leadership, thus authority is distributed throughout the village.

Change that is sustainable over time requires a commitment from people working together toward a shared vision, and the Sarvodaya model provides an example where understanding the system dynamics locally and nationally was critical to their success. Dr. Ari understood (early on) how the volatility in the country would impact village communities, and the importance of remaining neutral in politically motivated actions or warring factions, thus Sarvodaya developed largely outside of government control. When Dr. Ari began his initial work in 1958 with five villages and a small group of students, no one could have imagined the size and scale that is the Sarvodaya Movement today. This engagement of a small group of young people from wealthy families, working with villagers, turned out to be the first Shramadana work camp, and provided the example for what would be an essential component of the movement. Using Shramadana (*the sharing of labor, thought and energy*) to address infrastructure issues identified by the village, Dr. Ari put compassion and loving-kindness into actions that would bring together Buddhists, Hindus, Christians, Sinhalese, and Tamil; men and women; old and young, together. The Shramadana empowers villagers to make decisions about the specific needs of the village, and despite their differences people work together with a common goal of improving the living conditions for everyone in the village. This remains a central tenant of the Sarvodaya philosophy today.

Through a fluid and ever-emergent process that has had to adapt to changes and challenges due to war, economic hardship, and tensions between cultural and ethnic groups throughout the country; Sarvodaya has grown to be the largest nongovernmental organization in the country. While initially fully supported through donations from the West, today Sarvodaya has created several streams of funding including (1) a Finance Corporation that provides villages access to capital, is self-reliant and recognized by the Central Bank, (2) the development of rural cooperative businesses with the Sarvodaya as partial owner, and (3) renting many of their nationwide facilities for productive purposes. This self-financing model is augmented by some charitable contributions for relief and assistance programs. The organizational structure includes 1500 staff, most of them devoted to this work because they align with the purpose, or they came from villages where the connection to Sarvodaya enhanced their way of living. Over time, Sarvodaya has become a beacon of light for many Sri Lankans, and they maintain fluid systems as they adapt and continue to support the country when in need. For example, they were the first organization to assist after the December 2004 Sri Lanka Tsunami that killed over 35,000 people and left 500,000 villagers homeless. In the recent flooding caused by torrential rains that devastated the Colombo and Kegalle areas, taking thousands of homes and 200 lives, hundreds of Sarvodaya staff and volunteers are in the areas providing food, water, and temporary shelter for the thousands in need. In fact, Dr. Ari was out visiting the areas on the first day of the flood.

Leaving a Legacy: Inclusive and Generative Leadership

The Sarvodaya model is a powerful example of inclusive leadership that over time has grown to a national and international audience. In recent times, Dr. Ari has taken a new role in the larger organizational structure of Sarvodaya, as President he is considered the guide or spiritual leader, while his son, Dr. Vinya Ariyaratne has taken over as the General Secretary, responsible for the sustainable development of the Movement and others who hold positions in the organization continue to experiment with new ideas. For example, there is now a recognized education center, the Sarvodaya Institute of Higher Learning, created to provide a platform of training alternative to the formal education system in the country where rural community knowledge is formally recognized. The institute also draws people from around the world, from high school to college students, to other nonprofits all interested in the Sarvodaya model.

The staff works closely with Dr. V. Ariyaratne to develop programming that engages students and others in the ideals of Sarvodaya, while encouraging new and innovative ways to grow the organization. The work now is to ensure sustainability and growth of the Sarvodaya model, which requires adaptation to a rapidly changing political, and economic climate, as well as understanding new ways of learning and meaning-making for young adults in the 21st century. "Generative leadership is particularly relevant in situations of complexity when uncertainty and rapid change are dominant; since outcomes are not certain, the focus must be on the process" (Surie & Hazy, 2006, p. 15). The inclusive *process* is what the Sarvodaya model is predicated on, that all people have the capability to work together to benefit and enhance their own living conditions, and this process is enhanced by the organizational support that Sarvodaya provides. Yet, this process can be misunderstood, for instance, there are challenges with the shramadana as some people think organizing quickly and putting a group together for a project is sufficient, but as Macy (1983) notes, this does not allow for real learning and deep commitment from villagers (p. 62), which is necessary for long lasting change. When this occurs, the temptation is high to come up with a quick remedy, but with patience and some guidance from Sarvodaya staff, they continually trust the process. This unspoken yet tangible sense is also analogous to invisible leadership, where each person involved understands deeply that the organization's success depends not on single leaders as much as the purpose, the group's shared work, and the relationships formed in the "the space between" (Hickman & Sorenson, 2014, p. 13).

Dr. Ari and his colleagues understood this from the beginning, and implemented an emergent process that articulated a plan that remains fluid, yet always connected to a series of shared values. As noted earlier, Sarvodaya means the *awakening of all*, and there are four major tenants that underpin and support a philosophy that seeks far-reaching impact, that would impact the Sarvodaya and beyond. These six phases of awakening include: *purushodaya*: personal awakening, family awakening, *gramodaya*: village awakening, urban awakening, *deshodaya*: national awakening, and finally *vishvodaya*: world awakening. Today, Dr. Ari focuses much of his leadership on the emergent processes involved in national awakening, or the *Deshodaya Plan* (Fig. 1).

Each phase of awakening includes all members of society and is a slow deliberate process inclusive of each person and each community group. The model focuses on an integrative process that includes spiritual, moral principles, cultural norms, social development, economic systems, and political engagement.

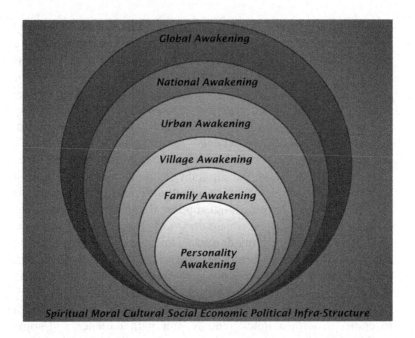

Fig. 1. Sarvodaya: Vision for the 21st Century. May 2004.

According to the *Sarvodaya Approach to the New Century Deshodaya National Assembly* document, the objective of the Movement is to evolve the horizontal network of cluster villages and create a coordinated national movement to continue to find lasting solutions to village, city, and country programs that affect daily life (Sarvodaya Approach, 2010, p. 2). Ultimately this assembly would address governance, where every citizen has fair and equitable treatment under the law, protection of basic human rights, a government that preserves and promotes, spiritual, moral, cultural, and social values and a government that consistently encourages continued conversations concerning national resources for the continued sustainability of humanity. The Sarvodaya Movement provides a prototype of a nonviolent process of action that would eventually pave the way for the evolution of a national system of good governance that guarantees and ensures lasting peace, unity, and development for the future (Sarvodaya Approach, 2010, p. 3).

Additionally, having intentionally avoided a formal role within the Sri Lankan government structure (for years), Dr. Ari recently agreed to serve as a civil representative on the Sri Lanka Constitutional Council, appointed by the President and then confirmed by Parliament again in September 2015 (Sri Lanka Brief, 2015). In these actions there is hope for generative leadership that materializes as a result of engagement with others on a national and global level, with the goal of creating a new social order that puts an end to capitalistic ventures that keep many people living in poverty.

While nearly 60 years old, the Sarvodaya philosophy has always been rooted in practical and universal human needs demonstrating how consciousness, economics, and power intersect and are inevitably connected. The art of understanding this and balancing these elements are the genius of Dr. Ari's work, and relevant to any dialog and any culture to create inclusive and transparent systems and leadership. For example, a quick review of the initial *United Nations 2015 Millennium Goals* (2015) reveals that most focus on basic human needs, and in some ways appear more concrete and to embrace a somewhat technical approach than the new *United Nations Sustainable Goals for 2030* (2016). These goals move beyond concrete, they embrace the planet as a whole, and they more fully incorporate goals such as the *well-being of humans and the planet* (consciousness) and *decent work* (economics) and *gender equality/human rights* (power). Remarkably, these goals are in perfect alignment with several aspects (consciousness, economics, and power) of the Sarvodaya vision for a new social order (Fig. 2). Dr. Ariyaratne had the foresight prior to the development of the original millennium goals, to recognize that a vision for a more just society and world would include these important dimensions. Furthermore, he and his colleagues recognized the importance of inclusion, and that all people should have a voice, from the earliest beginnings

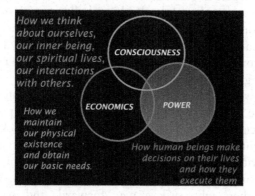

Fig. 2.   Sarvodaya: Vision for the 21st Century. May 2004.

of Sarvodaya, creating a philosophy and framework based on listening to the people, involving them and carrying their needs, and concerns to national and international stages.

Adaptations and partnerships of the Sarvodaya model exist in several places in the United States, and also in Nepal where local communities have followed the principles and philosophy to engage communities and seek solutions to community problems. "Sarvodaya USA was founded to support the Sri Lankan Sarvodaya Shramadana movement and to seek ways in which their methods of holistic human development could be emulated in other socioeconomic and geographical contexts" (Sarvodaya USA, 2016). Others have also been inspired by the Sarvodaya vision, for example, the Conscious community — Reno (2011) came together around Sarvodaya principles. And in Nepal collective efforts have been underway for 10 years to improve education, also based on community network models of Sarvodaya. Many more communities can benefit by creating adaptations of the Sarvodaya principles and comprehensive process.

There is much to be learned from the Sarvodaya philosophy and the many ways, large and small they have influenced people and organizations worldwide. This at a time when fear of the "other" is at an all time high around the globe, and we have all seen evidence of leaders using this fear to stroke hate and encourage violence between people who have different religious, ethnic, or cultural beliefs. We are at a critical juncture where we need to decide if we are going to build higher walls to keep us apart or bridges that will bring us closer to understanding each other. For centuries people have been fighting religious and cultural battles and it seems we are in the midst of this challenge today across the globe. When Dr. Ari says it is possible to eradicate many of the social and political leadership challenges of our time, he means throughout the world, not just in Sri Lanka. He exemplifies the idea that we must move beyond hatred and division, and seek generosity and trust, not competition, to solve many of our most vexing problems as human beings.

In his words, "It is my belief that we should courageously go beyond the narrow confines of conventional concepts and practices of social work and get to the roots of global sickness with a commitment to finding lasting remedies. After many years of working with and for people and learning from them, I have confidence in only one view" (Ariyaratne, 1998, p. 91). We join Dr. Ari and others who seek a way forward, and ask what our responsibility is as leader scholars and practitioners. Thus, in one example we see a way forward. The work of Dr. Ari and Sarvodaya may have started nearly 60 years ago during a different time, but thanks to Dr. Ari the framework and ideals from which this people's movement has grown, are more relevant today than perhaps they were in Sri Lanka 60 years ago.

Acknowledgments

We would like to thank Dr. Ari and the Sarvodaya staff for welcoming us into their communities and teaching us the importance of compassion, loving-kindness, and goodness in all leadership endeavors.

References

Anderson, R., & Williams, A. (2016). *Mastering leadership*. Hoboken, NJ: John Wiley & Sons.

Ariyaratne, A. T. (1998). A new social order. In E. Shapiro & D. Shapiro (Eds.), *Voices from the heart: A compassionate call for responsibility* (pp. 90–98) New York, NY: Jeremy P. Tarcher/Putnam.

Burns, J. M. G. (1978). *Leadership*. New York, NY: Harper & Row.

Conscious community – Reno. (2011). Retrieved from http://www.conscious-community-reno.org/. Accessed on August 2016.

Heifetz, R. A. (1994). *Leadership without easy answers*. Cambridge, MA: Belknap Press of Harvard University Press.

Heifetz, R., Linsky, M., & Grashow, A. (2009). *The practice of adaptive leadership: Tools and tactics for changing your organization and the world*. Boston, MA: Harvard Business Press.

Hickman, G., & Sorenson, G. (2014). *The power of invisible leadership: How a compelling common purpose inspires exceptional leadership*. Los Angeles, CA: Sage.

Hollander, E. P. (2009). *Inclusive leadership: The essential leader-follower relationship*. New York, NY: Routledge.

Horton, M., & Freire, P. (1990). *We make the road by walking: Conversations on education and social justice*. Philadelphia, PA. Temple University Press.

Macy, J. (1983). *Dharma and development: Religion as resource in the Sarvodaya self-help movement*. West Hartford, CT: Kumarian Press.

Rost, J. C. (1991). *Leadership for the twenty-first century*. New York, NY: Praeger.

Sarvodaya Approach to the New Century Deshodaya National Assembly. (March 2010). Lanka Jathika Sarvodaya Shramadana Sangamaya, No. 98, Rawathawatte Road, Moratuwa.

Sarvodaya USA. (2016). Retrieved from http://www.sarvodayausa.org/sarvo-daya-history-and-philosophy.html. Accessed on August 2016.

Sri Lanka Brief. (2015). *Sri Lanka Parliament Approves Civil Society Representatives of Constitutional Council*. Retrieved from Sri Lanka Brief Online. Retrieved from http://srilankabrief.org/2015/09/sri-lanka-parliament-approves-civil-ssciety-representatives-of-constitutional-council/. Accessed on August 2016.

Surie, S., & Hazy, J. (2006). Generative leadership: Nurturing innovation in complex systems. E:CO. 8(4), pp. 13–26.

United Nations Millenial Goals. (2015). Retrieved from http://www.un.org/mil-lenniumgoals/. Accessed on August 2016.

United Nations Sustainable Development Goals. (2016). Retrieved from http://www.un.org/sustainabledevelopment/sustainable-development-goals/. Accessed on August 2016.

Wijesingha, S. (2008). The boy from Unawatuna; the man from all the villages. In R. S. Brooks & D. A. Perera (Eds.), *A.T. Ariyaratne: Compassionate activist* (pp. 55–65) Sri Lanka: Sarvodaya Vishvalehka.

Mercy within Mercy: The Heart of Pope Francis' Inclusive Leadership in a Broken World

Dung Q. Tran and Michael R. Carey

Keywords: Pope Francis; Ignatius of Loyola; Jesuits; Ignatian spirituality; Mercy; inclusive leadership; the Catholic Church; Catholicism; servant leadership; spiritual leadership; Ignatian discernment

Introduction

Pope Francis, "the dynamic Argentinian leader of the world's 1.2 billion Catholics" (Hale, 2016, para. 5), has been praised by both leadership periodicals — *Harvard Business Review* (Hamel, 2015), *Forbes* (Loftus, 2015), *Fortune* (Colvin, 2017), *Fast Company* (Vanderbloemen, 2015) — and the mainstream media — *The Washington Post* (McGregor, 2015), *Time* (Rayman, 2015), and *The Wall Street Journal* (Rubenfire, 2014) — for his effective (Zetlin, 2014) and inclusive leadership (Yardley & Goodstein, 2016). Since his historic election as the first Jesuit pontiff, and first pope from the Americas, he has embodied and concretized inclusive leadership. For Hollander (2009), the successful practice of inclusive leadership requires a leader-follower relationship marked by "respect, recognition, responsiveness, and responsibility" (p. 3). Responding to the need for more life-affirming leader-follower relationships, Wuffli (2015) proposed a framework for inclusive leadership that should be:

- Dynamic and change oriented.
- Horizontal: to enable bridge-building across different sectors of society and across cultures.
- Holistic and broadly applicable: to involve as many people and diverse situations as possible.
- Explicitly normative: in terms of encouraging leaders to reflect on and take positions related to their underlying ethics and virtues (p. 3).

Pope Francis' counter cultural choices, call for mercy, concern for the marginalized of society, and man-of-the-people ways has distinguished him from his predecessors and electrified the media and the masses. Since the moment he stepped out on the balcony of Saint Peter's Square in 2013, his "top priority has been to make the church more inclusive" (Krames, 2015, p. 41). While Francis has not changed any doctrine, "he has moved the entire world with his compassion and inclusiveness" (Cahill, 2015, p. 69). For instance, in an interview with *America* magazine, Francis described his inclusive approach toward the lesbian, gay, bisexual, and transgender community:

... when God looks at a gay person, does he endorse the existence of this person with love, or reject and condemn this person? We must always consider the person. Here we enter into the mystery of the human being. In life, God accompanies persons, and we must accompany them, starting from their situation. It is necessary to accompany them with mercy. (Spadaro, 2013, para. 57)

Regardless of topic, the pope's plan for a more inclusive church is anchored by the virtue of mercy. As Allen (2015) asserted, "In all the ways that matter, mercy is the spiritual bedrock of this papacy" (p. 10). Former President Barack Obama (2015) recognized this at Pope Francis' White House arrival ceremony:

You remind us that "the Lord's most powerful message" [Francis, 2013b, para. 3] is mercy. And that means welcoming the stranger with empathy and a truly open heart— from the refugee who flees war-torn lands to the immigrant who leaves home in search of a better life. It means showing compassion and love for the marginalized and the outcast, to those who have suffered, and those who have caused suffering and seek redemption. (para. 7)

Pope Francis has sought to embody his mercy-filled message in his inclusive leadership practices: washing the feet of prisoners, embracing the physically disfigured, building shower facilities for homeless persons who sleep near Saint Peter's Square, and adopting Muslim refugees. For Lowney (2013), Francis is "doing what all good leaders do, jostling our imaginations when we become too complacent and stripping away the veneer of the familiar to expose the raw feel of a challenging truth" (p. 43). His merciful approach to leadership has "drawn widespread adulation from people around the world" (Levs & Pearson, 2013, para. 1). With man-of-the-year magazine covers from *Time*, *The Advocate*, and *Vanity Fair*, as well as over 27 million followers across multiple Twitter accounts (Vatican Radio, 2016), it is clear that Francis' message of mercy and inclusion has gone "viral." Pope Francis' inclusive leadership is transforming societies and merits more scholarly scrutiny.

As leadership scholars who are alert to questions of spirituality and how they impact inclusive leadership, we are interested in contributing to the enrichment of leadership theory and practice by engaging spiritual understandings of mercy and highlighting the importance of this virtue as an answer to the problems of the world we inhabit. To that end, the purpose of this chapter is to explore the role of mercy in Pope Francis' Ignatian-inspired spiritual vision and inclusive leadership for a broken world. This chapter is structured around two questions: (1) Who is Pope Francis? and (2) How does his Jesuit identity and message of mercy undergird his thinking, spirituality, and practice of inclusive leadership?

Who Is Pope Francis?

Pope Francis was born Jorge Mario Bergoglio on December 17, 1936, in Buenos Aires, Argentina. His parents had arrived in Buenos Aires 9 years prior, having come from Portacomaro, a village in northern Italy. The Bergoglio family left Italy for

Argentina to be nearer to relatives who had moved there in 1922. The Europe his parents left was reeling from the economic aftermath of World War I as well as the political problems epitomized by the rise of Benito Mussolini.

When Jorge began secondary school, he also began working in a hosiery factory. He started as a cleaner, eventually became an administrator, and finally worked in a local chemical laboratory, while he continued his studies. Bergoglio believed his work in the laboratory was one of the best things he ever did as he "got to see the good and bad of all human behavior" and learned the "seriousness of hard work" and about doing things properly from his supervisor, Esther Balestrino de Careaga, a "Paraguayan woman and communist sympathizer" (Ambrogetti & Rubin, 2013, pp. 14–15). Later in his life, the future Pope Francis reflected on her and the influence she had upon him: "I loved her very much …. Truly, I owe a huge amount to that great woman" (pp. 14–15).

At 21, Jorge came down with a severe case of pneumonia which resulted in the excision of the upper part of his right lung. Living with the limitations that such a disability entails and dealing with the resulting pain shaped his pastoral response to those who face a life-threatening illness: "What people need is to know that someone is with them, loves them, respects their silence, and prays that God may enter into this space that is pure solitude" (Ambrogetti & Rubin, 2013, p. 29).

Jorge Mario Bergoglio realized that he had a vocation to the priesthood after an encounter with a visiting priest during confession at his parish church. He entered the Society of Jesus as a novice in 1958 at the age of 22. Bergoglio studied the humanities at university, and then began to teach Psychology and Literature in a Jesuit secondary school. After his Jesuit formation, Pope Francis was ordained a priest in 1969, and soon after that he served as the provincial superior of the Jesuits in Argentina for the normal 6-year term of office from 1973 to 1979. Following that, he studied in Ireland and Germany, and in 1980 was appointed by the Society of Jesus to be the rector of the Philosophical and Theological Faculty of San Miguel. In 1992, he was appointed to the post of Auxiliary Bishop of the Archdiocese of Buenos Aires; in 1998, he became the Archbishop; and in 2001, he was named a cardinal by Pope John Paul II. On March 13, 2013, Jorge Mario Bergoglio became Pope Francis.

What Makes Pope Francis an Inclusive Leader?

Pope Francis' ability to authentically and emotionally connect with people has captured the collective imagination of humanity. The pontiff's pursuit of a more welcoming Catholic Church, "one that reaches out and embraces all, even when there are differences of opinion" (Crowley, 2014, p. xvi), has earned him international acclaim as an inclusive leader (Krames, 2015, p. 42). Francis' widespread appeal begs the following questions: Why does his inclusive leadership resonate with so many? What makes him effective as an inclusive leader? How have his identity, influences, and experiences shaped his approach to and embodiment of inclusive leadership? A study of his longstanding identity as a Jesuit priest and pastoral leader, and an examination of his message of mercy together reveal the guiding contexts that undergird his understanding and practice of inclusive leadership.

JESUIT IDENTITY AND TRAINING

In addition to being the first non-European pontiff in 1,300 years and the first pope since 913 CE to choose a name which had never been used by a predecessor (Bethune, 2013, p. 18), Pope Francis is "the first Jesuit pope in history" (O'Malley, 2014, p. 112). As he made clear during a press conference aboard a plane returning to Rome from Rio de Janeiro, the pontiff's identity as a Jesuit — and everything associated with that spiritual tradition — is a core context for understanding how he approaches life and leadership: "I feel a Jesuit in my spirituality; in the spirituality of the Exercises, the spirituality deep in my heart …. I feel a Jesuit and I think as a Jesuit" (Francis, 2013e, para. 63).

Founded in 1540 by Ignatius of Loyola, a Basque soldier-turned-mystic, the Jesuits (also called the Society of Jesus) are the largest religious order of priests and brothers in the Catholic Church (Giberti, 2015). During their own lifetime, Ignatius and the first Jesuits became a "worldwide missionary order, a major force in the sixteenth-century renewal of Catholicism, and created an educational system that transformed Europe and beyond" (Sparough, Manney, & Hipskind, 2010, p. 29).

In Lowney's (2003) view, Ignatius and the early Jesuits have much to "teach us twenty-first century sophisticates about leadership and coping with complex, changing environments" (pp. 4–5).

While he never uttered the word leadership, Ignatius and his colleagues built "the world's most influential company of its kind" (p. 7). The Jesuits' success is animated by Ignatius' *Spiritual Exercises*, a method for transformation known as Ignatian spirituality. This spiritual worldview is about finding "the freedom to become the person you're meant to be, to love and to accept love, to make good decisions, and to experience the beauty of creation and the mystery of God's love" (Martin, 2012, p. 1). As a worldview, Ignatian spirituality has not only shaped generations of Jesuits, their companions and colleagues, but, as several commentators have concluded (Bies, 2015; Lowney, 2013), Ignatius of Loyola, the Jesuits, and their Ignatian spiritual tradition are fundamental influences on Pope Francis' "thinking, spirituality, and leadership" (Ivereigh, 2014, p. xiv).

Attraction to the Jesuit community, missionary spirit, and concern for the poor. As a young man, the future pope was drawn to the Jesuits because of their sense of community: "I was always looking for a community. I did not see myself as a priest on my own. I need a community" (Spadaro, 2013, para. 14). Community living left such a lasting impression that it inspired Francis' decision to forgo the spacious, yet isolating, confines of the papal residence and live in a Vatican guesthouse, which is regularly inhabited by Vatican officials and visiting clergy:

> … when I took possession of the papal apartment, inside myself I distinctly heard a "no." The papal apartment … is big and spacious, but the entrance is really tight. People can come only in dribs and drabs, and I cannot live without people. I need to live my life with others. (para. 14)

Pope Francis also admired the Jesuits' missionary spirit and concern for the poor (Ivereigh, 2014, pp. 48–49). In many ways, working with the poor and those on the margins during Francis' Jesuit formation left an indelible mark on him. Regardless of leadership rank or role, the marginalized and disenfranchised were always a priority for him (Vallely, 2013, p. 50). When Francis served as the provincial leader of all the Jesuits in Argentina, he made direct contact with the poor an essential element of Jesuit formation (Ivereigh, 2014, p. 70). As Cardinal Archbishop of Buenos Aires, he was beloved for his availability, austere lifestyle, and closeness to the poor. For instance, as a cardinal, rather than be addressed using his formal title "Your

Eminence," he preferred to simply be called "Father Jorge" (Collazo & Rogak, 2013, p. xiii). He also lived in a simple apartment, cooked his own meals, and even established a direct phone line exclusively for priests to reach him (Lowney, 2013, p. 73). The future pontiff would spend his days traveling by bus to celebrate Mass in shantytowns, assist in soup kitchens, and visit those afflicted by Acquired Immunodeficiency Syndrome, or AIDS (Moynihan, 2013, pp. 150–151). Francis' closeness to the poor was especially embodied in his practice of washing the feet of marginalized people from Buenos Aires each year on Holy Thursday, a tradition he has carried into his papacy. After washing the feet of 12 young inmates — including a male Muslim and two women — from Casal del Marmo, a juvenile detention center in Rome, Pope Francis (2013c) told them (and the world), "This is a symbol, it is a sign ... Washing feet means 'I am at your service ...' As a priest and bishop, I must be at your service" (paras. 2–3).

Ignatian discernment. For all Jesuits, including Pope Francis, serving the marginalized must be preceded by a prayerful process of discernment which is "the overall term for the decision-making practices outlined by Ignatius in the Spiritual Exercises" (Martin, 2012, p. 305). Ignatius "developed a psychologically sophisticated system of spiritual discernment that... had the simple but profound insight that we can discern where God is calling or leading us through careful attention to the movements and inclinations of our own hearts" (Neafsey, 2006, p. 39). At the same time, Ignatius did not write "a step-by-step, follow-the-recipe sort of guide to making a decision. He knew that every decision carries with it so many variables that a cookie-cutter method would be contrived and clunky. Humans are simply too complex for a one-size-fits-all discernment manual" (Thibodeux, 2010, p. 6). Through his life experiences and observations about how God worked in the lives of others, Ignatius outlined a series of discernment practices in his *Spiritual Exercises* that used the concepts of desolation and consolation to reveal the workings of the evil spirit (Spitzer, 2008, p. 83).

According to Thibodeux (2010), desolation is when a person is empty of:

- Faith, hope, and love.
- The sense of God's being close to me.

and filled with some combination of the following:

- Restlessness and agitation.
- Boredom and apathy.
- Fear and worry.
- Secrecy (p. 16).

Conversely, consolation is operative when one has:

- Faith, hope, and love.
- The sense of God's closeness.
- Peace and tranquility.
- Great desires.
- Transparency (p. 44).

For Gula (1989), internal signs of consolation "open us to greater spiritual freedom and enable us to love God [and others] more" (p. 325). Instead of being able to do whatever one wants, spiritual freedom or interior freedom is "The ability to be detached from one's initial biases and to step back, the willingness to carefully balance the alternatives" (Martin, 2012, p. 306). Smith and Merz (2006) maintained that one's "awareness of interior freedom may be faint at first because many expectations, demands, biases, and sinful patterns" (p. 91) obscure it from view. As Martin (2012) noted, "Starting off by assuming that you should decide one way or the other is cheating yourself out of a good choice" (p. 307). Gula (2003) stated that "letting go of paralyzing attachments" (p. 207) such as fear of change, status, and the need for control is critical for obtaining interior freedom.

While finding freedom is an important part of the discernment process, it is also something that cannot be rushed. As Pope Francis experienced in the early days of his leadership, "discernment takes time. For example, many think that changes and reforms can take place in a short time. I believe that we always need time to lay the foundations for real, effective change" (Spadaro, 2013, para. 19). Furthermore, discernment can surprise as it "urges us to do precisely what you had at first thought you would do later" (para. 19). Most importantly, however, "Discernment is always done in the presence of the Lord, looking at the signs, listening to the things that happen, the feeling of the people, especially the poor" (para. 19). For Francis, all of his choices, "including those related to the day-to-day aspects of life, like the use of a modest car, are related to a spiritual discernment that responds to a need that arises from looking at things, at people and from reading the signs of the times. Discernment in the Lord guides [him] in [his] way of governing (para. 19).

As the future pope learned during a turbulent tenure as Jesuit provincial superior of Argentina, discernment must involve other people: "My style of government as a Jesuit at the beginning had many faults ... I had to deal with difficult situations, and I made my decisions abruptly and by myself ... eventually people get tired of authoritarianism" (Spadaro, 2013, para. 34).

Pope Francis learned his lesson and took a more collaborative and inclusive leadership approach as Archbishop of Buenos Aires:

> Over time I learned many things. The Lord has allowed this growth in knowledge of government through my faults and my sins. So as Archbishop of Buenos Aires, I had a meeting with the six auxiliary bishops every two weeks, and several times a year with the council of priests. They asked questions and we opened the floor for discussion. This greatly helped me to make the best decisions. (Spadaro, 2013, para. 36)

Francis' eventual embrace and positive experience with a more discerning, collaborative, and inclusive model of wielding authority led him to create a council of nine cardinal advisers after his election. This consultative body, comprised of cardinal archbishops from across the globe, is charged with advising him "in the governance of the universal Church and to plan the reform of the Roman Curia" (Ivereigh, 2014, p. 372).

While Francis attends most meetings, he does not speak. As he told Andrea Tornielli (2013), "I just listen, and that does me good" (para. 18). The pope's practice of listening affirmed Kasper's (2015) claim that, "Pope Francis wants a magisterium that listens" (p. 13). Francis' willingness to listen to the dialog among his advisers is reflective of an inclusive leadership process that is marked by values of mercy, respect, and involvement of others (Hollander, 2009, p. 4).

While Pope Francis consults and listens widely, he has been described as a charismatic leader with "strong convictions" (Vallely, 2013, p. 50), who, as a former Jesuit superior, is accustomed to making his own decisions. The dynamic tension that characterizes Francis' decision-making process is best described by Rabbi Abraham Shorka, a "brother and friend" (Bergoglio, 2013, p. xvi) of two decades, who said, "From his recent phone calls he is feeling very at peace with [himself]. He's in a very good established spiritual moment. He's listening and analyzing and meditating deeply. When he's arrived at a conclusion, he's unlikely to change his mind" (as cited in Vallely, 2013, p. 203).

Pope Francis' consultative discernment process is built on a method of proceeding that Jesuit superiors have employed for nearly 500 years. As Allen (2015) asserted,

> That's how things work within the Society of Jesus. A superior is expected to listen carefully to the views of the order's members and to consult widely among experts on the matter at hand. In the end, however, there's no vote before a decision is made and no veto power or referendum procedure once it's made. A superior is expected to decide alone and carry the weight of whatever choice he makes. (p. 195)

As evidenced in the discussion thus far, Francis' practice of deciding on his own after a period of consultation and discernment "coexist to some degree" (p. 195) in the pontiff's inclusive leadership approach to reforming the institutional church (Vallely, 2013, p. 182).

Pope Francis is a "church leader who from an early age felt called to be a reformer and was given the authority to do so" (Ivereigh, 2014, p. xv). Whether it was the Argentine Jesuit province, the Argentine Catholic Church, or now the global Catholic Church, Francis has always been driven by a desire to unite humanity through "a radical reform that… leads them to holiness" (p. xv). Francis is a values-driven community-oriented bridge builder who is on a mission to reform Catholicism in three ways: (1) shifting Catholicism toward the political and ecclesiastical center; (2) inspiring a deeper social commitment to defend the poor, oppose war, care for the environment, and protect people on the margins, especially immigrants, the elderly, and minorities; and (3) overhauling the Vatican's organizational bureaucracy (Allen, 2015, pp. 5–7).

With his prior leadership experiences and Ignatius of Loyola's decision making wisdom as his guide, Pope Francis recognizes that meaningful reform emerges out of an authentic spiritual discernment process that helps determine the "best way to act" (Martin, 2012, p. 309). For both Ignatius and Francis, "reform is ultimately about the courage to strip away the accrued layers of distraction to recover what has been lost. It is a going back in order to go forward. It is what makes them both great reformers" (Ivereigh, 2014, p. 55).

A MESSAGE OF MERCY

Along with his Jesuit identity, another critical component of Pope Francis' vision for reform and inclusive leadership is the theme of mercy. According to Jesuit theologian Jon Sobrino (1993), "Everything—absolutely everything—turns on the exercise of mercy" (p. 682). The concept of mercy is a core concern of sacred texts and has been developed by thought leaders such as Thomas Aquinas (Nowell, 1990, pp. 650–652), Catherine of Siena (Spinello, 2012, p. 80), Thomas Merton (1953/1981, 1955/ 1983), John Paul II (1980), Benedict XVI (2007), and Walter Kasper (2014). Drawing upon and developing Aristotelian and other classical sources, Aquinas (1912) conceptualized mercy as the "heartfelt sympathy for another's distress" (p. 1311). In his opening address at Vatican II, Pope John XXIII (1962), whom Robert Greenleaf (1996) considered one of the greatest servant leaders of all-time, urged the church to engage contemporary culture and society with the "medicine of mercy" (John XXIII, 1962, para. 32). More recently, Keenan (2010) defined mercy as "the willingness to enter into the chaos of another so as to answer them in their need" (p. 118). For Sobrino (1993), "Mercy is the primary and ultimate, the first and last of human reactions. It is that in terms of which all dimensions of the human being acquire meaning and without which nothing else attains to human status" (p. 682).

This understanding of mercy captures the underlying spirit of Pope Francis' inclusive leadership and,

> … expresses his conviction that mercy is the fundamental reality that structures … [divine activity], the perfection of the human person, and the mission of the church. It is the reality seen in… [the] freeing of the oppressed and welcoming of the prodigal, and it is the demand placed upon all who seek to authentically love their neighbor. (Walatka, 2016, p. 97)

In gestures inspired by mercy and reflective of inclusive leadership, Pope Francis started reaching out to his spiritual neighbors immediately after his 2013 election. For example, his papal installation was the first to be attended by the Chief Rabbi of Rome; Francis extended an invitation on his first full day in office.

He also invited Bartholomew, the Patriarch of Constantinople, "who became the first head of the Greek Orthodox Church in nearly a thousand years to attend the installation of a pope" (Vallely, 2013, p. 177).

In an effort to concretize his call for a poorer church for the poor (Francis, 2013a), the newly minted pontiff led by example. For instance, during Christmas 2013, he spent 3 hours visiting sick children and their families at a Roman hospital. A more dramatic gesture occurred during the 2014 Holy Thursday service at the Don Gnocchi center for the elderly and disabled, where Francis washed and kissed the feet of 12 patients whose age ranged from 16 to 86, several of whom were in wheelchairs with their feet severely swollen or disfigured (Allen, 2015, p. 140). Allen also noted that, "On all of these visits, Francis arrived in a blue Ford Focus that has become his trademark means of transportation around town, as opposed to the black Mercedes sedan that used to be the papal vehicle" (p. 140). Using more modest transportation was Francis' (2013d) way of modeling his invitation to priests and nuns to "choose a more humble car" (para. 9).

To help underscore the importance of mercy, Pope Francis also declared 2016 an Extraordinary Jubilee Year of Mercy. Francis' (2015) desire for the Jubilee is that all people of good will, "enter more deeply into the heart of the Gospel where the poor have a special experience of God's mercy" (para. 15). He is also encouraging people to reflect on the corporal and spiritual works of mercy — activities that involve one's "obligations to the neighbor in need" (McBrien, 1994, p. 942). While the tradition of the works of mercy is very rich, they are "considerably lost to the modern mind" (Keenan, 2008, p. 2). In many ways, Pope Francis is calling the global community to contemplate, rediscover, and lead with mercy — an essential human truth and a compelling answer to the spiritual and social questions of our time.

Conclusion

With the virtue of mercy, his Jesuit identity, and the tradition of Ignatian discernment as the foundation of Francis' inclusive leadership, one can better understand why the pope could utter his most famous words, "Who am I to judge?" (Francis, 2013e, para. 85) and allow the funeral of a transgender homeless person to take place at the mother church of the Jesuit order. While lengthy and emotionally challenging, the following vignette about Andrea Quintero, a Colombian who struggled with drug addiction and was often physically abused, beautifully describes the intersection and impact of Pope Francis' Jesuit identity, the role of mercy in his understanding and practice of inclusive leadership, and the new winds of change unleashed by his passion for social justice:

> On the evening of July 29, 2013, Quintero was beaten to death by unknown assailants; her body was later discovered alongside the tracks at the train station. Her remains were kept at the Roman morgue for four months in case any family members came forward to claim her for burial. No one did.

> Eventually, a city official reached out to Centro Astalli, a Jesuit-run center for migrants and refugees, to organize a respectful funeral for Quintero. Astalli's director, Fr. Giovanni La Manna, initially planned to put together a small service in the center's chapel, but it also occurred to him that the funeral could be a teaching moment. His idea was daring: Why don't we celebrate it at the Church of the Gesu, the mother ship of the entire Jesuit order?

> La Manna knew he would need an informal blessing from the Vatican, in part because with Francis being the first Jesuit pope in history, the leadership of the order wouldn't want to do anything to embarrass the pontiff. La Manna confessed that had the pope been anyone other than Francis, he never would have asked, as he could have imagined the reaction of the Vatican and Italian bishops; making a public spectacle out of the funeral would risk confusion about the Church's teaching on sexual morality, so better to do it in quiet. With Francis, however, La Manna said he felt the pope would "get it."

> Quintero's funeral took place in the Church of the Gesu on December 27, 2013, attracting a cross-section of street people as well as Rome's ecclesiastical and political elite. La Manna described it as a "signal for the entire Roman community that's distracted in the face of so many people who face discrimination and who live their difficulties to the indifference of our city." At one level, it may seem that because Francis didn't attend or ever

publicly extend his blessing to the event, his connection is marginal. One has to know Roman politics to appreciate that something this unusual would never have happened in a major Roman church before Francis, especially a church with a direct connection to the pope through his religious order, and thus how meaningful a symbol it is for the change he's inspiring. (Allen, 2015, pp. 141–142)

The above narrative dramatically demonstrates how Ignatian discernment, compassion, mercy, and the inclusive leadership of Pope Francis intersect and inspire. In both word and deed, Francis is urging all people of good will to embody merciful conduct, especially to those on the margins. As leadership scholars and practitioners who animate communities and organizations that long for more successful, sustainable, and satisfying outcomes, how might we appropriate Francis' practices of mercy and inclusive leadership in our personal and professional contexts? This question crosses the boundary of religious communities to apply to all organizational contexts: political, social, educational, nonprofit, and business. Regardless of context and the manner in which we translate Pope Francis' message of mercy and inclusive ideals into action, we, as leaders, ought to remain mindful of our relationships with others and the realities of our broken world, with an "explicit focus on ethics and virtues" (Wuffli, 2015, p. 5). Perhaps Robert Greenleaf (1977/2002), in his original definition of servant leadership, best expresses what Pope Francis challenges us to use as the measure of our inclusive leadership:

> Do those served grow as persons? Do they, while being served, become healthier, wiser, freer, more autonomous, more likely themselves to become servants? And, what is the effect on the least privileged in society; will they benefit or, at least, not be further deprived (p. 27)?

Acknowledgments

Thank you to Dr. Catherine Punsalan-Manlimos and Fr. Patrick Howell, S.J. of the Institute for Catholic Thought and Culture at Seattle University for funding this research project. The authors are also grateful to Tefi Ma'ake and Mary Ann Carey for their enduring support and expert editing of our work.

References

Allen, J. L. (2015). *The Francis miracle: Inside the transformation of the pope and the Church.* New York, NY: Time Books.

Ambrogetti, F., & Rubin, S. (2013). *Pope Francis: His life in his own words: Conversations with Jorge Bergoglio.* New York, NY: Putnam.

Aquinas, T. (1912). *Summa theological: Volume III-part II, second section.* (Fathers of the English Dominican Province, Trans.). New York, NY: Cosimo.

Benedict XVI. (2007). *Jesus of Nazareth.* New York, NY: Doubleday.

Bergoglio, J. M. (2013). The faÉade as a mirror. In J. M. Bergoglio & A. Skorka (Eds.), *Pope Francis on faith, family, and the church in the twenty-first century* (pp. xiii–xvi). New York, NY: Image.

Bethune, B. (2013). Suspension of disbelief. *Maclean's, 126*(13), 16–27.

Bies, R. J. (2015, September 22). What Pope Francis' U.S. stop says about his leadership. *Fortune.* Retrieved from http://fortune.com/2015/09/22/pope-francis-u-s-visit-leadership/. Accessed on July 15, 2016.

Cahill, B. (2015). Pope Francis, inclusiveness, and the LGBT community. In E. Brigham, D. E. DeCosse, & M. Duffy (Eds.), *Pope Francis and the future of Catholicism in the United States* (pp. 65–70). San Francisco, CA: Joan and Ralph Lane Center for Catholic Studies and Social Thought of the University of San Francisco.

Collazo, J. S., & Rogak, L. (Eds.), (2013). *Pope Francis in his own words.* Novato, CA: New World Library.

Colvin, G. (2017, March 22). The world's 50 greatest leaders. *Fortune.* Retrieved from http://fortune.com/2017/03/23/worlds-50-greatest-leaders-intro/. Accessed on July 15, 2016.

Crowley, P. (2014). Introduction: Beyond Vatican II: Toward a church of yes. In P. Crowley (Ed.), *From Vatican II to Pope Francis: Charting a Catholic future* (pp. xiii–xxv). Maryknoll, NY: Orbis.

Francis. (2013a, March 16). Audience to representatives of the communications media. Retrieved from http://w2.vatican.va/content/francesco/en/speeches/2013/march/documents/papa-francesco_20130316_rappresentanti-media.html. Accessed on July 15, 2016.

Francis. (2013b, March 17). Homily of Pope Francis. *Libreria Editrice Vaticana.* Retrieved from https://w2.vatican.va/content/francesco/en/homilies/2013/documents/papa-francesco_20130317_omelia-santa-anna.html. Accessed on July 15, 2016.

Francis. (2013c, March 28). Homily of Pope Francis. *Libreria Editrice Vaticana.* Retrieved https://w2.vatican.va/content/francesco/en/homilies/2013/documents/papa-francesco_20130328_coena-domini.html. Accessed on July 15, 2016.

Francis. (2013d, July 6). Meeting with seminarians and novices. *Libreria Editrice Vaticana.* Retrieved from http://w2.vatican.va/content/francesco/en/speeches/2013/july/documents/papa-francesco_20130706_incontro-seminaristi.html. Accessed on July 15, 2016.

Francis. (2013e, July 28). Press conference of Pope Francis during the return flight. *Libreria Editrice Vaticana.* Retrieved from https://w2.vatican.va/content/

francesco/en/speeches/2013/july/documents/papa-francesco_20130728_gmg-con-ferenza-stampa.html. Accessed on July 15, 2016.

Francis. (2015, April 11). *Misericordiae vultus: Bull of indiction of the extraor-dinary jubilee of mercy. Libreria Editrice Vaticana.* Retrieved https://w2.vatican.va/content/francesco/en/bulls/documents/papa-francesco_bolla_20150411_miser-icordiae-vultus.html. Accessed on July 15, 2016.

Giberti, C. N. (2015). Jesuits. In M. Odekon (Ed.), *The SAGE encyclopedia of world poverty* (pp. 857–858). Thousand Oaks, CA: Sage.

Greenleaf, R. K. (1996). *Seeker and servant: Reflections on religious leadership.* A. T. Fraker & L. C. Spears (Eds.). San Francisco, CA: Jossey-Bass.

Greenleaf, R. K. (2002). *Servant Leadership: A journey into the nature of legiti-mate power & greatness* (25th anniversary ed.). Mahwah, NJ: Paulist Press. (Original work published 1977).

Gula, R. M. (1989). *Reason informed by faith: Foundations of Catholic moral-ity.* Mahwah, NJ: Paulist Press.

Gula, R. M. (2003). *The call to holiness: Embracing a fully Christian life.* Mahwah, NJ: Paulist Press.

Hale, C. (2016, April 13). Could Pope Francis be a feminist pope? *Washington Post.* Retrieved from https://www.washingtonpost.com/news/acts-of-faith/wp/2016/04/13/could-pope-francis-be-a-feminist-pope/. Accessed on July 15, 2016.

Hamel, G. (2015, April 14). The 15 diseases of leadership, according to Pope Francis. *Harvard Business Review.* Retrieved from https://hbr.org/2015/04/the-15-diseases-of-leadershipaccording-to-pope-francis. Accessed on July 15, 2016.

Hollander, E. (2009). *Inclusive leadership: The essential leader-follower relation-ship.* New York, NY: Taylor and Francis.

Ivereigh, A. (2014). *The great reformer: Francis and the making of a radical pope.* New York, NY: Henry Holt.

John XXIII. (1962). Solenne apertura del concilio ecumenico vaticano II. *Libreria Editrice Vaticana.* Retrieved from http://w2.vatican.va/content/john-xxiii/it/speeches/1962/documents/hf_j-xxiii_spe_19621011_opening-council.html. Accessed on July 15, 2016.

John Paul II. (1980). Dives in misericordia. *Libreria Editrice Vaticana.* Retrieved from http://w2.vatican.va/content/john-paul-ii/en/encyclicals/documents/hf_jp-ii_enc_30111980_dives-in-misericordia.html. Accessed on July 15, 2016.

Kasper, W. (2014). *Mercy: The essence of the Gospel and the key to Christian life.* Mahwah, NJ: Paulist Press.

Kasper, W. (2015). Open house: How Pope Francis sees the church. *Commonweal, 7,* 12–15.

Keenan, J. F. (2008). *The works of mercy: The heart of Catholicism* (2nd ed.). Lanham, MD: Sheed & Ward.

Keenan, J. F. (2010). *Moral wisdom: Lessons and texts from the Catholic tradi-tion* (2nd ed.). Lanham, MD: Sheed & Ward.

Krames, J. A. (2015). *Lead with humility: 12 leadership lessons from Pope Francis.* New York, NY: AMACOM.

Levs, J., & Pearson, M. (2013, December 11). Pope Francis named *Time* Person of the Year 2013. CNN. Retrieved from http://www.cnn.com/2013/12/11/living/time-person-of-the-year/. Accessed on July 15, 2016.

Loftus, G. (2015, September 30). 3 Leadership lessons from Pope Francis. Forbes. Retrieved from http://www.forbes.com/sites/geoffloftus/2015/09/30/3-leadership-lessons-from-pope-francis/#34efa5444bd6. Accessed on July 15, 2016.

Lowney, C. (2003). *Heroic leadership: Best practices from a 450-year-old company that changed the world.* Chicago, IL: Loyola Press.

Lowney, C. (2013). *Pope Francis: Why he leads the way he leads.* Chicago, IL: Loyola Press.

Martin, J. (2012). *The Jesuit guide to (almost) everything: A spirituality for real life.* New York, NY: HarperCollins Publishers.

McBrien, R. P. (1994). *Catholicism* (New ed.). New York, NY: HarperCollins.

McGregor, J. (2015, September 24). How Pope Francis defines a good political leader. *Washington Post.* Retrieved from https://www.washingtonpost.com/news/onleadership/wp/2015/09/24/how-pope-francis-defines-a-good-political-leader/. Accessed on July 15, 2016.

Merton, T. (1981). *The sign of Jonas.* New York, NY: Harcourt Brace & Company. (Original work published 1955).

Merton, T. (1983). *No man is an island.* New York, NY: Harcourt Brace & Company. (Original work published 1953).

Moynihan, R. (2013). *Pray for me: The life and spiritual vision of Pope Francis, first pope from the Americas.* New York, NY: Image.

Neafsey, J. (2006). *A sacred voice is calling: Personal vocation and social conscience.* Maryknoll, NY: Orbis.

Nowell, I. (1990). Mercy. In J. A. Komonchak, M. Collins, & D. A. Lane (Eds.), *The new dictionary of theology* (pp. 650–652). Collegeville, MN: Michael Glazier.

O'Malley, J. W. (2014). *The Jesuits: A history from Ignatius to the present.* Lanham, MD: Rowman & Littlefield.

Obama, B. H. (2015, September 23). Remarks by President Obama and His Holiness Pope Francis at arrival ceremony. *Office of the White House Press Secretary.* Retrieved from https://www.whitehouse.gov/the-press-office/2015/09/23/remarks-president-obama-and-his-holiness-pope-francis-arrival-ceremony. Accessed on July 15, 2016.

Rayman, N. (2015, March 10). 5 Leadership lessons you can learn from Pope Francis. *Time.* Retrieved from http://time.com/3737887/pope-francis-leadership-lessons/. Accessed on July 15, 2016.

Rubenfire, A. (2014, August 14). Four leadership lessons from the pope. *The Wall Street Journal.* Retrieved from http://blogs.wsj.com/atwork/2014/08/14/four-leadership-lessons-from-the-pope/. Accessed on July 15, 2016.

Smith, C. A., & Merz, E. F. (2006). *Finding God in each moment.* Notre Dame, IN: Ave Maria Press.

Sobrino, J. (1993). Spirituality and the following of Jesus. In I. Ellacuría & J. Sobrino (Eds.), *Mysterium liberationis: Fundamental concepts of liberation theology* (pp. 677–701). Maryknoll, NY: Orbis.

Spadaro, A. (2013, September 30). A big heart open to God: The exclusive interview with Pope Francis. *America Magazine*. Retrieved from http://americamagazine.org/pope-interview. Accessed on July 15, 2016.

Sparough, J. M., Manney, J., & Hipskind, T. (2010). *What's your decision?: How to make choices with confidence and clarity*. Chicago, IL: Loyola Press.

Spinello, R. A. (2012). *The encyclicals of John Paul II: An introduction and commentary*. Landham, MD: Sheed & Ward.

Spitzer, R. (2008). *Five pillars of the spiritual life: A practical guide to prayer for active people*. San Francisco, CA: Ignatius Press.

Thibodeux, M. E. (2010). *God's voice within: The Ignatian way to discover God's will*. Chicago, IL: Loyola Press.

Tornielli, A. (2013, December 14). Never be afraid of tenderness. *La Stampa*. Retrieved from http://www.lastampa.it/2013/12/14/esteri/vatican-insider/en/never-be-afraid-of-tenderness-5BqUfVs9r7W1CJIMuHqNeI/pagina.html. Accessed on July 15, 2016.

Vallely, P. (2013). *Pope Francis: Untying the knots*. New York, NY: Bloomsbury.

Vanderbloemen, W. (2015, September 25). 5 Leadership lessons from Pope Francis. *Fast Company*. Retrieved from http://www.fastcompany.com/3051514/know-it-all/5-lessons-every-leader-can-learn-from-pope-francis. Accessed on July 15, 2016.

Vatican Radio. (2016, February 18). Pope Francis' followers on Twitter now exceed 27 million. Retrieved from http://en.radiovaticana.va/news/2016/02/18/pope_francis_followers_on_twitter_now_exceed_27_million/1209700. Accessed on July 15, 2016.

Walatka, T. (2016). The principle of mercy: Jon Sobrino and the Catholic theological tradition. *Theological Studies*, 77(1), 96–117.

Wuffli, P. A. (2015). *Inclusive leadership: A framework for the global era*. New York, NY: Springer.

Yardley, J., & Goodstein, L. (2016, April 8). Francis' message calls on church to be inclusive. *New York Times*. Retrieved from http://www.nytimes.com/2016/04/09/world/europe/pope-francis-amoris-laetitia.html?_r=0. Accessed on July 15, 2016.

Zetlin, M. (2014). Why Pope Francis is so effective: 8 lessons for every leader. *Inc*. Retrieved from http://www.inc.com/minda-zetlin/why-pope-francis-is-so-effective-8-lessons-for-every-leader.html. Accessed on July 15, 2016.

9

Harmony but Not Sameness: The Inclusive Leadership Style of the Chinese Profound Persons

Zhi Luan

Keywords: Confucianism; Daoism; Buddhism; inclusive leadership; profound persons; self-cultivation

Introduction

Former US Vice-President Albert Gore (2013) blamed the tradition of rationalist dichotomy for today's leadership crisis. He claimed that, with this cultural legacy, people in the West tend to separate the mind from body, nature from human being, and focus their attention on "ever narrower slices of the whole" while neglecting the whole (2013, p. xxi). He called on leaders to develop a global mind in order to think freshly and reclaim the control of our human destiny in the new area.

Similarly, the Confucian philosopher Tu Weiming (1998) argued that all the wicked problems of today are genetically connected with the "Enlightenment mentality," which holds that human history follows a linear progression from religion to philosophy to science (rationality) (p. 85). This prevailing ideology not only breeds the modern values such as liberty, individuality, and the rule of law but also causes "sharp difference, severe differentiation, drastic demarcation, thunderous dissonance, and outright discrimination" (Tu, 1998, p. 89). Tu and Ikeda (2011) urged that Enlightenment mentality be reoriented with new views of humanity so that the human race can shake off the crises.

Back in 1970s, the British philosopher of history Arnold Toynbee (1989) perceived the danger of the ever-disintegrating human society. He called an effective leadership to take on the mission of unifying the world. He reviewed the world history and anticipated that the Chinese nation would be able to shoulder such a leadership role. He said the Chinese culture is imbued with a unique ecumenical spirit of humanism, which has reared the nation's capability to make peace and harmony.

The Japanese Buddhist philosopher Daisaku Ikeda (2011) echoed Toynbee and said that the inclusive nature of the Chinese culture stems from "a philosophy of symbiosis" (p. 56). With this philosophy, people put themselves in the other's place and highlight mindfulness instead of selfishness (Tu & Ikeda, 2011). Ikeda believed that a leadership of wisdom and altruism cultivated from the symbiosis is essentially needed in the imminent global situation (Tu & Ikeda, 2011).

However, can China really meet the leadership call? Looking at the bewildering complication in China, this question is naturally controversial. Despite all the uncertainties, one thing seems positive, that since the late 1970s, the revival of the Chinese traditions has been noticeably strong (Chen, 2011). Numerous Chinese leaders from different walks of life are actively engaged in studying and promoting the traditional culture (Chen, 2011; Tu & Ikeda, 2011). Jing Kong, a Buddhist master, is one of the most accomplished and venerated. He is exemplary in revealing the quality of inclusive leadership in terms of advancing the ideals of religious cooperation, world peace, and racial harmony in China and throughout the world.

This study intends to explore the substance of inclusive leadership on the basis of the Chinese culture. It describes the style of leadership inclusiveness in the context of Chinese culture and conceptualizes its metaphysical foundation. It uses Master Jing Kong's example to illustrate the reality of this style of leadership and its expected universal significance. It is in the hope that some commonly shared values, deeply rooted in the Chinese cultural thought, can be revealed to constructively inform the leadership arena for making a better world.

Inclusive Leadership – The Way of Profound Persons

Chinese culture is characterized as a huge and complex system, yet its core values are firmly rooted in the teachings of three highly integrated philosophies or religions – Confucianism, Daoism, and Buddhism. Despite their philosophical emphasis, these three teachings have been reconciled with one another over the course of history and have jointly nurtured the cultural spirit of the Chinese nation (Nan, 2011). The leadership concept of *junzi* is a salient example. Although the concept was initiated in the Confucian project, its substance and efficacy have been nourished and strengthened also by Daoism and Buddhism.

The English translation of *junzi* frequently includes moral leader, exemplary person, and superior person. Tu (1989) recommended "profound person" as an alternative because it can avoid terminological ambiguity and "provide sufficient ground to cover the missing ramification of the original idea" (p. 16). In Tu's (1989) view, the meaning of *junzi* is broad and profound and covers the leadership roles in various dimensions of social engagement including political governance, organizational operation, education, and religious practice. Tu (1989) implied that the leadership function of a *junzi* optimally symbolizes the inclusiveness of the Confucian humanism. This study follows Tu's recommendation and uses "profound person" for the translation of *junzi*.

Ames and Rosemont (1998) noted that profound persons refer to those who work for the goal of human excellence through constant personal improvement. Tu and Ikeda (2011) indicated that the essential project of profound persons is to pursue the ancient Chinese ideal *datong*, or Great Harmony, as the eventual social end and highest human well-being. Profound persons usually engage themselves in three primary tasks: pursuing the Way, participating in politics, and undertaking constant and rigorous learning (Tu and Ikeda, 2011). Resonating with Ames, Rosemont, and Tu, this study identifies four characters that describe the inclusive leadership of the Chinese profound persons. They are humanity, mindfulness, transcendence, and self-cultivation.

HUMANITY

The concept of the term *ren* (仁) is the "foremost project" upheld in Confucianism (Ames & Rosemont, 1998, p. 48). Its translations in English prominently include benevolence, goodness, human-heartedness, and humanity. Confucius' definition of the term is multiangle, but basically centers on the meaning of deep and extensive human love (*Analects*, 12.22; Ames & Rosemont, 1998, trans.).[1] Ames and Rosemont (1998) commented that *ren* for humanity "suggests a shared, essential condition of being human owned by all members of the species"; the project of *ren* is to grow all those constitutive human relationships into "vital, robust, and healthy participation in the human community" (p. 49). Confucius specified that profound persons must "love the multitude broadly and be intimate with those of humanity" (*Analects*, 1.6; Ames & Rosemont, 1998). With Confucianism, humanity is most uniquely manifested in the project of extending family love.

The Chinese word *xiao* (孝) is a central concept of the Chinese traditions. It is usually translated as "filial piety" in English, which means one's duty and reverence for his or her parents. But according to Ames (2010), the proper translation of *xiao* should be "family feeling" instead because it accords Mencius' definition that the relationship between parents and children is essentially *qin*, or affection (p. 68). Regarding the significance of *xiao*, Confucius taught, "The Way of the profound person may be likened to traveling to a distant place; one must start from the nearest point. It may be likened to ascending a height of public responsibility; one must start from the lowest step, one's family" (*Zhongyong*, ch.15; Chan, 1973, trans.). Ames (2010) explained that family feeling serves as the very basic project for people to establish their moral life and as the ground for "Confucian role ethics" (p. 68). Tu (1989) affirmed that the Confucian family feeling refers to the most basic and natural human love, which needs to be preserved and extended for people to authentically embrace others and fulfill their community

---

[1]The translations of the classics in the text are based on one specific translator with reference to other translations.

duties. For achieved profound persons, "everyone in the world is their brother" (*Analects*, 12.5; Ames & Rosemont, 1998, trans.).

MINDFULNESS

The Chinese culture is characteristic of inward reflection (Tu, 1989). Inward reflection is a requisite daily practice of a profound person. Zengzi, a disciple of Confucius, would examine his person every day on three counts: his devotion to work, his loyalty to colleagues and friends, and his diligence to study. (*Analects*, 1.4; Ames & Rosemont, 1998, trans.).

Mencius specifically taught:

> If others do not respond to your love with love, look into your own benevolence; if others fail to respond to your attempts to govern them with order, look into your own wisdom; if others do not return your courtesy, look into your respect. In other words, look into yourself whenever you fail to achieve your purpose. (*Mencius*, 4A. 4; Lau, 2003, trans.)

Tu (1989) said that the mindfulness of profound persons "creatively establishes and enlarges itself (the true self) as an open system by entering into fruitful communication with an ever-expanding network of human-relatedness" (p. 117). Confucius stated, "Persons of humanity establishes others in seeking to establish themselves and promote others in seeking to get there themselves" (*Analects*, 6.29; Ames & Rosemont, 1998, trans.). The mindfulness of profound persons particularly manifests in two aspects: humility and tolerance.

Humility

Tu (1989) recognized that the mindfulness of profound persons exhibits a strong sense of humility, and a real profound person is "plain, simple, and amicable" in demeanor (p. 89). He identified three leadership aspects of a humble profound person: self-watchfulness, conscientiousness, and altruism. These three serve to guarantee that leaders overcome the ego and realize their humanity (Tu, 1989). Authentic leadership never functions to command but to show, suggest, and model the way for efficacy. Confucius remarked, "The excellence of the profound person is the wind, while that of the petty person is the grass. As the wind blows, the grass is sure to bend" (*Analects*, 12.19; Ames & Rosemont, 1998, trans.). Tu (1989) interpreted what Confucius really meant is that, instead of any coercive attempts, leaders should act out the way and transform the followers through exemplary teaching.

Tolerance

All-embracement is another feature of the Chinese culture (Qian, 2009), which is rooted the ancient vision of *datong*, or the Great Harmony. Regarding the essence of the Great Harmony, Tu explained:

> The Great Harmony does not impose a uniformity under which everybody must copy everyone else. Instead, it is the wisdom to integrate diversity.... It fully recognizes that difference is unavoidable and that dealing with difference in proper ways is necessary for peaceful co-existence among individuals and groups. (Tu & Ikeda, 2011, p. 62)

Addressing leadership practice, Confucius said, "Profound persons seek harmony not sameness; petty persons, then, are the opposite," and "Profound persons associating openly with others are not partisan; petty persons being partisan do not associate openly with others" (*Analects*, 13.23, 12.14; Ames & Rosemont, 1998, trans.). From a cosmological perspective, the tolerance of leadership is compared to the accommodating power of the nature in *Yijing* (*the Book of Changes*), "In accordance with the capacity and sustaining power of the earth, profound persons embrace and support people and things with their large virtue" (*Yijing, Kun* 1.3; Legge, trans.).

TRANSCENDENCE

The Chinese word *Dao* (道), or the Way, is the foundational concept of the entire system of Chinese culture. It metaphysically refers to the ultimate existence, which originates all things. Li Shen (2006) asserted that pursuing the Way is the ultimate project of the Confucians. Tu (1993) echoed Li and commented that profound persons cultivated a sense of mission and determined to seek the Way and transmit it for the continuation of human civilization. He characterized Confucianism as a system of humanism, which prepares profound persons to seek a "transcendental breakthrough" of "anthropocosmical" significance (Tu, 1993, p. 2).

Ames and Rosemont (1998) emphasized that the Confucian Way is primarily *rendao*, or a way for people to become "consummately and authoritatively human" (p. 46). Confucius expressed his perspective for leadership transcendence, "For a resolute intellectual-leader and a person of humanity, while they would not compromise their humanity to save their lives, they might well give up their lives in order to achieve it" (*Analects*, 15.9; Ames & Rosemont, 1998, trans.). Zengzi said the similar idea, "An intellectual-leader cannot but be strong and resolved, for they bear a heavy charge and their way is long. Where they take humanity as their charge, is it not a heavy one? And where their way ends only in death, is it not indeed long?" (*Analects*, 8.7; Ames & Rosemont, 1998, trans.).

Transcendence is prioritized in the Confucian classic *The Great Learning* as the three cardinal guidelines for leadership development, which include illustrating illustrious virtue, loving and serving the people, and resting in the highest excellence (*The Great Learning*, 1973; Chan, trans.). Nan (2003) pointed out that the three cardinal guidelines specify the transcendental leadership process through one's self-cultivation and actual social engagement towards the supreme humanity realization.

Mencius justified the possibility of fulfilling the transcendental breakthrough on the basis of self-cultivation (Tu, 1993). He depicted six stages for an ordinary person to work to reach the state of divinity:

> The desirable (humanity transcendence) is called 'good.' To have it in oneself is called 'true.' To possess it fully in oneself is called 'beautiful,' but to shine forth with this full possession is called 'great.' To be great and be transformed by this greatness is called 'sage;' to be sage and to transcend the understanding is called 'divine.' (*Mencius*, 7B.25; Lau, 2003, trans.)

Influenced by Mencius and Buddhism, there emerged a prevailing practice of self-cultivation among the Chinese leaders of the later generations. Those in the Song and Ming dynasties were especially remarkable in this line, who achieved preeminent attainments in academics and politics in seeking spiritual transcendence (Nan, 2003).

SELF-CULTIVATION

Learning is specifically highlighted in Confucianism for the development of human capacities. All the aforementioned aspects of inclusive leadership are necessarily derived from the profound persons' endeavor in their persistent and conscientious learning. Based on the eight stages prescribed in *The Great Learning* (1973; Chan, trans.) for leadership development,[2] the learning of a leader involves two substantive aspects: the broad learning for universal knowledge and the personal cultivation for self-knowledge (Tu, 1993). While extensive learning is widely applied in any leadership development project, the rigorous and systematic practice in self-cultivation is viewed as the salience with profound persons (Li, 2006; Nan, 2003; Senge, Scharmer, Jaworski, & Flowers, 2004; Tu, 1989; Tu & Ikeda, 2011).

Tu (1989) pointed out that self-cultivation serves to bridge the gap between one's universal knowledge and the actualization of his or her moral excellence for social ideal through the achieved self-knowledge. According to Tu (1989), there exists "a major difference between what one is and what one can become," and "For the profound person, self-knowledge is a prerequisite for a fruitful encounter with the external world" (p. 20). As such, self-cultivation for a profound person is by no means "a private affair" but an effort to reach universal relatedness as the great foundation for humanity (Tu, 1989, p. 8).

Self-cultivation is a very technically engaged system of personal training. In *The Great Learning*, six meditative spaces are laid out for such an exquisite process of training, which include stopping, settling down, calmness, light-heartedness, true and fine thinking, and attainment (*The Great Learning*, 1973; Chan, trans.). Senge et al. (2004) commented that, if one wants to be a great leader, he or she has to enter these six meditative spaces as a long process of self-cultivation. Mencius was exemplary as one of the early practitioners of technically backed self-cultivation for effective learning, who acknowledged that through personal endeavor, people can learn to become authentically human (Tu & Ikeda, 2011). Commenting on the Ming dynasty philosopher Wang Yangming's accomplishment in self-cultivation, Tu (1993) exalted:

---

[2]The eight stages include investigating all things, mastering all knowledge, developing sincere attitude, rectifying the heart, cultivating the person, regulating the family, ordering the state, and making peace and achieving harmony in the world.

As a result, his nature was strengthened and his deficiencies overcome so that he could bear witness to his faith in human perfectibility through self-effort. He philosophized about the import of pain and suffering for forming one body with heaven and earth and the myriad things because he had embodied it in his quest for ultimate self-transformation. (1993, p. 56)

The Metaphysical Foundation of the Chinese Inclusive Leadership

The Chinese cultural spirit is jointly nurtured by the teachings of Confucianism, Daoism, and Buddhism. Ikeda noted that the uniqueness of the Chinese cultural thought is its "wisdom of harmonious symbiosis," which fosters "an ethos of harmony rather than conflict, unity rather than division, us rather than me: spiritual tendency toward human-to-human and human-to-nature creative coexistence" (Tu & Ikeda, 2011, p. 105). This wisdom of symbiosis breeds the leadership inclusivity and is metaphysically grounded in the Confucian notion "the Unity of Heaven and Humanity," the Daoist belief "All Things in One," and the Buddhist philosophy of One-and-All.

THE UNITY OF HEAVEN AND HUMANITY

The Confucian Heaven refers to the supreme origin of everything (Nan, 2003). But unlike the usual religious tradition, the Chinese Heaven is not only the creator of the world, but is also the field of the creatures (Ames & Rosemont, 1998). Nan (1997) argued that, although not conventionally viewed as a religion, Confucianism shares the same message of old Indian religions that there is no duality between God and human.

The inseparable relationship between Heaven and humanity is unequivocally addressed in *Zhongyong* (*The Doctrine of Means*). *Zhongyong* starts with the words, "What Heaven imparts to man is called human nature. To follow human nature is called the Way. Cultivating the Way is called teaching. The Way cannot be separated from us for a moment. What can be separated from us is not the Way" (*Zhongyong*, ch.1; Chan, 1973, trans.). Here, cultivating the Way serves to link the Heaven-endowed human nature with Heaven.

Tu (1989) opined that the idea of Heaven-human unity provides the metaphysical stance for the understanding of universal integrity on the basis of diversity. As the Song dynasty philosopher Zhang Zai (1973) said:

> Heaven is my father and Earth is my mother, and even such a small creature as I find an intimate place in their midst. Therefore that which fills the universe I regard as my body and that which directs the universe I consider as my nature. All people are my brothers and sisters, and all things are my companions. (*The Western Inscription*; Chan, 1973, trans.)

Mencius suggested how to realize such inclusivity on the basis of self-cultivation. He said, "For a man to give full realization to his heart is for him to understand his own nature, and a man who knows his own nature will know Heaven. By retaining his heart and nurturing his nature he is serving Heaven" (*Mencius*, 7B.25; Lau, 2003, trans.). Tu (1989) explained that Mencius' idea of "serving Heaven" is as much as to say that profound persons are obliged to perceive and identify those hidden common experiences for the solidarity of human beings. The Unity of Heaven and Humanity fosters the idea of Great Harmony and signifies the feasibility of a "fiduciary community" on the basis of manifesting human naturalness. (Tu, 1989, p. 23).

All Things in One

Three classics primarily represent Daoism: *Yijing*, *Lao-tzu*, and *Zhaung-tzu*. Based on the cosmological principles drawn from the operation of the hexagram, *Yijing* defines the inseparable relationship between the three Powers of Heaven, Earth, and humanity. Lao Tzu, the founder of Daoism, advanced the metaphysics of *Yijing* and affirmed the integrity of humanity and the universe on the basis of Nature and Dao (the Way). In *Lao-tzu*, the text reads: "Man models himself after Earth. Earth models itself after Heaven. Heaven models itself after Dao. And Dao models itself after Nature" (*Lao-tzu*, ch.25; Chan, 1973, trans.). Predicated on this view, Lao Tzu requested leaders to emulate rivers and seas, which accommodate all mountain streams, and thus be their kings (*Lao-tzu*, ch.25; Chan, 1973, trans.).

The concept of All Things in One was most explicitly expressed by Zhuang Tzu, the co-founder of Daoism. In *Zhuang-tzu*, it is stated in chapter two *The Equality of Things* that "... The universe is but one mark, and all things are but a horse," and "The universe and I exist together, and all things and I are one" (*Zhuang-tzu*, ch.2; Chan, 1973, trans.). Nan (2007) commented that the theme of *The Equality of Things* is that things and phenomena in the world are seemingly different and unequal, but in actuality, they are fundamentally identical by sharing the same common Dao. However, people are usually discriminatory, only perceiving and focusing on the differences, which consequently causes complications and chaos; only those of wisdom know how to identify all things as one by abiding in the common principles of Dao (*Zhuang-tzu*, ch.2; Chan, 1973, trans.). Zhuang Tzu specifically addressed the importance of self-cultivation for leaders to transcend their selves in order to authentically serve the community without causing harm (*Zhuang-tzu*, ch.6; Chan, 1973, trans.).

Based on the metaphysical framework of Lao Tzu and Zhuang Tzu, the later Daoist practitioners developed techniques for their personal cultivation. The most popular practice is internal alchemy. Based on the recognition of *yin-yang* (female-male) interaction, the internal alchemy is a practice attempting to regulate essence, energy, and spirit in order for them to be highly integrated and concentrated for the purpose of improving an individual's physical, emotional and mental health, and ultimately returning to the primordial unity with Dao and everything (Nan, 2011). The principles of internal alchemy were widely employed as a source of effective leadership empowerment from self-cultivation.

One-and-All

When Buddhism arrived in China in the late Han dynasty (202 BC – 220 AD), it quickly became integrated with the indigenous religious beliefs and practices (Chew, 1993). Seng-chao, a renowned Buddhist monk in the Eastern Jin dynasty was highly esteemed for his effort in incorporating Daoism and Confucianism with Buddhism. In Chao *lun* (Chao's Treaties), Seng-chao (1973) wrote, "...things and I sprang from the same root, and right and wrong come out of the same breath. The principle is deep, subtle, abstruse, and hidden, and it is nigh impossible for ordinary people to understand completely" (Chao *lun*, ch.2; Chan, 1973, trans.).

Seng-chao's view is grounded in the One-and-All philosophy of the Hua-yen School of the Buddhism. Jing Kong (2012) said that the key message Hua-yen *jing* (Flowery Splendor Scripture) conveys is that all living and nonliving entities in the universe share the same True Nature; all beings have the same wisdom, abilities, and virtues as Buddha. Chan (1973) noted that, in addition to the Zen school, Hua-yen school is the most Sinicized part of Buddhism, and has exerted tremendous metaphysical and technical impact on the Neo-Confucians in Song and Ming dynasties.

The importance of Buddhism to the Chinese culture is beyond its mere metaphysical coherence with Confucianism and Daoism. Unlike Confucianism and Daoism, a major fabric of the wide spectrum of Buddhist belief-system is the epistemology, which emphasizes verification by practice and experience as an essential component of knowledge (Jing Kong, 2012; Nan, 2011). In this vein, assertions of Buddhism are supposed to be justified on "empirical" basis instead of only philosophical speculation or mystical intuition. The foundational Mahayana Buddhist concept of "thorough enlightenment" means the complete verification of the True Nature. In the *Platform Sutra*, Hui Neng (2007), the Sixth Patriarch of Zen Buddhism, describes what he really sees about the True Nature: it is intrinsically pure, intrinsically free from becoming or annihilation, intrinsically self-sufficient, intrinsically immovable, and manifests all things (*Platform Sutra*, 2007). Jing Kong (2012) noted that Buddhism claims 84,000 Dharma Doors for people to technically cultivate their selves and eradicate attachments, discrimination, and delusions in order to achieve enlightenments of different levels and realize the True Nature.

A Portrait of a Profound Person — Master Jing Kong[3]

Chinese culture experienced tremendous destruction over the past century. But since late 1970s, its revival has been steady and

---

[3]The information sources for this section include Master Jing Kong's several official websites (http://www.jingkongfashi.com/; http://www. amtb.cn/e-bud/e-bud.asp; http://www.amtfweb.org/english/master-html/ english-viewpoint; http://www.amtbweb.org/ebooks/Master_PeaceDevotion. pdf.) and the literature and DVDs for free distribution in my collection.

vibrant. Master Jing Kong is one of the dedicated Chinese leaders who assume the task of promoting the traditions and striving for world peace and unity.

Master Jing Kong was born in Anhui Province, China, in 1927. He went to Taiwan in 1949 and became a monk in 1959. Despite his greatest achievement in propagating Pure Land Buddhism, he is also known for his extensive studies of Confucianism, Daoism, Islam, Christianity, and other religions. He has been particularly praised and venerated for his dedication to the work of resolving conflict and promoting world peace by advocating multiculturalism and racial harmony. His accomplishments are many and diverse, which briefly include the following:

- On his journeys of propagating Buddhism overseas, he and his followers were able to establish amicable relationship with the local communities. He was awarded with a number of honorary citizenships in the United States, Australia, and Indonesia.
- When in Singapore, he took the initiative and interacted with the nine isolated major religions in this island city-state. A religious unity was thus achieved among the nine faiths through his efforts.
- He has frequently participated in various international peace-making and multicultural initiatives, which include the UN peace conferences, UNESCO programs, and Asia NGO summits.
- He joined in the national agenda for ethical unity and religious harmony launched by the Australian and Indonesian governments. He provided his advice and training programs for people of different cultures and religions to become united.
- He founded "Lujiang Cultural Education Center" in China and experimented on using the traditional Confucian values to improve the local morals and mores in his hometown. The experiment was a success, and was made the demonstration for UNESCO programs.

Four elements explain why Master Jing Kong has been steadily driven for 50 years to work for world peace and unity regardless of many setbacks and difficulties. They are great compassion, belief in multiculturalism, dedication to education, and self-cultivation.

GREAT COMPASSION

Master Jing Kong recognizes that people are split and conflicting because of the misconception of human nature. Once we become aware of the truth, we will be able to return to our natural goodness and establish peace and harmony. It is the very duty of a Buddhist practitioner to help people attain wisdom and relieve suffering.

BELIEF IN MULTICULTURALISM[4]

Master Jing Kong believes that we all share the same True Nature, but display multiple cultural qualities. He often compares different cultures and religions to the parts of our body, each having its own character and function, but organically serving the common and holistic interest. He proposed the concept that all religions are of the same origin, and are the compassionate and loving teachings of gods and sages.

DEDICATION TO EDUCATION

Master Jing Kong repeatedly underscores the importance of the traditional family education and religious education. He stressed that the world is dismantling because families are falling apart. Thus the traditional Chinese family education should be valued and promoted. He insisted that the essence of religion is educational rather than ritual and ceremonial; religious education is about resolving people's internal conflicts for the fundamental resolution of all the external conflicts.

---

[4]The recent British exit from the EU raised questions on the fate of multiculturalism. However, from the viewpoint of Master Jing Kong, it is not a problem with multiculturalism, per se, but an issue that people are not prepared for multiculturalism. The project of racial reconciliation and cultural accommodation is a long process in which wise and persistent efforts must be involved in terms of raising people's understanding of different cultures. The key point is the awareness and recognition of human commonality, which can serve to lay the foundation for a community of shared destiny and future. Brexit has once again rung the alarm bell that there is an urgent need for deepened multiculturalism in this ever more interrelated, yet still alienated world.

SELF-CULTIVATION

Master Jing Kong believes effective leadership lies in leader's cultivating the self and modeling the way. He would use any opportunity to temper himself, see through the true reality, and let go of attachments for liberation and enlightenment. He proposed ten principles for common self-cultivation practice: true sincerity, purity of mind, equality, proper understanding, compassion, seeing through, letting go, attaining freedom, according with proper conditions, and being mindful of Buddha.

Master Jing Kong exemplifies the way of a profound person and identifies with the four characters of humanity, mindfulness, transcendence, and self-cultivation in terms of leadership inclusivity. It indicates that inclusive leadership is a leadership style which fundamentally stems from our human nature and displays its intrinsically endowed wisdom and compassion; it requires the effort of self-cultivation for leaders to transcend the fortress of ego and authentically lead the community to realize its common benefit on the basis of peace and harmony; it comes from the heart and encourages the heart of others, so it resonates with people and empowers them to achieve positive personal and social transformation. The exemplary significance of Master Jing Kong's accomplishment for today's world is anticipated in three aspects:

First, peace and unity are the common human pursuit. However, the disintegration of reality requires a distinct perspective for the underlying problems and effective collaborative actions. A dialogical civilization needs to be built and advanced so that people across cultures get to deeply know each other and recognize the importance and feasibility of establishing a community with a shared identity and future.

Second, the wisdom of harmonious symbiosis is universally applicable and is specifically important in the time of globalization. In promoting multiculturalism based on the idea of the True Nature of everything, Master Jing Kong has proved to be able to unite people of cultural and religious diversity throughout the world. Chinese cultural thought once largely influenced political reform and social change in Europe (Ames, 2011; Creel, 1960), and may again exert its power in shaping the human condition of future (Ames & Rosemont, 1998; Bell & Chaibong, 2003; Tu & Ikeda, 2011). Giving voice to the undercurrent of human empathy, Chinese cultural thought may prove a particularly effective remedy to the prevalent instrumental rationality and excessive individualism, which have caused the current fragmenting human crises (Tu, 1998).

Third, self-cultivation is essential for making an authentic inclusive leader. As a Buddhist monk, Master Jing Kong shows the great potential of human goodness, which can be reached through conscientious learning for both universal knowledge and self-knowledge. Self-cultivation serves to sharpen our cognitive ability and, most importantly, turn it into the power of wisdom for effective actions in various social activities. The project of self-cultivation is always hard. However, as long as we are sincere about authentic leadership, rather than opportunism, profitable and efficacious self-development must be engaged to facilitate the process of leadership development.

All in all, Master Jing Kong sets a good example as an inclusive leader. He draws his passion and wisdom from his persistent study and practice of the teachings of saints and sages. His accomplishment indicates a path that people can follow to achieve the reality of inclusive leadership.

Conclusion

Across its 5000-year history, China has incorporated and contained multiple nations and cultures, and has substantially remained integrated, stable, and peaceful. This attainment significantly benefits from its cultural inclusiveness embodied in leadership pursuit and performance. The style of Chinese inclusive leadership has its solid metaphysical foundation laid upon the three interwoven teachings of Confucianism, Daoism, and Buddhism. With humanity, mindfulness, transcendence, and self-cultivation, the profound person exemplifies the spirit of such a leadership style. Self-cultivation is most essential of the four inclusive leadership characters because it is highly technically required and serves to ensure the authenticity of the other three. Master Jing Kong's success in his practice of the profound person's way illustrates that this seemingly obsolete ideal of leadership inclusivity still retains its validity and vitality and deserves attention and emulation. The world cannot afford unceasing competition and fragmentation. For the existence and continuation of the global village, efforts have to be made in terms of unity, peace, and harmony on the basis of our common humanity and the desire for excellence.

References

Ames, T. R. (2010). What is Confucianism? In W. Change & L. Kalmanson (Eds.), *Confucianism in context* (pp. 67–86). New York, NY: State University of New York Press.

Ames, T. R. (2011). *Confucian role ethics: A vocabulary*. Honolulu, HI: University of Hawaii Press.

Ames, T. R., & Rosemont, H. (1998). *The Analects of Confucius: A philosophical translation*. New York, NY: Ballantine Books.

Bell, A. D., & Chaibong, H. (2003). *Confucianism for the modern world*. Cambridge, UK: Cambridge University Press.

Chen, J. M. (2011). The national studies craze: The phenomena, the controversies, and some reflections. *China Perspectives*. Retrieved from http://chinaperspectives.revues.org. Accessed on March 15, 2016.

Chew, P. G. L. (1993). *The Chinese religion and the Baha'i Faith*. Welwyn, UK: George Ronald.

Creel, H. G. (1960). *Confucius and the Chinese way*. New York, NY: Harper & Row Publishers.

Gore, A. (2013). *The future: Six drivers of global change*. New York, NY: Random House. Information Age.

Hui Neng. (2007). *The Sutra of Hui Neng*. Taipei: The Corporate Body of the Buddha Educational Foundation.

Jingkong. (2012, December 29). Annotations on *Great Vehicle Sutra* of immeasurable longevity. Retrieved from http://blog.sina.com.cn/s/blog_6946398d0101cr6r.html. Accessed on March 22, 2016.

Lao Tzu. (1973). Lao Tzu. In W. T. Chan (Eds. & Trans.), *A source book in Chinese philosophy* (pp. 136–176). Princeton, NJ: Princeton University Press.

Li S. (2006). *A brief history of Confucianism*. Beijing, PRC: China People's University Press.

Mencius. (2003). *Mencius*. D. C. Lau (trans), London, UK: Penguin Classics.

Nan, H. (1997). *Basic Buddhism: Exploring Buddhism and Zen*. York Beach, Maine: Samuel Weiser, Inc.

Nan, H. (2003). *Reinterpretation of The Great Learning*. Shanghai, PRC: Fudan University Press.

Nan, H. (2007). *Commentaries on Zhuang Tzu*. Shanghai, PRC: Shanghai People's Publishing.

Nan, H. (2011). *Mencius and Gong Sunchou*. Beijing, PRC: Oriental Publications.

Qian, M. (2009). *The outline of Chinese history*. Beijing, PRC: Commercial Press.

Seng-chao. (1973). Chao lun. In W. T. Chan (Eds. & Trans.), *A source book in Chinese philosophy* (pp. 344–349). Princeton, NJ: Princeton University Press.

Senge, P., Scharmer, C. O., Jaworski, J., & Flowers, B. S. (2004). *Presence: Human purpose and the field of the future*. New York, NY: The Doubleday Broadway.

The Great Learning. (2013). In W. T. Chan (Eds. & Trans.), *A source book in Chinese philosophy* (pp. 85–94). Princeton, NJ: Princeton University Press.

Toynbee, A., & Ikeda, D. (1989). *Choose life*. Oxford, UK: Oxford University Press.

Tu, W. M. (1989). *Centrality and commonality*. Albany, NY: State University of New York Press.

Tu, W. M. (1993). *Way, learning, and politics: Essays on the Confucian intellectual*. Albany, NY: State University of New York Press.

Tu, W. M. (1998). Beyond the enlightenment mentality. In M. Tucker & J. Berthrong (Eds.), *Confucianism and ecology* (pp. 85–94). Cambridge, MA: Harvard University Press.

Tu, W. M., & Ikeda, D. (2011). *New horizons in eastern humanism*. New York, NY: I.B Tauris.

Yijing (The Book of Changes). (n.d.). J. Legge (trans), Retrieved from http://ctext.org/. Accessed on April 5, 2016.

Zhang, Z. (1973). The western inscription. In W. T. Chan (Eds. & Trans.), *A source book in Chinese philosophy* (pp. 497–499). Princeton, NJ: Princeton University Press.

Zhongyong (The Doctrine of the Mean). (1973). In W. T. Chan (Eds. & Trans.), *A source book in Chinese philosophy* (pp. 97–114). Princeton, NJ: Princeton University Press.

Zhuang Tzu. (1973). Zhuang Tzu. In W. T. Chan (Eds. & Trans.), *A source book in Chinese philosophy* (pp. 179–190). Princeton, NJ: Princeton University Press.

PART 3
Spiritual Inclusiveness

Introduction

Inclusive spirituality sounds almost oxymoronic. However, if we ponder more deeply than simply equating spirituality with religiosity, then we can open the door to the realm of inclusive universal faith and a sense of shared humanity. Spiritual inclusiveness is an awaking and invites others in.

A religious person might be spiritual, but a spiritual person is not necessarily religious. Spirituality, as we see it, connects the concepts of the "holy" with a notion of perfection in wholeness and goodness. Manifesting spiritual values means living ethically and morally daily in one's personal and professional endeavors.

Reflecting on the wisdom of the America theologian and philosopher Richard Mouw, who served for over twenty years as the president of Fuller Theological Seminar, Mouw's conviction of being open to and honoring others, doesn't weaken one's own faith, but in fact lives out the core principles in most Eastern and Western mainstream religions: to love as one would want to be loved themselves. Mouw calls for a new "convicted civility" based on his belief that those who are civil often lack strong convictions, and those with strong religious convictions often are not very civil.

What the various chapters in this section have in common is how spiritual inclusiveness comes alive in the practice of select spiritual leaders and their followers. Spiritual legitimacy is awarded, as Hollander rightly asserts through "idiosyncrasy credits" that people of faith engender in their trust and loyalty to charismatic and transformational spiritual leaders.

10 Rekindling the Legacy of Civil Rights: Leadership for an Inclusive, Just, and Compassionate Society

Juana Bordas

Keywords: Servant leadership; community; social action; coalitions; intergenerational; civil rights; multicultural leadership

---

Over 45 years ago, Robert Greenleaf in the *Servant as Leader* noted that leaders must be very right for the times in which they live. He urged Servant Leaders to address the critical issues of their day, which he described as: "an immoral and senseless war, destruction of the environment, poverty, alienation, overpopulation." Issues which are even more paramount for leaders today! Greenleaf defined leaders as *affirmative builders* of a better society (Greenleaf, 1970).

When I first started studying leadership, I found resonance with Greenleaf's writings. As a Latina who went to college during the civil rights movement, I have worked to promote social change and to creating a more diverse and equal society. I was in disbelief, then, when my publisher told me that my book on leadership in communities of color — a community-based, people-center, social activist form of leadership — was listed under business. I had been involved in leadership organizations, ran a woman's leadership institute, taught at the Center for Creative Leadership, and never knew there was no genre for community, multicultural, inclusive, or activist leadership. Well, I began to broadcast, "Leadership has been high jacked by corporations." Much of the leadership theory and concepts today have a predominately business orientation.

Even more disconcerting has been the advent of business and corporations into the public and government sectors. Now that corporations are financing elections we have the best government that money can buy! In the past 40 years lobbying and election funding by corporate interests have risen from $1.5 billion in 1998 to a high of $3.6 billion in 2010 (Rosiak, 2015). As the interests and profits of stockholders and corporate executives have taken precedent, the concerns of ordinary people, labor unions, and public interest groups have taken a back seat. Indicative of this was the Wall Street bailout in 2008 where public funds were used to sustain the very banks that drove the housing crisis in which 7 million American lost their homes (Sullivan, 2015).

In both leadership and the government sectors, corporations and money interests have become unduly influential overtaking the public good. Of course leaders should support strong businesses and a robust economy, this is essential to a good society. But the purpose of leadership must be much broader. Leadership must ensure that the public values that we hold dear — the common good, equality, pluralism, justice, and community are nurtured and permeate society. As Martin Luther King Jr. declared, "I do not think of political power...or economic power as an end. They are ingredients in the objective that we seek in life. And I think that end or that objective is a truly brotherly society, the creation of the beloved community" (King, 1983).

Preparing Many to Lead

Leadership in communities of color which grew into prominence during civil rights embraces this broader end, and focuses on advancing people's well-being. Former US Treasure and Latina leader Anna Escobedo Cabral captures this spirit, "What motivates people in our community who are doing great work and leading efforts is that they are looking out for the collective. *The collective good drives them*" (Bordas, 2012). Since historically resources, power, and influence were limited, leaders have relied on people power, empowerment strategies, and community organizing. The lack of economic power has required bringing people together and building partnerships and coalitions.

We will review five leadership principles that emerged out of communities of color since the civil rights movement. These principles are based on inclusive, collaborative, and democratic leadership and have a broad relevance and application to our increasingly diverse world. Leadership in communities of color holds the promise of revitalizing civic engagement and empowering people to tackle what Greenleaf termed, "the critical issues of our times."

Additionally, inclusive leadership today must be intergenerational and welcome involvement across age groups. This is a critical leadership challenge as we undergo the greatest generational shift in history and must engage millennials who are a diverse, connected, and activist generation (Madland & Teixeira, 2009). Intergenerational leadership is integral to communities of color whose unrelenting belief that the future would be better for their children fueled their continued activism. This is beautifully captured in the Iroquois Indian's great rule of leadership: "In every decision great leaders must consider the impact on their children, their children's children's children and unto seven generations" (Welker, 1996).

The five principles described below offer an integrated approach for utilizing inclusive and participatory leadership that can advance the just and compassionate society. These are: the leader as equal, leadership by the many, social activism and coalition leadership, the leader as the guardian of public values, leadership as community stewardship and service. Let us begin by exploring the role of the individual leader in communities of color and how she or he models inclusiveness and community commitment.

THE LEADER AS EQUAL

In many cultures, it is not correct to say, "I am a leader." Leadership is conferred on a person because of his or her abilities, good example, and service. The leader's power and respect come from being an integral part of the community and working side-by-side with people. A leader, then, is *one among equals*. Such leaders do not set themselves above others. In this way, people can identify with them easily and believe that they too can become leaders. The leader as equals play by the same rules as everyone else, refuses special privileges or favors, and treats everyone fairly. In short, a leader "walks their talk" demonstrating good character, honesty, humility, and keeping one's word. The leader as equal shatters the hierarchy and privilege that concentrated power and wealth in the hands of the few.

The leader as equal rolls up his or her sleeves, stuffs envelopes, serves food, attends community functions, and picks up people for meetings. Any type of elitisms or projection that one is above certain tasks lessens credibility and reestablishes hierarchy. Standing out too far out from others or calling too much attention to oneself can damage the group cohesion that is central to inclusive and community leadership. San Antonio's mayor Julián Castro the youngest mayor elected to head up a major American city exemplifies the leader as equal. "My values include family, service to others and a deep respect for other individuals. I need to be respectful and even deferential to others." This attitude connects people with their leaders and elevates their belief that they too can learn to lead.

For American Indians, inclusive leadership was integral to the way many tribes governed themselves. Benny Shendo was appointed to the Jemez Pueblo Council at a fairly young age. "I wasn't trying to be the leader. Since we don't have elections, at some point your name will be called ... Obviously, certain situations call for a particular type of leadership." After completing his council term, Benny returned to his role as an ordinary tribal member: "So now I'm among equals. I'm just a common man in the community. Other people will tell me what do. For us in Jemez, we are *leaders among equals* . . . at some point you are called and given certain responsibilities as a leader. People respect that. But, when your time is done, you are among equals again. So leadership rotates and no one is elevated above others."

When the leader assumes no special status and works side-by-side with people, this levels the playing field. The result is authentic collaboration where people work as equals to attain mutual goals. Since everyone can contribute, leadership is rotated depending on the task or function. Thus equity and reciprocity are the norm and many are prepared lead. In a truly inclusive environment where people feel connected and included — they reinforce each other's motivation and participation — and *leadership by the many* is cultivated. Creating a community of leaders is essential when a group's advancement depends on collective power and a critical mass of motivated people.

LEADERSHIP BY THE MANY

Leadership in communities of color historically represented people who grappled with discrimination and racism and needed to address the barriers that perpetuated inequality and economic disparity. As noted, leaders have had to rely on people's active participation and to utilize an inclusive process in order to engage them. During civil rights this could be a perilous process that required courage, discipline, and a strong belief that collective action would curtail discrimination and racism.

La Donna Harris who launched Americans for Indian Opportunity explains that participation and inclusion are central to Indian leadership: "Leadership is a communal responsibility with a concern for the welfare of the people or tribe and then sharing the work to be done based on skills and abilities. Leadership is shared responsibility and promoting people's well-being." Thus many are prepared to lead, are expected to contribute, and to do this in concert with others.

This form of leadership was learned at an early age by Arturo Vargas who is the executive director of The National Association of Latino Elected and Political Officials (NALEO). Vargas first appeared in the *Los Angeles Times* holding a picket sign when he was 10 years old. Because of overcrowding his elementary school had gone to half-day sessions. His immigrant parents who came to the United States seeking education and opportunities for their children joined a group called *Padres Unidos* (Parents United). Vargas saw for himself the power of "leadership by the many" as the school responded to the group's pressure and returned to full day classes.

Today Vargas through his work at NALEO is building a critical mass of Latino leaders to engage in the political and public policy process. Following the principle of leadership by the many, he believes, "We are not going to have this one charismatic leader that brings everyone together. It's thousands of leaders in thousands of communities across the country. It's a new style of leadership that is much more inclusive."

Leadership by the many encourages collaboration by promoting a shared vision that comes from the community or people; providing opportunities for meaningful participation, and dispersing authentic responsibility. These practices keep people motivated and moving forward while strengthening their leadership skills and ability to work together. Today in our ever increasingly divided world, encouraging many to lead can be an antidote to the continued disengagement of people in a political and economic system that seems stacked against them. When people experience the *power of many*, they understand that it has been through political and social movements, such as civil rights, that real change has been realized.

Social Action-Community Leadership

The leader as equal where everyone can contribute, and leadership by the many where many are encouraged to participate, are the prerequisites for developing a critical mass of people with the capacity and motivation to take action. The civil rights movement spurred a social activist form of leadership which centered on coalition building, community empowerment, and mass participation. The leader as community steward sustains this involvement by strengthening people's sense of identity, ability to work together, and commitment to a common purpose. Once these are in place, they are ready to take up the mantel of a more activism form of leadership.

SOCIAL ACTIVISM AND COALITION LEADERSHIP

In *Servants of the People: The 1960s Legacy of African American Leadership*, Dr. Lea Williams describes the lack of political equality, inadequate economic opportunity, racial segregation, and violence against the Black community as the genesis of a leadership form whose goals are social reform and the redistribution of power and resources. The shaping of leadership as social activism was a natural evolution for communities of color in which protecting and sustaining people were the heart of a leader's responsibility.

Ron Walters and Robert Smith describe how this approach has been fundamental to Black leadership: "One of the most important resources has been human power and this has required a concentration on the tactics and strategy of mass leadership, designed to effectively target the power of Blacks as a group to certain social objectives." They further note, "The leadership of a minority within a majority has implied the use of strategies of leverage and coalition rather than outright power" (Walters & Smith, 1999). When the Latino Policy Forum in Illinois strove to develop, "An American Agenda from a Latino Perspective" they brought together 11 organizations and 600 civic leaders, religious organizations, businesses, elected officials, and community activists. By listening to different points of view, communicating in an open, give-and-take fashion and welcoming new ideas, The Forum was able to weave common threads and integrate a collective vision and comprehensive agenda. Sylvia Puente, who heads up the Forum, understands the power of coalition and people working together: "Our strength lies in our numbers, in our collaborative work with hundreds and hundreds of community members. Every day we're working to train community members—more than five hundred this year—in parent education, fair housing, and to understand the complexities of immigration reform. Then they become community leaders in own right these areas."

Coalitions bring people and organizations together to address specific issues or to build new initiatives. For Latinos due to the grass roots, community focus of their organizations, coalition building has been the preferred strategy for advancing collective action. The most powerful national Latino organizations are coalitions. The National Council of La Raza, the largest Hispanic advocacy and civil rights organization represents a collation of over 300 community-based organizations. Realizing that one organization trying to influence corporate American would be like a voice crying in the wilderness. The Hispanic Association on Corporate brings together the 16 largest national Latino organizations to advocate for inclusion at all levels from employee hiring to the board room.

Coalition leadership unifies people with different interest by finding common ground, developing partnerships, and promoting a shared agenda. Coalition building is needed today to leverage the power ordinary people have to change the social and economic conditions that perpetuate inequality and exclusion. While coalition building and social action target specific issues, causes, or initiatives, the long-term commitment needed to work for change comes from a more integrated sense of community — one that is based on common values and a shared vision for the future. The leader as community steward demonstrates how serving others is instrumental to growing a community of leaders.

LEADERSHIP AS COMMUNITY STEWARDSHIP AND SERVICE

Community stewards follow the tradition of Robert Greenleaf in *The Servant as Leader* who designated leaders as those who sought to serve *first* and to do this by meeting people's highest priority needs. Greenleaf's litmus test for Servant Leaders was: do those served grow as persons, do they become healthier, freer, more autonomous, more likely to serve others (Greenleaf, 1970). Community stewards expand this focus on serving individuals to one of serving or being a good steward to the collective, the community, and society as a whole.

Unlike the dominant or mainstream culture, where the individual is central, communities of color have a collective identity where the family, community, or tribe takes precedent. Collectivist cultures are tightly woven, cooperative, and integrated. They cherish group welfare, unity, and working together. As "intact communities," they understand that their common struggles were only surmounted through collective efforts. This is reflected in the civil rights anthem "*We* shall overcome" or in the Hispanic rally, "¡Sí se puede!" (Yes! *We* can!) Community Stewardship reflects this collective orientation of communities of color.

The Jemez Pueblo's first principle of leadership, as described by Benny Shendo, speaks to this concept, "Leadership is responsibility and serving the community." Consequently, Shendo observes, people are willing to place their communities in their leader's hands. "There is profound trust in our leaders, a deep belief that they will always put people first. Leaders are guided by the question What's best for the people, for our community, for our way of life?"

The struggle for equity in communities of color has taken generations and required long-term perseverance and determination. Community stewardship is only sustainable when people continue their commitment decade-after-decade. A strategic way community stewards have kept people motivated, involved, and moving forward is using a step-by-step approach which has required careful planning, execution, and incrementally building on successes. A step-by-step approach reminds people that by staying the course, small contributions add up, and their joint efforts will eventually pay off.

Raul Yzaguirre, who helped forge many of the Latino community's organizations in the last century, advises, "We have to have a strategy of little victories. We can change things but in bite-size pieces. Leaders have to think big but it is the little success that builds people's confidence. As people succeed their vision of what is possible to accomplish becomes wider and more expansive." Each success makes people wiser, more resourceful, and sharpens their ability to work together.

Community stewards cultivate a shared identity, foster group consensus, and weave a common purpose among people by identifying and reinforcing common values. Values, explains Burt Nanus in *Visionary Leadership* shape our assumptions about the future, provide the content within which issues and goals are identified, and set standards for people's behavior and action. The Leader as Guardian of Public Values is the standard bearer for the values communities of color hold dear — values which are based on the very democratic principles that founded our country. Janet Murguía, President of The National Council of La Raza, emphasizes how critical values are in bringing people together: "There is this sense of connectedness across our ethnic roots and that connectedness is our strength. We have common bonds and values that we share."

The Purpose of Leadership

Inclusive leadership requires a shift from today's emphasis on the individual, business and profit, and competition to one where the collective welfare and the social good come first. To accomplish this, leaders must address issues and institutions that barricade people's full participation. By articulating values such as pluralism, justice, equality, and the public good, leaders beckon our society to live up to the *pubic values* on which our democracy was founded and to create institutions that reflect these values rather than individualistic ones.

Second, leaders bring together an intergenerational force of leaders to work for the community's advancement. This builds on a long-standing tradition of the civil rights movement when the Children's Crusade and young people demonstrated against desegregation in Birmingham, Alabama in 1963 (Cook & Racine, 2005). Intergenerational leadership is essential when a group's advancement depends on people power, long-term collaboration, and step-by-step progress.

GUARDIAN OF PUBLIC VALUES

Mainstream leadership is modeled on American individualism where self-interest takes precedent over needs of the group or community. Individualism promotes autonomy, competition, self-reliance, and control of one's circumstances. This is reflected in leadership theory that has concentrated on individuals, personal excellence, and competition.

In our society, individualism has resulted in an overemphasis on private values, personal behavior, and morality. The opposition to a woman's right to choose, the fight over gay marriage, treating drug abuse as a crime rather than a health issue, soaring incarceration rates as opposed to rehabilitation programs all indicate a concern with individual behavior, but not the responsibility to create a society where people's rights and equal opportunity are protected. Dr. Jim Joseph, distinguished author, activist, and leader explains, "Today the dominant society has moved away from communal responsibility and concentrates instead on individual values. This approach binds people to institutional racism and other social ills. It negates the mutual responsibility leaders have to support the good society based on the values this country was founded on."

In contrast, public morality and ethics incorporate *what is good for the whole*, and are not just concerned with personal behavior, private values, or blaming the individual (Joseph, 2015). Dr. Joseph continues, "We had to be concerned with the behavior of systems and institutions, or macro ethics that focused on public morality and community values. Because those systems and institutions oppressed the freedom of our citizens, our leaders have focused on *public values* and *institutional ethics*" (Bordas, 2012).

Public values are those we embrace as a nation on which our country was founded: justice, equality, the common good, democracy, freedom, and pluralism. The US Constitution even begins with "We, the people," reflecting inclusiveness and collectivism. Early Black leaders sought to realign America with these public values and to reposition leadership as responsibility for the supporting the common good.

Because of this, Dr. Joseph designates Black leaders as *guardians of public values*. "Our country's founders talked about justice and forming a more perfect union, so community was a high public value. African Americans are very concerned about community and justice. The Constitution promoted the common good and the general welfare. African Americans aspire to create a better life not only for their own people but to establish a society that cares for all people... Martin Luther King Jr. did this. Our founding fathers did this as well. They rallied people to seek 'justice for all' as a public value."

America's moral dilemma is that our society speaks the language of equality but does not fully incorporate our democratic values into our institutions or social structure. In fact, today's undue influence by corporations and money interest has set in course a trend where the interest of the few takes precedent of the interests of the many. Joseph summarizes how civil rights addressed this disparity: "In a segregated society, there was *intentional underdevelopment* that expressed itself *in* and was held in place *by* social institutions. Black leaders strove to humanize and sensitize these institutions in order to improve the lives of their people . . . incorporate the concept of our common humanity and open the doors to people of all colors, cultures and religions."

INTERGENERATIONAL LEADERSHIP

Life span doubled in the last century. Leaders today are challenged to work across four generations simultaneously and cultivate more lateral and equal relationships that bring out the unique perspectives, skills, and special contributions of each generation (American Management Association, 2014). Additionally, a huge generational shift is occurring. Millennials are the largest and most diverse generation in history. As the baby boomers retire it is imperative a new generation is prepared to take the helm of leadership and continue to create the inclusive, just, and compassionate society. Honorable Hilda Solis, former US Secretary of Labor, emphasizes this point: "We have to motivate our young people to build upon our legacies. We need to encourage them to reach out and include other people. We need to make sure there is a pathway to follow and that leadership is passed on from generation to generation."

Traditionally, as noted, communities of color have included all ages and stages of life. By grooming the younger generation, leaders ensure continuity and on-going community progress. Unlike societies where people retire, people of color honor their elders, who remain in leadership roles and continue contributing. Former San Antonio Mayor Julian Castro, who serves as US Secretary of Housing and Urban Affairs, speaks to this, "People from different generations need to work together. This way we can preserve our history, keep the integrity of those who came before, and young people will understand the sacrifices made in the past. Otherwise young people may compromise and lose their culture. Only by staying connected across generations can we keep moving forward together."

Millennials are uniquely suited to lead from an inclusive orientation. Forty-five percent were raised in collective cultures and identify as people of color or multicultural racial. Nine out of ten feel a responsibility to make a difference in the world and to be civically engaged. Millennials value connectivity and group welfare over individual reward (Keeter & Taylor, 2009). Leaders can capitalize on these preferences by treating young people as equal players with special contributions to make, providing opportunities for hands on and meaningful participation, and including them in the decision-making process.

Traditionally, mentoring implied an older leader teaching and guiding a younger one. Perhaps when change happened more slowly and young people were not as educated, technologically savvy, or experienced, passing knowledge in one direction might have worked. Today each generation has unique skills and contributions to make which requires more circular mentoring relationships where every age learns from the other. This underscores the leader as equal that fosters each person's capacity and reciprocal leadership.

Cooperation between generations requires older leaders to shake off previous beliefs that they know best or should be in charge. Young people must develop patience, learn from and respect the achievements of those who have come before them. Mutual learning requires listening across generations and being open to new ways of communication including technology. Dr. Antonia Pantoja, who started ASPIRA to empower Puerto Rican youth, had a knack for building intergenerational leadership and encouraging young people to share responsibility: "What do you do about the future? I make the future. You make the future. We make the future together."

Rekindling the Legacy of Civil Rights

The civil rights movement gave birth an inclusive leadership form which brought together communities of color, women, social activists, youth, and people of goodwill committed to creating a more just and equal society. Likewise, inclusive leadership can be a catalyst today for igniting a broad coalition of people from diverse backgrounds to address the critical social and economic issues of these times. Half a century later, we might consider the long-term impact — what are the contemporary movements that build on the legacy of the inclusive, collective, and activist leadership crafted during civil rights?

Let's look briefly at three of these: today's millennial activists, the Black lives Matter movement, and the fight for immigration reform that is the heart of Latino activism. Nine out of ten millennials believe they are responsible to make a difference in the world and believe that political engagement — getting involved — is an effective way to solve our national problems (Rainer & Rainer, 2011). Beginning with the Occupy Wall Street Movement in 2011, they are shining the spotlight on the growing wealth inequality where 1% of Americans own 40% of the wealth (Stiglitz, 2011). Millennials understand this discrepancy personally as they struggle to pay college loans that average $29,000 or cannot find good paying jobs in a global economy (Institute for College Access and Success, 2014).

African-American activism has been galvanized by the Black Lives Matters movement that protests the brutality and killing of Black men by police. Young Black men were nine times more likely than other Americans to be killed by police officers in 2015 (Swaine & Lartey, 2015). If current rates continue 1 out of 3 Black men will spend some time in prison in their life time (NAACP: Criminal Justice Fact Sheet). Black Lives Matters movement is building a coalition of people who are using the social protest strategies of civil rights to stand up against police brutality, an unjust criminal justice system, and to advocate for gun control legislation. They are following the legacy of "voting with your feet," demonstrating, and engaging people utilized in the civil rights movement.

On May 1, 2006 it is estimated that over two million people took to the streets to protest deportations, inhumane treatment of immigrants, and to seek immigration reform. Thus a new chapter in Latino activism was born. Young Latinos stand at the vanguard of this movement with the rise of *The Dreamers* — who take their name from the Dream Act, a bill before Congress that would have created a formal path to citizenship for young people here illegally who came to this country as children. United We Dream is the largest immigrant youth-led network in the nation with 47 affiliates in over 23 states that organize and advocate for access to higher education and legal status for all. Their slogan reflects their activist orientation: Immigrant youth building a movement for justice (United We Dream, 2013).

Movements such as these must work to pass legislation that institutionalizes the changes they are fighting for. Such was the case with the landmark Civil Rights Act of 1964 (Public Law 88-352, 78 Stat. 241) enacted July 2, 1964 that outlawed discrimination based on race, color, religion, sex, or national origin. The gay, lesbian, transgender, bisexual, and queer (GLTBQ) community has made historic gains using this tactic and challenging discriminatory laws from the steps of the US Supreme Court to statehouses around the country. While each of these movements target specific social injustices, most activists today understand that it is the growing gap between the rich and the poor and the continued concentration of power and resources that fuels the unjust society (Fry & Kochhar, 2014). Senator Bernie Sanders has brought together a broad and diverse coalition that champions his words: "The issue of wealth and income inequality, to my mind, is the great moral issue of our time. It is the great economic issue of our time and it is the great political issue of our time" (Sanders, 2016).

The divisions and disparities in today's world call for revitalizing the activist, inclusive, and collectivist leadership sown during civil rights that galvanized a whole generation into a collaborative force for change. By rekindling the inclusive leadership principles developed in these times and practiced by communities of color, we can advance a new social agenda that can build the more inclusive, just, and compassionate society. Dr. Martin Luther King Jr. believed that America had a date with destiny. America's destiny he proclaimed was to fulfill the democratic principles inherent in our country's founding and become a society that established equality and domestic tranquility for all people and generations to come. Today we are called to fulfill the dream of civil rights and to utilize the inclusive and activist leadership inherent in this struggle to move America to fulfill its true destiny. King also spoke of the *fierce urgency of now* — that we must act today, "Now is the time to make real the promises of democracy" (King, 1983). This call to action which is being heeded by people across America today is as relevant and critical as it was during the early civil rights struggle.

References

[*Note*: Unless otherwise noted, all quotations come from personal interviews which were transcribed verbatim that appear in the author's books *Salsa, Soul, and Spirit: Leadership for a Multicultural Age and The Power of Latino Leadership.*]

American Management Association. (2014, November 06). Leading the Four Generations at Work. Retrieved from http://www.amanet.org/training/articles/Leading-the-Four-Generations-at-Work.aspx. Accessed on May 06, 2016.

Bordas, J. (2012). *Salsa, soul, and spirit: Leadership for a multicultural age* (2nd ed.). San Francisco, CA: Berrett-Koehler.

Cook, E., & Racine, L. (2005). The children's crusade and the role of youth in the African American Freedom Struggle. *OAH Magazine of History, 19*(1), 31–36. doi:10.1093/maghis/19.1.31.

Fry, R., & Kochhar, R. (2014, December 17). America's wealth gap between middle-income and upper-income families is widest on record. Retrieved from http://www.pewresearch.org/fact-tank/2014/12/17/wealth-gap-upper-middle-income/. Accessed on May 09, 2016.

Greenleaf, R. K. (1970). *The servant as leader.* Indianapolis, IN: Robert K. Greenleaf Center.

Institute for College Access and Success. (2014). Project on student debt. Retrieved from Debt http://ticas.org/posd/hom. Accessed on July 27, 2016.

Joseph, J. A. (2015). *Saved for a purpose.* Durham, NC: Duke University Press.

Keeter, S., & Taylor, P. (2009, December 10). The Millennials. Retrieved from http://www.pewresearch.org/2009/12/10/the-millennials/. Accessed on May 03, 2016.

King, C. S. (1983). *The words of Martin Luther King, Jr.* New York, NY: Newmarket Press.

Madland, D., & Teixeira, R. (2009, May). New Progressive America: The Millennial Generation. Retrieved from https://www.americanprogress.org/wp-content/uploads/issues/2009/05/pdf/millennial_generation.pdf. Accessed on May 4, 2016.

National Association for the Advancement of Colored People: Criminal Justice Fact Sheet. Retrieved from NAACP http://www.naacp.org/pages/criminal-justice-fact-sheet. Accessed on July 27, 2016.

Rainer, T. S., & Rainer, J. W. (2011). *The Millennials: Connecting to America's Largest Generation.* Nashville, TN: B&H Publishing Group.

Rosiak, L. (2015, April 04). As government spending grows, special interest lobbyist paydays get bigger, too. Retrieved from http://www.washingtonexaminer.com/as-government-spending-grows-special-interest-lobbyist-paydays-get-bigger-too/article/2562926. Accessed on May 09, 2016.

Sanders, B. (2016). Retrieved from: https://berniesanders.com/issues/income-and-wealth-inequality/. Accessed on July 28, 2016.

Stiglitz, J E. (2011). Of the 1%, by the 1%, for the 1%. Retrieved from http://www.vanityfair.com/news/2011/05/top-one-percent-201105. Accessed on July 27, 2016.

Sullivan, B. (2015, April 23). Boomerang Buyers: Is There Homeownership After Foreclosure? | Credit.com. Retrieved from http://blog.credit.com/2015/04/boomerang-buyers-is-there-homeownership-after-foreclosure-114803/. Accessed on May 02, 2016.

Swaine, L., & Lartey. (2015). Young black men killed by US police at highest rate in year of 1,134 deaths. Retrieved from https://www.theguardian.com/us-news/2015/dec/31/the-counted-police-killings-2015-youngblack-men. Accessed on July 27, 2016.

United We Dream. (2013). Press release and information. Retrieved from http://unitedwedream.org/2015/ and http://unitedwedream.org/press-releases/dreamers-to-president-obama-deferred-action-delivers-the-latino-vote-president-obama-must-deliver-more/.

Walters, R. W., & Smith, R. C. (1999). *African American leadership*. Albany, NY: State University of New York Press.

Welker, G. (1996, February 8). The constitution of the Iroquois nations. Retrieved from http://www.indigenouspeople.net/iroqcon.htm. Accessed on May 01, 2016.

11

What Is "The Work" of Breaking the Zero-Sum Game?

Sarah Chace

Keywords: Group dynamics; inclusive leadership; basic assumptions

W e live in a time of *bouleversement*. A recent cover story of *Time* Magazine[1] suggested that 2015 was another 1968 — a year of ineluctable change. During the 50th annual Super Bowl game's half-time show the following year, pop star singer Beyoncé performed a radical new song, "Formation," simultaneously invoking the Black Lives Matter movement of today and the Black Panther movement of yesterday. A year after *Time*'s cover story appeared, a major trade press published *Witness to the Revolution*, an oral history of a pivotal 12 months in this country, from 1969 to 1970 — a time of social upheaval and political disturbance during which "America lost its mind and found its soul" (Bingham, 2016).

---

[1]See May 11, 2015 issue of *Time* Magazine.

These sorts of mainstream publications and events are representative of the current zeitgeist.[2]

Indicators of deep social forces engendering the inevitable crises that attend paradigm shifts (Kuhn, 1970) now include a widespread refusal to accept the notion of a "zero-sum game" as either sustainable or desirable. From the Arab Spring that began in the winter of 2010 to the Occupy Wall Street movement of 2011 to the current spate of demonstrations protesting race relations in America — all of these disruptions fall under the rubrics of *crisis* and *paradigm shift*. As Kuhn has written, "Novelty emerges only with difficulty, manifested by resistance, against a background provided by expectation" (Kuhn, 1970, p. 64). Each of the social movements cited above contains a kind of novelty, however painfully wrought — a novelty that seeks to disrupt a form of what economists have called "the zero-sum game" of limited resources, or a "fixed pie."

The shift that seeks to emerge in each of these cases also calls, in one way or another, for a more inclusive form of leadership. Such leadership would presumably break up the zero-sum game of inclusivity/exclusivity (cf. Leader-Member Exchange theory or LMX, in Graen & Uhl-Bien, 1998) by expanding the notion of leadership to include followers' input or episodes of leadership. Similarly, the notion of an expanded pie turns the construct on its head of a fixed amount of resources, material and otherwise.

Purpose

The purpose of this chapter is to examine three historic yet relatively contemporary movements for social and political change — the Arab Spring, Occupy Wall Street, and Black Lives Matter — through the lens of Wilfred Bion's basic assumptions (or "ba's") so as to illumine blind spots in what Kurt Lewin has articulated as "the field," where various forces are at play. In the three cases under discussion, these forces are defined as societal. The illumination provided by this analysis may render what

---

[2]As this chapter is being completed (July 2016), vigils are being held across the country to honor the deaths of two black men, Alton Sterling and Philando Castile, in the hands of police officers, as well as the deaths of five police officers shot by a sniper during a peaceful protest in Dallas, TX.

Lewin has called "certain conditions or forces" visible and, perhaps, more manageable for those who seek to lead inclusively. "One should view the present situation," Lewin has written, "... the *status quo*...as being maintained by certain conditions or forces" (Lewin, as cited in Burnes, 2004, p. 311, emphasis in the original). In order to ameliorate the status quo, such forces must be known.

Inclusive leadership — which, for the purposes of this discussion, is assumed to be the optimal way in which to exercise leadership so as to break up the zero-sum game — has been defined by Hollander (2012) as leadership that is exercised while having an "awareness of followers' needs" (Hollander, 2012, p. 196). Heifetz has suggested a way to accentuate this awareness by inviting the "deviant voice" in a group to be heard, and included, in a group (cf., Heifetz, 1994; Smith & Berg, 1987). French and Simpson (2010), in revisiting and analyzing Bion's notions of basic assumptions, regard "inclusiveness" in leadership as a kind of optimal dependency dynamic in what Bion has referred to as the driving "mentalities" of groups — either those of "basic assumptions" or those of "work groups" (French & Simpson, 2010). The proposition here presented is that inclusiveness leadership is both what the current swirl of events calls for, and the sort of leadership that would most benefit from the analysis of such events through the lens of Bion's group dynamics theory. In each of these cases the presence or absence of Bion's basic assumptions — Dependency, Fight/Flight, and Pairing — is analyzed. Table 1 outlines the cases of the three social movements and the arguments for their respective analyses.

BION'S BASIC ASSUMPTIONS

In a seminal study of group relations published more than 50 years ago, Wilfred R. Bion pioneered enduring ideas of what it means for a group to be on task — and, conversely, what forces are at play to distract it from its task. Bion's theory of "basic assumptions" or "ba's" has permeated the literature on the psychodynamics of groups for over 50 years (Cohen, Ettin, & Fidler, 1998; French & Simpson, 2010; Lafarge, 1990; Lawrence, Bain, & Gould, 1996; Smith & Berg, 1987). Such literature has, in turn, influenced the literature on leadership as it pertains to groups (Chace, 2013; Heifetz, 1994; O'Brien, 2016). This section briefly outlines the main tenets of Bion's theory of

Table 1. Basic Assumptions in Three Cases of Disruption.

Event	Basic assumption mentality	Work-group mentality	Example of basic assumption mentality as a diversion from purpose	Example of work-group mentality incorporating a basic assumption
Arab Spring	Dependency (baD)	None	Enduring support for el-Sisi	None
Occupy Wall Street	None	Fight/Flight (WF)	None	Refusal to create a platform with a spokesperson for a list of demands; disruption of public spaces.
Black Lives Matter (with focus on the death of Michael Brown)	Fight/Flight (baF)	Pairing (WP)	Violent protests following the death of Michael Brown, which included looting and vandalism	Prominence of two Black males in the quelling of protests following the death of Michael Brown in Ferguson, MO

Note: This table is inspired by Table 3 in French and Simpson (2010, p. 12).
Key:
baD = basic assumption of dependency as a distraction from purpose (French & Simpson, 2010, p. 3).
baF = basic assumption of fight/flight as a distraction from purpose (*ibid.*).
baP = basic assumption of pairing as a distraction from purpose (*ibid.*).
WD, WF, WP. Each of these basic assumptions — "D" (for dependency), "F" (for fight/flight), and "P" (for pairing) — is coupled with "W" for "work group." The implication of the each of these three acronyms in the context of this table is that the basic assumption is manifesting in a group's dynamic in a way that furthers the group's purpose. It should be noted that when referring to group dynamics the term "group mentalities" has also been used so as to provide more nuanced understanding of Bion's theory of group relations (French & Simpson, 2010, p. 3).

basic assumptions, as well as recent important proposed revisions to his theory — revisions to be incorporated into the discussion of the cases of attempts at breaking up the zero-sum game.

For every group to which a task is given, no matter how simple or complex it may be, according to Bion, three basic assumptions lurk in the background or, in a kind of "mission creep," take over the foreground (Bion, 1961). These ba's are: Dependency, Fight/Flight, and Pairing. In the literature, the shorthand for them is: baD, baF, and baP. If the inclination of the group is largely to veer away from its purpose or task — what Bion has called its "Work" — these basic assumptions will, singly or together (G. Fromm, personal communication, 2 May 2015), begin to preoccupy the group. Following are brief descriptions of each of the ba's.

Dependency
Bion's formulation of the basic assumption of Dependency (baD) has varied in its metaphors. At one time comparing the role of a group facilitator to that of a deity (Bion, 1961, p. 148), the fundamental "condition or force" that is often present in a group is to keep it intact at any cost. The "leader" or authority figure in the group is lionized or demonized, according to the group's perceptions. Another view of this relationship between group and leader articulates the phenomenon of dependency as analogous to that of a child upon a parent to keep one safe (Sher, 2003). As opposed to the basic assumptions of Fight/Flight and Pairing, where "the individuals function as adults," Sher has asserted, "in basic assumption [D]ependency, they do not" (p. 137). The group foists its own work upon the person to whom it designates authority — formal or informal. If the group perceives this individual as failing them, the individual will be ousted (Bion, 1961).

A contemporary example of a dependency dynamic gone awry (the positive aspects of dependency as well as of the other ba's are to be discussed below) is the prevailing attitude toward Barack Obama by many of his constituents when he assumed the presidency in 2009. Similar to a biopic created about Bill Clinton during his 1992 bid for the presidency, "The Man from Hope," the "Yes We Can" music video created by a number of artists and celebrities during the Obama presidential campaign captured a new brand of idealization placed on Obama's candidacy, and was downloaded 14 million times by the time of his election in 2008 (Ansley & Sellers, 2010, p. 95). Inevitably, Obama began to disappoint at least some of his constituents almost immediately.

Fight/Flight

The literature refers to the basic assumption of Fight/Flight as baF. Smith and Berg (1987) have written extensively on what they have called "the paradoxes of belonging." Building on Bion's construct and others', they have asserted that for every individual yearning to belong to a group that same individual contains within themselves a resistance to being swallowed up by the group, and of losing their individuality. Thus, the attitude of an individual belonging to the group takes on the dynamic of fight and/or flight (Lafarge, 1990; Smith & Berg, 1987).

Whole groups may also engage in this dynamic as they collectively resist belonging to a larger group. For example, the extraordinary rise of Donald Trump's candidacy in the Republican Party nomination process in 2016 owed much to the voters who perceived themselves as disenfranchised and rejected more conventional candidates during that year's primaries. One could reasonably surmise that the Trump voters were fighting those who disagreed with them (viz., the violence invoked and often acted out at Trump rallies) and fleeing from the Republican establishment, as one by one they rejected a string of more conventional and more qualified candidates.

Pairing

Pairing, or baP, occurs when groups call for the partnership of two to create a messianic third (Bion, 1961, pp. 151–152). The specter of sexuality that is present in all groups expresses itself through pairing (Torres, 2003, p. 97); yet in some situations the notion of pairing need not be that of the traditional male and female procreating a third entity, but simply $1 + 1 = 3$. The unborn third also embodies for the group the incipient notion of *hope* (Bion, 1961, pp. 151–152).

Again, an example from the 2008 presidential campaign offers a vivid example of pairing in the duo of presidential candidate Senator John McCain and vice presidential pick Governor Sarah Palin. The two politicians embodied atavistic symbols of pairing: The elder male warrior figure appears vigorous enough to sustain a demanding schedule and endure the tensions of a presidential bid while being juxtaposed with a younger charismatic, attractive female authority figure who had recently given birth. The symbolism of a recent pregnancy could be interpreted as containing the potential of a newborn child. For the group that voted for the McCain/Palin ticket, the drama of this pair may have symbolized the potential for the birth of a new Republican administration in the White House.

REVISITING THE BASIC ASSUMPTIONS

In an important journal article published in *Human Relations*, French and Simpson (2010) have "redressed" what might be called the over-dichotomized construct of Bion's basic assumptions. While these authors accept the notion of baD, baF, and baP, they have put aside the notion that the leaning of a group toward any given basic assumption is, in and of itself, necessarily suboptimal. Instead, they have construed what might be called "ba 2.0" — allowing for the idea that ba's may lean either toward or away from the work ("W") with which a given group is tasked. As an example, they discuss the idea of a positive pairing in the context of a friendship that is formed between two leaders of warring factions within an organization (French & Simpson, 2010, pp. 13–15). It is with this revised construct in mind that the following discussion of the three cases outlined below takes place.

Dependency: The Case of the Arab Spring

What Heifetz and others have called the "initial event" — a focus on the psychotherapeutic session's initiating moment — is not limited to the boundary of a single unit of an individual's or a small group's actions; it may be extrapolated to the dramas of institutional disruptions on the world stage. "The initial event," then, of the Arab Spring was based on notions of fairness, and the rage that ensues when the scales of fairness are deeply and obviously out of balance.[3] Mohammed Bouazizi, the iconic

---

[3]The driving idea of this book, *Breaking the Zero-Sum Game*, may be translated into the broad idea of bringing humanity together in a way that rejects the fundamental injustice that permeates a win/lose dichotomy when applied to a society.

Tunisian fruit vendor whose actions in December 2010 ignited the Arab Spring, could one day no longer tolerate daily acts of oppression at the hands of a corrupt system. In his own way he was calling for a breaking up of the zero-sum game to which he was subjected. As described by Taub (2016), this impoverished young man,

> ... fed up with a life of harassment and extortion by venal government officials, doused himself in paint thinner, struck a match, and unwittingly ignited the Arab Spring. Hundreds of thousands of citizens in the Middle East and in North Africa, sharing his rage and despair, rose up against an assortment of autocrats and kings. They demanded democratic reforms, economic opportunities, and an end to corruption. (Taub, 2016, p. 38)

In this gesture of anguished defiance, Bouazizi embodied what Bion might call the tendency toward Fight/Flight — fleeing from the existing system via self-immolation, in the ultimate act of fight in the form of resistance (resistance, of course, being a kind of fight).

As the Arab Spring has unfolded, however, the baF has been eclipsed by baD, as in the case of Egypt. In that country the healthy form of Fight/Flight, what French and Simpson would have referred to as Fight/Flight in the context of a "work mentality," has metamorphosed into a dependency upon an authoritarian figure as tyrannical as the one the Egyptian citizens deposed. Attempts to disrupt the balance of the zero-sum game via social media (a tool for inclusiveness leadership if ever there was one) and other more traditional forms of protest have resulted in futile revolutions, where the new status quo is no better than the old. The dangerous, somewhat leaderless mobs that deposed Mubarak in 18 days in January of 2011 eventually spawned an equally repressive dictator, Abdel Fattah el-Sisi. In the case of Egypt, the basic assumption mentality of dependency, devoid of positive tendencies toward the work of creating a more inclusive society, prevailed. By the light of some journalists (cf., Mekay, 2016; Wright, 2015), the current regime in Egypt is no better than that of Mubarak, and some have argued that it is worse. It is reasonable to speculate that the group of Egyptian citizens as a whole has in some ways unconsciously reached a consensus to endure a form of dependence once again on a single male authoritarian figure.

Fight/Flight: The Case of Occupy Wall Street

The three basic assumptions arrived at by Bion may intersect at any time. Depending on the context, one or another of these basic assumptions emerges as most appropriately salient. As the reader can see from Table 1, in the author's judgment the Occupy Wall Street movement was not a case of work avoidance but overall of work engagement, wherein a basic assumption could be discerned as a positive dynamic. The basic assumption of Fight/Flight appears to be the ba that best defined the situation. French and Simpson (2010) have stated that the mentalities of fight or flight could assist the group in its work. Such was the case in the episode of Occupy Wall Street.

Conceived in the wake of the 2008 financial meltdown, the Occupy Wall Street movement was the answer of United States to the Arab Spring. Beginning in the summer of 2011, within a matter of months the "Occupy" movement had spread from New York City to numerous other major cities, both in the United States and abroad — e.g., Occupy Boston, Occupy San Francisco, Occupy Madrid (Hardt & Negri, 2011). In a sense, the movement could also be viewed as a sort of meta-pairing: Those US citizens who were increasingly outraged by the economic inequities of a capitalist society "paired" with those citizens of repressive regimes in foreign countries. (Five years later, this revolutionary energy resurfaced in the 2016 presidential campaign of Vermont Senator Bernie Sanders, which held within these intensely felt aspirations for a more just society — especially in the context of income inequality.) Built on a platform that sought to make an intervention into a financial system perceived as systemically inequitable, the "Occupy" movement was comprised of a group formed to simultaneously fight a system and flee from it. In fact, the movement's platform was nebulous in its demands, a nebulousness that was perceived as the origin of the movement's collapse. Nonetheless, the Fight/Flight dynamic was purposeful, and thus belongs to the category of WF.

In psychological terms, the preservation of a group is its central preoccupation (Bion, 1961, p. 65). One way to preserve a group is to create or engage in turmoil with *casus belli* focused on another, or on some sort of external force. Certainly, the Occupy Wall Street movement was founded for the purpose of creating disequilibrium by the very fact of its existence (setting up tents and/or otherwise occupying public spaces, etc.). Another way for a group to maintain its integrity is to flee its "group-ness," thus acknowledging the ambivalence integral to all groups (Bion, 1961; Smith & Berg, 1987). In a manner markedly differ-ent from other societal interventions, the "Occupy" movement's refusal to create too much cohesion became a kind of flight from itself. Nonetheless its purposefulness in doing so weighted it on the positive side of the scales of Work mentality vs. Basic Assumptions mentality.

Pairing: Black Lives Matter

The case of 18-year-old Michael Brown's death by shooting on the streets of Ferguson, MO in August 2014 contains both basic assumptions and work-group mentalities. To a student of group dynamics, what unfolded in the immediate aftermath of Brown's death was symptomatic of conditions and forces in the larger field of race relations. This particular case reached its cli-max on the night of 24 November 2014 when an impaneled grand jury failed to indict the white police officer, Darren Wilson, who fatally shot Brown. Within minutes of the deci-sion, social media began circulating statistics on the unlikeli-hood of a grand jury's decision not to indict. With regard to failure of authority, events subsequent to the grand juries' fail-ures to indict both Darren Wilson in Ferguson, MO and other officers charged with similar acts have been both destructive and constructive. When the protests have devolved into rioting — as in Ferguson following the death of Michael Brown and in Baltimore following the death of Freddie Gray — it is inargu-able that the group of protesters has engaged in a basic assump-tion mentality of Fight/Flight in a way that did not contribute to the "work mentality." (It should be noted that many citizen protesters in both of these instances of rioting sought to inter-vene with the violence and serve as an example, for the pur-poses of this discussion, of WF.) More peaceful protests, however, such as those that took place in New York City immediately following the grand juries' failure to indict Darren Wilson, offer examples of reasonable cooperation on both the side of the protesters and the side of the police. In this instance, the group dynamic gravitated toward WF.

The most vivid example of a basic assumption evolving to further a work-group mentality occurred when the elevation of

Missouri's black Highway Patrol Captain Ron Johnson to take control of security at the time of the initial riots in Ferguson was quickly followed by the arrival of the top law enforcement officer in the land, Attorney General Eric Holder, another black man placed in a position of high authority. Images abounded in the media of Holder and Johnson conferring in public spaces. In the public imagination, an unconscious dynamic of hope was being born, or at least conceived (for some), in this pairing. This hope took the form of action symptomatic of a healthy work-group when a report was issued by the Justice Department approximately 6 months later, outlining the endemic injustices of the Ferguson, MO police department.

In sum, the Fight/Flight modality of violent protesters and looters was an example of a group whose purpose was derailed. Subsequent to this, however, with the appointment of highway patrol captain Ron Johnson to serve as an authority figure for security in Ferguson and the arrival of the top US law enforcement official, Attorney General Eric Holder, a work group dynamic was enhanced by the work-group mentality of pairing (WP).

Reflections on Leadership

Exercising leadership in groups that are overcome by one or another of the three basic assumptions is difficult if not impossible to do. In order for a group to escape its preoccupation with itself, it must have either a high awareness of its purpose and/or of its tendencies. Ideally, a work-group mentality will keep the suboptimal dynamics of the ba's in check. Yet a key insight of French and Simpson informs this discussion — that the basic assumption mentality and the work-group mentality "always co-exist" (French & Simpson, 2010, p. 5). In some cases, as in that of the Arab Spring, the basic assumption mentality has prevailed to the point where it has undermined the efforts to overcome the zero-sum game power that has caused so much human suffering. In the case of the Arab Spring, there is the chaos of Syria to look upon, or the tyranny of the el-Sisi regime in Egypt. While Tunis has given birth to a kind of democracy, it has also exported thousands of terrorists to the Islamic State organization. The Islamic State, in fact, is the ultimate purveyor of the most brutal kind of zero-sum game.

In terms of Occupy Wall Street, while its platform was never fully articulated, its statements were fairly clear: The zero-sum game of American capitalism is unsustainable. Of the three movements discussed in this chapter, this one seems to have functioned with the most vigilance concerning regression to a basic assumption (although the organizers may not have put it that way). The deliberate absence of leadership in the "Occupy" movement indicated a certain cognizance, and any amount of awareness will hinder the prevalence of a basic assumption mentality and foster a work-group mentality.

Finally, the Black Lives Matter movement, which is the most accentuated at the time of this writing, has the potential to seemingly hold to the purpose of making a difference to race relations in our society with regard to expanding the fixed pie of white privilege at the expense of black oppression into a new construct. The prevalence of peaceful demonstrations that have continued to occur under the aegis of this movement is noteworthy, despite the fact that some have devolved into destructive episodes, such as those following the death of Freddie Gray in Baltimore. As French and Simpson have noted when quoting Bion, the mentality of a work group may be furthered by the dynamic of a basic assumption. Such was the case in Ferguson, when Johnson and Holder became a pair.

Summary and Conclusions

This chapter has explored three cases in which inclusivity in leadership was the aspiration if not the final result of a social movement. All three of these movements were made up of people whose voices yearned to be heard, and who were tired of being relegated to the "out-group." The slices of the fixed pie had become increasingly thin, whether through a dearth of democracy, inequality of income, or a lack of social justice. This discussion has endeavored to offer a new set of lenses through which to analyze the situations inclusiveness leadership aspires to better as it aims to break up the zero-some game.

Acknowledgments

The seed idea for this chapter was sown at a conference presentation made in partnership with Rosie Lim Williams at the A.K.

Rice Institute's "Dialogues 2" conference in May 2015. I owe much to her insights and generative thinking. It also benefited from careful reading and thoughtful input from the following friends and colleagues: Linda Callahan, Nathan Harter, Naomi Rush Olsen, and H. Eric Schockman.

References

Ansley, T., & Sellers, P. J. (2010). Mobilizing to frame election campaigns. In B. F. Schaffner & P. J. Sellers (Eds.), *Winning with words: the origins and impact of political framing* (pp. 78–98). New York, NY: Routledge.

Bingham, C. (2016). *Witness to the revolution: Radicals, resisters, vets, hippies, and the year America lost its mind and found its soul.* New York, NY: Penguin Random House.

Bion, W. R. (1961). *Experiences in groups.* New York, NY: Routledge.

Burnes, B. (2004). Kurt Lewin and complexity theories: Back to the future? *Journal of Change Management,* 4(4), 309–325.

Chace, S. (2013). *Learning leadership: A case study on influences of a leadership training program on the practices of one group of urban school superintendents.* Unpublished doctoral dissertation, Teachers College, Columbia University, New York, NY.

Cohen, B. D., Ettin, M. F., & Fidler, J. W. (1998). Conceptions of leadership: The 'analytic stance' of the group psychotherapist. Group Dynamics: Theory, Research, and Practice, 2(2), 118–131. doi:10.1037/1089-2699.2.2.118

French, R. B., & Simpson, P. (2010). The 'work group': Redressing the balance in Bion's experiences in groups. *Human Relations,* 63(12). Retrieved from http://dx.doi.org/10.1177/0018726710365091. Accessed on January 7, 2016.

Graen, G. B., & Uhl-Bien, M. (1998). Relationship-based approach to leadership: Development of leader-member exchange (LMX) theory of leadership over 25 years: Applying a multi-level multi-domain perspective. *Monographs in organizational behavior and industrial relations,* 24, 103–134.

Hardt, M., & Negri, A. (2011, October 11). The fight for 'real democracy' at the heart of Occupy Wall Street. *Foreign Affairs.* Retrieved from: https://www.foreignaffairs.com/articles/north-america/2011-10-11/fight-real-democracy-heart-occupy-wall-street. Accessed on April 30, 2016.

Heifetz, R. A. (1994). *Leadership without easy answers.* Cambridge, MA: Harvard University Press.

Hollander, E. P. (2012). *Inclusive leadership: The essential leader-follower relationship.* New York, NY: Routledge.

Kuhn, T. S. (1970). *The structure of scientific revolutions.* Chicago, IL: University of Chicago Press.

Lafarge, V. (1990). Termination in groups. In J. Gillette & M. McCollom (Eds.), *Groups in context.* Lanham, MD: University of America Press.

Lawrence, W. G., Bain, A., & Gould, L. (1996). The fifth basic assumption. *Free Associations,* 6 Part I (37), 28–56.

Mekay, E. (2016). Five years on, talk of the Arab Spring survives in Egypt's cafés. *IBA Global Insight, 70*(1), 27–29.

O'Brien, T. J. (2016). *Looking for development in leadership development: Impacts of experiential and constructivist methods on graduate students and graduate schools.* Unpublished doctoral dissertation, Harvard Graduate School of Education, Harvard University, Cambridge, MA.

Sher, M. (2003). From groups to group relations: Bion's contribution to the Tavistock 'Leicester Conferences'. In R. M. Lipgar & M. Pines (Eds.), *Building on Bion: Branches* (pp. 109–144). London: Jessica Kingsley Publications.

Smith, K. K., & Berg, D. N. (1987). *Paradoxes of group life: Understanding conflict, paralysis, and movement in-group dynamics.* San Francisco, CA: Jossey-Bass.

Taub, B. (2016, April 18). The Assad files. *New Yorker*, 36–49.

Torres, N. (2003). Gregariousness and the mind: Wilfred Trotter and Wilfred Bion. In R. M. Lipgar & M. Pines (Eds.), *Building on Bion: Roots* (pp. 85–117). London: Jessica Kingsley Publishers.

Wright, R. (2015, December 15). How the Arab Spring became the Arab Cataclysm. *New Yorker*. Retrieved from http://www.newyorker.com/search?q=wright+how+the+arab+spring. Accessed on April 30, 2016.

12

Connective Leadership: From Zero-Sum to Inclusion

Jill Robinson, Maura Harrington,
Chris Cartwright and Kevin Walsh

Keywords: Nonprofit leaders; women leaders; connective leadership; youth leadership; intercultural leaders; Fulbright leaders

As leadership scholar Jean Lipman-Blumen (1996) asserts, we live in a world *where inclusion is critical and connection is inevitable* (p. xiii).

This chapter presents a leadership model grounded in ethics, accountability, and authenticity appropriate for building bridges of inclusion and understanding across diverse populations and sectors. We address questions about what it means to lead and provide practical lessons and behaviors to strive for pragmatic action. To illustrate the critical task of developing our future leaders, examples are provided through work with Fulbright students and International Youth

Ambassadors, along with research into leadership in different types of organizations and across gender lines.

In our exploration, we start at the beginning where early humans set the stage in a grueling, all or nothing world where the strongest man in the tribe rose, sometimes by default, to the top. Valiant leaders, most of them men, fought to overcome the hardship of physical boundaries and to protect their clan from an unforgiving landscape of enemies both of the wild and human ilk. Mere survival determined the winners and losers. It was a zero-sum game of winner-take-all; often the prize was food, land, or shelter, at the expense of life. This mentality continued to persist even as colonies and countries formed based on geography and political ideology.

This physical era gradually gave way to what Lipman-Blumen called the "Geopolitical Era." Characteristic of this time, leaders formed political alliances, competed at all echelons, and rule was absolute (Lipman-Blumen, 1996). Leaders, still mainly men, thought strategically by forming such coalitions as the New Deal, NATO, and the Warsaw Pact. This "progress" still noninclusive for many, left the world feeling fractured and longing for a different type of leadership which would allow previously disenfranchised groups to participate in the decisions that determined their future (Lipman-Blumen, 1996).

Partly due to the connective powers of transportation and technology, a new reality has slowly taken root. This new reality, the "Connective Era," teems with incongruity and discord created, both globally and within local communities, by the tension between interdependence and diversity (Lipman-Blumen, 1996). Such an era requires its leaders possess a unique understanding and wide-ranging skills to enable diverse constituents, who have differing perspectives on often multiple dimensions, to live and work collectively for their mutual benefit. Connective Leaders embark upon an important transformation by encouraging the emergence of our collective realities resulting from the inclusion of all stakeholders (Lipman-Blumen, 1996).

The Connective Era and its corresponding leadership model are particularly relevant to address such catalytic change by including individuals and groups with divergent identities and agendas who find themselves inevitably interconnected. Connective leaders can democratize conflicting individuals and groups who must live and work together productively and harmoniously to meld their divergent realities into a collective reality. In the last half century, various groups have learned to prize their distinctive identities, emphasizing their unique talents and values while demanding to have a voice. Thus, many diverse groups tend to favor acting autonomously, harnessing their unique gifts often through grassroots efforts. Concurrently, global interdependence, further connected through the internet and social media, is best served by collaborative relationships often bringing teams of people together for joint action. In this complex web of competing forces, no single behavioral response suffices, and no lone hero has all the answers. Leadership strategies of past eras fail in the Connective Era as a futile attempt to tackle new problems with old solutions. In this interdependent and diverse environment, Connective Leaders who can identify bridges of inclusion can help build the recognition of common goals and initiate productive collaboration fueled by commonality not realized in previous eras.

Model Description

Within this nascent era, the Connective Leadership™/Achieving Styles™ Model allows a differentiated, nuanced framework to uncover behavioral patterns that can be leveraged by Connective Leaders to address a complex, divergent, and interconnected reality (Lipman-Blumen, 1996).

The Model consists of three domains that describe behaviors leaders can draw from:

1. *The Direct domain*: achieving tasks *directly*.
2. *The Instrumental domain*: leveraging others and themselves as *instruments* to accomplish goals.
3. *The Relational domain*: establishing personal objectives in *relation* to the goals of others.

The following provides a breakdown of each of the nine individual styles embedded in the three domains listed above. An individual style is seen as neither good nor bad, but rather more germane for certain situations. Truly Connective Leaders can draw upon each of these nine styles depending on the relevant circumstances and constituents (see Fig. 1).

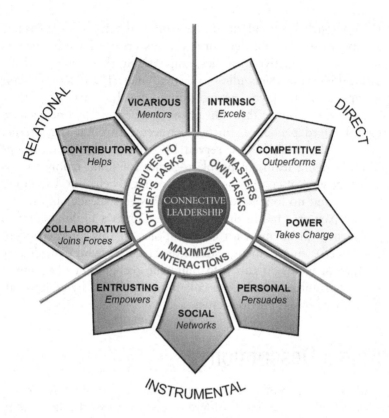

Fig. 1. Connective Leadership Model. *Source*: Reprinted with permission ©
Connective Leadership Institute.

THE DIRECT DOMAIN

The first Achieving Style, in the Direct domain, is *Intrinsic*.
Leaders who use this style are innately motivated to accomplish
their own tasks and goals. They tend to be perfectionists and rate
their work against their greatest competition, themselves.

For example, Stephen Hawking (2010) illustrates his intrinsic
love of his work.

> *Science is not only a discipline of reason but, also, one of*
> *romance and passion.*

The Intrinsic style is vital for leaders who are under pressure to
perform at high levels and those who are expected to consistently
showcase continuous improvement.

The second Achieving Style is *Competitive*. This style is leveraged by leaders who judge their own performance by ranking

their work against others. They take pride in being "number one." This quote made famous by Coach Vince Lombardi who identifies the ideology of the competitive style.[1]

Winning isn't everything, it's the only thing.

The skill of assessing competitors, both individuals and groups, and applying that knowledge to enhance organizational effectiveness is necessary to attain a sustainable competitive edge.

The third Achieving Style is Power. This style is used by leaders who prefer to be in charge. These leaders take control of most any situation.

Margaret Thatcher's (1982) quote shows her commitment to taking charge and being in control:

I am an extraordinarily patient, provided I get my own way in the end.

This style is imperative to take command or lead a team to success. People, in the midst of change, may look to such a leader willing to put herself/himself on the forefront of a challenge and forage toward victory.

THE INSTRUMENTAL DOMAIN

The first Achieving Style, in the Instrumental domain, is Personal. Such leaders often exhibit charismatic behaviors. They may use symbolism and rhetoric to sway followers into believing and internalizing in their vision.

This quote, often attributed to Martin Luther King Jr. (cited in a 2013 speech by Representative John Lewis, who worked with King (n.d.)), elicits emotion and symbolism to display the Personal style.

We may have all come on different ships, but we're in the same boat now.

In an era where change is the only constant, a leader's ability to persuade others through presence and communication is essential.

---

[1]This quote is thought to be first uttered by 11-year-old Sherry Jackson (Shavelson & Curtiz, 1953) in the film *Trouble Along the Way*.

The second Achieving Style, in this domain, is Social. This style leverages a large network of people to aid in the accomplishment of goals.

Mark Zuckerberg (2013), cited in the Business News Daily, shows that engaging his social network has been a successful practice for him.

> *The thing that we are trying to do at Facebook, is just help people connect and communicate more efficiently.*

Relationships are invaluable to Connective Leaders. The ability to strategically engage allies and adversaries can produce, otherwise, unattainable results.

The third Achieving Style is Entrusting. This style encourages others to contribute autonomously, with little supervision, by empowering and motivating them to achieve success and allowing them the freedom to ennoble themselves.

Here, Booker T. Washington (1901) shows his passion for entrusting others.

> *Few things can help an individual more than to place responsibility on him, and to let him know that you trust him.*

Research suggests this clear connection between autonomy and motivation (Pink, 2009). People tend to work harder for leaders who allow the freedom to create purpose through self-determination. Many high-performing individuals choose to be led by Entrusting leaders.

THE RELATIONAL DOMAIN

The first Achieving Style, in the Relational domain, is Collaborative. This style cooperates with others to accomplish tasks. They build trust to actualize the vision and goals that they create as a team.

Zainab Salbi (2010) depicts her collaborative leadership ideology in this quote.

> *Like life, peace begins with women. We are the first to forge lines of alliance and collaboration across conflict divides.*

The Connective Era is laden with opportunities to unite with other leaders, organizations, or regions for symbiotic goal implementation.

The second Achieving Style is Contributory. This leadership style devotes effort toward the tasks of others and relishes in the advancement of the significant other. Sheryl Sandberg (2011) shows her commitment to contributing.

It is the ultimate luxury to combine passion and contribution. It's also a very clear path to happiness.

As recognition of this style's importance, Servant leadership is emerging, as a powerful way to inspire others to drive toward aspirational goals.

The third Achieving Style, in this domain, is Vicarious. This style encourages others to attain greatness by behaving as a mentor. Vicarious leaders can embolden others to reach aspirational goals with words and actions that hearten their spirit.

Folorunsho Alakija (2012) shows her dedication to the encouragement of others.

I told as much of my life as I could to encourage people: to encourage others to get to where they should be, where they want to be.

In an age where organizations are "doing more with less" and "burn-out" is a real concern, Vicarious leaders provide reassurance needed to accomplish ambitious goals and subsequently, warranted recognition.

Connecting Across Cultural Difference

Improved technology, population growth, and globalization have made today's world increasingly interdependent. Therefore, putting your own country's interests first, at the expense of others, can have serious consequences. What we need to do is to think of humanity as a whole and develop a sense of concern on a global level. I refer to this as having a sense of "universal responsibility." (Dalai Lama, 2011)

In this section, we discuss how Connective Leadership addresses the need to lead across difference, specifically across world cultures and generations. By mitigating the pitfalls of negative ethnocentric attitudes and behaviors across difference (Bennett, 1993), we cultivate leaders ready for the Connective Era. In one case, we reveal the results of a study of incoming Fulbright graduate students from around the world arriving in the United States to pursue degrees in a variety of fields, and destined to leadership roles upon their return to their home countries. In the other case, we discuss international "Youth Ambassadors" from diverse backgrounds who were coached in the Connective Leadership Model by US-Based Doctoral Students. In both cases, the Connective Leadership Model and its corresponding Achieving Styles Inventory[2] (ASI) results offer insights into the potentiality of "Global Souls" (Bennett, 2008) to become inclusive leaders.

The Fulbright graduate student program offers a unique opportunity to observe future leaders in the making. Senator Fulbright founded the program, in 1946, to *Foster – leadership, learning, and empathy between cultures* (Fulbright Program, 2011a). Since its inception, 225,000 scholars have studied and researched around the world; annually 1,800 non-US students receive grants to study at US institution (Fulbright Program, 2011c). The Fulbright program alumni include 40 Nobel Prize recipients, three of whom were Peace Prize recipients. Many more have gone on to leadership roles in many contexts, with more than 330 alumni serving as current or past heads of state (Fulbright Program, 2011b).

When 120 international graduate students arrived, in 2010, in the United States, an orientation to cultural competency and leadership was conducted employing the Intercultural Effectiveness Scale (IES) (Kozai Group, 2008), for the intercultural competence assessment and the Achieving Styles Inventory (Lipman-Blumen, 1996) as the leadership assessment. Together the results reveal a unique pattern of correlations between the ability to work and lead effectively and appropriately across cultural difference (Cartwright, 2012).

With IES results, the Fulbright students displayed a high level of exploration of difference and self-awareness in the presence of difference. Their ability to make and maintain relationships, especially the ability to master another language was also high. Finally, their ability to self-manage the stresses of living,

---

[2]The Achieving Style Inventory allows participants to rank on a seven-point Likert scale how frequently they engage in a particular behavior corresponding to the nine styles described by the Connective Leadership Model (Lipman-Blumen, 2006; Lipman-Blumen, Handley-Isaksen, & Leavitt, 1983).

and in their case, studying across difference was also high (Mendenhall & Oddou, 1985).

Their ASI results were also unusually high, with a unique pattern of at least one high result in each of the three domains (Direct, Instrumental, and Relational). The Fulbright students displayed both strength in leadership acumen and the flexibility to employ different leadership styles to engage complex problems with diverse populations. Together their results displayed a strong foundation of curiosity as a means to learn about the diverse problems and populations and a willingness to take charge of complex leading and learning responsibilities. By looking at this highly sophisticated population, we can see the potentiality of cultivating leaders who can lead effectively and appropriately across difference.

Connective Leadership Training with Youth Ambassadors

In a cross-cultural study, the journeys of 10 Youth Ambassadors (YA), who were selected by The Change is Me International (CHIME-IN) based upon their passion, open-mindedness, and desire, were chronicled as they strived to develop their leadership capabilities (Walsh, 2015). The YAs were between 16 and 24 years old and were chosen to represent their generation as leaders. They hailed from Honduras, Australia, Bhutan/Nepal, Uganda, Guatemala, United States, United Kingdom, Dubai, Kenya, Mongolia, Pakistan, and United Arab Emirates. Each YA identified her/his goal-oriented behaviors through the Connective Leadership framework and chose two ASI styles, which she/he believed, would help them become more effective leaders.

Each YA was assigned a "Leadership Coach" (LC), either a Professor or Doctoral Candidate from Philips Graduate University. Prior to the coaching process, the YA participants engaged in a 60-min online training session to learn about the Connective Leadership Model. The LCs then worked with the YAs via Skype and provided a minimum of 180 minutes of individual leadership coaching for each participant over a 10-week period. At the conclusion of the coaching period, each YA participant retook the ASI with results compared to the previous ASI.

The project was designed with the ASI Model in mind, as it presented an opportunity to display behaviors in alignment with Connective Leaders.

The Project Vision: Cultivating world peace by coaching the YAs to become Connective Leaders.

The Project Goal: Enhance YA competencies in two self-selected Connective Leadership Achieving Styles.

The expected outcomes for the YAs:

- Improved leadership capabilities
- Enhanced leadership collaboration
- Increased self-confidence in leveraging the ASI Model

Each style of the Connective Leadership Model was exhibited at differing points throughout the project:

- The LC Team leveraged the Intrinsic Style by ensuring that YAs take initiative to meet their goals.
- The LC Team met regularly, and shared results in a constructive way, to motivate one another to advance, employing the Competitive Style regularly.
- Each YA worked on a project which required them to "take charge" as a leader and exhibit the Power Style.
- The YAs received international attention, which aided in the development of their savvy and charisma or Personal Style.
- The YAs developed relationships with one another and their coaches, which required flexing the Social Style.
- The LC Team leader selected the coaches as well as empowered and entrusted them, which was indicative of the Entrusting Style.
- YAs partnered with their coaches and worked together to develop goals using the Collaborative Style.
- The LC/YA team and YAs helped each other meet their goals utilized the Contributory Style.
- The YAs celebrated the success of one another, showcasing the Vicarious Style.

At the conclusion, the YAs' ASI scores showed an increase of 24.3% in styles chosen by the participants for development and an increase of 9.4% in styles that were not chosen by the YAs.

The following quotes were provided at the end of the study by YAs.

> A seventeen year old YA from Australia, stated, "this has been an invaluable tool in generating growth in my leadership abilities. I have greater confidence and willingness to solve any situation that enters my path."

> A sixteen year old YA from Dubai, said, "I not only saw a change in my Vicarious and Intrinsic styles, but I also saw a difference in all my other styles of leadership. Through coaching, I improved in nearly each style."

> A twenty-five year old YA from Guatemala, suggested, "I think that this process has made me a better leader. I feel like I have grown in becoming strategic and self-disciplined with my goals and that can be seen in other people's work."

From the Fulbright and Youth Ambassador research, we see both the potential and an actionable plan to develop Connective Leadership in diverse populations. These young leaders, from around the world, displayed higher levels of confidence and competence to reach within themselves and to reach out to diverse others to accomplish complex tasks.

Gender and Economic Sector Divides

In this section, the patterns of leadership styles across gender and economic sectors are examined. This highlights the need for the inclusion of both sexes across organizational boundaries as necessary in the Connective Era.

Research into sex differences in leadership grab the headlines as women's issues attract readers, but it also builds walls that separate the population squarely in half. The headlines report that out of the S&P 500 companies, women comprise 45% of the total workforce, yet only 4% of CEO positions, 19.2% of Board Seats, and 25.1% of management jobs (Diversity Inc., 2016). These statistics bring a visceral reaction in some women to demand exclusionary practices end and that *men* must be held responsible for this injustice. Others point to the differences in how men and women lead as the focus of such discrepancies, but are there really such divides?

Research into sex differences using the Connective Leadership Model across industries and decades consistently shows the similarities between men and women far out weight the differences. Such results suggest that rather than focusing on the small differences between the sexes, we should examine not only the *sex-role stereotypes*, but also *actual* changing *behavior*. In fact, the only substantial difference between the sexes is in competitive behavior, with not surprisingly, men reporting engaging in more competitive behavior than women (Robinson & Lipman-Blumen, 2003).

A more telling tale is when managers and supervisors were asked to rank order the nine Connective Leadership styles from those they used most frequently to those used less often (see Table 1). Examining the ASI data from the 1980s–2015 revealed that women consistently ranked the *Competitive* style at the bottom, nine out of nine, in their preference list. As for the stereotype of men having competition carved into their DNA, men ranked competitive behavior eighth of nine beginning in the 1980s, but by 2000, men also ranked competitive behavior last (ninth) (Robinson & Lipman-Blumen, 2017).

Based on these findings, treating women as a different type of leader, and encouraging them to be more competitive — to "lean in" (Sandberg, 2013) — reinforces the gender divide. In an inclusive world, instead of wasting resources teaching women how to

Table 1.   Leadership (Achieving) Styles Rankings by Sex.

U.S. Female Managers and Supervisors (N = 5,353)		U.S. Male Managers and Supervisors (N = 4,870)	
Style	Mean (SD)[a]	Style	Mean (SD)[a]
Intrinsic	5.57 (0.84)	Intrinsic	5.54 (0.81)
Contributory	5.34 (0.97)	Power	5.33 (0.99)
Power	5.23 (1.03)	Contributory	5.30 (0.92)
Collaborative	5.23 (1.12)	Collaborative	5.24 (1.07)
Vicarious	5.06 (1.02)	Vicarious	5.15 (0.97)
Entrusting	4.84 (0.99)	Entrusting	4.76 (1.00)
Personal	4.56 (1.23)	Personal	4.57 (1.22)
Social	4.39 (1.14)	Competitive	4.46 (1.15)
Competitive	3.90 (1.22)	Social	4.43 (1.11)

Source: Robinson and Lipman-Blumen (2017).
[a]Mean scores are calculated on a 7-point Likert Scale; SD = Standard Deviation.

behave like men, perhaps we could engage in more relevant leadership behaviors for *both* sexes. Emphasizing the broad spectrum of leadership behaviors in the Connective Leadership model offers one possibility.

The landscape is recrafting historic tales to include the contributions of women. The inclusion of Harriett Tubman and women suffrage demonstrators on US currency is but one example. While the statistics of women in leadership moves at a glacial pace, there are also pockets of inclusion for without the male half of the population also addressing these "human" equality issues, progress will all but halt. As feminist Gloria Steinem saw it "A feminist is anyone who recognizes the equality and full humanity of women and men." She stressed inclusion stating "Feminism has never been about getting a job for one woman. It's about making life more fair for women everywhere. It's not about a piece of the existing pie; there are too many of us for that. It's about baking a new pie" (Steinem, 2014).

Comparative Study of Achieving Styles and Connective Leadership Profiles among Leaders in the Nonprofit and for Profit Sectors

As our world becomes more interconnected and the needs of employees and the constituencies served are increasingly complex, the forces driving collaboration to achieve success, and in some instances survival, across the nonprofit and for profit sectors have grown exponentially. To identify points of connection, the Achieving Styles of leaders in senior and midlevel positions from US organizations in both the nonprofit and for profit sectors were examined to test commonly held beliefs that leaders in the nonprofit arena are far less competitive and task oriented than corporate leaders and to identify opportunities for partnership around "collective realities" with the ultimate goal of effecting change (Harrington, 2014).

Common misconceptions about nonprofit leaders include the assumption that nonprofit leaders, because they work for mission-driven organizations, tend to be less business oriented and task oriented and more people oriented. They, therefore, don't need to be as competitive. These assumptions require examination, as leaders in both sectors have come under fire recently, with a demand for more effective and ethical leadership strategies.

The nonprofit sector is well aware of the impending leadership transition due to the imminent retirement of Baby Boomers from high-level management positions and the value in developing the next generation of nonprofit leaders, which some feel should look like those from the business sector. Moreover, given the recent recession, the resounding drumbeat of funders has been that a leader must assure sustainability of the nonprofit, often defined as financial stability. Yet, to successfully run a nonprofit, a leader must be more agile and flexible, given extremely limited resources and the challenge of motivating staff, operating through creative solutions, leveraging relationships as well as being financially savvy. In addition, the nonprofit leader has the "double bottom line" of mission and finances, and must attain both while appeasing various stakeholders — including clients, boards of directors, funders, volunteers, elected officials, and staff.

Recent perspectives have now expanded the view of the nonprofit leader from a "do-gooder" to a well-rounded leader, able to flex leadership styles to meet the various challenges with decreasing resources and greater scrutiny from funders and governmental agencies, all too often with an overly stretched and underpaid staff that they must keep motivated. A recent review of organizational assessments of 700 nonprofits by the firm TCC concluded that "sustainability is not just about fundraising, but strong vision-centered leadership combined with intentional and formal learning practices, financial adaptability and good sense." Therefore, leadership is now considered by some as important as financial sustainability for the longer-term success of nonprofit organizations.

Research into Nonprofit and For-Profit Leaders

A comparison of nonprofit and for-profit leaders in the United States suggests that despite some expected and unexpected differences, the groups look similar in terms of many of their leadership styles. Both groups appear to rely on a mix of styles to support their leadership. Not surprisingly, however, for-profit leaders tend to score higher on Power while nonprofit leaders score themselves higher on Entrusting, supporting long-term assumptions that corporate leaders tend to rely on command and direct styles while nonprofit leaders tend to empower their employees. The data also suggest, however, that this is only part of the story, in that for-profit leaders also tend to favor Contributory behaviors which involve supporting the achievement of others with a hands-off approach as to defining the goals and direction. Surprising was that the nonprofit leaders did not favor the Personal style more than the for-profit, given their need to inspire a range of constituencies around their mission, most often without the resources of budgets for marketing support.

Most surprisingly is the low scores and ranking of the Competitive style for both groups. While the for-profit group did score higher as expected, it was ranked at or near the bottom for both similar to the low rankings when comparing men and women. This might be a result of the strong emphasis that has been seen in both the corporate and nonprofit worlds on teamwork and collaboration, over competitiveness, as a more effective means to achieve. It is also consistent with the values of Connective Leadership in working collaboratively and reaching out to others whom may have been competitors.

The results indicate that there are many commonalities between nonprofit and for-profit leaders. In addition, the concept of "Cross-over Leaders" as discussed by Phipps and Burbach (2010) as those who cross between the two sectors highlight the movement beyond zero-sum competition to the effectiveness of reaching across borders for nonprofit as well as for-profit leaders of both sexes.

Conclusion

The central theme of this chapter has been to emphasize that inclusive leadership is not a phenomenon found only in rare instances and enacted by only an even rarer charismatic few, but instead a process of effective engagement across a myriad of differences. We have offered examples of leadership styles being identified and developed in young people from around the world, as well as across gender, and finally across economic sectors. By bringing diverse populations together and motivating them to meet shared goals, Connective Leaders reduce the inherent tension around engaging diversity and activate the cognitive capacity to embrace their interconnectedness (Pettygrew & Tropp, 2011). We have employed the Connective Leadership Model as a means to identify leadership styles that can be learned in order to adapt to the complexity of our increasingly interconnected and interdependent world. As a shared model of leadership, one that values bringing in all stakeholders, supporting the tasks of others, as well as getting things done; we have offered a perspective on a way to lead that is inclusive as well as effective.

References

Alakija, F. (2012). Retrieved from http://www.cnn.com/2012/02/16/world/africa/folorunso-alakija-philanthropist-nigeria/. Accessed on May 4, 2016.

Bennett, J. M. (2008). On becoming a global soul. In V. Savicki (Ed.), *Developing intercultural competence and transformation: Theory, research, and application in international education* (pp. 13–31). Sterling, VA: Stylus.

Bennett, M. J. (1993). Towards ethnorelativism: A developmental model of intercultural sensitivity. In R. M. Paige (Ed.), *Education for the intercultural experience* (pp. 21–71). Yarmouth, ME: Intercultural Press.

Cartwright, C. T. (2012). *Assessing the relationship between intercultural competence and leadership styles: An empirical study of international Fulbright students in the U.S. Portland State University.* PSU Library Dissertations and Theses, paper 759, 206 p. Retrieved from http://pdxscholar.library.pdx.edu/cgi/viewcontent.cgi?article=1758&context=open_access_etds.

Dalai Lama. (2011, April 20). Retrieved from https://guillermorivarola.wordpress.com/category/mis-citas-favoritas/. Accessed on May 3, 2016.

Diversity Inc. (2016). Retrieved from http://www.diversityinc.com/2016-top-50-facts-figures/. Accessed on May 4, 2016.

Fulbright Program. (2011a). *About fulbright.* Retrieved from http://foreign.fulbrightonline.org/about.html. Accessed on August 1, 2011.

Fulbright Program. (2011b). *Legacy of leadership, the Nobel Prize winners.* Pamphlet by the Fulbright Program, Washington, DC.

Fulbright Program. (2011c). *State alumni, your global community.* Pamphlet by the Fulbright Program, Washington, DC.

Harrington, M. (2014, October). *Comparative study of Achieving Styles and Connective Leadership profiles among leaders in nonprofit and for profit sectors.* Paper presented at the International Leadership Association, San Diego, CA.

Hawkins, S. (2010). Retrieved from http://parade.com/37704/parade/12-inside-a-great-mind/. Accessed on May 4, 2016.

King, M. L. (n.d.). Retrieved from http://abcnews.go.com/blogs/politics/2013/08/rep-john-lewis-remembers-historic-march-on-washington/. Accessed on May 4, 2016.

Kozai Group. (2008). *Intercultural effectiveness scale.* St. Louis, MO: Kozai Group.

Lipman-Blumen, J. (1996). *The connective edge: Leading in an interdependent world*. San Francisco, CA: SAGE.

Lipman-Blumen, J. (2006). *Individual and organizational achieving styles: A conceptual handbook for researchers and human resource professionals*. Pasadena, CA: The Achieving Styles Institute.

Lipman-Blumen, J., Handley-Isaksen, A., & Leavitt, H. (1983). Achieving styles in men and women: A model, an instrument, and some findings. In J. Spence (Ed.), *Achievement and achievement motives: Psychological and sociological approaches* (pp. 151–204). San Francisco, CA: Freeman.

Mendenhall, M., & Oddou, G. (1985). The dimensions of expatriate acculturation: A review. *Academy of Management Review, 10*(1), 39–47.

Pettigrew, T. F., & Tropp, L. R. (2011). *When groups meet: The dynamics of intergroup contact*. New York, NY: Psychology Press.

Phipps, K. A., & Burbach, M. E. (2010). Strategic leadership in the nonprofit sector: Opportunities for research. *Journal of Behavioral and Applied Management, 11*(2), 137–154

Pink, D. H. (2009). *Drive: The surprising truth about what motivates us*. New York, NY: Riverhead Books.

Robinson, J. L., & Lipman-Blumen, J. (2003, September/October). Leadership behavior of male and female managers, 1984-2002. *Journal of Education for Business, 79*, 28–33.

Robinson, J. L., & Lipman-Blumen, J. (2017). Challenging our assumptions about male and female preferences for competition. *Journal of Leadership Studies, 10*(4), 66–74.

Salbi, Z. (2010). *The Daily Beast*. Retrieved from http://www.thedailybeast.com/articles/2010/03/07/our-fight-begins-today.html. Accessed on May 4, 2016.

Sandberg, S. (2011). Retrieved from http://www.huffingtonpost.com/2011/06/14/facebooks-sheryl-sandberg_n_876799.html. Accessed on May 4, 2016.

Sandberg, S. (2013). *Lean in: Women, work, and the will to lead*. New York, NY: Alfred A. Knopf, Random House.

Shavelson, M., & Curtiz, M. (1953). *Trouble along the way*. Burbank, CA: Warner Bros.

Steinem, G. (2014). Retrieved from http://www.huffingtonpost.com/2014/03/25/ways-gloria-steinem-taught-us-to-be-better-women_n_5022031.html. Accessed on May 4, 2016.

Thatcher, M. (1982). Retrieved from http://www.goodreads.com/author/quotes/198468.Margaret_Thatcher. Accessed on May 4, 2016.

Walsh, K. (2015). *Cross Cultural Millennial Behavior Transformation*. Paper presented at the International Leadership Conference, Barcelona, Spain.

Washington, B. T. (1901). Retrieved from http://thinkexist.com/quotation/few_things_can_help_an_individual_more_than_to/200601.html. Accessed on May 4, 2016.

Zuckerberg, M. (2013). *Business News Daily*. Retrieved from http://www.businessnewsdaily.com/4167-business-profile-mark-zuckerberg.html. Accessed on May 4, 2016.

13

Inclusive Leadership: A Western Concept or a Strategy That Will Transform the World?

Randal Joy Thompson

Keywords: Social inclusion; inclusive society; inclusive leadership; human rights; international aid

An inclusive society — or a society for all — in which all citizens, regardless of their differences, have equality of opportunity as well as a voice in determining the set of social and political institutions that govern them, has become a common goal of both international institutions as well as of groups pushing to change the current global order. Such a society, led by inclusive leaders distributed horizontally, would function on the basis of cooperation, on interactions and exchanges that would result in benefits for all — a positive sum game — rather than the zero-sum game that results from competition over scarce resources and is based on a view of humans as *homo economicus.* Inclusive societies led by inclusive leaders currently exist in communities around the world (Bollier & Helfrich, 2012; Gobillot, 2009). Indeed, the communities and organizations involved in the commons movement function by inclusiveness and posit a fundamentally different cooperative paradigm of being human and of humanity's relationship to the environment and resources, often called *homo reciprocans* (Bollier & Helfrich, 2012; Thompson, 2014; Wuffli, 2016). Some business leaders have posited that inclusive leadership is required in the emerging global order and propose a modified form of "new capitalism" that emphasizes human wellbeing and sustainability as much as profit as the driver of business (Wuffli, 2016).

International organizations such as the United Nations (UN), the World Bank, and the Organization for Economic Coopera-tion and Development as well as bilateral donor organizations such as the United States Agency for International Development (USAID), the British Aid Agency (DFID), and others have been issuing proclamations and strategies regarding inclusive societies for several decades. Donors and nongovernmental organizations (NGOs), in turn, have been channeling funds to foster inclusive-ness under the rubric of human rights. I will explore the evolution of the movement toward inclusiveness among interna-tional organizations, governments, and NGOs and argue that the theoretical framework of this movement continues to posit a world based on competition and the self-maximizing individual. Much of the narrative in discussions of inclusiveness in this domain stem from the intent to subdue conflicts between majori-ties and minorities and to maintain the semblance of world stability, rather than to foster shared decision making. Further, international discussions of inclusion rarely if ever discuss inclu-sive leadership. Rather, they assume that an inclusive society is possible without a drastic change in the way many global leaders lead and without a change in the socioeconomic system that thrives on competition more than collaboration.

I argue that although the proclamations regarding inclusive society and the progress made to include certain groups have fos-tered some movement toward a truly inclusive society, such a society cannot emerge without a fundamental shift in the world order. The way that international organizations are implementing inclusive societies appears largely as a Western concept, based mainly on liberal western contemporary political values. These values are secularized versions of a worldview originating in the philosophies of John Locke and Jean-Jacques Rousseau and further developed by the Protestant Reformation and initiation of capitalism and modified by postmodernism. Such values include a democratic system of governance, an emphasis on the individual and his or her rights, the right to private property, the notion that the concept of right and wrong is relative, and the belief that everyone should be treated equally despite their differences. Often, these values clash with the more traditional Eastern values that function with strong monarchical, dictatorial, or familial leadership, favor a collectivist, sometimes tribalist, rather than individualist society, national ownership of key industries, conservative values deriving from religious tradition, strong honor-shame societies which believe that certain behaviors should be kept private and certain individuals who exhibit these behaviors are justifiably excluded; and a stronger belief in rigid social structures in which individuals take their place by birth. Religious authorities and groups in the West join forces with those in the East when human rights ventures into areas considered questions of morality.

Human Rights

The global narrative on inclusive society emerged from several decades of issuing declarations and operationalizing human rights. In order to justify equal access to social opportunities and shared decision making, individuals from different races, ethnic groups, religions, ages, geographic location, socioeconomic level, sexual preference, gender, disabled, and other identities, needed to have rights derived from some universal, natural, or social standard.

The notion of human rights has been debated throughout history. Philosophers, politicians, and the populace have justified these rights by reference to God, to natural law, to universal principles, to cultural and religious imperatives, to social norms, and to individual preferences. The study of these rights has become contentious over the years with realist theorists arguing that human rights emerged to serve the interests of powerful states; critical theorists contending that such rights are used by the powerful states to suppress states in the South; and other theorists asserting that human rights have often been posited by weaker states to restrain more powerful states (Sikkint, 2015). In the world of foreign aid and international development, some efforts of donors to instill human rights in recipient countries have been viewed as cultural imperialism (Heard, 1997). Nonetheless, the recognition of human rights has served to allow marginalized groups a foundation upon which to base their demands for inclusion.

Contemporary discussions of human rights are generally traced back to several foundational documents, including the Magna Carta of 1215, the 1689 English Bill of Rights, US Declaration of Independence of 1776, the French Declaration on the Rights of Man and Citizen, written in 1789, and the US Constitution and Bill of Rights, that in 1791. The notion that humans have certain fundamental and self-evident rights that governments are required to secure can be found in the words of the US Declaration of Independence (Charters of Freedom, n.d.).

The foundational document that frames global human rights discussions today is the United Nations Universal Declaration of Human Rights (UDHR) adopted in 1948. Echoing much of the sentiment of the US Declaration of Independence, the UDHR begins by asserting that the "[r]ecognition of the inherent dignity and of the equal and inalienable rights of all members of the human family is the foundation of freedom, justice, and peace in the world" (Flowers, n.d., para 10). The 30 articles of the UDHR establish the principles and specific realms of human rights and many of them comprise the areas that define social inclusion (UN, 1948).

UDHR establishes that all individuals, equal before the law and provided equal protection by the law, have the right not to be held in slavery and not to be subject to torture or other inhumane treatment. Rule of law is an essential right granted by UDHR. Other rights elaborated in the UDHR include the freedoms: to marry by choice; religion, conscience, and thought; to own property; to social security; to choose work; to assemble; and others deemed fundamental. Furthermore, UDHR established that the basis of governmental authority is the will of the people as expressed through democratic process.

The Commission on Human Rights was formed by the Economic and Social Council of the UN (ECOSOC) to continue the dialog regarding universal and fundamental human rights. The Commission was reconstituted in 2006 as the UN Human Rights Council. The Council has 47 members who have been more carefully vetted than previously and it also conducts a universal periodic review of human rights abuses of all states, including those of the Council's memberships (Council on Foreign Relations, 2013).

Following in the footsteps of the UDHR, regional government organizations have ratified human rights declarations, such as the Charter of Human and People's Rights of African states (1981) and the Cairo Declaration on Human Rights in Islam (1990). The American Declaration of the Rights and Duties of Man, ratified in Bogota, Columbia in 1948, predated the UDHR and strongly influenced it (Sikkint, 2015). In 2000, the European Union (EU) followed suit and published *The Charter of the Fundamental Rights of the European Union*. The Vienna Declaration and Programme of Action (VDPA) was adopted at the World Conference on Human Rights held in Vienna in 1993. VDPA also proposed the creation of the UN High Commissioner for Human Rights, which was approved by the UN.

THE HELSINKI ACCORDS

The Helsinki Accords (also called The Final Act) were a series of agreements signed in 1975 between countries in the Western bloc and those in the Eastern bloc. Initiated at the request of Russia in order to secure their expanded borders secured at the conclusion of World War II, the Accords contained a section on human rights that served as the basis for increased criticism of Russia for violating of human rights by repressing dissent (Snyder, 2011).

THE HUMAN RIGHTS MOVEMENT

Generally considered to have begun in the 1960s, the human rights movement has been led predominantly by NGOs, which have, by and large, served as watchdogs to ensure that the foundational documents of human rights are implemented. Human rights groups pressure international organizations and governments to honor human rights and to punish those leaders who do not. War crimes have been prosecuted by the International Criminal Court largely as the result of pressure of these groups.

In recent years, human rights groups together with donors have increasingly pushed for women's rights as well as for the legal rights of Lesbians and Gays (LGBT). However, these groups have received a great deal of pushback in many parts of the world where traditional culture condones and forbids certain practices accepted by the liberal establishment in the West. For example, in Bangladesh in April 2016, a gay activist who was an employee of the USAID and his friend were bludgeoned to death because of their LGBT newspaper and public demonstrations for

LGBT rights. An Al Qaeda affiliated group claimed responsibility (McLaughlin, Melvin, & Ap, 2016).

US Department of State Deputy Assistant Secretary Richard Hoegland, himself gay, warned of a backlash against the US promotion of LGBT rights abroad. He recounted his personal experience promoting LGBT rights in Pakistan, which caused a violent backlash and accusations by some Pakistanis that this American-backed policy initiative was a form of the "worst social and cultural terrorism against Pakistan" (Goonenough, 2015, para. 10).

In countries such as Afghanistan, a backlash against women has erupted. Afghan women leaders have been harassed and murdered and laws oppressing women reenacted (Thompson, 2015). Many traditional men and women in Afghanistan and other Islamic countries view the Western support of women's rights and the portrayal of the *hijab* as a symbol of the oppression of women as political and cultural imperialism and as a strategy to achieve dominance (Thompson, 2015). The Institute of Human Rights (2016) held a forum at which women leaders of the International Women's Movement blamed the backlash on traditional and extremist religious groups worldwide, right wing political groups, and neo-liberal capitalism.

COORDINATION OF HUMAN RIGHTS GROUPS

Human rights groups continue to meet to issue declarations regarding human rights. The International Coordinating Committee on National Institutions for the Promotion and Protection of Human Rights has held 12 conferences. The most recent conference in Merida, Mexico on October 8–10, 2015 resulted in the Merida Declaration, which committed human rights organizations to support the United Nations Sustainable Development Goals, established in 2015 (OHCHR, 2015). The 17 sustainable development goals and 169 targets for 2030 include considerable discussion of human rights and creating an inclusive society (UN, 2015).

CRITIQUE OF HUMAN RIGHTS

Human rights have been criticized by scholars and politicians of a variety of persuasions. Many governments have complained that the human rights movement impinges on their sovereignty, as well as insults their culture. Many critiques have asserted that the entire concept of human rights stems from Western liberal political ideology and is not applicable globally (Heard, 1997). Others have claimed that human rights comprise an essential conversation that promotes the global neo-liberal capitalist project (Shemtob, n.d.). Still others have contended that human rights focus on the rights of individuals to seek pleasure at the expense of higher ideological causes and the obsession with such individual rights has weakened the fabric of social cohesion and responsibility (Shemtob, n.d.). The Council on Foreign Relations contended that many western countries, the United States above all, resist cooperation in international human rights because doing so "might harm business, infringe upon autonomy, or limit freedom of speech" (2013, para. 4).

As has been argued previously, not all rights are viewed globally as being universal, as evidenced in the backlash against LGBT and women's rights. Indeed, other rights, such as the right to bear arms, promoted by the National Rifle Association, and the right to have an abortion, promoted by Planned Parenthood, are highly contentious in the United States and are illegal in many countries around the world. In practice, western countries, or the global north, have emphasized civil and political rights whereas developing countries, or the global south, have emphasized economic, social, and cultural rights (Council on Foreign Relations, 2013).

ROLE OF NGOs

In general, NGOs are better positioned to promote many human rights more effectively than governments because they are viewed as less entwined with global power politics. This is especially true in regard to grassroots NGOs who advocate within their countries for protection of their own rights or rights of others who are less able to advocate. Efforts by miners, environmental groups, indigenous groups, women's groups, minority and ethnic groups, disabled groups, and others to fight within their own systems for human rights are often more effective than international governments because they are generally not tainted by outside association. The civil rights movement for African Americans and the movement for the rights of black in South Africa, as well the women's voting rights movement are examples of how effective NGOs, aligned with citizens, can force changes in government policy to ensure their rights are recognized. However, even in the case of these NGOs in the developing world, if they are heavily funded by international or bilateral donors organizations, they can be seen as the pawns of outside interests. Additionally, if these NGOs are perceived by their governments as threatening the power structure, they may be prohibited from operating.

From Human Rights to Inclusion

Concern by governments and international organizations over social exclusion and its complement social inclusion emerged in the 1970s in Europe in response to the radical restructuring of economic production caused by globalization and the influx of migrants. The catalyst for this concern was a fear that social cohesion, stability, and quality of life was being threatened by the exclusion of certain groups of individuals as a result of the economic restructuring and globalization (Atkinson & Marlier, 2010). During this period and subsequently, international organizations such as the UN, the World Bank, the Organization for Economic Cooperation and Development, and bilateral donor organizations posited a number of similar definitions of social exclusion centered around the notion that certain individuals are unfairly unable to participate in economic, social, political, and cultural activities that are considered the norm for a particular society. Exclusion, it was argued, was caused by excluded individuals' and groups' gender, economic status, religion, sexual preference, disability, race, ethnic group, age, customs or culture, or other defining characteristics that tend to marginalize them. Generally, exclusion is associated with lack of material resources (social necessities); income to acquire such necessities and/or state subsidies for their provision; access to formal labor markets; access to affordable/adequate housing; access to educational and health care opportunities; freedom from discrimination; opportunities for social participation (social networks); and power or voice to affect the policy choices (Labonte, Hadi, & Kauffman, 2011, p. 1).

There have been a number of theoretical frameworks posited for exclusion that serve as the basis for different strategies to include excluded or marginalized groups. Silver (2007) has proposed three paradigm of exclusion. The solidarity paradigm considers exclusion as the disintegration of social bonds between certain individuals and society because of differences in values and norms. Inclusion requires some type of moral reintegration of the excluded. The specialization paradigm sees exclusion as

the result of discrimination and consequent inability to participate in social exchange, education, and training. Inclusion in this
case is dependent on access to education, skills training, and hiring policies, in addition to strengthening social networks and
social capital. The monopoly paradigm considers that exclusion
stems from restriction to goods and services for those other than
the dominant group. Inclusion, in this case, might only be
achieved through citizen rights, often forcefully obtained through
protest and social unrest.

As in the case of human rights, the major international organizations have all published declarations, policies, and strategies
regarding inclusion. In recent years, poverty has been closely
associated with exclusion and the poverty reduction strategies of
organizations such as the World Bank and the EU have focused
on economic inclusion as their poverty reduction strategy
(Bennett, 2002; EU, 2000; World Bank, 2013).

The World Summit for Social Development convened by the
UN in Copenhagen in 1995 is considered to be the launching
point of the inclusion agenda of international organizations.
Member countries committed to promoting social integration to
create a "society for all" by fostering stable, safe, and just inclusive societies. Such societies would be based on the promotion
and protection of human rights, nondiscrimination, tolerance,
respect for diversity, equality of opportunity, solidarity, security,
and participation of all people, including those who are disadvantaged, marginalized, and vulnerable (UNESCO, 1995).

The declaration recognized the positive and negative impacts
of globalization and blamed increased poverty, unemployment,
and social disintegration on the rapid processes of change and
adjustment caused by the process. Environmental risks have also
been globalized as never before and the parameters of social
development have been profoundly changed, according to the
Declaration (UNESCO, 1995). The Declaration also recognized
increased inequality between rich and poor throughout the world
and the expanding gap between developed and developing countries, as well as increased instability and threats to peace
(UNESCO, 1995).

The United Nations Development Report of 2000 operatio-
nalized the focus on human rights and inclusion for the international development community (UN, 2000). This was the first
time the human rights and international development agendas
were merged with the recognition that they each fostered the
other. The right to dignity and adequate sustenance and freedom

from want entered into the now unified rights-development narrative (UN, 2000). Inclusive democracy was to be the universal model of political order and accountability of governments was to be stressed more than ever in addition to accountability of the private sector, especially multinational corporations (UN, 2000). The development community was encouraged to review the Universal Declaration of Human Rights and to include this perspective in all their work. From then on, the watchwords of development included accountability, transparency, participation, and inclusion (Carothers & Brechenmacher, 2014) with human rights activists encouraged to work side-by-side with development technical advisors.

Recognizing that cultural diversity was also becoming a global concept and that the objectives of development and security would require acceptance of this diversity, UNESCO issued a Universal Declaration on Cultural Diversity in 2001. This Declaration called on the international community to accept and respect cultural diversity and to regard economic advancement and human rights as compatible with this diversity (UNESCO, 2001).

There have been a number of policy papers published by international and bilateral organizations since 2000 that have pledged support for inclusive societies and a number of strategies for achieving them. Such inclusive societies do not guarantee equality of socioeconomic position nor of social status, nor do they mean equal political influence, nor inclusive leadership, but rather equal opportunity to social resources regardless on one's social identity. Social inclusion is also differentiated from social integration or social cohesion or social capital. Societies can be inclusive and not stable also, according to the international development literature, as long as barriers to entry on the basis of social identity have been lifted (UN, 2008, 2009, 2010, 2015, 2016; World Bank, 2013). Many societies have hierarchies of privilege cemented in, such as monarchies, dictatorships, caste-based systems, even achievement-oriented societies, so that equality of status is impossible in the current world order. Social inclusion is multidimensional and includes full access to the cultural, economic, environmental, physical, legal, political, relational, social, and spatial life and opportunities available in society (UN, 2009).

Social inclusion is generally pushed from grassroots, national, regional, and international groups fighting for their rights and for access to economic, social, and economic resources available to other groups, and facilitated by societal policies and institutions. Bennett (2002) argued that social inclusion is the responsibility of states while empowerment is the engine that allows individuals and groups to be included. She contended that States need to build the incentives and capacity within their institutions to respond to the demand of all citizens, regardless of social identity and create a level playing field, such that the identity of citizens overrides all other identities. On the other hand, individuals and groups need to be empowered to influence and hold institutions accountable (Bennett, 2002).

The most recent declaration on inclusive society is the Baku Declaration that emerged from the 7th meeting of the United Nations Alliance of Civilizations, held in Baku, Azerbaijan from April 25–27, 2016. The meeting was titled "Living Together in Inclusive Societies" and focused on the creation of inclusive society as a hedge against violent extremism, as a solution to disruptive migration, and the negative role of social media in instability and violence. On April 25, a group of youth met to discuss how to create an inclusive society and how to honor each other's diversity and culture while living together in harmony (UN News Center, 2016).

HOW TO CREATE AN INCLUSIVE SOCIETY

The UN (2009) argued that inclusive societies need to be founded upon a basic human rights principle that "all human beings are born free and equal in dignity and rights" (p. 9). The UN (2009) argued that States must ensure these fundamental rights are honored, that the rule of law is practiced justly, and that the security of all is ensured. A strong civil society that encourages the active participation of everyone is a prerequisite as well as universal access to public infrastructure and facilities and information, according to the UN report (2009). The UN (2009) also contended that education is the door to inclusion and that education for all should be provided.

The EU has taken action to move toward a more inclusive society. A major element of their strategy is the establishment of a Social Fund (ESF) directed at creating an inclusive society. The function of the fund is to increase employment in EU countries. ESF interventions focus on two types of assistance. The first assists people directly by "opening up comprehensive pathways to integration" (EU, 2010, p. 9) and includes training and education, guidance and counseling, and employment support. The second transforms systems and structures to establish more effective responses to individuals at risk of exclusion. These responses include removing societal barriers, improving services and changing attitudes, and raising awareness through public information campaigns and education (EU, 2010). It remains to be seen what the impact Brexit will have on the unity of the EU and on their strategy of inclusiveness. Certainly, Britain's exit will have significant ramifications on a number of key EU policies. Questions are already being asked about the fate of EU citizens living and working in Britain and immigrants hoping to enter Britain, as well as the impact of Brexit on EU governance systems and even global financial systems.

Steps toward social inclusion include changing the mindset of people by education and by leaders making everyone feel like they belong, achievements that are virtually impossible to attain given the fact that the world operates by power, fear, scarcity, and greed. States and individuals are compelled to compete for economic sustenance and wealth, to kill for power and security, and hence to justify their behavior by reference to religion, rights, and duties.

PROGRESS TOWARD INCLUSION

Significant progress toward inclusion has been made for certain groups. The standard of care for orphans, abandoned, and disabled children no longer is based on automatic institutionalization in most countries in the world. Community-based services, foster care, and family-like living arrangements have been established throughout Eastern Europe since 1990, as well as in the Middle East, and some Asian countries. Inclusive education for many physically and mentally disabled children, where children are taught in classrooms with so-called normal children has made significant progress in the world, although there is still much left to achieve (Artiles, Kozleski, & Waitoller, 2011). E-inclusion has progressed significantly with the expansion of connectivity and the smart phone.

A number of countries have established quotas for women and other marginalized groups to fill seats in Parliament and other elected and appointed political positions. Even with quotas, marginalized groups need to advocate to be included. Htun and Ossa (2012) discussed successful and less successful strategies for indigenous groups and women to be included in political positions in Bolivia. They found that women were more successful because they carved out a unified stance and strategy across diverse groups, whereas indigenous groups fought internecine battles and could not agree, but rather competed. They also found, which is also my experience, that even if quotas are met, the privileged groups still exercise the power within political institutions.

IMPACT OF THE INCLUSIVE SOCIETY APPROACH

Empirical evidence of the positive impact of the inclusive society approach is thus far sparse (Carter, 2015). Theoretical connections between inclusion and economic and social wellbeing are still stronger than the empirical evidence illustrating the causal linkage. Furthermore, the model explored continues to posit economic development as the ultimate goal, not even sustainable development or enhanced wellbeing.

INCLUSIVE LEADERSHIP

The international institution and donor literature is markedly devoid of discussions of inclusive leadership. In fact, there is little discussion of leadership in general. As stated previously, the focus is placed on accountability and transparency and anticorruption in terms of making government more responsive. Inclusiveness is generally worked toward by building active political parties, having free and fair elections, freedom of information laws, independent media, active NGOs and pushing education, and economic reform. The assumption appears to be that inclusiveness can be achieved with the existing leadership styles and with the current socioeconomic order and capitalist system. Given the scarce empirical evidence to prove this assumption, it thus far seems unlikely that the approach of donors will prove to be successful without some system of accountability for leaders and without the emergence of truly inclusive leaders. Further, without inclusive leadership, there is a missing element of an inclusive society. Such a society cannot be pieced together by policy changes and advocacy campaigns without leadership to set examples and lead the way. The Hofstede, Hofstede, and Minkov (2010) global study of leadership styles illustrates that authoritarian leadership is still commonly practiced in many countries of the world. Such leadership is incompatible with inclusive societies.

Conclusion

As I have argued, human rights conceptually establish the foundation of the notion of inclusive society and serve as the justification for excluded and marginalized groups to have equal access to and to be included in all social dimensions. The human rights movement has made significant strides in furthering the dialog about rights and progress has been made in a number of economic, political, and social realms, as discussed in this chapter. NGOs may be better positioned in the short term to advocate for human rights because multinational and bilateral government organizations are still viewed as imposing certain rights as a form of cultural imperialism. Many rights remain highly contentious. International organizations began the discussion regarding inclusive society primarily based upon the need to maintain stability and peace in heterogeneous societies caused by globalization and increased migration. However, these organizations developed policies for inclusion based on arguments for human rights. The EU has taken the lead to create inclusive societies among EU countries by implementing their social stabilization fund. Otherwise, the discussion regarding creating an inclusive world among international organizations remains abstract and without a global commitment to do so. Key international organizations do not discuss the need for inclusive leaders who will help establish inclusiveness as the overarching social paradigm. Still, many groups of people are beginning to discuss a shift in the underlying paradigm of being human, namely the cooperative *homo reciprocans*. Communities scattered across the globe are beginning to live more cooperatively. Despite the efforts that have been made to date, much more needs to be accomplished before society become inclusive and a major shift in the socioeconomic system and the global mindset needs to take place to enable increased cooperation and inclusiveness. However, the notion of inclusive society remains an important aspiration with enormous power to change the world.

Acknowledgments

I would like to thank Edin Ibrahimefendic, Attorney-at-Law, who works for the Office of the Human Rights Ombudsman in Sarajevo, Bosnia-Herzegovina for his suggestions for resources for my chapter and for his always brilliant perspective on global issues.

References

Artiles, A. J., Kozleski, E., & Waitoller, F. R. (Eds.), (2011). *Inclusive education: Examining equity on five continents*. Cambridge, MA: Harvard Education Press.

Atkinson, T., & Marlier, E. (2010). *Analysing and measuring social inclusion in a global context*, United Nations, New York, NY. Retrieved from http://www.un.org/esa/socdev/publications/measuring-social-inclusion.pdf. Accessed on March 4, 2016.

Bennett, L. (2002). Using empowerment and social inclusion for pro-growth: A theory of social change. Retrieved from http://siteresources.worldbank.org/INTEMPOWERMENT/Resources/486312-1095970750368/529763-1095971096030/bennet.pdf. Accessed on March 4, 2016.

Bollier, D., & Helfrich, S. (Eds.), (2012). *The wealth of the commons: A world beyond market and state*. Amherst, MA: Levellers Press.

Carothers, T., & Brechenmacher, S. (2014). Accountability, transparency, participation, and inclusion: A new development consensus? Carnegie Endowment for Peace.

Carter, B. (2015). Benefits to society of an inclusive societies approach. GSDRC. Retrieved from http://www.gsdrc.org/wp-content/uploads/2015/09/HDQ1232.pdf. Accessed on March 4, 2016.

Charters of Freedom. (n.d.). *The declaration of independence*. Retrieved from http://www.archives.gov/exhibits/charters/declaration_transcript.html. Accessed on March 5, 2016.

Council on Foreign Relations. (2013). The global human rights regime. Retrieved from http://www.cfr.org/human-rights/global-human-rights-regime/p27450. Accessed on March 5, 2016.

European Union (EU). (2000). *Charter of the fundamental rights of the European Union*. Retrieved from http://www.europarl.europa.eu/charter/pdf/text_en.pdf. Accessed on March 6, 2016.

European Union (EU). (2010). *The European social fund and social inclusion*. Retrieved from http://ec.europa.eu/employment_social/esf/docs/sf_social_inclusion_en.pdf. Accessed on April 10, 2016.

Flowers, N. (n.d.). *Human rights here and now: Celebrating the universal declaration of human rights*. Retrieved from https://www1.umn.edu/humanrts/edumat/hreduseries/hereandnow/Part-1/short-history.htm. Accessed on April 10, 2016.

Gobillot, E. (2009). *Leadershift: Reinventing leadership for the age of mass collaboration*. Philadelphia, PA: Kogan Page Limited.

Goonenough, P. (2015). State Department official warns of backlash in promoting LGBT rights abroad. *CNS News*. Retrieved from http://www.cnsnews.com/news/article/patrick-goodenough/state-dep-t-official-warns-backlash-promoting-lgbt-rights-abroad. Accessed on April 10, 2016.

Heard, A. (1997). *Human rights: Chimeras in sheep's clothing?* Retrieved from http://www.sfu.ca/~aheard/intro.html. Accessed on April 11, 2016.

Hofstede, G., Hofstede, G. J., & Minkov, M. (2010). *Culture and organizations: Software of the mind.* New York, NY: McGraw Hill.

Htun, M., & Ossa, J. P. (2012). Political inclusion of marginalized groups: Indigenous reservations and gender parity in Bolivia. *Politics, Groups, and Identities, 1*(1), 4–25.

Institute for Human Rights. (2016). *The backlash against women's rights.* Retrieved from http://www.iwm.at/events/event/the-backlash-against-womens-rights/. Accessed on April 6, 2016.

Labonte, R., Hadi, A., & Kauffman, X. E. (2011). Indicators of social exclusion and inclusion: A critical and comparative analysis of the literature. *Ei Exchange Working Papers, 2*(8). Retrieved from www.researchgate.net. Accessed on April 10, 2016.

McLaughlin, E. C., Melvin, D., & Ap, T. (2016). Al Qaeda group claims responsibility for Bangladesh LGBT hacking death. *CNN.* Retrieved from http://www.cnn.com/2016/04/25/asia/bangladesh-u-s-embassy-worker-killed/. Accessed on May 1, 2016.

OHCHR. (2015). *The Merrida Convention.* Retrieved from http://nhri.ohchr.org/EN/ICC/InternationalConference/12IC/Background%20Information/Merida%20Declaration%20FINAL.pdf. Accessed on April 15, 2016.

Shemtob, Z. (n.d.). *Human rights and wrongs: A critical overview of contemporary human rights skepticism.* Retrieved from http://zacharyshemtob.com/uploads/Human_Rights_and_Wrongs.pdf. Accessed on April 15, 2016.

Sikkink, K. (2015 December). Latin America's protagonist role in human rights: How the region shaped human rights norms post World War II and what it means for the field today. *International Journal on Human Rights.* Retrieved from http://sur.conectas.org/en/latin-americas-protagonist-role-human-rights/. Accessed on April 16, 2016.

Silver, H. (2007). *The Process of Social Exclusion: The Dynamics of an Evolving Concept,* Chronic Poverty Research Center, Working Paper No. 95, October 2007. [http://www.chronicpoverty.org/pdfs/95Silver.pdf].

Snyder, S. (2011). *Human rights activism and the end of the cold war: A transnational history of the Helsinki network.* New York, NY: Cambridge University Press.

Thompson, R. (2014). Commoning: Creating a New Socio-economic Order? *A Grounded Theory Study.* Ph.D. dissertation, Fielding Graduate University.

Thompson, R. (2015). Dying to lead: Women leaders in Afghanistan. In S. Madsen, F. Ngunjiri, K. Longman, & C. Cherrey (Eds.), *Women and leadership around the world.* Charlotte, NC: Information Age Publishers.

UNESCO. (1995). *Declaration and Programmme of Action of the World Summit for Social Development.* Retrieved from http://www.unesco.org/education/pdf/COPENHAG.PDF. Accessed on April 15, 2016.

UNESCO. (2001). Universal declaration on cultural diversity: Retrieved from http://unesdoc.unesco.org/images/0012/001271/127162e.pdf. Accessed on April 11, 2016.

United Nations (UN). (1948). *The UN universal declaration of human rights.* Retrieved from http://www.un.org/en/universal-declaration-human-rights/. Accessed on April 11, 2016.Accessed on April 11, 2016.

United Nations (UN). (2000). Human rights and human development. *UN Human Development Report 2000.* Retrieved from http://hdr.undp.org/sites/default/files/reports/261/hdr_2000_en.pdf. Accessed on April 11, 2016.

United Nations (UN). (2008). *Promoting social integration: Report of the expert group meeting.* Helsinki, July 8-9. Retrieved from http://www.un.org/esa/socdev/social/meetings/egm6_social_integration/documents/egm6.report.pdf. Accessed on April 12, 2016.

United Nations (UN). (2009). *Creating an inclusive society: Practical strategies for social integration.* Retrieved from http://www.un.org/esa/socdev/egms/docs/2009/Ghana/inclusive-society.pdf. Accessed on April 12, 2016.

United Nations (UN). (2010). Participatory dialogue: Towards a stable, safe, and just society for all. Retrieved from http://www.un.org/esa/socdev/publications/prtcptry_dlg(full_version).pdf. Accessed on April 13, 2016.

United Nations (UN). (2015). Transforming our world: The 2030 agenda for sustainable development. *Sustainable Development Knowledge Platform.* Retrieved from https://sustainabledevelopment.un.org/post2015/transformingourworld. Accessed on April 11, 2016.

United Nations (UN). (2016). *Baku: Youth stress vision of inclusive society at UN forum.* Retrieved from http://www.un.org/apps/news/story.asp?NewsID=53769#.Vx-Fabo7pUQ. Accessed on April 25, 2016.

UN News Center. (2016). *BAKU: UN global forum ends with renewed commitment to create inclusive societies.* Retrieved from http://www.un.org/apps/news/story.asp?NewsID=53802#.VyPxv7p2SbA. Accessed on April 25, 2016.

World Bank. (2013). Inclusion matters: The foundation for shared prosperity. Retrieved from http://www.worldbank.org/en/topic/socialdevelopment/brief/inclusionmatters. Accessed on April 20, 2016.

Wuffli, P. A. (2016). *Inclusive leadership: A framework for the global era.* New York, NY: Springer Publishers.

14

The Inclusive Leader at the Centre of an Interconnected World

Helen Caton-Hughes and Bob Hughes

Keywords: Inclusive leadership; diversity; inclusion; emotional intelligence; engagement; high-performance behaviours

Overview

Today we live in a world with the potential for more connections than we can possibly follow through in our lifetimes. The global village is now a global megacity of resources, technology, and ingenuity.

Yet war, famine and pestilence persist. As the UN Food and Agriculture Organisation (FAO) points out[1]; food production is sufficient for our global population; yet waste is high and distribution is inefficient. Just one example of the gap between what is possible today and what is practised today.

---

[1]Professor Fernando Figuerola, Professor of Food Science and Technology at the Austral University of Chile, Quoted in 'Knowledge@Wharton' 9 July 2008.

The same gap exists in leadership: talent is going to waste and our health is negatively impacted. It's costing financially too. There are gaps between organisations where leadership is practised along traditional western, white male, lines; and the prospect of greater prosperity and organisational success resulting from an inclusive workplace. There's also a generation gap: where older people hold power and young peoples' potential is hindered. If leadership is a resource, available to all, then its channel of distribution is being artificially narrowed, cutting the majority off from the benefits and resources good leadership brings.

Good leadership creates a more equal society for all of us. Where people genuinely believe they can advance their careers, tap into all available resources, and live better lives through applying their skills, talents and effort, everyone can prosper. Everyone can live well and educate their family, in a fair and transparent way.

Prevailing paradigms are what hold us back. In this chapter we address four key paradigms, that, when shifted, have the potential to open up organisational success through the better utilisation of all the skills and resources available to it.

These four paradigms are:

1. The hero-leader paradigm
2. The male over female leader paradigm
3. The monoculture over diversity in leadership paradigm
4. The older over younger leader paradigm

Combined together, this is an exclusive model of leadership. Older men, from the same background, keep leadership to themselves and feel heroic for so doing. The paradigm of exclusivity may not be intentional, but it's no longer in the best interests of the organisation, or of society.

The evidence for shifting away from these prevailing paradigms has been around for a while.

- The 'hero-leader' paradigm was challenged in 2004, in the Elsevier Leadership Quarterly[2] journal, which noted inverse correlation between performance and CEO charisma.

---

[2]'CEO charisma, compensation, and firm performance'; Henry L. Tosi, Vilmos F. Misangyi, Angelo Fanellid, David A. Waldmane, Francis J. Yammarino, The Leadership Quarterly 15 (2004) 405−420; ©2004 Elsevier Inc.

- A 2011 UK Parliament report quoted European research which showed that 'strong stock market growth among European companies is most likely to occur where there is a higher proportion of women in senior management teams[3], and that 'Companies with more women on their boards were found to outperform their rivals with a 42% higher return in sales, 66% higher return on invested capital and 53% higher return on equity'.[4]
- A 2014 Grant Thornton report[5] showed that companies with diverse executive boards outperform peers run by all-male boards, based on listed companies in India, the United Kingdom and the United States.
- As a 1994 US report[6] puts it: 'diversity in the workplace is profitable'. 'Organizations which excel at leveraging diversity ... will experience better financial performance in the long run than organizations which are not effective in managing diversity'.
- In 2010[7] and 2011[8] two authors highlighted the financial value of promoting from within the existing talent pool in the organisation; rather than paying lip service to developing talent then recruiting expensive and poor-performing outsiders. This means that ways need to be found to develop younger people and find leadership opportunities for them.

---

[3]Desvaux, Devillard-Hoellinger, and Baumgarten (2007).
[4]"The Bottom Line: Corporate Performance and Women's Representation on Boards", Lois Joy, Nancy M Carter, Harvey M Wagener, Sriram Narayanan, Catalyst, 2007
[5]Grant Thornton Report: The Value of Diversity, September 2015 by Francesca Lagerberg. http://www.grantthornton.global/en/insights/articles/diverse-boards-in-india-uk-and-us-outperform-male-only-peers-by-us$655bn/.
[6]Good for business: making full use of the nation's human capital: a fact-finding report of the Federal Glass Ceiling Commission [Washington, DC]: [United States Government Printing Office], [1995].
[7]Chasing Stars: The Myth of Talent and the Portability of Performance, Boris Groysberg, Princeton University Press.
[8]Paying More to Get Less: The Effects of External Hiring versus Internal Mobility, Matthew Bidwell, University of Pennsylvania, Administrative Science Quarterly, September 2011 vol. 56, no. 3, 369–407.

It's now time to take action to shift towards inclusive leadership and away from the outdated paradigm of leadership by exclusion.

One of the most powerful elements is the hero-leader paradigm, (typically) men who command in crisis and conflict, have people perform routine tasks, and reject input from inferiors; people who don't conform to the prevailing paradigm. These behaviours not only exclude others; they cut the organisation off from new ideas and better solutions. These are leaders judged by the power of their personality or the size of their pay packet; not by the effectiveness of their behaviours, or the example they give to future generations.

No single action will shift this, or the other paradigms. It requires concerted effort. And a connected society is an important lever. We can pilot different approaches and co-create a vision for what inclusive leadership looks like in an interconnected world.

This chapter contributes to that vision by setting out the leadership gaps and explores them. It offers a profile of an 'inclusive leader', suggests ways of countering specific gaps and considers how contribution, complexity and context impact on leadership. We conclude by offering an holistic model for inclusive leadership.

The paradigm needed in today's volatile, uncertain, complex and ambiguous world of leadership, is inclusive leadership. It needs a shift away from traditional leadership styles; away from a focus on the leader; towards developing others, as well as oneself.

It is a shift towards the consistent application of a combination of intellectual, managerial and emotional competencies (IQ, MQ and EQ). For this shift to be more enduring and inclusive, leadership needs to shift away from prioritising 'what' it achieves; towards a broader notion of 'purpose' that encompasses values-based performance, and leadership that draws on everyone's strengths and contributions.

Structural Leadership Gaps

The prevailing leadership paradigms hold everyone back — and create a leadership deficit. For companies, this is a huge lost opportunity in terms of return on assets, estimated at over $655 billion in 2014.[9]

---

[9]Grant Thornton Report, Ibid.

Structurally, the most obvious leadership gaps are in gender, culture and lack of age diversity. There are also the gaps between what is possible, what's practised in leadership development and the gap in our definition of 'leadership' itself.

The hero-leader paradigm currently prevails. One way of looking at prevailing paradigms is through the history of Hollywood. One hundred and forty-two films are listed as being of the Hollywood[10] 'superhero' genre, of which four mention women in the title (and just one features a 'black' superhero). Of these 84 were produced between 1920 and 1998; a further 58 between 2000 and 2016. This would indicate that, in popular culture, there's an increased attachment to the popular and dominant paradigm, even as women gradually open more boardroom doors.

Yet this 'hero charisma' has a cost. In 2004, a report evaluated the links between 'CEO charisma, compensation and performance'[11] and found that, while there was *no* correlation between charisma and performance, there *was* a significant correlation between a CEO's perceived charisma and their compensation package. So having charismatic white males at the head of organisations will cost more, has no performance impact and keeps other talented people out.

GENDER DIVERSITY

One way to fill the gap is to welcome in more talented women leaders, who are still in the minority. In March 2015, the UK newspaper *The Guardian*[12] reported that there were more men called John at the top of FTSE 100 companies than the *total* number of women at the top. Twenty-three per cent of boards included women and the goal was to have 25% representation by that date. In the United States, the organisation 20/20 Women on Boards[13] reported that, in 2015, '17.9% of corporate directors were women' (82.1% men); in Europe, all-male boards had fallen to 5.4% from 21% in 2011.[14]

---

[10]https://en.wikipedia.org/wiki/List_of_American_superhero_films 6 April 2016.
[11]The Leadership Quarterly Op. Cit.
[12]www.theguardian.com/business 6 March 2015.
[13]https://www.2020wob.com 6 April 2016.
[14]Guardian Newspaper, 27 April 2016 'Women Occupy Less than a Quarter of UK board positions'.

The argument in favour of women in these roles is that they bring diversity of thinking; some say they communicate more engagingly; they bring competitive advantage, they are certainly more representative of organisations' stakeholders, and organisations can tap into the greater pool of talent. These factors are also the benefit of more diversity generally, not just gender diversification.

Financially, the evidence for diverse gender leadership at board level is clear: They outperform their male-only-board rivals. 'In the US, S&P 500 companies with diverse boards outperformed rivals by 1.91%. In the UK FTSE 350 the gap was 0.53% and for the Indian CNX 200, 0.85%'.[15] The respective estimates for these gaps are $567 billion, $14 billion and $74 billion.

CULTURAL DIVERSITY

More diversity in terms of cultural leadership can also fill the gap. The UK National Health Service (NHS), available to every UK Citizen and one of the world's largest employers, has over 1.3 million staff. Not only would one expect these public service employees to reflect the diversity of the British population, but for its leadership to reflect that variety too.

This would be good for public health; as a diverse commissioning group helps ensure everyone's health needs are addressed. However, according to a 2014 report[16] 'The likelihood of white staff in London being senior or very senior managers is three times higher than it is for black and minority ethnic staff'. Yet, in a city like London, '41% of NHS staff, and 45% of the population are from black and minority ethnic backgrounds'.

AGE DIVERSITY

There's also a generational gap between older people holding power with the potential to hinder young peoples' career paths. In 2010, the average age of a FTSE 350 Board Director was 58. In 2013, the Harvard Law School[17] reported on the US situation,

---

[15]Grant Thornton, September 2015. Op. Cit.
[16]The 'snowy white peaks' of the NHS, Kline Roger. 2014, Middlesex University Research Repository.
[17]Harvard Law School, Taking a Fresh Look at Board Composition, post 9 September 2013.

where 'the average age of directors (68), average board tenure (8.7 years), and mandatory retirement age (72–75) have all risen'.

One solution is to explore opportunities for rotating leadership roles. The British academic and author Professor Mary Beard[18] wrote about how her own Cambridge Faculty rotates its Chair every 2 years. In Plan International, a child-centred community development organisation, people are promoted from Country to Regional Director, and revert after 4–5 years. This approach distributes wider experience of leadership amongst the group, and supports a collaborative and more cooperative way of working. This, of course, challenges the status quo, and has practical implications for how people are recognised and rewarded for what they contribute.

Intergenerational leadership matters because today's flatter organisational structures mean that traditional career paths are more nuanced than previously. Young people can't climb a ladder with each promotion taking them up a rung in the corporate hierarchy. They may not be looking for that traditional career route, but, in many organisations, the ladder may not even be available.

People say that 'millennials' (the generation born just before, or maturing in, the 2000s) want more from their job than just an income. People talk about their social values; about a greater expectation of involvement or consultation; about this generation being more socially networked than connected to institutions.[19] Whatever the reason, there's disconnect between their expectations and the opportunities society, as employers and policy makers, provides.

For people working in areas of the organisation that provide business support services, like HR, IT or marketing, these career paths are like walking through mountain paths to reach the summit. By contrast, professional and technical experts work increasingly in 'pyramid' career paths, where they either scramble up the sides to the top, or fall out of the organisation in the attempt. As the path becomes steeper and competition to get to the top gets

---

[18]https://www.goodreads.com/author/show/97783.Mary_Beard/blog. Accessed on July 24, 2016.
[19]See, for example, Forbes article, 25 September 2014, 'Have You Got Millennial Workforce Expectations All Wrong?'

tougher, more people opt out of the journey altogether. This is an unnecessary waste of talent.

The path millennials take matters, because of the opportunity cost to organisations. Not only in the churn of recruiting talented people, but in the lost leadership and development opportunities, damaging organisations today. Developing and retaining leaders within organisations is a more reliable and cost-effective route to better leadership.[20] So by not understanding, and meeting the needs of, younger people, this leadership gap is of our own creation.

Three Shifts

Three shifts that organisations can make today, without reference to role longevity, gender or cultural contributions, will increase diversity in leadership tasks:

- Recognise people for the skills they contribute
- Provide leadership development and experience
- Progress from hierarchical to networked organisations

There's an often-repeated maxim that we reward people for their increasing experience and role longevity, but what if that's not 20 years of experience, just 1 years' experience repeated 20 times? When we shift recognition and reward systems away from annual pay-rises (which reward loyalty but little else) to rewarding technical leadership, based on skills and contribution, factors such as age cease to matter. Recognising technical leadership has the added advantage of *not* promoting people unsuitable to people management into those types of leadership roles.

Providing leadership opportunities means designing in work shadowing, opportunities to 'act up' (for example, by attending meetings with the necessary decision-making powers, or undertaking holiday cover at the senior level). All these opportunities rely on the willingness and ability of senior people to trust and respect others; to delegate, and properly hand off, tasks to them.

---

[20]'Why Promoting From Within Usually Beats Hiring From Outside', Susan Adams, Forbes — http://www.forbes.com/sites/susanadams/2012/04/05/why-promoting-from-within-usually-beats-hiring-from-outside/#3b6686893fb2 2 May 2016.

When well organised and prepared for, these leadership opportunities offer greater stability and continuity for the organisation.

This delayering and moving away from a strongly hierarchical structure may seem radical. Yet networked organisations, where team members self-organise, are common in the fast-moving world of digital technologies. Buzzwords like 'Agile' and 'Scrum' abound, but at the heart of this movement is a simple premise. A job is just a job.

A role is merely a collection of tasks, which can be moved around. Tasks making up a manager's role today can be distributed around the team; playing to peoples' skills and strengths. This is not the same as saying that a self-organising team doesn't need direction, or clear compelling, vision, mission and purpose — fully connected to the wider organisational purpose.

This evolution still requires boundaries, so that the limits around self-organisation are clear. This requires management — rather than a role of 'manager'. It also needs leadership: people with a strong sense of responsibility; ready to be accountable for the tasks they've taken on.

When intelligent people lack drive and challenge in their role, they look around for it; and if they don't find opportunities to stretch themselves in their current roles, they often leave the organisation — at great cost to employers.

The costs of replacing lost employees is fourfold[21]:

- 'Stars' bought in from outside tend to cost 18% more than their replacement.
- There may be additional costs in raising pay for the team members who receive the new leader: they are crucial to ensuring the new hire gets up to speed.
- There is an overall decline in team performance during this period.
- At the end of all this cost in time and effort, the new star is 61% more likely to be let go than internally developed leaders.

This waste in talent and resources is unnecessary. As well as improving performance and return on assets by filling the

---

[21]Forbes article, September 2014, op. cit., Quoting the work of Prof. Matthew Bidwell.

leadership gap with a more inclusive and diverse pool of leadership talent, there is still an opportunity to achieve value, even if people — such as the young rising stars are (temporarily) leaving the organisation.

For example, if people can leave thinking and talking well of their former employer, an organisation's reputation can benefit. Giving people the chance to develop their talents internally is one way to demonstrate good employment practices. Supporting people to develop outside of the organisation may be another, as acceptance of churn offers the possibility for the employee to return at a later date, already familiar with the organisational culture.

The Leadership Paradigm Shift Needed

There's a fourth, more abstract, leadership gap: between what's possible today and what's practised today. Clear measures exist against which to evaluate 'better leadership' behaviours, but our expectations, stereotypes, prevailing paradigms and outright biases prevent us from getting the best out of people.

Put simply, the application of the right combination of appropriate leadership competence and style, applied in any given situation, will result in higher performance and better outcomes.

Because leadership is context specific, the need to develop flexible leadership styles, to suit different situations, is vital. Key scholarship includes work by people like Howard Gardner[22] who first set out the notion of multiple intelligences; then developed by Daniel Goleman,[23] from whom we understand the importance of applied EQ as an ability in leaders; and Dulwicz and Higgs,[24] who show how organisations can be more effective when EQ competences are embedded in organisational cultures.

This scholarship has led to the development of emotionally resonant leadership styles, which in some contexts can replace

---

[22]Gardner H. (1983). Frames of mind: The theory of multiple intelligences.
[23]Daniel Goleman, Emotional Intelligence 1995 (1996 in the UK) Bloomsbury.
[24]Victor Dulewicz, Malcolm Higgs (2000) 'Emotional intelligence — A review and evaluation study', *Journal of Managerial Psychology*, 15(4), 341–372.

traditional commanding and pacesetting styles. It has also led to the recognition that it is a combination of competences that create better leadership and higher performing organisations:

- Traditional IQ (intellectual competence)
- Managerial competences (MQ)
- Emotional intelligence (EQ)

The paradigm shift, still needed in the leadership development field, is for a conscious shift away from traditional leadership styles, for an attitudinal shift away from a focus on the leader, towards developing others, as well as developing oneself, and for the consistent application of this combination of competencies (IQ, MQ and EQ).

Additionally, for this shift to be more enduring and inclusive, leadership needs to shift its focus away from what it achieves — successful performance — to a broader notion of purpose that encompasses the 'why', or values-based performance and to the 'who': leadership that consciously models the ideal of success which includes everyone's strengths and contributions.

Traditional leadership styles tend to focus on the leader and his/her direction and energy; typically 'commanding' or 'pacesetting' in the Goleman et al.[25] terminology.

The challenge with the commanding style is that it relies on orders flowing in one direction (from top to bottom). It is useful in emergency situations. However, overuse results in a dependent workforce and a leader/deputy leader structure. Team members — who in today's world expect their contribution to be made, listened to and responded to — become frustrated in structures which don't take their expertise, education and strengths into account. It makes no sense to develop frustrated and dependent teams.

The pacesetting style may have its merits in providing effort and energy to get new projects off the ground. The challenge is that in a world heavily reliant on the expertise of knowledge workers — as distinct from 'makers' — predictability is no longer a given.

---

[25]See 'Primal Leadership/The New Leaders' where the six styles are: Commanding, Pacesetting, Democratic, Coaching, Visionary and Affiliative (Goleman, Boyatzis, & McKee, 2002).

The key leadership challenges of the 21st century workforce include volatility, uncertainty, complexity and ambiguity (VUCA). Each of these forces contributes to unpredictability; so leadership has to orientate itself around those factors, and no longer assume that a predictable pace can be set.

The most expensive examples of trying to force out of date thinking through pacesetting leadership is in the world of IT projects. In the United Kingdom, it's estimated that the Government lost £10 billion on the National Health Service IT project alone.[26] In the United States,[27] it's estimated that the Department of Defense has lost over four times as much money to cancelled projects as the $20 billion lost by NASA in research and development programmes. It's unlikely that these countries are alone in their experiences.

By contrast, products such as 'Skype' — the world's most downloaded software — have been developed more organically, where the actual product and customer base, emerge from the interests of its developers. In the case of Skype, 5 people: 2 Swedes and 3 Estonians were the founding team.

Methods such as 'Agile' and 'Scrum' have arisen in the place of a top-down, pacesetting leadership style. Summed up by such statements as: 'Build projects around motivated individuals'. 'Give them the environment and support they need', and 'trust them to get the job done'.[28]

Having a portfolio of leadership styles to call upon addresses the need to be more flexible in a complex and unpredictable world. EQ competencies underpin these styles and can be measured at individual and group levels.

The work of Harold Schroder and his team at Princeton University provided a clear high-performance framework which identifies high-performing management and leadership competencies (MQ).

Four clusters summarise the competences: Thinking, Involving, Inspiring and Achieving, 'based on factorial studies of competency ratings for a number of managers'.[29] However, Schroder makes

---

[26]Guardian online — Abandoned NHS IT system has cost £10 billion so far.
[27]Popular Science — http://www.popsci.com/science/article/2012-09/infographic-nasas-canceled-projects.
[28]'Agile Manifesto' Principles — see http://agilemanifesto.org.
[29]Harold M. Schroder, 'Managerial Competence: The Key to Excellence' Kendall/Hunt, April 1989.

clear that excellence does not rely on an individual alone: 'Excellence is optimizing the range of competency contributions in a workgroup'. So this combination of high-performing behaviours and applied emotional intelligence supports team building, better performance and interdepartmental collaboration.

We know that these leadership attitudes and behaviours work to deliver better leadership. Yet what is practised is often a result of what today's leaders experienced in their own development, the role models around them, and how those people behaved.

Definition Gap

There's also a definition gap — of what we mean by 'leadership'. So far, we've been describing 'leaders' as people at the top of organisations, typically in positions of power. It's not necessarily about position or power. In our model, 'leadership' is based on personal success — and the development of the whole team; team success supports organisation success, which, in turn, contributes to a more successful society. It's more about influence than power. Where positional power was predicated on the value of budgets controlled, the number of people reporting, or the number of departments or offices under the leader's control, today's leadership is about how well a leader enables others to be successful and unlocks their potential.

The authors' vision is for a world of work that grows leadership and supports a new type of leader:

> *People who role model authentic leadership — which springs from their values — who have a sense of vision and purpose. People who take ownership and responsibility — who engage others — who listen and share a spirit of innovation and enquiry. People who lead — not because it's in their job title — because they take ownership, contribute and deliver more. This new type of leadership is one that makes the world of work a more fulfilled and effective experience.*

In this definition, what makes a leadership role is the assumption of responsibility — stepping forward and driving decisions and actions; and being accountable — to the team and the wider organisation — for their successful application.

TWO KEY BARRIERS

Yet this points to two key barriers in the dominant paradigm: individual ego and the perceived threat to it from others. In studies, people are, in theory, open to others and welcome their intelligence, but close to, they prefer being with people less intelligent than themselves.

For example 'Six studies revealed that when evaluating psychologically distant targets, men showed greater attraction toward women who displayed more (vs. less) intelligence than themselves. In contrast, when targets were psychologically near, men showed less attraction toward women who outsmarted them'.[30]

These studies focused on personal relationships, but in the close working proximity of many organisations, it's easy to see how these behaviours might create unconscious bias in who a leader surrounds themselves with.

The second barrier is fear: the perceived threat of stepping out of line, being made to look foolish or doing things differently. If the status quo rewards fitting in; going with the majority or improving what already exists, then paradigm shifts won't happen. Supporting people to take calculated risks; to look at situations with fresh eyes and do things differently — even to fail — need to be key elements of leadership development.

Creating a Culture of Inclusive Leadership

We have the knowledge and the opportunity, today, to break out of the old paradigms, diversify leadership and hold leaders to account against measurable competences and behaviours.

This approach is based on the work of Ken Wilber and his 'whole systems' model.[31] It acknowledges the need for willingness to shift — in individuals and in the wider culture; the need to understand the behavioural shifts needed, and the structural readiness within which those shifts can be embedded.

---

[30](Psychological) Distance Makes the Heart Grow Fonder: Effects of Psychological Distance and Relative Intelligence on Men's Attraction to Women; Lora E. Park, Ariana F. Young, Paul W. Eastwick, *Personality & Social Psychology Bulletin* (November 2015) 41(11), 1459–1473; http://psp.sagepub.com/content/41/11/1459.
[31]A Brief History of Everything, Ken Wilber, 2nd ed., Shambhala, 2007.

The paradigm shift towards inclusive leadership is needed on four levels:

1. The individual, internal, attitudinal shift — away from the dominant paradigm and towards the paradigm of inclusivity
2. The individual, external, behavioural shift, where leaders model inclusive, high-performance, behaviours
3. The collective, internal, attitudinal shift — away from business as before and towards a willingness to include diverse strengths and competences
4. The collective, external, structural shifts — which groups, teams, organisations and societies can take together

At an individual level, the work of James Autry (The Servant Leader[32]) points to this link between the individual human condition and team building, morale building and bottom-line performance. Autry specifically states that his goal is to develop 'a leader who serves, rather than one who expects to be served' for higher performance to occur. This, in itself, may be a paradigm shift for some people.

Autry's work is echoed by the UK business leader John Timpson and his notion of 'Upside Down Management'.[33] He's quoted as putting the success of his own (family run, United Kingdom) business down to one factor: 'It's the people who serve our customers who run the business and everyone including me are just there to help'. Timpson is also concerned with developing the next generation and wrote a book to his son[34] on how to navigate the minefield of running a successful business.

This shift from leader as director/pacesetter to leader as enabler means that teams and individual team members are in a better position to access, and tap into, all the resources available to them. Just as 'knowledge' was previously seen as the source of power, so withholding or granting access to other resources is a way of exerting power. However, in today's knowledge economy, power is held at every level in the organisation. Better distribution resources, and empowering people to feel equipped and resourceful, will pay better dividends.

---

[32]The Servant Leader, James Autry, Prima Publishing 2001.
[33]Upside Down Management, John Timpson, Wiley & Sons, 2010.
[34]Dear James, John Timpson, Caspian Publishing, 2000.

These authors explore the values and underlying morality of better leadership, how to deliver it as an individual leader, and how to structure organisations such that these leadership methods translate into more successful organisations.

If the shift at an internal, attitudinal level, is to make the effort to remove ego and reduce the feeling of threat from those who are different from ourselves, the individual external action or behaviour is to develop others. This may mean

- Nominating the best people for a project
- Surrounding older leaders with younger, better-educated people
- Recognising and rewarding leaders for developing others

Developing others is a key cluster in the Schroder high-performing behaviours and includes the behaviours of giving feedback to stimulate better performance, coaching people and ensuring they have access to training and development — which creates greater consistency and more sustained excellence.

However, inclusive leadership is not the role of one individual. No single action or individual effort will shift this paradigm; it requires concerted effort by groups and a connected society. Using the Wilber model, the collective, internal shift required is to agree new models that value this generosity of individual leaders; applauds the success of others and creates a sense of group pride.

As well as basing leadership development on evidence-based competencies, those new models must include ways of changing the recruitment, retention and reward systems at a collective level, such that it is high performance and better leadership that is rewarded, objectively, rather than the subjective reward given to charisma or one-off interview performance.

This means individuals and organisations addressing their own, conscious and unconscious, biases. Examples include professional firms, such as Deloitte, hiding the name of applicants' universities, or an algorithm 'to consider "contextual" information alongside academic results.'[35] Or the BBC[36] introducing

---

[35]'Firm "hides" University when Recruits Apply'; http://www.bbc.co.uk/news/education-34384668.
[36]'Who, What, Why: What is name-blind recruitment?' http://www.bbc.co.uk/news/magazine-34636464 accessed 2nd May 2016.

'name-blind' recruitment to reduce unconscious bias against minority ethnic applicants.

In his book 'Drive', Dan Pink points to the shift in importance towards intrinsic motivation and away from extrinsic rewards (Pink, 2009). He points out the gap between what's known about motivating people and current practice in the workplace. By tapping into peoples' own intrinsic values and sense of purpose at a personal and individual level, leaders are better able to motivate their teams successfully. This means, however, shifting away from an assumption that what motivates one individual works for everyone; and, particularly, what motivates an individual leader may not motivate his or her team members.

As the Wilber model implies, however, individual shifts in attitude and behaviour alone are not enough. Inclusive leadership as a paradigm shift needs concerted effort, attitudinal and behaviour change at collective levels too. In his book Under New Management,[37] David Burkus explores a number of prevailing management behaviours that could and should be changed, as well as exploring the underlying need for these changes to achieve organisational improvements.

Two examples from this work go to the heart of leadership development: the need to hire as a team and the need to reduce 'managers' and increase 'leadership'. For the former, Burkus argues that successful performance is more of a team, than an individual, effort. And for this reason, it's better to hire as a team to get the best fit. The evidence is based on the comparison between hiring an individual star performer or 'lift-outs', where a whole team relocates to a new company. By extension, this organisational attitude to hiring requires a very different method and approach. Trial periods and team panels, as distinct from HR-specialist panels, are two examples.

Burkus describes the process of distributive leadership as pushing management functions down the line or 'firing the managers'. This requires a higher level of personal responsibility and accountability on everyone's part. It also requires greater transparency in roles and reduced hierarchy. Management mobility was also translated into physical mobility in one company, where desks need only two cords to be unplugged before they can be rolled to wherever they are needed.

---

[37]Under New Management, David Burkus, 2016, Houghton Mifflin Harcourt.

Again, at the heart of these shifts in organisational beha-viours are shifts in understanding as to what drives autonomy and intrinsic motivation. For people to perform well, they need the organisation to 'cede control over what to do and how to do it'. Burkus shows how these 'autonomy-related policies' delivered a 9% increase in total value-add per employee.

The good news, therefore, is that inclusive leadership works for everyone in the system. It delivers more for organisations at board level and adds value on the shop floor or the coal face, without overloading any one part of the system.

Developing Inclusive Leaders

There are leadership models which separate 'technical' from 'project' leadership, or 'people' from 'general' leadership. Our argument is that every team member should develop their leader-ship qualities and apply them to their role.

We argue for a behavioural model of leadership: a skill set that can be developed by anyone who is willing to learn and apply the skills. Additionally, leadership behaviours are based on a foundation of self-awareness; of willingness to shift attitudes and grow skills.

While traditional organisations separate out their communi-cation departments, or their learning and development, we argue that every manager or leader should develop high-level communi-cation skills, and be equipped to support team learning and development. An inclusive leader is an engaging leader: willing to engage not just in performance and delivery (the 'what'), but in system improvements (the 'how') and personal, and people, development (the 'who').

Context and position do matter in terms of leadership devel-opment. In order to make inclusive leadership achievable, we look at 'inclusive leaders' in four ways:

1. Leaders as people in responsible positions
2. Team leaders distributing leadership
3. Individuals contributing leadership
4. Leadership as engagement with society

Whilst we may agree with Burkus' proposal to 'Fire the Managers' in principle, many leaders are still people with responsi-ble positions. With high levels of responsibility and accountability:

to the public, to shareholders and to regulators. From a starting point of technical leadership, these people need to understand their governance responsibilities and demonstrate competence and trustworthiness.

Project management calls for a more distributive leadership approach: where technical experts within the project can be invited to contribute their expertise and encouraged to step forward with solutions and new possibilities. However, this form of leadership still relies on the person at the top 'distributing' or bestowing leadership on the team. It requires a high level of transparency and role definition — or at least a definition of what 'distributive leadership' means within the particular context. 'Choosing partnership over patriarchy' is how Peter Block[38] described it in his seminal work on 'Stewardship'.

When the approach to leadership is turned upside and team members are invited to contribute from a position of their strengths, talents and experience (as distinct from having leadership distributed down to them), a more enabling or inclusive model is achieved. This method requires an understanding of every team members contribution, and an expectation of visible leadership: that all team members will contribute, speak up and speak out.

Many organisations are already showing greater leadership in society through their corporate social responsibility (CSR) activities. Offering coaching, mentoring and educational support schemes are typical examples. Providing work experience, internships and work shadowing are all ways to raise young peoples' aspirations, as well as support people returning to work, or changing careers in midlife.

Beyond this application of leadership in specific contexts, there are a number of consistent and measurable ways to develop inclusive leadership.

Inclusive leader profiling draws on Harold Schroder's work on high-performance behaviours; and on diverse qualities, experience and strengths (e.g. Gallup[39]). Not relying on 'expert leaders', inclusive leadership is also emotionally intelligent. We can develop leaders who create better working environments through influence and relationships, not power.

---

[38]Stewardship by Peter Block, Berrett-Koehler Publishers, 1996, 2nd ed., 2013.
[39]Gallup Strengthsfinder Technical Report 2007.

THE COMPLEXITY OF DEVELOPING INCLUSIVE LEADERS

At its essence, leadership is a series of visible, measurable, behaviours, driven by invisible impulses: internal conscious and subconscious thoughts, attitudes and feelings, which can only be accessed through self-awareness, reflection and insight.

If we are to make inclusive leadership a reality, then both the visible behaviours and the invisible impulses need to be addressed and developed. The challenge is not to overcomplicate leadership development, nor oversimplify. As Einstein warns us 'Everything should be made as simple as possible, but not simpler'. Or, as Wilber's whole systems model demonstrates, the further from the central idea one goes, the more complicated things become. His work creates new terminologies to explain the ideas — which encompass galaxies and planets in one sphere, sensations and concepts in another. And, if it were written today, it would have to encompass interplanetary travel too.

The risk is that inclusive leadership development becomes so overcomplicated that people use the complexity as a reason not to take action. Rotter's locus of control model[40] is one example. The notion of an intrinsic or external locus of control is important. It points to the need to make conscious choices — whether about careers, business decisions, or responding in different situations. Understanding such a topic will certainly support a leader to understand themselves and others, yet a pithy report title sums up the situation in 2011[41] '28 Measures of Locus of Control'. The author intended to 'paint a picture of the complexity of the construct' and in this he succeeded.

Similarly, the list of unconscious biases found on Wikipedia[42] grows. Again, it's an important concept to understand; it supports better decision taking, directly improves inclusivity and reminds us that our memories sometimes play tricks. But learning a list of 72 (to date) biases is not the solution.

---

[40]Rotter, J. B. (1966). Generalized expectancies for internal versus external control of reinforcement. *Psychological Monographs: General & Applied* 80(1), 1–28.

[41]The Locus of Control Construct's Various Means of Measurement: A researcher's guide to some of the more commonly used Locus of Control scales; Copyright © 2011 by Russ Hill. ISBN 978-0-9833464-3-2, Will to Power Press, Beach Haven, NJ.

[42]https://en.wikipedia.org/wiki/List_of_cognitive_biases. Accessed on May 5, 2016.

Ironically, Wikipedia has its own biases, such as the entry for Hedy Lamarr.[43] Best known for her film work, she was also the inventor of radio guidance technology (the forerunner of WiFi and Bluetooth), but her entry was mainly about films. It took concerted effort for Wikipedia to recognise its own bias, and include the scientific contribution of her work and induction into the Inventors Hall of Fame in 2014.

The question in developmental terms is, what does support a person to become a more inclusive, engaging, leader? While we may live in a complex world, the solution to handling complexity is not always more complexity. Additionally, when we create an environment of inclusive leadership around us, we create more resources to tap into. More potential answers and possibilities; not just from people, but from the wider range of available internal and external, visible and invisible resources.

Conclusions

Inclusive leadership behaviours can be developed. They are not just the preserve of older people, the well educated or the wealthy. They can be made available through our digitally connected world. Thanks to the power of the internet we can hold live video conversations across the world; or tap into self-paced learning resources at a convenient place and time. This approach (known as 'blended learning') means that the cost of leadership development can fall dramatically, and puts it within the reach of everyone.

If there's a model for an inclusive leader it's the combination of intellectual intelligence, emotional and management intelligence. Someone willing to switch attitudes away from 20th century leadership behaviours to embrace inclusivity. Willing to explore their own attitudes and feelings, they will appreciate the value of others' strengths, motivations, values and contributions. Their communication styles will orient towards listening rather than just talking and asking rather than just telling. They will judge, and be judged, on observed high-performing behaviours; rather than 'flavour of the month' leadership fads. They will take employee engagement seriously and turn plans into actions, to benefit both team spirit and the bottom line.

---

[43]https://en.wikipedia.org/wiki/Hedy_Lamarr accessed 24/7/16

Whilst some people may have natural strengths amongst this skill set, these are developable skills. And today's technologies make them more affordable for organisations who see the need to develop their inclusive leaders.

This is not a proposal for a 'one size fits all' model of leadership. Rather for a process of leadership development that starts with the organisation's needs, and assumes that, within it, already exist many untapped resources. Tapping into these resources requires four key steps:

1. Define the leadership need — through consultation and research
2. Discover the existing talent — regardless of age, gender or culture
3. Develop people to meet the need
4. Deploy them, while supporting them to deliver on their leadership potential

Inclusive leadership is not just a rationale for bringing more women into the boardroom, opening up to a more culturally diverse leadership team or supporting young people to develop their talent. It's not just about improved performance or better results. It's a rational step with an ethical and moral base. It makes sense to deploy and develop the most talented people in the team, regardless of their culture, gender or age.

References

Adams, S. (2012). Why Promoting From Within Usually Beats Hiring From Outside (Report). Forbes.

Autry, J. (2001). *The servant leader*. New York, NY: Prima Publishing.

Bidwell, M. (2011, September). Paying more to get less: The effects of external hiring versus internal mobility. *Administrative Science Quarterly*, 56(3), 369–407, University of Pennsylvania.

Block, P. (1996). *Stewardship: Choosing service over self-interest*. San Francisco, CA: Berrett-Koehler Publishers.

Burkus, D. (2016). *Under new management*. Boston: Houghton Mifflin Harcourt.

Desvaux, G., Devillard-Hoellinger, S., & Baumgarten, P. (2007). *Women matter: Gender diversity, a corporate performance driver*, Report, McKinsey & Company.

Dulewicz, V., & Higgs, M. (2000). Emotional intelligence — A review and evaluation study. *Journal of Managerial Psychology*, 15(4), 341–372.

Figuerola, F. (9 July 2008). Quoted in 'Knowledge@Wharton'.

Gardner, H. (1983). *Frames of mind: The theory of multiple intelligences.* New York, NY: Perseus Books.

Goleman, D. (1995). *Emotional intelligence.* New York, NY: Bloomsbury.

Goleman, D., Boyatzis, R., & McKee, A. (2002). *Primal leadership.* New York, NY: Little, Brown.

Good for business: Making full use of the nation's human capital: A fact-finding report of the Federal Glass Ceiling Commission, [Washington, DC], 1995, United States Government Printing Office.

Groysberg, B. (2010). *Chasing stars: The myth of talent and the portability of performance.* Princeton, NJ: Princeton University Press.

Hill, R. (2011). *The locus of control construct's various means of measurement: A researcher's guide to some of the more commonly used locus of control scales.* Beach Haven, NJ: Will to Power Press.

Joy, L., Carter, N. M., Wagener, H. M., & Narayanan, S. (2007). The Bottom Line: Corporate Performance and Women's Representation on Boards. *Catalyst, 3*, 1.

Kline, R. (2014). *The "snowy white peaks" of the NHS.* London: Middlesex University Research Repository.

Lagerberg, F. (September 2015). The Value of Diversity (Report). Grant Thornton.

Park, L. E., Young, A. F., & Eastwick, P. W. (November 2015). (Psychological) Distance makes the heart grow fonder: Effects of psychological distance and relative intelligence on men's attraction to women. *Personality and Social Psychology Bulletin, 41*(11), 1459–1473.

Pink, H. M. (2009). Drive: The surprising truth about what motivates us. New York: Riverhead Books.

Rotter, J. B. (1966). Generalized expectancies for internal versus external control of reinforcement. *Psychological Monographs: General & Applied, 80*(1), 1–28.

Schroder, H. M. (1989). *Managerial competence: The key to excellence.* Iowa. IM: Kendall/Hunt Publishing Company.

Timpson, J. (2000). *Dear James.* London: Caspian Publishing.

Timpson, J. (2010). *Upside down management.* Oxford: Wiley & Sons.

Tosi, H. L., Misangyi, V. F., Fanellid, A., Waldmane, D. A., & Yammarino, F. J. (2004). CEO charisma, compensation, and firm performance. *The Leadership Quarterly, 15*, 405–420. Elsevier.

Wilber, K. (2007). *A brief history of everything.* Colorado: Shambhala.

PART 4
Inclusiveness and Diversity in Higher Education

Introduction

For many, higher education institutions today represent a beacon of hope for a world desperately in need of deep change regarding inclusiveness. They have the potential to be that special place where faculty, students, and the community in general can meet to reflect and dialogue about both the current, pressing issues of the world and the deeper, more philosophical, fundamental questions, and to do so with respect and openness to each other's ideas. Furthermore, higher education institutions have proven to be an invaluable tool for social mobility and equity in the overall society.

Although some steps have been taken to improve inclusiveness in this field, much remains to be done, particularly because the challenge is multi-faceted. Inclusiveness in higher education not only refers to what happens once a person is inside the institution but also to what happens before, helping potential students and candidates make the right choices, and to what happens after graduation, assisting students to succeed in their chosen career.

Unfortunately, in the past few years higher education institutions have been shocked by a series of scandals, ranging from admissions favoritism to widespread racism and incidents of sexual assault. To make matters worse, quite often institutions have been too slow to change, with some even going into full-fledged denial. Some of these cases gained notoriety and caused irate reactions from students and the general society, which ended with very high-ranking officials, including presidents and deans losing their jobs.

After the dust settles, no magical solution appears on the horizon, but one thing remains clear: higher education institutions still have a long way to go toward inclusiveness.

The chapters in this section explore some very enlightening examples of institutions embracing the challenge of fostering inclusiveness, in the most creative ways. In each chapter, readers will experience the transformational impact that inclusive leadership has over all of the stakeholders of such institutions. From this perspective, higher education institutions could be taken as an example of what an inclusive society should look like: a place where different people and different ideas can meet, instead of fight; a place where everyone is welcome; and a place where particular care is put to ensure that all the voices are heard.

15 Neighbors, Allies, and Partners in Inclusion: An HBCU and an SEC Land Grant Institution

Barbara A. Baker and Joyce de Vries

Keywords: Relational leadership; bottom-up collaboration; diversity; equity; inclusion

Background

Academic institutions tend to be large, hierarchical behemoths in which change sometimes occurs excruciatingly slowly. It often takes a crisis or a seismic event to affect a quick response in an academic setting. Such a seismic event occurred at the end of 2015 at the University of Missouri, when a graduate student, Jonathan Butler, stopped eating, demanding that the president of the university system, Tim Wolfe, step down because he and other school leaders had failed to act in dealing with racism on the overwhelmingly white Columbia campus. University leaders at Missouri were seemingly unmoved by an individual student's hunger strike, but when several campus organizations including the football team joined Butler in protest and threatened not to play in an upcoming game, the behemoth moved quickly.

The result was that both the president and the chancellor of the university, R. Bowen Loftin, stepped down. In his resignation speech, Loftin asked that the university community listen to each other's problems and "stop intimidating each other." He said that this was not "the way change should come about. Change comes from listening, learning, caring, and conversation" (McLaughlin, 2015). Thus began a watershed moment when universities all over the United States suddenly noticed that swift change can be instigated by members of an academic community who are not at the top of the organizational hierarchy, perhaps even drawing into question the power of the hierarchy itself. The time for the business-as-usual approach to issues of diversity, equity, and inclusion abruptly ended on college campuses across the country.

About 2 years before the cases in Missouri and elsewhere led to many universities' overtly articulating their commitment to diversity, equity, and inclusion, advanced career women faculty members at Auburn and Tuskegee Universities had already begun the process of listening, learning, caring conversations about the palpable lack of inclusion that we had all experienced in our careers within two separate and different work environments in rural Alabama. Auburn University is a predominately white land grant university and member of the Southeastern Conference primarily recognized for its football program; Tuskegee University is a renowned historically black college founded by Booker T. Washington some 20 miles from Auburn. A long and storied history of the muddy relationship between these two institutions had precluded much lasting cooperation between them, even though the university communities share members such as professors and faculty spouses who had been educated or worked at both institutions.

The Tuskegee Auburn Women's Leadership Alliance

The Tuskegee Auburn Women's Leadership Alliance (TAWLA) began humbly among a few women faculty members who casually convened to talk about shared experiences. Most of us had had significant experiences on both campuses; so we already knew that the situations on our campuses were not unalike. We knew that neither university had ever had a woman president and had almost no women leaders in their upper administrations nor on their boards of trustees. (To be fair, a woman briefly served as interim president of Tuskegee University, but the record tellingly fails to acknowledge her term.) Both universities also have male provosts, and men are overrepresented on both boards of trustees. Auburn University's board is comprised of fourteen members, two of whom are women, and Tuskegee's board includes four women among nineteen members. We knew that the satisfaction, retention, and advancement rates among women at both universities were abysmal, and we did not kid ourselves about the causal relationship between these two points: few women leaders and abysmal advancement rates for women. We recognized and spoke freely about the double-edged irony of a history of exclusion in which the leadership of the universities has neither reflected our images, nor had the mostly male leadership understood or seriously considered the circumstances of women, even when they purportedly were setting out to address issues of difference, fairness, and belonging.

We knew well the intricacies and complexities of the challenges we face in the historical, cultural, and traditionally conservative southern environment in which we operate. We knew from decades of experience that the overused and worn out rhetoric of diversity, equity, and inclusion had not included us in any realistic and lasting ways. We knew that the chances of any of us, whether white women at a historically black university, or black women at a majority white university, or simply, women at either Alabama university, would ever experience the comfort of inclusion that often opens the pathway to the top of the hierarchy.

We agreed that the time for business-as-usual approaches had long passed and that it was in our best interests to make the time to find realistic ways to come together and create tangible and lasting progress towards inclusivity. We agreed that we would need a long-term plan that would strike at the core of the problem, which we defined as a lack of belonging within the highest echelons of academic leadership. To honestly address our sense of exclusion from the decision-making spheres of our universities, we would need to spend time together relentlessly listening, caring, and conversing. Thoughtful listening seemed the only possible way to disentangle the perplexing mystery of the career-life stalemate in which we found ourselves collectively bound.

The Relational Leadership Model

None of the members of our alliance had been granted the type of positional authority within our institutions that lends itself to opportunities to affect policy and thereby permanently change the culture that had consistently closed to women the pathways to the top of the academic hierarchy. We subscribed, instead, to the idea that we could address the issue of our own inclusion through our relationships with each other. Thus, we entered into a relational leadership process, setting as our purpose the goal of improving the academic climates of our institutions so that they might become more inclusive and equitable, particularly for women.

According to Komives, Lucas, and McMahon (2009), the relational leadership model focuses on five primary components, all of which apply to the work of the TAWLA. The relational approach "to leadership is purposeful and builds commitment toward positive purposes that are inclusive of people and diverse points of view, empowers those involved, is ethical, and recognizes that all four of these elements are accomplished by being process-oriented" (p. 74). The relational leadership model is aspirational in that it does not describe the way leadership has been practiced in the past, but rather looks to shared purpose among group members in order to drive an organization forward.

Our alliance illustrates the relational leadership model in its emphasis on inclusion, the achievement of which, inside both academic institutions, is our main purpose. Just as those at the University of Missouri who had shown that change can be precipitated outside of the traditional hierarchy of authority, we intended to call into question the power of traditional hierarchical thinking and embrace our circumstances as non-positional leaders. In doing so, we accepted our shared feelings of exclusion from positional authority as a means to our desired outcome of eventual full inclusion in a different kind of academic environment which we intended to co-create through an ongoing process.

The relationships among the members of TAWLA would be central to the process and fundamental in achieving our purpose. As women so often do, we agreed to be co-creators of our organizational structure by giving equal voice to each member of the alliance. The model that we followed is highly feminine in the way that it values the process of our co-creation over any end product (e.g., Aries, 1977; Kahn & Gaeddert, 1985; Rosener, 1990; Sweeney & McFarlin, 1993). While we value our purpose — a sense of belonging in the highest echelons of academic leadership — we also value the process through which we intend to achieve it. As Komives *et al.* (2009) argue, "How that purpose is achieved (the process) is just as important as the outcome" (p. 75).

The network that our relationships formed also reflects a feminized conceptualization of the process of inclusion. Komives *et al.* (2009) define "inclusion" as "thinking of networks and webs of connection instead of seeing issues and problems as isolated" (p. 86). Our problems were not isolated incidents; rather they were historic and institutionalized trajectories that seemed immutable. We countered that immutability with positivity and civility embodied in communication strategies that facilitated the inclusion of each other in our interactions.

Just as "Listening with empathy and communicating with civility are communication skills that facilitate the inclusion of others" (Komives *et al.* 2009, p. 86), they are also typically considered assets of a feminized leadership style. Marie C. Wilson argues in *Closing the Leadership Gap: Add Women, Change Everything* (2007), for instance, that "a tendency toward greater inclusiveness, empathy, communication up and down hierarchies" is at the core of what women bring to leadership (p. 6). In co-creating a process of inclusion, we would have to listen empathetically in a fashion that dissipated the perception of any hierarchical authority among us. If our alliance was to succeed in leading others towards inclusion, it would be through relationships built on communication.

As we began carefully listening to each other, we were forced to recognize our complicity in our situations of powerlessness and immobility. We agreed that we needed to look inward instead of only casting blame outward. Had we taken on too many responsibilities? Had we failed to say "no" when forced into traditional (and often feminine) roles that impeded our career trajectories, for example? Research shows that "Women are asked to engage in more service to their departments, universities, and professions than their male colleagues," and that women who choose to say no "pay a penalty in terms of likeability" (Chenoweth et al., 2016). That penalty further hinders achievement of decision-making and policy-setting authority in academe. Persons of color, who are typically underrepresented in academic institution, often have even more demands made on their time than their counterparts in terms of service.

None of the members of our alliance thought that serving on one more committee or in another organization would improve our chances of achieving inclusion or a sense of belonging in the highest echelons of decision-making authority within our institutions. We decided that we could not let our newly formed alliance become yet another time-draining duty that would distract us from our research and teaching and thrust us further into the back of the line. We would need to establish a vision and mission focused on collectively moving our academic careers forward.

Socialized Vision, Motivating Mission

The relational leadership model offers a definition of vision building that acknowledges that "each person must be involved in the process of building a vision with others" (Komives *et al.* 2009, p. 81). According to Komives *et al.* (2009), a socialized vision is a sustainable vision because it is co-created among committed group members. Members of the TAWLA shared a strong commitment to the organization because we found ourselves collectively bound in career paralysis that results from institutional and personal impediments such as time constraints, heavy teaching loads, work-family obligations, and a host of related obstacles. Honest discussions of our individual inabilities to circumvent systems historically embedded in our institutions motivated us to co-create "a realistic, credible," and "attractive future" (p. 81), and that future needed to embody the ongoing momentum of continuous co-creation. We formulated a simple, twofold vision reflecting the process of shared momentum: "Forward Together."

With that vision, we set out to realize a series of concrete initiatives that would lead one to the other, attracting more members to the vision as we progressed. The ethical standard for each initiative would be measured by its capacity to provide a sense of self-esteem and affirmation for the members of our alliance, something that our traditional university settings had failed to provide us. According to Komives *et al.* (2009), "To be motivating, a vision must be a source of self-esteem and common purpose" (p. 82). The initiatives of our alliance should perpetuate a sense of fairness and belonging among us that would stand in contrast to the entrenched sense of exclusion from the decision-making arenas we had all experienced.

Next we co-created a realistic mission to match our socialized vision. Our motivating mission is "to build on work already underway, combine efforts, share resources, talents, and strengths to bring about the strongest outcome for women in our area, Tuskegee, Auburn, and Macon and Lee counties." We intended to perpetuate continuing motivation by focusing on the work each one of us is required to do and brainstorming ways that we might be able to assist each other in fulfilling ongoing professional obligations. This helped us commit to regular meetings and enticed us to invite others to join us. We began expanding, reaching out to graduate students and former students who had experiences at both universities and to men and women at all ranks within our organizations. While the alliance was created specifically to advance women toward equality in leadership, well-attended, lively meetings quickly revealed a shared legacy of exclusion and homogeneity at both institutions that reaches beyond issues of gender into a myriad of complexities historically entangled and in paralysis.

Making Empowering Meaning

As our alliance matured, we realized that a shared experience of exclusion from decision-making arenas frequently hampers academic output and further hinders advancement within academe. To transform our academic cultures into inviting environments in which all stakeholders can perform, we identified together key concepts about which we could speak from experience: professional balance, self-awareness, confrontation with injustice, micro-aggressions, career ladder challenges, historical perspectives, engagement with community, sense of obligation and responsibility, leadership and path clearing for others, and confidence issues, among many others.

Most importantly, we recognized the value of discussing our personal experiences with these topics. Although we had all been professionally trained to mute or to disregard the personal in our academic work, we acknowledged that speaking with authority from our personal experiences held significant potential in helping us formulate a different kind of academic content, and that a personally-infused experiential tack towards our respective discipline content might actually move the needle in terms of diversity, equity, and inclusion within our work situations, not just for us personally, but especially for the next generations of academics who will serve our respective institutions.

To facilitate discussions that would lead us towards this new kind of content — experientially infused discipline content — we turned to an article published by a group of African American women counselor educators called "Having Our Say: African American Women, Diversity, and Counseling" (2005). In the meetings of the TAWLA, we distributed points from the article and discussed how what these counselor educators described resonated with our own experiences and institutions.

Taking as a beginning premise the possibility that indicators of racial and gender discrimination can be strikingly similar, we asked each other, for example, the following questions about the relationship between the professional and the personal: Are we expected to be a superwoman — an ever-nurturing role model? Do those expectations conflict with the fortitude, assertiveness, and frankness required for success in academe? Is there a relationship between these competing challenges and our health and home life? Do we feel that we are pitted in competition for resources against those who should be closest to us? Do we experience incongruence between policies and actions related to our identity? (Bryant et al. p. 315–317).

By asking each other these questions, we entered into a meaning-making experience. Our conversations flourished as we became wrapped in liberating discussions about the truth of our situations. Whether we were African American or non-African American, female or male, student or staff, as long as we felt our difference from those who hold positional authority in our academic environments or we had experienced a lack of belonging in decision-making arenas, we found meaning through freely discussing the points that Bryant et al. had named in "Having Our Say" (2005). Meaning making is a key to the relational leadership model which relies on "truly understanding" shared experience. According to Komives *et al.* (2009), "the relational empathy skill of trying to see things from the perspective of another" validates that meaning (p. 108-109). In our example, we built meaning from our experiences of a myriad of historic and cultural complexities, all bound up with the most personal facets of the humanness we bring to our academic careers, that is, the genders and races with which we identify.

With the personal aspects of our careers in mind, we set out to accomplish the sense of congruence between our work and ourselves that the authors of "Having Our Say" (2005) suggest we might find by taking ownership of personal beliefs, values, attitudes, and feelings that help us make sense of the world (Bryant et al. p. 317). Bryant et al. suggest that we might fulfill the mandates of tenure and promotion guidelines, for example, by finding likeminded people with whom to collaborate, and that we should search out relevant and publishable research that mitigates alienation and devaluation that we so often feel (p. 318).

We embraced the idea of entering a collaborative process that could lead to passionate publishing about experientially infused discipline content. Put another way, we could rely on one another as resources to create areas of research that we are passionate about because they resonate with the academic lives that we are living. We agreed that the best way to fulfill our mission of combining efforts, sharing resources, talents, and strengths to bring about the strongest outcome for ourselves and future generations of academics was to apply our new found liberation within the professional arenas in which we are regularly measured and evaluated. The process of co-creation led us to a concrete initiative that provided pragmatic action towards a realistic future that we all desired.

The bottom-up collaboration in which we participated generated an idea for a symposium, and that symposium would contribute to our ongoing conversation at the same time it presented the opportunity to fulfill the mandates of our work that are prescribed within the current hierarchical order. We gave ourselves the gift of professional presentations about topics that are personal and meaningful at the same time they are useful to the institutions we serve. We created a space to value our work, and to present on topics that we wanted to share, but that are often ignored and undervalued in academe.

We distributed widely the following call for papers for the symposium which was held February, 2016 on the campus of Auburn University. Call for papers: "The papers in the Tuskegee Auburn Women's Leadership Alliance project will explore voices from the margins of academe, particularly the situation of women, both past and present, within higher education and the professions, and especially within the university and community settings of Tuskegee and Auburn. Through this main thread we will address larger issues such as fostering multicultural competence, combatting racism and sexism, and mentoring the next generation."

Many of the members of our alliance presented papers at the symposium, and we also attracted many other members of our academic communities to our project. Most significantly, the project continues to expand as more people awaken to its potential. The papers that we have gathered so far are organized thematically into the following sections: health and the workplace, international and transnational implications, literary resonance, and historical context.

Forward Together: Beyond the Rhetoric

The process of relational leadership that we are engaged in is intended to move us beyond the rhetoric of diversity, equity, and inclusion to tangible objectives that embody our shared values and purpose. The symposium that the TAWLA successfully planned and executed brought the voices of an exceptionally inclusive group of women, men, students, and staff together to apply our personal stories to the content of our diverse disciplines. In speaking together in a bottom-up collaborative forum, we claimed agency over our contributions to our disciplines in a manner that grants each of us the kind of self-esteem that we seek in our academic careers.

Plans are underway to revise and edit the conversations that made up our symposium into a cogent narrative about the work of an inclusive and diverse group of scholars, students, and staff, who, while from different universities, share experiences, particularly experiences related to our sense of exclusion. We envision this narrative as the core of a collaborative book tentatively called *Outside In: Voices from the Margins*. The intention of the book is to open a space for passionate publishing that creates congruence between the often excluded academic practitioner and her professional mission, thereby demonstrating forward momentum toward inclusivity at all levels, forging the possibility for truly inclusive leadership.

Beyond our book project, we have been able to provide support for one another by embracing our collective agency through individual efforts on the behalf of one another. For example, we have begun purposefully recommending and nominating one another for important service assignments rather than simply accepting university imposed decisions about what service is appropriate for us.

Furthermore, we are committed to intentional support of one another in terms of awards and prestigious appointments.

Finally, when the TAWLA gathers, we see inclusion at work. Rather than gathering to discuss what a diverse and inclusive body of committed academics might accomplish, we actualized the realities of that promise. We are relational leaders moving forward towards self-defined purpose.

We remain committed to the idea that we will achieve a sense of belonging within the larger academic environments of which we are a part when we see ourselves reflected in the leadership of our academic institutions. Similarly, when we see our images reflected in leadership, the sense of difference among all of us will begin to dissipate. Our passionate publishing project, support of one another, and future plans are only the beginning of pragmatic actions that the TAWLA will take to build bottom-up collaboration among seemingly unlikely partners in inclusion.

References

Aries, E. (1977). Male-female interpersonal styles in all male, all female, and mixed groups. In A. Sargent (Ed.), *Beyond sex roles*. New York, NY: West.

Bryant, R. M., Coker, A. D., Durodoye, B. A., & McCollum, V. J. (2005). Having our say: African American women, diversity, and counseling. *Journal of Counseling and Development: JCD, 83*(3), 313–319.

Chenoweth, E., Fortna, P., Mitchell, S., Savun, B., Weeks, J., & Cunningham, K. (April, 2016). How to get tenure (if you're a woman). *Foreign Policy*. Retrieved from https://foreignpolicy.com/2016/04/19/how-to-get-tenure-if-youre-a-woman-academia-stephen-walt/. Accessed on June 27, 2017.

Kahn, A. S., & Gaeddert, W. P. (1985). From theories of equity to theories of justice: The consequences of studying women. In V. E. O'Leary, R. K. Unger, & B. S. Wallston (Eds.), *Women, gender, and social psychology*. Hillsdale, NJ: Erlbaum.

Komives, S. R., Lucas, N., & McMahon, T. R. (2009). *Exploring leadership: For college students who want to make a difference*. Hoboken, NJ: John Wiley & Sons.

McLaughlin, E. C. (November, 2015). University of Missouri president and chancellor step down amid race row. CNN. Retrieved from http://www.cnn.com/2015/11/09/us/missouri-football-players-protest-president-resigns/.

Rosener, J. (1990). How women lead. *Harvard Business Review, 68*(6), 119–125.

Sweeney, P. D., & McFarlin, D. B. (1993). Workers' evaluations of the "Ends" and the "Means": An examination of four models of distributive and procedural justice. *Organizational Behavior and Human Decision Processes, 55*(1), 23–40. doi:10.1006/obhd.1993.1022.

Wilson, M. C. (2007). *Closing the leadership gap: Add women, change everything*. (2nd ed.) New York, NY: Penguin.

16

From Institutional Diversity and Inclusion to Societal Equity and Justice: Higher Education as a Leadership Training Ground for the Public Good

Brighid Dwyer and Ralph A. Gigliotti

Keywords: Intergroup dialogue; leadership; diversity; student protest; crisis; higher education

Institutions of higher education are often described as distinct from the "real world," despite their pertinence in preparing students for life after graduation. In many ways, universities serve as microcosms of the larger society, providing a living laboratory for team building, leadership, dialogue, and critical thinking. Situated in a fractured world that faces ongoing and systemic dilemmas of inequality and injustice, colleges occupy an important role in advancing the public good across local, national, and international contexts (Savior & Cooper, 2015).

In reaction to recent student protests across the globe, the varied responses from leaders in higher education have either furthered or damaged inclusivity efforts on college and university campuses. These responses have, in large part, been isomorphic and informed by environmental pressures that encourage similar institutional responses (DiMaggio & Powell, 1983). Yet we believe this normative isometric pattern can be interrupted by leaders being proactive, rather than reactive, to campus diversity and inclusion efforts, developing allies, and utilizing dialogue as a thoughtful and intentional tool when conflict arises (Gurin, Nagda, & Zúñiga, 2013; Kendall, 2003).

Overview of Contemporary Campus Protests

Until recently, the US academy has, in large part, retreated to the "ivory tower" and abandoned its activist history — a history rooted in protests against segregation, the Vietnam War, affirmative action policies, and a wide array of global and domestic injustices (Thelin, 2011). There has also been a dramatic increase in the quantity and scope of protests across colleges and universities that have gained national and international attention. Some recent examples include race-related protests at the University of Missouri, University of North Carolina, Chapel Hill, Emory University, Yale University, Ithaca College, Amherst College, various campuses at the University of California, and elsewhere. In addition to these domestic cases, the scope of international student protests in recent years is fairly extensive, including those student-led protests in China, Spain, South Africa, Nigeria, and India. The reasons for these protests are widespread; yet in all instances, college and university students demonstrated a willingness to stand up for issues of collective concern.

The responses to these protests are critical incidents in the life of the college or university dealing with the protest. In many cases, protestors seek to radically change the systems of oppression and injustice within their respective organization, and society more broadly. These ongoing situations provide valuable cases for better understanding the issues impacting various stakeholders, particularly those most marginalized within the institution. Additionally, in response to the protests, the various cases point to the critical role of dialogue and inclusive leadership in order to both strengthen the student experience and collectively work toward the advancement of the common good.

This apparent resurgence of domestic and international student activism is consistent with the findings of the annual Cooperative Institutional Research Program survey of first year students conducted by UCLA's Higher Education Research Institute. According to the survey results, interest in political and civic engagement has reached the highest levels since the study began 50 years ago. Specifically, nearly 1 in 10 incoming first year students expect to participate in student protests while in college (Higher Education Research Institute, 2016). In an attempt to form and transform organizations and societies around principles of inclusive leadership, these protests have the potential to build upon the talking, writing, and thinking about diversity, which have become more common in contemporary higher education (Hurtado, Alvarado, & Guillermo-Wann, 2015; Jayakumar, 2015; Williams, 2013). Sustainable and systemic change is necessary and only occurs as a by-product of inclusive practices that are reflective of strategic diversity leadership (Williams, 2013).

Campus protests point to a variety of issues associated with institutional diversity and equity. Johnson (2015) acknowledges the following characteristics of the protests:

> Contemporary student protest has arisen in response to myriad issues, both local and national, but three main topics stand out: racial discrimination, sexual assault and harassment, and rising tuition and student debt. In each case, longstanding grievances of traditionally underrepresented students have been brought to a crisis (para. 10).

These points of crisis are also critical opportunities for strategic diversity leadership, as will be discussed below.

In his writing on diversity strategic planning, Williams (2013) emphasizes that diversity planning often occurs as the result of a crisis. As such, diversity planning is often reactive and limited in that the response primarily addresses the immediate needs, and it does not lay out a proactive approach for the future. A thoughtfully crafted, proactive, and strategic approach to diversity planning can help to prevent future crises (Williams, 2013) and also better address the immediate concerns that affect key internal and external stakeholders. Specifically, developing a deliberate and thoughtful response and adopting strategic measures can mitigate the future alienation of minoritized groups.

The surge in student activism, coupled with the need for more intentional responses, extends beyond US institutions of higher education. An understanding of student protests across an international context is instructive for higher education leaders both within and beyond the United States. This exploration of student protests and the various responses by senior leaders to these protests points to the importance of inclusive leadership practices by higher education leaders. The broader public good, as illustrated by a society of tolerance and inclusivity, very much hinges upon the use of effective civil strategies by students in protesting issues on their campus and the use of effective leadership responses to these student concerns.

Isomorphism: Peer Learning Across Institutions

Institutions respond in similar ways because they are influenced by one another. This phenomena, institutional isomorphism, or institutionalism (DiMaggio & Powell, 1983), is, in essence, peer pressure on an institutional level. Mimetic isomorphism suggests that environmental pressure plays an active role in encouraging institutions to copy peer and aspirant institutions. In the case of student protests, higher education leaders look to one another to see how others respond. These responses provide examples for how one's own institution might respond and then create and reinforce a climate of reactivity, deniability, and in a select few cases, ownership and dialogue. By demonstrating inclusive leadership practices, leaders have an opportunity to step outside of the isomorphic pressures and assess situations in ways that allow for meaningful and equitable decision-making. The notion of isomorphism could be advantageous or beneficial if organizations and their leaders mimic behaviors of inclusivity and compassion.

According to Carmeli, Reiter-Palmon, and Ziv (2010), "inclusive leadership is at the core of relational leadership and focuses on whether followers feel that leaders are available to them, as well as whether the leader listens and is paying attention to the follower needs" (p. 254). These inclusive leaders demonstrate the integrity to do what is just and right, and these leaders are also the ones who demonstrate a willingness to change stagnant institutions and implement different isomorphic pressures that have the potential to radically change the expected institutional norms, such that diversity and inclusion become normatively institutionalized and professionalized within educational settings and beyond (Williams & Wade-Golden, 2013). As such, the learning that occurs across institutions may lead to a cascading set of institutional leadership decisions that promote diversity and inclusion across colleges and universities.

A Summary of Recent Incidents at the University of Missouri

Institutional leaders have responded to the aforementioned student protests in a variety of ways, ranging from avoidance and aversion to embracement and encouragement. One recent case that has attracted widespread public attention involves the University of Missouri.[1] In the fall of 2015, the group, Concerned Student 1950, at University of Missouri staged a series of protests to demonstrate their frustration with the University's inattention to serve the needs of underrepresented students, specifically, low-income and black students. The protests included blocking the president's car during the homecoming parade, a hunger strike by a graduate student, and a boycott by the football team. In addition, there were threats of a campuswide faculty walkout and the executive cabinet of the Missouri Student Association demanded President Wolfe resign. This frustration of feeling ignored, particularly related to racial incidents, was compounded by the widely publicized shooting of an unarmed black teenager, Michael Brown, about 120 miles away in Ferguson, Missouri.

Despite the subsequent implementation of diversity and inclusion training, an issued statement from Chancellor Loftin deploring "recent incidents of bias and discrimination," and a formal

---

[1]For a more detailed description of the historical events that preceded the protests at the University of Missouri, see Pearson (2015), Landsbaum and Weber (2015), and Woodhouse (2015).

apology from Wolfe acknowledging, "racism does exist at our university and it is unacceptable," a response that was perceived to be inadequate by many across the institution. Wolfe announced his resignation in November, 2015, followed by the decision of Loftin to step down at the end of the year.

The antecedent conditions and historical context of racial hostility at the University of Missouri are important to consider in this particular case (Fortunato, Gigliotti, & Ruben, 2017). Criticism of this magnitude does not manifest overnight, but rather builds over time until the pressure explodes. The perceived inability of the university administration to identify the connections between local racial issues with the death of Michael Brown, the nationwide outcry of the threat of death and dehumanization of black bodies, and campus racial tensions at the University of Missouri, as reported on by numerous news outlets, led to the escalation of the issues on campus.

Inclusive leadership certainly involves the incorporation of diverse and wide-ranging social identities into the decision-making process, but it also requires reaching beyond the immediate community. As Nembhard and Edmondson (2006) state, "leader inclusiveness captures attempts by leaders to include others in discussions and decisions in which their voices and perspectives might otherwise be absent" (p. 947). Colleges and universities are a societal microcosm and exist to create knowledge from society and for society. It is this nexus of university and societal events that collectively transforms communities and creates a sense of the public good. When this nexus is forgotten or broken, societies remain stagnant or are transformed in negative ways.

The Mizzou case is illustrative of the damage that can occur due to failures in inclusive leadership. Maintaining strong relationships with the many stakeholders who have an interest in the organization, particularly during times of organizational crisis, is crucial (Fortunato et al., 2017; Gigliotti & Fortunato, 2017). In this case, the stakeholders who were being ignored were students of color. Historically, students and particularly students of color have been underestimated and not fully considered stakeholders. Utilizing an inclusive and strategic diversity leadership frame positions all students, and particularly underrepresented students, as valuable members of the campus community who are listened to and consulted as agents of change and necessary to the stability of the university. Moreover, strategic diversity leadership requires that leaders navigate the complex and rugged terrain of racial tensions on college and university campuses in ways that are truly inclusive. By modeling practices of inclusive leadership, college and university leaders can help to advance institutions in pursuit of a collective good — one that is inclusive of a multitude of perspectives, open to dialogue, and oriented toward the advancement of all people, in particular, those who have historically been underserved.

Strategic Diversity Leadership

Recognizing that many recent student protests are in response to institutional and environmental issues of diversity and inclusion, the effectiveness of leaders in higher education will reflect one's ability to engage in what Williams (2013) calls strategic diversity leadership. Over the past decade, inclusive and strategic diversity leadership have begun to receive long overdue attention by both scholars and practitioners. Research has generated new conversations about the need for more diverse and inclusive campuses (Dwyer, 2012; Smith, 2015; Solorzano, Ceja, & Yosso, 2000). This research has expanded beyond the concepts of diversity and campus racial climate, often focusing more specifically on the ways in which the deliberate use of dialogue and dialogue programs can develop inclusive leadership practices among students. Proactive campus leaders have advocated for and implemented more inclusive diversity practices across institutions, including greater intentionality around student, staff, and faculty recruitment and retention (Moody, 2012; Smith, 2015), the adoption of intensive interpersonal work, such as the growth of campus-wide intergroup dialogue programs (Dessel & Rogge, 2008), and the increased attention and focus on the professionalization of institutional diversity, including the encouragement of campus members to join professional organizations that focus on enhancing diversity competencies (Williams & Wade-Golden, 2013). As the responses to various student protests indicate, strategic diversity leadership in higher education remains of timely importance.

The events at the University of Missouri highlight the need for inclusive leadership to guide one's response to the surge of student activism on college and university campuses. These very real concerns on university campuses deserve careful, authentic, and honest responses from leaders in higher education. Dillon and Bourke (2016), for example, present the following six traits of inclusive leadership, all of which seem useful for effectively responding to student protests and campus unrest: commitment, courage, cognizance of bias, curiosity, cultural intelligence, and collaboration. Within each of these six areas, the authors identify 15 elements associated with inclusive leadership, including a commitment to personal values, humility, empowerment, and perspective-taking.

Beyond the ineffective response at Missouri, there are a number of effective responses from senior higher education administrators from which we can all learn. Based on the reporting that has followed the incidents in Missouri, the "listening tour" and empathetic support for the demands of the students from the newly appointed interim president of the University of Missouri system, Michael Middleton, has been met with widespread support. Following the protests at the University of Missouri and Yale University, students at Emory University staged similar protests and issued demands of their own. As Ajay Nair, senior vice president and dean of campus life, indicated, his initial reaction to student demands was "defensive" (Brown, 2016). He went on to note that "our students are seeking change. They mean for the demands to be provocative and jarring. If we look at the demands just at face value, we're missing something." His careful "sense-making" of the protests allowed him to examine the situation at a deeper level; moving beyond the protests, Nair oversaw the institution's response which included the initiation of working groups to assess each of the demands, the solicitation of all campus stakeholders to weigh in on possible solutions, and the development of a racial-justice retreat for students and members of the faculty and staff (Brown, 2016).

In her study of student and administrator perceptions of student protests at the University of California, Atkinson (2014) found that both students and administrators emphasized the value of communication, listening, and safety as key characteristics of effective responses to student protests. Atkinson also noted that despite the administrators' perception of being effective communicators and listeners during the protests, student activists tended to disagree with this sentiment. As we contrast the responses at the University of Missouri and Emory University, for example, it seems that in the case of Missouri, leaders inadequately recognized the severity of the issues on their campus until it was too late, unlike the reported proactive and inclusive response by leaders at Emory. The situations at Missouri and Emory are quite different; yet the different responses capture the critical role of communication and dialogue in building inclusive environments, even given the ongoing protests from student activists. Inclusive leadership, as noted earlier, moves the response to these protests from one of avoidance and aversion to embracement and encouragement. In many ways, the juxtaposition of responses to campus protests across the country and internationally provides a variety of responses for others to model when dealing with similar circumstances. In essence, we see mimetic isomorphism taking root.

From the perspective of leaders at three University of California campuses, the following tools were most useful in navigating the various challenges associated with the student protests: relationship building, knowledge of student development theory, trust, and patience (Atkinson, 2014). Building upon these themes and tools, the notion of inclusive leadership provides a fitting description of what is most needed during this period of racial hostility and campus unrest. Hollander (2009) asserts that inclusive leadership is a two-way relationship that is grounded in respect, recognition, responsiveness, and responsibility; and it is about "doing things with people, rather than to people" (p. 3). Taking such a stance when it comes to conducting everyday business on college and university campuses often can prevent the emergence of campus protests.

The Role of Dialogue in Inclusive Leadership

When inclusive leadership is adopted and dialogue is used to engage in conversations where people disagree with one another, productive solutions can often be found. The role of dialogue in leading during these difficult times cannot be underestimated. In much the same way as dialogue is a central imperative for servant leadership (Gigliotti & Dwyer, 2016), necessitating that leaders think of others before themselves, dialogue is also critical for inclusive leadership. Inclusive leadership relies on dialogue in that it helps leaders assess who is present and who is not, and whose needs are being attended to and whose are absent from consideration. If conversation is not occurring, and more importantly, if leaders are not listening, there is arguably an absence of inclusive considerations.

Dialogue is defined in a variety of ways. Employing its basic definition, dialogue is the exchange of verbal and nonverbal messages between two or more people and is often used as a synonym for discussion or conversation. Bohm (1996) shares that dialogue is about creating a collective and shared meaning between people where they create "something new together" (p. 3). As a result of making something new, a shared understanding results from dialogic interactions. Cuentas and Méndez (2013) expand on this stating:

> dialogue is a process of genuine interaction in which human beings listen deeply and respectfully to each other in a way that what they learn changes them…No participant gives up his or her identity, but each recognizes the human value of the claims of the others and therefore acts differently towards others. (p. 9)

This conceptualization of dialogue that highlights the dignity of the whole person remains fundamental to inclusive leadership. At its core, dialogue is a process that engages people to thoughtfully engage with others such that they develop a greater understanding of perspectives different from their own. Dialogue is an essential part of inclusive leadership, in that inclusive leadership must actively take into account a variety of perspectives in making decisions. This approach is not an ancillary maneuver used for political correctness; but rather it is a fundamental and authentic approach to leadership that seeks to cultivate relationships of trust and care. This use of dialogue is arguably the most advantageous and direct way to cultivate inclusive leadership that meets the needs of multiple perspectives. As Gigliotti and Dwyer (2016) state, "dialogue occupies an important role in the co-construction of leadership between leaders and followers," and this is especially the case as it relates to practices of inclusive leadership (p. 70). The leader's ability to utilize dialogue in order to hear others' perspectives, advocate for marginalized voices, and implement inclusive strategic decisions hinges on the leader's willingness to engage in dialogue with followers.

Moreover, dialogue is an effective tool for effectively engaging with the core issues that are central to the problems on college and university campuses which have led to recent student protests. In fact, the Intergroup Dialogue Program at the University of Michigan arose more than 25 years ago out of the third wave of the Black Action Movement (BAM). During a time of high significant racial tensions in the 1980s, many campus protests emerged in response to discriminatory and racist actions against black students (Glenn, 2010). The dialogue program began as a way to transition from protests to talking and listening to one another in order to better understand different points of view.

Given the contemporary climate, dialogue programs continue to grow in size and scope across college and university campuses (Cannara, 2016; Maxwell, Nagda, Thompson, 2012; Roldan, 2016; Zúñiga, Nagda, Chesler, & Cytron-Walker, 2007). For example, as a way of deepening their diversity efforts, the Intergroup Relations Program (IGR) at Villanova University offers courses for undergraduate students. While Villanova strives to have a more racially diverse population of students, diversity efforts also recognize that simply having a broad array of students on campus is not enough; rather, embracing inclusive excellence throughout the university is also essential.[2] In concert with other initiatives focused on inclusion, equity and justice, IGR at Villanova utilizes dialogue among students and faculty, and staff in order use dialogue to engage deeply in conversations about race, sexual orientation, socio-economic status, gender, religion, and more (Aloi, 2014). Moreover, IGR is the place where conversations begin and yet they also continue outside of class in ways that have begun to create a more inclusive and equitable campus.

Cornell has a similar approach to Villanova with their Intergroup Dialogue Project (IDP). At Cornell, 48% of undergraduates are US domestic students of color and international students (combined) (NCES, 2016). The advancement of a campus-wide dialogue program is illustrative of an institutional commitment to inclusive leadership. In IDP students engage in difficult conversation about a variety of social identities, but their engagement with these topics does not end there. In addition, the skills learned in IDP class have led to justice projects being acted out in the local community and have fostered an expectation that equity is normative in society (Aloi, 2014). At both Villanova and Cornell, dialogue is one part of an expansive diversity strategic plan that is proactive in nature and requires thoughtful and continual engagement with others about diversity.

---

[2]For a more about inclusive excellence, see https://www.aacu.org/making-excellence-inclusive

Strategies for Advancing Institutional Diversity

As we consider the critical role of leaders in higher education, the strategies suggested here are also relevant for leaders beyond higher education, especially given the complexities and challenges associated with diversity across institutional types. The purpose of highlighting and understanding inclusive leadership is to empower courageous and dynamic leaders to create equitable and just organizations that have the potential to radically transform societies. This is to say they have a place, they are valuable, and they matter. In the spirit of inclusive leadership, an understanding of and appreciation for all kinds of diversity is a critical competency for leaders in higher education (Ruben, 2012). As Chen and Van Velsor (1996) state, it is imperative that "the diversity leader develop the capacity to be an open-minded, continuous learner, a relationship builder, and a people developer" (p. 299). Recent protests challenge leaders in higher education to demonstrate these behaviors; and in many instances, the responses to these protests are on display for a wider audience that extends beyond the walls of the institution.

In order to create inclusive universities that will foster acts of public good inclusive leaders must recognize that all behavior is communicative (Barge, 2013; Bateson, 1972) and leaders must critically assess the messages being sent as a result of their behaviors, both intentionally and unintentionally (Ruben, De Lisi, & Gigliotti, 2017). Modeling inclusive behavior, building empathetic relationships, and serving as an ally, advocate, and champion for the most marginalized of the community are critical strategies for any and all leaders who wish to be inclusive. Leadership without considerations of inclusivity marks an unsuccessful leader.

Moving beyond compliance thinking (doing only enough to comply with laws and regulations) (Smith, 2015), effective inclusive leadership addresses the opportunity for growth and development that can come from an emphasis on equity at all levels of the organization. The role of higher education in serving the public good includes strategic diversity leadership that emphasizes not simply tolerance, but also inclusion in new and innovative ways. Pasque (2010) suggests that a key to connecting higher education to the public good is to include traditionally silenced voices and to adopt "multiple frames for considering the relationship between higher education and society" (p. 166). These "non-traditional" frames for leadership, such as an Ecological Impact Model (Pasque, 2010, p. 118) and Dialogic Process Model (Pasque, 2010, p. 119) decenter traditional hierarchical notions of leadership. In fact, Pasque (2016) finds that by utilizing these frameworks in a leadership convening, it allows for underrepresented leaders to challenge the dominant narrative. Pasque (2010) lifts up this perspective and situates this dynamic within the contemporary higher education landscape that calls upon leaders to "change their current trajectory that perpetuates educational stratification academic capitalism" (p. 191). In her research on connections between higher education and the public good, Pasque advocates for an Interconnected/Advocacy Frame that, at its core, highlights "cultural exclusions and develop[ing] inclusive space for emancipatory change" (p. 170). As such, this perspective empowers the voices of the underrepresented, specifically women and people to color, so they are heard and valued as central to the conversation.

Although Pasque presents a framework that creates deeper connections between higher education and the public good, other researchers such as Kezar, Chambers, and Burkhardt (2005) acknowledge that the social charter between higher education and the public "is being lost as public policy and institutional divisions unintentionally focus more on revenue generation and the individual benefits of higher education rather than on its broader social role and benefits" (p. xiii). While these connections are sometimes muddied, by looking to Pasque and others, we can see how focusing on inclusion solidifies the connection between higher education and the public good. Also, Smith (2015) provides a way for us to more clearly see the connections between higher education, inclusion, and the public good. As she acknowledges, "it is time to move beyond old questions [about whether or not to accommodate diversity] and to ask instead how we can build diversity into the center of higher education, where it can serve as a powerful *facilitator* of institutional mission and societal purpose" (p. 3).

The intentional strategies of college and university leaders, coupled with the engagement and activism of college students, are moving conversations from campus diversity and inclusion efforts to those of societal equity and justice. This movement toward equity and justice is a moral obligation of higher education and is consistent with what Williams (2013) describes as an essential function of the modern college and university. At the core of this chapter is that diversity and inclusion higher education decision making will not only strengthen institutions of higher education, but will also advance the public good.

Institutions are strengthened by moving from compliance to inclusive excellence (AAC&U, 2016). The dialogic and inclusive leadership practices emphasized in this chapter can help advance institutions and move them from compliance-oriented thinking through a series of stages and toward becoming models of inclusive excellence. First institutions must identify how they are implicated in institutional isomorphism (DiMaggio & Powell, 1983; Williams & Wade-Golden, 2013), recognizing when they simply copy the compliance work on diversity and inclusion from other institutions, rather than creating innovative and institution specific diversity initiatives. In order to move closer to inclusive excellence, colleges and university must shift away from a sole emphasis on compliance thinking. This requires campus leaders to authentically listen to marginalized parties (Gigliotti & Dwyer, 2016) and cultivate inclusive leadership traits such as cognizance, courage, commitment, curiosity, cultural intelligence, and collaboration (Dillon & Bourke, 2016). The next step toward embracing inclusive excellence is to embrace equity and justice. This involves leaders modeling inclusive behavior which can achieved by engaging others in conversation. We especially recommend engaging in structured opportunities for dialogue where the power dynamics are minimized (Bohm, 1996; Dwyer, Gigliotti, & Lee, 2014). The last stage, to move toward inclusive excellence, is changing institutional systems and structures so that they become inclusive, equitable, and just. This involves building empathetic relationships with other leaders who can also change their policies to become more equitable (Williams, 2013). In order to truly demonstrate inclusive excellence, leaders must serve as allies, advocates, and champions for the underrepresented and marginalized members of their community. Promoting inclusive excellence includes all of the items described above and summarized in Fig. 1. Yet, pursuits of inclusive excellence will not be without error — perfection is elusive in this realm. However, leaders must continue to engage in these practices and conduct audits (Patton, 2010) to ensure that they are vigilant in the pursuit of inclusive excellence.

Conclusion

The many pressing issues facing our colleges and universities, along with the protests that emerge in response to these issues,

Fig. 1. Engaging Inclusive and Strategic Diversity Leadership.

are often cast as a "zero-sum" game. By breaking the zero-sum logic of winners and losers, leaders in higher education can use the protests as an opportunity to create transformative institutional change. The use of inclusive leadership practices demonstrates a commitment to student concerns and models proactive strategies for other leaders. The strategies and concepts associated with strategic diversity leadership presented in this chapter emerge within the context of higher education, yet the principles for and emphasis on inclusive leadership cut across sectors and societies. In line with the other chapters in this volume, this approach to inclusive leadership is available to all leaders across all sectors, and truly transcends industries, cultures, disciplines, and boundaries.

A recent report by researchers at the Research Center for Leadership in Action at New York University's Robert F. Wagner Graduate School of Public Service noted the following:

> The literature about inclusion and the multiple perspectives on diversity seems to agree that it is not enough to have representatives of diverse groups within organizations but to create an overall environment that celebrates and leverages multiplicity and pluralism. (Research Center for Leadership in Action, 2011, p. 10)

We would extend this thinking further to point to the specific role that dialogue can play in helping to elevate and actualize inclusive leadership, particularly on college and university campuses. The topic remains timely and important for domestic and international audiences. Future responses to student protests will not only provide a model for other leaders and organizations to mimic, but they will also contribute to the role of higher education in achieving their purpose of contributing to a broader public good.

References

Aloi, D. (2014). What we talk about when we talk about 'diversity.' *EZRA: Cornell's Quarterly Magazine*. Spring, 2014. (VI) 3. Retrieved from http://ezramagazine.cornell.edu/SPRING14/cover.html. Accessed on May 4, 2016

American Association of Colleges and Universities. (2016). Without diversity, equity, and engagement, there is no true educational excellence. Retrieved from https://www.aacu.org/about/statements/2016/ut-fisher. Accessed on June 30, 2016

Atkinson, S. (2014). Bridging the divide: Perceptions of effective responses to student protests as perceived by administrators and student activists. Unpublished doctoral dissertation, University of California, Davis, CA.

Barge, J. K. (2013). Pivotal leadership and the art of conversation. *Leadership*, *10*(1), 56–78.

Bateson, G. (1972). *Steps to an ecology of the mind*. New York, NY: Ballentine.

Bohm, D. (1996). *On dialogue*. New York, NY: Routledge.

Brown, S. (2016, March 15). How one university took its student protesters seriously. *The Chronicle of Higher Education*. Retrieved from http://www.chronicle.com/article/Video-How-One-University-Took/235834. Accessed on June 27, 2017.

Cannara, R. E. (2016). Intergroup dialogue with pre-service teachers: Measuring attitudes, comfort and action among social justice educators. Doctoral Dissertation. Retrieved from https://escholarship.org/uc/item/4tm4q72n. Accessed on July 10, 2016

Carmeli, A., Reiter-Palmon, R., & Ziv, E. (2010). Inclusive leadership and employee involvement in creative tasks in the workplace: The mediating role of psychological safety. *Creativity Research Journal*, *22*(3), 250–260.

Chen, C., & Van Velsor, E. (1996). New directions for research and practice in diversity leadership. *Leadership Quarterly*, *7*(2), 285–302.

Cuentas, M. A., & Méndez, A. L. (2013). Practical guide on democratic dialogue. Crisis Prevention and Recovery Practice Area of the UNDP Regional Centre for Latin America and the Caribbean, and the Department of Sustainable Democracy and Special Missions (DSDSM) of the Secretariat for Political Affairs of the GS/OAS. Clayton, Panama City, Panama. Retrieved from https://www.oas.org/es/sap/dsdme/pubs/guia_e.pdf. Accessed on April 14, 2015.

Dessel, A., & Rogge, M. E. (2008). Evaluation of intergroup dialogue: A review of the empirical literature. *Conflict Resolution Quarterly*, *26*(2), 199–238.

Dillon, B., & Bourke, J. (2016, April 14). The six signature traits of inclusive leadership. Deloitte University Press. Retrieved from http://dupress.com/articles/six-signature-traits-of-inclusive-leadership/. Accessed on July 6, 2016

DiMaggio, P., & Powell, W. (1983). The iron cage revisited: Institutional isomorphism and collective rationality in organizational fields. *American Sociological Review*, *48*, 147–160.

Dwyer, B. M. (2012). *Students' cross-racial interactions at an emerging Hispanic-serving institution.* Unpublished doctoral dissertation, University of Michigan, Ann Arbor.

Dwyer, B., Gigliotti, R. A., & Lee, H. H. (2014). Mindfulness & authentic leadership development for social change: The intergroup dialogue program at Villanova University. In K. Goldman Schuyler, J. E. Baugher, K. Jironet, & L. Lid-Falkman (Eds.) *Leading with spirit, presence, and authenticity* (pp. 125–146). San Francisco, CA: Jossey-Bass/Wiley.

Fortunato, J. A., Gigliotti, R. A., & Ruben, B. D. (2017). Racial incidents at the University of Missouri: The value of leadership communication and stakeholder relationships. *International Journal of Business Communication, 54*(2), 199–209.

Gigliotti, R. A., & Dwyer, B. (2016). Cultivating dialogue: A central imperative for servant leadership. *Servant Leadership: Theory and Practice, 3*(1), 69–88.

Gigliotti, R. A., & Fortunato, J. A. (2017). Crisis leadership: Upholding institutional values. In B. D. Ruben, R. De Lisi, & R. A. Gigliotti (Eds.), *A guide for leaders in higher education: Core concepts, competencies, and tools.* Sterling, VA: Stylus Publishing.

Glenn, A. (2010). Open it up or shut it down: The 1970 Black action movement strike at Michigan. *Ann Arbor Chronicle.* (March 30, 2010). Retrieved from http://annarborchronicle.com/2010/03/30/open-it-up-or-shut-it-down/. Accessed on May 4, 2016.

Gurin, P., Nagda, B. R. A., & Zúñiga, X. (2013). *Dialogue across difference: Practice, theory, and research on intergroup dialogue.* New York: Russell Sage Foundation.

Higher Education Research Institute. (2016). The American freshman: National norms of Fall 2015. Retrieved from http://heri.ucla.edu/monographs/TheAmericanFreshman2015.pdf. Accessed on May 3, 2016.

Hollander, E. P. (2009). *Inclusive leadership: The essential leader-follower relationship.* New York, NY: Taylor & Francis Group.

Hurtado, S., Alvarado, A. R., & Guillermo-Wann, C. (2015). The salience of racial identity at two-and four-year colleges and the climate for diversity. *Journal of Higher Education, 86*(1), 127–155.

Jayakumar, U. M. (2015). The shaping of postcollege colorblind orientation among Whites: residential segregation and campus diversity experiences. *Harvard Educational Review, 85*(4), 609–645.

Johnson, A. (2015, December 11). Student Protests, Then and Now From 'Hey, hey, LBJ!' to 'Black lives matter!' *Chronicle of Higher Education.* Retrieved from http://www.chronicle.com/article/Student-Protests-ThenNow/234542. Accessed on March 15, 2016.

Kendall, F. E. (2003). *How to be an ally if you are a person with privilege.* Retrieved from http://www.scn.org/friends/ally.html. Accessed on July 14, 2016.

Kezar, A. J., Chambers, T. C., & Burkhardt, J. C. (2005). *Higher education for the public good: Emerging voices from a national movement.* San Francisco, CA: Jossey-Bass.

Landsbaum, C., & Weber, G. (2015, November 9). *What happened at University of Missouri? Slate.* Retrieved from http://www.slate.com/blogs/the_slatest/2015/11/09/timeline_of_u_of_missouri_protests_and_president_resignation.html. Accessed on March 20, 2016.

Maxwell, K. E., Nagda, B. R., & Thompson, M. C. (2012). *Facilitating intergroup dialogues: Bridging differences, catalyzing change.* Sterling, VA: Stylus Publishing, LLC.

Moody, J. (2012). *Faculty diversity: Removing the barriers* (2nd ed.). London: Routledge.

Natation Center for Education Statistics. (2016). Retrieved from http://nces.ed.gov/collegenavigator/?q=cornel&s=all&id=190415. Accessed on May 4, 2016.

Nembhard, I. M., & Edmondson, A. C. (2006). Making it safe: The effects of leader inclusiveness and professional status on psychological safety and improvement efforts in health care teams. *Journal of Organizational Behavior, 27*(7), 941–966.

Pearson, M. (2015, November 10). *A timeline of the University of Missouri protests. CNN Online.* Retrieved from http://www.cnn.com/2015/11/09/us/missouri-protest-timeline/index.html. Accessed on March 20, 2016.

Pasque, P. (2010). *American higher education, leadership, and policy: Critical issues and the public good.* New York: Springer.

Patton, L. D. (2010). Best Practices for examining and evaluating campus culture centers and multicultural affairs offices. In L. D. Patton (Ed.), *Cultural centers in higher education: Perspectives on identity, theory, and practice* (pp. 194–200). Sterling, VA: Stylus.

Research Center for Leadership in Action. (2011). Leadership, diversity, and inclusion: Insights from scholarship. NYU Wagner. Retrieved from https://wagner.nyu.edu/files/leadership/LeadershipDiversityInclusionScholarship.pdf. Accessed on May 3, 2016

Roldan, C. (2016). Intergroup Dialogue at Colgate University: Student outcomes and effects senior honors theses. Paper 1. Retrieved from http://commons.colgate.edu/theses/1. Accessed on July 12, 2016.

Ruben, B. D. (2012). *What leaders need to know and do: A leadership competencies scorecard.* (2nd ed.). Washington, DC: National Association of College and University Business Officers.

Ruben, B. D., De Lisi, R., & Gigliotti, R. A. (2017). *A guide for leaders in higher education: Core concepts, competencies, and tools.* Sterling, VA: Stylus.

Savior, R. D., & Cooper, B. S. (2015). Lessons in university leadership: Reports from religious and secular university presidents. *Journal of Higher Education Management, 30*(1), 102–109.

Smith, D. G. (2015). *Diversity's promise for higher education: Making it work* (2nd ed.). Baltimore, MD: Johns Hopkins Press.

Solorzano, D., Ceja, M., & Yosso, T. (2000). Critical race theory, racial microaggressions, and campus racial climate: The experiences of African American college students. *Journal of Negro Education,* 60–73.

Thelin, J. R. (2011). *A history of American higher education* (2nd ed.). Baltimore, MD: The Johns Hopkins University Press.

Williams, D. A. (2013). *Strategic diversity leadership: Activating change and transformation in higher education*. Sterling, VA: Stylus.

Williams, D. A., & Wade-Golden, K. C. (2013). *The chief diversity officer: Strategy, structure, and change management*. Sterling, VA: Stylus.

Woodhouse, K. (2015, November, 10). *Activists oust two leaders. Inside Higher Ed*. Retrieved from https://www.insidehighered.com/news/2015/11/10/u-mis-souri-leaders-resign-amid-student-concerns-over-racism-and-diversity. Accessed on March 20, 2016.

Zúñiga, X., Nagda, B. R. A., Chesler, M., & Cytron-Walker, A. (2007). Intergroup Dialogue in Higher Education: Meaningful Learning About Social Justice: ASHE Higher Education Report, Volume 32, Number 4. Sterling, VA: John Wiley & Sons.

17 Dialogic Change and the Practice of Inclusive Leadership

Niels Agger-Gupta and Brigitte Harris

Keywords: Inclusion; post-heroic leadership; social construction; dialogic change; leadership education; generative metaphor

The Turn Toward Inclusion

Royal Roads University (RRU), in Victoria, British Columbia, Canada, was founded in 1996 to serve mid-career adults and focus on applied research. RRU is distinguished by its use of adult education principles and practice-focused experiential learning. The University attracted faculty with similar pedagogical/androgogical interests (Knowles, Holton, & Swanson, 2005), and students commonly described their learning experience at RRU as "life-changing" (Agger-Gupta & Etmanski, 2014; Walinga & Harris, 2016).

In 2012 three faculty members, curious about what characterized teaching and learning at RRU, held a series of consultations to which all members of the university community were invited. The process brought together faculty, staff from the library, IT services, registrar's office, student services, and students to share perspectives about RRU's essential learning and teaching elements and practices. The result was a white paper on RRU's learning and teaching model (LTM) (Hamilton, Márquez, & Agger-Gupta, 2013). As important, however, was that the process built a community identity, pride in the University and engaged people in discussions about what matters to them.

Included in the University's 2014–15 academic plan, the LTM has had a prominent role in the direction of the University and has inspired faculty, staff, and student inquiries into aspects of their own practices. Many of these studies were recently published in a book, Engaging Students in Life-Changing Learning: The Royal Roads University Learning and Teaching Model in Practice (Hamilton et al., 2016). This process has led to more projects, research, and excitement about current and future directions at RRU. The inclusive process increased the capacity of the University to serve its mission and built new relationships across the University, all with the aim of helping students succeed.

Ours is a story of inclusive leadership of people cocreating and leading from wherever they are in an organization. We are two leadership educators. Inclusive leadership approaches and practices guide how we work with colleagues and students as well as our teaching of leadership. This chapter examines the theoretical underpinnings of inclusive leadership, and the role of social construction and dialogic change in creating an inclusive organizational culture. We also describe four key principles based on inclusion and dialogic processes that provide a foundation for our practice of inclusive leadership.

Several years ago, faculty and staff at the School of Leadership Studies embarked on a series of facilitated dialogues that aimed to bring us together as a team and to find the commonalities in our perspectives on leadership (Harris & Agger-Gupta, 2015). While inclusive leadership approaches have long been part of our practice, this process identified the inclusive leadership values and practices we held in common, and the robustness of the approach to build relationships, mediate divisive forces, and increase our capacity to serve our students. Our leadership journey from theory to practice is of interest to leadership educators, scholars, and practitioners seeking to better understand and apply the concept of inclusive leadership in their particular settings. While the setting is Canadian, the theoretical discussion and principles have application beyond Canada, as study on inclusion in organizations in Australia, China, India, Mexico, and the United States demonstrated (Prime & Salib, 2014).

What Is Inclusion in Organizations?

Sally Helgesen, first to write about inclusion as a critical element of leadership, described it as, "draw[ing] on leadership skills from throughout the organization, while at the same time providing opportunities for people to develop those skills" (1995, p. 110). Inclusion is about sharing ownership of issues, opportunities, and processes, and includes a shared implementation of cocreated solutions. This shared ownership is very different from organizational stakeholders acquiescing ("buying-in") to a leader's process or solution, and is what Zimmerman et al. (2013), in a healthcare context, called, "front-line ownership."

Keimei Sugiyama, Kevin Cavanagh, Chantal van Esch, Diana Bilimoria, and Cara Brown (2016) framed inclusion as, "enhancing the relational self-awareness necessary to consider multiple identities and perhaps even intersectionality of identities in meeting belonging and uniqueness needs" (p. 256). Thus, the key benefit of inclusive leadership is in "relating to others in a way that makes them feel valued for their unique talents and backgrounds" (p. 257). Similarly, Jennifer Thorpe-Moscone's (2015) study of inclusive leadership in Canada identified that feeling valued as a part of a team led to a sense of belongingness, which, in turn, led employees to feel valued for their uniqueness. These two characteristics were essential to employees feeling included. Sugiyama et al. (2016) found that leadership development needs to balance building relationships and accomplishing business objectives but, critically, one cannot be done without the other (p. 258).

So, if inclusion and building relationships across an organization are an essential part of leadership, leadership theory needs to reflect these ideas. Joseph Raelin (2003, 2006, 2016) contrasted a historical model of leadership as dispassionate, autocratic control with "leadership-as-practice," or the concept of "leaderfulness." This concept proposed leadership in an effective organization necessarily occurs among all members, who work together collaboratively, and compassionately, as a collective (2003, pp. 14–18). A "leaderful" organization encourages leadership from anywhere in the organization. In this conception, leadership is about agency, and becomes a shared and expected aspect of organizational or community citizenship (Raelin, 2014, 2016). "Collaborative leaders realize that everyone counts; every opinion and contribution sincerely matters" (Raelin, 2003, p. 16). Steve Rayner (2009), who framed agency and inclusion from the perspective of learning, also understood leadership as inclusive, "involv[ing] every member of the learning community in some form of 'learning leadership'" (p. 439). He also noted "an inclusive leader aims to facilitate the transforming and transformative effect of learning in the work of making provision for the most vulnerable in the learning community" (p. 445). This turn toward inclusive leadership is about creating contexts that welcome the wisdom and engagement of all stakeholders, and away from autocratic, top-down direction.

Inclusion is also embedded in Marilyn Taylor's (2011) characterization of "post-conventional" and "post-heroic" leadership discourse. Such leaders have "personal purpose and responsibility, are values-focused, and practice shared leadership and collaboration, authenticity, and transparency" (p. 189). Thus, leadership goes well beyond strategic decision making, to advocating an inspirational purpose and, a profoundly respectful appreciation for and engagement of all organizational stakeholders across diversities (Quinn & Thakor, 2014). The intention is to make the workplace a center of dignity, meaning, and community (Weisbord, 2012). Leaders, therefore, harness the hearts and minds of all organizational members, forging new directions by listening deeply, understanding and engaging others in dialogue to create shared meanings. Inclusive leadership strategies include motivating others through humble respect for their experiences and perspectives, supporting, requesting and sharing authentic feedback (Schein, 2013), and inspiring, coaching, and mentoring others to build understanding and competence (Kouzes & Posner, 2007; Quinn & Thakor, 2014). Thus, the turn from heroic leadership is simultaneously the turn toward inclusion as a core part of leadership.

From Individualism to Relational and Group Constructs of Innovation

Lev Vygotsky (1986) demonstrated that knowledge is developed socially. He coined the term "proximal zone of development" to refer to the difference between what a child could accomplish on a test by him/herself, and the increased knowledge the child could demonstrate when in conversation with a trusted older student or teacher on the tested topic (p. 102). However, until relatively recently, the structure of assignments, courses, and evaluation methods have reflected the tacit assumption that invention and learning are private, asocial acts (LeFevre, 1986, p. 13). Similarly, conceptions of the individual heroic leader are based on an assumption that leadership, innovation, and education are solitary acts.

Karen LeFevre (1986) attributed the origin of individualistic approaches to invention as the desired and ideal state to the Greek philosopher Plato. Plato's *The Phaedrus* describes invention as a solitary, individual act of recall to the perfect state prior to birth (LeFevre, 1986; Plato & Jowett, 2001). LeFevre argued that the belief that truth and knowledge is entirely within, and accessible only by purely individual efforts, has had a substantial impact on the creative act — and for scholarship as a whole — where the rewards for invention have traditionally focused on the individual. This individualistic way of thinking, said LeFevre, has dominated our models of intellectual thought and led to confusion between independent thinking and solitary thinking (thinking "for" as opposed to "by" yourself), even if teachers with the best of intentions believe they are encouraging self-reliance and self-expression (1986, pp. 12–13).

The move to inclusive leadership through dialogic approaches reflects a change in thinking about innovation and change. LeFevre identified seven aspects of invention that are social and relational (1986, pp. 33–35). First, the "self" that does the inventing is socially influenced, and even socially and culturally constituted (also see Gergen & Gergen, 2008). Second, invention is done through language or other symbolic systems that are created and shared among a discourse community. Third, invention is built upon the foundation of knowledge accumulated from previous generations and "each creative act is given to another generation of thinkers who may dismiss, confirm, or build on it" (p. 34). Fourth, an internal dialogue with an imagined other or an audience that supplies premises or beliefs may enable invention. Fifth, writers often use editors or others whose feedback comments support further creativity. Sixth, invention is powerfully influenced by professional or scholarly institutions, regulatory bodies, or governments, which set expectations, scope, and acceptable and unacceptable frames for invention (see, for example, Jane Jorgensen & Frederick Steier's article on frames and framing, 2013). Seventh, the social context of the inventor (or writer) plays a large role in determining the reception or evaluation of the invention (LeFevre, 1986, pp. 33–35). The last two aspects of LeFevre's invention as a social act seem to echo Jürgen Habermas's "validity claim" of normative legitimacy for a communicative act, whereby a listener (or audience) needs to accept both the communication itself, and the speaker, as legitimate within a particular context, in addition to the other validity claims of comprehensibility, truthfulness (or honesty), and factual accuracy (1985, pp. 305–319). Like invention, leadership is relational and dialogic.

Dialogic Change and Inclusion

Gervais Bushe and Robert Marshak (2015) describe organizational change as a socially constructed process, in that "change" is essentially a realignment of how the key stakeholders see themselves and their perspectives on an issue. As organizational stakeholders become more skillful in reflection and considering alternatives to their original position, conversations can lead to new ideas more easily in organizations. Chris Argyris (1990) demonstrated organizations that created "safe" spaces for dialogue were able to make progress in addressing issues and opportunities with greater consensus, while organizations in which workers and staff felt unsafe or unsupported in being authentic, or where bosses resented such openness, were unsuccessful in moving forward (Schein, 2015, pp. xi–xii). Both alone (1990), and with his coauthor, Donald Schön, (Argyris & Schön, 1978), Argyris described "defensive routines" within organizations that created "undiscussable" issues. Simply calling for "openness" within an organization does not make it so, particularly when subordinates feel psychologically unsafe in speaking their minds in the presence of their bosses (Bushe & Marshak, 2009). More recently, Bushe and Marshak (2015) identified 40 dialogic organizational development methods that help to create psychological safety and authentic dialogue, such as Open Space Technology (Owen, 2008), Interview Matrix (Chartier, 2002; Harrison, 1999; O'Sullivan, Corneil, Kuziemsky, & Toal-Sullivan, 2015), and World Café (Brown & Isaacs, 2005). In part, these approaches involve learning new ways to communicate, or "think together," including "suspending" one's initial reaction to what someone says, considering alternative explanations, and reflecting on one's own reactions, rather than blurting out knee-jerk response (Isaacs, 1999, pp. 134–158). William Isaacs argued that these dialogue strategies allowed for a greater number of ideas to surface, individuals had greater opportunity to qualify their comments and explain their thinking, and group consensus was more frequent. Frank J. Barrett, Gail Fann Thomas, and Susan P. Hocevar (1995) described dialogue and relationship as the heart and core of any change process:

> For it is through patterns of discourse that we form relational bonds with one another; that we create, transform, and maintain structure; and that we reinforce or challenge our beliefs. The very act of communicating is the process through which we constitute experience. (p. 353)

If conversations build relationships and construct our subjective and intersubjective worlds, then being a participant in the ongoing discourse of an organization or community is an essential part of being seen to be — and feeling oneself to be — included.

The Turn to Social Construction in Leadership

The turn to social construction (see Berger & Luckmann, 1967; Gergen & Gergen, 2008) is another way of understanding the dialogical nature of social invention. The dialogue between and among peers in a safe environment is how new concepts take root. Social relations and language are context-based and interdependent:

> The meaning of "strike" and "home run" do not only depend on the rules of baseball talk, but on their function within a form of life that includes balls, bats, bases,

fields, players, umpires, hotdogs, and so on. Broadly speaking, the ways in which we walk, talk, laugh, cry, worship, engage in warfare, and virtually everything else we do, become sensible — or not — by virtue of collaborative action. (Gergen & Hersted, 2016, p. 182)

According to Bushe and Marshak (2015), cultures and whole worlds are built based on collective meaning making, and that different metaphors produce a resulting dialogue where personal and organizational changes are simultaneous. They suggest one or more of three change processes take place in dialogic change. First, a disruption in the normal socially constructed reality stimulates or results in a more complex reorganization of that reality (see, for example, Prigogine & Stengers, 1984). Second, a change to one or more core narratives takes place — for example, a change in purpose, vision, mission, who has influence or not, important challenges and opportunities, or normative behaviors in the organizational culture — resulting in new, socially agreed upon narratives that support the new order. Third, a generative image or symbol is created that provides a new way of thinking about social interactions and the organization as a whole (Bushe & Marshak, 2015, pp. 20−24). For example, the phrase, "sustainable development," is a generative image that, when introduced in 1987, led to new relationships between organizations and environmentalists (Bushe, 2013, p. 93). Gervais Bushe and Aniq F. Kassam (2005) found change efforts that developed such generative images were more likely to have long-term success.

In our experience, positive, inclusive change comes about from the collective wisdom of the stakeholders to the change, especially those who are going to be affected by it. Ultimately, any given change is negotiated through a learning process centered on the dialogue between parties who hold different models of reality in their minds as a result of their unique life experiences. Bushe and Marshak (2015) describe this emergent conversational process as "dialogic change," because it results in a socially constructed new organizational reality that is first conceptualized and almost simultaneously developed as the new norm, through the conversation among stakeholders about an issue, problem, or opportunity (see, for example, Ford, 1999; Gergen & Thatchenkery, 1996). These conversations and inclusion in decision making directly relate to the success of change initiatives. Good ideas can come from anyone, if one is willing to listen to the diverse voices, and recognize the power of articulated lived experience to describe new perspectives but recognizing the power of emergent new ideas requires letting go of rationally predetermined outcomes (Bushe & Marshak, 2015, p. 18). This inclusive leadership approach can have a dramatic impact on the kinds of stories people tell about their organization, on the organizational culture and climate of encouraging diverse perspectives, and, ultimately, on organizational effectiveness.

Fostering Inclusive Leadership in Leadership Education

The new understanding of leadership has implications for universities in their critical role of educating professionals. What should the role of universities be in the face of serious and seemingly intractable problems, including growing economic disparity, climate change, and a global context of (v)olatility, (u)ncertainty, (c)omplexity, and (a)mbiguity, with the first letter of these words also forming the acronym, VUCA (see, for example, Euchner, 2013). Michael Fullan and Geoff Scott (2006) argue that universities must prepare students to become leaders who can work effectively with others to solve the complex and divisive problems that confront the world (p. 42). In fact, if universities do not rise to this challenge, they risk becoming marginalized or even irrelevant. Implicit in their argument is the need for inclusive leaders who can work to harness the wisdom of others to solve problems. Given the need for inclusive leaders to address such problems, how should we, as leadership educators, teach and model inclusive leadership values and practices? In the School of Leadership Studies, faculty members engaged in dialogues over several years to identify commonly held values and principles that constitute the unifying foundation of our programs. These interlocking and overlapping inclusive principles are leadership as engagement, engaged scholarship, orientation to possibility, and learning as transformation (Harris & Agger-Gupta, 2015). These four principles serve as a generative image for the School, and have had a dramatic impact on our work. Each of these principles is defined below, and explicitly linked to the support and development of inclusive leaders engaged in dialogic change.

Four Principles for Inclusion

LEADERSHIP AS ENGAGEMENT

Inclusive leaders help others to work together effectively, creating in followers both sense of belonging and that their unique contributions are recognized and valued (Sugiyama et al., 2016). This relational work entails leaders engaging others to work toward a common purpose, facilitating inclusive processes, and removing barriers. Including the people who will be impacted by or are responsible for implementing change is critical for creating a sense of ownership (Wheatley, 2006, p. 69). The principle of leadership as engagement implies the inclusive leadership behaviors of empowering others, and humility, for example, seeking and listening to the input of others (Prime & Salib, 2014), acknowledging the need to learn about others' perspectives.

Leadership as engagement requires "social intelligence," in which leaders engage in "humble inquiry," being curious about and seeking to understand the perspectives of others (Schein, 2013) and distinguishing what is known from what is assumed and what is unknown (Schein, 1997, p. 206). Inclusive and engaging leaders value their own ongoing and "emergent learning" (Taylor, 2011), with which they navigate unfamiliar or previously not experienced landscapes, issues, challenges, and turbulence in their environments. Critically, they also support the development and learning of others. They help people to grow and thrive through creating opportunities for meaningful conversations, maintaining an orientation to possibility, and recognizing that change and learning are transformative experiences (Harris & Agger-Gupta, 2015). In this way, they build an organization's capacity to respond effectively to the challenges it encounters (Senge, 1990).

ENGAGED SCHOLARSHIP

Our practice of "engaged scholarship" is an extension to knowledge creation of the principles of leadership for engagement. Engaged scholarship removes barriers between those who create knowledge (i.e., do research) and those served by knowledge creation (i.e., practitioners). Engaged scholars bring together people with different perspectives — primarily scholars and practitioners — to cocreate knowledge (Barge et al., 2008). Diverse perspectives can foster "a much deeper understanding of a phenomenon" (Van de Ven, 2011, p. 43) than researchers or practitioners could achieve by themselves. Just as inclusive leaders seek to include a wide range of perspectives in problem solving, learning, and confronting new and emerging situations, engaged scholarship calls on scholars to practice inclusion of various stakeholders in research. Thus, scholar-practitioners need to invite those who are not normally part of the conversation to the table, and make this kind of leadership the organizational norm, creating opportunities for increased insight, positive connection, inclusion, and change (Wheatley, 2002; Woods, 2016, p. 81).

In engaged scholarship, students are also partners in knowledge creation, particularly in action research and service learning projects. Hillary Bradbury and Peter Reason (2003) characterize action research projects as: "(1) grounded in lived experience, (2) developed in partnership, (3) addressing significant problems, (4) working with, rather than simply studying, people, (5) developing new ways of seeing/theorizing the world, and (6) leaving infrastructure in [their] wake" (p. 155). Similarly, service learning involves real-world community or organizational projects as vehicles for learning, with benefit for students and their institutions and communities and/or organizations. These projects involve: (1) learning goals or outcomes for students, and the aim of benefitting a community; (2) collaboration of students, faculty/staff, and community/organization members and/or community organizations and educational institutions; and (3) critical reflection and assessment processes that document both meaningful learning and community outcomes (Felten & Clayton, 2011).

Students in our programs engage in action research, and service learning in their masters' research. They engage stakeholders to plan and carry out an action research project within an organization, often the one in which the students work, to address an actual problem or opportunity of significance. We support our students in research that aims to make a positive difference in organizations, communities, and professional groups. We work with our students as "cocreators of knowledge" (Fretz & Longo, 2010, p. 317) and positive change, learning to apply inclusive and dialogic principles through an inquiry approach to problem solving. Through their research, our students learn the benefit of including diverse perspectives to generate new perspectives and solutions for social benefit. We see our students as cocreators of "an engaged academy," helping to increase both student engagement in their learning and university engagement in communities (Fretz & Longo, 2010, p. 313).

ORIENTATION TO POSSIBILITY

Inclusive leaders need to maintain an orientation to possibility, open to changing their minds through learning and dialogue. "When the leader is able to abide in ambiguity and not defend against the accompanying feelings of fear and anxiety, new opportunities for learning and creativity open up" (Skjei, 2014, p. 218). Changing their thinking about barriers, and problems can help leaders become unstuck. For example, rather than fighting resistance, inclusive leaders welcome such differences as an opportunity to understand the diversity of perspectives involved in an issue (Allen, 2012, p. 71). Holman (2010) urges leaders to "call forth 'what could be'" (p. 62) and use problems as "a doorway to opportunity" (p. 63). Thus, leaders can reframe perceived or actual barriers as motivators for creativity through moving beyond discouragement and blame to taking an evidence-informed basis for determining next steps (Adams, 2009). As leadership educators, we foster this orientation in our students as a means of developing leaders who can respond effectively in volatile and uncertain contexts (Euchner, 2013).

LEARNING AS TRANSFORMATION

Inclusive leadership, and leadership education, requires an understanding of transformative learning. Such learning goes beyond "facts," or "first order learning" (Bateson, 2000), to learning how to learn ("second-order learning") and an understanding of how inclusive values and relating to the world have an impact on learning ("third-order learning"). Thus, in addition to teaching knowledge and application of skills, we believe that leadership educators need to create a learning environment and activities in which students can engage in second- and third-order learning to enable them to "transform themselves and society" (UNESCO, 2009). Second- and third-order learning are also characteristic of "emergent learning" (Taylor, 2011), which helps leaders "to engage constructively with the unfamiliar, and to adapt and learn in a continuously emergent context" (p. 27). Such transformative learning challenges leaders to be inquirers to create the potential of seeing things anew, and even to "know how to construct new knowledge when faced with problems for which there is no known solution or even for which there is no known conceptual lens" (Raelin, 2006, p. 7).

We have more than anecdotal evidence that our students experience "transformative learning" (Mezirow, 2000). Jennifer

Walinga and Brigitte Harris (2016) examined the learning narratives of 45 students in four RRU masters-level programs. They documented students' transformative learning processes from the initial disorienting dilemma to the emergence of new and enduring state of insight or consciousness. These transformations changed how students learned and had lasting application in both their professional and personal lives. As leadership educators, we have come to believe that learning with the specific goals of individual and collective transformation is critical to inclusive leadership, but we also see the challenges of doing so, since transformative change requires students, and sometimes faculty, to accept and adopt emergence, and letting go of preconceived outcomes (see, for example, Bushe, 2013).

Conclusion

This chapter discussed "the turn to inclusive leadership" to address the challenges that confront leaders. It examined the theoretical grounding of social construction in the shift from individualism to relational and group constructs of innovation as well as the role of dialogic change in creating an inclusive culture. We also described four key principles, which were the outcomes of the School of Leadership Studies' inclusive and dialogic processes.

While we both work to practice inclusive leadership and teach it in our graduate programs, we recognize this approach to leadership is not easy. In our own, and in our students', applied research we have witnessed frequent organizational churn, resulting in changed priorities and strategic direction that decreases engagement and the withdrawal of support for these projects. Stakeholders in such research may feel change is necessary and want to be consulted, but find it difficult to take the time to engage in dialogue. Yet, when we ask our graduates about the most valuable learning experiences in our program, the answer is consistently that the research project provided their richest learning.

The literature tells us that inclusive leadership focused on dialogic change results in better outcomes (Bushe & Marshak, 2015; Helgesen, 1995), increased ownership (Wheatley, 2006; Zimmerman et al., 2013) and a sense of belonging and being valued (Sugiyama et al., 2016). Our experiences of inclusive leadership, and our students' feedback tell us that, despite the challenges, the outcomes are worth it.

Acknowledgments

The authors would like to thank their colleagues in the School of Leadership Studies at Royal Roads University for the generative dialog — including numerous disagreements — over the last 5 years. These have led to our organization's inclusive and collaborative culture that has sparked our understanding and teaching of leadership. We would also like to thank the many Leadership students for countless stimulating dialogues that have also helped forge our leadership understandings, and with whom we hope we have demonstrated a continuous orientation to possibility. As well, we would like to thank our respective partners for their support and encouragement.

References

Adams, M. G. (2009). *Change your questions, change your life: 10 powerful tools for life and work* (2nd ed.). San Francisco, CA: Berrett-Koehler Publishers and Books24x7, Inc.

Agger-Gupta, N., & Etmanski, C. (2014). The paradox of transformative learning among mid-career professionals. *International Journal of Adult Vocational Education and Technology (IJAVET)*, 5(1), 35–47. doi:10.4018/ijavet.2014010104

Allen, K. (2012). Dancing on a slippery floor: Transforming systems, transforming leadership. In C. Pearson (Ed.), *The transforming leader: New approaches to leadership for the twenty-first century* (pp. 64–74). San Francisco, CA: Berrett-Koehler Publishers.

Argyris, C. (1990). *Overcoming organizational defenses: Facilitating organizational learning*. New York, NY: Prentice Hall.

Argyris, C., & Schön, D. A. (1978). *Organizational learning: A theory of action perspective (Later Printing)*. New York, NY: Addison-Wesley.

Barge, J. K., Jones, K. E., Kensler, M., Polok, N., Rianoshek, R., Simpson, J. L., & Schockley-Zalabak, P. (2008). A practitioner view toward engaged scholarship. *Journal of Applied Communication Research*, 36(3), 245–250.

Barrett, F. J., Thomas, G. F., & Hocevar, S. P. (1995). The central role of discourse in large-scale change: A social construction perspective. *The Journal of Applied Behavioral Science*, 31(3), 352–372. doi:10.1177/0021886395313007

Bateson, G. (2000). *Steps to an ecology of mind: Collected essays in anthropology, psychiatry, evolution, and epistemology* (1st ed.). Chicago, IL: University of Chicago Press.

Berger, P. L., & Luckmann, T. (1967). *The social construction of reality: A treatise in the sociology of knowledge.* New York, NY: Anchor Books.

Bradbury, H., & Reason, P. (2003). Action research: An opportunity for revitalizing research purpose and practices. *Qualitative Social Work, 2*(2), 155–175. doi:10.1177/1473325003002002003.

Brown, J., Isaacs, D., & World Cafe Community. (2005). *The world cafe: Shaping our futures through conversations that matter* (eBook 1). San Francisco, CA: Berrett-Koehler Publishers. Retrieved from http://site.ebrary.com.ezproxy.royalroads.ca/lib/royalroads/detail.action?docID=10315429.

Bushe, G. R. (2013). Generative process, generative outcome: The transformational potential of appreciative inquiry. In D. L. Cooperrider, D. P. Zandee, L. N. Godwin, M. Avital, & B. Boland (Eds.), *Organizational generativity: The appreciative inquiry summit and a scholarship of transformation* (Vol. 4, pp. 89–113). Bingley, UK: Emerald Group Publishing Limited. Retrieved from http://www.gervasebushe.ca/AI_generativity.pdf. Accessed on September 16, 2015.

Bushe, G. R., & Kassam, A. F. (2005). When is appreciative inquiry transformational? A meta-case analysis. *The Journal of Applied Behavioral Science, 41*(2), 161–181. doi:10.1177/0021886304270337 Accessed on May 30, 2014.

Bushe, G. R., & Marshak, R. J. (2009). Revisioning organization development: Diagnostic and dialogic premises and patterns of practice. *The Journal of Applied Behavioral Science, 45*(3), 348–368. doi:10.1177/0021886309335070 Accessed on February 24, 2014.

Bushe, G. R., & Marshak, R. J. (2015). Chapter 1: Introduction to the dialogic organization development mindset. In G. Bushe & R. J. Marshak (Eds.), *Dialogic organization development: The theory and practice of transformational change* (pp. 11–32). San Francisco, CA: Berrett-Koehler Publishers.

Chartier, B. (2002). Tools for leadership and learning: Building a learning organization. Retrieved from http://managers-gestionnaires.gc.ca/tools-outils/tools_for_leadership-trousse_du_leadership-eng.php. Accessed on March 29, 2013.

Euchner, J. (2013). Navigating the VUCA world: An interview with Bob Johansen. *Research Technology Management, 56*(1), 10–15.

Felten, P., & Clayton, P. H. (2011). Service-learning. *New Directions for Teaching and Learning, 2011*(128), 75–84. doi:10.1002/tl.470

Ford, J. D. (1999). Organizational change as shifting conversations. *Journal of Organizational Change Management, 12*(6), 480–500.

Fretz, E. J., & Longo, N. V. (2010). Students co-creating an engaged academy. In H. Fitzgerald, C. Burack, & S. D. Seifer (Eds.), *Transformation in higher education: Handbook of engaged scholarship* (Vol. 1, pp. 313–335). East Lansing, MI: Michigan State University Press.

Fullan, M., & Scott, G. (2006). *Turnaround leadership.* San Francisco, CA: Jossey-Bass. Retrieved from http://catalog.hathitrust.org/Record/005288094. Accessed on August 31, 2016.

Gergen, K. J., & Gergen, M. M. (2008). Chapter 10: Social construction and research as action. In P. Reason & H. Bradbury (Eds.), *The SAGE handbook of action research* (pp. 159–171). London: SAGE Publications Ltd. Retrieved from http://srmo.sagepub.com/view/the-sage-handbook-of-action-research/d16.xml. Accessed on April 1, 2014.

Gergen, K. J., & Hersted, L. (2016). Chapter 9: Developing leadership as dialogic practice. In J. A. Raelin (Ed.), *Leadership-as-practice: Theory and application*. New York, NY: Routledge.

Gergen, K. J., & Thatchenkery, T. J. (1996). Organization science as social construction: Postmodern potentials. *The Journal of Applied Behavioral Science*, 32(4), 356–377. doi:10.1177/0021886396324002 Accessed on October 13, 2014.

Habermas, J. (1985). *The theory of communicative action, volume 1: Reason and the rationalization of society* (T. McCarthy, Trans.). Boston, MA: Beacon Press.

Hamilton, D., Márquez, P., & Agger-Gupta, N. (2013). RRU Learning & Teaching Model. Retrieved from http://media.royalroads.ca/media/marketing/viewbooks/2013/learning-model/?pageNumber=1. Accessed on October 20, 2013.

Hamilton, D., Marquez, P., Agger-Gupta, N., Grundy, S., Veletsianos, G., Forssmann, V., & LeGault, M. (Eds.). (2016). *Engaging students in life-changing learning: The Royal Roads University learning and teaching model in practice*. Victoria, BC, Canada: Royal Roads University. Retrieved from https://learningandteachingmodel.pressbooks.com/. Accessed on April 22, 2017.

Harris, B., & Agger-Gupta, N. (2015). The long and winding road: Leadership and learning principles that transform. *Integral Leadership Review*. January-February. Retrieved from http://integralleadershipreview.com/12569-115-long-winding-roadleadership-learning-principles-transform/

Harrison, T. (1999, February 22). Instructions for interview matrix [manual]. Retrieved from http://www.chriscorrigan.com/facilitation/matrice_e.pdf. Accessed on September 20, 2015.

Helgesen, S. (1995). *The web of inclusion*. New York, NY: Doubleday Business.

Holman, P. (2010). *Engaging emergence: Turning upheaval into opportunity*. San Francisco, CA: Berrett-Koehler.

Isaacs, W. (1999). *Dialogue: The art of thinking together* (1st ed.). New York, NY: Crown Business.

Jorgenson, J., & Steier, F. (2013). Frames, framing, and designed conversational processes: Lessons from the world café. *The Journal of Applied Behavioral Science*, 49(3), 388–405. doi:10.1177/0021886313484511. Accessed on December 17, 2013.

Knowles, M. S., Holton, E. F., & Swanson, R. A. (2005). *The adult learner: The definitive classic in adult education and human resource development* (6th ed.). Oxford, UK: Butterworth-Heinemann/Routledge.

Kouzes, J. M., & Posner, B. Z. (2007). *The leadership challenge* (4th ed.). San Francisco, CA: Jossey-Bass, J. Wiley.

LeFevre, K. B. (1986). *Invention as a social act*. Carbondale, IL: Southern Illinois University Press.

Mezirow, J. (2000). *Learning as transformation: Critical perspectives on a theory in progress*. San Francisco, CA: Jossey-Bass/Wiley.

O'Sullivan, T. L., Corneil, W., Kuziemsky, C. E., & Toal-Sullivan, D. (2015). Use of the structured interview matrix to enhance community resilience through collaboration and inclusive engagement. *Systems Research and Behavioral Science, 32*(6), 616–628. doi:10.1002/sres.2250. Accessed on January 28, 2016.

Owen, H. (2008). *Open space technology: A user's guide* (3rd ed.). San Francisco, CA: Berrett-Koehler Publishers.

Plato, & Jowett, B. (2001). *Phaedrus.* Blacksburg, VA: Virginia Tech.

Prigogine, I., & Stengers, I. (1984). *Order out of chaos: Man's new dialogue with nature.* Toronto: Bantam Books.

Prime, J., & Salib, E. R. (2014, February 11). Inclusive leadership: The view from six countries [Text]. Retrieved from http://www.catalyst.org/knowledge/inclusive-leadership-view-six-countries. Accessed on May 13, 2016.

Quinn, R. E., & Thakor, A. V. (2014). Chapter 9: Imbue the organization with a higher purpose. In J. E. Dutton & G. M. Spreitzer (Eds.), *How to be a positive leader: Small actions, big impact.* San Francisco, CA: Berrett-Koehler Publishers and Books24X7.

Raelin, J. A. (2003). *Creating leaderful organizations: How to bring out leadership in everyone.* San Francisco, CA: Berrett-Koehler.

Raelin, J. A. (2006). Taking the charisma out: Teaching as facilitation. *Organization Management Journal, "First Person", 3*(1), 4–12.

Raelin, J. A. (2014). Imagine there are no leaders: Reframing leadership as collaborative agency. Leadership, 1742715014558076. doi:10.1177/1742715014558076

Raelin, J. A. (Ed.). (2016). *Leadership-as-practice: Theory and application.* New York, NY: Routledge.

Rayner, S. (2009). Educational diversity and learning leadership: a proposition, some principles and a model of inclusive leadership? *Educational Review, 61*(4), 433–447. doi:10.1080/00131910903404004. Accessed on May 20, 2016.

Schein, E. H. (1997). The concept of "client" from a process consultation perspective: A guide for change agents. *Journal of Organizational Change Management, 10*(3), 202–216. doi:10.1108/09534819710171077. Accessed on January 31, 2016.

Schein, E. H. (2013). *Humble inquiry: The gentle art of asking instead of telling.* San Francisco, CA: Berrett-Koehler Publishers and Books24X7.

Schein, E. H. (2015). Foreword: Dialogic organization development: Past, present, and future. In G. Bushe & R. J. Marshak (Eds.), *Dialogic organization development: The theory and practice of transformational change* (pp. vii–xiv). San Francisco, CA: Berrett-Koehler Publishers.

Senge, P. M. (1990). *The fifth discipline: The art & practice of the learning organization* (1st ed.). New York, NY: Doubleday.

Skjei, S. (2014). Leaders' lived experience of authentic moments. In K. Goldman Schuyler, J. E. Baugher, K. Jironet, & L. Lid-Falkman (Eds.), *Leading with spirit, presence, and authenticity* (pp. 213–231). San Francisco, CA: Jossey-Bass.

Sugiyama, K., Cavanagh, K. V., van Esch, C., Bilimoria, D., & Brown, C. (2016). Inclusive leadership development drawing from pedagogies of women's and general leadership development programs. *Journal of Management*

Education, *40*(3), 253–292. doi:10.1177/1052562916632553. Accessed on May 20, 2016.

Taylor, M. M. (2011). *Emergent learning for wisdom*. New York, NY: Palgrave Macmillan.

Thorpe-Moscon, J. (2015). Inclusion is key to keeping Canadian high potentials (Research Report). Toronto, ON, Canada: Catalyst Research Centers. Retrieved from http://www.catalyst.org/system/files/inclusion_is_key_to_keeping_cana-dian_high_potentials.pdf. Accessed on May 20, 2016.

UNESCO. (2009). Education and the search for a sustainable future (Policy dialogue: ESD and development policy). (Vol.: 1; 2009-179121e). Paris. Retrieved from http://unesdoc.unesco.org/images/0017/001791/179121e.pdf. Accessed on July 13, 2016.

Van de Ven, A. H. (2011). Engaged scholarship: Stepping out. *Business Strategy Review*, *2*, 43–45.

Vygotsky, L. S. (1986). *Thought and language – Revised edition* (Original 1962). Cambridge, MA: The MIT Press.

Walinga, J., & Harris, B. (2016). Chapter 1: From barriers to breakthroughs: Student experiences of the RRU learning model. In D. Hamilton, P. Márquez, N. Agger-Gupta, S. Grundy, G. Veletsianos, V. Forssmann, & M. LeGault (Eds.), *Engaging students in life-changing learning: The Royal Roads University learning and teaching model in practice*. Victoria, BC, Canada: Royal Roads University. Retrieved from https://learningandteachingmodel.pressbooks.com/chapter/tocheck-from-barriers-to-breakthroughs-student-experiences-of-the-rrulearning-model/. Accessed on July 13, 2016.

Weisbord, M. R. (2012). Productive workplaces: Dignity, meaning, and community in the 21st century (3rd (25th Anniversary) ed.). New York, NY: Pfeiffer and Books24X7.

Wheatley, M. (2006). *Leadership and the new science: Discovering order in a chaotic world*. San Francisco, CA: Berrett-Koehler.

Wheatley, M. J. (2002). The work of servant-leadership. In L. C. Spears & M. Lawrence (Eds.), *Focus on leadership: Servant-leadership for the twenty-first century*. New York, NY: Wiley.

Woods, P. A. (2016). Chapter 4: Democratic roots: Feeding the multiple dimensions of leadership-as-practice. In J. A. Raelin (Ed.), *Leadership-as-practice: Theory and application* (pp. 70–87). New York, NY: Routledge.

Zimmerman, B., Reason, P., Rykert, L., Gitterman, L., Christian, J., & Gardam, M. (2013). Front-line ownership: generating a cure mindset for patient safety. *Healthcare Papers*, *13*(1), 6.

18

Building Inclusive Leaders: A Critical Framework for Leadership Education

Leonard D. Taylor, Jr. and
Ethan Brownell

Keywords: Leadership education; leadership development; leadership studies; Critical Race Theory; Intersectionality Theory; TribalCrit

Changing How We Educate on Leadership

Locally, nationally, internationally; formally and informally; leaders everywhere are working to navigate a changing world. Today's leaders have had varying success in creating sustainable, effective, and inclusive change. Tensions exist about who should lead, how they should lead, and to what end. More than ever, countries and communities across the globe need leaders who are well equipped to facilitate change, while navigating and addressing historical, political, and interpersonal tensions. Leadership education spaces, especially in higher education, are well suited to meet these needs.

Leadership education curriculum has gained ascendance globally, with many education spaces being dedicated to delivering leadership education and training for social change (Brown, 2004). The field of leadership education shoulders a responsibility to develop leaders to "...take action against the oppressive political elements of reality" (Freire, 1994, p. 17). A challenge, however, is the lack of guiding leadership frameworks that consider the complexity, history, and indemnity of societal issues (Haber & Komives, 2009; Patterson, 2013). A critical leadership framework stands to inform leadership education by empowering emerging leaders with the capacities and skills necessary to engender change.

LEADERSHIP CORNERSTONES: A BRIEF REVIEW OF LITERATURE

In efforts to assert the saliency of the literature referenced here, without overstating the contributions, the works referenced are considered *cornerstones* of the leadership literature used for students' leadership learning and development. The literature included here represents widely referenced theories and studies guiding leadership education efforts in college settings. Peter Northouse (2015) offers a catalog of leadership theories, highlighting dominant categories of leadership literature. The Multi-Institutional Study of Leadership has also helped to outline cornerstones of leadership literature (Dugan, Komives, & Owen, 2006). This brief review highlights several key areas of leadership literature.

Helen Astin (1996) developed a leadership development model to address the need for new approaches to cultivating student leadership capacity in higher education. This Social Change Model of Leadership Development focuses on the personal and interpersonal aspects of leadership development, a departure from previous literature focused almost exclusively on skill building (Astin, 1996). This model has seven core values focused in three areas: personal, group, and societal. The concept of citizenship is used to advance communal understandings of leadership.

The Leadership Challenge model emerged from leadership in the private sector, but has been adapted for use in leadership development in collegiate settings. The Leadership Challenge model asserts five key traits or behaviors to be emphasized in leadership development. This model encourages empowerment as an approach to leadership development (Kouzes & Posner, 2006).

The Authentic Leadership Model emphasizes self-awareness related to values, identity, emotions, goals, and motives, and sustainable relationships with followers. This model challenges leaders to be confident in themselves and their values, and display behaviors that reflect those values (Avolio & Gardner, 2005). The authors address temporal considerations, such as the sustainability of leadership, which have not surfaced in previous leadership literature.

Researchers recognized the limitations of leadership literature more than a decade ago, when they set out to understand how leaders develop in college settings, "Leadership theories that rely on traits, behaviors, and situations to explain leadership worked well in an industrial era when the predominant goals of leadership were production and efficiency" (Komives, Owen, Longerbeam, Mainella, & Osteen, 2005, p. 593). They called attention to the need of leadership theories and approaches that respond to the new and emerging needs based on a postindustrial society (Komives et al., 2005). Through a grounded theory study of small and diverse sample of students and recent graduates, the authors were able to map and catalog their participants' developmental processes and trajectories. This work explores how students' experiences influence their development as leaders.

Several theories identified here follow the goal of responding to new and emerging needs in postindustrial society. Servant leadership is founded on the principle that a leader considers the needs of the organization and its members before their own needs (Greenleaf, 1977). In this theory, leaders serve the goals of the organization while simultaneously developing leadership skills and traits. Transformational leadership emerged in the early 1990s from a survey of graduate students in business (Bass & Riggio, 2006). The authors set out to address the limitations of transactional approaches to leadership by promoting transformational interactions, thus stimulating followers to achieve extraordinary outcomes (Bass & Riggio, 2006). Transformation is achieved through the empowerment of followers, and by aligning the goals of followers, leaders, and the organization. This model introduces the concept of caring as a leadership performance. While this theory has been contended, the term is widely used in contemporary leadership discourses.

MOVING LEADERSHIP FORWARD

The works presented above are notable for their respective contributions to leadership literature in higher education. This body of work also reveals areas for continued study. The Inclusive Leadership concept emerges as a promising framework to refine some of the cornerstone leadership discourses. Edwin Hollander (2012) considers the role that power plays in contemporary leadership theories, particularly in the relationship between followers and leaders. Hollander (2012) begins to challenge the leader-follower dialectic as he highlights (1) the utility of leader-follower interdependence, (2) the notion that leaders are also followers, and (3) seeks to move away from leader-centric models. Hollander (2012) touches on a variety of important topics including but not limited to: decision making and power sharing, ethics, and legitimacy. Hollander (2012) also offers thoughtful critique on popular models of leadership (transactional leadership, transformational leadership, and charismatic leadership), as well as the limitations of Inclusive Leadership.

The Social Change Model very intentionally challenges organizational boundaries of leadership with its focus on societal and community values (Astin, 1996). Although the context need not be constrained to one particular environment, more intentional considerations of context are necessary in the application of leadership theories and models. This guards against overstating the utility of any particular theory or approach. For example, transformational leadership is used as a part of countless university leadership programs and initiatives with little consideration of its business origins. Higher education scholars emphasize the need to consider context in the application of theories and best practices, to ensure successful translation into institutional practice (Bensimon, 2007).

An additional opportunity for continued study is how leadership exists and how leaders develop in noninstitutional contexts. Literature about leadership used for college students is almost exclusively oriented in institutional contexts. There is little work done to understand the leadership development and experiences that students have in their lives outside of institutions. It is not that these things are completely absent. Some scholars have advanced leadership discourses through their considerations of community contexts and students' lived experiences (Astin, 1996; Komives et al., 2005). In Astin (1996), citizenship takes the form of social responsibility and collective impact. Komives et al. (2005)

invite discourses from interview participants about the leadership experiences that have contributed to their development, some of which happen before college, outside of college campuses, and are related to social issues. Both of these studies contribute to increasingly comprehensive understandings of students' leadership experiences. More needs to be done, however, to intentionally and explicitly explore leadership development in students' lives outside of campus (Avolio & Gardner, 2005; Bass & Riggio, 2006). For example, a student from an agrarian background could have a wealth of leadership experiences accumulated in rural settings but not see them as relevant based on the institutional nature of leadership discourses. Educators need to be skilled at inviting learners to find examples of leadership in all parts of their lives, especially outside of formal institutional contexts. There is opportunity to explore how leadership takes shape in informal settings, communities, and especially within indigenous cultures.

Theories of servant leadership and transformational leadership have stimulated an increased interest in discussing followers and followership, greatly enriching leadership literature and discourse (Avolio & Gardner, 2005; Bass & Riggio, 2006; Greenleaf, 1977; Kouzes & Posner, 2006). Work needs to be done to complicate the dynamic further by moving beyond static leader and follower roles. An exploration of: (1) the simultaneity of leadership and followership, (2) the role of dissent, and (3) the roles of dissenters in leadership situations are three areas that could contribute to more robust understanding of actors in leadership situations. European scholars have started to address this, asserting that leadership roles like followership and leadership are mutually constructed and coproduced (Collinson, 2005), inviting more critical perspectives on traditional conceptions of leadership. This also suggests the utility of international leadership literature, especially perspectives from outside of the global west.

The concept of Inclusive Leadership and the questions that it invites serve as a fitting point of departure for continued interrogation and subsequent development of leadership theories. A particularly salient critique of the Inclusive Leadership Model is that it assumes the leader and follower relationships exist in an open system, not informed or constrained by pressures from authority and politics (Hollander, 2012). Additional considerations to add to this critique are related to the social identities of people performing in these relationships, and the history of these relationships. How are the relationships and dynamics in leader and follower roles different for different people based on their social identities? Roya Ayman and Karen Korabik (2010) assert the importance of considering social identity in leadership performance, as well as the absence of these considerations in many of the widely used leadership theories. As work to develop leaders and advance leadership education continues, increasingly nuanced perspectives and theories on leadership are necessary, especially those that consider the complexity and intersection of social identities.

Additionally, it is important to consider the history of leadership environments, and the histories of the people within them. History is often overlooked, or when considered, is seen as an innocuous or immutable contextual aspect. Individual, organizational, societal histories, and the authors of those histories are vital for leaders and leadership educators to consider for movement toward more inclusive and socially responsible approaches to leadership.

The works of David Collinson and Dennis Tourish (2015) and Shawna Patterson (2013) begin to introduce critical and poststructural considerations as they explore how power is constructed in the context of leadership and leadership education. Critical Leadership Studies raise questions about power, largely in formal organizations and institutions outside of higher education (Collinson, 2005), and are slowly beginning to address leadership education (Collinson & Tourish, 2015). For example, there has been a significant attention to gender differences in leadership development and performance, but limited exploration of feminist perspectives in leadership practice (Eagly & Chin, 2010). Building on the work of Critical Leadership Studies scholars, well-developed critical theories contribute to the formation of a framework to be used to guide curriculum and pedagogy in leadership education.

Critical Times Call for Critical Theories

Diversity education literature is useful but often seen as separate, leading to the overreliance on isolated diversity lessons and trainings to understand the relationship of leadership to social issues. Separating leadership from diversity and social justice suggests that leadership only sometimes needs to attend to these issues, or the people affected by these issues. If leaders and leadership education seek to promote change toward more inclusive, equitable, and libratory spaces, then they should be informed by theories, paradigms, and practices that are rooted in creating that same change.

A critical stance brings attention to issues of power, privilege, and oppression in preparing emerging leaders. A critical approach to leadership education can invigorate the field, challenging educators to "retool their teaching and trainings to address issues of power and privilege," to ultimately "...weave social justice into the fabric of educational leadership curriculum, pedagogy, programs, and policies" (Brown, 2004, p. 78). Critical theories can help educators to interrogate, understand, deconstruct, and reconstruct leadership education curriculum, pedagogies, cultures, and trajectory. The framework below leverages critical theories to attend to the reproduction of social inequality, addresses marginalization based on social identity, and develops strategies that empower people to create change.

ORIGINS OF CRITICAL THEORY

Critical Theory grew from the contributions of several founding and contemporary scholars. Although more contemporary critical theories are used to guide the development of a leadership education framework here, it is helpful to explore the emergence of Critical Theory to understand the longstanding commitment to disrupting human injustice. Max Horkheimer (1972) asserts the goal of Critical Theory is to interrupt domination across societies and within communities through the development of interdisciplinary research that is both empirical and historical. Founding theorists assert that this research must "...identify and explain the underlying causes of social problems in order to make positive transformation possible" (Martínez-Alemán, Pusser, & Bensimon, 2015, p. 8). Critical Theory seeks to address human subjugation through rigorous and thoughtful investigation and interrogation of social issues, the histories of those issues, and the structures and cultures that maintain them (Horkheimer, 1972; Martínez-Alemán et al., 2015).

Moving beyond interrogation and critique, some theorists and theories assert the need for the resistance to and dismantling of unjust systems (Flyvbjerg, 2000). Critical Theory is widely used by feminists, critical race theorists, and others to "...identify[sic] and locate the ways in which societies produce and preserve specific inequalities through social, cultural, and economic systems" (Martínez-Alemán et al., 2015, p. 8). Tenets and constructs from several critical theories are considered in the creation and delivery of curriculum through this framework.

CRITICAL RACE THEORY

The emergence of Critical Race Theory (CRT) is most directly associated with Critical Legal Studies (CLS), although it is continually evolving through varied and innovative application. CLS seek to expose and challenge the purported neutrality of law and legal reasoning, asserting that it is value-laden and influenced by social, economic, political, and cultural phenomena (McCoy & Rodricks, 2015). CRT focuses intently on exposing, interrogating, and challenging structural and systemic racialized oppression to support social transformation. CRT builds on CLS as it works to disrupt ahistorical perspectives through the use of voice and counternarrative (Lynn & Dixson, 2013; Matsuda, Lawrence, Delgado, & Crenshaw, 1993; McCoy & Rodricks, 2015; Yosso, 2005). Specifically in higher education policy and practice, CRT is a theoretical framework and analytical tool to understand, investigate, interpret, and deconstruct oppressive educational structures and systems (McCoy & Rodricks, 2015). The tenets of CRT help to frame the theory and understand its utility. CRT:

(1) recognizes that racism is endemic to American life;
(2) expresses skepticism toward dominant legal claims of neutrality, objectivity, colorblindness, and meritocracy;
(3) challenges ahistoricism and insists on a contextual/historical analysis of the law;
(4) presumes that racism has contributed to all contemporary manifestations of group advantage and disadvantage;
(5) insists on recognition of the experiential knowledge of people of color and our communities of origin in analyzing law and society;
(6) is interdisciplinary and eclectic; and
(7) works toward the end of eliminating racial oppression as part of the broader goal of ending all forms of oppression (Matsuda et al., 1993, p. 6).

Critical Race Theory is particularly useful in that: (1) it considers the indemnity of racism and other social ills; (2) it challenges ahistorical interpretations of social issues in favor of historical, contextual analysis; and (3) it values interdisciplinary knowledge and approaches (Lynn & Dixson, 2013).

TRIBAL CRITICAL RACE THEORY

Tribal Critical Race Theory (TribalCrit) challenges longstanding perspectives on Native Americans by positioning them as both racial and political groups (Bartlett & Brayboy, 2005; Brayboy, 2005). This is important, as it acknowledges the history of these groups' nationhood. Other critical theories centered on social identity discuss various types of oppression as they emerge *within* US context while TribalCrit engages issues that emerged from the *imposition* of European and US context through colonialism and imperialism. Brayboy (2005) outlines the tenets of TribalCrit:

(1) colonization is endemic to society;
(2) US policies toward Indigenous peoples are rooted in imperialism, White supremacy, and a desire for material gain;
(3) Indigenous peoples occupy a liminal space that accounts for both the political and racialized natures of their identities;
(4) Indigenous peoples have a desire to obtain and forge tribal sovereignty, tribal autonomy, self-determination, and self-identification;
(5) the concepts of culture, knowledge, and power take on new meaning when examined through an Indigenous lens;
(6) governmental and educational policies toward Indigenous peoples are intimately linked around the problematic goal of assimilation;
(7) tribal philosophies, beliefs, customs, traditions, and visions for the future are central to understanding the lived realities of Indigenous peoples, but they also illustrate the differences and adaptability among individuals and groups;
(8) stories are not separate from theory, but they make up theory and are real and legitimate sources of data and ways of being; and
(9) theory and practice are connected in deep and explicit ways such that scholars must work toward social change (pp. 429–430).

While TribalCrit centers on the experiences of Native Americans, particularly those impacted by European and US colonialism, it can be applied to understand the effects of colonialism and imperialism on conquered people globally. The TribalCrit tenets above and other scholars' work help us to consider: (1) the centrality of culture, values, and beliefs in understanding people's lived experiences, (2) the role of institutional structures and policies in assimilation and social reproduction,

(3) the importance of personal stories and narratives in informing theory, and (4) the necessity of connecting theory and practice in working toward social change (Brayboy, 2005; Lynn & Dixson, 2013).

INTERSECTIONALITY THEORY

Intersectional Theory is derived from critical feminist work and challenges essentialism, particularly assumptions of universality of the experiences of women of color (Carbado, Crenshaw, Mays, & Tomlinson, 2013). It is noted for the thoughtful exploration of the intersections of marginalized social identities and the subsequent, compounded impact (Carbado et al., 2013; Crenshaw, 1991). McCoy and Rodricks (2015) explain:

> ...People of Color often solidarize based on shared characteristics or experiences as a means to cultivate agency and gain greater access against their ongoing marginalization by those in power. Such efforts, while worthy, still silence and erase the unique experiences of specific communities under the People of Color umbrella (p. 63).

McCoy and Rodricks (2015) explain this through the convergence of race and class: "With race and access to capital historically connected, different structures (capitalism, patriarchy, hegemony) converge with law and policy to exclude individuals and communities within a specific nation state" (p. 63). This reveals how, even in the efforts to liberate, ignoring the uniqueness of people's experiences can invite different type of oppression. Intersectionality Theory invites additional nuance to critical theories and perspectives, by creating more space for the variety of identities that inform and impact people's lived experiences.

A Working Framework

EMERGING DIMENSIONS OF A CRITICAL LEADERSHIP FRAMEWORK

The following dimensions are offered as focal points for a critical leadership education framework: internal discourses on social experiences and issues, interpersonal interactions, contextual understandings of leadership theories and concepts, theoretical perspectives, and histories and historical perspectives of societies and social issues. The emergence of these areas is influenced by the work of Collinson and Tourish (2015), Patterson (2013), and the critical theories and theorists presented above.

Internal discourses. A number of widely used leadership theories center on the individuals practicing leadership, and offer prescriptive sets of individualistic leadership behaviors and traits (Astin, 1996; Collinson & Tourish, 2015). Servant Leadership and the Social Change Model begin to consider collectivist perspectives as they discuss larger societal needs. Whether an individualistic or collectivist approach, attention should be paid to the way individuals make sense of their engagement as leaders, as well as the values and perspectives that inform their sensemaking. Understanding privately held beliefs, uncovering unconscious biases, and exploring perspectives on self, others, and social issues are necessary undertakings for leaders, especially those committed to social change (Brayboy, 2005; Horkheimer, 1972; McCoy & Rodricks, 2015). Leadership education is poised to help students and instructors unearth, explore, and understand their internal discourses and how they influence their perspectives.

Teaching about leadership and social change requires a complex, nuanced, varied, historical understanding of systems. Critical Theory, CRT, Intersectionality Theory, and TribalCrit emphasize the value of experiential knowledge from people historically ignored or pushed to the margins. Globally, people of color and others have been socialized to see Eurocentric approaches to leadership as ideal or most valuable. A focus on internal discourses can help people invite their experiential knowledge, especially from their own cultural paradigms, and potentially disrupt monolithic leadership paradigms. For example, CRT challenges notions of neutrality, objectivity, and meritocracy within oppressive systems and structures. To mount this challenge successfully, the individuals in organizations must be examined as well as the systems and structures themselves (Bensimon, 2005).

Interpersonal interactions. Several theories and models of leadership focus on the interpersonal exchanges between leaders and others. Efforts to discuss interpersonal interactions in leadership education often overlook the importance of understanding the complexity of others' lived experiences. People's identities, histories, and lived experiences are important to understanding and navigating the complexities of interpersonal interactions, especially in leadership roles (Collinson & Tourish, 2015).

Intersectionality invites people to consider others in nuanced and complex ways. Groups of people collectively working toward change may acknowledge the group's shared interests and identities but take for granted the intersections of other identities and the impact of those intersections. The early feminist movement, for example, is critiqued for being exclusively focused on the experiences of upper class white women. The voices and experiences of queer women, working class and poor women, and women of color were largely overlooked. Acknowledging the intersection of identity is necessary to mitigate the emergence of oppressive sentiments even within like-minded or similarly identifying groups (Carbado et al., 2013; Crenshaw, 1991; McCoy & Rodricks, 2015).

Interpersonal interaction is not just about interactions across difference. Understanding the implications for our interactions with similar peers is necessary, as these are many of the spaces where problematic biases and prejudice emerge and are reinforced. Resistance and dissent are often characterized as the responsibility of the oppressed. Practices of allyship and solidarity with oppressed groups have helped to diversify resistance efforts, take, for example, non-Black participants in the Black Lives Matter Movement in the United States. An additional responsibility of allied leaders, through this framework, is to leverage their social and political capital for advocacy in spaces where the oppressed are often absent.

Concepts in context. When context is ignored, intentionally or unintentionally, concepts are taken to be universal. This begins to move toward the types of essentialism that critical theories, like Intersectionality Theory, seek to dismantle. It is important to understand how leadership, power, and other concepts exist and operate in different contexts. A number of leadership theories have essentialized leadership to what UK scholars have coined as "heroic individualism," circumscribing leadership into very narrow and prescribed roles and behaviors (Collinson & Tourish, 2015; Lipman-Blumen, 2000). This is arguably due to the overwhelming presence of US authors in leadership literature as well as a predominant focus on leadership for business and industry, "[Because] most studies are conducted by U.S. researchers in U.S. companies about U.S. employees, informed by U.S. perspectives and methods it is perhaps unsurprising that leadership research articulates primarily U.S. values" (Collinson & Tourish, 2015, p. 20). This demonstrates the need for an acute understanding of from what context leadership theories originate, and the need for more and varied perspectives of leadership from different contexts.

People's value of, response to, and use of power are largely influenced by their personal experiences and contexts, particularly in how they respond to others in power. Following many of the cornerstone theories mentioned above, leaders are taught to perform based on their own style and comfort. A considerable amount of leadership literature focuses on the behaviors and dispositions of leaders, but significantly fewer pieces explore the impact of those styles from the lenses of followers. Leaders should also be trained to consider how people might respond to different styles and approaches, and in a variety of contexts.

The consideration of power in interpersonal interactions, organizations, and society, is a valuable nuance offered by UK critical leadership scholars. Collinson and Tourish (2015) assert, "...for good or ill, leaders exert significant power and influence over contemporary organizational processes. Whilst the exercise of power and authority is sometimes necessary and may deliver desirable ends, CLS also addresses the dangers of concentrating control in the hands of a few" (p. 21). These perspectives challenge the assumptions espoused by many leadership theories that: (1) leaders must navigate and act within structural and hierarchal power, (2) that power structures and patterns are ubiquitous and immutable, and (3) leadership should be measured based on the successful use of power (Collinson & Tourish, 2015). These parts help to more intentionally and explicitly consider power in leadership contexts, in how we explore and deconstruct leadership phenomena, and how to more intentionally cultivate context-responsive philosophies and approaches to leadership.

Theoretical perspectives. Experiential components of leadership education have continued to proliferate and evolve, allowing people to learn from situations through direct experience and reflection. While practicality is paramount, the utility of theory is also important. Leadership education should empower those learning about leadership with the skills to thoughtfully consume, apply, critique, and create leadership theories. Comprehensive exploration and interpretation of theories, their guiding epistemologies, ontologies, and underlying constructs can help to advance and complicate leaders' consumption and application of leadership literature and teachings. Empowering leaders with the skills to inform leadership theories invites more voices and perspectives on leadership, congruent with calls from scholars in Critical Leadership Studies (Collinson & Tourish, 2015).

Critical theorists and scholars promote interdisciplinary scholarship to disrupt monolithic narratives in scholarship by diversifying the paradigms used to inform curriculum and practice. This approach invites leadership educators and scholars to mine a variety of leadership spaces for wisdom, especially unexplored spaces outside of business and management paradigms.

Histories and historical perspectives. Attention to history in this context calls attention to problematic histories or the absence of histories all together, especially in recounting stories of the oppressed. This ahistoricism contributes to the promulgation of social issues by ignoring the decisions and policies that have contributed to injustices. Ahistoricism induces people to see the past as neutral, natural, and inevitable, as opposed to a series of imperfect, biased decisions made by fallible people (Lynn & Dixson, 2013; Matsuda et al., 1993; McCoy & Rodricks, 2015; Yosso, 2005). As a result of ahistoricism, "master narratives" emerge and mask power and subjectivity in the capturing, maintaining, and retelling of history, particularly the histories of oppressed or conquered people (Ladson-Billings, 1998).

An example of this comes in the historical accounts of the American Civil Rights Movement. Rosa Parks was characterized as a Black woman, physically tired from work, and refusing to obey segregationist laws that required her to move to the back of the bus she was riding. Years later, narratives surfaced that revealed her refusal to move to the back of the bus was an act of political resistance, and part of a larger strategy to enact the Montgomery Bus Boycott orchestrated by the National Association for the Advancement of Colored People. The later perspective conveys intentionality, collective strategy, and complexity on the part of Parks and other civil rights leaders. This moves beyond passive disobedience to characterize Parks's action as an active resistance to injustice. An intentional focus on history not only challenges master scripting, but also supports thoughtful capturing, maintaining, and retelling of history moving forward. Whether a CEO or civil rights activist (or both), leaders benefit from an enhanced historical understanding of the organization or society they are working within.

LEVELS OF APPLICATION

To effectively inculcate these critical perspectives and practices into curriculum and pedagogy and sustain their usage, leadership educators and their organizations must also be examined through these lenses. Robert Rhoads and William Tierney (1992) and Patterson (2013) are used as a structure to attend to the institutional considerations necessary for effective support of these efforts. Their work asserts the importance the actors and structures involved in creating and disseminating leadership education training and curriculum. The overall goal is to support leaders and educators in translating theories of leadership into practice and action in ways that will effect inclusive and sustainable change.

Instructors, educators, and trainers. Patterson (2013) encourages educators to reflect on their own biases and how they may influence their work in the classroom. This reflection is important for educators to ensure congruence between delivery of course content and their performance in the classroom. For example, instructors who invite students to be vulnerable but do not demonstrate vulnerability in their teaching may be perceived as inauthentic or engender distrust. Demonstrating content in practice can offer students contextual and real-time examples of course concepts: "Students require faculty and staff who can coach them in working through discomfort and independently identifying techniques that will lead toward self-initiated relationships. Educators should therefore provide students with spaces to learn how to develop these skill sets" (Patterson, 2013, p. 14).

Departments, organizations, and institutions. Leadership education is often facilitated through formal institutions, organizations, and structures. Those institutions, organizations, and structures should also be considered through a critical lens to understand if organizations perform in congruence with the values and perspectives they teach. Critical theories make clear the precarious nature of organizations, particularly in how problematic practices and perspectives may be subtly and intentionally maintained (Lynn & Dixson, 2013; McCoy & Rodricks, 2015). Collinson and Tourish (2015) bring attention to this phenomena; "Studies have also revealed profound patterns of leadership dysfunctionality in some radical social change organizations…" (p. 20).

Intentionally examining the structures, policies, and cultures of the institutions, organizations, or departments can help establish spaces to develop and facilitate leadership education experiences. Organizations that teach leadership and commit to creating change in local or global contexts should work to inculcate critical perspectives into their polices, structures, cultures, practices, and people, helping to establish the permanence and longevity of these efforts.

Conclusion

The dimensions considered for this framework offer important areas of focus for efforts seeking to develop thoughtful and inclusive leaders. Moving toward a critical leadership framework can help unearth and interrupt the subtle but pervasive hegemony under the surface of leadership education discourses. Diverse and international perspectives are invited to challenge dominant voices, paradigms, ontologies, and epistemologies.

Critical Theory, CRT, TribalCrit, and Intersectionality Theory, all offer thoughtful and necessary contributions to the development of a critical leadership framework, but this work should not be limited to these theories. Wisdom from other critical theories, both well established and emerging, can also be used to this end. As scholars and practitioners continue to develop critical lenses for their own leadership contributions, they are encouraged to draw from paradigms and traditions that fit their needs and those of the people they seek to impact.

Acknowledgments

Thanks to the University of Minnesota — Twin Cities, Leadership Minor for convening leadership educators around critical topics in the field.

References

Astin, H. S. (1996). Leadership for social change. *About Campus*, *1*(3), 4–10.

Avolio, B. J., & Gardner, W. L. (2005). Authentic leadership development: Getting to the root of positive forms of leadership. *The Leadership Quarterly*, *16*(3), 315–338.

Ayman, R., & Korabik, K. (2010). Leadership: Why gender and culture matter. *American Psychologist*, *65*(3), 157.

Bartlett, L., & Brayboy, B. M. J. (2005). Race and schooling: Theories and ethnographies. *The Urban Review*, *37*(5), 361–374.

Bass, B. M., & Riggio, R. E. (2006). *Transformational leadership.* Mahwah, NJ: Psychology Press.

Bensimon, E. M. (2005). Closing the achievement gap in higher education: An organizational learning perspective. In A. Kezar (Ed.), *New directions for higher education* (Vol. 131, pp. 99–111). San Francisco, CA: Jossey-Bass/Wiley.

Bensimon, E. M. (2007). The underestimated significance of practitioner knowledge in the scholarship on student success. *The Review of Higher Education, 30*(4), 441–469.

Brayboy, B. M. J. (2005). Toward a tribal critical race theory in education. *The Urban Review, 37*(5), 425–446.

Brown, K. M. (2004). Leadership for social justice equity: Weaving a transformative framework and pedagogy. *Educational Administration Quarterly, 40*(1), 77–108.

Carbado, D. W., Crenshaw, K. W., Mays, V. M., & Tomlinson, B. (2013). Intersectionality. *Du Bois Review: Social Science Research on Race, 10*(02), 303–312.

Collinson, D. (2005). Dialectics of leadership. *Human Relations, 58*(11), 1419–1442.

Collinson, D., & Tourish, D. (2015). Teaching leadership critically: New directions for leadership pedagogy. *Academy of Management Learning & Education, 14*(4), 576–594.

Crenshaw, K. (1991). Mapping the margins: Intersectionality, identity politics, and violence against women of color. *Stanford Law Review, 43*(6), 1241–1299.

Dugan, J. P., Komives, S. R., & Owen, J. E. (November, 2006). *Multi-institutional study of leadership.* Retrieved on from the National Clearinghouse for Leadership Programs https://nclp.umd.edu/include/pdfs/ILA%202006.pdf. Accessed on December 10, 2015.

Eagly, A. H., & Chin, J. L. (2010). Diversity and leadership in a changing world. *American Psychologist, 65*(3), 216.

Flyvbjerg, B. (April, 2000). Ideal theory, real rationality: Habermas versus Foucault and Nietzsche. Paper presented to the Political Studies Association's 50th Annual Conference, The Challenges for Democracy in the 21st Century, London School of Economics and Political Science, pp. 10–13. Retrieved from flyvbjerg.plan.aau.dk/IdealTheory.pdf

Freire, P. (1994). *Pedagogy of the oppressed* (Rev. ed.). New York, NY: Continuum.

Greenleaf, R. K. (1977). *Servant leadership.* New York, NY: Paulist Press.

Haber, P., & Komives, S. R. (2009). Predicting the individual values of the social change model of leadership development: The role of college students' leadership and involvement experiences. *Journal of Leadership Education, 7*(3), 133–166.

Hollander, E. (2012). *Inclusive leadership: The essential leader–follower relationship.* New York, NY: Routledge.

Horkheimer, M. (1972). *Critical theory: Selected essays* (Vol. 1). London, UK: A & C Black.

Komives, S. R., Owen, J. E., Longerbeam, S. D., Mainella, F. C., & Osteen, L. (2005). Developing a leadership identity: A grounded theory. *Journal of College Student Development*, 46(6), 593–611.

Kouzes, J. M., & Posner, B. Z. (2006). *The leadership challenge* (Vol. 3). Hoboken, NJ: John Wiley & Sons.

Ladson-Billings, G. (1998). Just what is critical race theory and what's it doing in a nice field like education? *International Journal of Qualitative Studies in Education*, 11(1), 7–24.

Lipman-Blumen, J. (2000). *Connective leadership: Managing in a changing world*. Oxford, UK: Oxford University Press.

Lynn, M., & Dixson, A. D. (Eds.). (2013). *Handbook of critical race theory in education*. New York, NY: Routledge.

Matsuda, M. J., Lawrence, C. R., Delgado, R., & Crenshaw, K. W. (1993). *Words that wound. Critical race theory, assaultive speech, and the first amendment*. Berkley, CA: Westview Press.

Martínez-Alemán, A. M., Pusser, B., & Bensimon, E. M. (Eds.). (2015). *Critical approaches to the study of higher education: A practical introduction*. Baltimore, MD: JHU Press.

McCoy, D. L., & Rodricks, D. J. (2015). Critical race theory in higher education: 20 years of theoretical and research innovations. *ASHE Higher Education Report*, 41(3), 1–117.

Northouse, P. G. (2015). *Leadership: Theory and practice*. Thousand Oaks, CA: Sage publications.

Patterson, S. M. (2013). Layers of critical engagement: Exploring the intersections of leadership, critical theory, and learning. *About Campus*, 18(1), 9–15.

Rhoads, R. A., & Tierney, W. G. (1992). *Cultural leadership in higher education*. University Park, PA: National Center of Postsecondary Teaching, Learning, and Assessment.

Yosso, T. J. (2005). Whose culture has capital? A critical race theory discussion of community cultural wealth. *Race Ethnicity and Education*, 8(1), 69–91.

PART 5
Inclusiveness in the Field

Introduction

"We are going to construct a more inclusive society. We are trying to build a country in which no one is left out." Franklin Delano Roosevelt In 1942, in the middle of World War II, President Roosevelt was fully aware of the sacrifices the American people were making fighting the war in Europe and in the Pacific, and he needed them to understand why. At that moment, he appealed to inclusiveness as one of the pillars of the new society they were fighting for.

While inclusive leadership is thought by some to be a theoretical concept developed by people with little contact with the "real world," evidence shows that even the most practical people (and perhaps *especially* the most practical people) develop very creative and concrete ways to make inclusive leadership a reality.

From diverse parts of the world, involving educated and noneducated people, across socioeconomic and demographic categories, leaders completely different in personal traits and personal backgrounds can be found implementing their own particular ways of inclusive leadership.

At a time when "bad news" takes up the overwhelming majority of the front pages, and at a time when, more than ever, the case seems to be being made for selfishness and a culture of "every person for themselves" or "you're on your own," it is imperative that these real examples of inclusive leaders be put in the spotlight, as a message of what we can do and what we can be when we open ourselves to others.

Readers of these chapters will learn that inclusive leadership is not the realm of specially gifted individuals that were able to find complex solutions to complex issues. Inclusive leaders are normal people. Perhaps the biggest surprise is how simple the solutions to complex problems are, once we change our perspective.

Readers shouldn't be surprised if they feel themselves questioning and reflecting on what they should be doing to foster inclusiveness in their respective communities. Of course we can't change everything. But couldn't we change *something*?

Perhaps it's time to go back to F.D.R.'s words, and understand what is really at stake.

19 Transforming Leadership through Village Outreach: Women as Change Agents in Sub-Saharan Africa

Mecca Antonia Burns, Bernard Mukisa, Lydia Sanyu and Denis Muwanguzi

Keywords: Budondo; Suubi; Forum Theatre; Uganda; maternal health; PHE

Someone acts ... Who is this 'someone'? She could be called a leader. I prefer to call her an initiator who, because of certain motivations of her own combined with a certain self-confidence, takes the first step toward change ... She breaks the ice. And what is this act? To communicate with other potential actors ... In my view this is the crucial leadership act lying at the very heart of the process of change and always necessary to that process. (Burns, 1996)

Introduction

This is the story of Budondo, a village in Uganda where inclusive, transformational leadership has fostered change on a grassroots level for 20 years. We will describe how an American family joined with a Ugandan family to spark the creation of a rural health center, through an arts-based leadership process.

Budondo village has found its way onto the map through a blend of indigenous and Western leadership, placing female empowerment foremost and demonstrating that everyone benefits when "women lift the world up" (B. Beti, personal communication, May 3, 2016.). Budondo Intercultural Center (BI Center) was started by the family of Bernard Mukisa, in a village not far from the equator and the source of the Nile. In 1999, Mukisa returned to Budondo village after 6 years at the University of Minsk in Russia where he studied theater for social transformation. Grateful to find his wife Teopista and their children well cared for by the community, he has dedicated himself to his village ever since.

According to Mukisa, "Women in villages like Budondo rarely possess authority, even within the family. Communities are entrenched in corruption, domestic violence, land wrangles, and school dropout due to pregnancy. Attempting change may be seen by those in power as a threat. Theatre is a traditional tool for exhorting African leaders to be more responsive to the people."

In this chapter, we will situate the BI Center within a cultural context of collective leadership and informal education. We will offer Forum Theatre as a method of inclusive dialogue and show how it is used for social transformation in Budondo village and beyond, through BI Center and Presence Center for Applied Theatre Arts.

TRANSACTIONAL, TRANSFORMATIONAL, INCLUSIVE

Transactional and transformational leadership are familiar concepts in the social sciences (Bass, 2006; Burns, 1978, 1994). Transactional leadership works when leaders and followers agree about what is essential. Transactional leaders emphasize fairness, operating within a given framework. Transformational leaders seek to change the framework — to transform followers into leaders who can see beyond their own self-interest, achieve results greater than originally planned, and embrace the unknown.

Inclusive leadership integrates transformational and transactional leadership, recognizing that followers' needs are fundamental to both approaches (Hollander, 2007).

TRANSFORMING LEADERSHIP IN AFRICA

African-led initiatives tend to grow directly from the felt needs of a given community. Despite a scarcity of financial capital, an abundance of *social* capital may attract Westerners who become moved by the courage and creativity they see happening in the field. Relationships deepen when insiders and outsiders share stories and listen to social concerns, letting their values and motivations coalesce.

Before I (Mecca Antonia Burns) ever heard of Budondo, Åse Eliason Bjurström and her Swedish colleagues were leading workshops there on sustainable development and theater. According to Mukisa and Teopista' s son, Muwanguzi Denis, "[Åse] has been that taproot right from germination."

What is catalyzed when outsiders "throw themselves into a relationship with followers"? (Burns, 1978, p. 20). The outsiders' empathy deepens, and the villagers begin to see their community through fresh eyes and ears upon realizing that it matters to someone besides themselves. Outsiders become followers — validating felt needs, supporting indigenous leadership, and imagining possibilities together. As values and motivations merge, both groups become aware of mutual wants and needs and the potential to become agents of social transformation.

What keeps this system egalitarian; what allows collective, inclusive leadership? Listening processes must balance cohesion with differentiation. We authors favor Forum Theatre, a theatrical dialogue that was invented in Brazil 50 years ago and has spread across the globe, putting inclusive, transformational leadership into action. Budondo provides a remarkable example (Box 1).

Budondo Village: A Case Study in Population, Health and Environment

Lush and verdant year round from rich sunshine and rainfall and deep fertile soil, Uganda has been called "the pearl of Africa." Perhaps because of these blessings, when you walk through a

Box 1: A Daughter's Remembrance of James MacGregor Burns

While Mukisa and Teopista were already using theater as a tool for social transformation in Uganda, I was in America doing research for my father's next book on leadership.

One afternoon in 1993, my father and I were relaxing in a paddleboat in the Tidal Basin, encircled by Washington DC's iconic architecture. Our oarswomen were my tiny daughters — his granddaughters — who were paddling strenuously under the founding fathers' marble gaze. He and I were discussing my contribution to his new book, Transforming Leadership, *a long-overdue follow-up to* Leadership *(Burns, 1978), I was researching two topics: theater as change agent and population policy in rural India.*

Suddenly he pronounced words that stung me — but ultimately transfigured my life. "You know, Antonia ... I just don't feel you've really penetrated those villages." How could he say this to me? I had spent months searching through dusty libraries.

Later I wondered if he was speaking of himself as well. Was he transferring his own regrets onto me? I recalled my mother telling me of their trip to India decades earlier, and the scenes of poverty that haunted him all his life — a life devoted to studying the American presidency. Now as a grandfather perhaps he recognized the impossibility of "penetrating" those villages himself.

The mantle slipped so subtly onto my shoulders that I didn't notice it until 2005, when my father, brother, and sister-in-law began planning a Global Poverty Leadership Initiative (GPLI), to empower indigenous leaders in Sub-Saharan Africa (Sachs, 2005). By now, Transforming Leadership *was published, with its bold antipoverty manifesto. While planning the GPLI, we Burnses met with Tom Fox, longtime family friend and international development specialist. Suddenly it seemed naive to think that hierarchical village systems would support female leadership. Ultimately we discovered that in Budondo women and girls were already finding their voices, with participatory theater as a powerful strategy for inclusion.*

At the time I didn't yet see how I, a drama therapist and theater activist, could approach poverty in Africa. I dreaded feeling like an outsider. Yet now my daughters were older and I could picture myself working internationally. Though the GPLI remained unfunded, I had already contacted Bernard Mukisa, who offered to host my husband and myself in his village in exchange for Forum Theatre training. Mukisa was already educating his children to carry the work into the future. Reflecting on this 10 years later, I see how fulfilling the unfinished tasks of our forebears can "clothe the nakedness of our hearts" (Ubalijoro, Uwizeyimana, & Verghis, 2016, p. 306).

village like Budondo, you see children everywhere you turn. You can glimpse them through gaps in the vegetation where deforestation has occurred. They are climbing trees to find fruit, gathering discarded plastic bags to bind into soccer balls, laughing, singing, or just sitting and gazing at you as you walk by their huts. More than half the population is under age 15. What will the village be like when these children become parents?

Imagine a woman named Rose, 21 years old, already with four children, who serves on her community's Village Health Team. In villages like Budondo, the average woman has seven children before turning 30. Rose and her husband plow other people's gardens to fend for their young, to keep them healthy and in school. Uganda has one of the fastest-growing populations on earth, and many women would like to space births or limit family size but lack the information and resources to do so.

As I learned from my research on India, people do not like being told not to have babies. "Population control" is a touchy, loaded issue, and studies across the globe affirm that education of girl children is the gentlest and strongest "contraceptive." Girls who attend secondary school delay childbearing and have more choice over their destinies (Bbaale & Mpuga, 2011).

THEATER CULTIVATES EMPATHY

Sanyu Lydia, the middle daughter in the Mukisa family, grew up acting in Atuwa Troupe. She acknowledges, "girl-child education in Africa is on a standstill in many fathers' thoughts. A boy has more favor in families than girls. The mother cannot help much since mothers have no say in society."

"Still, through theatre many are convinced that women can be great in society if given chance. Theatre is a way to feel and bring out other people's emotions in real life. For example, in 2002, our troupe sensitized people about HIV/AIDs."

"In the play, we see a girl child of about 12 years. Her step-mother abuses her and she decides to run to her only grand-father, who forcefully marries her to a rich man in favor of wealth. She deeply falls into tears seeing the world coming to an end. She rejects the idea but the grandfather insists "what I want is to see you married before I die." She has no alternative but to accept. After 15 years in marriage, she is HIV positive.

"In this play, I performed as the girl. I really thought as if the world wasn't fair, because how could it be that I was born alone, without a mother. I wondered how could it be that my mother died while giving birth to me. Why should the person I considered to be mother handle me rudely? Oh!! I understand that she is a stepmother but even my grandfather, how could he just give me away, why didn't he accept my choice? Why did he match me with an HIV infected person? I would really feel moved by the emotions and this made more perfection in playing my part." In both theater and life, emotions can move us toward meaningful action.

TRADITIONS OF INFORMAL EDUCATION AND COLLECTIVE LEADERSHIP

According to Mukisa, "largely informal schooling existed in Uganda until 1893, when Europeans introduced formal education. Parents and other relatives taught their children through game, song, dance and oral literature, forming a foundation for morals that are still cherished. In these traditional performances, there was no distinction between audience and performers: All participated.

"In the evening during gatherings around the fire, elders would teach the young; there was rarely a story that did not have a lesson. Fathers, grandfathers and uncles taught boys their responsibilities: to support their family, to care for their wives when they were sick, and proper roles for men and women. Songs were sung to show the consequences if people didn't fulfill roles. Stories might poke fun at a man who failed to care for his family, or who was captured with his neighbor's wife — or a man who beat his wife until she said enough is enough and beat him back."

Lydia adds, "When we were young, our elders used to tell us stories, teach us songs; theater was the best means of passing clear information to the young. Local instruments were played, dances and songs amidst the buzzing, to gather people and inform them about danger in the society. Theater is still the quickest means of sensitizing people."

Through Forum Theatre, women who are silent in mixed company can find their voices as protagonists: a bride beaten for going to school, a pregnant girl driven off or sold into marriage, a mother dying in childbirth. And watching these portrayals, the audience is motivated to change the outcome.

ATUWA TROUPE

In 1999, Mukisa and Teopista began to organize young village performers — all school dropouts — into Atuwa Troupe. Mukisa recalls: "Teopista had been home for six years while I was in Russia. On the ground as a "local expert," she knew the problems and challenges people faced. We thought maybe we could work with children to stop men from beating their families. We could find an entry point that way, as it was difficult to form a troupe of married women, since husbands would forbid it — especially if we were talking about them!

"If their children were in school, parents would say theatre was a waste of time. So Teopista suggested working with school dropouts, who tend to be a headache to their parents. Girls often leave school when they become pregnant and are forced to marry. A year later they might return home after being chased away by their husbands. So we would bring them into a perform-ing group, and we saw how this would change their attitude. Previously they didn't have a vision of the future or ability to imagine what is possible. After all, the rest of the community thinks their lives are wasted. The girls were considered "second hand" — who will marry them now?

"When the youth were first brought to the group, some were miserable, unwanted, and did not have soap or cream for their skin. They were pale and slept badly, on mats covered with their mum's dresses from the day. By the end of the first year they were smart and clean, and no longer timid. According to Teopista, these changes opened the eyes of parents ... Children who had been shy were now able to stand before crowds, to sen-sitize them and even educate the leaders. Backstage afterwards they would be heard to say: "Yes, we've told them!"

Lydia adds: "Girls who dreamed of being professionals got the message: You can go back to school, even though you've given birth. Women realized they didn't have to sit and wait for their husbands to provide for them; they saw that they themselves could work to buy paraffin and school books. Instead of feeling sorry for themselves, they began to act."

The Transformative Power of Participatory Theater

Forum Theatre is a branch of Theatre of the Oppressed, invented by Augusto Boal during Brazil's military dictatorship of the 1960s. Boal was a colleague and compatriot of Paulo Freire, whose popular education model helps people reclaim their roles as active, transformative agents in the world (Freire 1970).

In a Forum Theatre skit, spectators are invited to replace the protagonist to propose solutions. This artful disruption of power dynamics transforms citizens into change agents. According to James MacGregor Burns, Boal defines oppression as "a power dynamic based on monologue rather than dialogue. His goal was to inject a second voice — the voice of the people — that would open the system to question and challenge" (Burns, 2003, p. 165).

In 2007, my husband and I stayed with Mukisa's family for 2 weeks and led Forum Theatre sessions in the courtyard. Mukisa recalls that "After a few days' work, participants came out of their shells to tell their untold stories and enacted them on stage." Initially we brainstormed many issues: corruption, child abuse, polygamy, environmental degradation, theft, and inheritance laws, finally settling on three areas — poverty, education, and sanitation — to perform for secondary school students in Iganga town.

As Mukisa describes the outreach, "Many of the youths who came up to replace the protagonist spoke out words they had all along kept to themselves. This was a unique opportunity for their voices to be heard. At first it looked like it was not going to work. All of a sudden, I realized that the students were meeting this form of theater for the first time, and they were not used to being alone in front and talking. When I looked around, my whole group was watching me to see what was next. Then I remembered what a good mobilizer I was and thought of ways of instilling confidence in the audience.

"When the first person, a girl, came up, the rest laughed. I read it that they laughed because, 'What was she going to act; she was never an actress.' I caught the opportunity to encourage her and tell her that whatever she was doing was right. This was the breakthrough. Hands competed to be chosen to come forward."

HOW FORUM THEATRE WORKS

Forum Theatre is not an esoteric, elitist phenomenon, meant only for those who self-identify as artists. While artistic splendor is prized, there is faith that art resides in every human as our birthright. Mirroring society onstage lets people become actors in the process of transformation, encouraging them to open up and find lasting solutions to the challenges they face (Rafiki Theatre, 2014). Forum Theatre makes everyone the artists, the creators of their own true lives.

A Forum Theatre skit is devised by people who share a common problem. But the actors do not solve the problem; it is up to the spectators to intervene. Hence they are called *spectactors* — activated spectators.

Once a spectactor steps in, the play continues, as the actors try to move the plot toward its typical dismal conclusion and the spectactors try to make it turn out differently. It is empowering and engaging for the audience to see their own peers intervene in the role of change agent. The theater work shows multiple perspectives, always recognizing the humanity of the opponent. The goal is not to defeat the adversary, rather to uplift and edify. Theater games vividly demonstrate how to strengthen opponents rather than crush them (Burns, Beti, Okuto, Muwanguzi, & Sanyu, 2015).

SUUBI HEALTH PROJECT: A GLIMMER OF HOPE

In 2010 my husband and I returned to Budondo village. We had received messages while on the bus from Kenya indicating that the family wanted to continue foregrounding girls and women. Next morning the group gathered under a mango tree, where Muwanguzi Denis spoke prophetic words, "What we need is a women's reproductive health center." Suddenly our way forward was clear.

That same day, however, I learned that my younger daughter, Alethea, had fallen ill while working with AIDS orphans in

Kenya. During my 12-hour bus ride back to Nairobi, I promised myself I'd return to Budondo later that year.

In Alethea's hospital room, she and I mapped out plans for the health center, seeing "women's reproductive health" as a nexus for numerous social issues. Foremost was maternal and infant mortality — not a controversial issue. Everyone wants babies and mothers to survive. We could include teen pregnancy prevention, HIV screening, family planning, domestic violence, child nutrition, sanitation, education for girls, and economic opportunities for women.

Later that week, Mukisa, Dia, Denis, and Brad showed up in Alethea's hospital room and we celebrated her recovery — and Suubi's inception. Mukisa owned a hut that could be renovated into a birth center. How much would that cost? He estimated $1,200. Alethea began organizing music events at her college. A colleague told me about Mama Hope, an organization that mobilizes African communities through indigenous and external leadership, providing global advocates who listen, organize, and fundraise. In time, Mama Hope staff visited Budondo and fell in love with the family and their village, and the building of the clinic was underway.

MATERNAL FORUM

In January 2011, I kept my vow, returning to Budondo alone to help the troupe devise Forum Theatre on reproductive health. During 2 weeks of rehearsal, villagers often dropped by to watch, in the deep shade of the mango tree. Many told the same true story: a mother lost her life because a traditional birth attendant (TBA) didn't recognize a complicated delivery in time, and the hospital was far away. We presented our Forum Theatre piece in a nearby trading center to assess community support for building a clinic. A hundred villagers attended, and several stepped into the action to pose solutions.

Afterward, the audience sat for 2 hours on rickety wooden benches to envision building a clinic, which would take years to materialize. Meanwhile, outreach was already happening.

Outreach Programs

Even before the Suubi Center was constructed, it began operating as a base for two outreach organizations, the Village Health

Workers (VHW) and Twogere ("Speak Out") Girls Club. Muwanguzi Denis describes how Suubi projects epitomize inclusive leadership. "Goals are shared in weekly meetings where staff members present developments in their field, building a fund of common knowledge and wisdom, strengthening team cohesion while clarifying each member's contribution."

TWOGERE GIRLS CLUB

The Twogere Girls Club is for schoolgirls wishing to avoid early pregnancy and further their education. In a rural society where women are expected to give birth early and often, the club is an unusual opportunity for girls to organize around their own hopes and dreams. Girls train in theatrical storytelling to share their challenges as young women.

Twogere originated with girls who had dropped out because of pregnancy, lack of school fees or supplies for menstruation, negative family attitude toward girl-child education, or long distances to schools. Twogere means, "Let us speak out," suggesting that women can be leaders. Money from acting enables girls to go back to school and even higher institutions of learning.

"Twogere outreach to secondary schools tackles obstacles to girls' education. A health worker, opinion leader, or entrepreneur in poultry keeping may speak during workshops interlinked with theatre practice. Girls learn to make schoolbags and reusable sanitary pads and then instruct their schoolmates. From girl-to-girl chats, we now rarely hear of girls missing classes due to menstrual flow. The schools exchange ideas and stories which are performed as Forum Theatre to pass on messages and pose solutions."

SUUBI WOMEN

According to Muwanguzi Denis, "The Suubi Health Center was built to address the insufficient health services surrounding Budondo. Existing clinics have poor hygiene, unqualified personnel, and only pain-relieving drugs. The nearest government health center is 20 km away from Budondo and often has drug stockouts. Most maternal deaths in Budondo have occurred during the transportation of expectant mothers to the health unit. When complications are serious, it is often too late to relocate the patient to the hospital. Time slips away while those involved must decide whether to go to hospital, seek transportation, and negotiate fees with medical staff. These delays create a triad of risky points at a time when the lives of the mother and the unborn baby are at stake.

"Several interlinked issues keep families in a vicious cycle of poverty and ill health. The single biggest threat to health and the environment is the cutting of trees for charcoal and firewood, and to make room for sugarcane plantations. Sugarcane depletes soil nutrients, risking food security in homes, letting malnutrition and related complications set in. BI Center develops strategies to address population, health, and environment (PHE) at a household level."

"The Suubi Women have trained for three years as a Village Health Team (VHT) providing basic services, they can become medically certified through coursework in nearby Jinja. On outreaches, they use Forum Theatre to educate the community on prevention and healing."

When I heard that the Suubi clinic would form a VHT, my India research leapt off the dusty shelves and sprang to life. In *Transforming Leadership*, we described how Indira Gandhi's policy of forced sterilizations had brought down her government — but failed to bring down the birth rate. Meanwhile, in a village in Jamhked, a husband-and-wife team of doctors had trained local women as a VHT, spreading knowledge and eradicating disease. The women addressed social ills, locked out abusive husbands, and started small businesses. Astonishingly, the region's fertility rate dropped by more than half. How did a couple of country doctors succeed? They addressed authentic needs, empowering women as natural leaders (Burns, 2003).

Gretchen Steidle, founder of Global Grassroots, describes the female leadership she has seen emerge "among the ranks of undereducated subsistence farmers, war widows, the rural poor and survivors of horrific violence." When women have a chance to apply their own insights and instincts for how societies can evolve, they grow their capacity to address the needs of the most marginalized and vulnerable (Steidle, 2014).

Beyond Budondo Village: Suubi Outreaches

Muwanguzi Denis describes his challenges as an outsider. "One of the 12 Suubi women disclosed to me after the first week of our three-year training, 'Well, you are not a woman or a girl; neither are you married nor old enough to understand sexuality issues affecting us. It took a while for me to feel comfortable discussing reproductive health with you.' Not only did this statement give me insights into gender-related perceptions, but also showed the importance of building the capacity of local women to deal with their own problems."

In 2013, Denis asked me to teach the Suubi women counseling skills. We used mirroring games (Burns, Beti, & Okuto, 2017) for reflective listening and empathy. Then in three groups the women shared stories and devised Forum skits. One story recounted how a health worker had to walk several hours a day to participate in the training, and her husband became suspicious and beat her. Women stepped into the scene to pose a range of solutions, including arising 2 hours earlier to hoe the garden. Teopista enacted a soft conversation persuading the husband, while still in bed, that the free training she was receiving was beneficial for their whole family — showing once again how women lift the world.

According to Denis, "The eight Suubi Women and 24 Twogere Girls' Club members are our two main community engagement and entry platforms. In secondary schools, we perform skits about stereotypical gender roles in a family setting. One audience included 1,200 students, teachers, and parents. Boys, girls, teachers, and parents got involved as spectactors, disclosing attitudes on how daily house chores influence school outcomes among girls. A monologue depicted how it feels to get tired before even beginning the school day."

"One man shared this reaction with the project team during the post-forum dialogue: 'We men are hardly at home during the day as we try to fend for our families. We who attended today got a chance to experience our daughters' voices of what they go through. My question is, how do we get such messages to our fellow men?'"

EXTENDING OUTREACH FURTHER AFIELD

How indeed do these ideas and values radiate out from Budondo? In 2014, the authors embarked on what we affectionately called the "journey mercies tour," working in Western Kenya, the Great Rift Valley, the coast of the Indian Ocean, Nairobi, and a war-torn mountain dividing Kenya and Uganda. Whenever people heard about Suubi, they asked how they could start a health center. They assumed if they got a pile of money everything would fall into place. Denis explained that they didn't have to wait for funding; lives can be saved right away by forming a VHT. Furthermore, funders prefer to support working projects.

FROM TRANSACTING TO TRANSFORMING

During 10 visits to East Africa, I have interacted with people on streets, in vehicles, in villages. I ask someone where to buy fruit and I end up hearing all about their project back in their home village. Is this purely transactional — or are we mutually seeking to engage on a moral plane? Do they desire social transformation, or mainly to bring home a few shillings to their families in the evening? How do transactional and transformational leadership augment each other?

In our 2007 cultural exchange, we traded hosting for theater training, and were treated as fellow artists, not potential funders. Feasting on homegrown food, we learned about rural Ugandan life and how drama, dance, and music foster change there. As theater happened and friendships flourished, our motives coalesced; work and pleasure blended through art. Transactions conducted in a fair and loving fashion can help facilitate the emergence of transformational leadership.

THE WORLD'S PAIN

Back in the USA when I spoke of my travels, my father would inevitably ask me: "So, are you *writing* about your work in Africa?" Writing was the way he knew — his attempt to banish specters of poverty and injustice. Some westerners wonder if their service can help mitigate the shame of global inequity. Is this then a simple transaction: exchanging service for imagined relief from guilt? Or can this kind of "empathic immersion" (Palus, Harrison, & Prasad, 2016, p.185) genuinely unite leaders and followers in mobilizing social transformation?

"Politics is not about dividing one into two. It is the opposite: it is to bring two into one, where everyone is present with his/her own dignity and differences." (Ganguly, 2011, p. 96). This is the view of Jana Sanskriti — a grassroots movement in India, bringing Forum Theatre outreach to thousands of people each month, highlighting women's issues.

Budondo Intercultural Center demonstrates how a continuum of transactional, transformational, and inclusive leadership is necessary and relevant in Africa. Building trust in community out-reach calls for a response to immediate felt needs — coupled with a long-range vision of transformation that includes everyone.

A Call to Action

Budondo has emerged as a model sustainable village and leader-ship center in rural Uganda. People come there to educate each other about best practices, creating a ripple effect as followers become leaders. The Suubi Women's VHT is poised to continue Forum Theatre outreach — as long as they can also provide for their families at home.

Budondo Intercultural Center is a labor of love and a work in progress in which there is room for everyone. We invite you to help spread the word, visit the village, write, donate, volunteer, and contact your representative. Above all, we welcome your empathy and your creativity.

> A family started by a 16 year old girl and an 18 year old boy [Teopista and Mukisa] has taken a path down the valleys, plateaus and hills ... instilling hope in those who had lost it. (Muwanguzi, 2015)

Budondo Intercultural Center   http://bicenter.wixsite.com/bicenteruganda

Facebook page https://www.facebook.com/BudondoIntercultural Center/

Mama Hope (partner organization) — http://www.mamahope.org/communities/uganda/

Video documentation https://www.youtube.com/watch?v=fWJW 4444piY&list=PLt5zY35ckp-In22uTIvwaa4mG4ptRXPCl

Acknowledgments

The authors wish to acknowledge their families, through whom this work thrives even across generations.

Ugandan family: Teopista Kwikiriza Mukisa, Sofia Namwase, Mukisa Charles, Kinawa Modest, Mirembe Clare, Atuwa Hannah Gorrety, and Dr. Sam Magada.

American family: Brad Stoller, Alethea and Chelsea Leventhal, Stewart and Deborah Burns, and the late David Burns, James MacGregor Burns, and Janet Rose Dismorr Thompson Burns Keep.

Special thanks to Amy Taylor for editorial assistance.

References

Bass, M. B., & Riggio, E. G. (2006). *Transformational leadership*. Mahwah, NJ: L. Erlbaum Associates.

Bbaale, E., & Mpuga, P. (2011). Female education, contraceptive use, and fertility: Evidence from Uganda. *Consilience: The Journal of Sustainable Development*, 6(1), 20–47.

Burns, J. M. (1978). *Leadership*. New York, NY: Harper & Row.

Burns, J. M. (1996). Retrieved from http://www.hawaii.edu/intlrel/pols635f/s98stuff/jburn_p1.htm. Accessed on August 3, 2015.

Burns, J. M. (2003). *Transforming leadership: The pursuit of happiness*. New York, NY: Grove Press.

Burns, M., Beti, B., & Okuto, M. (2017). Truth comes in many colors: Theatre of the oppressed for conflict transformation and trauma healing in Kenya. *Grassroots Leadership and the Arts for Social Change*. Bingley: Emerald.

Burns, M., Beti, B., Okuto, M., Muwanguzi, D., & Sanyu, L. (2015). Forum theatre for conflict transformation in East Africa: The domain of the possible. *African Conflict and Peacebuilding Review*, 5(1), 136–151.

Freire, P. (1970). *Pedagogy of the oppressed*. New York: Continuum.

Ganguli, S. (2011). Theatre is hope; theatre is freedom. Schonmann, S. *Key Concepts in Theatre/Drama Education*. Berlin: Springer.

Hollander, E. (2007). *Inclusive leadership: The essential leader-follower relationship (Applied Psychology Series)*. New York, NY: Routledge

Muwanguzi. (2015). Retrieved from https://othernessproject.org/2015/03/19/birth/. Accessed on May 7, 2015.

Palus, J., Harrison, S., & Prasad, J. (2016). Developing relational leadership in Africa. In K. G. Schuyler (Ed.), *Creative social change: Leadership for a healthy world*. Bingley: Emerald.

Rafiki Theatre. (2014). Retrieved from: www.rafiki-theatre.org. Accessed on March 23, 2016.

Sachs, J. (2005). *The end of poverty* (pp. 238–243). New York, NY: Penguin.

Steidle, G. (2014). Global grassroots. Retrieved from: http://www.globalgrassroots.org/blog/tag/leadership/. Accessed on November 26, 2015.

Ubalijoro, E., Uwizeyimana, B., & Verghis, M. (2016). Women and leadership in Rwanda, emerging transformation: The spiritual, social, and political dimensions of transmuting suffering. IN K. G. Schuyler (Ed.), *Creative social change: Leadership for a healthy world*. Bingley: Emerald.

20 Congo Calling — Blood on Our Hands

Miriam Gosling

Keywords: Inclusive leadership; Democratic Republic of Congo (DRC); nongovernment organization (NGO); conflict minerals

T his chapter explores Inclusive Leadership in a nongovernmental organization (NGO): Congo Calling, and I hope it will be a voice for those suffering atrocities that are occurring daily to the people in the Democratic Republic of Congo. I further hope that readers might be inspired to join — to be included — in the campaign. This chapter is therefore an invitation to inclusion.

Congo Calling is a United Kingdom (UK)-based campaign founded by Director Bandi Mbubi, a refugee to the UK after he spoke at TEDx Exeter in 2012. It fights for conflict-free technology minerals from the Democratic Republic of Congo (hereafter known as the DRC) and in particular lobbies for the adoption and implementation of political, legal and commercial frameworks to promote ethical mining practices there. Illegal mining in the eastern part of the DRC fuels a continuing war which denies local people the peace, stability and prosperity which could flow from the ethical management of the Congo's natural resources.

To date an estimated 5.4 million people have died from war-related causes and 2 million have been displaced.[1] Femicide is a distinctive feature of the conflict and due to the high prevalence of sexual violence and use of rape as a weapon of war, the DRC has been referred to as the 'Rape Capital of the World' as well as the 'World's Worst Place to be a Woman'.

The mining industry is intricately caught up in the violent economy as militias seek to control the mines, the minerals and the trade in order to fund their wars. Congo Calling's aim is to make a difference in the DRC by inspiring consumers around the world to demand that technology companies develop conflict-free mineral products, and to commit to buying them once they are available. This is an effective method for making a change in an industry that is consumer led.

History

The DRC is the third largest country in Africa and has a population of 67 million people; it is one of the wealthiest countries in the world with an estimated wealth of $24 trillion.[2] However, it consistently scores dreadfully low in the UN poverty rankings. In 1960, the Congo gained independence from Belgium and in 1971 was renamed Zaire by President Mobutu. In 1996 the country split into Zaire (then the Congo) and the Democratic Republic of Congo, which is currently led by President Joseph Kabila.

There has been constant violence in the country, but two wars to note; 1996–1997 between Rwanda and Zaire (then the DRC) and 1998–2003 known as the Great War of Africa and was fought between nine African nations and 20 rebel groups. These wars saw the deaths of over 5 million people,[3] though the majority of these were due to malnutrition and disease. In 2014 one of the major rebel groups, the M23, withdrew from the war, reducing the violence, although several other groups and factions remained. One rebel group to note is the Mai Mai, which means water in Kiswahili, who believe that bullets will rain on them like

---

[1](United Nations Human Development Report — http://hdr.undp.org/en/countries/profiles/COD).
[2]http://www.forbescustom.com/EmergingMarketsPgs/DRCongoP1.html
[3]https://www.rescue.org/country/democratic-republic-congo#what-caused-the-current-crisis-in-congo

drops of water when they are shot and pride themselves on supplying their groups with approximately 300,000 child soldiers.[4]

The main source of income in the DRC is from agriculture and the mining of gold and cobalt. The mines can mostly be found on the eastern side of the country in North and South Kivu provinces that border the Great Lakes, Rwanda, Burundi and Uganda. There are between 500,000 and 2 million people employed by the mines, of which, according to the charity organization World Vision, 40% are children as young as 8.[5] The mines are a lucrative source of income for the corrupt military and rebel groups, earning them around $44 million a year. They must control the mining population with violence, fear and rape to continue to grow financially.

Conditions faced by miners are brutal for men, women (many pregnant) and children who work long hours in deep holes, collect minerals, crush them and carry them down the mountains. Alongside the ever-present threat of rape, there is a severe lack of basic safety — miners are often crushed or stuck in collapsed mines with no way of rescue (Side Bar 1).

The Campaign Team

Congo Calling's Director Bandi Mbubi first arrived in the UK in 1991 as a political refugee from the DRC and gained asylum in 1992. During this period he met Claire Kennedy, his solicitor assigned to helping with his case. The two remained close friends and when Claire set up TEDx Exeter in 2012 she asked Bandi to speak, knowing as she did of his desire to influence change in his home country. Bandi came to champion the issue of conflict minerals in technology as he felt he was able to create a direct, tangible link for the international community with the technology in their homes (laptops, phones, TVs, washing machines etc.) to the atrocities occurring in the DRC. Successful campaigns have been run throughout Africa by international NGOs, for example the campaign to end blood diamonds in South Africa, and he knew it was possible to approach the issues at ground level and drive change.

---

[4]https://www.essex.ac.uk/armedcon/story_id/000910.pdf
[5]http://www.worldvision.org/child-protection-news-stories/child-labor-children-reveal-horror-working-mine

Side Bar 1

An anonymous tin digger describes an attack he lived through at a tin mine in Mwenga territory in March 2015:

> The attack happened because there is a conflict between two armed groups that's linked to the heritage of the local throne. They came and circled the camp and began firing bullets. After the attack they grouped us together because they had already taken all of our belongings - our tin, our clothes, our solar panels, food. We had to carry the pillaged goods to a place in the forest. We walked for a whole day. They took everything. I had 300 kilos of tin in my house, which took me two months to amass, which they took. I feel really distressed because I worked for two months and now my family will have nothing.

Charles, a gold miner from Mwenga was quoted as stating:

> I was attacked by armed men who stabbed me with a knife in my legs. They cut me here and here [indicates the top of his thighs]. I was asleep in my bed and the men came – they forced the door open. They took everything – all that I had. They were military, they wore military clothes and all four of them were carrying guns. As soon as they arrived they attacked me – they cut me – so I lay there crying out. I didn't see their faces. The whole thing lasted for an hour or so. Afterwards I went to hospital. I was there for one and a half months.

https://www.globalwitness.org/mining-for-our-minerals/

In his first TEDx Exeter talk in 2012, Bandi called for action against mobile phones that 'leave a bloody trail'.[6] In explaining that the minerals found in mobile devices (tin, tantalum, tungsten and gold) are primarily mined in the DRC and how the quest for these minerals fuels the conflict in the DRC, Bandi forged a clear

---

[6]https://www.ted.com/talks/bandi_mbubi_demand_a_fair_trade_cell_phone

link between an everyday communication tool and its contribution to the bloodiest war since World War II. He explained how mobile phones are intrinsically linked to atrocities in the DRC, yet could easily be turned around to bring about positive change. This was a tangible focus for the public on how the phones held in their hands were the products of actions happening thousands of miles away.

Following his TEDx talk, Bandi established 'Congo Calling' as a UK-based campaign, eventually registered as a charity, with four other trustees drawn from the TEDx organizing committee: Claire Kennedy as Chair (Bandi's advocate for his asylum case 20 years earlier), Tim Harlow as Bursar, Sara Gibbs and Bandi as Director. One would assume the role of Director is a full-time paid position, but the organization still lacks sufficient funding to enable Bandi to do this. His 'daytime' job is that of Director for the Manna Society — a day centre for about 200 homeless people per day (since 2009), in central London.

I joined the Congo Calling campaign in 2013 as a Programme Coordinator and Bandi's Personal Assistant in an organizational role, which required identifying leaders in various entities throughout the UK willing to adopt tightly controlled procurement policies. I also had to ensure that Congo Calling was fully engaged in the norms and regulations of the UK voluntary sector, to help the political movement of the campaign, as well as the politics amongst the international community of sister organizations.

I needed to seek people to lead internal campaigns that would persuade senior managers to reform their procurement policies. Often these potential campaign leaders were not in positions of power, and did not have resources or influence by means of their position. My job was to identify talented people who were inspired by the mission and cause, teach them the campaigning practices and include them in a wider network so that they could leverage more influence. Students are excellent examples: an individual student has very little positional power, but by working with Congo Calling they could have a significant degree of influence. I should also note that Congo Calling is not the only organization in the field, in fact the global leaders in this campaign is the US-based 'Enough Project'[7] that specifically targets the world's youth (16–25 years old) and who thrive on

---

[7]http://www.enoughproject.org

technology's possibilities, through the Conflict-Free Campus Initiative.[8]

Student Inclusiveness

Students are, in fact, an ideal target because universities are primed to listen to their opinions, and most have been brought up in a society where equality, justice and the future of the planet matter.

In 2012 Congo Calling assumed responsibility to work with UK universities, including Exeter, St Andrews, Kingston, Essex, Glasgow and the NUS (National Union of Students), campaigning for conflict-free technology procurement policies. These campaigns successfully put pressure on the technology companies to take better care of how and where they source minerals, and provided support for the International Conference on the Great Lakes Region mineral tracking system,[9] a certification that recognizes safer mining environments and working conditions. Crucially, this certification has begun to prove persuasive in relationships with the rebel groups that have a strong hold on (or strongholds in) the mining areas. A joint statement posted on Intel's website stated that alongside the (US banking reform) Dodd-Frank Act 1502 the certification process resulted in 'a 55 percent reduction in armed-group profits from tin, tungsten and tantalum mined in the region',[10] though there is still some way to go (Side Bar 2).

The campaign took on the form of a formal organization when students combined their efforts and it faced questions about its inclusiveness. On one hand, the desire for skilled and enthusiastic campaigners at UK universities was a fairly straightforward job description, but behind this were a number of difficult questions:

---

[8]By encouraging university officials and stakeholders, both of whom are large purchasers of electronics and powerful spokespersons, to commit to measures that pressure electronics companies to responsibly invest in Congo's mineral sector, students are voicing the demand for conflict-free products from Congo (http://www.conflictfreecampus.org/).

[9]http://www.oecd.org/investment/mne/47892582.pdf

[10]http://iq.intel.com/what-intel-is-doing-in-the-congo-working-to-make-products-conflict-free/

Side Bar 2

The Dodd-Frank Act 1502 'is a disclosure requirement only and places no ban or penalty on the use of conflict minerals. If companies discover they have been sourcing conflict minerals from DRC or adjoining countries, it is not illegal for them to continue doing so; however, they must report this to the SEC'.

https://www.globalwitness.org/en/archive/dodd-frank-acts-section-1502-conflict-minerals/

(a) Who is to say that a self-nominating volunteer is capable, is respected or will be seen as a legitimate representative of the student body?

(b) As the ultimate beneficiaries of the campaign are miners, villagers and women in the DRC, should they be included in Congo Calling's strategy or governance processes? How might this be affected?

(c) Congo Calling campaigns to change consumer choices, in order to put pressure on tech companies to reform their supply chain policies. (As it turned out, the United States and World Trade Organization's (WTO) policies and regulations did much of this job for us.) Once this message gets through to tech companies, should the campaign continue to include students? Or should it shift to an industry and regulator focus?

These were questions of strategy, and each had important consequences for the leadership of the campaign and the organization. In turn — who should be included in which aspects, and how might this be ensured?

Inclusive Leadership

Inclusive leadership is defined by Edwin P. Hollander as:

> 'doing things with people, rather than to people', which is the essence of inclusion. Improving decision making and achieving desired ends are among its goals, without relying on one person's capabilities alone. It also provides

an atmosphere that promotes fairness of input and output to all. (Hollander, 2012)

The problem for a campaign group, however, is precisely who counts as 'us'? Who should be included? In the case of Congo Calling we knew that our evolving strategy would have implications for who should be included in this sense of engagement; we also wanted to expand inclusiveness to cover the intended beneficiaries of our work — those caught up in the mining operations in the DRC. We were also mindful of the competition amongst NGOs active in this area, keen that they should not become 'outgroups' to each other, but that we should foster a cooperative set of strategies. Leadership was to play a vital part in this.

Leadership can be considered with respect to its position, processes, person, performance or purposes (Case, 2013; Grint, 2001), and each of these might be qualified by degree of inclusiveness — although there may be apparent contradictions between them. For example, if we define leadership by reference to 'position' in the organization, we would identify the CEO, President or Chairperson as holding the highest leadership, and others in the hierarchy afforded leadership responsibility and (potentially) authority according to their position. Here inclusiveness might be assessed by the degree to which access to leadership positions is open and fairly administered. However, we might understand leadership in terms of processes such as envisioning a desired future, garnering support, aligning diverse interests, articulating a strategy. People regardless of their formal position might accomplish any of these; in fact some might be carried out by groups of people as a collective effort, with no identifiable leader; by informal cultural norms or by formal practices such as 'away-days', 'brain-storming' or speech making. That is not to say that such practices are necessarily inclusive — they could be carried out by a cabal of insiders, an exclusive elite or a quasi-political interest group. Alternatively, inclusive leadership practices could explicitly and intentionally solicit contributions from all stakeholders.

Looking to leadership as qualities of the person — probably the most common assumption in leadership development theory — is the focus on individuals' attitudes towards diversity, 'otherness' and collaboration. Psychometric assessments offer a means to describe a person according to the qualities that any particular test deems to be important. For example, the popular 'Big Five' test measures Openness, Conscientiousness, Extroversion, Agreeableness and Neuroticism (Gosling, Rentfrow, & Swann,

2003). Openness is a measure of attitude towards new experiences, which might relate to a willingness to include people and views that would challenge one's own, and agreeableness is a result of empathy and sensitivity to others. Both of these might be traits that contribute to the willingness and ability of a leader to be inclusive. However, it also appears that these two traits are negatively associated with task performance (Neal & Yeo, 2011), suggesting that if 'being inclusive' becomes an overriding concern for a leader, progress on the task may suffer. One might speculate that in such circumstances colleagues would become disenchanted — after all, they join a campaign in order to have impact, not just for the social club. This is just one reason that focus on the leader can be important in understanding how an organization develops, but it's not enough on its own because most collective efforts give rise to 'checks and balances', whereby team members compensate for the weaknesses of others — including the leader(s). Often, however, leadership is judged on the basis of performance — what is achieved. Regardless of the personal attitudes, the formal positions or the practices of so-called leaders, if they succeed in inclusive outcomes, it counts as inclusive leadership. Conversely, if the most open-minded people in the most enlightened organization practicing participative methods nonetheless fail to include stakeholders, this should not (in this perspective) be counted as inclusive leadership. Finally, where leadership is defined in terms of purpose, we look at the extent to which that purpose expresses the interests of a narrow group of actors. An inclusive purpose would be one that encompasses the interests and ideals of a broad segment of society, and even where well focused, such as on the conflict-based economy of Congolese mining, is amenable to encompassing related aspects such as femicide, land rights and so forth.

These five possible framings can thus be differentiated as inclusive personal leadership, inclusive positional leadership, inclusive leadership processes, inclusive leadership performance or results, inclusive leadership purposes. Neither one of these is 'correct'; nor is it necessary to refer to all of them in relation to every leadership question. But in analysing the development of Congo Calling, I will refer to leadership sometimes in terms of the personal qualities of key people, sometimes in terms of processes, outcomes, purposes or practices. My intention is to locate inclusive leadership, however defined, in relation to the three key operational and strategic issues identified above.

Congo Calling started with a call to activism in the charismatic setting of a TEDx talk, something like a summons to the audience. Because of the emotional and forethought response to Bandi's talk, the TEDx organizers moved quickly to support him in establishing a formal organization that could build a campaign based on locally organized pressure groups. The core team was formed of four Trustees (from the committee that organized TEDx Exeter), Director Bandi Mbubi and myself as a Programme Coordinator. In the early days it relied heavily on the self-organizing zeal and instinctive cooperative spirit of volunteers and donors to promote the movement, enthused by Bandi's articulate personal message. Subtle guidance by the four trustees, especially the Chair, ensured sufficient coordination amongst initiatives at various universities, media presence and relations with other campaign organizations in the UK, Europe, Africa and the United States. The spirit of the organization was happily inclusive: we welcomed volunteer activists from universities and some secondary schools across the UK, provided campaign support and materials, and often relied on volunteers to develop local strategies and represent the wider campaign. This was an organization that was enthusiastically inclusive because it fitted our strategy; and the inspirational talks, videos and vision offered by Bandi bound us together in a shared purpose, no matter what other political, religious, national or other identities we might each have.

However, with success came complexity and more demands on our resources — especially Bandi's time and presence. The US campaign, the Enough Project, was making significant progress and European policy makers could be persuaded to legislate on supply chain certification. As the focus expanded from young consumers of technology to cosmopolitan bureaucrats and international procurement professionals, the decision-making demands on the Trustees became more pressing. But they were part-time volunteers, Bandi had a full-time job in another sector, and my attention was spread thinly. The natural self-help inclusiveness of a consumer campaign could not be relied on for the subtle political manoeuvring needed in Brussels, Westminster and Washington DC. Who to include, how to include them, over which kinds of decisions and actions, emerged as a critical issue for Congo Calling. The personal competencies of Bandi, the Chair of the Trustees, the other Trustees and some of the key volunteers was crucial, and sometimes difficult. We stretched the processes by which we sought funds, set priorities, decided on priorities and spent our budgets; the distributed, emergent leadership that had worked in a student campaigning organization came into tension with the fiduciary leadership of the NGO and the discrete behind the scenes leadership required in the policy debates. Leadership practices had concentrated on Bandi's inspiring communication skills; but his time was limited and the Board struggled to find a way of operating that could give sufficient attention to crucial financial and strategic matters. Inclusion of more and varied interests was certainly not at the forefront of their concerns. Into this context Bandi brought a new challenge: could we directly include women in the DRC — and the people currently living and working in the mines. Thus as the challenges shifted, so did our strategy; and with it our understanding and aspirations for inclusive leadership. In the next section we will address this relationship between strategy, operations and leadership.

Key Operational and Strategic Issues

SELF-NOMINATED VOLUNTEERS

Congo Calling primarily wanted to create positive change agents through working with university and school students, to inspire change and to create a clear space and path for those changes to take place. Practically the campaign would be invited to speak by the universities' NUS/Amnesty Group or Sustainability panel, reinforced by connections made through social media, TED talks, word of mouth or conference networking.

Informed students were supported by Congo Calling to call on their university to make reduction in the use of conflict minerals a priority in its investment and procurement policy. Once aware of how technology had been created and how it had impacted lives in the DRC and other mining countries such as Colombia, students were keen for training and campaign support; they could see themselves as 'change makers' in stopping the flow of blood associated with everyday technology. The tangible possibility of such impact was demonstrated by the launch of the world's first fair-trade mobile phone, the Fairphone, in 2013.[11] By educating students and faculty members alike, Congo Calling created a sense of power through change from the students as they could see what they could do, and make the change

---

[11] www.fairphone.com

themselves. Importantly, they found that they were able, by taking action, to be included in the campaign.

St Andrews was the first university to connect with the campaign when student Desre Hancocks invited Bandi to speak at a conference on the current situation in the Eastern Democratic Republic of Congo. Hancocks said 'from the moment I first heard Bandi speak at the panel discussion ... I desired to be part of a group of people who create a platform for a people who have had their voices brutally taken away to be heard....Bandi is so approachable. He doesn't make you feel like you're a criminal. He makes you think you can actually do something. You can have a phone and still be ethical'. After much hard work, their conflict-free procurement policy campaign came into place.[12]

This evolved into a familiar pattern; Bandi as the one who inspired, then the organizer (myself) would enable connections to networks and for the organization to function on a daily basis and the doers (of which there were many and local students) would tackle governmental issues on the ground. This process was repeated at university level as Bandi spoke and inspired students and staff to organize and create change within their own organizations.

Paul Regan (2006) demonstrates how to build coalitions through organizing around common interests — even when those groups see each other as in some ways 'opposed'. We know that universities are in constant competition and graduating students find their curriculum vitae's and resumes under scrutiny, not only to include high grades, but also extracurricular activities. Many students join activities at least in part for the purpose of standing out, but Congo Calling found that its members and advocates stood apart. They often worked anonymously, clearly enthused by the purpose of fighting for an issue that was not only tangible to manage but mattered. Some students were rewarded for their hard work and total inclusion within the organization by speaking at Port Cullis House in 2014. At this prestigious address British MPs joined the students with direct influence over procurement policies (Side Bar 3).

Throughout the university visits, students stated that Bandi was 'so inspirational, the way he carries himself. He's a gentle giant. He had no hatred, even though he had experienced so much trauma'; however, the campaign struggled to build

---

[12]http://conflictfreestandrews.org

Side Bar 3

Desre Hancocks, former student at St Andrews University, Scotland and student activist said:

'At the end of the Conference held at St Andrews University, Marie-Therese Nlandu called us to her and said that for the first time in the many years, that because of what we had done by organizing this Conference she believed her peoples voice had finally been heard. It was a deeply profound and emotional moment for me. When I think about the struggles we faced to gain the vast amount of funding required and the logistics of organizing an event that was of the highest professional standard it all paled in the immense struggle the people of the DRC are going through day in and day out.' 'It became clear that my days of "student" activism needed to translate into a life of activism. This was for me, never a "fad", something to do because it was "the thing to be seen doing"'.

successful projects which required prolonged organization and specific pressure points because it became clear that the NGO needed to build a power base from which to act. In addition to this, it ran initially through the public's generosity in funds, skills and time the organization later struggled with funding as the campaign lacked a specialty fundraiser.

ON THE GROUND BENEFICIARIES

Some of Congo Calling's core team members felt that the ultimate beneficiaries of the campaign — the population of the DRC: primarily women, children and miners — should be included in the campaign's strategy process because inclusive leadership should surely extend to those it has the greatest effect on and arguably the reason the campaign started in the first place. We know working in diverse teams can be both frustrating and rewarding: If a team works for a goal greater than its individual parts then the outcome benefits all. If divided due to conflict or discourse, the result is wasted energy from individuals with a poor output. As Paul Regan questions 'How can individuals and institutions be part of a collective response?' (2006, pp. 183–203). The team, however, was split on the decision to extend its decision making to the beneficiaries. Some felt that the organization had reached its limits in time, finances and people power and to extend Congo Calling's resources to the DRC would be at the detriment to the campaign. Many of us argued that this was just an excuse to keep the camping local so that the founders could still hold the majority control, very much a method of leading from the top down and one that was not helping the campaign grow and have a greater impact.

CONSUMER CHOICES

In 2010 the Dodd-Frank Wall Street/Banking Reform and Consumer Protection Act highlighted the trade of conflict minerals to electronic and other industries. The law states that any company trading through the American stock market had to state whether or not their minerals originated in the DRC or a country supporting armed conflict. Since the European Union (EU) currently does not provide such a comparative piece of legislation, the consumers rely on companies providing freely unrestricted auditing information. Companies that are at the forefront of this movement include Intel, which committed to only using conflict-free technology minerals in 2015.[13] For the reason that there is little or no regulation in the EU, it is primarily up to the consumer to act as the enforcer and those in charge of procuring technology for organizations to make informed decisions. These decisions cannot be made without clear and instructive information that can be made to feel part of a wider network: inclusive to a greater cause. The pressure to make this change must come not only from those governing, but also from the workers/users.

To the point where the Congo Calling campaign began to make a real difference with the help of students and to discard them would seem meaningless and least of all naive to believe that a shift to industry-regulated focus could happen without them. The campaign was arguably at its strongest united with a mix of cross-generational and multicultural volunteers, found in students and younger people.

---

[13]http://www.intel.com/content/www/us/en/corporate-responsibility/conflict-free-minerals.html

The State of Civil Society Report 2016 by CIVICUS[14] raises the issue that most civil society organizations (CSOs) use inclusive leadership to amplify the voices of those who are marginalized and by doing so promotes the unheard, unequal, those living in poverty and those discriminated against. Congo Calling with other CSOs follow these common threads and are therefore seeing a need for recognizing a collective effort to fight global issues. We should note that the 'wealth gap', which sees 62 people owning the same wealth as half the world,[15] has a direct link to the corporations and governments benefiting from the trade in conflict minerals. A shrinking political space has meant a larger effort in teamwork across NGOs and CSOs is required to tackle this (Side Bar 4).

For this NGO, inclusive leadership was vital and required to work, not only with a younger population but also with the Congolese people. The diversity in the movement is key, and consideration of race, ethnicities, gender and class when appealing to the volunteers was necessary. Inclusive leadership invites a systemic nature of change where we, the people, the inclusive cohort cannot rely on the world governments and international corporations to do the right thing in ending the trade and supply of con-

---

Side Bar 4

In Civil Society Report 2016-CIVICUS, page 66, Jenny Ricks, Head of Inequality Initiative, ActionAid International states:

> the experience of inequalities is lived on a day to day basis, and where struggles are already being fought and won, and fought and lost. It is meant to build from here and elevate the struggle.

http://www.civicus.org/images/documents/SOCS2016/summaries/SoCS-full-review.pdf

---

[14] www.civicus.org/images/documents/SOCS2016/summaries/SoCS-full-review.pdf

[15] www.oxfam.org.uk/media-centre/press-releases/2016/01/62-people-own-same-as-half-world-says-oxfam-inequality-report-davos-world-economic-forum

flict minerals. The power has and will always lie with the people being held to account on all levels including governments. The strongest alliances are built on shared visions. With the Enough Project in the United States successfully lobbying for new legislation and the Dodd-Frank Act clamping down on more corporations, perhaps Congo Calling should embrace its inclusive nature and work with them to push the EU to create its own conflict minerals legislation, not to mention to help battle the fallout from Brexit.

Call to Action

Throughout this chapter we have explored the direct link that the international community has with the DRC on a daily basis (even the computer that has been used to type this chapter) and examined the necessity of inclusion in NGO work that penetrates at the grassroots levels. If we champion the new Sustainable Development Goals (set forth by the UN), then, by default, we should address the issue of diversity to promote peaceful and inclusive societies for sustainable development and provide access to justice for all and build effective, accountable and inclusive institutions at all levels. The facts are clear: 48 women an hour or four in every 5 minutes are raped in the DRC every day.[16] There is blood on our hands, our mobile devices, tablets and TVs. We must put an end to this.

So what can you do?

1. Put pressure on and boycott the international technology giants and ask them to clean up their supply chains.
2. Spread the word; the more people who know about this, the more we can affect women, children and men in the mines.
3. Write to your representative and ensure that unethical trading standards are not allowed to enter our supply chains.
4. Work with you colleges, universities, schools and companies to account for where their technology comes from. You will be supported by the Enough Project's Conflict-Free Campus Initiative[17] (in the United States) or Congo Calling[18] (in Europe).

---

[16]http://www.ncbi.nlm.nih.gov/pmc/articles/PMC3093289/
[17]http://www.conflictfreecampus.org
[18]http://www.congocalling.org

In the meantime, Congo Calling's goal is to work with NGOs on the ground that provide valuable information to the growing population obsessed with new technology on the methods used to create it and to perhaps achieve a sustainable planet and a generation that cares more for human rights than that of the next Xbox. There is still a long way to go to seeing real change in the DRC. It raises the question that if this method of inclusive leadership could be put into practice on the ground in the DRC with local communities and mining companies, could war be reduced and a greater chance of sustainable mining methods put into practise?

Acknowledgements

I would like to express my gratitude to the many people who helped create this chapter, in addition to the hard work and commitment that Congo Calling and other such NGOs have shown for creating significant change to the DRC.

References

Case, P. (2013). Review essay: Grint K. The arts of leadership & leadership. *Leadership and the Humanities*, *1*(1), 59–62.

Gosling, S. D., Rentfrow, P. J., & Swann, W. B. (2003). A very brief measure of the Big-Five personality domains. *Journal of Research in Personality*, *37*(6), 504–528. doi:10.1016/S0092-6566(03)00046-1. ISSN 0092-6566.

Grint, K. (2001). *The arts of leadership*. Oxford: Oxford University Press.

Hollander, E. P. (2012, August). *Inclusive leadership: The essential leader-follower relationship* (p. 3). New York, NY: Routledge.

Neal, A., & Yeo, K. X. (2011). Predicting the form and direction of work role performance from the Big 5 model of personality traits. *Journal of Organizational Behavior*, *33*, 175–192.

Regan, P. (2006). Broad based organizing — Reflective citizenship and political action. *Organizational and Social Dynamics*, *6*, 183–203.

Websites:

- http://conflictfreestandrews.org
- http://hdr.undp.org/en/countries/profiles/COD
- http://iq.intel.com/what-intel-is-doing-in-the-congo-working-to-make-products-conflict-free/

- www.civicus.org/images/documents/SOCS2016/summaries/SoCS-full-review.pdf
- www.conflictfreecampus.org
- www.congocalling.org
- www.enoughproject.org
- www.essex.ac.uk/armedcon/story_id/000910.pdf
- www.fairphone.com
- www.forbescustom.com/EmergingMarketsPgs/DRCongoP1.html
- www.globalwitness.org/en/archive/dodd-frank-acts-section-1502-conflict-minerals/
- www.globalwitness.org/mining-for-our-minerals/
- www.intel.com/content/www/us/en/corporate-responsibility/conflict-free-minerals.htmlState
- www.ncbi.nlm.nih.gov/pmc/articles/PMC3093289/
- www.oecd.org/investment/mne/47892582.pdf
- www.oxfam.org.uk/media-centre/press-releases/2016/01/62-people-own-same-as-half-world-says-oxfam-inequality-report-davos-world-economic-forum
- www.rescue.org/country/democratic-republic-congo#what-caused-the-current-crisis-in-congo
- www.ted.com/talks/bandi_mbubi_demand_a_fair_trade_cell_phone
- http://www.worldvision.org/child-protection-news-stories/child-labor-children-reveal-horror-working-mine

21 Unpacking Inclusivity: Lessons from *Ubuntu* Leadership

Gloria J. Burgess

Keywords: Leadership; *Ubuntu*; Inclusivity; Values; Disproportionality; Leadership Development

---

The legacy you leave is the life you live.
— J. Kouzes and B. Posner

Although much has been written about leading and leadership practice, education, and development, there is a profound imbalance, an imbalance that venerates leaders in the corporate sector, particularly business leaders. The dearth of models, research, and resources for and about leaders and leadership practice, education, and development outside of the corporate sector is frustrating, at best, and at times downright disheartening. Transcending the traditional logic and paradigm that privileges the focus on business leaders, this chapter offers a more inclusive perspective on leading, an approach that is infused

379

with the ethos of *Ubuntu*, an African way of viewing and living in the world and that pervades the formation, values, and practices of many persons of African heritage. For those who choose leadership, this African perspective and way of being informs their leadership — who they are, what they know, what they do, and how they do what they do.

One such person who transcends the traditional template for leading is Joyce James. A champion for children of color in the child welfare system, James is a human-services executive in Texas. An inclusive leader, her approach prizes community and equity, and it is infused with compassion, dignity, humility, and respect — an approach that is often referred to as *Ubuntu* leadership (Burgess, 2016; Elkington, 2015; Ndlovu, 2015; van der Cloff, 2003; van Hooft, 2013).

For several years during the past decade, I had the opportunity to work directly with James. As a trusted advisor, I observed and witnessed her leadership and its impact first-hand. This chapter provides an overview of her leadership and key lessons that comprise a framework for *Ubuntu* leadership. As a prelude to the lessons and framework, I will provide more context about *Ubuntu*, an operational definition of this unique way of being, and a summary of James's leadership.

Ubuntu — Context and Definition

A shift in scenery often yields a shift in perspective. As a result of shifting our scenery, we can return to our normal living and leading routines and relationships with fresh eyes and new insights. To change our scenery, we can take a walk, read a book, hike, snorkel, watch a great movie, garden, golf, go fishing, meditate, listen to music, ride our bike to work, or travel to another city or country. I love to travel. When I do, I invariably gain new insights and perspectives.

> Many years ago, one of my mentors asked if I'd ever visited Africa. At that time, I'd only dreamed about such a journey. "Why do you ask?"
>
> "When you do, your work will be different."
>
> "How so?"
>
> "Your soul will be transformed."

Years later, when I visited Africa for the first time, I came to fully understand and live into my mentor's prescient words. As the Boeing 747 descended through the bright blush of Kenya's equatorial sunrise, vast expanses of land came into view at a scale that humans could comprehend. During our approach to Nairobi, I surveyed mile after mile of rust-red earth flanked by voluptuous green hills. As the plane continued its descent, I noticed that many of the hillsides were terraced beneath a heavy overgrowth of vines.

Just as the wheels touched the runway, I felt a burst of energy course through my entire body. Unlike the typical jolt one experiences when a jetliner touches down, mine was the shock of recognition and deep remembrance. The shock of my body awakening to what my soul already knew. The specter of red clay dirt and vine-shrouded hills was not unlike the terrain of my childhood home in rural Mississippi — some 10,000 miles across the Atlantic. Little did I know that this landscape of red roads and green hills would be the first of many instances of my soul remembering my motherland of Africa. During my month-long stay in Kenya, I discovered the origins of what I'd known and experienced all my life. In Mississippi, my experience had a name: community. In Kenya and in many other parts of Africa, community had another name — *Ubuntu*. Not only had my perspective shifted, I was inspired!

Although most Westerners are unfamiliar with the term *Ubuntu*, we are actually quite familiar with many of its aspects. In the lovely, inspirational book *Believe*, Archbishop Emeritus Desmond Tutu defines *Ubuntu*. Read the honorable archbishop's words and notice what's already familiar to you about this way of being, this way of life.

> The definition of *Ubuntu* has two parts. The first is that the person is friendly, hospitable, generous, gentle, caring, and compassionate. In other words, someone who will use his or her strengths on behalf of others — the weak and the poor and the ill — and not take advantage of anyone. This person treats others as he or she would be treated. And because of this, they express the second part of the concept, which concerns openness, largeheartedness. They share their worth. In doing so my humanity is recognized and becomes inextricably bound to theirs.

Providing contextual dimension to this way of being, living, and moving through the world, Archbishop Tutu elaborates:

> People with *Ubuntu* are approachable and welcoming; their attitude is kindly and well-disposed; they are not threatened by the goodness in others because their own esteem and self-worth is generated by knowing they belong to a greater whole. To recast the Cartesian proposition, "I think, therefore I am," *Ubuntu* would say, "I am human because I belong." Put another way, a person is a person through other people, a concept captured by the phrase "me we."

In my travels to various parts of Africa, I have experienced many people with *Ubuntu*. One of my dear friends and traveling companions has traveled to many more countries in Africa than I have, and her experiences echo mine. Recently, she sent me this lovely story that delves deeper into the heart of *Ubuntu*.

> An anthropologist studying the habits and customs of an African tribe found himself surrounded by children most days. So, he decided to play a little game with them. He managed to get candy from the nearest town and put it all in a decorated basket at the foot of a tree. Then he called the children and suggested they play the game. When the anthropologist said "Now," the children had to run to the tree. He told them that the first one to get there could have all the candy for him or herself. So the children all lined up waiting for the signal. When the anthropologist said "Now," the children took each other by the hand and together they ran towards the tree. They all arrived at the same time, divided up the candy, sat down, and began to happily munch away. The anthropologist went over to them and asked why they had all run together when any one of them could have had all the candy to themselves. The children responded: "*Ubuntu*. How could any one of us be happy if all the others were sad?"

Clearly, *Ubuntu* is not only a quality. Epitomized by a unique way of viewing and being in the world, *Ubuntu* is considered to be the essence of what it means to be human. This way of being, living, and moving through the world is imbued with a high degree of relational awareness, inviting us to honor others *while* honoring ourselves. In many African cultures, to acknowledge and appreciate someone for their *Ubuntu* nature is regarded as the highest praise.

What I learned about *Ubuntu* in Kenya and elsewhere reaffirmed what I already knew about aboriginal and indigenous cultures, including African, American, Australian, Chinese and the many cultures that emerged from China, and Pacific Islanders (Burgess, 2016). Called by different names in these diverse cultures, the cultural inflections of *Ubuntu* and *Ubuntu* leadership, its progeny, are similar to what many Westerners variously refer to as selfless leadership, servant-leadership, and legacy leadership (Arrien, 1993; Block, 2003; Burgess, 2015, 2016; Elkington, 2015; Kegan, 1983; Kouzes & Posner, 2006; Maluga, 2009; Ndlovu, 2015; van Hooft, 2013; Visser, 2009). By any name, this approach to inclusive leadership is inspired and calls us to live and lead in a way that is focused, at once, on both the collective and the individual.

Like any other way of being, knowing, and doing, *Ubuntu* comprises many dimensions. Key among them are worldview, principal tenets, relational focus, and signature qualities, which are briefly defined below:

- *Worldview.* The frame of reference, or mental model, which powerfully influences our perceptions of how the world works and how we live in it.
- *Principal tenets.* The guiding values, assumptions, beliefs, principles, and practices that are embedded in worldview.
- *Relational focus.* The person or persons to whom we direct our primary attention and emphasis.
- *Signature qualities.* The distinguishing assets, characteristics, and traits that infuse our behaviors.

As with every aspect of life, how we live is how we lead. In other words, leaders take their worldview, values, practices, and qualities of being from one area of their life, embodying and applying them in other areas including their leadership. Table 1 highlights the essential dimensions of *Ubuntu* and how they manifest in everyday life and in leadership. Following this table is a diagram that shows a visual model for *Ubuntu* leadership.

Table 1.   Dimensions of *Ubuntu* Leadership

How *Ubuntu* Manifests In...	
Everyday Life	Leadership
Worldview	
Unifies three core aspects of being human: being, knowing, and doing. These core aspects are the locus and central departure point for living.	These core aspects are the dominant, driving influence in the leader's formation, comprising the "control center" for their values, beliefs, choices, and actions.
Principal Tenets	
"I am human because I belong." In other words, I am a person through other persons. Thought and action are centered on we *and* me — *at the same time.*	The leader's essential aim is to cultivate a strong collective through a shared sense of belonging, mutual regard, and concern.
Relational Focus	
The primary attitude is other focused. At the same time, a person honors herself or himself. Concern and caring for others is fundamental; both are given.	The leader's focus is directed toward the wellbeing, functioning, and sustainability of the whole, or the collective — i.e., family, village, tribe, group, team, organization, community, and nation.
Signature Qualities	
Friendly, generous, caring, compassionate; open to others; large-hearted; giving; shares their strengths; treats others as they would be treated; recognizes others' humanity.	These qualities infuse and are consistently evident in the leader's motives, choices, and actions, whether the leader is acting on behalf of the group, or herself or himself.

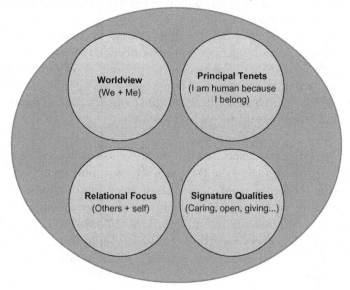

Framework: *Ubuntu* Leadership

There are many lessons to be learned from *Ubuntu*. Later, I will explore some of the key lessons, viewing them through the lens of Joyce James's leadership.

An *Ubuntu* Leader in Action: Summary of Joyce James's Leadership

Throughout her accomplished career, Joyce James has dedicated herself to working on behalf of children and youth in the child welfare system. With a vision to significantly impact the lives of children of color in the system, as Assistant Commissioner for Texas Child Protective Services, James was finally in the right leadership position at the right time. Her mission: to confront and dismantle one of the biggest systemic issues in child welfare – disproportionality – the condition of overrepresentation and disparity in the treatment of children of color in the child welfare system. No small feat, for disproportionality is deeply ingrained in the child welfare system not only in Texas but throughout the United States. It is embedded in its policies, practices, and procedures and compounded by disproportionality in other systems that are connected to child welfare, including our education, judicial, and mental health systems.

In her own words, James declared, "We must have a vision that says everyone is entitled to be treated with dignity and respect." Taking the radical position that children should not grow up in foster care, her vision asserts: "...as social workers, we can work to change the factors that contribute to poverty and disparate outcomes for African-American families and children" (James, 2006). In Casey Family Programs (Casey), a privately endowed foundation, James found a collaborator that shared her bold vision. Like James, Casey's mission was also focused on eliminating disproportionality. James and her leadership team worked closely with the foundation's social work and leadership development teams to realize their bold vision. Collectively, as the Child Welfare Team (CWT), they challenged the status quo, using an inclusive leadership approach, characterized by specific, time-honored, African-centric values and practices.

Lessons from *Ubuntu*: A Leadership Framework for the Future

Together, the values and practices of the CWT comprise elements that are foundational to *Ubuntu* leadership. As previously mentioned, persons with the spirit of *Ubuntu* are imbued with signature qualities of what it means to be human, including the qualities of being caring, open, and giving. They are approachable, welcoming, kindly, and well-disposed. Driven by the concept of "we me," such persons also understand that they belong to a greater whole. *Ubuntu* leadership is characterized by the very same qualities and attitude, or disposition, toward living. Specific values and practices of the CWT provide numerous lessons in leading and leadership. These are discussed in the following subsections.

LEAD FROM A POSITION OF VALUES

As the CWT knew, values undergird every aspect of work. In fact, values shape everything leaders are and do. The shared values embraced by the CWT included respect for culture, ensuring that cultural resonance and competence informed their work at every level; inclusion of families, youth, and community members, so that all decisions, policies, and procedures were informed by the radiance of the persons within the communities being served; integrity in decision-making; compassion for all; and a passionate commitment to eradicating disproportionality.

From the outset, it was evident that the CWT had a deep desire to excel, a desire that was most fervently and visibly revealed in their passion for igniting, actualizing, and celebrating the hopes and dreams of young people, and of their families and communities. Together, these values and those mentioned above became the touchstone for informing, shaping, and aligning all aspects of the CWT's planning, problem-solving, decision-making, and social work practices (Seymour, 2007).

LEAD FROM A POINT OF VIEW THAT ELEVATES THE WHOLE, OR THE COLLECTIVE

Early on, the CWT surfaced challenges, issues, and problems, making them visible not only to community leaders, as is traditional, but to all community stakeholders. The CWT was careful to make the invisible visible, using practices that included sharing the data and telling community stories in ways that included constituents. In so doing, they gained buy-in from community leaders, forging allies in the process. The CWT's practices align with the value of cultural resonance and competence, which favors and privileges the community.

To most contemporary Westerners, favoring and privileging the community rather than the individual is a radical notion. Furthermore, privileging the community is an unconventional way of leading relative to the worldview shaped by many Western, Northern hemisphere ways of being and knowing. Robert Elkington founder of Global Leadership Initiatives asserts, "The *Descartian* notion of individuality has informed so much of our Western epistemology..." and Descartes' "famous *cogito ergo sum* [or] '*I think therefore I am*,' gave rise to a notion of leadership that, in the main, may have been much more self-focused, transactional, and by virtue of its ontology, self-serving." By contrast, *Ubuntu* leadership offers a very different perspective and ontology. Shaped and informed by a dissimilar worldview, it offers an orientation to living and leading that is uncommon in terms of Western concepts of leadership, ways of leading, and leadership formation.

As previously mentioned, *Ubuntu* honors relational awareness to the highest degree, ensuring that every aspect of culture, including leading, is simultaneously viewed, embodied, and enacted through the lens of "we" *and* "me." This African perspective essentially states, "I am, because you are." In other words, I exist in relationship *with* you not in relationship *to* you. This subtle difference in language translates into significant differences in terms of how leaders actually lead. In the *Ubuntu* worldview, the group, or collective, is not subordinate to the individual. Indeed, the collective is prized, prioritized, and privileged. This means that every person and indeed every other "part of the system" [i.e., community, village, team, organization, nation, etc.] "holds merit and value" (Elkington, 2015). The ethos of *Ubuntu* leadership means that everyone and everything — sentient and non-sentient — is viewed as holistic, as integral, as essential.

LEAD WITH COMPASSION

Compassion is "sympathetic pity and concern for the sufferings or misfortunes of others." The CWT extended this definition of compassion to include the concept of leading *with*, or leading on *behalf of*. For the CWT, leading with compassion was expressed as "so that" leadership, which was evident in several areas, including community leadership, community organization, and community accountability (Seymour, 2007).

Community leadership expanded the notion of leadership beyond the usual arenas – i.e., institutions, organizations, and systems. In addition, community leadership actually included community members, *so that* leadership was placed where it rightly belonged – within and with the families and community. In this way, community leadership became synonymous with community ownership. To shore up community members' awareness and skills, they were invited to participate in a rigorous training program that included *Undoing Racism*, to better equip them as agents of social change and transformation.

Community organization and community accountability meant going to and engaging with community members, *so that* the CWT could be mentored and guided by community members to learn what strengths were present in the community as a whole and in community members. Community organization and community accountability also included welcoming community residents to the table not only as key informants, but also as agents of change, *so that* they could address and deal with their own concerns and issues. Rather than being viewed as problems to be solved or as hapless, helpless victims, the CWT viewed the community as an asset. And community members were viewed as abundant, resilient, and resourceful; they were seen as persons who could and would take charge to create innovative, sustainable solutions.

LEAD WITH PASSION

One of the key processes used by the foundation's leadership development experts was to invite CWT leaders and members to reflect on and declare their passion, to surface privately and publically what fueled their investment in children, youth, and families. Why? When a leader, or anyone else for that matter, articulates and declares their passion, that action creates personal and professional accountability while reinforcing their commitment to stay the course in the arduous, exhausting work of confronting and challenging discriminatory systemic policies, practices, and procedures.

Leaders ignited by the fire of passion, purpose, and perseverance understand that they lead, *so that* they can ably serve others. They lead *so that* others can benefit from their investment of spiritual, physical, emotional, and intellectual energy. The CWT provides numerous and diverse examples of those who lead with passion, purpose, and perseverance; those who have a dream, a marvelous vision of possibility; those who keep their eyes on the prize; those who make necessary adjustments along the way. Such leaders refuse to take "no" for an answer. They see failure as valuable feedback, as merely another opportunity to course correct and begin again. These leaders are entrained to transmute *Impossible* to *I'm possible* (Burgess, 2016).

LEAD FROM A POSITION OF CHARACTER

James instinctively knew that leading begins from within. Others on the CWT also understood either from their early leadership formation or their subsequent development as a leader that leading begins from within, beginning with who you are, beginning with your being. That leading begins from within runs contrary to the popular belief that leading begins with what you know or what you do. Of the thousands of articles, books, and monographs about leading and leadership, most focus on what leaders must know or do to ignite, influence, and inspire others (Burgess, 2015, 2016). *Ubuntu* leadership focuses on who you are – first and foremost.

Ubuntu leadership recognizes that knowing and doing are indeed vital aspects of leading. Each facet of leading – knowing, doing, and being – is critical. In fact, if one facet is muted or missing, the integrity of the whole is compromised, making it impossible to lead in a way that is trustworthy, just, or sustainable. But knowing and doing must be undergirded by being – the inner essence of who we are – for it is the most fundamental facet of leadership formation and leading.

Ubuntu leadership recognizes that in today's complex, hyperconnected world, it is no longer acceptable to marginalize our being, this essential dimension of character, leadership formation, and leading. Indeed, if we are to fulfill our promise as enlightened and responsible global leaders, it is essential to attend to this foundational aspect of who we are. One of the key lessons of *Ubuntu* leadership is an invitation to acknowledge the imperative to devote ourselves to forming, equipping, and developing leaders from the inside out (Burgess, 2016).

SHAPE THE FUTURE THROUGH CHOICES AND ACTIONS IN THE PRESENT

The CWT left an indelible imprint on the children, youth, and families involved in the child welfare system, and the communities in which they lived. At the end of the day, their imprint is their legacy.

Many years ago, I coined the term *legacy consciousness*, which means to embrace an attitude of living, learning, and leading in deep relationship with ourselves, others, and our world. Furthermore, it is an invitation to be true to our authentic self, to bring forth our signature presence, and to be of service as an instrument of healing and transformation. *Legacy consciousness* declares, "When we get clear about who we are and who and what we value, we can stand up and use our voice to agitate and make a difference, no matter what" (Burgess, 2006). *Ubuntu* leadership is grounded in the values of *legacy consciousness*, values that are essential for ensuring that you leave a positive legacy — not as something you think about and deliberately construct at the end of your life, but by your way of being here and now, by the choices you make and actions you take here and now.

Consciously or unconsciously, we all leave a legacy. *Ubuntu* leadership is about becoming, being, and staying conscious about how you lead today, tomorrow, and every moment, because every choice, every decision leaves an imprint, impacting the collective, including you.

CONNECT ONE'S VOICE AND TOUCH

Like an increasing number of contemporary thought leaders, James and the CWT understood that one of the key responsibilities of a leader is to connect her voice and touch (Arrien, 1993; Bennis, 1989; Burgess, 2006, 2008, 2015, 2016; De Pree, 1989, 1992; Graham, 1991; Intrator & Scribner, 2007; Kunitz, 1995; Palmer, 1997, 1999; Scharmer, 2009; Visser, 2009; Wheatley, 2010, 2014; Whyte, 1996, 2007; Zander & Zander, 2000). In other words, she must connect who she is with who and what she cares about and how she leads, aligning her walk with her talk (Burgess, 2015, 2016). In today's chaotic, fissured, and polarized families, tribes, communities, organizations, and nations, connecting one's voice and touch is not a luxury. It is an imperative. Now more than ever, it is a precondition to leading inclusively, nimbly, and sustainably in our complex, interdependent, pluralistic world (Burgess, 2006, 2008, 2016).

Leaders who neglect or ignore connecting their voice and touch do so at their own peril. Currently, a significant proportion of the world is shaped and governed by a "we me" worldview. And this percentage will likely increase over time. Within the next 30 years, our population will increase by almost 30 percent – from 7 billion to 9 billion. Not only will there be more persons on the planet, in some countries the population will shift from being predominantly white to being predominantly persons of color. Also, between now and 2047, a significant percentage of the population will experience some kind of dislocation due to geo-socio-political shifts, war, resource depletion, and extreme natural disasters. In ways that we cannot predict or even fathom, many of us will experience disruption of life as we know it today. It behooves leaders to be proactive in learning new approaches, new models, and new frameworks for leadership. It behooves them to shift their focus and point of view, so they can situate themselves to rethink, reconsider, and reimagine our world, our nations, our communities, our organizations – and themselves.

Viewed through the lens of James's leadership, there are many lessons to be gleaned from *Ubuntu*, lessons that comprise a leadership framework for the future. Table 2 summarizes the key practices and lessons explored in this chapter.

Resources for Leaders

Whatever your leadership role – as advocate, coach, developer, educator, mentor, organizer, peacemaker, or policy-maker – ask yourself: what might I learn about *Ubuntu* cultures and *Ubuntu* leadership? As you contemplate this critical question, consider the lessons discussed previously as resources for your ongoing personal and professional learning, growth, and development. In addition to the lessons explored, consider the books, articles, and links that are included in the references listed at the end of the chapter. These resources have been and continue to be helpful to me as a leader, leadership educator, leadership coach, and as I mentor current and emerging leaders.

Closing

When you think about inclusive leadership, I trust that you will turn not only to the latest cognitive, social, and cultural research,

Table 2.   Key Lessons from *Ubuntu* Leadership.

Focus	Lesson
Values	*Ubuntu* leaders understand that their values undergird and shape everything they are and do. They understand and appreciate that just as they have been served by the women and men on whose shoulders they stand, they have a responsibility to serve others. This is a time-honored practice of gratitude.
Collective	*Ubuntu* leaders begin with and elevate the collective – their team, family, tribe, community, village, organization, or nation. They are genuinely curious about others and are open to being mentored by and learning from and about others, *so that* they can serve them honorably and well.
Compassion	*Ubuntu* leaders lead with compassion. They understand that we are not here to have dominion over others, but to value, honor, and serve one another, *so that* we can benefit others through our spiritual, physical, emotional, and intellectual energy.
Passion	*Ubuntu* leaders lead with passion and conviction. They are fueled by their passion, purpose, and perseverance, *so that* they can ably serve others. Where others see barriers, they see possibilities. Refusing to take "no" for an answer, they favor and follow the energy of "yes."
Character	*Ubuntu* leaders lead with an understanding that your character shapes who you are, who you include, and how you lead. They do not blindly impose themselves or their ways of knowing, thinking, doing, and being on others.
Legacy Consciousness	*Ubuntu* leaders consciously shape the future by how they lead here and now. They do not wait until the end of their career or life to construct their legacy. They are keenly aware that their choices and decisions make an impact here and now, impacting others today and creating a ripple effect into the future.
Voice and Touch	*Ubuntu* leaders connect their voice and touch. In other words, they connect who they are with who and what they care about and how they lead. They know and demonstrate the value and significance of aligning their walk with their talk.

but that you will also turn to research that prizes the ethos of *Ubuntu* and *Ubuntu* leadership. In doing so, you can equip yourself and others to value, understand, and unpack inclusion and reap the bounty of its beauty, diversity, and richness. Furthermore, by turning to this inclusive, appreciative worldview and approach to living and leading, you can inspire and equip yourself to create the conditions for environments in teams, families, communities, tribes, villages, organizations, governments, and nations where dignity, respect, humaneness, gratitude, generosity of spirit, passion, compassion, faith, collaboration, and trust are normative rather than the exception. By turning to *Ubuntu* leadership, you can inspire and equip yourself to be a leader who is in step with the future.

References

Arrien, A. (1993). *The four-fold way: Walking the paths of the warrior, teacher, healer, and visionary.* New York, NY: Harper Collins.

Bennis, W. (1989). *On becoming a leader.* Reading, MA: Perseus Books.

Block, P. (2003). *The answer to how is yes: Acting on what matters.* San Francisco, CA: Berrett-Koehler.

Burgess, G. (2006). *Legacy living: The six covenants for personal & professional excellence.* Provo, UT: Executive Excellence Publishing.

Burgess, G. (2008). *Dare to wear your soul on the outside: Live your legacy now.* San Francisco, CA: Jossey-Bass/Wiley.

Burgess, G. (2015). Reflections on leadership formation and the arts. In The International Network for Arts Education (Ed.), *The wisdom of the many: Key issues in arts education.* Münster: Waxmann Publishing.

Burgess, G. (2016). *Flawless leadership: Connecting who you are with what you know and do.* Edmonds, WA: Red Oak Press.

De Pree, M. (1989). *Leadership is an art.* New York, NY: Crown Business.

De Pree, M. (1992). *Leadership jazz: The essential elements of a great leader.* New York, NY: Dell Publishing.

Elkington, R. (2015). *The art of humility in leadership.* Blog post.

Graham, M. (1991). *Blood memory: An autobiography.* New York, NY: Doubleday.

Intrator, S., & Scribner, M. (2007). *Leading from within: Poetry that sustains the courage to lead.* San Francisco, CA: Jossey-Bass.

James, J. (2006). Black history month keynote address. Texas.

Kegan, R. (1983). *The evolving self: Problem and process in human development.* Cambridge, MA: Harvard University Press.

Kouzes, J., & Posner, B. (2006). *A leader's legacy.* San Francisco, CA: Jossey-Bass.

Kunitz, S. (1995). Touch me. In *Passing through: The later and new poems* (pp. 158–159). New York, NY: W. W. Norton & Company.

Maluga, C. (2009). *Understanding organizational leadership through* Ubuntu. London, UK: Adonis & Abbey Publishers.

Ndlovu, P. M. (2015). *Discovering the spirit of* Ubuntu: *Compassion, community, and respect.* London, UK: Palgrave McMillan.

Palmer, P. (1997). *The courage to teach: Exploring the inner landscape of a teacher's life*. San Francisco, CA: Jossey-Bass.

Palmer, P. (1999). *Let your life speak: Listening for the voice of vocation*. San Francisco, CA: Jossey-Bass.

Scharmer, O. (2009). *Theory U: Learning from the future as it emerges*. San Francisco, CA: Berrett-Koehler.

Seymour, J. (2007). *Engaging communities in taking a stand for children & families: Leadership development and strategic planning in the Texas Child Welfare System*. Seattle, WA: Casey Family Programs.

van der Cloff, L. (2003). Leadership lessons from the African tree. *Management Decision, 41*(3), 257–261.

van Hooft, L. (2013). *The power of African thinking: About Ubuntu, unifying leadership in a new world*. The Netherlands: Green Dream Works.

Visser, M. (2009). *The gift of thanks: The roots and rituals of gratitude*. New York, NY: Houghton Mifflin Harcourt.

Wheatley, M. (2010). *Perseverance*. San Francisco, CA: Berrett-Koehler.

Wheatley, M. (2014). *How does raven know? Entering sacred world, a meditative memoir*. Provo, UT: Margaret J. Wheatley, Inc.

Whyte, D. (1996). *The heart aroused: Poetry and the preservation of the soul in corporate America*. New York, NY: Crown Business.

Whyte, D. (2007). *Crossing the unknown sea: Work as a pilgrimage of identity*. New York, NY: Riverhead Books.

Zander, B., & Zander, R. (2000). *The art of possibility: Transforming professional and personal life*. New York, NY: Penguin Books.

22

From Barriers to Breakthroughs: Leading Others Past Wicked Problems to Inclusive Practice Using Integrated Focus

Jennifer Walinga

Keywords: Creative insight; leadership; problem solving; inclusion; culture

E ffective leadership hinges upon problem solving ability. Effective problem-solving results in solutions that are inclusive, systemic, and sustainable — the marks of great leadership. Likewise, the skills of leadership are also problem-solving skills: discerning and communicating an inspiring vision, facilitating collaborative processes, designing integral communication systems and mechanisms, building a culture of thriving, and fostering sustainable and systemic decisions. For instance, Liberal leader Justin Trudeau, elected prime minister of Canada in 2015, discerned the needs and aspirations of the Canadian populace to return to a values-oriented vision of Canada and to find security and grounding in the values of peace and diversity rather than in the Conservative party's platform of control. The best solutions are sustainable, systemic, and elegant — the result of a holistic problem-solving process that succeeds in solving the 'whole' problem and hinges on inclusive, collaborative, and systems-oriented leadership practice involving all stakeholders. Trudeau relied on collaborative and inclusive processes, swiftly followed up on campaign promises with integrated and far reaching communications, and restored Canada's cultural values and practices with a gender-balanced cabinet, a pledge to welcome 25,000 refugees, support for the middle class, and investment in research, education, and development. This chapter illustrates how an integrated focus approach to leadership problem solving "breaks the zero-sum game logic of winners and losers, and enables leaders to create environments where the norm is collaboration, generosity and trust instead of competition, selfishness and control."

For a leader to be capable of "building bridges of inclusion and understanding, and inspiring others to focus on common goals rather than on opposite interests," s/he must develop a capacity for holistic and integrative problem solving. Just as the leadership literature prefers to broadcast the image and myth of the leader as a "winner," a "hero," either in business, sports, or even the military, so does the problem-solving literature prefer to focus on linear, rational, and zero-sum approaches in these same realms (Durand-Bush & Salmela, 2002; D'Zurilla & Sheedy, 1992; Ketchen, Snow, & Street, 2004; Kovác, 1998; Nutt, 2002, 2004; Pugh, 1991; Smith, Carlsson, Sandström, 1985; Vance, Groves, Paik, & Kindler, 2007; Wang & Horng, 2002; Wanish, 2000). In their research on problem solving and leadership practice, Walinga et al. built a conceptual model of integrative problem solving, called "integrated focus" (Walinga, Cunningham, & MacGregor, 2010; Walinga, 2011), designed to enhance performance in a variety of realms including leadership practice. An integrated focus approach extends problem-solving theory beyond linear, rational models, demands a more holistic, inclusive process, and results in more systemic, sustainable solutions.

This chapter describes and discusses several cases of leadership practice from a variety of contexts that mirror the integrated focus problem-solving model and process in order to showcase, capture, and illustrate how the process of integrated focus problem solving forms the basis of integrative leadership as a model for inclusive and effective leadership practices. The chapter begins with an overview of problem-solving theory including creative problem solving, insight problem solving, and the particular challenges of complex or "wicked" problems. This will be followed by a description of insight as well as related concepts of constraint relaxation, problem framing, restructuring and reformulation, and problem finding leading to the integrated focus conceptual model and its cognitive, psychological, and physiological underpinnings with reference to studies conducted on the integrated focus process in a variety of contexts including sport, education, business, and aesthetics. Finally, the author identifies several cases of the integrated focus process in action from a variety of scenarios including political, medical, corporate, environmental, media, arts, and sport. Each case will be introduced, providing some background and contextual details and will then trace the integrated focus process through the actions of the leader profiled in order to provide a variety of exemplary templates for the reader to follow in developing their own leadership practice.

Overview of Insight Problem Solving, and the Particular Challenges of Complex or "Wicked" Problems

Integrative problem solving elaborates upon the principles of insight — the "out of the box" or "aha!" solution to what is perceived to be an intractable or "wicked" problem (Knoblich, Ohlsson, Haider, & Rhenius, 1999; Knoblich & Oellinger, 2006; Ohlsson, 1984). Walinga (2011) expands upon insight problem solving theory by proposing that achieving insight relies on restructuring the problem frame to be more integrative and holistic. The insightful solution differs from a merely creative solution or idea by being sustainable, systemic, and elegant: an integrative solution shows insight by illustrating a profound understanding of the problem at its core, elegance through simplicity, and sustainability by offering a practical and enduring application that is systemic in nature (Walinga, 2011). Implementing an integrated focus approach demands inclusive, collaborative, participative processes.

Systemic "wicked" problems (cf. Rittel & Webber, 1973), where the solutions remain elusive and the problems cannot be resolved with traditional modes of mechanistic and reductionist inquiry and decision making (Lovelock, 2007), demand a particular type of problem-solving process, capability, and leadership. Linear and rational problem-solving processes (e.g., specify the problem, gather and analyze data, formulate a solution and then implement the solution) are insufficient for generating radical, disruptive, or breakthrough innovations (Steiner, 2009). For leaders to evolve beyond the zero-sum, problem-solving approach requires a capacity to integrate multiple interacting factors and involve holistic, integrative, systemic, and long-term thinking (Gharajedaghi, 1999; Lozano, 2014; Wheatley, 1992). Integrative problem solving requires a capacity to think in paradoxes (cf. Westenholz, 1993), consider opposing views, and adopt different perspectives (Ryan, Tilbury, Corcoran, Abe & Nomura, 2010). The evolved leader for the future must lead more systemically and sustainably. Society has come to realize that there can be no winners in the zero-sum game because the world is an intricate, interconnected, interdependent system.

Wicked problems demand leadership capable of organizational transformation in order to shift institutional logic, values, and beliefs (Moss Kanter, 2011, p. 68). For instance, making products more recyclable or reducing the carbon footprint addresses only a part of the whole sustainability challenge and does not address the complexity of the issue. Likewise, current practices based on eco-efficiency "....work within the same system that caused the problem in the first place," measures like these "present little more than an illusion of change" (McDonough & Braungart, 2001, p. 4). Wicked problems require us to confront how we are reproducing the "dominant social paradigm" and how we view ourselves in relation to the larger societal and natural domain. Solving wicked problems requires a frame of mind that can grasp the interplay between humans and society, between self and the world (Wright Mills, 2000). Our approach to problem solving is impacted by our frame of reference, which derives from our mechanistic, reductionist worldview (Gladwin, Kennelly, & Krause, 1995;

Shrivastava, 1995; Shrivastava, Ivanaj, & Ivanaj, 2012). Our existing frame of reference is problematic as Westenholz (1993) writes: "as social beings, we are creating these pictures to defend our identity against a chaotic world," and these in turn "become a prison into which we are locked, so what we cannot view the world 'afresh'" (p. 39). Individuals will often relapse into old frames of reference before they have time to construct a new understanding of the situation. One of the major barriers to more integrative thinking is that it requires us to break through existing mental models (Lozano, 2014; Senge, 1990).

The entrenched cognitive, social, economic, institutional, and technological barriers "lock us into trajectories and lock out more systemic and integrative alternatives" resulting in incremental change (Seyfang & Smith, p. 588). Existing organizational structures (e.g., institutional silos) and processes (e.g., lack of tools) signal a lack of organizational capability and a tendency toward organizational inertia (Shrivastava, 1995). Some work has been done on identifying ways in which barriers may be overcome or even transformed into enablers of action (Burch, 2009). Burch identifies the key challenge as facilitating existing capacity into action and emphasizes the importance of institutional structures, organizational culture, and policy. Building on the sentiment of Ehrenfeld and his question "can anything be done to radically transform the way businesses work?" (2005), I argue that we need to understand how we think and problem-solve, and how we value thinking. We need to foster the ability to think deeply (Ehrenfeld, 2005) and divergently (Guilford, 1967) in order to rethink past perceptions and practices and produce the right kind of innovative solutions (Ehrenfeld, 2005). Organizations can waste a great deal of time, energy, and resources attempting to solve the wrong problems. Defining organizational challenges in a systemic and insightful manner leads to solutions that are more systemic and sustainable. Walinga et al. show that the capacity for systemic thinking, insight into the true nature of a problem, and sustainable solution generation demands the capacity to see past perceived barriers and threats (Walinga, 2007, 2008). In order to solve complex, "wicked" problems, and avoid the zero-sum game, leaders need to develop their understanding of the emotional, psychological, and structural mechanisms that allow for insightful problem definition and integrative solution generation.

Insight and Related Concepts of Impasse, Constraint Relaxation, Problem Framing, Restructuring and Reformulation, and Problem Finding

The "aha!" or Eureka effect stems from a story about the ancient Greek polymath Archimedes (ca. 250 BC) who was asked by the local king to determine whether a crown was made of pure gold. During a trip to a public bath, Archimedes noted that water was displaced when his body sank into the bath, and particularly that the volume of water displaced equaled the volume of his body immersed in the water. Having discovered how to measure the volume of an irregular object, and conceiving of a method to solve the king's problem, Archimedes allegedly leaped out and ran home naked, shouting "eureka!" (I have found it). Similarly, Sir Isaac Newton is said to have "discovered" gravity when an apple fell from a tree onto his head thus sparking the insight. Both stories capture well the rumination or feelings of frustration typical of a seemingly intractable, or "wicked" problem, the suddenness of the insight itself, as well as the spark or prompt that seems to catalyze the solution.

The Eureka effect was first described by Pamela Auble, Jeffrey Franks, and Salvatore Soraci in 1979. The essence of the "aha!" feeling underling insight problem solving was empirically investigated by Shen, Yuan, Liu, and Luo (2015). Stellan Ohlsson suggests that some salient features of the problem are incorporated into a mental representation of the problem at the beginning of the problem-solving process. In the first step of solving the problem, the problem is considered in the light of previous experience. Eventually, an impasse is reached, where all approaches to the problem have failed, and the person becomes frustrated. Kershaw and Ohlsson believe that this impasse drives unconscious processes which change the mental representation of a problem, and cause novel solutions to occur (2004).

Currently there are two theories for how people arrive at the solution for insight problems. The first is the progress monitoring theory (MacGregor, Ormerod, & Chronicle, 2001). The person will analyze the distance from their current state to the goal state. Once a person realizes that they cannot solve the problem while on their current path, they will seek alternative solutions. In insight problems this usually occurs late in the puzzle. The second way that people attempt to solve these puzzles is the representational change theory (Knoblich, Ohlsson, & Raney, 2001). The problem solver initially has a low probability for success because they use inappropriate knowledge as they set unnecessary constraints on the problem. Once the person relaxes his or her constraints, they can bring previously unavailable knowledge into working memory to solve the problem. The person also utilizes chunk decomposition (Knoblich et al., 1999), where s/he will separate meaningful chunks into their component pieces. Both constraint relaxation and chunk decomposition allow for a change in representation, that is, a change in the distribution of activation across working memory, at which point the solver may exclaim "aha!." Currently both theories have support, with the progress monitoring theory being more suited to multiple step problems, and the representational change theory more suited to single-step problems. Klein and Jarosz (2011) found multiple pathways to solving insight problems: One pathway triggered by detecting a contradiction. A second pathway is triggered by a need to break through an impasse. The third pathway gets triggered by seeing a connection.

Integrated Focus Conceptual Model and Its Cognitive, Psychological, and Physiological Underpinnings

Researchers investigating leadership approaches for solving wicked problems have discussed the principles of holistic framing but omit the path for reaching a more specific integrated frame. For instance, Manolis et al. (2009) proposed eight leadership principles modified from adaptive leadership concepts in Heifetz (1994), Heifetz and Laurie (2001), and Heifetz and Linsky (2002a, 2002b) when proposing integrative leadership principles in order to advance the integration of conservation science into policy, management, and society at large. The eight principles described by them reflect and honor the importance of diversity and holism when framing a problem: in particular the principles of (1) recognizing the social dimension of the problem, (4) combining strengths of multiple leaders, (5) extending influence through networks of relationships, (7) nurturing productive conflict, and (8) cultivating diversity (p. 345), reflect a divergent approach to problem framing. Likewise, Alban-Metcalfe and Alimo-Metcalfe (2010) propose "integrative leadership principles" which include: Engaging as an effective team, constructive challenge, ensuring shared vision, promoting quality and improvement, connecting and influencing, effective performance and risk management, clarity and accountability and personal qualities and values, and align with Yukl's (2009) demand for permeability, a culture with strong values for learning, innovation, experimentation, flexibility, and continuous improvement, social networks, differentiation among major subunits balanced against greater information sharing, conflict.

However, what we have discovered in our careful tracing of the insight problem-solving process (Walinga, 2008, 2011) is that divergent thinking alone does not result in a problem frame that will unlock the insightful solution. We have discovered that barriers are the key to completing the whole "wicked" problem frame and unlocking the insightful solution. Generating many or complex problem frames does not necessarily result in a more productive problem frame or more insightful solutions. Divergent problem framing is not as intentional and therefore not as productive. There must be a divergent quality in that we must expand the problem frame, but there must also be an intentional convergence regarding what is included in the problem frame, a convergent divergence if you will. Through our research on insight problem solving we discovered that failure, feeling stuck, or hitting barriers, the true "intractability" of the intractable problem holds the most enlightening clues to a more productive problem frame (Walinga, 2008; Walinga et al., 2010). It is these barriers that, when explored and understood, lead the solver down a path to the core values and goals most at stake — both a route and root finding process. Once these core values and goals are revealed and brought back into focus — for they tend to disappear when we are too focused on barriers and failure for multiple cognitive and physiological reasons — they can be combined with the "intractabilities" or barriers themselves to complete the integrated problem frame and bring to mind the "aha!" solution that is characteristic of insight. For instance, the barriers to conservation may be financial imperatives or conflict. We might find ourselves protesting this barrier, expending great energy in fighting the system, "big oil," or the government to remove or reduce this barrier or threat. If instead we trace this barrier to the core value it protects, we discover that human sustainability is also central to these financial concerns. The reason "big oil" persists because the industry sustains jobs, human beings, families, and communities. The problem frame is at once expanded to include both the sustainability of the fish and ecosystem and the sustainability of the human, social, and economic systems.

For some, a more holistic problem frame is the leader's moral responsibility or imperative: West Churchman (1967, p. 142) warned "that whoever attempts to tame a part of a wicked problem, but not the whole, is morally wrong." One could argue that leaders are irresponsible when they solve only a part of a wicked problem or fail to admit the limitations of their strategies and processes. Ansell and Gash (2008) point out that most collaborative efforts arise from previous failed attempts to find solutions through adversarial or managerial approaches. In Haubold's study (2015) on the application of adaptive leadership to conservation challenges in Florida, she concurs with our findings on the power of failure and barriers, citing that:

> ...it is likely that the development of Florida's imperiled species management system would not have occurred had it not been for the continuing controversy and interest of the stakeholders. Identification and understanding of the issue and its context by a multidisciplinary team resulted in the first ever articulated desired future conditions for imperiled species in Florida. Stakeholder concern about impacts, specifically impacts that could result from management of imperiled species in Florida such as improving conservation for imperiled species and effects of new regulations on industry or homeowners, led to Commission staff re-framing the issue in a way that inspired all stakeholders to engage in difficult work. Adaptive leadership principles were used to frame the wicked problem and address the impacts that needed to be managed (pp. 354–55).

Juzwishin and Bond (2012) in their paper discussing moral leadership in healthcare contribute further aspects to the insight problem solving framing stage including "the moral courage to challenge conventional wisdom, the generosity to involve those affected in finding solutions, and the humility to work within the paradox of failure being part of the solution" (p. 3022). Through our research on values-based leadership and integrative problem-solving processes, I call for an evolution in leadership practice from simple, linear, top-down, and zero-sum models to complex, integrative, holistic models demanding tools and approaches that can accommodate complexity, intractabilities, and unpredictability — otherwise known as the natural universe.

Based on previous research (2010, 2011) in both experimental and applied settings, Walinga et al. have found that the integrated focus problem-solving process followed the following phases in order to result in insight:

Cases of the Integrated Focus Process in Action from a Variety of Leadership Scenarios

What follows are several examples of leadership decision making governed by the integrated focus problem-solving approach. These scenarios illustrate the process and provide real-life examples as templates for leadership practice. Leaders using the integrated focus process follow the primary appraisal, initial representation, impasse (this is a complex, wicked problem for which there seems no solution), secondary appraisal (I accept that I do not have the resources so how can I achieve my goal despite the barrier/reality?), integrated focus (aha!).

A famed "wicked" problem was that facing the leadership team at National Aeronautics and Space Administration (NASA) prior to the Challenger disaster. Volkema (1995) cites the Challenge Shuttle disaster when explaining the importance of problem formulation as a means to effective problem solving:

> Preceding the fatal launch, there was considerable discussion regarding the technical performance of Challenger's O-rings in cold temperatures. Key decision makers, however, were concerned about several previous launch delays and about jeopardizing other scheduled missions. Furthermore, political support for the space shuttle program could be bolstered if the launch was to coincide with the president's State-of-the-Union message. The problem quickly became how to convince those engineers concerned with the O-rings to go along with the launch, the corrupting lie, rather than exploring ways to gain favorable publicity and ensure future missions (pp. 82–83).

The Challenger case has often been utilized to illustrate the features and negative outcomes of Janus' theory of Groupthink; however, the case also illustrates human problem-solving tendencies when confronting wicked problems, in this case including multiple stakeholders and associated pressures. The NASA program was under the microscope in terms of media, public, and federal scrutiny due to a series of failed launches prior to the disaster. This pressure, coupled with economic, political, and reputational factors for all partners (NASA, Thiokol, US Government), caused NASA to be very anxious to proceed with the launch. To justify its budget NASA had scheduled a large number of missions in 1986. It was vital for the Challenger to be launched so that there would be enough time to refurbish the launch pad to prepare it for the next launch. The European Space Agency was providing added competition and there was political pressure for the Challenger to be in space when the president of the United States gave the State of the Union address. Under duress, the leaders framed the problem as whether to launch or not to launch. In actuality, if the group had drilled down through the barriers to the core values at stake, it would have become apparent that the threats included negative media which was causing public and government doubt. Funding threats would ultimately threaten NASA's future as a space agency and program. What the leaders should have then focused on is how to creatively communicate the value of the space program to the public, the government, and the media. Innovation, discovery, education, sustainability, exploration, and the future could all highlight the value of the program and the importance of protecting the shuttle if a delay is necessary. Communications that center on such values would have made the decision to not launch that much more imperative and obvious. Instead, the decision was framed around a lack of data and the credibility of Thiokol.

Another example of insight occurred within NASA during the early days of the space program. Scientists tried to solve the problem of heat of reentry by devising a substance that could withstand heat, and met with repeated failure. Their ultimate solution — the ablative heat shield that burns away as the space vehicle penetrates the atmosphere, taking the heat with it — turned upside down their original problem definition of "how to withstand the heat" and reframed the problem more integratively as "how can we protect the space vehicle on re-entry given that no re-entry induced heat resistant material exists?" It became clear that the real problem that NASA engineers were attempting to solve was that of diverting the heat. Heat can be addressed in many ways: captured, consumed, diverted, and dissipated.

A historical example of creative insight occurred within the Mann Gulch fire of 1949 and demonstrates aspects of the insight problem-solving process. The issue of heat was a prominent feature of the Mann Gulch forest fire which was later made famous through Karl Wieck's work on "sensemaking" (2001) and captured in author Norman McLean's book *Young Men and Fire* (1992). Mann Gulch occurred when a wildfire in the Helena National Forest, Montana, United States spread out of control and ultimately claimed the lives of 13 firefighters who had parachuted into the fire. Foreman Wagner Dodge led the team of "smokejumpers" toward the Missouri River. The fire, however, spread faster than anticipated and had already cut off their path to safety. The men had to turn around but the fire was quickly gaining on them. When Dodge realized that they would not be able to outrun the fire, he started an escape fire and motioned amidst the roar of the flames for everyone to lie down in the area he was about to burn down. The other team members, thinking him crazy, hurried toward the ridge of Mann Gulch instead (achieving heroic speeds in their desperate attempts to escape!). Only two of them, Bob Sallee and Walter Rumsey, managed to escape through a crevice and find a safe location — a rock slide with little vegetation to fuel the fire. Two other members survived with heavy injuries but died within a day. Only Dodge had the insight to remove fuel so as to reduce the chance of being burned by the fire. Ironically, the two other survivors benefitted from the same principle that Dodge applied in his solution: though they reached it purely by chance, the rocky slope they reached had no fuel for the fire. Insight appears to require the ability to "shake loose" from assumptions and prior knowledge (that the problem was "how to outrun or escape the fire") but, perhaps most importantly, the ability to clearly define the problem ("how do we avoid being burned by the fire?"). Like the NASA ablative shield, the insight was to provide alternative fuel for the fire so as to divert it from whatever is at stake — person or spacecraft.

In an organizational setting, Caldwell et al. describe a large healthcare facility which was operating with success in a large urban center (2007). The center employed over 1000 doctors and several thousand nurses and staff. A smaller health center opened within the same area, offering good care at a reduced rate, and soon lured a good portion of the clientele away from the larger center. One can imagine the implications that attempting cost cutting would have upon both employee and client satisfaction. A more insightful solution found the larger center focusing instead upon quality. Their new mandate of offering "quality care at a moderate rate" found commitment from organizational members and was implemented over 2 years with a positive response from clientele.

In a sport setting, a coach of a university soccer team with whom I consulted over many years was problem solving the barriers she faced in leading her team to a national championship. After many sessions working with individual athletes to cogenerate insights and strategies in the face of various performance barriers, she then identified a barrier of her own: the goalie. For several years, her starting goalie, though an effective, skilled, and reliable performer, had been wreaking emotional havoc within the team. Her angry outbursts, passive aggressive comments, and generally negative actions and attitudes were having an impact on the team dynamic and culture. In clarifying the barrier further, the coach was able to crystalize the barrier as the goalie's personality. Her personality was indeed a reality that did not seem to be changeable. The coach had spent many hours counseling and coaching the goalie off the field with little success or impact. I drilled down further on the barrier asking what concerned the coach most about the goalie's personality (comments, attitude, outbursts, and actions). The coach described the tenuous atmosphere of athletes on tenterhooks, the discouraged climate, the uncertainty and fear that permeated the girls' interactions and energy: they never knew when they would be attacked, any positive energy or momentum was eventually punctured by a negative comment; during a goal setting session she remarked "this is all useless, we just need to do it, we just need to stop making stupid mistakes and get on with it." I asked what concerned the coach about that and she described the importance of positive energy, confidence, connection, and trust as fundamental to performance. If the girls were afraid, or even just distracted, by the goalie's negativity, it would hurt their confidence and thus their performance. The coach's dilemma was that the goalie was excellent and they relied on her. The second goalie was a rookie, inexperienced, raw. However, as we drilled down further, she revealed that confidence, trust, and positivity were essential. Though the goalie was critical to their success, there would be no success with her on the team.

We framed the challenge as: given that the coach is not able to change the goalie's attitude, how can she facilitate optimal performance in her team? She looked at me and calmly said: she has to go. The coach had a tough conversation with the goalie and cut her from the team a few weeks before Nationals. The team went on to the semifinals of their division championships where they faced their arch nemesis in a shootout. The young goalie was rising but did not know the tendencies of all of the players on the opposing team, critical information to help her anticipate the shots they would be firing. The coach called the former goalie who shared the information. In this way, the former goalie was also a critical part of the team's success in winning the division semifinal and qualifying for the National championship. The team was on a mission and, at the Nationals, they strolled through the single elimination quarterfinals with a shutout win of 1-0 and then qualified for the gold medal game with a semifinal win of 2-1. The soccer team then captured their first-ever Canadian Interuniversity Sport (CIS) National title with an impressive and convincing 3-0 victory in the final. They young goalie recorded her 6th shutout.

Kidney Chain originator and founder of the National Kidney Registry, Garet Hil, inspired by his 10-year-old daughter's illness, generated the idea of a kidney chain as a "pay it forward" solution to long donor waiting lists. When his attempt to donate a kidney to his daughter was called off at the last moment due to exorbitant levels of antibodies in her blood, he "panicked" and entered his and her names in every paired kidney exchange program possible across the country. After 15 relatives were tested, a 23-year-old cousin was finally identified as a match. Hil soon realized that the barrier was the limited number of matches available. When he drilled down on this barrier further he realized that the problem with limited matches was that not enough donors were made visible, the pool was too limited lowering the statistical probability of finding a match. The real challenge was to expand the pool of donors, not to find a match. Hil created the National Kidney Registry which operates more like a chain, linking together incompatible donors and recipients with other incompatible pairs, so that patients in renal failure can receive life-altering transplants. With the help of a grant from Aetna, an insurance company, and his colleague, Rich Marta, Hil spent months devising and testing and revising what eventually became BestMatch, a program designed to execute chains in real time. Based on algorithms used to make trades on the New York

Stock Exchange, the principle behind BestMatch is surprisingly simple: the more pairs in the pool, the more possible chains. To create a three-way exchange, a pool of 100 incompatible pairs will generate 10 billion possible combinations. With a pool of 500 incompatible pairs, the number of possible combinations jumps exponentially to 31 trillion. Hil used both insight to reframe the challenge facing kidney transplant patients, and remote association in linking the stock exchange trading principle with a challenge within the field of medical science, to generate a truly elegant and enduring solution to a "wicked" problem.

Next, I share an example of problem solving within the complex field of Human Resources and hiring processes. In discussion with a leader of an executive education department at a university, she described and contrasted for me two complex and risky personnel decisions — one that endured and one that failed: in the first more enduring decision, a decision to hire "somebody new and green" — she considered the risks immediately and thereby constructed the barrier of failure by asking herself "what is the worst that can happen?." In this way, she imagined the barrier and experienced the impasse of failure — letting the organization down, costing time and resources, negatively impacting her reputation. Once she was able to imagine these barriers and experienced the impasse, she accepted that she could not control the potential for failure and instead prepared her approach to the new hire with the barriers and her goals in mind: "what am I trying to achieve, what is this place all about, how long do we have to get there (and) at the end of the day what are the really key elements in the context of the achievement and which ones could you actually not achieve and the world wouldn't come to an end." She also described her decision as "holistic": "hopefully all my decisions have an ethical component to them, and a people and relationship component to them, sometimes it is probably something that causes me problems. But they are also about believing in people that build teams to be successful."

Relating the second, failed decision, she described a more linear decision making process: She had "collected some information previous to making that decision. Information about the person we were going to hire. Reference kind of information. Contextual information, and then made the decision." But she also described a barrier focus typical of a linear problem-solving approach in that she felt constrained by the context and history of this person's role and position and was in a dilemma which she described as: "If I do not appoint this person to this job she will lose face, what are you going to do with her, because she is already working in your department, what are the implications for everyone else in the unit if she is not appointed to this job?" A more systemic and integrated focus would have found her acknowledging the barriers and constraints (status quo, history, group expectations) while keeping the goal in view. Her strategy would have been one of managing the constraints while still achieving the goal of what is best for the future of the organization. The integrative solution demands deep thinking and creativity but will ultimately result in a more enduring and satisfactory solution for all including, even, the person not hired for the position for she would certainly be happier avoiding failure and performing in a role more suitable to her strengths.

Open source innovation, information, and services are taking the world by storm and one can argue that the open source concept emerged from this same integrated focus, insight problem-solving process of identifying the barriers (lack of resources to keep up with demand for information/product/service), accepting that we have a lack of or finite resources (we can't possibly connect with or educate infinite clients or customers), revealing the values or goals (service/support/access is important), and reframing the challenge to include both the goals and values and the barriers (how do we supply access and support with limited resources?). The insight of open sourcing is to flip the equation by inviting the public to join the problem-solving process. The City of Vancouver opened their databases to the public to create a more efficient and economical model of self-service. Dog licenses, property tax payments, business forms, can be downloaded and applications or processes completed online without the intervention of municipal staff. InnoCentive is an open source organization that showcases challenges for various companies and organizations inviting solution proposals from the public for a preset award. Uber and AirBnb, ride and accommodation sharing apps, are pushing society toward an espoused "sharing economy." However, with the advent of these open, social innovations, as a society we find ourselves wrestling with these conceptualizations of open source and facing new challenges. The open model sits in tension with social, cultural, and economic models thereby creating a "wicked" problem unto itself and challenging leaders to navigate the complexities of competing values and systems. Applying the integrated focus model, we could that open models threaten our existing capitalist framework creating antagonisms and tensions, that is, between taxi drivers and Uber because the new model threatens the livelihoods of the taxi drivers. However, the new models, though perceived as barriers to some, are a reality; some would argue the new open and shared models are an evolutionary inevitability. The path forward will demand that we drill down to the values that are under threat: livelihoods, sustainability, and efficiency. In the case of Uber, the reframed challenge becomes "how can society change and evolve in a way that transitions from, yet supports the needs and values of, the old models?"

Companies seeking to implement more sustainable (human, environmental, and financial) practices are wise to employ the integrated focus model of insight problem solving for addressing the complex, systemic, "wicked" problem of sustainability. Integrative solutions include such out of the box and inspiring business approaches such as IKEA's aggressive commitment to "future proofing" its company (Kelly-Detwiler, 2014). CEO Steve Howard emphasizes that sustainability must involve "a rational business decision with a decent payback but that values are critical to the entire endeavor" (para. 5). The company is isolating itself from the volatilities of electric power markets by focusing on what delivers long-term energy security, a macro hedge on energy price rises, and addresses carbon. IKEA also has a long-term business philosophy to own most of their stores, factories, and land — essentially, building out a long-term "green" hedge, which will allow them to much more accurately forecast future energy operating costs. As a consequence, IKEA owns as many renewable energy resources as some energy companies and is the second largest private commercial solar owner. The company is also working on a geothermal system to heat and cool a soon-to-be-constructed store near Kansas City. The IKEA example illustrates how the three-phase approach of (1) a values-based focus, (2) an integrative, systemic problem frame, and (3) creative thinking strategies can lead to insightful and sustainable solutions that solve the whole challenge of sustainability. As Howard articulates:

> If you start with a values-driven point of view, you can make a business case. Climate change and energy security mean you have to have a radical approach. We need a six, seven, or eight-fold decrease in carbon intensity. That's not business as usual. Energy efficiency only gets you so far. You have to decouple your business from

carbon. Then you have to look at what's commercially scalable (2014, para. 3).

Systems thinking, governed by a values focus and acknowledging existing barriers and constraints, leads to an integrative framing of the problem which fosters more insightful (complete, systemic, elegant, and sustainable) solutions.

In this chapter, I have provided a description and discussion of "wicked" problems, an overview of insight problem-solving, a description of the integrated focus model for insight problem solving, and a series of "wicked problem" cases to illustrate the integrated focus model in a variety of contexts. The model was generated from a series of experimental and qualitative investigations with a variety of populations and problem-solving scenarios, both realistic and laboratory. The model provides insight into the insight problem-solving process by teasing apart the problem-framing phase and illustrating the value of accepting the barriers as a means to revealing the core values underlying the problem. In "wicked" problems, the complexity itself may prove a barrier to seeing the whole problem as well as the values inherently driving its solution leaving the problem frame incomplete and therefore unproductive. When a complex problem is framed more integratively to include both barriers and values, the integrative frame proves more productive in generating truly sustainable, systemic, and elegant solutions to what would otherwise appear to be intractable problems. As in most situations, when two otherwise remote concepts are combined, the result can often be both surprising and pleasing.

The model of integrated focus (Table 1) builds on theories of stress and cognition to propose that, we primarily appraise a problem or stressor as a threat or not a threat, and if deemed a

Table 1. *The Integrated Focus Model for Leveraging Insight.*

(a) Primary appraisal (is this a problem?)
(b) Secondary appraisal (do I have the resources?)
(c) Problem rerepresentation:
    a. I don't have the resources — resign, there is no solution.
    b. I don't have the resources — deny, I will just keep trying!
    c. I don't have the resources — accept, how do I achieve my goal despite this barrier?
(d) Solution generation
    a. Give up — no focus — no solution
    b. Fixation, rumination — barrier focus — stuck/impasse
    c. Reframe — integrated focus — insight

threat, we conduct a secondary appraisal which determines whether we have the resources to address the threat. If we do not have the resources, we primarily appraise whether that lack of resources is a threat and, if our lack of resources is deemed a threat we either shut down (flight/freeze), deny, and continue to confront the threat or attempt to change the fact that we lack resources (fight). Or we can accept our lack of resources and include this reality within our problem frame: given our constraints, barriers, and/or lack of resources, what is the problem? In this way, we reveal the core values that are at stake and under threat in the first place. We are then able to reframe the challenge in a new way: given our constraints, barriers, and/or lack resources, what are some creative ways through which we can achieve our goals and values? In this way, the process is iterative and recursive with opportunities to spin off into a new path and breakthrough after each point of appraisal (Fig. 1).

The When implications of the integrated focus approach to insight problem solving are, in my mind, far reaching. Leaders able to facilitate and conjure an "integrated focus" are better able to "break the zero-sum game logic of winners and losers, and … create environments where the norm is collaboration, generosity and trust instead of competition, selfishness and control." Faced with "wicked" problems, we must first clearly distinguish between barriers that we cannot change or control for the moment, and the actual values and goals these barriers threaten. The challenge is not always to overcome the barrier. Often, the

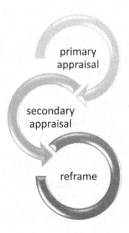

Fig. 1. Integrated Focus Insight Problem Solving Flow Pattern: Appraisal/Reappraisal, Frame/Reframe.

challenge is first to accept the barrier and then to follow that barrier as a clue or pathway to the values at stake. Once brought back into the focus, the values can now combine with the barriers in a more integrative framing of the problem: given the barrier, how might we still achieve our goals and values? In this integrative reframing of the challenge comes the "eureka," "aha," epiphany moment of insight. Insightful solutions to wicked problems are not magic, and need not be elusive. This chapter argues that the challenge of "wicked" problems is not insurmountable; the challenge rests not at the solution generation stage but at the problem-framing stage. Human beings have the capacity and power to understand our cognitive, emotional, and physiological systems in order to frame problems more systemically and integratively. Human beings also have the creative capacity to then generate creative, sustainable, elegant solutions to our complex problems.

References

Alban-Metcalfe, J., & Alimo-Metcalfe, B. (2010). Integrative leadership, partnership working and wicked problems: A conceptual analysis. *The International Journal of Leadership in Public Services*, 6(3), 3–13.

Ansell, C., & Gash, A. (2008). Collaborative governance in theory and practice. *Journal of Public Administration Research and Theory*, 18(4), 543–571.

Burch, S. (2009). In pursuit of resilient, low carbon communities: An examination of barriers to action in three Canadian cities. *Energy Policy*, doi:10.1016/j.enpol.2009.06.070.

D'Zurilla, T. J., & Sheedy, C. F. (1992). Relation between social problem solving ability and subsequent level psychological stress in college students. *Cognitiue therapy psycgology*, 61(5), 841–846

Durand-Bush, N., & Salmela, J. H. (2002).The development and maintenance of expert athletic performance: Perceptions of world and Olympic champions. *Journal of Applied Sport Psychology*, 14(3), 154–171.

Ehrenfeld, D. (2005). Sustainability: Living with the imperfections. *Conservation Biology*, 19, 33–35. doi:10.1111/j.1523-1739.2005.0456a.x.

Gladwin, T., Kennelly, J., & Krause, T. S. (1995). Shifting paradigm for sustainable development: Implications for management theory and research. *The Academy of Management Review*, 20(4), 874–907.

Gharajedaghi, J. (1999). *Systems thinking: Managing chaos and complexity.* Burlington, MA: Butterworth-Heinemann.

Guilford, J. P. (1967). *The nature of human intelligence.* New York, NY: McGraw-Hill.

Heifetz, R. A. (1994). *Leadership without easy answers.* Cambridge, MA: The Belknap Press of Harvard University Press.

Heifetz, R. A., & Laurie, D. L. (2001). The work of leadership. *Harvard Business Review*, 79, 131–140.

Heifetz, R. A., & Linsky, M. (2002a). *Leadership on the line: Staying alive through the dangers of leading*. Boston, MA: Harvard School Business Press.

Heifetz, R. A., & Linsky, M. (2002b). A survival guide for leaders. *Harvard Business Review*, 80, 65–72.

Juzwishin, D., & Bond, K. (2012). Cultivating excellence in leadership: Wicked problems and virtues. *Healthcare Management Forum*, 25, 161–164.

Kershaw, T., & Ohlsson, S. (2004). Multiple causes of difficulty in insight: The case of nine-dot problem. *Journal of Experimental Psychology: Learning, Memory, and Cognition*, 30, 3–13.

Ketchen, D. J., Snow, C. C., & Street, V. L. (2004). Improving firm performance by matching strategic decision-making processes to competitive dynamics. *Academy of Management Executive*, 18(4), 29–43.

Klein, G., & Jarosz, A. (2011). A naturalistic study of insight. *Journal of Cognitive Engineering and Decision Making*, 5(4), 335–351.

Knoblich, G., & Oellinger, M. (2006). AHA! The eureka moment. *Scientific American Mind*, 17(5), 38–43.

Knoblich, G., Ohlsson, S., & Raney, G. E. (2001). An eye movement study of insight problem solving. *Memory & Cognition*, 29, 1000–1009.

Knoblich, G., Ohlsson, S., Haider, H., & Rhenius, D. (1999). Constraint relaxation and chunk decomposition in insight problem solving. *Journal of Experimental Psychology: Leaning, Memory, and Cognition*, 25(6), 1534–1555.

Kovác, T. (1998). Effects of creativity training in young soccer talents. *Studia Psychologica*, 40(3), 211–217.

Kelly-Detwiler, P. (2014). IKEA's aggressive approach to sustainability creates enormous business opportunities. *Forbes*. Retrieved from http://www.forbes.com/sites/peterdetwiler/2014/02/07/ikeas-aggressive-approach-to-sustainability-creates-enormous-business-opportunities/. Accessed on June 2015.

Lozano, R. (2014). Creativity and organizational learning as means to foster sustainability. *Sustainable Development*, 22(3), 205–216.

Lovelock, J. (2007). *The revenge of Gaia*. London: Penguin Group.

McDonough, W., & Braungart, M. (2001). The next industrial revolution. In M. Charter & U. Tischner (Eds.), *Sustainable solutions: Developing products and services for the future* (pp. 139–150). Sheffield: Greenleaf Publishing Ltd.

Moss Kanter, R. (2011). How great companies think differently. *Harvard Business Review*, 89(11), 66–78.

MacGregor, J., Ormerod, T., & Chronicle, E. (2001). Information processing and insight: A process model of performance on the nine-dot and related problems. *Journal of Experimental Psychology: Learning, Memory, and Cognition*, 27, 176–201.

Manolis, J. C., Chan, K. M., Finkelstein, M. E., Stephens, S., Nelson, C. R., Grant, J. B., & Dombeck, M. P. (2009). Leadership: A new frontier in conservation science. *Conservation Biology*, 23, 879–886.

McLean, N. (1992). *Young men and fire*. Chicago, MA: University of Chicago Press.

Nutt, P. C. (2002). Averting decision debacles. *Technological Forecasting and Social Change*, 71(3), 239–265.

Nutt, P. C. (2004). Averting decision debacles. Technological Forecasting and Social Change.

Ohlsson, S. (1984). Restructuring revisited: An information processing theory of restructuring and insight. *Scandinavian Journal of Psychology*, 25, 117–129.

Pugh, M. B. (1991). The effects of teaching problem solving on academic performance and retention. *Community/Junior College Quarterly of Research and Practice*, 15(3), 339–349.

Rittel, H. W., & Webber, M. M. (1973). Dilemmas in a general theory of planning. *Policy Sciences*, 4(2), 155–169.

Ryan, A., Tilbury, D., Corcoran, P. B., Abe, O., & Nomura, K. (2010). Sustainability in higher education in the Asia-Pacific: Developments, challenges, and prospects. *International Journal of Sustainability in Higher Education*, 11(2), 106–119.

Shrivastava, P. (1995). The role of corporations in achieving ecological sustainability. *Academy of Management Review*, 20, 936–960.

Shrivastava, P., Ivanaj, V., & Ivanaj, S. (2012). Sustainable development and the arts. *International Journal of Technology Management*, 60(1/2), 23–43.

Steiner, G. (2009). The concept of open creativity: Collaborative creative problem solving for innovation generation – A systems approach. *Journal of Business & Management*, 15(1), 5–33.

Senge, P. M. (1990). *The fifth discipline*. New York, NY: Doubleday/Currency.

Shen, W., Yuan, Y., Liu, C., & Luo, J. (2015). In search of the 'Aha!' experience: Elucidating the emotionality of insight problem-solving. *British Journal of Psychology*, doi:10.1111/bjop.12142.

Smith, G. J. W., Carlsson, I., & Sandström, S. (1985). Artists and artistic creativity. *Psychological Research Bulletin*, 25, 1–26.

Westenholz, A. (1993). Paradoxical thinking and change in frame of reference. *Organizational Studies*, 14, 37–58.

Wheatley, M. J. (1992). *Leadership and the new science: Learning about organization from an orderly universe*. Oakland, CA: Berrett-Koehler Publishers.

Wright-Mills, C. (2000). *Sociological imagination*. New York: Oxford University Press.

Walinga, J. (2008). Change readiness: The roles of appraisal, focus, and perceived control. *Journal of Applied Behavioral Science*, 44(3), 315–347.

Walinga, J. (2011). From walls to windows: Using barriers as keys to unlock insightful solutions. *Journal of Creative Behavior*, 44(3), 1–25.

Walinga, J., Cunningham, J. B., & MacGregor, J. (2010). Improving performance in solving insight problems: The roles of assumptions, barriers and goals. *Journal of Creative Behavior*, 45(1) 47–58.

Wang, C.-W., & Horng, R.-Y. (2002). The effects of creative problem solving training on creativity, cognitive type and R&D performance. *R&D Management*, 32(1), 35–41.

Wanish, J. A. (2000). An investigation of student development, life values, athletic identity, and the use of the center for enhanced performance among selected cadets at West Point. *Dissertation Abstracts International Section A: Humanities and Social Sciences*, 61(3-A), 933.

Weisberg, R. W. (1995). Prolegomena to the theories of insight in problem solving: A taxonomy of problems. In R. J. Sternberg & J. E. Davidson (Eds.), *The nature of insight* (pp. 157–196). Cambridge, MA: MIT Press.

Wertheimer, M. (1959). *Productive thinking*. New York, NY: Harper & Row.

West Churchman, C. (1967). Wicked problems. *Management Science*, 14, 141–142.

CHAPTER

23

Striving for Horizontality by Addressing Power Differentials in Radical Organizing

Claire Delisle, Maria Basualdo,
Adina Ilea and Andrea Hughes

Keywords: ICOPA; leadership; horizontality;
penal abolition; social movement;
radical organizing

Introduction

Social justice organizing is different from typical objects of leadership studies, because the category "leadership" is highly contentious. Activists either consider leadership to be intrinsically authoritarian, and thus reject it out of hand (Diani, 2003, pp. 105–106), or espouse notions of horizontality and anti-authoritarianism (Gordon, 2005; Heckert, 2010; Juris, 2008; Routledge, 2009; Sitrin, 2006) and therefore have a more collective view of how leadership is manifested. Horizontality is "…a flat plane for organizing [involving] …non-hierarchical relationships in which people no longer make decisions for others" (Sitrin, 2006, p. vi). Horizontality here denotes a lack of authoritarian top-down leadership thus allowing more people to be included in conversations and decisions.[1] Horizontality challenges the Europeans' "...long history of hierarchical and highly structured government and legal systems" (Kuyek, 2011, p. 60) which can be oppressive for others (ibid, p. 61). As activists and anti-oppression advocates, "...our work for change should try wherever possible to encourage, create space for and accept leadership from other racial and cultural groups... It does mean allowing the space and time for cultural forms to emerge, to take leadership and power" (ibid.). By transforming traditional structures, a space can be created whereby oppressed people can be "for themselves" in a way that is empowering for them, instead of being relegated to the margins, or forced into the oppressive structure. It also connotes a striving for consensus and building relationships (ibid.).[2] Achieving non-authoritarian and egalitarian dynamics implies being mindful of hegemonic Western patterns of domination and variations in the resources that participants in a collective endeavor bring to the table. We focus here on a penal abolitionist movement, and the organization of one of its conferences, in order to examine the possibilities and limits of breaking the zero-sum game in radical organizing when organizers bring different levels of zero-sum and non-zero-sum resources to the exercise.

Since the 1970s, a body of literature has developed, critiquing penal frameworks, and theorizing and strategizing the abolition of prisons and penal structures (see for instance, Hulsman, 1986; Mathiesen, 1974, 2015; Pepinsky & Quinney, 1991; West & Morris, 2000). Around the world, people work toward this, including prisoners, ex-prisoners, survivors of social harm, their loved ones, activists of various stripes and scholars.[3] Penal abolitionists adopt a radical posture vis-à-vis the punishment framework in regard to the prison, the police, courts, and

---

[1] "Inclusive" is a contentious qualifier. Some feel that the positionality whence one is inclusive is indicative of unequal relations of power. It suggests that one group can decide on the other group's participation.
[2] Sitrin (2006) stresses that these terms do not convey the fulsomeness of the Spanish term "horizontalidad."
[3] These categories are porous, for example, some belong to more than one group.

corrections, respectively.[4] The only international entity devoted exclusively to their eradication is the International Conference on Penal Abolition (ICOPA) (Actionicopa.org).[5] This conference-movement has held 16 conferences in a different part of the world where survivors of state or social harm,[6] activists and scholars gather to share critiques of penal structures and to collectively develop strategies for moving the struggle forward (see actionicopa.org).[7] ICOPA is a valuable entity to explore for its continuity and resilience. It is characterized by a lack of governance structures or designated leaders and an openness to valuing and respecting the many voices that flow in and out of its space.

Given the composition of ICOPA (survivors of state or social harm, activists and academics), attention is given to its power dynamics. Considerable effort is made to place survivors at the center of the deliberations and have them play a role in organizing and contributing to the conference. For those currently imprisoned and otherwise not able to attend, sessions are devoted to reading their written works (Fiander, Chen, & Piché, 2014; Larsen, 2008). Grassroots activists also bring key experiential and theoretical knowledge to the table. Conversations about theory and strategy benefit from these inputs and "keep it real." It is therefore key to be attentive to the way the conference unfolds so that all types of participants can benefit from the exchanges. A perceived problem is that academics are a resource-heavy contingent, and are often over-represented in conference organization. ICOPAs are often held on university campuses which are still considered by some to be bastions of white male upper-middle-class privilege (Brownlee, 2015; Cannon, 2013; Coté, Dey, & de Peuter,

---

[4]Abolitionists first targeted the prison. Later, they broadened their target because all the appendages of the criminal justice system are part and parcel of the punishment framework, and the existence of prison relies on other parts of the system for its survival (i.e., police and courts).

[5]There are other anti-prison and anti-penal organizations, such as the Anarchist Black Cross internationally whose mandate is broader than penal abolition, and Critical Resistance, whose purview is the US, for instance.

[6]This includes prisoners, ex-prisoners and victims, as well as their loved ones.

[7]A small fund set up by ICOPA co-founder, Ruth Morris provides limited monies for the conference.

2007; Haiven & Khasnabish, 2014). Professors[8] often fall into one or the other of these categories, while the bulk of criminalized individuals has a tendency to emanate from poor, marginalized and often racialized communities. Activists come from all backgrounds. The nature of academic conferences is sometimes perceived as punctilious and unimaginative. Some think that attending ICOPAs on university campuses is oppressive (Delisle et al., 2015a, Interview, June 24, 2014[9]). Yet, the benefits of holding such conferences on campus are that the institution's resources are often free.

This chapter explores challenges and the measures taken to organize ICOPA 15 along horizontal principles. It stems from data collectively gathered and inter-subjectively analyzed from the local organizing committee of ICOPA 15 (See Delisle et al., 2015b). It is the result of an organic conversation before, during and after the conference. We seized the opportunity of hosting ICOPA 15 to engage in a self-reflexive exercise of our own leadership dynamics. We asked what makes ICOPA work, what impinges on its fluid functioning, and examined possibilities for how we can grow our awareness about privilege, horizontality, and how the possession of zero-sum and non-zero-sum resources impacts organizational dynamics and the empowerment of individuals.

Organizing the conference is a multi-faceted endeavor involving tasks ranging from logistics to vetting contribution submissions. We explore three elements that we believe made it difficult to engage in horizontality during the organization of ICOPA 15: The structure of the academy; unaddressed power differentials among organizers; and non-reflexivity. Then, we focus on elements that were conducive to beginning a more horizontal way of doing things: Discussion of leadership and process; self-reflexive meetings; mindfulness about horizontality and collective action; and we propose anti-oppression measures and practices. We address the zero-sum resources of one member (the lead) of the committee, and how this impacted committee meetings. We also look at the positive aspects of our endeavor, including ways that resources were shared, and the mindfulness with which some organizers undertook the process.

---

[8]We use the term "professor" here instead of "academic," in order to differentiate from students who do not necessarily have the same privileges (race, gender, class).

[9]For this research, we also had conversations (semistructured interviews) with international participants about leadership in ICOPA. To preserve anonymity, interviews are identified by date.

A Guiding Theoretical Basis for Analysis

We use three theoretical lenses to analyze leadership dynamics in ICOPA. First, we are attentive to the need for "decolonizing"[10] (Brown & Strega, 2005; Cannon, 2013; Estrella, 2015; Smith, n.d.) the academy by building bridges with the community, lest the former believe it is the only place where meaningful knowledge can emerge. Second, we use an anti-oppression framework that enables us to consider oppression and unearned privilege (see Pease, 2010; Smith, n.d.; Bishop, 2015; Estrella, 2015). The anti-oppression framework includes a deconstruction of oppression (racism, patriarchy, and so on), an exploration of the meaning and impact of unearned privilege based on these oppressions, and a consideration of liberation strategies, some of which include autonomous organizing principles (Estrella, 2015). Third, we draw understanding from anarchist principles of organizing that are based on a conceptualization of zero-sum and non-zero-sum resources, and relational ethics (See Gordon, 2005; Routledge, 2009, respectively).

Gordon (2005) argues that concerns about leadership are really about the distribution of power, as well as autonomy and solidarity (p. 131). He borrows Starhawk's (1987) three-pronged conceptualization of power: power over, achieved through domination (p. 9); power-from-within, akin to power-to, which has to do with the sense of mastery that extends to realms of creativity and connection to others (*ibid.*); and power-with, "the influence we can exert in a group of equals, our power to shape the group's course and shift its direction" (pp. 10, 268).[11] Equality among members is the essential aspect of this type of power. Gordon suggests, however, that it is wrong to assume such an equality (p. 155). To do so would mean to ignore the differential in "skills, resources, recognition and support [activists] need in order to be effective and feel valued" (p. 156). Differences in resources affect the ability to have power-with (p. 160). He develops a typology of resources: "zero-sum" resources being things like money, space, time and logistical equipment. These are difficult to

---

[10]To decolonize means to actively resist colonialism, which perpetuates the subjugation and exploitation of oppressed groups such as the indigenous peoples, see Wilson and Yellow Bird (2005, p. 2).
[11]VeneKlasen and Miller (2002) also have a fourth category: "power within, meaning personal self-confidence." (p. 45).

duplicate or share; information, skills, access to networks and publicity are one category of "non-zero-sum" resources which are easily duplicated or shared; and finally, issues such as commitment, energy and personality traits, which though also "non-zero-sum" resources, are nonetheless harder to duplicate (p. 161).

In terms of relational ethics, Routledge (2009) teases out an approach for the considered relationship between the activist-academic and resisting others, and the ensuing possibility of active resistance to oppression and domination. Such collaboration between activist-academics and resisting others involves participating in "spaces of action which are inclusive and anti-hierarchical" (p. 83). He proposes a methodological manifesto that incorporates activism (which he characterizes as living theory beyond words), affinity, emotion and relational ethics (p. 87).

In addition, Routledge says that "...relations of honesty, truth and interpersonal acknowledgement" allow us "...to build a genuine moral language"; and it helps us "...become more fully conscious human beings" (Routledge, 2009, p. 88). Self-consciousness, we are reminded, is self-knowledge, understanding one's past and one's present, desires, fears and needs, and "one's relationship to the larger world" (*ibid.*). This is helpful in the "... articulation of a temporary common ground, wherein relations of difference and power (e.g., concerning gender, age, ethnicity, class, and sexuality) are negotiated across distances of culture, space, and positionality in the search for mutual understanding" (p. 88). Undertaking a process of decolonizing one's self and getting used to not flaunting expertise is one of the benefits of retaining relational ethics as part of our ongoing demeanor in struggle.

Organizing ICOPA 15

Although the lead organizer had begun the process earlier, organizing ICOPA 15 began in earnest in September 2013. Having recruited people to compose the organizing committee, monthly meetings were held at the University of Ottawa to set about staging the international event that June. The lead organizer is a full-time professor who benefits from a recognition of his legitimacy by the university and the ensuing support and assistance from the institution, his own office, grant money to support the work for organizing the conference and paid time to devote to such a venture. He is in fact an academic-activist, familiar with, and mindful of, the tensions around privilege and oppression. The other members of the committee consisted of a number of activists from community organizations, several graduate and undergraduate students, and an adjunct professor.[12] Of the group, the full-time faculty member disposed of an abundance of zero-sum resources compared to most others on the committee. Because of the nature of the academy, there was an unequal power differential between the professor and the students, between him and the adjunct professor,[13] and between him and the community activists.

The lead took on the drafting of the agenda and the chairpersonship of the meetings. Dates and times for meetings were decided with the people present at the meeting, so there was no consultation with those absent. Meetings were held at the university usually on week-nights. This may have contributed to the limited involvement of those who were unavailable to meet in the evenings or unwilling to come to the university. There may have been mobility and transportation issues because meetings were held on campus. Speculatively, potential community participants may have considered the university to be an intimidating environment. This may have had a bearing on the participation (or lack) of some community members. Even though systematic outreach efforts were initiated, more could have been done. Ongoing engagement with grassroots organizations is necessary for meaningful participation to take place. Area activists are, however, as elsewhere, spread notoriously thin, which can also explain the absence of some players.

At the start and well into the process, the lead organizer managed most of the aspects of the conference organization. This can in part be explained by the fact that he had attended ICOPAs and was therefore knowledgeable about many aspects of the conference; and because he had a relationship with some international ICOPA figures, who informed him about process and know-how. Typically, he arrived at meetings with an agenda crafted by himself, having circulated it ahead of the meeting to solicit input from committee members. During the process of organizing the conference, at least at the beginning, the lead role was key, since everything that was unfolding needed his say. He disposed of grant money, and negotiated with the University regarding space and technical support for the conference. As the

---

[12] The authors are part of this group.

[13] Adjunct professors do not have the same zero-sum resources as full-time professors.

months went by and sub-committees formed — tasked with such things as fundraising, grant applications and registration — others began to take responsibility for specific tasks; gradually, the lead organizer was able to let go of more tasks and duties as others stepped up and trust developed in people's level of commitment. ICOPA 15 featured, beyond the opening and closing plenaries, 36 panels, 90 presenters, films on two evenings, and a demonstration against immigration detention. Over 350 delegates from around the world were in attendance.

Factors that Impinge Horizontal Leadership Dynamics

THE STRUCTURE OF THE ACADEMY

Considered by many to be a noble institution, the university has been subjected recently to harsh critiques. In a neoliberal context, the university is seen by some as being at the service of the interests of capital, by its enterprise in commodifying knowledge "products," by its recourse to disciplinary controls and by its partnerships with corporations for profit-geared knowledge production (see Brownlee, 2015; Bousquet, 2008; Haiven & Khasnabish, 2014). Some qualify the academy as the University Industrial Complex (See Giroux, 2015). These critiques encompass an analysis of the professoriate. In a neoliberal division of labor reminiscent of the patriarchal dichotomy of highly-paid male executives and their low-paid female clerical counterparts,[14] at the top of the academic pecking order, full-time faculty are under pressure to produce more research findings but are relatively well paid, while part-time professors, the professoriate's poor cousins, are tasked with intense teaching loads at poor pay and poor conditions (Brownlee, 2015, pp. 45–51).

In this context, the tendency not to share information and knowledge, a non-zero-sum resource, and the tendency to take on official communications with an assumed mandate from the organizing committee can save time, are in keeping with the

---

[14]In Canada, women, though representing 44% of all PhD graduates in 2008 (Statcan, 2011), represent only 30% of faculty in the social sciences (all ranks included) and at all levels, women earn only 88.8% of the salary of their male counterparts ("The Changing Academy", *CAUT Education Review, 12*(1), January 2010, pp. 1-6).

competitive environment of the corporatized university, and may be actions that are taken for granted by members of the academy. After all, it is difficult to see how others without the right credentials associated with the title "professor" could take on the role of negotiating the terms of the space allocation and so forth with the University bureaucracy. For instance, the adjunct professor has no easy communication route with the administration, and did not possess an account for the management of grant money. Some community members can and do take on these roles within the University and one community member is experienced in these roles, but her input was not sought for this, most likely in part because she was not well-known to the group. It follows that this is not a context conducive to collaboration with community counterparts, which, in the context of organizing ICOPAs, is problematic. So while information and knowledge are non-zero-sum resources that are relatively easy to share, the structural obstacles in the academy render it unlikely; yet, doing so is one way to counter hierarchical practices in organizing.

UNADDRESSED POWER DIFFERENTIALS AMONG ORGANIZERS

In order to make possible the use of horizontal principles in organizing, it stands to reason that resource-sharing is one important facet. As Gordon (2005) reminds us, zero-sum resources are difficult to share, and even some non-zero-sum resources may be difficult to duplicate (pp. 155–156). In the organizing dynamic for ICOPA 15, it was clear that the full-time professor had an abundance of resources while the other members of the committee were not as well-equipped. Again, one community participant did have resources, but the organizing committee seemed unaware of this. Moreover, even in realms where graduate students had more knowledge (of the content of submissions, for instance) they still had a tendency to defer to the lead's assessment of the quality of submissions; primarily, because he was seen as having more general and ICOPA knowledge. A certain amount of sharing by the lead was undertaken in the form of access to offices for some of the students, for instance, and co-authoring an article about the conference. But upon reflection, a more systematic sharing of information and knowledge would have helped make others feel more at ease with ICOPA's workings.

NON-REFLEXIVITY

Members of the organizing committee who were not part of the research group have reported being very satisfied with the unfolding of the organizing process. Through a questionnaire they filled out after the conference, and which they participated in reviewing, it was evident that many considered the committee a fairly flat structure where everybody had an equal say in decisions. They found meetings respectful, they felt rewarded in their organizing tasks, and they were trusting of fellow organizers both in terms of the follow-through on their respective responsibilities and in terms of feeling safe enough to speak up in the group. This perception on the part of many organizers speaks to the efforts made by the lead organizer and others to be considerate, re-affirm their contributions and voice their acknowledgment of others' work. This disposition was readily emulated by others in the group, and three months before the conference, the tenor of the frequent emails sent around suddenly contained more fulsome recognition and gratitude for others' work. However, the fact that participants felt this way does not mean that veritable horizontal relations were established. We suggest that on the contrary, people were comfortable with a top-down approach where final responsibility would lay with someone else. This may be indicative of a state of disempowerment that cannot be altered without purposeful action. On the other hand, it is also possible that individuals came to make a specific contribution without the desire to take on a more robust commitment, or without any awareness of organizing leadership. For members outside the research group, there was no space for reflexivity that may have permitted entertaining a different conception of how organizing took place.

Steps toward Horizontality in ICOPA Organizing

DISCUSSION OF LEADERSHIP AND PROCESS

One element that can enhance the process of collective organizing is to have a conversation early on about the dynamics of the group process. It is never too early to begin organizing. It is possible and preferable to begin having conversations with those likely to be part of the group (even if others are not yet present), prior to the time when organizing begins. This provides the necessary space, devoid of stress and time-limitations, to calmly converse about the principles and ideals for the action group.

In order to consciously engage in a horizontal action group, it is critical that the members involved address the issue of leadership. A conversation about expectations around leadership is necessary. Once a consensus is reached on the preferred type of group dynamics (horizontal, in this case), then it becomes the group's responsibility to stay mindful of the dynamics. It becomes incumbent on all members to be attentive to slippages toward hierarchy (that can manifest in a number of ways such as taking on an unexpressed mandate, not sharing information, acting solo) and point these out when they occur.

There would have been sufficient time prior to forming the organizing committee when people interested in participating could have met on an informal basis to share ideas about how to proceed. In such an open environment, the lead's role could have been discussed and proposals made to alter the perceived and actual top-down structure of the committee. The obstacles to doing this are twofold: in the first instance, it is unclear how and to what extent individuals are aware or even care about group dynamics and their involvement in them. In the second instance, given the formality of the university, the deference with which people (mostly students) treat faculty, (because of grading or thesis supervision, for instance), is a challenge to breaking down hierarchical patterns of social engagement. Nonetheless, it is one way of subverting structurally imposed conditions that promote obeisance.

SELF-REFLEXIVE MEETINGS

The research portion of the organizing committee (which included the lead) met after committee meetings to reflect on how the meeting unfolded. We began a process of journaling and the regular meetings fostered a self-reflection that brought to the fore the lack of horizontality in the larger organizing meetings. Initially conceptualized as a study of horizontal leadership, which stemmed from a perception of ICOPA as an entity that espoused such principles,[15] it came as a surprise to some of the research

---

[15]Witnessing the horizontality of closing plenaries in ICOPAs can lead to this understanding. In 2014, interviews with international participants revealed that the question of who guides or leads ICOPA is murky. Some refer to a bygone "steering committee," while others believe that there are no leaders in ICOPA.

group members as they saw the dynamics of the organizing committee unfold, that this was not the case. The lead organizer identified as the lead and others openly said they were at ease with
this state of affairs. This became a subject of discussion when one
of the members challenged the others about horizontality and
what it would mean for this group to adopt such an approach. A
consideration of these dynamics, over time, had an effect on the
research group and on the organizing committee as a whole. As
it turns out, the lead had purposefully engaged in the research
portion of the group, specifically in order to undertake a self-
reflexive exercise about organizing dynamics.

MINDFULNESS ABOUT HORIZONTALITY AND COLLECTIVE ACTION

The research sub-committee was made up of six members of the
larger organizing committee and comprised two professors (full-
time and adjunct), two graduate students and two community
members. It had its own dynamic, different from the larger committee in some ways. The lead still looked like the lead. One community member, steeped in horizontality and decolonization
principles, regularly brought up the problem of the absence of horizontality at organizing meetings and asked the others to reflect on
the dynamics at work. The other members of the sub-committee
seemed in the middle between the lead and the community member. Most of those in the middle said they had no problem with
how these dynamics functioned. It was difficult to change a situation in which the lead was taking the lead, when others in the
group offered such support for his leadership. One explanation is
that others were unwilling to take on more responsibility because
of lack of time or energy; another may be that they trusted the
abilities of the lead; a third explanation is that, faced with such
apparent competence on the part of the lead, others felt disempow-
ered to take on more responsibility. Having discussed these issues
at the research sub-committee, the lead became more mindful
about his role. As sub-committees charged with different aspects
of the conference were set in motion, he was able to trust that
things were getting done as they should be. This manifested in people taking responsibility to organize different facets of the conference. Leadership became less stringently hierarchical though the
extent to which this was fact or mere impression remains unclear.
It is certainly the perception among some, that horizontality was
not achieved to the extent desired. It can be surmised, however,
that the exercise did create an awareness of these issues.

ADOPTING ANTI-OPPRESSION MEASURES AND PRACTICES

A central plank of horizontality is an awareness and a conscious-ness of the positionality of one's self and others. As a matter of course, anti-oppression and decolonization training for social jus-tice activities, especially those that bring together people from the academy and the broader community, is a positive step in alter-ing relations of power, increasing empowerment and addressing privilege. However, even training sessions are fraught with oppressive tendencies because typically, it falls on the marginal-ized groups to have to make the privileged aware of their lack of consciousness. We are reminded by hooks (1988),

> Where [black] people are called upon to take primary responsibility for sharing experiences, ideas, and infor-mation [they are placed] once again in a service position, meeting the needs of whites. (hooks, 1988, p. 47, in Cannon, 2013, p. 21)

To address this problem, it is key that those with privilege responsibilize themselves and not wait until people from tradi-tionally oppressed groups to "educate" them on this. Such train-ing allows people to learn their relative unearned privilege and find a safe way to recognize and address it (Estrella, 2015). The work of confronting one's unearned privilege in ongoing and reg-ular anti-oppression sessions is helpful as a refresher in keeping the awareness of one's privilege in the forefront. Doing so helps people share power, step away from monopolizing leadership roles and be more understanding of the many ways that oppres-sion wreaks havoc on social relations, and interferes with the full expression of people's potential.

In *The Pedagogy of the Oppressed*, Paul Freire reminds us that liberation is achieved through a praxis (action + reflection) and it "...implies no dichotomy by which this praxis could be divided into a prior stage of reflection and a subsequent stage of action. Action and reflection occur simultaneously." He also says that "critical reflection is also action" (Freire, 1972, p. 123). This is why anti-oppression training is a priority and invites us to engage fully in a "...cycle of theory, application, evaluation, reflection, and then back to theory" (Foster, n.d.). Social trans-formation is the product of praxis.

Those with an abundance of zero-sum (money, space, speed and capacity) and non-zero-sum resources (information, knowl-edge, attitudes) are often cast, or take initiative to be, in "leadership" roles. Such was the case in our group. The lead was conscious of these dynamics and collaboratively worked to intentionally change the group dynamics, though success was limited. Decolonization and anti-oppression training can help some people become aware of their privilege and keep it in check by sharing those resources that are easy to share, and remaining mindful of ways to increase sharing with others in the group. It also enables subjugated voices to emerge once a language is discovered that can make sense of the oppression they experience.

It is more likely that the playing field will be flattened when people recognize their privilege and address it by taking up a less central position at meetings, thus making a space for those who are less apt to speak up. There also times when intentional steps can be taken to create a space where people feel empowered to participate more fully (see Juris, 2008, on "intentional space").

Conclusion

Different leadership "games" can emerge depending on the type of leadership process engaged. Experience tells us that, in many circumstances, leadership and organizing are emulated. Traditional ways of leading (chairing, being the lead, proposing, showing expertise, appropriating mandates, speaking on behalf of others) are understood as sound ways to get things done. However, other types of organizing and leading afforded by horizontal processes, can serve to build capacity for the organization and be a more empowering experience for organizers.

For ICOPA 15 and its group dynamics, the larger organizing committee had a hierarchical leadership structure, with the leadership role coming from the academic contingent. This speaks loudly to Gordon's (2005) notion that power-with can be unevenly distributed depending on the resources at people's disposal (pp. 155–156). In particular, it is difficult for others who do not have the same array of resources (both "zero-sum" and "non-zero-sum") to feel completely empowered and self-confident to undertake more robust participation. Nonetheless, a degree of prefiguration[16] and solidarity was achieved by

---

[16]Prefiguation is a principle of anarchist organization that refers to affinity groups espousing the change or the ideal they wish to see. Typically, it means doing ourselves and actively countering oppression in group dynamics. For more, see Heckert, 2010.

the group, largely because a portion of the committee was engaged in a self-reflexive exercise.

Purposeful action undertaken to share knowledge, be open to the quality of non-academic knowledge and know-how, and reaching out to non-academics are first steps in addressing the tendency toward lop-sidedness in ICOPA organizing. The inclusion of the prisoners' works session is an important testament to outreach. But more fulsome and systematic efforts to create an "intentional space" (Juris, 2008) may be one of the few tangible ways to gain more participation from survivors of state or social harm, or community-based activists.

It is often the case that ICOPA is unknown to the locality in which the conference is set to take place. Hosting an ICOPA is an opportunity to introduce to local anti-prison and anti-penal groups, other international participants and their research and action. Knowledge sharing among this contingent is a crucial aspect of abolition strategizing. As took place in the run-up to ICOPA 16 in Ecuador, events can be held well ahead of the conference date to workshop anti-prison or anti-penal issues and use these moments to introduce ICOPA to various peoples and groups.

We have explored power dynamics and how resources can be shared to promote horizontality in organizing. By analyzing the organization of one ICOPA we learn that reflexivity, mindfulness and liberation practices are key steps in addressing power differentials. This type of work builds capacity, creates relationship and increases solidarity. This approach is viable for many different contexts in which we are active, including other social justice groups, unions and cooperatives. Making our experience known can spark a conversation about power dynamics in social justice organizing more broadly, and build sustainable bridges between the academy and the community. Further investigation into how other groups organize ICOPA on their territory can more fully corral progressive radical courses of action in organizing conferences, and in staging campaigns to abolish punishment practices in their myriad forms. We also believe that addressing oppression and unearned privilege, and developing allyship can alter social dynamics and leadership processes for the better, and this can be put to the service of social justice organizing more broadly.

References

Bishop, A. (2015). *Becoming an ally: Breaking the cycle of oppression in people*. Black Point, NS: Fernwood.

Bousquet, M. (2008). *How the university works: Higher education and the low-wage nation*. New York, NY: New York University Press.

Brown, L., & Strega, S. (2005). *Research as resistance: Critical Indigenous and anti-oppressive approaches*. Toronto, ON: Canadian Scholars Press.

Brownlee, J. (2015). *Academia, Inc.: How corporatization is transforming Canadian universities*. Black Point, NS: Fernwood.

Canadian Association of University Teachers (CAUT). (2010). The changing academy? A portrait of Canada's university teachers. *CAUT Education Review*, 12(1), 1–6. Retrieved from http://www.caut.ca/docs/education-review/the-changing-academy-a-portrait-of-canada-rsquo-s-university-teachers-%28jan-2010%29.pdf?sfvrsn=14. Accessed on May 23, 2016.

Cannon, M. J. (2013). Changing the subject in teacher education: Centering indigenous, diasporic, and settler colonial relations. *Cultural and Pedagogical Inquiry*, 4(2), 21–37.

Coté, M., Dey, R. J. F., & de Peuter, G. (2007). *Utopian pedagogy*. Toronto: University of Toronto Press.

Delisle, C., Basualdo, M., Ilea, A., & Hughes, A. (2015a). "Research project on ICOPA, September 2013 to August 2014". Interview, June 24, 2014.

Delisle, C., Basualdo, M., Ilea, A., & Hughes, A. (2015b). The International Conference on Penal Abolition (ICOPA): Exploring dynamics and controversies as observed at ICOPA 15 on Algonquin Territory, Penal Field, XII. Retrieved from https://champpenal.revues.org/9146. Accessed on June 13, 2017.

Diani, M. (2003). 'Leaders' or brokers? Positions and influence in social movement networks. In M. Diani & D. McAdam (Eds.), *Social movements and networks: Relational approaches to collective action* (pp. 105–122). Oxford, UK: Oxford University Press.

Diani, M., & McAdam, D. (Eds.). (2003). *Social movements and networks: Relational approaches to collective action*. Oxford, UK: Oxford University Press.

Estrella, L. (2015). The Taking Tree. Retrieved from https://prezi.com/k_e7roi3wl-h/the-taking-tree/. Accessed on August 14, 2016.

Fiander, S., Chen, A., & Piché, J. (2014). Prisoners of state repression and writing for social justice. *Journal of Prisoners on Prisons*, 23(2), 1–5.

Foster, M. (n.d.). Critical or radical pedagogy: An application of critical theory. Retrieved from http://www.markfoster.net/struc/criticalpedagogy.html. Accessed on April 16, 2016.

Freire, P. (1972). In Bergman Ramos, M. (transl.), *The pedagogy of the oppressed*. New York NY: Herder & Herder.

Giroux, H. (2015). *University in chains: Confronting the military-industrial-academic complex*. New York, NY: Routledge.

Gordon, U. (2005). Anarchism and political theory: Contemporary problems. PhD Dissertation (Unpublished). Oxford, UK: Trinity College.

Haiven, M., & Khasnabish, A. (2014). *The radical imagination*. Black Point, NS: Fernwood.

Heckert, J. (2010). Listening, caring, becoming: Anarchism as an ethics of direct relationships. In B. Franks & M. Wilson (Eds.), *Anarchism and moral philosophy* (pp. 186–207). Basing stoke, UK: Palgrave Macmillan.

hooks, b. (1988). *Talking back: Thinking feminist, thinking black*. Toronto, ON: Between the Lines.

Hulsman, L. (1986). Critical criminology and the concept of crime. *Contemporary Crises*, *10*(3-4), 63–80.

The International Conference on Penal Abolition (ICOPA). Retrieved fromwww.actionicopa.org. Accessed on December 28, 2015.

Juris, J. (2008). Spaces of intentionality: Race, class and horizontality at the United States Social Forum. *Mobilization: An International Quarterly*, *13*(4), 353–372.

Kuyek, J. (2011). *Community organizing: A holistic approach*. Black Point, NS: Fernwood.

Larsen, M. (2008). Abolition and the universal carceral. *Journal of Prisoners on Prisons*, *17*(2), 1–5.

Mathiesen, T. (1974). *The politics of abolition*. New York, NY: Wiley.

Mathiesen, T. (2015). *The politics of abolition revisited*. New York, NY: Routledge.

Pepinsky, H., & Quinney, R. (Eds.). (1991). *Criminology as peacemaking*. Indianapolis, IN: University of Indiana Press.

Routledge, P. (2009). Toward a relational ethics of struggle: Embodiment, affinity and affect. In R. Amster, A. DeLeon, L. Fernandez, A. J. Nocella II, & D. Shannon (Eds.), Contemporary anarchist studies: An introductory anthology of anarchy in the academy (pp. 82–92). N.p.: Routledge, e-book.

Sitrin, M. (Ed.). (2006). *Horizontalism: Voices of popular power in Argentina*. Oakland, CA: AK Press.

Smith, A. (n.d.). Heteropatriarchy and the three pillars of white supremacy: Rethinking women of color organizing. Retrieved from http://www.cpt.org/files/Undoing%20Racism%20-%20Three%20Pillars%20-%20Smith.pdf. Accessed on April 13, 2015.

Starhawk. (1987). *Truth or dare: Encounters with power, authority and mystery*. San Francisco, CA: Harper SanFrancisco.

Statcan. (2011). Doctoral students and university teaching staff: February 2011. In Education Indicators in Canada: Fact Sheets. Retrieved from http://www.statcan.gc.ca/pub/81-599-x/81-599-x2011006-eng.htm. Accessed on May 14, 2016.

VeneKlasen, L., & Miller, V. (2002). Power and empowerment. PLA Notes, 43, 39–41. Retrieved from http://pubs.iied.org/pdfs/G01985.pdf. Accessed on May 21, 2016.

West, W. G., & Morris, R. (2000). *The case for penal abolition*. Toronto, ON: Canadian Scholars Press.

Wilson, W. A., & Yellow Bird, M. (2005). *For Indigenous eyes only: A decolonization handbook*. Santa Fe, NM: School of American Research.

24 Cross-Cultural Collaborators: Expatriate and Host Country National Inclusive Relationships

Tami J. France

Keywords: Expatriates; coaching; women's leadership; mentoring; growth mindset

Introduction

Individuals and groups often rely on partnerships with other individuals and/or organizations with different cultural norms and leadership preferences. Leadership is a cultural construct, as such differences in values, norms, and attitudes (culture) may lead members of different cultural groups (i.e., expatriate and host country nationals [HCNs]) to disparate understandings of the nature and purpose of leadership, and divergent expectations (Northouse, 2007). These differences could perpetuate a state of unknown-ness between individuals and groups; reinforcing a sense of threat, thus creating a perceived need to be in competition with others for resources as a means to overcome the perceived threat. This dynamic is experienced by many individuals leading in cross-cultural environments wherein stakeholders engage with a win—lose mindset.

The development of formal and informal coaching and mentoring relationships is one strategy that has been successfully employed by expatriates and HCNs to surmount these differences and balance the zero-sum equation. In the context of coaching and mentoring relationships, the HCN teaches the expatriate about the organizational and national cultures so that the expatriate can more accurately understand their core values, ontology, and epistemology. This aids the expatriate's adjustment, promotes culturally appropriate behavior, and facilitates the building of trust, collaboration, and constructive relationships. In turn, the expatriate teaches the HCN about the area of expertise for which s/he was retained, thus promoting the efficiency, effectiveness, and self-efficacy of the HCN and the organization. Through reciprocal mentoring and coaching relationships collaboration and knowledge exchange between HCNs and expatriates is enhanced as they iteratively share the roles of leader and follower, expert, and learner. As a result, power and status are equalized thus shifting the orientation from competition to collaboration.

The examples in this chapter illustrate how female expatriates and HCNs have used coaching and mentoring relationships to overcome the zero-sum dynamic. This is demonstrated through a case study outlining the importance of formal and informal mentoring and coach-like relationships to support expatriate success in private sector businesses in Hong Kong and China. The real-life examples presented by female expatriates in this chapter are evidence that the ever-present win: lose orientation encountered by HCNs and expatriates leading in the global environment is not inevitable. When organizational actors assume a growth mindset and employ reciprocal mentoring and coaching relationships, the power dynamic is equalized and the zero-sum equation is balanced.

The overall purpose of this chapter is threefold. First purpose is to expand the conversation about inclusive leadership and individuals working across cultures as collaborators not competitors; second purpose is to be a resource to better prepare expatriates as cross-cultural professionals and leaders; and third purpose is to provide organizations with a deeper understanding of those relationships that lead to and support cross-cultural collaboration and professional success. By way of these three objectives, this chapter aligns with the purpose of this book to enhance leadership knowledge and practice around the world.

Review of Literature

CULTURE AND LEADERSHIP

Formal and informal leaders will continue to build relationships while working across cultures in this world of global interconnectedness. These relationships are affected by culture and the perceived value of leaders in cultural contexts. Cross-cultural experiences, including expatriate assignments, are becoming more important for a successful professional career and leadership role (Chura, 2006; Judge, Cable, Boudreau, & Bretz, 1995; Ng, Eby, Sorensen, & Feldman, 2005). The ways that the cultural environment of a country affect the success of expatriates, and for female expatriates in particular, has continued to be a topic of study and exploration (Sinangil & Ones, 2003; Stroh, Varma, & Valy-Durbin, 2000; Vance & Paik, 2001; Varma, Toh, & Budhwar, 2006).

Leadership is a behavior that is influenced by culture and identity. Culture influences the way leaders and followers practice and behave. The GLOBE definition of leadership is "the ability of an individual to influence, motivate, and enable others to contribute toward the effectiveness and success of the organizations of which they are members" (House, Hanges, Javidan, Dorfman, & Gupta, 2004, p. 15). Almost all definitions of leadership involve influence and it can be noted that "leaders influence others to help accomplish group or organizational objectives" (p. 15). Followership is also a behavior and good followership helps leaders to see and reach their own blind spots. HCN followers are critical in helping expatriate leaders be conscious of cross-cultural blind spots and behaviors that would derail their professional success when working across cultures. Chaleff (2009) posits that this conscious behavior can occur at any point when an individual understands his or her own power to effect change, tap into the courage to take the stand required, and display or develop the skills to effectively reflect back to the positional leaders the consequences of their behaviors. In cross-cultural collaboration, a shared understanding of this ability to effect relationships and outcomes allows leaders and followers to confront complex cross-cultural situations in new and more effective ways.

> Given the increasing globalization of industrial organizations and the growing interdependencies among nations, the need for a better understanding of cultural influences on leadership and organizational practice has never been greater. Leaders confront situations that are highly complex, constantly evolving, and difficult to interpret. (House et al., 2004, p. 10)

How leadership and followership are influenced by culture and then how expatriates and HCNs flow between leadership and followership are crucial to successful to cross-cultural collaborations and partnerships. "While leaders [and expatriates] do not need to know or understand cross-cultural research and theory, they do need to be aware of the effect that culture has on their own leadership and that of others" (Booysen, 2015, p. 244). The same can be said about expanding self-awareness of the effect that culture has on one's ability to follow.

EXPATRIATION

The amount of literature related to expatriate assignments and collaborating across cultures continues to grow. There is a focus on the role of mentors, expatriate socialization, adjustment, and career development in a different culture (Chao, Watz, & Gardner, 1992; Feldman & Bolino, 1999; Harvey, Buckley, Novicevic, & Wiese, 1999; Johnson, Kristoff-Brown, Van Vianen, & De Pater, 2003; Mezias & Scandura, 2005; Ragins, Cotton, & Miller, 2000; Sanchez, Spector, & Cooper, 2000; Shaffer, Harrison, & Gilley, 1999). The challenges faced by expatriates as they focus on their mission of leading and working cross-culturally include socialization to the new environment, concerns related to career development, and a constant struggle with new and very different cultural norms (Adler, 2008; Caligiuri & Tung, 1999; Hofstede, 1999, 2005; Javidan & House, 2001; Woodall, 2005). Multinational organizations as well as individual expatriates face the challenge of assignment completion and retention (Black, Mendenhall, & Oddou, 1991; Carraher, Sullivan, & Crocitto, 2008; Mezias & Scandura, 2005).

Expatriates, as cross-cultural leaders, are faced with the "greatest number and kind of professional and personal challenges" when they take on an international career assignment

(Crocitto, Sullivan, & Carraher, 2005, p. 528). Being an expatriate and leading and following with HCNs adds to importance of collaboration within professional and personal experiences. Currently, more is known about why expatriates fail than why they succeed (Crocitto et al., 2005) and research has found that organizations in certain countries pay more attention to expatriates and acknowledge the importance of cultural awareness in international business better than others (Carraher et al., 2008; Tung, 1997). This consideration is increasingly important as more expatriates enter the global workforce and define what success means to them when developing relationships, building partnerships, and collaborating across cultures.

RELATIONSHIPS AND COLLABORATION

A variety of relationships are needed to create and maintain professional expatriate success through collaboration. Essential relationships can be either formal or informal and exist across multiple nationalities. Finding a balance inside the matrix of types of relationships; between formal and informal, local and foreigner, professional and personal can add value to the expatriate experience. The findings from the cases and stories presented corroborate with the extant literature and research about the need for social and relationship support for expatriates (Caligiuri, Joshi, & Lazarova, 1999; Caligiuri & Lazarova, 2002; Dupuis, Haines, & Saba, 2008; van der Velde, Bossink, & Jansen, 2005). The studies that focus on mentoring and similar types of relationships that support the success of expatriates offer a framework as well (Harvey, McIntyre, Heames, & Moeller, 2009; Shortland, 2011). Opportunities for expatriates to spend time with other expatriates from the same home country, same gender, and/or similar cultural framework, are helpful. Such relationships, with those who have successfully worked across cultures, will afford them the space to discuss their in-country experiences and cross-cultural experiences (Owen, Javalgi, & Scherer, 2007) with an individual with shared understanding.

In addition to relationships where the individuals involved are both from the same nationality or cultural framework, there should also be multiple relationships with local individuals from the host country, HCNs, who act as cultural liaisons. These individuals are essential to interpreting local behaviors, cultural norms, and expectations. Maintaining balanced network of relationships and a balanced flow of roles between leadership and followership builds the strong framework for success through support and opportunity. An American based in China in the consulting/professional services industry commented on how helpful and important it was to have both an expatriate mentor and a HCN mentor in their network of relationships,

> I don't know how else to phrase it, but you need a [local national] mentor who's going to hang out with you and do [local] things with you. And I also think you need an expat mentor, somebody who's been there before you, who can help you find things, like somebody to cut your hair who speaks English. I never found that and I don't know why, but I had my hair cut by someone [at a place] down the street who only spoke Chinese. And the same person was never there twice in a row. I just sort of gave up and said, [I can't communicate], so I'm going to have bad hair for two years, I can live with that. But really, for most people that's not going to work. So I think an expat mentor and a [HCN] mentor are key to really becoming comfortable.

An expatriate mentor can help find expatriate-friendly services and allows for a mutual cultural understanding and aligned perspectives on situations. A HCN mentor allows the expatriate to experience the culture from a local perspective. According to Zhuang, Wu, and Wen (2013), "if an international enterprise can effectively establish a comprehensive mentor-protégé plan then the expatriate can achieve the goals of [the] assignment successfully" (p. 37). This type of plan to build relationships is centered around the components of successful collaborations.

Collaboration begins around a problem or issue, and in this setting cross-cultural collaboration begins around expatriation and acculturation. As an expatriate and HCN dyad forms these two members of the collaboration belong to a new in-group with one another. As the role of the dyad becomes more important, the strength of the relationship increases. This is of particular importance in creating collaboration across cultures, since membership to an in-group is one component of a socially constructed boundary and the relationship is centered around collaboration, not competition created by the actions of the dyad (McGreavy, Hutchins, Smith, Lindenfeld, & Silka, 2013). Identity can affect how individuals collaborate across cultures. Social Identity Theory describes how people connect to others, and what might drive individual behavior in social settings. Thomas, Mavor, and

McGarty (2012) suggested that social identification, along with the perception of collective efficacy, lead to collective action, an outcome of collaboration. Social identity requires a personal feeling of belonging to a relationship, which motivates people to participate in collective behavior to support one another. Collaboration is enhanced by the understanding of when to lead and when to follow.

There are four processes that enhance collaboration; social categorization, forming an awareness of social identity, social comparison, and a search for uniqueness or psychological distinctness (McNamara, 1997). In a social context, where relationships form between expatriates and HCNs, the individuals will go through these four processes to experience themselves as members of the collaborative relationship. They each determine their own purpose in collaboration, and the similarities or differences between them. This is why social identities are important to understand, they affect each person's perceptions, motivations, and behaviors during the collaboration process (Stoner, Perrewé, & Hofacker, 2011). There is individual identity, including how each member interprets themselves as a unique individual, and collective identity, or how each member interprets themselves as part of the collaborative dyad relationship (Stümer, Simon, & Loewy, 2008).

Collective identity as part of social identification shapes how each person behaves and contributes resources, information, and time, based on the sense of how each connects to the relationship (Greer, 2017). With collective identity, the members switch from individual self-interest to collective interest, creating the context where goals, ideas, and resources are shared (De Cremer & van Knippenberg, 2005; Veal & Mouzas, 2010). Collective identity defines the willingness of participants to "engage in collective behavior" (Kramer, 2006, p. 30), such as develop a shared goal, spend time in conversations and dialogue, and work through conflicts and difficulties. When the collective identity is developed, the expatriate and HCN act with more of a collective sense of "us" and remove any need to compete and thus enhances interactions that support the needs of each member of the dyad.

Developing a shared goal or vision within the cross-cultural collaborative relationship is a critical element for successful outcomes. The shared goal or vision intentionally provides energy to the collaborative process and removes the focus on competition. The creation of the shared goal or vision also generates a deeper collective identity, by going through the process of deciding and defining the shared goal or vision it moves the collaboration forward. Actions that support the success of each person in the relationship are acted upon.

MENTORING AND COACHING

Mentoring has been a focus in the literature because it can be a means to shape the knowledge, skills, attitudes, and behaviors of expatriates (Harvey et al., 1999; Mezias & Scandura, 2005). The specific role of mentors in the international context is in need of further development (Allen, Eby, Poteet, Lentz, & Lima, 2004) and mentoring relationships in expatriate assignments are under-examined (Mezias & Scandura, 2005). Mentor/coach relationships contain certain behaviors, actions, and ideal components. An ideal mentor/coach has an understanding of the expatriate experience and the conditions created within the specific cultural environment. They help the expatriate remove cultural barriers and provide a deeper level of cultural understanding through intuitive listening and focusing on the individual expatriate's needs. The mentor/coach can normalize confusing cultural experiences and validate these experiences to remove feelings of isolation. They offer advice about the culture, provide support with the local language, and give insights into the cultural context surrounding situations. They may be more knowledgeable about the local policies, business processes and norms, and offer guidance through ambiguous cultural and professional situations.

A mentor/coach is willing to help the expatriate by focusing on the needs of the individual and not telling or directing them what to do. The mentor/coach helps to create feelings of comfort through appreciative reflection and goal setting. They coach them in the process of letting go of deeply embedded assumptions. Booysen (2015) summarizes the cross-cultural coaching experience:

> In cross-cultural coaching, the [mentor]/coach helps the coachee through a process of assessment, challenge, reflective and reflexive questioning, and support to make sense of how culture influences [her] own beliefs and behaviors and that of others [she] works with. It also addresses how new cultural-rich meaning can be integrated into existing paradigms to enhance learning, understanding, and sense making to develop new ways of seeing (p. 242).

This cross-cultural coaching offers an opportunity for deep personal growth and development. An American based in Hong

Kong working in the academic/education industry shared her story about how her mentor/coach was able to support her to reflect on her experiences during a challenging time:

> One day, I was particularly distraught and [my mentor] sat down and listened to me and asked me questions, never trying to make a connection to his life [or offer advice]. That was the first time that I felt truly listened to and I valued his ability to hold his life at bay and make it entirely about my own experiences. The most important thing a mentor can do is validate that your experiences are meaningful to you, sure they can normalize [your experiences] with comparing it to their experiences, but once they make the relationship about them, the [mentor/ coach] relationship suffers.

An informal or formal mentor/coach can also provide professional career support by sharing their experience and wisdom related to industry trends and professional networking by demonstrating how to build relationships across cultures. They have the interest and the ability to encourage exploration about what professional success means for the individual expatriate. They listen to the expatriate's career objectives, observe their behaviors, and offer constructive feedback. A formal mentor/coach inside the same organization can foster trusting relationships between the expatriate and the organization bridging the cultural divide by developing knowledgeable and informed global insights by and with the organization.

In addition to finding a mentor/coach for themselves, expatriates can benefit from being a mentor/coach to others, or having a mentee/coachee. Supporting others has a positive relationship with perceived expatriate success as well as resilience and explains a significant amount of expatriate cultural adaptation success. Therefore, this is a key strategy to put into practice as a female expatriate or as an organization updating global programming. An American formerly working in Hong Kong in the business development/professional services industry experienced this sense of duty toward others,

> The initial adjustment was very difficult, and then once I got through it I had such a sense of accomplishment and appreciated it so much that I wanted to help others who were coming in new [to Hong Kong] to adjust ...

this is because of the empathy I developed during [my own] initial adjustment.

Another way to support others is by co-creating development plans with local nationals. By sharing their own industry expertise and global knowledge the expatriate can leave their own legacy within the global context.

Cross-Cultural Collaboration in Practice

Cross-cultural professional success is enhanced through collaborative relationships for expatriates in China, Hong Kong, Taiwan, and Macau. The case study ($n = 102$) findings corroborate with the literature that focuses on the role of mentors, expatriate socialization, adjustment, and career development in a different culture (Chao et al., 1992; Feldman & Bolino, 1999; Harvey et al., 1999; Johnson et al., 2003; Mezias & Scandura, 2005; Ragins et al., 2000; Sanchez et al., 2000; Shaffer et al., 1999). The challenges faced by expatriates as they focus on their mission of leading and working cross-culturally include socialization to the new environment, concerns related to career development, and a constant struggle with new and very different cultural norms (Adler, 2008; Caligiuri et al., 1999; Hofstede, 1999, 2005; Javidan & House, 2001; Woodall, 2005).

It is evident that a variety of relationships support success and having access to multiple types of relationships is essential for individuals working across cultures. The definition of mentor/coach used is: a relationship (either formal or informal) with individuals who acted as mentors *(experienced, gave advice)* or coaches *(future-focused, challenged you to overcome barriers)* while working across cultures. An Australian formerly working in China in the automotive/advertising industry commented on the need for multiple mentor/coach relationships to support her success as an expatriate,

> I had two key mentors while working in China, one supported me in life and assimilating into life as an expatriate, the other was a professional colleague who bridged the [cultural knowledge] gap and was an exceptional support ... he had lived in Asia for so long [he shared so much knowledge] ...if I had only had one of those mentors the outcome would have been different ...I needed that balance [and support of both mentors].

The types of relationships that are relied on most by female expatriates are described in Table 1 according to the two cultural perspectives (western and eastern) and the two categories of relationships (personal and professional).

Table 1. Expatriate Multiple Essential Relationships Matrix.

	Local National	Foreigner Expatriate	Virtual	Other
Formal (Professional) Relationship	Supervisor/ Manager	Supervisor/ Manager	Supervisor/ Manager	Networks or Associations
	Team Members	Team Members	Team Members	
	Colleagues	Colleagues	Colleagues	
Informal (Personal) Relationship	Friendships	Friendships	Friendships	Children or other family
	Spouse	Spouse		

Any combination of the multiple essential relationships can be approached with a mentor/coach-like mindset. The findings show that just over half (58.8%) of the individuals who participated in the study had access to a relationship that they considered as either an informal or formal mentor/coach-like relationship. Close to one third (29.3%) of those who had access to a mentor/coach relationship found real value in this relationship and heavily relied on this mentor/coach to support their success. Of those who had access to this type of relationship (41.4%) relied on this mentor/coach relationship to support their success. Therefore, if there are multiple mentors, at least one HCN mentor and one home country mentor the mentoring process can be more beneficial to supporting quicker adjustment of the expatriate and more collaboration between each dyad.

In a study conducted by Zhuang et al. (2013), the findings indicate that the assistance provided by mentors, from both home and host countries, facilitates expatriate adjustment in the host country. Through mentoring and coaching relationships, higher levels of perceived success are created. Female expatriate perceived success is highly correlated with and can be explained by having access to mentor/coach relationships while working across cultures. This finding is also aligned with previous research (Jassawalla, Asgary, & Sashittal, 2006; Mezias & Scandura, 2005).

An American based in Hong Kong from the academic/ education industry told a story about meeting a local HCN who had also traveled abroad to the United States. They were able to exchange stories and discuss the differences between each of their cultures and the associated norms:

> We compared experiences and bonded over the shared frustrations and culture shocks. I think it was a unique exchange because we were both "venting" about the opposite culture in a respectful, comical way. We both were able to laugh and say, "Yep that is my culture!" as a response to our gripes about the opposite culture.

A Canadian formerly based in China in the business administration/human resources industry commented on the importance of being open, having a learning mindset, and respecting the host country and culture:

> Successful expatriates are there to have an experience and to learn and to transfer knowledge and to be part of an experience and to be open-minded and want to learn more about a culture, not cause others to lose face and not embarrass people and be respectful of cultures.

Thus, having a growth and learning mindset, a vision of what collaboration means, and a plan for developing collaborative mentor/coach relationships are elements that shift focus from competition to cooperation. The extant literature also suggest that when individuals are working across cultures they go through transformations in their identity. These changes affect the expatriate's sense of self and their behaviors and actions (Andreason & Kinner, 2005; Boies & Rothstein, 2002; Nasholm, 2009; Starr, 2009). The findings in this current research suggest that an informed view of self-supports perceived success of female expatriates and this informed view could alleviate the emotional demands related to transformations in identity and corroborates previous studies on the role of self-reflection and cross-cultural awareness as factors influencing success of expatriate assignments (Cole & McNulty, 2011; Fischlmayr, 2002; Janssens, Cappellen, & Zanoni, 2006; Selmer & Leung, 2003a, 2003b; Tung, 2004).

This informed view is developed through several exercises the expatriate and HCN take part in together, or as a self-reflection activity. Cross-cultural self-awareness is an aspect of this informed view of self. Having an informed view of self allows the individual to internalize the new behaviors and norms and let go of several that have become unnecessary as their relationships change and collaboration becomes a primary focus. According to Selmer (1999), using problem-focused coping strategies such as having a better understanding of one's feelings and reactions helps to alleviate misunderstandings. This aligns with the need for an informed view of self to support understanding during interactions between expatriates and HCNs and an acceptance that misunderstandings will occur.

By using the cross-cultural collaboration process with an HCN colleague or friend, the expatriate can determine which personal and professional values to preserve, which values define them at the core. Holding these elements close through challenging cultural dynamics supports their cross-cultural success. This act of maintaining core values and letting go of irrelevant thoughts or behaviors is a delicate balance that can be best managed with an informed view of self and through dialogue in the expatriate–HCN relationships. An American based in China in the consulting/professional services industry commented on the intentional focus on maintaining personal values and activities:

> Whatever it is you liked doing in your regular life, if you like to read, if you like to paint, if you like to walk, if you like to run, find a way to keep doing that, but with a Chinese twist to it. So that you get an appreciation for whatever that hobby or that love you have in your life, find out how that works in the [new] Chinese [context of] life.

Multiple international assignments and exposure to multiple cultures can enhance the development of an informed view of self and the following related competencies: crystallized view of values and identity, an understanding of personal strengths and weaknesses, clearer career interests, and enhanced self-awareness (Dickmann & Harris, 2005; Makela & Suutari, 2011). An Australian formerly working in China in the automotive/advertising industry commented on assumptions and self-awareness,

> Never ever ever ever assume anything in a culturally foreign environment ... because if you do, you will be wrong. Your basic [cultural and behavioral] assumptions based on your upbringing and your [cultural] intuition are always going to be wrong ... you are coming [into the new cultural environment] from a completely different place and completely different upbringing.

Along with maintaining personal values and letting go of norms, there is also significance in defining what personal success means inside this new cultural context. Spending time defining and understanding emotional triggers and defining and understanding oneself inside the new cultural context is valuable. Defining what it means to feel validated and creating and understanding of what it means to stay motivated as an expatriate is also key. An American based in China in the academic/education industry commented: "If you're waiting for external validation, particularly, I think, on an international assignment, that's a tough thing because culturally, it's a completely different expectation. It has to come from within [through an informed view of self]."

The ability to lead and follow across cultures is enhanced through humility and an understanding of the role of identity (Thomas, 2002). The ability to maintain personal identity and humility demonstrates a sense of self-efficacy. Self-efficacy is defined as the persistence in attempting to attain a desired outcome in the face of obstacles and mistakes (Vroom, 1976) and continue to persist in accomplishing a goal. A conscious focus on mindfulness and self-reflection is helpful to keep the expatriate balanced and on a path toward desired outcomes for a successful international assignment. An American formerly working in China in the consulting/professional services industry utilized this process of reflection, advocacy and inquiry, and noticed that China felt "softer" to her because of her previous international experience working in a different culture. She recommended the use of a quarterly reflection journal and recounts how this helped her,

> It helped me keep [reflecting on experiences and then keep] looking forward [toward the future] and not get stuck only in the moment … and it really pushed me to think about [and advocate for change] about what wasn't going well. Then I could seek out someone locally and [inquire and] say, "Hey tell me what this means or has this ever happened to you?" and I was able to continue making forward progress [through the iterative process of reflection, advocacy, and inquiry].

An informed view of self and an understanding of how to develop collaborative relationships across cultures can also be built on the frameworks of courageous followership. Just as followers stand up to and for their leaders in the organizational context, this model is transferrable to the expatriate–HCN collaborative dyad context.

Chaleff (2009) recommends six strategies to develop trust and collaboration in leader—follower relationships and these six strategies can be used in expatriate—HCN dyads to build reciprocal coaching—mentoring relationships.

1. Place people around you who *tell you what they see*, not what they think you want to see.
2. Always pose your ideas for change by saying "This is what I'm considering" not "This is what we're going to do."
3. Always ask for what you may "be missing" or "not seeing" that could pose additional risks to manage.
4. Listen to responses carefully. Give others full latitude to advise you how to manage the risk or not take the risk.
5. Question their reasoning respectfully. Seek to understand and verify their data and reasoning, not to humiliate.
6. Make your decision based on the data in this situation, not on risks you have gotten away with.

There is evidence through the extant literature and theory that an individual's ability to adapt and appreciate another culture is trainable. Development and growth happens through experience with customs, norms, and beliefs of other cultures, and is based on social learning theory (Bandura, 1977; Black & Mendenhall, 1990). Findings from this research state that successful expatriates focus on always observing and always learning. Adopting a growth mindset is one way to continue to develop an informed view of self as an expatriate. Dweck (2006) defines the difference between a fixed mindset and a growth mindset. The fixed mindset measures ability right now (fixed) and projects it into the future. The growth mindset is based on the belief that individual qualities are cultivated and developed through effort. Expatriates can change and adapt by adopting a growth mindset about their cross-cultural experiences.

Fig. 1 illustrates the emergent dimensions of cross-cultural professional success. France (2015) introduced the model, which was influenced by extant literature and case study findings. This model can be applied to many different cultural contexts and the perceived success of each individual is an iterative integrated process that is continually redefined according to changes in each of the four dimensions of cross-cultural professional success. The information shared in this chapter was based on the two dimensions on the right side of the model (1) informed view of self and (2) multiple essential relationships.

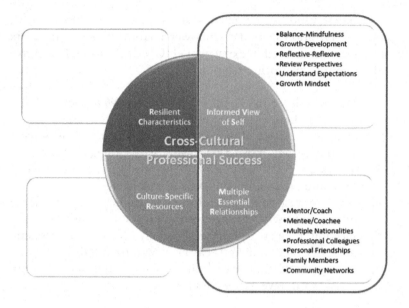

Fig. 1.   Dimensions of Cross-Cultural Professional Success.

The need to focus on each of the four dimensions of cross-cultural professional success will look slightly different for each expatriate, each leader, each individual, and each cultural context. The need to rely on of the four dimensions either heavily or slightly will greatly depend on prior cross-cultural experience or exposure to the host culture and access to collaborative relationships.

Closing

The exploration of relationships and resources that support the success of professional expatriates leading and working across cultures builds a strong case for breaking the zero-sum game and focusing on collaborative intent. Positive sustainable change is created, adding to and expanding upon the current scholarship and global leadership and organizational practices.

All of the stories and layers of experiences in this study are inspiring because the participants represent leaders and future leaders in the global workforce. Their willingness to participate in this study, reflect on their experiences around success, and discuss their engagement in learning about relationships that support success is encouraging. There is not an exact formula for success and it is a personal journey based on the individual and an interest in collaborating across cultures. This chapter allowed for the sharing of new knowledge, offered a critical view of theory alongside practice, and provided a new way of thinking about cross-cultural collaborators and their professional success. The information shared offers an opportunity to reflect and search for a deeper understanding of inclusive leadership inside global experiences.

References

Adler, N. (2008). *International dimensions of organizational behavior.* Mason, OH: Thomson-Southwestern.

Allen, T. D., Eby, L. T., Poteet, M. L., Lentz, E., & Lima, L. (2004). Career benefits associated with mentoring for protege's: A meta-analysis. *Journal of Applied Psychology*, 89(1), 127–136. doi:10.1037/0021-9010.89.1.127

Andreason, A. W., & Kinner, K. D. (2005). Repatriation adjustment problems and the successful reintegration of expatriates and their families. *Journal of Behavioral and Applied Psychology*, 6, 109–126.

Bandura, A. J. (1977). *Social learning theory.* Englewood Cliffs, NJ: Prentice Hall.

Black, J. S., & Mendenhall, M. (1990). Cross-cultural training effectiveness: A review and theoretical framework for future research. *Academy of Management Review*, 15, 113–136. doi:10.5465/amr.1990.11591834

Black, J. S., Mendenhall, M., & Oddou, G. (1991). Toward a comprehensive model of international adjustment: An integration of multiple theoretical perspectives. *Academy of Management Review*, 16(2), 291–317. doi:10.5465/amr.1991.4278938

Boies, K., & Rothstein, M. G. (2002). Managers' interest in international assignments: The role of work and career satisfaction. *International Journal of Intercultural Relations*, 26(3), 233–253. doi:10.1016/S0147-1767(02)00002-0

Booysen, L. (2015). Cross-cultural coaching. In D. Riddle, E. Hoole, & E. Gullette (Eds.), *Center for creative leadership handbook of coaching in organizations* (pp. 241–288). San Francisco, CA: Jossey-Bass.

Caligiuri, P., & Lazarova, M. (2002). A model for the influence of social interaction and social support on female expatriates' cross-cultural adjustment. *International Journal of Human Resource Management*, 13(5), 761–772. doi:10.1080/09585190210125903

Caligiuri, P. M., Joshi, A., & Lazarova, M. (1999). Factors influencing the adjustment of women on global assignments. *International Journal of Human Resource Management*, 10(2), 163–179. doi:10.1080/095851999340495

Caligiuri, P., & Tung, R. (1999). Comparing the success of male and female expatriates from a United States-based multinational company. *International Journal of Human Resource Management*, 10(5), 763–782. doi:10.1080/095851999340143

Carraher, S. M., Sullivan, S. E., & Crocitto, M. M. (2008). Mentoring across global boundaries: An empirical examination of home-and host-country mentors on expatriate career outcomes. *Journal of International Business Studies, 39,* 1310–1326. doi:10.1057/palgrave.jibs.8400407

Chaleff, I. (2009). *The courageous follower: Standing up to & for our leaders.* San Francisco, CA: Berrett-Koehler.

Chao, G., Watz, P. M., & Gardner, P. (1992). Formal and informal mentorships: A comparison of mentoring functions and contrast with non-mentored counterparts. *Personnel Psychology, 45,* 619–636. doi:10.1111/j.1744-6570.1992.tb00863.x

Chura, H. (2006). A year abroad (or 3) as a career move. *New York Times.* Retrieved from http://www.nytimes.com/2006/02/25/business/worldbusiness/25abroad.html?pagewanted=all. Accessed on March 27, 2016.

Cole, N., & McNulty, Y. (2011). Why do female expatriates "fit-in" better than males? An analysis of self-transcendence and socio-cultural adjustment. *Cross Cultural Management-An International Journal, 18*(2), 144–164. doi:10.1108/13527601111125996

Crocitto, M., Sullivan, S., & Carraher, S. (2005). Global mentoring as a means of career development and knowledge creation: A learning-based framework and agenda for future research. *Career Development International, 10*(6), 522–535. doi:10.1108/13620430510620593

De Cremer, D., & van Knippenberg, D. (2005). Cooperation as a function of leader self-sacrifice, trust, and identification. *Leadership & Organizational Development Journal, 26*(5/6), 355–369. doi:10.1106/01437730510607833

Dickmann, M., & Harris, H. (2005). Developing career capital for global careers: The role of international assignments. *Journal of World Business, 40,* 399–408. doi:10.1080/09585190801953749

Dupuis, M., Haines, V. Y., & Saba, T. (2008). Gender, family ties, and international mobility: Cultural distance matters. *International Journal of Human Resource Management, 19*(2), 274–295. doi:10.1080/09585190701799846

Dweck, C. (2006). *Mindset: The new psychology of success.* New York, NY: Ballantine Books.

Feldman, D. C., & Bolino, M. (1999). The impact of on-site mentoring on expatriate socialization: A structural equation modeling approach. *The International Journal of Human Resource Management, 10*(1), 54–71. doi:10.1080/095851999340639

Fischlmayr, I. C. (2002). Female self-perception as barrier to international careers? *International Journal of Human Resource Management, 13*(5), 773–783. doi:10.1080/09585190210125912

France, T. (2015). *A mixed methods study: Dimensions of cross-cultural professional success: Experiences of Western women living and working in Eastern cultures.* Unpublished doctoral dissertation, Antioch University, Yellow Springs, OH.

Greer, P. (2017). *Elements of effective interorganizational collaboration: A mixed methods study.* Unpublished doctoral dissertation, Antioch University, Yellow Springs, OH.

Harvey, M., Buckley, M., Novicevic, M., & Wiese, D. (1999). Mentoring dual-career expatriates a sense-making and sense-giving social support process. *International Journal of Human Resource Management, 19*(5), 808−827. doi:10.1111/j.1559-1816.2009.00571.x

Harvey, M., McIntyre, N., Heames, J. T., & Moeller, M. (2009). Mentoring global female managers in the global marketplace: Traditional, reverse, and reciprocal mentoring. *The International Journal of Human Resource Management, 20*(6), 1344−1361. doi:10.1080/09585190902909863

Hofstede, G. (1999). Problems remain, but theories will change. *Organizational Dynamics, 28*, 34−44. doi:10.9707/2307-0919.1014

Hofstede, G. (2005). *Cultures and organizations: Software of the mind* (2nd ed.). New York, NY: McGraw-Hill.

House, R. J., Hanges, P. J., Javidan, M., Dorfman, P. W., & Gupta, V. (2004). *Culture, leadership, and organizations: The GLOBE study of 62 societies*. Palo Alto, CA: Sage.

Janssens, M., Cappellen, T., & Zanoni, P. (2006). Successful female expatriates as agents: Positioning oneself through gender, hierarchy, and culture. *Journal of World Business, 41*(2), 133−148. doi:10.1016/j.jwb.2006.01.001

Jassawalla, A. R., Asgary, N., & Sashittal, H. C. (2006). Managing expatriates: The role of mentors. *International Journal of Commerce & Management, 16*(2), 130−140. doi:10.1108/10569210680000212

Javidan, M., & House, R. J. (2001). Cultural acumen for the global manager: Lessons from project GLOBE. *Organizational Dynamics, 29*, 289−305. doi:10.1016/s0090-2616(01)00034-1

Johnson, E. C., Kristoff-Brown, A. I., Van Vianen, A. E. M., & De Pater, I. E. (2003). Expatriate social ties: Personality antecedents and consequences for adjustment. *Journal of International Selection and Assessment, 11*(4), 277−288. doi:10.1111/j.0965-075x.2003.00251.xFel

Judge, T. A., Cable, D. M., Boudreau, J. W., & Bretz, R. D. (1995). An empirical investigation of the predictors of executive career success. *Personnel Psychology, 48*, 485−519. doi:10.1111/j.1744-6570.1995.tb01767.x

Kramer, R. (2006). Social identity and social capital: The collective self at work. *International Public Management Journal, 9*(1), 25−45. doi:10.1080/10967490600625316.

Makela, L., & Suutari, V. (2011). Coping with work-family conflicts in the global career context. *Thunderbird International Business Review, 53*, 365−375. doi:10.1002/tie.20414

McGreavy, B., Hutchins, K., Smith, H., Lindenfield, L., & Silka, L. (2013). Addressing the complexities of boundary work in sustainability science through communication. *Sustainability, 5*, 4195−4221. doi:10.3390/su5104195

McNamara, T. (1997). Theorizing social identity: What do we mean by social identity? Competing frameworks, competing discourses. *Teachers of English to Speakers of Other Languages, 31*(3), 561−567.

Mezias, J. M., & Scandura, T. A. (2005). A needs-driven approach to expatriate adjustment and career development: A multiple mentoring perspective. *Journal of International Business Studies, 36*(5), 519−538. doi:10.1057/palgrave.jibs.8400159

Nasholm, M. (2009). An identity construction perspective on careers of Swedish international itinerants. *Management Review*, 20, 53–69. doi:10.1108/17538371211269068

Ng, T. W., Eby, L. T., Sorensen, K. L., & Feldman, D. C. (2005). Predictors of objective career success. A meta-analysis. *Personnel Psychology*, 58, 367–408. doi:10.1111/j.1744-6570.2005.00515.x

Northouse, P. (2007). *Leadership: Theory and practice* (4th ed.), Thousand Oaks, CA: Sage Publications.

Owen, C. L., Javalgi, R. G., & Scherer, R. F. (2007). Success strategies for expatriate women managers in China. *Review of Business*, 27(3), 24–31. doi:10.1108/09649420210416813

Ragins, B. R., Cotton, J. L., & Miller, J. S. (2000). Marginal mentoring: The effects of type mentor, quality of relationship, and program design on work and career attitudes. *Academy of Management Journal*, 43(6), 1177–1194. doi:10.2307/1556344

Sanchez, J. I., Spector, P. E., & Cooper, C. L. (2000). Adapting to a boundaryless world: A developmental expatriate model. *The Academy of Management Executive*, 14(2), 96–106. doi:10.5465/ame.2000.3819309

Selmer, J. (1999). Effects of coping strategies on sociocultural and psychological adjustment of western expatriate managers in the PRC. *Journal of World Business*, 34(1), 41–51. doi:10.1016/S1090-9516(99)00006-1

Selmer, J., & Leung, A. (2003a). Are corporate career development activities less available to female than to male expatriates? *Journal of Business Ethics*, 43(1–2), 125–136. doi:10.1023/a:1022979619747

Selmer, J., & Leung, A. (2003b). International adjustment of female vs male business expatriates. *International Journal of Human Resource Management*, 14(7), 1117–1131. doi:10.1080/0958519032000114237

Shaffer, M. A., Harrison, D. A., & Gilley, K. M. (1999). Dimensions, determinants, and differences in the expatriate adjustment process. *Journal of International Business Studies*, 30(3), 557–583. doi:10.1057/palgrave.jibs.8490083

Shortland, S. (2011). Networking: A valuable career intervention for women expatriates? *The Career Development International*, 16(3), 271–292. doi:10.1108/13620431111140165

Sinangil, H. K., & Ones, D. S. (2003). Gender differences in expatriate job performance. *Applied Psychology: An International Review*, 52(3), 461–475. doi:10.1111/1464-0597.00144

Starr, T. L. (2009). Repatriation and short-term assignments: An exploration into expectations, change and dilemmas. *International Journal of Human Resource Management*, 20(2), 286–300. doi:10.1080/09585190802670557

Stoner, J., Perrewé, P. L., & Hofacker, C. (2011). The development and validation of the multi-dimensional identification scale (MDIS). *Journal of Applied Social Psychology*, 41, 1632–1658. doi:10.1111/j.1559-1816.2011.00770.x

Stroh, L. K., Varma, A., & Valy-Durbin, S. (2000). Why are women left at home: Are they unwilling to go on international assignments? *Journal of World Business*, 35(3), 241–255. doi:10.1016/s1090-9516(00)00037-7

Stümer, S., Simon, B., & Loewy, M. I. (2008). Intraorganizational respect and organizational perspective: The mediating role of collective identity. *Group Processes Intergroup Relations*, *11*(5), 5–20. doi:10.1177/1368430207084842

Thomas, D. C. (2002). *The essentials of international management*. Thousand Oaks, CA: Sage.

Thomas, E. F., Mavor, K. I., & McGarty, C. (2012). Social identities facilitate and encapsulate action-relevant constructs: A test of the social identity model of collective action. *Group Processes Intergroup Relations*, *15*(1), 75–88. doi:10.1177/1368430211413619

Tung, R. (2004). Female expatriates: The model global manager? *Organizational Dynamics*, *33*(3), 243–253. doi:10.1016/j.orgdyn.2004.06.002

Tung, R. L. (1997, April). *Canadian expatriates in Asia-Pacific: An analysis of their attitude toward and experience in international assignments*. Paper presented at the meeting of the Society for Industrial and Organizational Psychology, St Louis, MO.

van der Velde, M., Bossink, C. J. H., & Jansen, P. G. W. (2005). Gender differences in the determinants of the willingness to accept an international assignment. *Journal of Vocational Behavior*, *66*(1), 81–103. doi:10.1016/j.jvb.2003.12.002

Vance, C. M., & Paik, Y. (2001). Where do American women face their biggest obstacle to expatriate career success? Back in their own backyard. *Cross Cultural Management*, *8*(3–4), 98–116. doi:10.1108/13527600110797308

Varma, A., Toh, S. M., & Budhwar, P. (2006). A new perspective on the female expatriate experience: The role of host country national categorization. *Journal of World Business*, *41*(2), 112–120. doi:10.1016/j.jwb.2006.01.010

Veal, G., & Mouzas, S. (2010). Learning to collaborate: A study of business networks. *Journal of Business & Industrial Marketing*, *25*(6), 420–434. doi:10.1108/08858621011066017

Vroom, V. (1976). *Motivation and work*. New York, NY: Prentice Hall.

Woodall, J. (2005). Convergence and diversity in HRD. *Human Resource Development International*, *8*(1), 1–4. doi:10.1080/1367886052000342582

Zhuang, W., Wu, M., & Wen, S. (2013). Relationship of mentoring functions to expatriate adjustments: Comparing home country mentorship and host country mentorship. *The International Journal of Human Resource Management*, *24*(1), 35–49. doi:10.1080/09585192.2012.669784

25

Inclusive, Authentic, Values-Based or Opportunistic — What Counts as Leadership Today? A Case Study of Angela, Donald, Francis and Helen

Lorraine Stefani

Keywords: Inclusive leaders/leadership; authentic leadership; transformational leadership; societal change

Introduction

It may be asking much of any leader to transform society, for that is a major task requiring the commitment of leaders at many different levels in society. However, those who are in powerful global leadership roles can do much to create more inclusive societies if they have an inclusive mindset. The plight of the poor and the disenfranchised is a social concern and should surely be a concern for our chosen leaders in the contexts within which they operate. An inclusive society would seek to eliminate child poverty and address the gaping inequalities we can see all around us. Inclusive societies would be those in which all parties are treated with equal respect and afforded the freedoms to choose to live the lives that we value, access to education, healthcare, food and shelter.

Given that our four chosen leaders are in positions which give them the potential to create the conditions for more inclusive societies to evolve, we can ask how each of them 'measures up'. A defining moment for Angela was her response to the plight of millions of refugees fleeing from war-torn Syria (Gibbs, 2015). She did the best she could to enable access to the living conditions most of us take for granted. Donald Trump has set himself up as the champion of white working class America, but fails to show an inclusive mindset through the ways in which he denigrates immigrants of all nationalities and persuasions, and indeed anyone he considers to be inferior such as women, Muslims, his own compatriots (Allen, 2016). Pope Francis shows compassion and concern for the poor, the marginalized and the dispossessed (Chua-Eoan & Dias, 2013). Helen Clark has a strong but by no means exclusive focus on women recognizing and acknowledging that women 'hold up half the sky' and suffer disproportionately because of their general lack of empowerment. She has a mission to eradicate child poverty (Pilkington, 2016). The legacy of these four leaders will most likely mirror the attributes charted throughout this chapter. How will we 'calibrate' them on the key theme of 'inclusive leadership'?

The intention of this chapter is to interrogate leadership for our times through the lens of *inclusion* and the extent to which four key figures are contributing to meaningful, positive societal change. During the years 2015–2016 the above four leaders, each recognized for different reasons and with appeal to very different audiences, have been dominant in the news for their impact and influence at a global level. The idea of *'leadership'* often seems to have become aligned with the notion of *'power'* with many of our political leaders in supposedly model democracies forgetting that their role is to serve their nation, not dictate how people should live their lives and constantly ignore the wishes of their electorate.

Angela Merkel, Chancellor of Germany and leader of the Christian Democratic Union political party, appears to transcend the level of power-play shown by so many of her political peers. Her compassion during the woeful refugee crisis in 2015, created primarily by the ongoing war in Syria, showed a level of leadership that shamed the political leaders of many surrounding countries albeit her actions in asking Germany to open its doors to the refugees jeopardized her own popularity within her country.

Donald Trump, a wealthy American businessman, politician and reality television personality, personifies the traits of self-importance, egotism and arrogance and yet he currently tops the media charts in the USA for exposure. In his campaign to become the Republican Party nominee for the office of President of the United States of America, he clearly speaks to many Americans with his rabid outbursts about women, Mexicans, Muslims and indeed key members of his own political party. While some of his recent opponents for the Republican Party candidacy are embarrassed by Donald Trump's rhetoric, some surprising political figures are supportive of him becoming leader of the 'world's greatest democracy'.

Religion is an increasingly troublesome matter in the 21st century, or rather, the way that religion is being used as a tool of power or a tool of oppression is creating increasingly dangerous divisions in society. Pope Francis, elected 266th leader of the Roman Catholic Church in 2013 is a beacon of light in a very dark time. On taking on his role Pope Francis very quickly became renowned for his humility, emphasis on God's mercy, concern for the poor and promotion of interfaith dialogue. Pope Francis shows his leadership by living his values.

Every year *Forbes* Magazine publishes an article entitled 100 women who lead the world. Helen Clark, the former Prime Minister and leader of the Labour Party in New Zealand and current Administrator for the United Nations Development Programme (UNDP), makes it into the top 25 of this list of highly prestigious women (McNamara & Howard, 2016). She is the first female UNDP head and she is a favoured candidate to succeed Ban Ki-Moon as Secretary General of the United Nations.

What do these four very different leaders have in common and what makes them truly individualistic as leaders? What impact are they making in the world as leaders? What will be their legacy? Can they be role models for a brave new world of meaningful authentic and inclusive leadership in the 21st century? Given that little scholarly research currently exists on the leadership characteristics and attributes of the four chosen leaders, this case study draws on articles in the popular media to explore the above questions.

The chapter will also offer a schema for evaluating leadership and using the ever popular framework presented by Jim Kouzes and Barry Posner (2012), determine whether the leaders in question live up to their 'five practices of exemplary leadership'.

The Challenge of Leadership

Despite the many thousand books and articles on the topic, there is no agreed definition of the term leadership. It is in essence a contested concept. The many different frameworks offered by scholars, CEOs and business leaders are, however, indicative of the characteristics of leadership we may seek for the complex world of the 21st century. Terms such as authenticity, integrity, courage, service to society, dedication to a shared purpose are common themes in the leadership literature (e.g., George, 2003; Grint, 2005; Greenleaf, 1977). I would add to these key characteristics: the ability and strength of character to challenge the status quo, as leaders are rarely in place to maintain the existing state of affairs; the ability to engage constructively across borders, boundaries and cultures. Global leaders do not have the luxury of operating within a narrow sphere of influence; rather, they must understand the consequences and complexities of a highly interconnected world. Another significant challenge to global leaders is the ability to build trust and respect. In the past decade many leaders have spectacularly lost the trust of their constituents.

The challenge of leading for the purpose of transforming societies is considerable but we can only imagine what the world would look like if the leaders of today lived up to the above attributes. The remainder of this chapter explores the extent to which our four chosen leaders live up to the tenets of inclusive leadership and have making the world a better place as their primary focus.

Leaders and Leadership for the Times

Angela Merkel, the first woman Chancellor of Germany, is at first sight an unlikely character to inspire the world. She does not exude the charisma so favoured in the age of reality television and sound-bites masquerading as informed comment, nor the oratory powers of some of our world leaders (Orth, 2015). What she does exude is a sharp intellect, a strong grasp of 'big picture' global politics and thoughtfulness in her actions. In an extraordinary show of leadership during the Syrian refugee crisis, Angela Merkel asked a great deal of her country by asking her countrymen and women to show a welcoming face to over a million refugees, casualties of what has come to be termed 'radical Islam brutality'. Expressing her belief that great civilizations build bridges, and that wars are won both on and off the battlefield, Angela Merkel displays admirable values: she shows humanity, generosity and tolerance to demonstrate how Germany's great strength could be used to save rather than destroy (Gibbs, 2015). Angela Merkel lives up to a number of positive attributes including having the courage to offer an authentic response to an immediate crisis, communicating with her constituency to try to build a climate of trust, respect and dignity towards the refugees. She understood the importance of showing compassion and humanity, giving 'refuge' to people whose lives and freedom are at risk in their own country (UNHCR, 2016). Was this a transformative moment for German society?

Compare Angela Merkel's show of courageous leadership to the level of debate in the United States of America over the Republican candidate who could become the next President. It has become perfectly acceptable to many to have Donald Trump stand up on a daily basis and exploit a divided country (Allen, 2016). For example, in contrast to Angela Merkel, Trump is using immigration and the current refugee crises as a mainstay of his electioneering platform, exploiting people's fear of difference. He has suggested a total shutdown on Muslims entering the United States and stated he would kill the families of terrorist suspects and carpet bomb Syria to demolish ISIS. He has declared that Mexican immigrants to the United States are rapists, drug addicts and criminal types and that he will force Mexico to pay for a wall to be built across the border to keep Mexicans out of the USA. He diminished and verbally abused all of his opponents in his campaign to become the presidential candidate (Scherer, 2015) and thinks nothing of using abusive language about women. It is not a show of courage to use abusive and offensive language against any group of people and doing so does not build trust or respect or foster connections in troubled societies.

Trump's behaviours would appear to tend towards the antithesis of the positive attributes of inclusive leadership.

However, while Donald Trump cannot be considered an *inclusive* leader, given his obvious popularity amongst a significant sector of American society uncomfortable questions can be raised relating to the shifts in collective consciousness he may be effecting through his narrative. Is he effecting transformation within the American psyche by means of a narrative that is appealing to a critical mass?

While it is not expected of the person holding the highest office of the Roman Catholic Church to engage in political commentary, we are living in unusual times. Pope Francis is unusual in his visibility, level of social and political engagement, dedication to the poor and articulation of his vocation as being to work for a more just and united society (Chua-Eoan & Dias, 2013; Address to the Council of Europe, 2014). But even Pope Francis has been drawn to comment on Donald Trump's extreme views particularly on immigration. Like Angela Merkel, Pope Francis believes we must build bridges and create homes for the excluded, in contrast to Donald Trump who believes we must build walls and build them quickly to keep people out (Hale, 2015). Pope Francis has articulated that 'the biggest threat to hope is when you feel that you don't matter to anybody or that you have been left aside. He is explicit in his view that that all lives matter (Dias, 2016). Pope Francis is engaged in a project to transform the Roman Catholic Church from a cleric-centred, inward looking bureaucracy to an outward facing organization focusing on social teaching and empowerment (Verhoye, 2015). He is attempting to take the church back to its Catholic tradition of supporting the poor, the marginalized and the oppressed. His reaching out to divorcees, to gays and lesbians (Greene, 2016), those previously marginalized by the Catholic Church are signs of his efforts to turn the organization around from its judgmental and critical stance to a more inclusive ethos.

It is a courageous move to take on the challenge of rebuilding trust around a powerful organization which has for so long been closed, secretive and dishonourable around the issue of sexual abuse and misconduct (Chua-Eoan et al., 2013). Will Francis come to be seen as the Pope who transformed the Catholic Church in such a way as to impact positively on the lives of many millions of people around the world?

Pope Francis is not alone in his quest to alleviate the suffering of the poorest people on earth and indeed his agenda aligns with that of the United Nations Development Group. Helen Clark whose leadership credentials include: her current role as Chair of the United Nations Development Group, the first woman to hold this prestigious post; former leader of the New Zealand Labour Party and first woman Prime Minister of New Zealand from 1999 to 2008 (Clark, 2015). As a potential successor to Ban Ki-Moon leader of the United Nations, Helen Clark has put to us the scale of the challenge of eradicating poverty, of aiming for a future of peace, prosperity and dignity for all (Clark & Solheim, 2015). One of Helen Clark's strengths as a leader is her advocacy for women in leadership and putting women's issues on the global development agenda (Clark, 2014). It is her contention that in the many struggles in poor nations arising from global challenges such as climate change, perpetual wars, droughts and floods, lack of education and basics such as clean drinking water, women bear the brunt of the many social and economic challenges.

'Women hold up more than half the sky' (Kristof & Wu-Dunn, 2009), and represent much of the world's unrealized potential. They are the educators. They raise the children. They hold families together and increasingly drive economies. They are natural leaders. We need their full engagement... in government, business and civil society (Ban Ki-Moon, 2016). It is clear in her many speeches and presentations that Helen Clark shares these sentiments and sees the potential for transformation in global society in the empowerment of women. In a changing and challenging world Clark's advocacy for women is critical (Rogers, 2014; Watkins, 2015).

The next section offers further exploration of the dispositions of these four leaders and examines their potential to effect positive and sustainable transformation within the complex contexts within which they operate.

Leadership Dispositions

Leadership does not occur in a vacuum; it is context dependent and that context is rarely static and thus leaders and leadership might be said to evolve depending on changing circumstances. Leadership is often understood as the interaction between the leaders, the followers and the social task and environment (Stefani, 2015). In this time of fundamental change and challenge our lives are being transformed through technological change, through

geopolitical challenges, and through the changing needs of societies and new generations. We need leaders who can operate
within such complex environments and who can quickly adapt to
the changing needs of the societies they lead.

Angela Merkel is something of an enigma as a leader. The
woman who grew up in the German Democratic Republic has
risen up the ranks of the German Christian Democratic Union
party and led that party and her country in her own
inimitable style since 2005. The Christian Democratic Party that
Merkel leads is largely comprised of Roman Catholics, yet she
herself is a Protestant. This in itself is testimony to her ability to
work across religious divides (Wiliarty, 2008). While much of the
Western world appears to have been seduced by the idea that
charisma is a key attribute of leaders, most commentary on
Merkel describes her as 'bland', or 'frumpy' (Orth, 2015). If we
are shaped by our history, growing up in the GDR would have
taught her to be careful of her words and of how she presented
herself. As Chancellor of Germany she has in the past few years
'evolved' as a highly visible and influential leader on the world
stage. She has had to manage through the 'euro crisis', the complex financial situation within the Euro zone countries which
arose after the global economic crisis of 2008 (Shambaugh,
2012; Williams, 2012) making what seemed like unreasonable
demands on countries such as Greece, Italy, Portugal and Spain
to mend their spendthrift ways. She has had to deal with
Vladimir Putin and his potentially threatening and destabilizing
interventions manifested in for example his 'war' with the
Ukraine in 2014 (Petrou, 2015). Perhaps most spectacularly of
all her actions was her response to the apocalyptic refugee crisis
of 2015 with hundreds and thousands of victims of the civil war
in Syria fleeing their war-torn world by whatever means possible.
Angela Merkel, horrified by what the world was seeing, asked
her country to be welcoming, to be unafraid, and to view the
sea of refugees as victims to be rescued rather than invaders to
be repelled. It was a moment in which Merkel showed great
moral courage. In the words of Nancy Gibbs of Time magazine,
*'leaders are tested only when people don't want to follow; for
asking more of her country than most politicians would dare,
for standing firm against tyranny as well as expedience and for
providing steadfast moral leadership in a world where it is in
short supply Angela Merkel is Times's Person of the Year'*
(Gibbs, 2015).

In her actions Merkel showed her strong belief that the way forward was not to build walls and fences but to give people the chance of freedom. She does not openly display the baubles of office and may well be considered bland but she has shown great courage over the years of her Chancellorship, making tough decisions that are not necessarily always popular, but are generally well thought out. According to *Time* magazine in one of Merkel's speeches she stated that *'the heart and soul of Europe is tolerance.......the worst period of hatred, devastation and destruction happened not even a generation ago. It was done in the name of my own people'* (Gibbs, 2015). She is engaged in a project which may transform Germany and Germans' view of themselves, and is in her own way contributing to the emotional healing of a country with a dark past. Merkel may well come to be viewed as the leader who took a step back, viewed the terrain, the prevailing psyche of the German people, the current reality, and took action which may re-orientate or reset the values by which the country is viewed. Will we come to view Angela Merkel as a truly authentic, inclusive and transformative leader of the 21st century, a role model for those who come behind her?

Where Angela Merkel is meticulously careful in her pronouncements, Donald Trump is a leader of whom it is said by many commentators 'appeals improperly to emotion and prejudice to gain power' (e.g., Scherer, 2015). Apparently, Trump's appeal to hundreds and thousands of Americans including many notable figures in the Republican Party, is his understanding and empathy regarding the frustrations and fears that currently grip those same Americans (Baltz, 2016). Many of Donald Trump's supporters express concern about rising healthcare costs, low wages, bankrupt political leadership and of course there is the more or less constant threat of terrorism which currently grips the world from the Middle East to Asia, Africa and Europe which in turn creates fear in America. Donald Trump considered Angela Merkel to be 'insane', for example, over her stance on immigration and continues to whip up fear amongst his followers that America is being taken over by people 'not like us' (Scherer, 2015).

Is Donald Trump a product of the darker side of the times in which we live? Ideas such as banning Muslims from entering into America, building a fence along the Mexican border, re-introducing torture techniques, are only some of the ideas he has put forward (Obeidallah, 2016) and his followers love what they are hearing.

Even though Trump stokes the flames of hate towards Latinos and Muslims, mocks the disabled, endorses violence against people who disagree with him and uses the most derogatory, misogynistic language to describe women, support for him continues to grow. How can we describe Donald Trump in leadership terms with such a track record?

Narcissistic is a term applied to people who are extremely pre-occupied with personal adequacy, power, prestige and vanity and can't see beyond their own sense of self-importance. Is Donald Trump a narcissist? Is he more concerned with his own agenda and his ego than about America's future? Michael Maccoby a renowned psychoanalyst writing in the *Harvard Business Review* (Maccoby, 2004) suggests that 'narcissistic individuals can be especially suited to act as a support to others, to take on the role of leader and to give fresh stimulus to cultural development, or they can damage the established state of affairs'. Donald Trump's growing popularity seems to spring from his willingness to challenge the status quo of American politics and political leadership, which might be considered to be no bad thing! With his charismatic appeal to a sizeable and vocal block of predominantly white working class voters, he displays much of the dark side of narcissism. He gives the impression of invincibility, and behaves in a ruthless and relentless manner towards his opponents. But these are not courageous acts of leadership rather they are egotistical and cowardly behaviours. Despite the apparent popularity of his rhetoric, this cannot be seen as a display of steadfast moral leadership. Narcissistic leaders often thrive in times of great chaos (Maccoby, 2004) and we are without doubt, living in a time of chaos and seemingly intractable challenges. Trump is surely damaging the current state of affairs. To a certain sector of the population of the United States of America, he might appear to be promising transformation through his slogan of *Make America Great Again* (Cadei, 2016). However, to others his reckless and inappropriate rhetoric might be extremely damaging not just within American society but also regarding the global reputation of the USA.

While Donald Trump comes across as aggressive and authoritative, Pope Francis appears as empathetic and collaborative (Buchanan, 2015). The organizational culture of the Roman Catholic Church might in the eyes of many be seen to be cleric-centred with an emphasis on power, bureaucracy and conservatism. Pope Francis is taking on the challenge of turning around this culture towards a social teaching-centric orientation, with a particular emphasis on social justice and supporting the poor, the marginalized and the oppressed (Verhoye, 2015). His actions to date, his eschewing of the wealthy trappings of his position, his ability to connect with his followers, his visibility and his humility have led some to call him a transformational and charismatic leader (Verhoye, 2015). Pope Francis' leadership orientation would appear to align with the idea of *servant leadership* (Greenleaf, 1977). He is true to his purpose, to call people to God. A key principle of servant leadership is to promote emotional healing in people and the organization (Wheeler, 2012). Within a matter of months of taking office Pope Francis elevated the healing mission of the church—the church as servant and comforter of hurting people in an often harsh world, above the doctrinal police work so important to his recent predecessors (Chue-Eoan & Dias, 2013). For Pope Francis to take on the challenge of addressing in a meaningful way, the highly publicized transgressions of priests and bishops, to look to ways of healing those affected by the paedophilia from within the Church instead of using all of the legal prowess at the disposal of the Church to whitewash the sinful behaviours, shows a high level of moral courage and leadership. We might borrow the words of Max DePree (2004) in suggesting that Pope Francis is showing the moral courage and leadership to ask the question of the Roman Catholic Church: 'who do we intend to be'? And the journey of response may well be one of transformation of the 'establishment'. Perhaps to a greater extent than the other leaders under discussion Pope Francis will leave a profound legacy to the global society he serves.

Like Angela Merkel, Helen Clark is liked, admired and respected for her high level of intellect. She served 9 years as Prime Minister of New Zealand and under her leadership New Zealand achieved significant levels of economic growth, low levels of unemployment and high levels of investment in health and education (Clark, 2015).

To achieve these positive outcomes required bringing people from different political persuasions together because it is rare for any single political party in New Zealand to have an overall majority, meaning that coalitions must be built. It is a credit to Helen Clark's negotiation skills and her integrity and her powers of persuasion and collaboration that she achieved so much.

It is obviously a considerable achievement to be nominated and considered for the challenging role of United Nations Secretary General. To fulfil the role requires of the incumbent that they have the skills to engender the support of the member states of the UN. 'The Secretary-General would fail if they did not take careful account of the concerns of Member States, but they must also uphold the values and moral authority of the United Nations, and speak and act for peace, even at the risk, from time to time, of challenging or disagreeing with those same Member States' (UN, 2016). Clark's nomination therefore is indicative of her having the skills to build connections, promote and support a climate of trust and respect and indeed the courage to consider such a global leadership role. In her presentation to the United Nations General Assembly (2016) she made a strong pitch as a 'unifier' of a diffuse and fragmented organization, as someone who would like the UN to be anticipatory of global crises and take explicit and decisive action, and a pitch for the United Nations to work harder on developmental interventions which will promote inclusive societies. In her current role in the UNDP, she gives her commitment to enabling and empowering the marginalized and the impoverished. During her time as Prime Minister of New Zealand, Helen Clark always gave positive consideration to, for example, the indigenous Maori population of New Zealand, the sizeable population of Pasifika peoples, women, children and the elderly, in other words making a positive difference for the marginalized in society.

Towards a Framework for Inclusive Leadership for the 21st Century

In general terms there is a stronger tendency towards partisan politics both in the USA and in the UK and to some extent in Australasia. The public is seeing stronger ideological divisions between major political parties. This was seen very clearly in the bitter debate over Brexit, the referendum held in the UK to decide Britain's relationship with the European Union (Asthana, Quinn, & Mason, 2016). We have seen strengthening ideological divides in the USA during Barack Obama's presidency (Bump, 2016). We saw the divisions between political parties in Europe over the issue of mass immigration (Gibbs, 2015). Such chronic divisions and political partisanship is not conducive to 'ending the zero-sum game' whereby it becomes inevitable that some must lose out where others make great gains. In the 21st century, the major issues impacting on societies are poverty and inequality of income which in turn erode the potential for inclusive societies. Social mobility is at risk and the potential for children of the poor to become the best they can be is severely limited. Do our four chosen individuals show the leadership traits, the inclusive mindsets necessary to set the societies within their respective spheres of influence on the pathway towards ending this zero-sum game and helping the transformation required to give everyone a meaningful stake in their society?

Table 1 below shows a framework that incorporates the desirable attributes for inclusive leadership which were articulated earlier in this chapter and a tentative evaluation of Angela, Donald, Francis and Helen within this framework.

It is suggested that Angela Merkel and Pope Francis perform strongly on all eight of these desirable leadership attributes. Helen Clark has perhaps had less high profile exposure than the other leaders, but there is nevertheless growing positive commentary on her transformational potential. Donald Trump does not rate highly in many of these attributes and we might speculate what this will mean should he become president of the USA.

Table 1.   Eight Attributes of Inclusive Leadership.

Leadership Characteristic	Angela Merkel	Donald Trump	Pope Francis	Helen Clark
Moral Courage	√	X	√	√
Authenticity of Purpose	√	?	√	√
Ability to Challenge Status Quo	√	√	√	√
Moral Integrity	√	X	√	√
Inclusive	√	X	√	√
Builds Trust & Respect	√	X	√	√
Engagement Across Borders, Boundaries and Cultures	√	X	√	√
Transformational Potential	√	X	√	?

Reconfiguring the above table into a renowned leadership framework, that of Posner and Kouzes (2012) it is possible to align the 'Five Practices of The Leadership Challenge' with key attributes of inclusive leadership as follows:

• Model the Way	Show moral courage and integrity
• Inspire a Shared Vision	Show authenticity of purpose
• Challenge the Process	Ability to challenge the status quo
• Enable Others to act	Positive inclusive engagement
• Encourage the Heart	Build trust and respect

Leadership Characteristic	Angela Merkel	Donald Trump	Pope Francis	Helen Clark
Model the Way	√	X	√	√
Inspire a Shared Vision	√	?	√	?
Challenge the Process	√	√	√	√
Enable Others to Act	√	X	√	√
Encourage the Heart	√	X	√	√

In this speculative evaluation of the four selected leaders the outcome using Posner & Kouzes framework tends towards similar results. Donald Trump stands out as being different from the other three in terms of the frame of reference of inclusive leadership. His leadership behaviours seem less likely to effect the transformational change required to create a more inclusive society.

From the analyses throughout this chapter we can only hope that Donald Trump is not given the leeway he so desires to make America in his distorted image of 'great again' while we can speculate that Angela Merkel, Pope Francis and Helen Clark will become 21st century role models for ending the zero-sum game and transforming societies through Inclusive Leadership.

Acknowledgements

I would like to thank Eric Schockman and Raul Lagomarsino for their constructive feedback on the early drafts of this chapter and their ongoing positive encouragement.

References

Allen, D. (2016). *The moment of truth: We must stop Trump.* Washington Post, 21 February 2016. Retrieved from https://www.washingtonpost.com/opinions/moment-of-truth-we-must-stop-trump/2016/02/21/0172e788-d8a7-11e5-925f-1d10062cc82d_story.html. Accessed on March 24, 2016.

Asthana, A., Quinn, B., & Mason, R. (2016). UK votes to leave EU after dramatic night divides nation. *The Guardian,* June 24, 2016. Retrieved from https://www.theguardian.com/politics/2016/jun/24/britain-votes-for-brexit-eu-referendum-david-cameron. Accessed on August 9, 2016.

Baltz, D. (2016). *Behind the rise of Donald Trump, long standing grievances among left out voters.* The New Zealand Herald, 8 March, 2016. Retrieved from http://www.nzherald.co.nz/world/news/article.cfm?c_id=2&objectid=11601347. Accessed on March 9, 2016.

Buchanan, L. (2015). *6 Key leadership traits Pope Francis and Donald Trump Share* Inc. Magazine September 25, 2015. Retrieved from http://www.inc.com/leigh-buchanan/6-leadership-traits-pope-francis-donald-trump-share.html. Accessed on April 14, 2016.

Bump, P. (2016). The unprecedented partisanship of Congress explained. Retrieved from https://www.washingtonpost.com/news/the-fix/wp/2016/01/13/heres-why-president-obama-failed-to-bridge-the-partisan-divide-graphed/. Accessed on July 11, 2016.

Cadei, E. (2016). Make America Grande Again! *Newsweek Global, 166*(19), 12–16.

Chua-Eoan, H., & Dias, E. (2013). Pope Francis – The People's Pope TIMEs Magazine December 2013. Retrieved from http://poy.time.com/2013/12/11/person-of-the-year-pope-francis-the-peoples-pope. Accessed on April 1, 2016.

Clark, H. (2014). Inaugural address at the UNDP Global Centre for Public Service Excellence in Singapore on "Women's Equal Participation and Leadership in Decision-Making: A Global Development Priority." Retrieved from http://www.undp.org/content/undp/en/home/presscenter/speeches/2014/06/03/helen-clark-inaugural-address-at-the-undp-global-centre-for-public-service-excellence-in-singapore-on-women-s-equal-participation-and-leadership-in-decision-making-a-global-development-priority-.html. Accessed on February 2, 2016..

Clark, H. (2015). *Why women's leadership matters* Pierhead Session, National Assembly of Wales. Retrieved from http://www.undp.org/content/undp/en/home/presscenter/speeches/2012/04/10/helen-clark-inclusion-and-equality-why-women-s-leadership-matters.html. Accessed on February 2, 2016.

Clark, H., & Solheim, E. (2015). Refugee crisis must not deflect us from our long term development aims. The Guardian 16 November 2015. Retrieved from http://www.guardian.com/global-development/2015/nov/16/refugee-crisis-must-not-deflect-us-from-our-long-term-development-aims. Accessed on April 15, 2016.

DePree, M. (2004). *Leadership is an art.* New York, NY: Dell Publishing.

Dias, E. (2016). Why Pope Francis is on the Mexican Side of the Border, TIME Magazine February 17, 2016. Retrieved from http://time.com/4226808/pope-francis-border-mass/. Accessed on April 16, 2016.

George, B. (2003). Authentic leadership: Rediscovering the secrets to creating lasting value. San Francisco, CA: Jossey Bass.

Gibbs, N. (2015). The choice-person of the year Angela Merkel: Leader of the free world. *TIME Magazine*, 22–51.

Greene, R. A. (2016). Pope to church: Be more accepting of divorced Catholics, gays and lesbians CNN News April 8 2016. Retrieved from http://edition.cnn.com/2016/04/08/europe/vatican-pope-family/. Accessed on May 15, 2016.

Greenleaf, R. K. (1977). *Servant leadership: A journey into the nature of legitimate power and greatness*. Mahwah, New Jersey: Paulist Press.

Grint, K. (2005). *Leadership: Limits and possibilities*. Hampshire, UK and New York: Palgrave Macmillan.

Hale, C. (2015). Donald Trump has a Pope Francis Problem, CRUX August 11, 2015. Retrieved from http://www.cruxnow.com/life/2015/08/11/donald-trump-has-a-pope-francis-problem/. Accessed on April 14, 2016.

Kouzes, J., & Posner, B. (2012). *The leadership challenge: How to make extraordinary things happen in organizations*. San Francisco, CA: Jossey-Bass.

Ki-Moon, B. (2016). Retrieved from http://www.brainyquote.com/quotes/quotes/b/bankimoon643814.html. Accessed on June 8, 2016.

Kristof, N., & WuDunn, S. (2009). *Half the sky: Turning oppression into opportunity for women worldwide*. New York and Toronto: Alfred A Knopf.

Maccoby, M. (2004). Narcissistic leaders: The incredible pros, the inevitable cons Harvard Business Review. Retrieved from https://hbr.org/2004/01/narcissistic-leaders-the-incredible-pros-the-inevitable-cons. Accessed on March 23, 2016.

McNamara, A., & Howard, C. (Eds.). (2016). The World's 100 most powerful women. *Forbes Magazine*. Retrieved from https://www.forbes.com/power-women/. Accessed on June 25, 2017

Obeidallah, D. (2016). *Donald Trump: A vote for GOP front-runner is a vote for bigotry* (Opinion). Retrieved from CNN.com http://edition.cnn.com/2016/02/24/opinions/support-trump-support-bigotry-obeidallah/. Accessed on March 25, 2016.

Orth, M. (2015). *Angela's Assets* Vanity Fair. Retrieved from http://www.vanityfair.com/news/2015/01/angela-merkel-profile. Accessed on April 15, 2016.

Petrou, M. (2015). The real leader of the free world: how the reluctant Angela Merkel became the one person capable of stopping Putin and bringing peace and security back to Europe. *MacLean's*, *128*(8) 22–30.

Pilkington, E. (2016). Helen Clark, Former New Zealand Prime Minister Confirms Bid for United Nations Top Job. Retrieved from https://www.theguardian.com/world/2016/apr/05/helen-clark-former-new-zealand-prime-minister-confirms-bid-for-united-nations-top-job. Accessed on July 11, 2016.

Rogers, D. (2014). *Opinion: Is Helen Clark UN Secretary-General number nine?* Retrieved from http://www.massey.ac.nz/massey/about/massey/news/article.cfm?mnarticle_uuid=C50CF0A-9E95-CA4F-4A94-BBAAA37C3C65. Accessed on April 6, 2016.

Shambaugh, C. J. (2012). *The Euro's 3 crises*. Retrieved from https://www.brookings.edu/wp-content/uploads/2012/03/2012a_Shambaugh.pdf. Accessed on June 23, 2017.

Scherer, M. (2015). Donald Trump. *TIME Magazine*, 56–63.

Stefani, L. (2015). Stepping up to leadership in higher education. *Journal of All Ireland Society for Higher Education*, 7(1). Retrieved from http://citeseerx.ist. psu.edu/viewdoc/download?doi=10.1.1.684.4781&rep=rep1&type=pdf. Accessed on April 14, 2016.

UNHCR. United Nations Refugee Agency. Retrieved from http://unhcr.org. Accessed on September 8, 2016.

Verhoye, A. M. (2015). Unfreezing the organizational culture of the catholic church: A case study of Pope Francis' organizational culture change initiative using the transformational leadership theoretical framework. Doctoral Dissertation, University of Minnesota. Retrieved from http://conservancy.umn. edu/bitstream/handle/11299/175357/Verhoye_umn_0130E_15994.pdf?sequence= 1&isAllowed=y. Accessed on April 15, 2016.

Watkins, T. (2015). Posing the question – Can Helen Clark lead the United Nations? Retrieved from http://www.stuff.co.nz/national/politics/opinion/ 70729847/Posing-the-question-can-Helen-Clark-lead-the-United-Nations. Accessed on April 6, 2016.

Wheeler, D. (2012). *Servant leadership for higher education: Principles and practice*. San Francisco, CA: Jossey Bass.

Wiliarty, S. (2008) Angela Merkel's path to power: The role of internal party dynamics and leadership. *German Politics*, 17(1), 81–96.

Williams, C. J. (2012). Euro crisis imperils recovering global economy, OECD warns. *Los Angeles Times*. Retrieved from http://latimesblogs.latimes.com/ world_now/2012/05/eurozone-crisis-global-economy.html. Accessed on June 25, 2017.

26

Global Interdependence: The Inclusive Nature of Humanitarian Leaders at Heifer International

Malcolm E. Glover

Keywords: Leadership; Humanitarian Aid; Global Nonprofit; Inclusion; Interdependence; Heifer International

I n an era when human interaction is shaped by various social, environmental, and economic forces, leaders of global nonprofit organizations are finding new ways to meet the challenges of an interdependent world by harnessing the power that comes from diverse perspectives, disciplines, and cultures. Global nonprofit organizations are dynamic entities that are hubs for inclusion, transformation, collaboration, and change. International nongovernmental organizations, or NGOs, are essentially types of nonprofit organizations that are not part of a government entity or operated through a government program (Davies, 2014). Both global nonprofits and NGOs are highly diverse institutions with a multicultural workforce prone to collaborative behaviors (Austin, 2000; Putnam, 2000; Skocpol, 2003). The deliberative actions of humanitarian leaders at these transnational organizations are shaped by their cooperative habits and varied experiences in communities. As confirmed by Rose (2010), the human understanding of and actions toward inclusion, or egalitarian policies and practices, is derived from societal traditions, as well as socio-economic, political, and cultural influences.

"Inclusion" is a multifaceted concept often related to terms such as equity, equality, mutuality, and fairness (Precey, 2011, p. 37). Leader inclusiveness is an idea that speaks to the actions of a manager or change agent whose "words and deeds invite contributions from others and who demonstrates appreciation of those contributions" (Bowers, Robertson, & Parchman, 2012, p. 8). Nembhard and Edmondson (2006) suggest inclusive leaders value input from others and inspire followers by encouraging both the outspoken and reserved to voice their opinions and share problem-solving strategies without fear of reprisal. The interconnected nature of the modern world requires leaders to operate in an inclusive manner, appreciate societal changes, and adapt to complex situations.

Global Leader Inclusiveness

Scholars have suggested employee engagement and organizational effectiveness are inextricably linked to inclusive leadership practices (Bakker, Albrecht, & Leiter, 2011; Choi, Tran, & Park, 2015; Strom, Sears, & Kelly, 2014). According to Shuck and Herd (2012), leaders who are inherently concerned with the needs of their followers tend to create collaborative work environments with personnel who are committed to team objectives and the organizational mission. The advancement of more inclusive practices across the global development sector is a product of system-wide efforts to improve accountability, promote democratic reforms, and foster sustainable solutions to persistent problems.

Leader inclusiveness encourages and values the different viewpoints expressed by diverse team members and has the potential to surmount barriers to team performance goals in professional settings (Mitchell et al., 2015). In a global context, Nishii and Mayer (2009) suggest leader inclusiveness is a vital relational leadership style that necessitates consultation with followers and the use of procedures and tools that enhance shared decision-making processes. Leader inclusiveness often reveals one's penchant for exhibiting behaviors that value cultural diversity, ideological differences, and conflicting viewpoints or ideas within team interactions, especially at times when the majority attempts to overrule or marginalize minority opinions without due process (Nembhard & Edmondson, 2006).

Thompson and Byrnes (2011) observed inclusiveness has cultural overtones, expressed in both communal and environmental conditions, that can contribute to increasing acceptance, as well as productive interactions among people who observe different customs or hail from different communities. Findings from previous multinational studies indicate high levels of perceived cultural inclusiveness lead to an increase in positive attitudes, intercultural interactions, and rewarding relationships among diverse peoples (Ward & Masgoret, 2004; Ward et al., 2005). Culturally inclusive workplaces, particularly in the humanitarian sector, acknowledge, value, and promote diversity so that various worldviews and experiences can be expressed in a constructive manner and yield positive employee attitudes that provide space for equitable treatment and the pursuit of common goals (McLoughlin, 2011; Tawagi & Mak, 2014).

The Inclusive Nature of Global Nonprofits

Global nonprofit organizations reflect and address communal concerns, and the extent to which leaders are inclusive has an impact on the social and psychological needs, aspirations, and well-being of followers (Bok, 2010). Routinely, these humanitarian entities offer programs and services that empower marginalized peoples around the world. Global nonprofits meet the needs of diverse communities by functioning as collective action institutions that represent specialized policy interests (Leroux & Goerdel, 2009).

A considerable increase in the number of NGOs operating across the globe is partially a product of new technological advancements and communication capabilities that connect disparate groups to a common purpose and transform the ways nonprofits interact with their publics (Andreasen & Kotler, 2002). The changing roles of national governments and the private sector, as well as the evolving nature of philanthropy, increasing social needs, and emerging international crises, also contribute to the proliferation of these multinational institutions that require the skills of inclusive leaders (Lindenberg & Bryant, 2001).

Many nonprofit organizations have become more international in mission and scope, due to the forces of globalization that have increased partnerships, fostered alliances, and created new challenges (Austin, 2000). For nearly two decades, scholars have assessed international nonprofit organizations and discovered the entities command unprecedented levels of trust (Laidler-Kylander, Quelch, & Simonin, 2007; Wootliff & Deri, 2001). The number of global nonprofit organizations has risen sharply in recent years fostering both competition and collaboration among these humanitarian groups, their employees, and stakeholders (Laidler-Kylander et al., 2007). As entities that often have a peace and conflict resolution orientation (Gidron, Katz, & Hasenfeld, 2002), global nonprofits tend to merge the ideas and experiences of a culturally diverse workforce to increase public awareness of important issues and promote civic engagement (Putnam, 2000; Skocpol, 2003).

The shifting landscape for transnational advocacy and relief organizations has, as stated by Laidler-Kylander et al. (2007), "profoundly altered the mind-set and duties of nonprofit managers and leaders, propelling them into new competitive arenas..." (p. 254). In addition to adequate supervision of personnel and the accurate fulfillment of stakeholder needs, Brunham (2002) suggested modern nonprofit leaders, particularly in the global arena, now have to be concerned with building the organization's brand identity, or the representation of a reputation through the communication of an entity's attributes, values, purpose, strengths, and mission (Aaker, 1996). Moreover, the sound stewardship of global nonprofit organizations is complicated by the tensions that inevitably exist when leaders and managers try to balance responsibilities, seize opportunities, and address predicaments.

Laidler-Kylander et al. (2007) observed current research in nonprofit management, coupled with their detailed interviews of close to 100 executives at 10 international nonprofit organizations, resulted in findings that suggest the multiple roles personnel play and the varied requests of stakeholders affect a global nonprofit's ability to leverage resources, tackle complex challenges, and communicate complicated matters to the public. While the literature lacks consensus with regard to performance outcomes, scholars have affirmed that the actions of global nonprofit leaders must reflect the organization's current mission, build trust with consumers, include the broader public, and address the needs of multiple stakeholders in a way that fulfills program implementation benchmarks (Bosc, 2002; Letts, Ryan, & Grossman, 1998; Oster, 1995; Richie, Swami, & Weinberg, 1999).

The Heifer International Model

One organization in the vanguard of agencies and institutions that use inclusive leadership strategies to address communal and environmental crises in the developing world is Heifer International. According to Heifer International's *Annual Report* (2012), the multinational charitable organization works with communities in need around the world to end hunger and poverty in a sustainable fashion and care for the Earth. The global nonprofit also envisions "a world of communities living together in peace and harmony and equitably sharing the resources of a healthy planet" (p. 2). [Through agricultural and educational initiatives], the Heifer team seeks to empower families and "turn hunger and poverty into hope and prosperity" by making meaningful connections between communities and helping develop sustainable agriculture and commerce to historically and chronically impoverished areas (Heifer International, 2013, p. 1).

Heifer's commitment to principles that engage the public in global development projects is a product of inclusive leadership precepts that promote the inherent value of people and encourage the development of personal relationships with stakeholders through networks of acceptance and trust (Covey & Merrill, 2006; Fink, 2005; Precey, 2011). As the starting point of any relationship, trust is often nurtured by inclusive leaders and collaborative managers who want to build a rapport with others and enhance organizational outcomes (Fink, 2005). Heifer's participatory approaches to rural development are steeped in the organization's faith-based origins.

HEIFER INTERNATIONAL'S RELIGIOUS ROOTS

Heifer International began as Heifers for Relief in 1944 under the leadership of Dan West, a Church of the Brethren peace activist (Moser, 2010). As a relief worker during the Spanish Civil War, West directed a program that provided rations of milk to hungry refugee children. The humanitarian experience West gained during that time gave him the idea that the children he served in war-torn communities needed a cow rather than a cup of milk (Kerby, 2006; Moser, 2010). Working with church members, West founded Heifers for Relief so cows could be donated to impoverished families. Church of the Brethren leaders and local farmers in the United States supplied pregnant dairy cows for the outreach projects and recipient families had to promise that they would donate the first female calf to another poor family (Kerby, 2006; Moser, 2010).

A Christian denomination whose origins date back to the 1700s, the Church of the Brethren has historically taken a strong stance for principled nonviolence, pacifism, and conflict resolution around the world (Kreider, 2001). The church's teachings inspired West to serve the poor. Brethren doctrine and structure embraces an egalitarian ideal that, like inclusive leadership, invites and appreciates the contributions of others (Bowers et al., 2012). As clergy, Brethren ministers serve in a functional capacity rather than a hierarchical position of authority and both preachers and parishioners consider inclusion and acceptance fundamental aspects of church life (Church of the Brethren, 2008; Kreider, 2001).

Writings from the denomination's governing body, or General Board, suggest Church of the Brethren members uphold the belief of "unity in diversity," a concept of unity without uniformity and diversity without fragmentation that transcends mere tolerance of physical, cultural, linguistic, social, religious, political, ideological or psychological differences and establishes a more complex unity based on the understanding that differences enrich human interactions (Church of the Brethren, 2008; Lalonde, 1994). Although Church of the Brethren dogma helped define the genesis of Heifer's mission and purpose under Dan West's leadership in the early years, the transnational nonprofit is no longer a mere religious charity. Heifer has transformed into a more inclusive and secular global enterprise that is influenced by the collaborative ethos set forth in Brethren doctrine without being beholden to religious proselytizing.

HEIFER INTERNATIONAL'S MODERN MISSION

After reforms in the 1950s and consolidation efforts in the early 1970s, Heifer International broadened its scope to distribute fish, chickens, pigs, goats, sheep, oxen, water buffaloes, and other livestock to poor rural communities around the world (Kerby, 2006; Moser, 2010). The animals that Heifer sends to developing communities in need of support are a source of food and provide the recipients with reliable income, as agricultural products such as milk, eggs, and honey are traded or sold at market. "When many families gain this new sustainable income [from Heifer's animals and the organization's community-based educational programs], it brings new opportunities for building schools, creating agricultural cooperatives, forming community savings and funding small businesses" (Heifer International, 2013, p. 1).

As a world hunger relief charity, Heifer International has made a measurable impact, as documented by Ferrari (2013); in the 70 years of Heifer's existence, 20.7 million families have achieved lives of self-reliance and sustainability through the non-profit's initiatives in more than 125 countries. As a result of Heifer's projects and programs, "more mothers and fathers are able to feed their children and those children are healthy and able to go to school" and "where once, whole communities were living in poverty — lacking adequate nutrition, income and resources — those communities are now strong and successful economies" (Ferrari, 2013, p. 2). In fiscal year 2013, Heifer employees working on the ground in various locations across the globe directly and indirectly helped 2,140,263 families move out of poverty (Heifer International, 2013, pp. 2–9).

Through collaborations with residents, stakeholders, donor groups, and partners, Heifer's scope of work helps communities realize higher incomes, retain healthier livestock, and raise standards that improve access to education in the developing world. To date, 105.1 million men, women, and children have received tools and training from the organization to help sustain their lives and create a prosperous future (Heifer International, 2014a). When implementing projects in Africa, the Americas, Asia and the South Pacific, and Central and Eastern Europe, Heifer adheres to a core principle, known as "Passing on the Gift," which enables recipients of Heifer livestock and services to become donors. For instance, after projects are established, families that received resources from Heifer — such as livestock, seeds or training — pass on these gifts to other families in need in their community, allowing them to help others as they have been helped. Practicing this core tenet can be transformative. "On average, Passing on the Gift lasts for at least six generations, no matter the project" (Heifer International, 2013, p. 7).

Inclusive Leadership Across Cultures

Currently, Heifer staff members work with residents in over 30 countries and implement programs that have minimal long-term effects on the environment and natural resources (Heifer International, 2014b). The nonprofit also operates within the precepts of a community model that ensures families and villages make their own decisions about what crops, animals, and market strategies make sense for conditions on the ground in their area. Heifer International's focus on confronting social challenges to further community-based efforts for ending hunger and poverty in a sustainable way, coupled with its initiatives that seek to build parity among men and women, made the inner workings of the global nonprofit organization a suitable setting for the exploration of inclusive leadership in diverse settings.

CULTIVATING INCLUSION THROUGH HUMAN INTERACTION

In Southeast Asia, when typhoons buffet the Philippines and other natural disasters wreak havoc across that island country's pastoral communities, the employees of Heifer Philippines are often on the front lines of outreach efforts helping the Filipino people recover and rebuild. Whether providing humanitarian assistance or creating new programs that empower local residents, Karla Rodulfo and her Heifer colleagues are constantly working together to improve the lives of the Filipinos they serve in cities and tribal areas. Rodulfo has worked with Heifer for eight years. During that time, she has only been involved with the global organization's initiatives in the Philippines. Rodulfo was born in the Philippines and she currently lives there. As the planning, monitoring, and evaluation manager for Heifer's programs in the Philippines, Rodulfo regularly monitors and evaluates active projects to determine their effectiveness. "I do most of the progress reports on our initiatives and submit those findings to officials at headquarters, as well as our different stakeholders and funders," Rodulfo said.

Rodulfo is governed by a simple belief that sharing ideas and bringing people together to solve their own problems is a necessity when attempting to alleviate hunger and poverty. "One of the challenges we face is how to make our projects more sustainable so families can have higher incomes and communities can thrive without direct involvement from Heifer staff," Rodulfo said. "Since we have ventured into the area of disaster reduction and developed programs to improve preparedness, our work is even more centered on organizing communities, giving people the skills that add value to their lives, and empowering them to confront natural disasters so they can be more resilient during hazardous events."

Consistent with earlier research findings (Bowers et al., 2012), events on the ground in the Philippines suggest when broad cross sections of Heifer personnel and other key stakeholders are included in decision-making processes, teams tend to implement changes with ease. Ongoing development work in the country has taught Rodulfo that people in "partner communities" who receive training and services often want to connect with providers on a personal level first. She stresses that the success of any collaborative endeavor requires that Heifer employees build trust and develop a rapport with local residents. "If you are going to move forward on any project, people want to know that you understand their concerns," Rodulfo stated. "In every community, there are people who want to be a part of efforts to solve local problems and increase opportunities for their families." She says true collaboration that harnesses the best ideas from native residents can create avenues for honest dialogue and sustainable development.

As a person who seeks compromise, Rodulfo is prone to tackle concerns by finding agreement or common ground, between the extreme positions of others in an effort to remove any impediments to progress. "I try to address issues directly and bring people together to solve problems," admitted Rodulfo. "Part of my management style is to try and find a win-win solution for both parties as much as possible." Through various experiences, she has discovered mutually beneficial solutions can be the best balm to heal old wounds and bridge divides.

Rodulfo says her perspectives on global development have evolved during her eight years working for Heifer International. "Before Heifer, I worked as a monitoring officer for several government projects funded by the World Bank. In my earlier work, whenever I would go to the field, I always thought that as someone from the government I had all the answers to the community's problems. You know, we had this view that we are the light and we guide the people," said Rodulfo. "However, when I joined Heifer my perspective changed. Now, I know that you are really supposed to go to a community as a facilitator and let the families themselves find solutions to their concerns and their problems."

CULTIVATING INCLUSION THROUGH GRASSROOTS INITIATIVES

Uganda is home to one of Heifer International's more than 30 country field offices around the world that work in partnership with a sizeable network of local nongovernmental organizations and grassroots groups. For many decades, Ugandans endured civil wars, terrorist attacks, and grave human rights abuses, including genocide, sex slavery, and the forcing of children to become soldiers. Before officially joining Heifer International in 2007, Dan Bazira worked on development projects in the Northern region of Uganda that addressed the needs of civilians who were forced to live in makeshift camps due to war and other atrocities.

Most of Bazira's earlier work in that region focused on humanitarian relief. He decided to join the staff of Heifer Uganda, in order to develop long-term solutions to the vexing problems that were plaguing his country. "I wanted to use the skills that I had learned to work with an organization that would ensure sustainability in the community right from a household level," Bazira explained.

From his office in Kampala, Dan Bazira oversees the evaluation of Heifer projects in Uganda and he provides support for performance and program monitoring efforts. Bazira focuses on team building to enhance organizational and communal outcomes. When necessary, he convenes people to tackle major concerns. Through a methodical process, he assigns certain individuals specific tasks and those same colleagues then look at the particular components of an activity or create strategies that will contribute to the successful completion of projects. "There has to be sharing of information and cooperation among the team to ensure collaboration and overall effectiveness," Bazira said.

Traditionally, Ugandans who live in some of the most vulnerable communities lack adequate sleeping facilities and housing made of good quality materials, according to extensive conversations with Bazira. Many villagers live in grass hut houses that are prone to destruction due to changes in weather. Bazira considers his work in the development arena to be part of wide-ranging humanitarian efforts that transform communities, build civil society, and inspire collective action. "Through our efforts, some people have transitioned from these temporary structures to more permanent homes and many are living more comfortable lives and are in a position to provide for their children who previously lived in extreme poverty and did not have access to education," Bazira said. "I see all of these outcomes as important and it excites me, because we are helping communities and changing lives." Bazira admits engaging community members in the development and implementation of reform initiatives is a necessity, as Heifer personnel work to build communal trust and encourage the type of grassroots participation that helps guarantee projects and services meet the needs of local people.

Heifer International began its operations in Uganda in 1982 in an effort to improve the country's economy and overhaul an agricultural sector that was left in ruins as a result of civil wars in the late 1970s and early 1980s. Currently, the direct beneficiaries of Heifer's services in the country are people who come from diverse cultural backgrounds and communities. As a result of these various interest groups, Dan Bazira and other members of the Heifer Uganda staff have to make sure the organization's outreach activities involve input from stakeholders at the community level, the country level, and even the global level. "One of the constant challenges we face is ensuring there is a balance of perspectives, experiences, and talents within the organization, because different communities have different needs," Bazira said. "There are always different requirements at different times, but I try to bring balance to most situations by providing opportunities for constant communication among colleagues and stakeholders so all involved know what services we can and cannot provide." Bazira's quest for balance fosters inclusion, which bolsters camaraderie and facilitates democratic governance (Feldman, Khademian, Ingram, & Schneider, 2006).

Heifer Uganda continues to implement initiatives that improve food security and nutrition; increase employment opportunities and income; reduce cases of HIV/AIDS; decrease environmental degradation; and enhance gender equity and women's empowerment. In addition, Dan Bazira admits comprehensive efforts that support the aspirations of farmers are having a lasting impact. "Right now, farmers have even testified to me that because of [Heifer projects] they no longer see themselves as beggars and lowly receivers of support, but they now consider themselves to be donors and helpers in the community who have passed on agricultural skills training, food, and monetary resources to other people in their area," Bazira said.

Overcoming Barriers to Inclusion

Although Karla Rodulfo, Dan Bazira, and other Heifer personnel rely on collaboration, accommodation, and compromise to fulfill personal and institutional objectives, there are various factors and circumstances that hinder efforts to create an inclusive atmosphere. In the Philippines, Heifer International staffers have learned project success often depends on adapting their strategies and adjusting program timelines to meet the challenges of unforeseen circumstances in the field. "We have to make changes to plans along the way to suit the realities of situations that happen in the communities we serve," said Karla Rodulfo, who evaluates programs for Heifer Philippines. "As changes happen, we usually do consultation meetings with the project partners and even the community so everyone understands new objectives."

Rodulfo's comments suggest modifications to program timelines and goals are very common for field-based projects and with any change community members have to be informed before Heifer staffers implement a new strategy. In order to overcome budgetary constraints and adequately address local concerns when there is a shortage of long-term funds, Karla Rodulfo and her colleagues have relied on guidance and support from area residents who benefit from Heifer's initiatives. "One of our innovative approaches to development is we consult the community, ask them for solutions to local problems, and let them decide the steps to take to confront the issue," Rodulfo said.

For instance, Rodulfo recounts an example of community-driven innovation that helped Filipino families fulfill their commitment of "passing on the gift" even after the death of their livestock. Some villagers, who accepted the responsibility of giving the offspring of their livestock to another poor family, were deeply concerned about how they would fulfill their promises if and when cattle die. "Local people came up with the great idea to set up a livestock insurance fund to help families with dead livestock shoulder the expense of buying more livestock through the contributions of fund members in the community," Rodulfo said. "The community also set up a mortuary fund to help livestock insurance fund members who have a loved one that dies.... it's like a mutual aid fund for families."

Researchers have suggested informal relationships and casual communications spur collaboration that significantly enhances access to resources, improves employee expertise, and increases human socialization by giving people the skills and habits necessary to understand social norms and fully participate in society (Bozeman & Corley, 2004). However, collaborative efforts among diverse teams or a multicultural workforce are inherently complicated because even though collaboration promotes inclusion and fosters a sense of egalitarianism those joint efforts also create space for conflict, competition, communication difficulties, increased project expenses, and bureaucratic constraints (Cummings & Kiesler, 2005; Hara, Solomon, Kim, & Sonnenwald, 2003; Katz & Martin, 1997; Walsh & Maloney, 2007). Collaboration can even affect the time it takes to complete certain tasks, because joint initiatives usually require building a consensus among partners before any concerted action is taken (Aguilar et al., 2013).

In addition to cooperative concerns, competent governance remains a challenge for initiatives promoting inclusivity in some of the communities Heifer serves, because of learning deficits. "Most of the community-based groups in Uganda that have formed from Heifer projects are dealing with issues of good leadership and self-governance," said Dan Bazira, a monitoring manager for Heifer programs. "You find that some groups still have leadership concerns or problems with management effectiveness, which can partially be attributed to low literacy levels among leaders and a lack of opportunities for these same leaders to be exposed to different environments where they can receive proper mentoring and education."

Carmeli, Reiter-Palmon, and Ziv (2010) insist openness, accessibility, and availability are hallmarks of inclusive leadership that foster employee cooperation and creativity in the workplace. Consequently, Heifer International employees are constantly implementing reforms, overseeing structural changes within departments, and overhauling services in a concerted effort to meet the needs of diverse stakeholders. Analyses indicate effective communication and human engagement are emerging factors that influence the work of global practitioners (Cummings & Kiesler, 2005; Shrum, Genuth, & Chompalov, 2007). Effective communication requires listening and candor, inclusive principles.

Parties must be willing to speak freely and act authentically, in order to increase mutual understanding.

Honest communication with partner families is a hallmark of the relationship between Heifer employees and the communities where they work. Karla Rodulfo says, whenever projects in the Philippines face financial constraints, her colleagues let local families know the situation and Heifer staff also encourage local residents to develop plans at the grassroots level so they can help themselves and develop solutions to their own problems rather than always coming to Heifer for help. Rodulfo is adamant when she states "sustainable solutions can come from the community."

From his vantage point in Uganda, Dan Bazira admits open dialogue is an investment in public relations that often leads to improved outreach and raises Heifer's visibility. "When we listen to local people and speak to their concerns, we also have a chance to communicate the success stories from our programs and our work to the broader public," Bazira said. "Communication with villages and the government keeps us informed and helps us promote all of the research and development that has taken place in Uganda because of our projects."

The perspectives of Karla Rodulfo and Dan Bazira exemplify the work habits and wise counsel exhibited by inclusive leaders. Openness, availability, and accessibility are inclusionary qualities that allow leaders to set high expectations, listen to employees, discuss strategies for work goals, and pay attention to new opportunities (Carmeli et al., 2010). Through collaborative efforts, the inclusive leader is able to defy passé hierarchical norms and increase trust among followers through the direct expression of a benevolent style of leadership that authentically conveys care and concern for followers (Burke, Sims, Lazzara, & Salas, 2007; Edmondson, 2004).

The Promise of Inclusion for Global Development Practitioners

Harnessing the power of inclusive leadership often yields sustainable coalitions and influences social change by incorporating the ideas of diverse staff and community members in the planning and execution of organizational goals. As suggested by Hollander (2009), as well as Choi et al. (2015), leaders who use an inclusive management style are likely to exert considerable influence on employee behavior and team participation due to distinct supervisory efforts that enhance relationships and fulfill the job-related needs of workers.

At its best, inclusive leadership amplifies the communicative and collaborative exchanges that occur between professionals and the people they serve. In an interdependent world, the organizations that survive and thrive are often products of inclusive leaders who support and reward their employees, while also encouraging the kinds of cooperation and information sharing that inspires followers to share their opinions, participate in creative tasks, and embrace the prevailing organizational ethos (Carmeli et al., 2010; Lin & Liu, 2012). In order to adequately address social, cultural, financial, environmental, institutional, and economic concerns, organizations and individuals must be willing to seek consensus when creating policies and implementing programs. Developing comprehensive protocols that promote inclusion can aid efforts by global nonprofit leaders to solve complex problems, empower oppressed populations, overcome cultural differences, and create programs that endure.

Acknowledgments

I would like to thank Heifer International, especially Heifer Philippines and Heifer Uganda, for allowing personnel to participate in this research. In particular, I appreciate the fact that Karla Rodulfo and Dan Bazira were willing to take part in thorough interviews that explored their personal and professional lives.

References

Aaker, D. (1996). *Building strong brands*. New York, NY: Free Press.

Aguilar, S. M., Ynalvez, M. A., Kilburn, J. C., Hara, N., Ynalvez, R. A., Chen, K., & Kamo, Y. (2013). Research productivity of East Asian scientists: Does cosmopolitanism in professional networking, research collaboration, and scientific conference attendance matter?. *Asia-Pacific Social Science Review*, 13(2), 41–62.

Andreasen, A., & Kotler, P. (2002). *Strategic marketing for nonprofit organizations*. (6th ed.). Upper Saddle River, NJ: Prentice Hall.

Austin, J. (2000). Strategic collaboration between nonprofits and businesses. *Nonprofit and Voluntary Sector Quarterly*, 29(1), 69–97.

Bakker, A. B., Albrecht, S. L., & Leiter, M. P. (2011). Key questions regarding work engagement. *European Journal of Work and Organizational Psychology*, 20, 4–28.

Bok, D. (2010). *The politics of happiness*. Princeton, NJ: Princeton University Press.

Bosc, J. (2002). Brands: They need to work just as hard as you do!. *Nonprofit World*, 20(1), 29–30.

Bowers, K. W., Robertson, M., & Parchman, M. L. (2012). How inclusive leadership can help your practice adapt to change. *Family Practice Management*, 19(1), 8–11.

Bozeman, B., & Corley, E. (2004). Scientists' collaboration strategies: Implications for scientific and technical human capital. *Research Policy*, 33(4), 599–616.

Brunham, K. (2002). What skills will nonprofit leaders need in the future? *Nonprofit World*, 20(3), 33–35.

Burke, C. S., Sims, D. E., Lazzara, E. H., & Salas, E. (2007). Trust in leadership: A multi-level review and integration. *Leadership Quarterly*, 18, 606–632.

Carmeli, A., Reiter-Palmon, R., & Ziv, E. (2010). Inclusive leadership and employee involvement in creative tasks in the workplace: The mediating role of psychological safety. *Creativity Research Journal*, 22, 250–260.

Choi, S. B., Tran, T. B. H., & Park, B. I. (2015). Inclusive leadership and work engagement: Mediating roles of affective organizational commitment and creativity. *Social Behavior and Personality*, 43(6), 931–944.

Church of the Brethren. (2008). *A resolution urging forbearance*. Retrieved from http://www.brethren.org/about/statements/2008-forbearance.pdf. Accessed in 2016.

Covey, S. M. R., & Merrill, R. R. (2006). *The speed of trust: The one thing that changes everything*. New York, NY: Simon & Schuster.

Cummings, J. N., & Kiesler, S. (2005). Collaborative research across disciplinary and organizational boundaries. *Social Studies of Science*, 35(5), 703–722.

Davies, T. (2014). *NGOs: A new history of transnational civil society*. New York, NY: Oxford University Press.

Edmondson, A. C. (2004). Psychological safety, trust, and learning in organizations: A group-level lens. In R. M. Kramer & K. S. Cook (Eds.), *Trust and distrust in organizations: Dilemmas and approaches* (pp. 239–272). New York, NY: Russell Sage Foundation.

Feldman, M. S., Khademian, A. M., Ingram, H., & Schneider, A. S. (2006). Ways of knowing and inclusive management practices. *Public Administration Review*, 66, 89–99.

Ferrari, P. U. (2013). *Heifer International 2013 annual report*. Little Rock, AR: Heifer International.

Fink, D. (2005). *Leadership for mortals*. London, UK: Sage.

Gidron, B., Katz, S. N., & Hasenfeld, Y. (2002). *Mobilizing for peace: Conflict resolution in Northern Ireland, Israel/Palestine, and South Africa*. New York, NY: Oxford University Press. 2002. In N. Nair & D. Bhatnagar, D. (2011, Spring). Understanding workplace deviant behavior in nonprofit organizations:

Toward an integrative conceptual framework. Nonprofit Management & Leadership, 21(3). doi: 10.1002/nml.20026.

Hara, N., Solomon, P., Kim, S. L., & Sonnenwald, D. H. (2003). An emerging view of scientific collaboration: Scientists' perspectives on collaboration and factors that impact collaboration. *Journal of the American Society for Information Science & Technology*, 54(10), 952–965.

Heifer International. (2012). *Heifer International 2012 annual report*. Little Rock, AR: Heifer International.

Heifer International. (2013). *Heifer International 2013 annual report*. Little Rock, AR: Heifer International.

Heifer International. (2014a). *Our impact*. Retrieved from http://www.heifer. org/ending-hunger/accomplishments/index.html. Accessed in 2016.

Heifer International. (2014b). *Our work*. Retrieved from http://www.heifer.org/ ending-hunger/our-work/index.html. Accessed in 2016.

Hollander, E. P. (2009). *Inclusive leadership: The essential leader-follower relationship*. New York, NY: Routledge.

Katz, J. S., & Martin, B. R. (1997). What is research collaboration? *Research Policy*, 26(1), 1–18.

Kerby, R. (2006). Heifer project. In M. Odekon (Ed.), *Encyclopedia of world poverty* (pp. 476–477). London, UK: Sage.

Kreider, J. K. (2001). *A cup of cold water: The story of brethren service*. Elgin, IL: Brethren Press.

Laidler-Kylander, N., Quelch, J. A., & Simonin, B. L. (2007). Building and valuing global brands in the nonprofit sector. *Nonprofit Management & Leadership*, 17(3), 253–277. doi:10.1002/nml.

Lalonde, R. (1994). Unity in diversity: Acceptance and integration in an era of intolerance and fragmentation. Retrieved from http://bahai-library.com/lalonde_ unity_diversity. Accessed in 2016.

Leroux, K., & Goerdel, H. T. (2009). Political advocacy by nonprofit organizations: A strategic management explanation. *Public Performance & Management Review*, 32(4), 514–536. doi:10.2753/PMR1530-9576320402.

Letts, C., Ryan, W., & Grossman, A. (1998). *High performance nonprofit organizations: Managing upstream for greater impact*. Hoboken, NJ: Wiley.

Lin, C. Y. Y., & Liu, F. C. (2012). A cross-level analysis of organizational creativity climate and perceived innovation: The mediating effect of work motivation. *European Journal of Innovation Management*, 15, 55–76.

Lindenberg, M., & Bryant, C. (2001). *Going global: Transforming relief and development NGOs*. Bloomfield, CT: Kumarian Press.

McLoughlin, C. (2011). Inclusivity and alignment: Principles of pedagogy, task and assessment design for effective cross-cultural online learning. *Distance Education*, 22, 7–29.

Mitchell, R., Boyle, B., Parker, V., Giles, M., Chiang, V., & Joyce, P. (2015). Managing inclusiveness and diversity in teams: How leader inclusiveness affects performance through status and team identity. *Human Resource Management*, 54(2), 217–239.

Moser, M. L. (2010). Heifer Project International. In D. Jacques & P. Kepos (Eds.), *International directory of company histories* (pp. 207–210). Detroit, MI: St. James Press.

Nembhard, I. M., & Edmondson, A. C. (2006). Making it safe: The effects of leader inclusiveness and professional status on psychological safety and improvement efforts in health care teams. *Journal of Organizational Behavior, 27*(7), 941–966.

Nishii, L. H., & Mayer, D. M. (2009). Do inclusive leaders help to reduce turnover in diverse groups? The moderating role of leader-member exchange in the diversity to turnover relationship. *Journal of Applied Psychology, 94*(6), 1412–1426.

Oster, S. (1995). *Strategic management for nonprofit organizations.* New York, NY: Oxford University Press.

Precey, R. (2011). Inclusive leadership for inclusive education – The Utopia worth working towards. *Contemporary Management Quarterly, 2*(20), 35–44.

Putnam, R. D. (2000). *Bowling alone: The collapse and revival of community in America.* New York, NY: Simon and Schuster. In K. Leroux & H. T. Goerdel (2009). Political advocacy by Nonprofit organizations: A strategic management explanation. Public Performance & Management Review, 32(4), pp. 514-536. doi: 10.2753/PMR1530-9576320402.

Richie, R., Swami, S., & Weinberg, C. (1999). A brand new world for nonprofits. *International Journal of Nonprofit and Voluntary Sector Marketing, 4*(1), 26–42.

Rose, R. (2010). *Confronting obstacles to inclusion: International responses to developing inclusive education.* New York, NY: Routledge.

Shrum, W., Genuth, J., & Chompalov, I. (2007). *Structures of scientific collaboration.* Cambridge, MA: The MIT Press.

Shuck, B., & Herd, A. M. (2012). Employee engagement and leadership: Exploring the convergence of two frameworks and implications for leadership development in HRD. *Human Resource Development Review, 11*, 156–181.

Skocpol, T. (2003). *Diminished democracy: From membership to management in American civic life.* Norman, OK: University of Oklahoma Press.

Strom, D. L., Sears, K. L., & Kelly, K. M. (2014). Work engagement: The roles of organizational justice and leadership style in predicting engagement among employees. *Journal of Leadership & Organizational Studies, 21*, 71–182.

Tawagi, A. L., & Mak, A. S. (2014). Cultural inclusiveness contributing to international students' intercultural attitudes: Mediating role of intergroup contact variables. *Journal of Community & Applied Social Psychology, 25*, 340–354.

Thompson, J., & Byrnes, D. (2011). A more diverse circle of friends. *Multicultural Perspectives, 13*, 93–99.

Walsh, J., & Maloney, N. (2007). Collaboration structure, communication media, and problems in scientific work teams. *Journal of Computer-Mediated Communication, 12*(2), 712–732.

Ward, C., & Masgoret, A. M. (2004). *The experiences of international students in New Zealand: Report on the results of the national survey.* Wellington, NZ: Victoria University of Wellington.

Ward, C., Masgoret, A. M., Ho, E., Holmes, P., Cooper, J., Newton, J., & Crabbe, D. (2005). *Interactions with international students.* Wellington, NZ: Victoria University of Wellington.

Wootliff, J., & Deri, C. (2001). NGOs: The new super brands. *Corporate Reputation Review, 4*(2), 157–164.

About the Authors

Niels Agger-Gupta, PhD, is Associate Professor and Program Head of the Graduate Certificate in Leadership at Royal Roads University in Victoria, Canada. A former Program Head, MA-Leadership, Niels maintains his "orientation to possibility" through supervising Leadership students engaged in transformative capstone projects. Research interests include action research, dialogic change, appreciative inquiry, and group methods, including world café. He holds a PhD in Human and Organizational Systems from Fielding Graduate University (Santa Barbara, California).

Barbara A. Baker, Executive Director of the Women's Leadership Institute at Auburn University, has published and taught in African American and Southern literature and music, women's leadership, and community and civic engagement. She is the author of *The Blues Aesthetic and the Making of American Identity*, and the editor of *Scholarship in Action: Communities, Leaders, and Citizens, Albert Murray and the Aesthetic Imagination* and *Lewis Nordan: Humor, Heartbreak, and Hope*.

Maria Basualdo has extensive experience in community-based research using participatory methodologies, and forming partnerships with community partners, faculty members, and student researchers. She has been involved with community development strategies that support activities to engage and reconnect people, and contribute to justice issues, environmental sustainability, socioeconomic development, and cultural revitalization.

Aldo Boitano de Moras, educated in Spain, Germany, Chile, and the United States where he received the National Honor Society Award in High School. Aldo received a Bachelor and Masters in Industrial Civil Engineering in December 1992 (Universidad de Chile) and an MBA in December 2006 (UNC-Charlotte Belk School of Business). He has 20 years of experience in top management, marketing and sales positions with a strong leadership and teamwork emphasis. Over this extended period, he has hold strong leadership positions such as CEO of Vertical Chile, CEO of El-Colorado/Farellones Ski resorts, CEO of Vertical USA, and General Manager of Drillco Tools USA that show a broad International experience and very successful work in various fields.

Aldo is a World-class Mountaineer and active philanthropist as well as a seasoned lecturer and consultant to companies and world forums. He is also an active member of board of directors of German Climbing Club (DAV) and founder of ski patrol group. He is a certified Mountaineering and climbing instructor and guide. He is also a Mountaineer with over 25 years of experience leading expeditions in Africa, Alaska, Antarctica, the Chilean, Peruvian and Ecuadorian Andes, USA, Patagonia (both in Chile and Argentina), and the Himalayas. Currently, he is an associate producer of the TV Series Patagonia Adventures filmed with renowned artists and a Canadian film crew.

Aldo received "Chile's Best Sports Annual Activity Award 1996" for participation in K2 expedition. He is the organizer of the first two climbing competitions of Chile (1990, 1991) and finished third in the national swimming competitions in 1978, 1979, and 1980. He also enjoys tennis, running, biking, baseball, reading, poetry, photography, carpentry, and computers. He has travelled through Latin America, most of US states (42), Canada, Europe, Africa, Oceania, Asia, and Antarctica.

As a university professor, he has taught at Wharton Executive education and at UNC-Charlotte School of Business. He currently teaches on International Business, Leadership and Building High Performance teams at ESE-Universidad Los Andes and at School of Business Universidad de Chile both at corporate programs and at post-graduate and MBA level. He normally lectures and consults on leadership, team-work, business models, environmental protection, social enterprise, and technology topics. He is also the editor of the upcoming book to be published by Emerald: *Breaking the Zero-Sum Game: Transforming Societies Through Inclusive Leadership*; A Volume in the International Leadership Association series *Building Leadership Bridges*. Research team on Leadership Dispatches: Chile's extraordinary comeback from disaster (27-F earthquake) published by Stanford Business Books.

He is a partner of Vertical (the largest experiential learning consulting firm in LA), Electra (a solar energy development company with three large-scale projects in northern Chile), Origenes (represents large mining and lithium projects), and Boretek (a high tech IoT endeavor with world patents on deep drilling and representative of IoT solutions) and serves the boards of Electra and the International Leadership Association.

Aldo is currently the Executive Director of Executive Development (ED), an organization dedicated to consulting and world-class Taylor-made in company education. His latest endeavor is the co-creation of an Australian Company: Chilean Lithium Salars.

Juana Bordas is author of two-award winning books *The Power of Latino Leadership* and *Salsa, Soul, and Spirit: Leadership for a Multicultural Age*. In 2015 she was a contributor to the new edition of *Peter Drucker's Five Most Important Questions*. Juana served as advisor to Harvard's Hispanic Journal on Public Policy, the Kellogg National Fellows Program, vice chair of Greenleaf Center for Servant Leadership, trustee of the International Leadership Association and Union Institute and University.

Ethan Brownell is an undergraduate student at the University of Minnesota – Twin Cities studying Mechanical Engineering and Leadership Development. His research interests are related to how improved leadership development in engineering fields may help to inform international development efforts.

Gloria J. Burgess, a pioneering innovator, is an acclaimed leadership consultant, author, and speaker. She serves as faculty for executive leaders at University of Washington, University of Southern California, Trinity Clergy Project, and Seattle University. Many years ago, she coined the term *legacy consciousness*, which she writes about in her books *Legacy Leadership* and *Dare to Wear Your Soul on the Outside*. Dr. Warren Bennis declared her books as "original, powerful, and inspirational work that should be required reading for all serious students and practitioners of leadership."

Mecca Antonia Burns holds a master's degree in Counseling Psychology and is a Registered Drama Therapist and board-certified trainer. She co-founded Presence Center for Applied Theatre Arts in Charlottesville, Virginia, USA. She trains groups in East Africa in Theatre of the Oppressed and has led work-shops in Spain, Senegal, Finland, Puerto Rico, and Romania. She contributed to *Transforming Leadership, African Conflict & Peacebuilding Review,* and *Grassroots Leadership and the Arts for Social Change.*

Michael R. Carey received his B.A. from Loyola Marymount University and both MA and PhD from Gonzaga University. His master's thesis and doctoral dissertation were both on the topic of Jesuit education. He has also published articles and books about transforming leadership and servant-leadership, and has served as a consultant for a variety of organizations.

He has made a pilgrimage to Pamplona, Loyola, Montserrat, Manresa, Barcelona, and Rome to visit the key sites related to Jesuit founder Ignatius of Loyola's own conversion experience and the development of his guide for personal transformation called the Spiritual Exercises. He works with faculty at Gonzaga in use of what is called Ignatian Pedagogy, i.e., a method of teaching that is based on Ignatius of Loyola's guide for transfor-mation. Currently, he is the Dean of the Virtual Campus and Associate Professor of Organizational Leadership at Gonzaga University.

Robin E. S. Carter is a cubicle dweller wayfinding between mind-less busyness and abstract leadership and followership concepts as a PhD student at Alvernia University, Reading, PA. She per-sists in an effort to escape what she believes will one day be viewed as a personal and cultural twentieth-century anomaly called corporate America. This sense making shift informs her ideas around self, servant, place, anticipatory, authentic, aes-thetic, and visionary leadership as researcher, writer, and artist.

Chris Cartwright, MPA, Ed.D., is the Director of Intercultural Assessment for the Intercultural Communication Institute where he supports individuals and organizations from around the world in assessing and developing global leadership and intercultural competence. He is also the Associate Director of Graduate Programs, serving as faculty adviser, instructor, and thesis/cap-stone director. He teaches, trains, consults, and researches in the areas of intercultural competency, assessment of student learning, leadership, service-learning, and social justice.

Helen Caton-Hughes is MD of the Forton Group, which specia-lizes in leadership development and leadership coaching, internationally. A qualified marketing consultant, holding "Chartered Marketer" status, she also holds an International Coach Federation (IC) professional accreditation (PCC) and is a qualified Team and Leadership coach. She is an accredited assessor for the Chartered Management Institute (UK) and the ICF. What interests her is what it takes to be a leader, and the different thinking, behaviors, and skills that enable leaders to implement change successfully. Helen is the creator of the unique Leadership and Leadership Coaching Routemaps™.

Sarah Chace, Ed.D., is an assistant professor in the Department of Leadership and American Studies at Christopher Newport University. Her research interests explore the intersection of group dynamics, adult development, and adaptive leadership. She has recently authored articles on the emergence of leadership in moments of political crisis and cultural disruption. She is currently at work on a book for Routledge.

William Clark has over 15 years of experience working in government operations, nonprofit management, and public housing management. Prior to launching Eli Patrick, he joined Workforce Solutions Collaborative as its Director. He manages the development and day-to-day operations of the collaborative. He previously served as Director of Special Projects for the City of Philadelphia's Office of Economic Opportunity where he was responsible for over $4.5 billion of Economic Opportunity Plans (EOPs), ensuring supplier, employment, and job seeker diversity for major construction projects. He leverages his expert knowledge and years of experience in meeting facilitation and coaching to help clients develop leaders, manage change, launch new ventures, innovate, solve problems, and become financial sustainable. He holds a Doctor of Strategic Leadership degree from Regent University and a Master of Leadership Development degree from Penn State University.

Claire Delisle is a critical pedagogue and teaches criminology and sociology at the University of Ottawa. She conducts one research project on social and leadership dynamics in social movements; and another on the issue of statelessness and its consequences. She utilizes collaborative participant-action methods in her research.

Raúl Lagomarsino Dutra has more than 18 years of experience as a Business School professor and management consultant, specialized in Leadership, Strategic Human Resources Management and Innovative Cultures. He started his academic career at IEEM Business School (Uruguay) and then he moved to Colombia, where he was Academic Dean of INALDE Business School. He is currently a full-time professor of Human Capital at ESE Business School (Chile), from where he participates as visiting faculty with some of the most prestigious Business Schools in Latin America, such as IPADE (México), INALDE (Colombia), PAD (Perú), IDE (Ecuador), ISE (Brazil) among others. As a management consultant, he has collaborated with more than 100 companies in 11 countries, and currently sits in the Board of companies that operate in real estate, utilities, and consulting. In 2010, he co-founded Emergap (www.emergap.com), a consulting firm specialized in innovation and organizational culture transformation. He has an MBA and a PhD from IESE Business School.

Brighid Dwyer, PhD is the Director of the Program on Intergroup Relations at Villanova University and an Assistant Professor in the Communication and Education and Counseling Departments. Her research explores dialogue, diversity and inclusion, leadership, Minority-Serving Institutions, and students' cross-racial interactions in college. Her work has been published in several edited books and journals including: *Creating inclusive campuses for cross-cultural learning and student engagement* (NASPA, 2007), *Today's college students: A reader* (Peter Lang, 2014), *Educational Foundations, and the Journal of Peace and Justice Studies*.

Leigh E. Fine is an Assistant Professor in the Staley School of Leadership Studies at Kansas State University. His scholarly interests include leadership pedagogy, assessment, queer theory, social construction, and intersections of gender and sexual identity. He has taught graduate and undergraduate courses related to multicultural leadership, ethics in leadership, peer leader development, and foundations of leadership.

Tami J. France, PhD focuses her time on leadership development initiatives through curriculum design, coaching, facilitation, research, writing, and program management. Her role at the Mayo Clinic is based in Leadership and Organization Development. She is also an adjunct faculty member at the University of Minnesota — Carlson School of Management. She earned her PhD in Leadership and Change from Antioch University with a research focus on cross-cultural leadership and professional success. She has a passion for diversity and inclusion initiatives, has lived in three countries, and has traveled extensively to speak and share her research findings in Europe, Asia, and the Americas. She has a Professional in Human Resources (PHR) certification, Silver Quality Fellow certificate from the Mayo Clinic Quality Academy, is certified in Immunity to Change and Flawless Consulting coaching and consulting techniques, and is pursuing International Coach Federation (IFC) coaching credentials.

Christopher Gergen is CEO of Forward Impact (http://www.forwardimpact.info/) which develops entrepreneurial working and living communities including HQ Raleigh, HQ Greensboro, HQ Charlotte, Think House, and the Duke TeachHouse. He is also the co-founder of Forward Cities (www.forwardcities.org) – a national learning collaborative between cities focused on building more inclusive innovation economies. He also co-founded InnovateNC (www.innovatenc.org) – a similar multicity learning collaborative in North Carolina. Additionally, he is Innovator in Residence with the Center for Creative Leadership, a fellow with Duke University's Innovation & Entrepreneurship initiative, and co-author of the nationally acclaimed book *Life Entrepreneurs: Ordinary People Creating Extraordinary Lives*, as well as a biweekly column for the *Raleigh News & Observer* and *Charlotte Observer* on "Doing Better at Doing Good." He is a 2013 Henry Crown Fellow at the Aspen Institute and lives with his wife and two children in Durham, NC.

Cheryl Getz is an Associate Professor of Leadership Studies and the Director of the Leadership Minor in the Department of Leadership Studies at the University of San Diego. She teaches undergraduate and graduate leadership courses in group dynamics, college student development, and action research. She has also taught several global study courses in South Africa, Qatar, and a village immersion course in Sri Lanka. Her areas of expertise include nontraditional leadership pedagogies, application of adaptive leadership to higher education, development of inclusive and integrated leadership development programs.

Ralph A. Gigliotti, PhD, is assistant director of leadership programs for the Center for Organizational Development & Leadership at Rutgers University, where he oversees a number of faculty and staff leadership development initiatives and leads several research projects related to leadership and communication in higher education. He also serves as the co-director of the Rutgers

Leadership Academy and co-director of the Distinction in Leadership in Academic Healthcare Program. His research interests explore the intersection of organizational communication, leadership, and crisis communication, particularly in the context of higher education. His research appears in numerous books and journals, including the *Journal of Leadership and Organizational Studies*, *Journal of Leadership Education*, and the *Atlantic Journal of Communication*. He is also the co-author of *A Guide for Leaders in Higher Education: Core Concepts, Competencies, and Tools* (Stylus Publishing, 2017).

Malcolm E. Glover, PhD is a global leadership scholar and humanitarian who travels the world helping people solve problems. As a crisis manager, communication analyst, educator, and award-winning journalist, he has worked with governments and grassroots organizations in over eleven countries on five continents. He has a PhD from the University of Central Arkansas and is founder and CEO of Glover Global, an innovative consulting firm offering strategies that empower individuals, engage communities, and enhance institutions. He has worked with NPR, MSNBC, MTV, USAID, and the Clinton Foundation, among others. He is a program coordinator for the National Archives and Kettering Foundation's *Advise the President* book series that explores the strategic decisions of U.S. presidents on domestic and foreign policy matters. Whether managing strategic partnerships, conducting scholarly research, teaching students, or crafting ground-breaking projects, he builds coalitions and improves outcomes for initiatives in the public and private sectors.

Miriam Gosling is the Director for the Centre for Peace and Global Studies at a Quaker school in south England, runs a management consultancy, is trustee of a charity providing care for brain-injured children, and has led campaigns for conflict-free minerals in consumer electronics for "Congo calling". She is a member of the Civicus UN young leaders community and is based in the UK.

Maura Harrington is widely recognized for her expertise in leadership development, evaluation design and strategy, and in all aspects of organizational development with a focus on strategic planning. At the Center for Nonprofit Management, she oversees the provision of client services to organizations across sectors. She teaches courses on Research, Evaluation, and Organizational

Psychology in the USC departments of Social Work and Psychology. She has been an affiliate of the Connective Leadership Institute for more than 25 years.

Brigitte Harris, PhD, is Professor and Dean of the College of Social and Applied Science at Royal Roads University. She embraces the University's key role of educating, and transforming leaders who can engage others to create positive change. Her research interests include action research and narrative inquiry as a means of engaging others, women in leadership and transformative education. She holds a PhD from the Ontario Institute for Studies in Education (University of Toronto).

Andrea Hughes has a Master's degree in Criminology from the University of Ottawa and is a social justice activist. She has been involved in several groups in the Ottawa area. She currently works for an academic journal.

Bob Hughes is the CEO of the Forton Group, which specializes in leadership development and leadership coaching A PCC-credentialed coach, he is an accredited assessor for the Chartered Management Institute (UK) and the International Coach Federation (ICF). With a track record in people motivation and project delivery, he has the personal experience of what it takes to transform corporate cultures to be more inclusive, effective and coach-like. He is an acknowledged expert in the fields of leadership, talent management, and employee engagement and coaches the C-Suite across all sectors. He has delivered leadership development, coaching, and transformation to clients around the world and is in demand as an inspiring public speaker.

Adina Ilea is a doctoral candidate in the department of criminology at University of Ottawa. Her research examines cultural and self-constructed conceptualizations of identity as they relate to sexual offending and victimization. She has been an active member of various front line and social justice groups, including Circles of Support and Accountability (CoSA), The Criminalization and Punishment Education Project (CPEP) and The International Conference on Penal Abolition (ICOPA).

Zhi Luan has a PhD in Interdisciplinary Leadership Studies. He graduated and received his degree from the doctoral program in leadership studies at the University of Central Arkansas in April, 2016. Before he came to study in the United States, he was a college instructor teaching a variety of courses in cultural studies and business management and a leader of several educational and legal organizations in China. His research interests lie in leadership development from the perspectives of Chinese philosophy.

Ebere Morgan, PhD, is a successful and well-seasoned professional with decades of diverse experient lead engagements on both local and international platforms. He is a consummate strategist, author, educator, consultant, and leadership communicator, he holds a PhD in Leadership & Strategic Change. He advances thought leadership in various professional disciplines including Healthcare, Leadership Development, Organizational Leadership, and Strategic Foresight. He is the President & CEO of Deztiny Inc., and is passionate about people, organizations and all things Leadership — one entity at a time!

Bernard Mukisa studied Music, Dance, and Drama at Makerere University and received an MA in Theatre Directing from the Byelorussian University of Culture in Minsk. He taught Directing and People's Theatre at Makerere from 1997 to 2000 and helped the East African Theatre Institute link countries through cultural exchange for grassroots empowerment and democratization. He and his family founded Budondo Intercultural Center and Suubi Health Project in their home village of Budondo where he resides.

Denis Muwanguzi received his B.S in Public Health from Mountains of the Moon University in Uganda and a master's degree in Public Health from Lund University, Malmo, Sweden. He co-founded Suubi Health Project in Budondo village, Uganda. He has worked as a theatre practitioner, sensitizing and educating communities about health and human rights since he was 12, and has co-facilitated Forum Theatre outreach in Uganda and Kenya.

Lyndon Rego is the Director of Innovation and Global Director of Leadership Beyond Boundaries at the Center for Creative Leadership® (http://www.ccl.org/). In this role, he heads up CCL innovation efforts and the global Leadership Beyond Boundaries initiative to make leadership development more affordable and accessible around the world. He has delivered leadership development, innovation, and train-the-trainer programs in the United States, Latin America, Africa, India, and Asia for audiences including corporate leaders, social entrepreneurs, rural communities, and youth leaders. He writes and speaks on issues at the intersection of leadership, complexity, innovation, and social change. He and the LBB team were the recipients of the 2014 Global Work Award from the Organizational Development Network. He lives with his wife and daughter in Winston-Salem, NC.

Colleen Rigby, in the role as MBA Director at the University of Waikato, focuses on transforming the careers of leaders and managers. She is responsible for the leadership development of MBA students and has published and presented papers in the domains of leadership, ethics, and entrepreneurship. She is a registered psychologist, who applies her profession to the assessment and coaching of managers and leaders.

Jill Robinson is a Professor at the University of Redlands teaching courses in Human Resource Management, Leadership, and Business Strategy and is a certified Practitioner for the Connective Leadership Institute. She holds a PhD and MA in Organizational Behavior and an MBA in Human Resources. Her industry background is in HR Management in the Healthcare Industry where she has worked in Employee Relations, Training, and Safety. Her research interests are in leadership and gender issues.

Elisa Sabatini serves as the Executive Director for Via International. Program areas include family health, nutrition, micro-finance, sustainable agriculture, community leadership education, and volunteerism. She formerly served World SHARE as the Regional Director for Latin America. She coordinated participatory processes to create an autonomous SHARE organization in Guatemala as well as develop self-funding food distribution in Mexico and a rural agricultural loan fund. In Mexico, the Compartamos (SHARE) program is now the largest micro finance initiative in Latin America. She has lived in Spain, Guatemala, Mexico, Hawaii, and San Diego, CA.

Lydia Sanyu holds a BA in Business Administration from St. Lawrence University, Kampala, Uganda and has served as administrator for Budondo Intercultural Center and Suubi Health Project. Her community organizing skills evolved through theater and she has trained in Forum Theatre since 2007. As program manager for Twogere Girls club, she coordinates skills development trainings and Forum Theatre outreach for young girls and community health workers.

H. Eric Schockman, PhD is an Associate Professor and Chair of the Leadership Department and Director of the Center for Leadership at Woodbury University. He also teaches in the PhD program in Global Leadership and Change at Pepperdine University.

A public policy expert, Schockman previously served as Associate Dean and Associate Adjunct Professor at the Sol Price School of Public Policy at the University of Southern California. He is the President and founder of the Global Hunger Foundation, dedicated to helping women in the developing world, brake the chains of poverty by funding projects designed to provide sustainable development and organic farming. He served as CEO and President of a prestigious international anti-hunger organization for over a decade pumping some $60 million in grants into the field. Schockman served as Vice President of the California League of Conservation Voters Educational Fund where he supervised environmental public opinion polling and statewide voter engagement. He was a top consultant to the California State Assembly and the Los Angeles City Council. Eric also served as Policy Director for the City of Los Angeles' Elected Charter Reform Commission. Schockman was the founder of the national anti-hunger organizations (NAHO), an alliance of all major national anti-hunger organizations in the United States. Additionally, Schockman was a member the National Interfaith Hunger Director's Committee. He was on the founding board of directors of the Global Food Banking Network. The Senate Rules Committee has recently appointed him to the California State Library Commission. He was the former Chair of the California Postsecondary Education Commission, an appointment made by Governor Arnold Schwarzenegger. Appointed by California State Assembly Speaker Emeritus Antonio Villaraigosa, Eric has also served on the Little Hoover Commission, a bipartisan, independent body whose function is to promote efficiency, effectiveness, and economy in state programs. He served in the Peace Corps in Sierra Leone, West Africa, and taught agricultural and sustainable development.

Schockman speaks before elected officials, professional, and community organizations across the country and is frequently quoted in *The Los Angeles Times, The Chicago Tribune, The Dallas Morning News*, CNN, NPR, and other national publications and electronic media.

He has also written several books and edited many articles on leadership and politics in California, the nation and international affairs, and presented on panels on these same topic.

Schockman holds a PhD in Political Science and International Relations from the University of California.

Lorraine Stefani is Professor of Higher Education Strategic Engagement at the University of Auckland. Her Higher Education Strategic Engagement role has led to her involvement in projects with the NZ Ministry of Health, the Ministry of Higher Education in Saudi Arabia, and a six-month consultancy period at Princess Nora University in Saudi Arabia. Her research interests include interrogation of leadership models in complex organizations, pedagogy for the 21st century, and the changing nature of higher education provision. She has published widely on topical issues relevant to leading change in higher education and presented keynote lectures at many national and has international conferences. She currently holds the position of President of the Higher Education Teaching and Learning Association (HETL).

Leonard D. Taylor, Jr. is an Assistant Professor of Educational Leadership at Mississippi State University. His research focuses on how institutions enhance their student success efforts using research knowledge, institutional data, and best practices. He is also focused on advancing the dialogue about power and systems of oppression in leadership education spaces, to inform current and future efforts for social change.

Randal Joy Thompson is a scholar-practitioner who has spent her career as a Foreign Service Officer in international development, working in countries in all regions of the world. She has advised governments and helped to change systems that impact women's health, child welfare, education, social science research, and program evaluation. Her research interests include leadership, organization development, and the commons. She is the Founder and Principal of Dream Connect Global, a social networking corporation, and its subsidiary, Excellence, Equity, and Empowerment.

Dung Q. Tran earned his doctorate in Leadership Studies at Gonzaga University and completed his master's degree in Theological Studies — with emphases in Spirituality and Catholic Higher Education — at the Jesuit School of Theology of Santa

Clara University. He also obtained a master's degree in Secondary Education as well as two bachelor's degrees in Communication Studies and Theological Studies from Loyola Marymount University. His research interests include servant-leadership, spiritual leadership, Ignatian spirituality, Jesuit higher education, hermeneutics, Vietnamese history, and the intersection of communication, leadership, and theology. His work has been published in *Communication Research Trends* and *The International Journal of Servant-Leadership* (SUNY Press). He is currently an Instructor in Organizational Leadership at Seattle University.

Rouxelle de Villiers is a senior lecturer and executive business mentor at the University of Waikato. She specializes in the development of executive decision competencies and inter-personal leadership skills. She has many years of experience as business liaison and management consultant. Her research interests include persuasion, mentorship, feedback and leadership styles.

Joyce de Vries is an associate professor of Art History at Auburn University and served as Director of the Women's Studies Program at Auburn, 2011-2017. Her research focuses on women, diversity, and inclusion in academia; feminist analysis of contemporary visual culture; and gender, material culture, and the domestic realm in Early Modern Italy. She published the book *Caterina Sforza and the Art of Appearances: Gender, Art and Culture in Early Modern Italy* with Ashgate, 2010.

Jennifer Walinga is a Professor in the School of Communication and Culture at Royal Roads University. Her research and consulting work investigates and addresses the need for more sustainable practice in our work and life spaces. She is a two-time Olympian, and the experience she gained training and competing at an elite level forms the basis for her practice, teaching, and facilitation. She helps leaders and groups to refine their organizational design, enhance their organizational culture, and develop their creative problem solving and communication skills in order to thrive, not just survive, in the complex, fast-paced, chaotic workplaces of today. She is a mother of three and an active member of the athletic and educational communities in Victoria, BC.

Kevin Walsh is a Professor at Phillips Graduate University and an accomplished leadership development facilitator/coach. He is a trainer for Living As A Leader and The Ken Blanchard

Companies. His consulting practice specialties include a wide range of training and development solutions. He has trained over 10,000 employees from the front line to the C-suite, across the globe. He has earned Doctorate of Psychology in Organizational Management and Consulting and is a Professional Certified Coach.

Index